FEMALE RELIGIOUS AUTHORITY IN SHI'I ISLAM

FEMALE RELIGIOUS AUTHORITY IN SHI'I ISLAM

PAST AND PRESENT

♦ ♦ ♦

EDITED BY MIRJAM KÜNKLER AND
DEVIN J. STEWART

EDINBURGH
University Press

Edinburgh University Press is one of the leading university presses in the UK. Publishing new research in the arts and humanities, EUP connects people and ideas to inspire creative thinking, open new perspectives and shape the world we live in. For more information, visit www.edinburghuniversitypress.com.

This book has been made Open Access through funding from the Persian Heritage Foundation, Fresno CA.

Edinburgh University Press Ltd
13 Infirmary Street, Edinburgh EH1 1LT

Typeset in 10/12 Book Antiqua by
IDSUK (DataConnection) Ltd

A CIP record for this book is available from the British Library

ISBN 978 1 4744 2660 2 (hardback)
ISBN 978 1 4744 2662 6 (webready PDF)
ISBN 978 1 4744 2663 3 (epub)

Published with the suport of the University of Edinburgh Scholarly Publishing Initiatives Fund.

EU Authorised Representative:
Easy Access System Europe
Mustamäe tee 50, 10621 Tallinn, Estonia
gpsr.requests@easproject.com

CONTENTS

List of Tables and Figures vii
Note on Transliteration viii
Notes on the Contributors ix
Acknowledgements xiii

1. Introduction – Female Religious Authority in Shi'i Islam: Past and Present 1
   Mirjam Künkler and Devin J. Stewart
2. Forgotten Histories of Female Religious Authority in Islam 18
   Mirjam Künkler
3. Umm Salama: A Female Authority Legitimating the Authorities 47
   Yasmin Amin
4. Heiress to the Prophet: Fatima's *Khuṭba* as an Early Case of Female Religious Authority in Islam 78
   Alyssa Gabbay
5. Female Authority in the Times of the Shiʿi Imams 105
   Liyakat Takim
6. 'She Should Not Raise Her Voice When among Men': Imāmī Arguments against (and for) Women Judges 121
   Robert Gleave
7. Husniyya's Debate at the Court of Harun al-Rashid: Sectarian Polemics and Female Religious Authority 138
   Devin J. Stewart
8. Layli as Queen of Heaven by Muhammadi of Herat, *c.* 1565 193
   Michael Barry

9. Princesses, Patronage and the Production of Knowledge in Safavid Iran 211
Yusuf Ünal

10. The Lives of Two *Mujtahidāt*: Female Religious Authority in Twentieth-century Iran 271
Mirjam Künkler and Roja Fazaeli

11. The Other Half of the Mission: Amina 'Bint al-Huda' as a Representative (*Wakīla*) of Muhammad Baqir al-Sadr 298
Raffaele Mauriello

12. The '*Ālimāt* of Sayyida Zaynab: Female Shi'i Religious Authority in a Syrian Seminary 325
Edith Szanto

13. Women's Religious Seminaries in Iran: A Diversified System Despite State Attempts at Unification and Standardisation 341
Maryam Rutner

Index 395

TABLES AND FIGURES

Tables

13.1 Student Capacity, Academic Year 2012–2013 368
13.2 Number of Seminaries and Students in Iran for the Academic Year 2017–2018 369
13.3 Women's Religious Seminaries in Fars, 2012–2013 370
13.4 Five-year Programme, Second Level, 2010–2011 371
13.5 Curriculum: Jurisprudence and Principles of Jurisprudence, Third Level, 2011–2012 381
13.6 Exegesis and Qur'anic Studies, Third Level, 2011–2012 386
13.7 Seminaries, Fourth Level, 2018–2019 390
13.8 General Knowledge for Admission to Fourth Level 391
13.9 Specialised Knowledge for Admission to Fourth Level 391

Figures

8.1 'Seated Princess', by Muhammadi, probably Herat, *c.* 1565 194
8.2 'Seated Princess', by Mirza Ali, Tabriz, *c.* 1540 195
8.3 'Layli and Majnun in School', illustration to Nizami's *Khamseh* by Bihzad and Qasim Ali, Herat, 1494 198
8.4 'The Angels Bow Before Adam and Eve': illustration to a *Fāl-Nāmeh* or 'Book of Omens' for Shah Tahmasp, Qazvin, *c.* 1560 206
13.1 Rayhaneh al-Nabi in Shiraz und al-Zahra in Estahban 344
13.2 Women's Religious Seminaries in 2011 345

NOTE ON TRANSLITERATION

Chapters either follow the *IJMES* style guide (where Arabic predominates) or that of the *Journal of Persianate Studies* (where Persian expressions predominate). The EUP house style requires that diacritics be omitted in personal names, except for ʿayn and hamza.

NOTES ON THE CONTRIBUTORS

Yasmin Amin received a doctorate in Islamic studies from the University of Exeter's Institute of Arab and Islamic Studies, for a thesis titled 'Humour and Laughter in the Ḥadīth'. She obtained a postgraduate diploma in Islamic studies in 2006 and an MA in Islamic studies in 2010, both from the American University in Cairo. She is co-translator of *The Sorrowful Muslim's Guide* (Edinburgh University Press, 2018), co-editor of *Islamic Interpretive Tradition and Gender Justice Processes of Canonization, Subversion and Change* (2020) and the author of the forthcoming *Musnad Umm Salama and the Factors Shaping its Evolution*.

Michael Barry is Distinguished Professor at the American University of Afghanistan. He taught in the Department of Near Eastern Studies at Princeton University (2004–2015), served as consultative chairman of the Department of Islamic Art at the Metropolitan Museum of Art (2005–2009), and has been a special consultant to the Aga Khan Trust for Culture since 2009.

Roja Fazaeli is Lecturer in Islamic Civilisation(s) at Trinity College Dublin. Her PhD thesis was a comparative study of Islamic law and international human rights law concerning women in the Shi'a tradition and was funded by the Irish Research Council for Humanities and Social Sciences. She serves on the editorial board of the *Journal for Religion and Human Rights*. Previously she served on the boards of the Association of Persianate Studies, the Irish Refugee Council, and UNIFEM (UN Women) Ireland.

Alyssa Gabbay is associate professor in the Department of Religious Studies at the University of North Carolina at Greensboro. She received her PhD in Classical Persian Literature and Medieval Islamic History from the University of Chicago in 2007 and is the author of *Islamic Tolerance: Amir Khusraw and Pluralism* (2010), as well as several book chapters and journal articles. She is currently at work on two book projects: *The New Moon of Perfection and*

Other Prefaces (under advance contract), a series of translations and critical editions of the prefaces to Amir Khusraw's books of poetry; and *Gender and Succession in Medieval Islam: Bilateral Descent and the Legacy of Fatima*, which traces the development and impact of the belief among medieval Shi'ites that Fatimah, daughter of the Prophet Muhammad, perpetuated her father's lineage through her sons. Gabbay received the Foundation for Iranian Studies' Award for Best PhD Dissertation on a Topic of Iranian Studies in 2007.

Robert Gleave is Professor of Arabic Studies, University of Exeter. His main area of research interest is the history of Shi'i *fiqh*, particularly legal theory and jurisprudence (*uṣūl al-fiqh*). He is author of *Inevitable Doubt: Two Theories of Shī'ī Jurisprudence* (2000), *Scripturalist Islam: The History and Doctrines of the Shī'ī Akhbārī School* (2007) and *Islam and Literalism: Literal Meaning and Interpretation in Islamic Legal Theory* (Edinburgh University Press, 2012). He is currently Director of the Islamic Reformulations project, examining changing patterns of Islamic thought in the classical and modern period.

Mirjam Künkler (PhD, Columbia University) is a senior research fellow at the Swedish Collegium for Advanced Study (SCAS). Before joining SCAS, she taught Near Eastern Studies at Princeton University, where she also directed the Oxford-Princeton research cluster on 'Traditional authority and transnational religious networks in contemporary Shi'i Islam' and co-directed the Luce Program on 'Religion and International Affairs' for several years. Her books include *Democracy and Islam in Indonesia* (with Alfred Stepan, 2013), *A Secular Age Beyond the West* (with John Madeley and Shylashri Shankar, 2018), and *The Rule of Law in the Islamic Republic of Iran: Power, Institutions, and Prospects for Reform* (with Hadi Enayat, 2021). Her articles have appeared in, inter alia, *Comparative Studies of Society and History*, the *Asian Studies Review*, the *British Journal of Middle Eastern Studies*, *Constellations*, the *Journal of Law and Religion*, *Democratization*, the *Oxford Encyclopedia of Islam and Women*, and *the Princeton Encyclopedia for Islamic Political Thought*. Künkler is co-founder and PI of the 'Iran Social Science Data Portal' (http://irandataportal.syr.edu).

Raffaele Mauriello is an Assistant Professor at the Faculty of Persian Literature and Foreign Languages, Allameh Tabaṭaba'i University, Tehran (Iran), where he also teaches at the Faculty of Theology and Islamic Knowledge. Moreover, he is an Adjunct Professor at the Master's programme in Geopolitics and Global Security at the Sapienza University of Rome. Previously, he was a Postdoctoral Research Fellow at the Faculty of World Studies, University of Tehran. Dr Mauriello is a historian and linguist, specialising in Global Studies, Shi'ite Islam, the Near East, Iran and Latin America. In 2013, he was awarded *The World Prize for the Book of the Year of the Islamic Republic of Iran* in the field of Islamic Studies for his monograph *Descendants of the Family of the Prophet in Contemporary History: A Case Study, the Šī'ī Religious Establishment of al-Nağaf (Iraq)*.

Maryam Rutner received a PhD from the Middle Eastern and Islamic Studies Department at New York University. Her dissertation dealt with the life and work of Nosrat Amin (d. 1983), the most prominent female mojtahed in twentieth-century Iran. Rutner's broader research deals with the relationship between politics and religion, women and gender, religious authority, as well as Shi'ism in the modern Middle East. Her articles include 'Religious Authority, Gendered Recognition, and Instrumentalization of Nusrat Amin in Life and after Death' *Journal of Middle East Women's Studies* 11.1 (2015), 24–41; and 'A Survey of the Content and Purpose of Political Science in Iran and its Significance for the Iranian Society', *Journal of Persianate Studies* 3.1 (2010), 104–127.

Devin J. Stewart earned a BA *magna cum laude* in Near Eastern Studies from Princeton University in 1984 and a PhD with distinction in Arabic and Islamic Studies from the University of Pennsylvania in 1991. He has been teaching at Emory in the Department of Middle Eastern and South Asian Studies since 1990. His research has focused on Shi'ite Islam, the Qur'an, Islamic law and legal education, biography, autobiography, speech genres, and other topics in Arabic and Islamic studies. He is the author of *Islamic Legal Orthodoxy* (1998) and *Disagreements of the Jurists* (2015) and a co-author of *Interpreting the Self* (2002). He has written a number of studies on dissimulation in Shi'ite and Sunni Islam, polemics between Sunnis and Shi'ites, Islamic legal scholarship and education, and Islamic biographical writings. Articles include: 'The Identity of "the Mufti of Oran": Abu al-`Abbas Ahmad b. Abi Jum`ah al-Maghrawi al-Wahrani (d. 917/1511)', *Al-Qantara: Revista de Estudios Árabes* 27.2 (2006), 265–301; 'The Students' Representative in the Law Colleges of Fourteenth-Century Damascus', *Islamic Law and Society* 15.2 (2008), 185–218; 'The Ottoman Execution of Zayn al-Din al-`Amili', *Die Welt des Islams* 48 (2008), 289–347; 'The *Maqamat* of Ahmad b. Abi Bakr al-Razi al-Ḥanafī and the Ideology of the Counter-Crusade in Twelfth-Century Syria', *Middle Eastern Literatures* 11.2 (2008), 211–232; 'Ibn al-Nadim's Isma`ili Contacts', *Journal of the Royal Asiatic Society*, Series 3, 19.1 (2008), 21–40; 'Polemics and Patronage in Safavid Iran: The Debate on Friday Prayer during the Reign of Shah Tahmasb', *Bulletin of the School of Oriental and African Studies* 72.3 (2009), 425–457; and 'Poetic License in the Qur'an: Ibn al-Sa'igh al-Hanafi's *Ihkam al-Ray fi Ahkam al-Ay*', *Journal of Qur'anic Studies* 11.1 (2009), 1–54.

Edith Szanto is an Assistant Professor in the Department of Religious Studies at the University of Alabama. Prior to coming to Alabama in 2019, she taught for eight years at the American University of Iraq, Sulaimani, allowing her to pursue a variety of research topics related to contemporary religion in Iraq and Iraqi Kurdistan. Dr. Szanto received her PhD in Religious Studies from the University of Toronto in 2012. Her dissertation examined Twelver Shi'ite practices in Syria, where she spent three years as a Fulbright scholar researching popular Islamic practices and working for the United Nations (UN). She is the author of 'Sayyida Zaynab in the State of Exception: Shi'i Sainthood as "Qualified Life" in Contemporary Syria' (*IJMES*, 2012), and 'Challenging Transnational Shi'i Authority in Ba'th Syria' (*BJMES*, 2018).

Liyakat Takim is the Sharjah Chair in Global Islam at McMaster University in Hamilton, Canada. A native of Zanzibar, Tanzania, he has authored numerous scholarly works on diverse topics including reformation in the Islamic world, the treatment of women in Islamic law, Islam in America, the indigenisation of the Muslim community in America, dialogue in post-911 America, war and peace in the Islamic tradition, Islamic law, Islamic biographical literature, the charisma of the holy man and shrine culture, and Islamic mystical traditions. He teaches a wide range of courses on Islam and offers a course on comparative religions. His second book, titled *Shi'ism in America,* was published in 2009. His first book, *The Heirs of the Prophet: Charisma and Religious Authority in Shi'ite Islam,* was published in 2006. He is currently working on his third book, *Ijtihad and Reformation in Islam.*

Yusuf Ünal is a PhD student at Emory University, Atlanta, GA, in the Islamic Civilizations Studies Program. His areas of research include Safavid intellectual and religious history, Ottoman–Safavid relations, Sunni–Shi'i polemics, conversion narratives, and translation movements in early modern and modern times.

ACKNOWLEDGEMENTS

The idea for this volume was born several years ago in Qom when Mirjam Künkler conducted field research on the women's *ḥawza* Jāmi'at al-Zahrā'. Keiko Sakurai of Waseda University and Mirjam Künkler then set out to convene a conference on female religious authority in modern Iran, which was held at Princeton University in 2015. We acknowledge with deep gratitude the support by the Japanese Society for the Promotion of the Sciences (JSPS), which funded the conference, and thank the Center for the Study of Religion (CSR) at Princeton University for providing a congenial environment for our comparative discussions. The work here also benefited from the graduate course 'Female Religious Authority in Islam' that Mirjam Künkler taught on the topic at Princeton University.

The volume set out to take stock of the research developments in the field of female religious authority in Shi'ism, to identify lacunae requiring further research, and to further the development of comparative and interdisciplinary research projects incorporating the findings developed there. We thank Abbas Amanat, Karen Bauer, Nelly van Doorn, Khaled Abou El Fadl, Rozaliya Garipova, Meriem el Haitami, Renate Jacobi, Mohsen Kadivar, Anwar al-Khalili, Lilia Labidi, Katie Manbachi, Hossein Modarressi, Roy Mottahedeh, Masoud Noori, Ruth Roded, Keiko Sakurai, Asma Sayeed, Irene Schneider, Sedigheh Vasmaghi, and Qasim Zaman for spirited conversations that shaped our way of thinking on the matter.

Only once we have a better account of the variations in female religious authority across space and time, as well as in comparison to their male counterparts in a given context, will we be able to formulate hypotheses as to which conditions and developments – theological, jurisprudential, social, economic, political – particularly enhanced, promoted, or, conversely, stifled the phenomenon.

Mirjam Künkler and Devin J. Stewart, April 2018

CHAPTER

1

INTRODUCTION FEMALE RELIGIOUS AUTHORITY IN SHI'I ISLAM: PAST AND PRESENT

Mirjam Künkler and Devin J. Stewart

Recent decades have witnessed an explosion of scholarly output focusing on women in Islamic societies. A salient milestone in this development is represented by the publication of the *Encyclopedia of Women and Islamic Cultures*, whose six weighty volumes present an overview of a tremendous amount of scholarship on women in the various regions of the Islamic world and in various historical periods, conducted by scholars of literature, history, sociology, anthropology, and other fields, in Europe, North America, the Middle East, and elsewhere.[1] This survey reveals certain major biases in scholarly coverage to date, some of which the editors have endeavoured to address. Overall, scholarship has been skewed towards the Middle East and the Arab world, in comparison with work on Muslim societies in sub-Saharan Africa, South Asia, Central Asia, China, Indonesia, Malaysia, Muslim minorities in the West and elsewhere, and the editors of the *Encyclopedia* made significant efforts to rectify this imbalance, in particular by commissioning entries devoted to specific regions in many of the *Encyclopedia*'s various topical sections. Scholarship on women in Islamic societies also shows a significant predilection for the modern period, in part because of the availability of sources, in part because of the training of the scholars involved, but also in part because of the motivation to address current politics and societal restrictions on women. Accordingly, there has been a significant emphasis on national laws and constitutions, women's status, education, entrance into the workforce, and political participation. Topics in family law, veiling, barriers to education, child marriage, and other legal restrictions on women have received particular attention. With the exception of some focus on revered women of the early Muslim community, such as the wives of the Prophet, scholarship

[1] Suad Joseph (general ed.), *Encyclopedia of Women and Islamic Cultures*, 6 vols (Leiden: Brill, 2003–7).

has relatively ignored women in medieval and pre-modern Islamic societies, although this is changing rapidly at present. Moreover, scholarship on women in the modern period has often presented a flat, undifferentiated view of the status of women in Islamic societies prior to the advent of modern nationalisms, in many cases based not on serious investigation of the topic but rather on assumptions of the radical break between modernity and traditional societies. One area of research that the *Encyclopedia* marks as salient but that clearly remains underdeveloped is the roles women have played in traditional structures of learning and religious authority in the Islamic world.[2]

Islamic Religious Authority

The studies in this volume stand at the intersection of three large areas of investigation in Islamic studies: Islamic religious authority, Shi'ism, and the role of women in the Islamic tradition. Debates about who enjoys legitimate religious authority are of course as old as the Islamic tradition itself. Moreover, the question goes to the very heart of the formation of different groups and sects, many of which identified themselves over the question of religious leadership. The very distinction between orthodoxy and heresy depends on what is recognised as legitimate religious authority.

An understanding of women's religious authority in Islamic contexts requires a general conception of Islamic religious authority, something that has been contested in the literature. Scholarship on this question reveals an abundance of diverse opinions, not few of which remain overly simplistic by positing that the sole form of religious authority is that of the Imamate or Caliphate.[3] Others assume that the theologians are the sole wielders of authority in Islamic society.[4] George Makdisi has argued that Muslim jurists have exclusive religious authority from the eleventh century onward, although he admits that their claims were formulated against the Caliphs and theologians in particular.[5] A slightly more complex view recognises two forms of religious authority in actual or potential conflict. Ash'ari theology has long been recognised as a compromise between Hanbali traditionalism and Mu'tazili rationalism that became Islamic orthodoxy.[6] Abu Hamid

---

[2] See, for example, the following entries: Ruth Roded, 'Islamic Biographical Dictionaries: 9th to 10th Century', *Encyclopedia of Women and Islamic Cultures*, 1:29–31; Asma Afsaruddin, 'Islamic Biographical Dictionaries: 11th to 15th Century', *Encyclopedia of Women and Islamic Cultures*, 1:32–36.

[3] Henri Laoust, *Les schismes dans l'Islam* (Paris: Payot 1965).

[4] John B. Henderson, *The Construction of Orthodoxy and Heresy* (Albany: State University of New York Press, 1998).

[5] George Makdisi, *The Rise of Colleges* (Edinburgh: Edinburgh University Press, 1981).

[6] Duncan Black MacDonald, *Development of Muslim Theology, Jurisprudence, and Constitutional Theory* (New York: Charles Scribners' Sons, 1903), 186–192; Ignaz Goldziher, *Introduction to Islamic Theology and Law* (Princeton: Princeton University Press, 1981), 100–111. Goldziher, however, notes al-Ash'arī's traditionalist leanings later on in his career and holds that it is the later school of Ash'arism rather than al-Ash'ari himself who formed and promoted this middle position.

al-Ghazali (d. 505/1111) is seen as the creator of an orthodoxy based on the synthesis of Islamic law and mysticism, or, in other terms, of incorporating mysticism into orthodox Islam. This interpretation amounts to a claim that Sufi masters and jurists constitute the dual religious authorities of the Muslim world.[7] In the anthropology of Islam in North Africa in particular, scholars long recognised that two systems of religious authority existed in a potentially antagonistic but nevertheless stable symbiosis, essentially dividing up society according to jurisdiction. In their view, jurists and a highly literate form of Islam held sway in urban centres, while the countryside was under the control of mystical masters and Sufi brotherhoods, who presided over vernacular forms of Islam. This corresponded to a political division between areas controlled by tribes (*sibā*) and areas controlled by the central, royal government (*makhzan*).[8] Yet even recognition of two modes of religious authority does not provide an adequate model for the workings of religious authority, orthodoxy, and heresy over the vast expanse of the Islamic world in both time and space. A more realistic model of religious authority in Islam would include at least the following groups as potential claimants to authority: imams or caliphs, kings or sultans, theologians, hadith experts, jurists, philosophers, Sufi masters, and preachers. In fact, medieval Muslim scholars saw Islamic religious authority as involving several distinct 'categories' – social or professional 'groups' termed *ṭā'ifa*, pl. *ṭawā'if* – eternally jockeying for position in the market of religious ideas.[9] According to this view, authority resides in jurists as a class, in theologians, hadith experts, caliphs/imams, Sufi masters, preachers, philosophers, and so on. Views of this type are replacing the models traditionally adhered to in Islamic studies, and these have the potential to make better sense of the available data concerning religious movements and change in the course of Islamic history. This is of course by no means guaranteed: the overly simplistic models positing a single mode of religious authority, or at most two, have also persisted, and they remain embedded in most introductory textbooks on Islam and on Middle Eastern history, thus failing to capture the social, intellectual, and religious realities of Islamic history.

If one attempts to incorporate Muslim women, and women in the Twelver Shi'i tradition in particular, into this model, the question then becomes to which 'classes' of claimants of authority can women belong? The answer is

---

[7] MacDonald, *The Development of Muslim Theology, Jurisprudence and Constitutional Theory*, 215–241.

[8] For an overview, see Edmund Burke, *The Ethnographic State: France and the Invention of Moroccan Islam* (Berkeley: University of California Press, 2014), 106–107, 169–182. Michael Brett expands the model to include four types of holy men, and thus religious authority, in 'Mufti, Murabit, Marabout and Mahdi: 4 Types in the Islamic History of North Africa', *Revue des Mondes Musulmans et de la Méditerranée* 29 (1980): 5–15.

[9] Michael Cooperson, *Classical Arabic Biography: The Heirs of the Prophet in the Age of al-Ma'mūn* (Cambridge: Cambridge University Press, 2000).

to almost all of them, despite the fact that scholarship and public perception have only begun to recognise this as a possibility. Nearly all classic accounts of religious authority in Islam assume that the holders of religious authority are male.[10] Yet, while women have never been Imams in the Islamic tradition, they have been rulers, jurists, theologians, and hadith experts, and they have played significant roles in shaping Islamic scholarly traditions throughout the centuries. Furthermore, even if they have not been very prevalent within a particular category, it is important to realize that they are not theoretically excluded. Of women's participation in these classes of claimants to religious authority, their role as scholars of hadith is that which has been emphasised in research to date.[11] Ruth Roded, Jonathan Berkey, Renate Jacobi, and Mohammad Akram Nadwi have surveyed biographical dictionaries of the tenth to fifteenth centuries, bringing to light evidence of hundreds of women who participated in the transmission of hadith. Some of these were accomplished and erudite, and some gained great fame, being recognised as *musnidas*, that is, 'supports' or 'anchors' who guaranteed the transmission of revered texts to entire subsequent generations.[12] Irene Schneider and Asma Sayeed have also drawn attention to the hundreds of women identified as

---

[10] For an overview of the literature, indicative of the assumed male gender of Islamic authority, see Gudrun Krämer and Sabine Schmidtke (eds), *Speaking for Islam: Religious Authorities in Muslim Societies* (Leiden: Brill, 2006); Nikki R. Keddie (ed.), *Scholars, Saints, and Sufis. Muslim Religious Institutions in the Middle East since 1500* (Berkeley: University of California Press, 1972) (with the exception of the chapter by Fernea and Fernea); Hamid Dabashi, *Authority in Islam. From the Rise of Muhammad to the Establishment of the Umayyads* (New Brunswick, NJ: Transaction Publishers, 1989); Stephen Humphreys, 'A Cultural Elite. The Role and Status of the 'Ulama in Islamic Society', in *Islamic History. A Framework for Inquiry*, rev. edn (Princeton: Princeton University Press, 1991), 187–208; Muhammad Qasim Zaman, *The Ulama in Contemporary Islam. Custodians of Change* (Princeton: Princeton University Press, 2002); Wael B. Hallaq, *Authority, Continuity, and Change in Islamic Law* (New York: Cambridge University Press, 2001).

[11] For an early review by twentieth-century scholars on women as *muhaddithat*, see Ignaz Goldziher, 'Women in Hadith Literature', in *Muslim Studies*, vol. II, ed. S. M. Stern (Chicago: Aldine Publications Co., 1968), 366–368, who notes that '*musnidas* are common up to about the tenth [sixteenth CE] century, and [that] this title occurs very frequently in the lists of authentications in manuscripts and in *ijazas*.'

[12] Khaled Abou El Fadl, for example, notes, 'it appears that certain families from Damascus, Cairo, and Baghdad made a virtual tradition of training female transmitters and narrators, and that these female scholars regularly trained and certified male and female jurists and therefore played a major contributing role in the preservation and transmission of Islamic traditions'. Khaled Abou El Fadl, 'Legal and Jurisprudential Literature: 9th to 15th Century', *Encyclopedia of Women & Islamic Cultures*, 1: 27–41. In his overview of the history of women as hadith scholars, Mohammad Akram Nadwi shows that 'in the formative period of Islam, the period of the Companions and Successors, women scholars are not only great in number but also great in prominence [and] great in their authority. Men go to them to learn, and doing so is normal.' Mohammad Akram Nadwi, *Al-Muhaddithat: The Women Scholars in Islam* (London: Interface Publications, 2007).

outstanding teachers and scholars of hadith and have examined their roles and accomplishments in the transmission of knowledge.[13]

Less attention has been accorded to women's historical role as jurists in Islamic societies.[14] Khaled Abou El Fadl has called attention to women who are described as jurists (*faqīhāt*) by later sources, and who authored works and became fully qualified legal authorities.[15] Most legal literature, both in Shi'i and Sunni Islam, does not restrict women from reaching the status of a *mujtahida* or *muftiya*, a fully qualified jurist capable of granting legal opinions to lay believers.[16] This may be surprising to outsiders, who expect the system to be entirely patriarchal and repressive of women on principle. A recent textbook, for example, claims that the legal term *ijmā'* 'refers solely to the consensus of male scholars'.[17] A more accurate definition would be 'the consensus of fully qualified jurists' – women are not excluded, for Islamic legal theorists across the board hold that they may indeed become fully qualified jurists. The Sunni jurists Ibn Hazm (d. 1064), Abu Ishaq al-Shirazi (d. 1083), Abu Hamid al-Ghazali, and others do not include masculinity (*dhukūra*) as a requirement for *ijtihād*. In the history of Shi'i jurisprudence, al-Sharif al-Murtada (d. 1044), al-Shaykh al-Tusi (d. 1067), al-Muhaqqiq

---

[13] See Ruth Roded, *Women in Islamic Biographical Collections. From Ibn Sa'd to Who's Who* (Boulder: Lynne Rienner Publishers, 1994); Irene Schneider, 'Gelehrte Frauen des 5./11. bis 7./13. Jh.s nach dem biographischen Werk des Dhahabi (st. 748/1347)', in *Philosophy und Arts in the Islamic World. Proceedings of the 18th Congress of L'Union Européenne des Arabisants et Islamisants held at the Katholieke Universiteit Leuven (Sept. 3–9, 1996)*, eds U. Vermeulen and D. de Smet (Leuven: Peeters, 1998), 107–121; Jonathan Berkey, *The Transmission of Knowledge in Medieval Cairo: A Social History of Islamic Education* (Princeton: Princeton University Press, 1992); Richard W. Bulliet, 'Women and the Urban Religious Elite in the Pre-Mongol Period', in *Women in Iran, From the Rise of Islam to 1800*, eds Guity Neshat and Lois Beck (Champaign: University of Illinois Press, 2003), 68–79; Renate Jacobi, 'Der Gelehrte und die Dichterin. Eine Seelenfreundschaft im mamlukischen Ägypten', in *Studien zur Semitistik und Arabistik. Festschrift für Hartmut Bobzin*, eds Otto Jastrow, Shabo Talay, and Herta Hafenrichter (Wiesbaden: Harrassowitz, 2008), 183–203; Renate Jacobi, 'Gelehrte Frauen im islamischen Spätmittelalter', in *Nonne, Königin, Kurtisane: Wissen, Bildung und Gelehrsamkeit von Frauen in der frühen Neuzeit*, eds Michaela Hohkamp and Gabriele Jancke (Königstein: Helmer, 2004), 225–246; and Roswitha Badry, 'Zum Profil weiblicher 'Ulama' in Iran: Neue Rollenmodelle für "islamische Feministinnen"?', *Die Welt des Islams* XL.1 (March 2000), 7–40.

[14] Note that women's role here is comparatively unparalleled in the other Abrahamic religions, specifically in the redaction of Hebrew Bible, Talmud, and New Testament.

[15] See Abou El Fadl, 'Legal and Jurisprudential Literature', 40.

[16] Karen Bauer, *Gender Hierarchy in the Qurān: Medieval Interpretations, Modern Responses* (Cambridge: Cambridge University Press, 2013). For juristic opinions on whom women may lead in prayer, see Christopher Melchert, 'Whether to Keep Women Out of the Mosque: A Survey of Medieval Islamic Law', in *Authority, Privacy and Public Order in Islam. Proceedings of the 22nd Congress of L'Union Européenne des Arabisants et Islamisants*, eds B. Michalak-Pikulska and A. Pikulski (Leuven: Peeters, 2006), 59–69.

[17] Aaron Hughes, *Muslim Identities: An Introduction to Islam* (New York: Columbia University Press, 2013), 145.

al-Hilli (d. 1325), Muhammad Baqir al-Wahid al-Bihbahani (d. 1791), al-Shaykh Murtada al-Ansari (d. 1864) and Muhammad Kazim al-Khorasani (d. 1911) all did not include masculinity as a requirement for *ijtihād*. The same is true in the twentieth century for al-Muhaqqiq al-Isfahani (d. 1946), Muhsin al-Hakim (d. 1970), and Muhammad Mahdi Shams al-Din (d. 2001). It is only a number of Shi'i jurists from the twentieth century who stipulate that a fully qualified jurist must be male, such as Muhammad Kazim al-Yazdi (d. 1919), Shaykh Abdul-Karim Haeri Yazdi (d. 1937), and Sayyid Hossein Borujerdi (d. 1961). Despite this new trend, the original opinion, according to which a fully qualified jurist need not be male, continues to be the dominant opinion to date.[18] The story of women's involvement in the history of Islamic legal scholarship is only beginning to be told, and so are those of women's roles as rulers, preachers, Sufi masters, and so on.

Women's Religious Leadership, Women's Islamic Authority

To date, no monograph or collection exists on the topic of Women's Religious Authority in Shi'i Islam. While questions concerning the conceptualisation of authority in Islam have been one of the focal points of the discipline of Islamic Studies in recent years (see footnote 10), the present state of research does not allow for broader conclusions about women's religious authority in Shi'i Islam or in Islam more generally. There has been a significant growth in publications on aspects of female religious authority in modern Islam over the past ten years, however. The most comprehensive of these has been a volume edited by Masooda Bano and Hilary Kalmbach, *Women, Leadership and Mosques: Changes in Contemporary Islamic Authority* (Leiden: Brill, 2012), which brought together case studies on (mostly Sunni) female religious authorities from Asia, the Middle East, Europe, North America, and Africa in the twentieth century. Also mostly dealing with examples from the Sunni world and with a focus on contemporary figures is a special issue on 'Muslim women and the challenge of authority', edited by Juliane Hammer and Riem Spielhaus, in *The Muslim World* 103.3 (2013), 287–431. Both collections, particularly the very substantial first one, have covered previously blank spots on the map of Islamic female authority. Yet, neither engages with examples of female religious authority from the classical and medieval periods (other than contemporary appropriations of these). Furthermore, neither study attempts to formulate hypotheses as to why female religious authorities are to be found more in some geographic and temporal contexts than in others.

---

[18] See Haydar Hubb Allah, 'al-Mar'a wa-marja'iyyat al-iftā': Dirāsa fiqhiyya istidlāliyya ḥawl shar'iyyat taqlīd al-mar'a', in Haydar Hubb Allah, *Dirāsāt fi al-fi qh al-islāmi al-mu'āsīr,* 5 vols (Beirut: Dar al-Fiqh al-Islami al-Mu'asir, 2011), 1:203–1:255.

Beside the two mentioned collections, a number of scholars have undertaken case studies of individual women who exerted Islamic authority or were held up as authoritative figures in particular time periods. In the field of anthropology, recent examples include Azam Torab, who has studied women prayer leaders in post-1980 Tehran, Faried Saenong, who has examined female preachers in contemporary Jakarta, and Nor Ismah, whose research has focused on Indonesia's newly instituted educational programmes in training women to issue fatwas.[19] In the field of Islamic Studies, Mona Hassan has written on women *vaizler* (preachers) in contemporary Turkey, Meriem el Haitami on the *murshidat* of Morocco, and Maryam Rutner on Iran's foremost *mujtahida* in the twentieth century, Nosrat Amin (d. 1983).[20] In religious studies, Juliane Hammer has written about female prayer leaders among American Muslims, and Nelly van Doorn on the women's wings of Indonesia's large Islamic organisations.[21] With regard to pre-modern women, some significant studies have appeared, including Asma Sayeed's examination of the evidence regarding Shi'i female hadith transmitters between the eleventh and eighteenth centuries; Behnam Sadeghi's study of juristic opinions on whether, when, and whom women may lead in prayer; and Khalid A. Sindawi's study of the figure of Fidda, the slave-servant of Fatima.[22]

Apart from the growing scholarly interest in examples of women exercising religious authority in Islam, recent policy initiatives add to the growing interest in the phenomenon of female religious authority. Over the last fifteen years, a number of Muslim states have initiated programmes that

---

[19] Azam Torab, *Performing Islam: Gender and Ritual in Iran* (Leiden: Brill, 2006); Faried Saenong, 'Women's Religious Education: Indonesia', *Encyclopedia of Women and Islamic Cultures,* first published online: 2016. Consulted online on 14 January 2017 <http://dx.doi.org/10.1163/1872-5309_ewic_COM_002089>; Nor Ismah, 'Destabilising Male Domination: Building Community-Based Authority among Indonesian Female Ulama', *Asian Studies Review* 40.4 (2016), 491–509.

[20] Mona Hassan, 'Women Preaching for the Secular State: Official Female Preachers (Bayan Vaizler) in Contemporary Turkey', *International Journal of Middle East Studies* 40.3 (2001), 451–473; Meriem el-Haitami, 'Women in Morocco: Reconceptualizing Religious Activism', *American Journal of Islamic Social Sciences,* 30.4 (2014); Maryam Rutner, 'Religious Authority, Gendered Recognition, and Instrumentalization of Nusrat Amin in Life and after Death', *Journal of Middle East Women's Studies* 11.1 (2015), 24–41.

[21] Juliane Hammer, *American Muslim Women, Religious Authority, and Activism: More Than a Prayer* (Austin: University of Texas Press, 2013); Nelly van Doorn, *Women Shaping Islam: Indonesian Muslim Women Reading the Qur'an* (Champaign-Urbana: University of Illinois Press, 2006).

[22] Asma Sayeed, 'Women in Imāmī Biographical Collections', pp. 81–97 in Michael Cook, Najam Haider, Intisar Rabb, and Asma Sayeed (eds), *Law and Tradition in Classical Islamic Thought: Studies in Honor of Professor Hossein Modarressi* (New York: Palgrave Macmillan, 2013); Asma Sayeed, *Women and the Transmission of Religious Knowledge in Islam* (Cambridge: Cambridge University Press, 2013); Behnam Sadeghi, *The Logic of Law-Making. Women and Prayer in the Islamic Legal Tradition* (Cambridge: Cambridge University Press, 2013); Khalid A. Sindawi, 'Fiḍḍa l-Nūbiyya: The Woman and her Role in Early Shī'ite History', *Al-Masāq: Journal of the Medieval Mediterranean* 21.3 (2009), 269–287.

train women in aspects of religious authority: cases in point are the *murshidat* programme in Morocco, the appointment of female judges in religious courts of the West Bank, in Israel, as well as in Malaysia, and the proclamation of grand muftis in several Gulf states that women should be trained in *iftā'* with the goal of eventually appointing them to national *iftā'-councils.*[23] Mirjam Künkler and David Kloos published a special issue in the *Asian Studies Review* that compares such recent state initiatives with longer running community programmes that train and certify female Islamic leaders in Southeast Asia.[24]

A shortcoming of extant studies is that they focus nearly exclusively on women in one place (typically Cairo, Damascus, Baghdad, or Nishapur) and usually around a relatively short time frame (about thirty to 100 years), and thus can offer neither diachronic accounts nor analyses of geographic variation. For example, cursory evidence suggests that – unlike their Mamluk counterparts – women in the Persianate world were not excluded from the *madrasa* environment and that they also more frequently engaged in juristic scholarship than their Arab contemporaries. For the case of modern Shi'ism, evidence suggests that women were referred to as jurists in the Iranian context from the sixteenth century onwards, but only more rarely in the Shi'i communities of what are today Iraq, Lebanon, and Bahrain, raising the question of whether the Iranian context, and not necessarily the Shi'i context, may be more accepting of, or conducive to, female participation in scholarship in the religious sciences.

This Volume

This volume comprises, in addition to this introduction, a general overview of the issue of female religious authority in Islamic history and eleven focused studies that treat specific instances or aspects of female religious authority in Twelver Shi'i contexts. In 'Forgotten Histories of Female Religious Authority in Islam', Mirjam Künkler presents a survey of various instances in which Muslim women, both Sunni and Shi'i, have become learned in the Islamic religious sciences and wielded religious authority, concentrating on women hadith experts and women jurists, although she refers as well to women rulers such as Gawhar Shad Bigum (d. 1457), the sovereign famous for construction of Herat's Friday Mosque. Overall, she makes the point that the frequent near-complete neglect of women as religious authorities throughout the Islamic world during the various historical periods is belied by an objective consideration of the evidence on the ground, whether historical

[23] Mirjam Künkler, *Women as Religious Authorities: What A Forgotten History Means for the Modern Middle East.* Issue brief no. 10.02.18. Rice University's Baker Institute for Public Policy, Houston, Texas, October 2018.

[24] Mirjam Künkler and David Kloos (eds), *Asian Studies Review* 40.4 [Special Issue: Studying Female Islamic authority: From Top-Down to Bottom-Up Modes of Certification] (2016), 479–599.

or contemporary. Rather than a general absence of the phenomenon, there is great diversity across time and space regarding the question of whether women were regarded as religious authorities, and if so, in what function precisely and to what effect. She ends with a plea for the programmatic examination of the factors that enable women to wield authority in some Islamic contexts but not in others.

The remaining chapters of this volume address specific episodes, instances, or portrayals of female religious authority in the Twelver Shiʿi tradition, organized in approximate chronological order. Yasmin Amin examines the figure of Umm Salama, one of the Prophet's wives who is lauded in the Shiʿi tradition for her devotion to the *ahl al-bayt*, the Prophet's descendants. She plays a key role in establishing the legitimate succession of ʿAli b. Abi Talib to the position of leadership of the Muslim community, as well as subsequent successions. Her case is one of many instances in which the women associated with the *ahl al-bayt* play a vital part in preserving the *naṣṣ* or explicit designation of a successor that guaranteed the proper unfolding of the historical Imamate.

Alyssa Gabbay discusses Fatima's *khuṭba* or oration, a manifesto of protest against the historical injustice inflicted on her and her descendants by the Caliph Abu Bakr (632–634) when he decided not to grant her the right to inherit the oasis of Fadak from her father's – the Prophet Muhammad's – property. The text is likely apocryphal but nevertheless old, being attributed to the eighth-century historian Abu Mikhnaf (d. 773–774) and also preserved in the ninth-century anthology *Balāghāt al-nisā'* by Ibn Abi Tahir Tayfur (d. 893). This text portrays Fatima not only as a staunch defender of the rights of the *ahl al-bayt* but also as an astute interpreter of Islamic scripture and law. It is indeed on the basis of this text that Fatima has been held up as a model of female religious authority in subsequent Shiʿi tradition.

Liyakat Takim's contribution focuses on female companions of the Imams. Ironically, the companions of the Imams, designated by the technical term *rijāl* (literally 'men'), also include women, who number among the revered figures whose biographical notices are recorded by authors of the tenth and eleventh centuries. These female companions serve important roles as witnesses to the historical events connected with the unfolding of the Imamate, as actors privy to the Imams' intimate intentions regarding succession, as custodians of the Imams' secret possessions, and especially as transmitters of the Imams' knowledge and therefore bearers of Islamic canonical tradition and embodiments of correct juridical praxis.

Robert Gleave discusses the historical debates in the Twelver Shiʿi legal tradition over the question of whether women can serve as judges. While it is agreed by many Twelver authorities that women are able to attain the rank of fully qualified jurists and to grant legal opinions, the majority opinion has been that, even if they reach the level of fully qualified jurists, women may not serve as judges in the courtroom. After examining Shiʿi arguments against women's right to serve as judges, Gleave finds that though the

Twelver Shi'i position differs little from that of Sunni jurists, the manner in which they frame their discussion differs considerably, for they are much more reluctant to state outright that women are fundamentally deficient in their intellect, something their Sunni counterparts do quite frequently. This may suggest a sensitivity to the topic of female religious authority in the Shi'i tradition, based on an awareness of outstanding examples of women's historical performance of legal authority, such as the example of Fatima's *khuṭba* discussed above.

Devin J. Stewart analyses the debate of Husniyya, a text that was composed in Safavid Iran in the sixteenth century but attributed to the twelfth-century scholar Abu al-Futuh al-Razi, who is best known for his Persian commentary on the Qur'an, *Rawḍ al-jinān wa-rawḥ al-janān*. The text, a clever adaptation from the story of the slave-girl Tawaddud in *One Thousand and One Nights*, portrays a debate between Husniyya, a slave-girl who belonged to a third party but worked as a servant in the house of Ja'far al-Sadiq and became very learned through the instruction of the Imam, and the leading Sunni scholars during the time of the Abbasid Caliph Harun al-Rashid. Her resounding victory shows that even a slave woman could be imagined as taking on the role of expert theologian and jurist, proving the truth and superiority of Shi'i doctrine against Sunni opponents.

Michael Barry's chapter provides a commentary on the cover illustration of this book, which has been excerpted from a sixteenth-century painting by the Safavid master-painter Muhammadi of Herat. Inspired by the works of Bihzad, who rose to fame at the Timurid capital of Herat and went on to set the foundations of the artistic traditions of the Safavid court, Muhammadi produced his 'Seated Princess' *c.* 1565, probably for the Safavid prince Ibrahim, then governor of Khurasan. Barry argues that Layli, the princess in Muhammadi's painting and the beloved of Majnun, is portrayed here as the queen of heaven, a manifestation of the divine, in keeping with Ibn Arabi's theology of the feminine nature of God's essence (*dhāt*). Barry suggests that this is one of the rare examples in Islamic art in which a woman is portrayed as a figure possessing religious authority.

Yusuf Ünal examines works dedicated to princesses of the Safavid dynasty, finding that the authors and translators of these works regularly portrayed the princesses as religious and temporal authorities, supplementing their being cast – those who were unmarried, in any case – as brides of the Twelfth Imam in other contexts, connecting their own authority with that of the Imam of the Age while also allowing them to maintain autonomy, being free of obligations to an ordinary husband that their peers did not enjoy. The writers repeatedly styled the princesses as modern incarnations of Bilqis, the Queen of Sheba, and Mary, the mother of Jesus, and furthermore granted them titles such as *murawwij al-madhhab*, 'propagator of the sect', which ordinarily were reserved for the Safavid kings. These perhaps surprising titles and epithets, which cannot be dismissed as frivolous hyperbole, indicate an acceptance of female members of the Safavid dynasty as participants in the divinely sanctioned sovereignty accorded to the Shahs.

Mirjam Künkler and Roja Fazaeli discuss the lives and works of two prominent modern Iranian female *mujtahidāt*, Nosrat Amin (1886–1983) and Zohreh Sefati (1948–), asking how the status of a *mujtahida* compares to that of a *mujtahid* and how both have been affected by changes in religious education over the course of the twentieth century. Although these women are not alone, they are among a limited number of women who have completed a traditional education in Islamic jurisprudence and have been recognised by male scholars as having attained the rank of *ijtihād*. Both scholars have written extensively on Islamic topics, including law, hadith, and ethics, and both have granted certificates of study, or *ijāza*s, to female and male students. Overall, their examples show that there is a relatively strong tradition of female learning in the religious sciences in Iran, especially in comparison with the situation in most Sunni societies, and the opinions of Sefati are occasionally invoked in public debate over religious issues. Nevertheless, the accomplishments of Nosrat Amin and Zohreh Sefati were only possible because of extraordinary efforts in learning they both made, defying predominant educational policies. Indeed, the fact that Iran's largest contemporary women's *ḥawza*, Jāmi'at al-Zahrā', originally designed to produce graduates who had completed all three levels of the *ḥawza* curriculum, was subsequently demoted to an institution devoted to the production of women graduates focused on *tablīgh* or proselytisation, suggests a restriction of opportunities for women to attain juristic authority.

Raffaele Mauriello discusses the figure of Amina Bint al-Huda, the sister of the Iraqi Shi'i scholar Muhammad Baqir al-Sadr, who was executed along with her brother by Saddam Husayn on 8 April 1980. Amina was not only a religious teacher and author on Islamic topics. Mauriello makes the provocative argument that, besides becoming Iraq's leading female social movement leader in the twentieth century, Bint al-Huda functioned de facto as a *wakīl*, or agent, for her brother's aspiring *marja'iyya*. Her learning and her choice of career path, along with her decision not to marry, made it possible for her to work closely with her brother in a capacity generally reserved for male authority figures.

Edith Szanto examines the case of female teachers in a contemporary women's seminary in the shrine-town of Sayyida Zaynab, fifteen kilometres south of Damascus, Syria. Having conducted ethnographic research at the Zaynabiyya, a Shi'i religious educational institution dedicated to the teaching of women that was founded in 1973 by the Iraqi scholar Sayyid Hasan Shirazi, Szanto asks what determines whether the path of becoming a teacher in one of the seminaries was available to a woman or not. Her study shows an important distinction between women teachers, termed *'ālimāt*, and women religious performers, termed *mullayāt*. The former have significant potential to act as scholarly authorities, while the latter do not. Her analysis of education and behaviour in the Zaynabiyya suggests that women's capacity to act as effective religious authorities hinges on their embodiment of *'aql kāmil*, 'perfect reason', or 'fully developed rational capacity', which entails not just rational or scholastic understanding but also sensitivity, practicality, and ethics. Against the background of this particular understanding of reason, female religious authority must be traditional and charismatic and is restricted to female members of scholarly families who do not challenge male authority, because their relationship with male authorities is itself taken as evidence of their general qualifications.

Maryam Rutner discusses two women's seminaries in contemporary Iran, the Rayhaneh al-Nabi Seminary in Shiraz and the al-Zahra Seminary in Estehban, a small town about 200 kilometres southeast of Shiraz, which are both part of what may be the largest programme for women's religious education in the world, built up by the Islamic Republic of Iran since the 1990s. Examining administration, curriculum, and organization, she provides valuable documentation regarding the content and design of education at these institutions, revealing that they include four levels of instruction, each with distinct goals in terms of thematic focus, societal function, and politics. Most graduates of the first two levels do not continue their studies in the Islamic Sciences and are rather intent on getting a general education. Fewer than 10 per cent of the students continue on to the third level, in which they pursue focused study on religious topics and concentrate on particular branches of Islamic knowledge, including law, theology, and Qur'anic commentary. The fourth level involves advanced training in Islamic law, paralleling the studies undertaken by male students who intend to become *mujtahids*, or fully qualified jurists. Rutner reports that the students and staff intend to produce female jurists or *mujtahidāt* at this level, but the number of students who reach it is currently small, and it is too early to evaluate the effectiveness of this programme. Finally, Rutner discusses the expansion and reform of women's education in the Shi'i seminaries. Despite state attempts to standardise curricula and control the substantive content of women's religious training, she suggests that these have been successful only to a limited degree. She further demonstrates that assessments of women's Islamic authority cannot be divorced from the interpretations that they propagate.

The essays included in this volume cover a wide range in terms of time, space, source material investigated, and forms of religious authority. Chronologically, they cover all of Islamic history, from the time of the Prophet Muhammad and the nascent Muslim community until the present day. Geographically, they are concentrated in the central lands of the Islamic world, treating historical episodes that unfold in the Hejaz, Iraq, Iran, and Syria. They draw on hadith literature, biographical works, anthologies, legal compendia, polemical texts, dedicated treatises, modern institutional records, participant observation, and paintings. They treat women members of the Family of the Prophet, other women who are associated with the households of the Imams, companions of the Imams, women as hadith-transmitters, judges, jurists, and theologians, women as royal members of Shi'i dynasties, women as religious teachers and guides, and women as agents of leading jurists.

Overall, the studies assembled here demonstrate that Twelver Shi'ism presents a long and variegated tradition of prominent women figures, whether revered religious icons, historical personages, fictional characters, or combinations of all three, that played important roles with regard to religious authority. Like their male counterparts, these women fall into several societal categories that have claimed and wielded different types of religious authority, except the Imamate itself. They range from being a source of hadith (Fatima), to preserving and transmitting hadith (for example, Fatima, 'A'isha, Umm Hani, Umm Aslam, and Hakima, daughter of the ninth Imam), narrating esoteric secrets (for example, Umm Sa'id), delivering a *khuṭba* (for example, Fatima), serving as a leader of the caravan for hajj (for example, Bint al Huda), teaching women (for example, Amina Begum, Bint al-Huda, Nosrat Amin, Zohreh Sefati), representing a *marja' al-taqlid* as a *wakil* (Bint al-Huda), engaging in scholarly works (for example, Amina Begum, Nosrat Amin, Sedigheh Vasmaghi), establishing religious schools for women (Nosrat Amin), and holding important positions in religio-political institutions (for example, Zohreh Sefati and Fariba 'Alasvand).

The study of these figures reveals a number of recurrent themes with regard to female religious authority. Access to education, networks of influence, and religious authority itself is often gained through or facilitated by male relatives and family connections. Women who belong to important scholarly families and can be taught by their fathers or brothers are much more likely to become scholars themselves than women without such ties. Historically, religious knowledge was transmitted from a master to a disciple, and it was the responsibility of a master to verify that his or her knowledge was passed on to the disciple. This interpersonal transmission system, together with the lack of public places for women to learn, discouraged many from studying. Inevitably, women's learning seldom took place outside the boundaries of a family, which is why the female scholars whose names appear in the biographical literature are primarily the daughters or wives of established male scholars. The situation significantly changed in the late twentieth century. The introduction of female seminaries since the 1980s has opened up new opportunities for women who seek Islamic knowledge (for example, in Iran and Syria). Nevertheless, in most cases the deficient quality of the type of training offered in these seminaries has meant that religious authority and the prevalent culture of learning remain male-dominated.

Beside facilitating access to educational programmes, family connections emerge as an important factor for two other reasons. First, they can endow women with a pious, devout, and faithful reputation by association with male family members who are themselves reputed to have these qualities. To develop a voice and gather a following and/or students is impossible without an immaculate reputation. Second, gaining religious authority depends on having one's expertise recognised by the predominantly male body of contemporary scholars. Under a system constituted by the interpersonal transmission of knowledge, it is the responsibility of a master to vouch for and certify the acquisition of certain knowledge by the disciple. This limits women's opportunities to be recognised as possessors of knowledge, simply because, with the exception of those women in scholarly clerical families, few others have the type of access such relationships require.

The studies in this volume also bring out the important point that even within one mode of authority, subsidiary authorities exist. As Liyakat Takim shows, the companions of the Imams are recognised as loci of authority because of their close contact with the Imam. This is a type of authority, even if it is understood to be derivative from and subordinate to that of the living, present Imam. Yasmin Amin's study of Umm Salama, Alyssa Gabbay's study of Fatima's oration, Liyakat Takim's discussion of the female companions of the Imams, and Devin J. Stewart's discussion of the debate of Husniyya show that women were able to gain this type of subsidiary authority and were closely allied with and supported the Imamate, in addition to gaining authority on account of their knowledge of law and other fields. One may argue that there existed an expanded conception of the Imamate in which other members of the Holy Family participated, including female members, most obviously Fatima, but also some of the wives of the Prophet such as Umm Salama, other relatives and members of the extended family such as Fatima's servant Fidda, and other wives, slaves, and servants of later Imams. In addition, because of various societal institutions, the authority that women attained was often mediated through men and subordinate to them. This subordination was not categorical, and women sometimes came to the fore, particularly during crises or trying circumstances. It is striking that after women were able to become learned, they often worked to teach other women, establishing female-to-female educational institutions or networks of learning.

To formulate some tentative comparative conclusions, it appears that – at least judging from what we know at present – women's participation in religious authority as jurists has been significantly more important in the Twelver Shiʿi tradition, particularly in modern history, and especially in Iran, than it has in Sunni societies, while their participation in the transmission of hadith during the medieval period was significantly less substantial than that of their Sunni counterparts. The main reason for this difference has to do with relative differences between Twelver Shiʿi and Sunni Islam with regard to the cultivation of the various religious sciences. For many centuries in the medieval period, the study of hadith was relatively ignored in Twelver Shiʿi circles, and scholars focused on the study of the law per se, making do with consultation of the canonical Shi'i works of the *akhbār* as source material. Interest in the focused study of hadith was only revived in the sixteenth and seventeenth centuries. In contrast, the study of hadith was highly developed in many Sunni societies in the medieval and early modern periods, particularly in Iraq, Syria, Egypt, and the Hejaz, and even came to have a substantial social presence in public performances and dictation sessions, the likes of which are unknown in Shi'i contexts. The social capital associated with the acquisition of hadith expertise in Sunni societies was not matched by equivalent concern in Shi'i societies.

In contrast, the Shi'i tradition of legal study has shown remarkable strength and continuity over time, and it has maintained a social role and presence that surpasses those of its Sunni counterparts, particularly from the nineteenth century to the present day, and especially in Iran. The Twelver Shi'i legal system of education has survived into modern times more intact than it has in Sunni environments, and has by and large been spared the ravages wreaked by the confiscation of endowment properties by the modern nation-states of the Sunni Islamic world, mainly because the Shi'i institutions depended more on *khums* funds - essentially an income tax on the believers - than on endowments, and so could not be controlled as directly by governments.

It is reasonable to argue that the importance of the figure of Fatima in Shi'i tradition sets the stage for an enhanced emphasis on female religious authority. This is not surprising, given the evidence that the role of Fatima in Shi'i history has had specific effects on the Shi'i law of inheritance, so that a sole surviving daughter will inherit all of her father's wealth, whereas according to Sunni inheritance law she will inherit only half. Although Sunni religious tradition also accords a place to revered women of the early Muslim community, such as 'A'isha, the prophet's youngest and most influential wife, the legacy of Fatima is somewhat different because of her intimate connection with the legitimacy of the historical Imamate. It is through Fatima that the bloodline between the prophet and the later Shi'i imams is established, and it is for this reason that Shi'i traditions portray her as the one who transmits the Muhammadan light to them. Characteristically, her traditions and commentary on the Qur'an are considered to embody an authority comparable to that of the Imams. The issue of Fadak (a tract of land claimed by Fatima and her descendants) is not merely about Fatima's rights as a daughter of the Prophet but about the position of the *ahl al-bayt* in the Muslim community after the Prophet's passing, as well as the injustice of those members of the community who opposed and mistreated them. This pattern continued with other women descendants of the Prophet who played key roles in the succession of the Imams upon the demise of their predecessors. It may be argued that these revered women provided a salient model of religious authority for Shi'i women in general. Nevertheless, one should not exaggerate the social effects of this emphasis on women in the Shi'i tradition, for it was usually not so powerful that it overcame the social restrictions on women in Shi'i societies that limited their access to education and positions of power. Nevertheless, the legacy of Fatima, Zaynab, and other women of the *ahl al-bayt* made their stories available to the Shiʿi public, such that their examples could be invoked under the right circumstances and serve as inspiration to women of later generations. In addition, the fact that the holy family revered by Shiʿi believers expanded to include such figures as Fidda, the slave-servant of Fatima, who was the female counterpart of ʿAli's slave-servant Qanbar, and Husniyya, the servant of Jaʿfar al-Sadiq, allowed non-*sayyid* and non-Arab Shiʿi women to find inspiration in revered historical models as well.

The authority of noble women or women involved with royal courts may have been influenced by Mongol or Turkic dynastic models. It is known that Iran experienced the highest levels of Mongol influence in the Middle East. It bore the brunt of Hulagu's invasion, and the Ilkhanid dynasty (1258–1349), with its capital in Tabriz, lasted for nearly a century. In the Mongol and Turkic traditions, women in ruling families often participated openly and intensively in politics and were instrumental in succession disputes and other political conflicts.[25] In some senses, the Safavids, who entered onto the world stage when they conquered the former Ilkhanid capital from the Aqqoyunlu in 1501, kept up the Ilkhanid legacy in many ways, including adoption of the combined 'hijri-Turki' calendar with a cycle of twelve named years and the maintenance of an itinerant court. The pivotal roles played by certain women such as Pari Khan Khanum, the sister of Shah Tahmasb, may be linked to a tradition of political activity by noble women indebted to earlier Mongol and Turkic legacies.[26]

In envisaging the most promising areas for future research, one must confront the problem of sources. A survey of the biographical dictionaries of Twelver scholarly tradition leaves the impression that they provide only limited information about women scholars and that this has been extensively, if perhaps not exhaustively, explored by Asma Sayeed, Liyakat Takim, and Devin J. Stewart. It is clear that some of the women to whom entries were devoted engaged in teaching other women and serving as advisors to them on legal issues, but it must be admitted that the sources available to date do not allow investigators to determine anything more about their lives or activities. Unless new, less reticent sources are discovered, it is unlikely that this will change. The religious authority of Fatima and other women of the *ahl al-bayt* is a fertile area for further research because of the vast devotional and polemical literature devoted to the lives of the Imams and the early

---

[25] See Bruno De Nicola (ed.), *Women in Mongol Iran: The Khatuns, 1206–1335* (Edinburgh: Edinburgh University Press, 2017).

[26] Maria Szuppe, 'La participation des femmes de la famille royale à l'exercice du pouvoir en Iran safavide au XVIe siècle (Première Partie)', *Studia Iranica* 23.2 (1994), 211–258; Szuppe, 'La participation des femmes de la famille royale à l'exercice du pouvoir en Iran safavide au XVIe siècle (Seconde Partie)', *Studia Iranica* 24.1 (1995), 61–109.

history of the Islamic community. Even if many of the accounts are apocryphal, they reveal a great deal about the conceptions and contours of religious authority during the times when the accounts were created or compiled. The situation is somewhat different when one examines women scholars of the nineteenth and twentieth centuries, for more detailed sources on a number of women scholars from these periods exist, including their own writings. In the Iranian context, references to individual *mujtahidāt* and other women of extensive juristic authority point to potentially rich case studies that yet remain to be written, such as about the mother of Grand Ayatollah Borujerdi, a *mujtahida* in her own right, and the women of the Qazvini Baraqani family. Such case studies will benefit from drawing on sources that remain outside the public realm, such as oral histories and family archives. The investigation of royal or noble women, whether of the Safavid, Qajar, or other Shiʿi dynasties is also very promising, because of their relatively frequent appearance in court chronicles and other documents. Furthermore, as Yusuf Ünal's study shows, much information about them stems from works they sponsored or treatises dedicated to them. Information about women's religious authority in the Shiʿi tradition may also be derived from Sufi literature within the Shiʿi tradition and poetic works, including the biographical genre of *tadhkirat al-shuʿarāʾ*, two significant sub-traditions that have not been addressed in this volume. Moreover, Twelver Shiʿi legal literature is so vast that it is very likely that substantial discussions having to do with women and various questions related to legal authority have not yet been examined. Finally, modern institutions intended to provide a religious education to women and to form future women leaders in the field of religion present significant opportunities for future research.

To close, although the nineteenth and twentieth centuries have seen an increase in the number of women scholars who acquired *ijāza*s of *ijtihād*, and excelling in juristic thinking, the question remains open as to whether women can attain the highest religious statuses equal to those attained by men. In the Twelver Shiʿi tradition, religious authority hinges to a large extent also on the number of followers one succeeds in gathering, and women religious leaders still by and large lack a social following. Followers (*muqallid*s) not only enhance one's scholarly reputation but also contribute *khums* funds, which the religious leader may use to fund social and educational projects, and these in turn enhance his religio-social authority. Most believers, whether male or female, not only prefer male leaders; they also find the idea of following a female jurist unheard of. Muhammad Hussein Fadlallah of Lebanon and Grand Ayatollah Yousef Saneʿi of Iran number among the few scholars to have argued that women, too, can aspire to the *marjaʿiyya*.

CHAPTER

2

FORGOTTEN HISTORIES OF FEMALE RELIGIOUS AUTHORITY IN ISLAM

Mirjam Künkler

Introduction

Women are rarely associated with religious authority. As far as the Abrahamic religions are concerned, although women are known to have exercised religious authority at various points in the histories of Judaism, Christianity, and Islam, ruling orthodoxies have, for the most part, precluded women from obtaining the qualifications necessary for textual exegesis, as well as the authority to interpret religious law.

It is only in particular branches of these religions that women are recognised today as religious authorities. Among Jewish communities, the last few decades have witnessed an increase in the number of rabbinic schools that train women and prepare them for religious leadership.[1] Female rabbis have been ordained in Reform, Reconstructionist, and Conservative, but not Orthodox, Judaism.[2] In today's Roman Catholic Church, women

---

[1] An early Jewish community that permitted women to engage in higher scholarship was the Therapeutae, founded in Egypt before the first century CE. Some of its female members formed their own monastic establishments. See Julia Clancy Smith, 'Exemplary Women and Sacred Journeys: Women and Gender in Judaism, Christianity and Islam from late Antiquity to the Eve of Modernity', in *Women's History in Global Perspective*, vol. I, ed. Bonnie G. Smith (Champaign: University of Illinois Press, 2004), 107. Smith also writes of individual Jewish women in the Middle Ages who attained some rank of scholarship, such as 'the wives of rabbis Dulce and Urania of Worms [who in the twelfth and thirteenth century CE Germany] achieved considerable learning and acted as prayer leaders for circles of Jewish women, although both were empowered by association with revered religious leaders'. Ibid., 108.

[2] The reform movement began to ordain women as rabbis in 1972, the reconstructionist in 1977 and conservative communities in 1983. See Simon Greenberg (ed.), *The Ordination of Women as Rabbis: Studies and Response* (New York: The Jewish Theological Seminary of America, 1988); and Pamela Nadell, *Women Who Would be Rabbis: A History of Women's Ordination 1889–1985* (Boston: Beacon Press, 1998).

are excluded from priestly authority,[3] although according to literary and epigraphic evidence, women did serve as priests during the fourth and fifth centuries CE.[4] Moreover, until at least the ninth century CE, the Western Church knew ordained female deacons, and in the Eastern Church the ordination of female deacons was in place for even longer. In the twentieth century, several Anglican churches started to open the ministry for women, as did – at the end of the twentieth century – the Old Catholic Churches of the Union of Utrecht.[5] Many Protestant denominations have since the 1970s started to train and certify women as pastors, and opened leadership positions to women, such as seats of bishoprics.[6]

In most contemporary Muslim societies, women face great obstacles to serve as religious leaders – be it as fatwa-issuing muftis, judges of religious law, teachers in institutions of higher religious learning, or scholars

---

[3] Women's role within the emerging Christian church became restricted very early. As Julia Clancy Smith writes, 'by the end of the first Christian century, bishops and laymen increasingly restricted women's church roles. Orthodoxy rested upon eliminating female preaching and teaching, an idea found in the contested Deutero-Pauline letters, which also negatively portray women's nature.' Smith, 'Exemplary Women and Sacred Journeys', 114.

[4] Although the Roman Catholic Church since then never again recognised women as priests, the Second Vatican Council (1962–1965) had an empowering effect on women serving in the Catholic Church, in so far as women have since been permitted to 'act as Eucharistic ministers, as chancellors of dioceses, and as lectors'. There is of course also a more recent history of intra-Catholic advocacy in favour of women's ordination. The Pontifical Biblical Commission in 1976 concluded that there is no biblical reason to prohibit women's ordination. See Gary Macy, *The Hidden History of Women's Ordination: Female Clergy in the Medieval West* (Oxford: Oxford University Press, 2008). In response, the Sacred Congregation for the Doctrine of the Faith during the same year issued a document ('Inter Insigniores') that explicated the reasons why ordination should be reserved to men. In 1994, Pope John Paul II tried to silence the discussion with 'Ordinatio Sacerdotalis' in that he once again affirmed the doctrinal position of the Church. To finally put the advocacy for female priesthood to rest, the Congregation for the Doctrine of the Faith on 29 May 2008 issued a statement reaffirming 'women priests and the bishops who ordain them will be excommunicated *latae sententiae*'. See 'Catholic Women March in Rome for Female Priesthood', *The New York Times*, 15 October 2008. In 2002, the Argentine Bishop Romulo Braschi ordained seven women and at least three others have been ordained since. All ordained women have since been excommunicated by the Roman Catholic Church. See *Roman Catholic Womenpriests* <http://www.romancatholicwomenpriests.org/index.htm>, last accessed 10 July 2009. Braschi had already distanced himself from the Roman Catholic Church in the 1970s and in 1975 set up an independent Catholic church.

[5] I thank Angela Berlis for pointing me to these developments. See also Angela Berlis, 'Women's Ordination in the Old Catholic Churches of the Union of Utrecht', in *Women and Ordination in the Christian Churches: International Perspectives*, eds Ian Jones, Kirsty Thorpe and Janet Wootton (London: T. & T. Clark – Continuum, 2008), 144–154.

[6] Even here one finds large variation. While the German Lutheran church, for instance, does not discriminate between men and women for any office within the church, the Lutheran church in Poland continues to exclude women from all clerical offices, although both Lutheran churches subscribe to the same theological tradition and see each other as part of the same interpretive school. Similarly, the Missouri Synod of the Lutheran church in the United States still does not ordain women, while most other North American Lutheran synods began ordination of female pastors in the 1970s.

of Islam – despite the fact that most schools of jurisprudence recognise women as muftis, and despite the fact that local Muslim cultures did recognise women as religious scholars and leaders over sometimes substantial periods of time. From the eighth to sixteenth centuries CE, women had a particularly prominent role to play as transmitters of hadiths, and although most schools of jurisprudence do not recognise women as judges, we know of female jurists who authored juristic treatises and were sought after as teachers and scholars of jurisprudence throughout Islamic history. More recently, governments of Muslim-majority countries have turned to promote women again as religious leaders through state-funded or state-supported programmes that train women as prayer leaders, muftis, or scholars.

This article highlights the diverse roles that women played in the transmission and production of religious knowledge over the course of Islamic history, and gives an overview of female religious leadership in modern Iran. The significant role of women in sustaining and shaping the scholarly tradition through the centuries is still little reflected in both scholarly and public perceptions. Nearly all classic accounts of religious authority in Islam proceed from the assumption that this authority is male.[7] The possibility that women might exercise various aspects of religious authority is usually not discussed. Yet, when we break down religious authority into its various manifestations (e.g., leading prayer, preaching, issuing fatwas, transmitting hadith, judging in court, shaping the Islamic scholarly tradition), nuances emerge that call the exclusively male character of religious authority in Islam into question. By drawing attention to and sketching the biographies of women in some of these roles with a focus on modern Iran, this article is motivated by the hope that more research will be dedicated in the future to the examination of their works and lives, in order to arrive at a more accurate and comprehensive picture of the contribution of women to the Islamic tradition, as well as the limits of this contribution.

---

[7] For an overview of the literature, see Gudrun Krämer and Sabine Schmidtke, 'Introduction' in *Speaking for Islam: Religious Authorities in Muslim Societies*, eds Gudrun Krämer and Sabine Schmidtke (Leiden: Brill, 2006); Hamid Dabashi, *Authority in Islam. From the Rise of Muhammad to the Establishment of the Umayyads* (New Brunswick, NJ: Transaction Publishers, 1989); Nikki R. Keddie (ed.), *Scholars, Saints, and Sufis. Muslim Religious Institutions in the Middle East since 1500* (Berkeley: University of California Press, 1972); Wael B. Hallaq, *Authority, Continuity, and Change in Islamic Law* (Cambridge: Cambridge University Press, 2001); Stephen Humphreys, 'A Cultural Elite. The Role and Status of the 'Ulama in Islamic Society', in *Islamic History. A Framework for Inquiry*, rev. edn (Princeton: Princeton University Press, 1991), 187–208; Muhammad Qasim Zaman, *The Ulama in Contemporary Islam. Custodians of Change* (Princeton: Princeton University Press, 2002).

Women Transmitting and Preserving the Tradition

Out of all the roles that women could occupy that relate to religious authority, their role as transmitters of hadiths is most thoroughly researched.[8] The in-depth studies of the biographical dictionaries of the tenth to fifteenth centuries by scholars such as Ruth Roded, Jonathan Berkey, Renate Jacobi, Mohammad Akram Nadwi, Khaled Abou El Fadl, Muhammad Zubayr Siddiqi, Devin Stewart, Irene Schneider, and Asma Sayeed, have catalogued the hundreds of women identified as outstanding teachers and scholars of hadith.[9] As Khaled Abou El Fadl notes, 'it appears that certain families from Damascus, Cairo, and Baghdad made a virtual tradition of training female transmitters and narrators, and that these female scholars regularly trained and certified male and female jurists and therefore played a major contributing role in the preservation and transmission of Islamic traditions'.[10]

---

[8] For an early review by twentieth-century scholars on women as *muḥaddithāt*, see Ignaz Goldziher, 'Women in Hadith Literature', in *Muslim Studies*, vol. II, ed. S. M. Stern (Chicago: Aldine Publications Co., 1968), 366–368, who notes that '*musnidas* are common up to about the tenth century [AH], and this title occurs very frequently in the lists of authentications in manuscripts and in *ijāzas*'. For other works on women as traditionists, see Huda Lutfi, 'Al-Sakhawi's Kitab al-Nisa as a Source for the Social and Economic History of Muslim Women during the Fifteenth Century, AD', *Muslim World* LXXI (1981), 104–124; Richard W. Bulliet, 'Women and the Urban Religious Elite in the Pre-Mongol Period', in *Women in Iran, From the Rise of Islam to 1800*, eds Guity Neshat and Lois Beck (Champaign: University of Illinois Press, 2003), 68–79; Elizabeth Sartain, *Jalal al-Din al-Suyuti: Biography and Background* (New York: Cambridge University Press, 1975), 125–127; Asma Sayeed, 'Women and Hadith Transmission Two Case Studies from Mamluk Damascus', *Studia Islamica* 95 (2002), 71–94.

[9] See Ruth Roded, *Women in Islamic Biographical Collections. From Ibn Sa'd to Who's Who* (Boulder: Lynne Rienner Publishers, 1994); Mohammad Akram Nadwi, *Al-Muḥaddithāt: The Women Scholars in Islam* (Oxford and London: Interface Publications, 2007); Irene Schneider, 'Gelehrte Frauen des 5./11. bis 7./13.Jh.s nach dem biographischen Werk des Dahabi (st. 748/1347)', in *Philosophy und Arts in the Islamic World. Proceedings of the 18th Congress of L'Union Européenne des Arabisants et Islamisants held at the Katholieke Universiteit Leuven (Sept. 3–9, 1996)*, eds U. Vermeulen and D. de Smet. (Leuven: Peeters, 1998), 107–121; Jonathan Berkey, *The Transmission of Knowledge in Medieval Cairo, A Social History of Islamic Education* (Princeton: Princeton University Press, 1992); Renate Jacobi, 'Der Gelehrte und die Dichterin. Eine Seelenfreundschaft im mamlukischen Ägypten' in *Studien zur Semitistik und Arabistik. Festschrift für Hartmut Bobzin*, eds Otto Jastrow, Shabo Talay, and Herta Hafenrichter (Wiesbaden: Harrassowitz, 2008), 183–203; Renate Jacobi, 'Gelehrte Frauen im islamischen Spätmittelalter', in *Nonne, Königin, Kurtisane: Wissen, Bildung und Gelehrsamkeit von Frauen in der frühen Neuzeit*, eds Michaela Hohkamp and Gabriele Jancke (Königstein: Ulrike Helme Verlag, 2004), 225–246; Muhammad Zubayr Siddiqi, *Hadith Literature: Its Origins, Development, and Special Features* (Cambridge: Islamic Texts Society, 1993), 117–123; Devin Stewart, 'Women's Biographies in Islamic Societies: Mirza 'Abd Allah al-Isfahani's Riyad al-'Ulama', in *Rhetoric of Biography: Narrating Lives in Persianate Societies*, ed. L. Marlow (Cambridge, MA: Harvard University Press, 2011); and Asma Sayeed, *Women and the Transmission of Religious Knowledge in Islam* (Cambridge: Cambridge University Press, 2013).

[10] Khaled Abou El Fadl, 'Legal and Jurisprudential Literature', *Encyclopedia of Women and Islamic Cultures*, 6 vols, ed. Souad Joseph (Leiden: Brill, 2003–2007), 1: 27–41, here p. 40.

Women's role of transmitting hadiths had its model in 'A'isha, the prophet's youngest wife, who had been such a prolific transmitter that Muhammad is said to have told followers they would receive 'half their religion' from a woman.[11] In his overview of the history of women as hadith scholars, *al-Muḥaddithāt,* Mohammad Akram Nadwi, shows that

> in the formative period of Islam, the period of the Companions and Successors, women scholars are not only great in number but also great in prominence [and] great in their authority. Men go to them to learn, and doing so is normal.[12]

The biographical dictionaries of the Damascene hadith scholar Muhammad Shams al-Din al-Dhahabi (d. 1347), the Cairene (Shafi'i) scholar Ibn Hajar al-'Asqalani (d. 1449), and of the Cairene historian Shams al-Din Muhammad ibn 'Abd al-Rahman al-Sakhawi (d. 1497) are particularly instructive.[13] The latter devoted an entire volume of his twelve-volume work *al-Ḍaw' al-lāmi' li-ahl al-qarn al-tāsi'* to female scholars, featuring 1,075 biographical entries.[14] By comparison, the compilations of al-Dhahabi and Ibn Hajar are modest in scope. In his work *Dhayl al-Durar al-kāmina,* Ibn Hajar includes 170 prominent women of the fourteenth century CE, under many of whom the author himself had studied.[15] Al-Dhahabi included in his twenty-four volume work *Siyar a'lām al-nubalā'* (The Lives of Noble Figures) the

---

[11] Some other female descendants of the prophet, such as his granddaughter Zaynab and his great-great-great-great-granddaughter Nafisah, are recognised as women of learning and wisdom.

[12] Mohammad Akram Nadwi, *Al-Muḥaddithāt: The Women Scholars in Islam* (Oxford and London: Interface Publications, 2007). Nadwi is in the process of writing a biographical dictionary of some 8,000 women scholars across the centuries in the field of hadith. His work shows that the phenomenon of female *muḥaddithāt* intensified in the thirteenth to fifteenth centuries CE. After the sixteenth century far fewer biographies are available of both female and male hadith scholars. According to Siddiqi, the last known female traditionist 'of the first rank who is known to us was Fatima al-Fudayliya, also known as al-Shaykha al-Fudayliya [d. 1831] . . . Towards the end of her life, she settled at Mecca, where she founded a rich public library. In the Holy City she was attended by many eminent traditionists, who attended her lectures and received certificates from her. Among them, one could mention in particular Shaykh Umar al-Hanafi and Shaykh Muhammad Sali.' See Muhammad Zubayr Siddiqi, *Hadith Literature* (Cambridge: Islamic Texts Society, 1993), 117–123, here 122–123.

[13] According to Berkey, at least 411 of these can be assumed to have received *ijāzas* or have been otherwise highly educated. See Jonathan Berkey, 'Women and Islamic Education in the Mamluk Period', in *Women in Middle Eastern History*, eds Nikkie Keddie and Beth Baron (New Haven: Yale University Press, 1991), 146.

[14] There is an unpublished MA thesis, written in 1982 at the University of Saarbrücken, Germany, by Angela Degand on Sakhawi's twelfth volume alone. The thesis was supervised by Renate Jacobi. To the best of my knowledge, until today Degand's is the most extensive analysis of Sakhawi's twelfth volume. Angela Degand, 'Untersuchungen zu einer Geschichte der Frauenbildung im islamischen Spätmittelalter anhand des 12. Bandes von as-Saḫāwī's biographischem Lexikon, *aḍ-Ḍau' al-lāmi' li-ahl al-qarn at-tāsi*'', Universität des Saarlandes, Saarbrücken, 1982.

[15] Ibn Hajar al-'Asqalani, *Dhayl al-Durar al-kāminah fī a'yān al-mi'ah al-thāminah* (Beirut: Dār al-Kutub al-'Ilmīyah, 1998).

biographies of ninety-three women, who served as teachers and transmitters of the tradition from the eleventh to the fifteenth centuries CE.[16]

Irene Schneider, who has studied al-Dhahabi's biographies of the women of the eleventh to thirteenth centuries CE, suggests that one can assume that *all* of the women portrayed were regarded in their lifetime as authoritative transmitters.[17] One woman, Fatima bint al-Zahid al-Nishaburiyya of Nishapur (d. 1087), is mentioned explicitly as having taught hadith sciences in the *madrasa* of her father. In this, she presents a remarkable exception for in the large majority of accounts women are known as teachers outside the *madrasa* system to which they usually did not have access. According to Wiebke Walther, she disputed with the most revered mystics of her time.[18] Others are described as important teachers of both male and female students, and detailed descriptions of seating orders suggest that genders were not spatially segregated, but that men and women, teacher and student, frequently sat side by side – an account that contrasts with Berkey's work on Cairo. There is also no evidence that these women transmitted or taught only gender-specific themes only.[19] Further, two of the Iranian traditionists are also explicitly mentioned as preachers: 'A'isha bint Hasan from Isfahan (d. 1068) and Fatima bint al-Baghdadi from Isfahan (d. 1144). While 'A'isha is described to have preached only in front of women, the same is not noted about Fatima, raising the question whether she may have preached in front of men, too.[20] One of the two most important

---

[16] See Schneider, 'Gelehrte Frauen des 5./11', 107–121. The biographies of women included amount to 2 per cent of all biographies that al-Dhahabi reviewed, most of which were of male contemporaries of the prophet. None of the twenty women studied served in official offices, such as administrators or judges.

[17] To illustrate this, Schneider, for instance, quotes Dhahabi as referring to Safiyya of Damascus (d. 1248) as *uḥtīja ilayha* – she was one 'who was needed' (for the transmission of the tradition).

[18] Wiebke Walther, *Die Frau im Islam* (Leipzig: Verlag Edition Leipzig, 1980), 80. Also available in English: Wiebke Walther, *Women in Islam* (Princeton: Markus Wiener., 1993).

[19] In translation, 'There is no evidence of gender-segregated training, or that women would have transmitted only "women-specific" knowledge.' Schneider, 'Gelehrte Frauen des 5./11', 118. Also: 'All enumerated facts therefore suggest that the mentioned women in this period did not only study in private, but that they indeed taught lessons that numerous male and female students took part in.' Ibid., 119. Schneider argues that the biographies indicate that the initiative to seek education usually stemmed from the father rather than the daughter/woman herself. Of the twenty women studied, seven hailed from Damascus and Baghdad, while most lived and worked in Iran, especially in Isfahan and Nishapur. Ibid., 108ff.

[20] For the case of Iran, Roswitha Badry notes that in Rajabi's compilation of 600 outstanding women in Persianate history, about 10 to 15 per cent are scholars and 20 per cent *muḥaddithāt* (and 35 per cent poetesses). Compare Muhammad Hasan Rajabi, *Mashahir-i Zanan-i Irani va Parsi-guyi az Aghaz ta Mashrutih.* (Tehran: Surush Press, 1995). More than half of the traditionists in this compilation lived in the eleventh/twelfth centuries CE. Many of these are mentioned in the travelogues of the Shafi'ite al-Sam'ani (1113–1166) – women whom he met in his travels to Isfahan and Nishapur. At least ten of these women are mentioned to have granted *ijāzas.* See Roswitha Badry, 'Zum Profil weiblicher "Ulama" in Iran: Neue Rollenmodelle für "islamische Feministinnen"?', *Die Welt des Islams* XL.1 (March 2000), 7–40.

teachers of hadith for al-Dhahabi was a woman herself: Zainab bint 'Umar b. al-Kindi.[21] The literature on women and Islamic education in Mamluk Egypt emphasises that women were known as teachers outside the *madrasa* system to which they usually did not have access.[22] The example of Fatima bint al-Zahid al-Nishaburiyya raises the question of whether the Iranian context was different from the Egyptian, and perhaps different from the rest of the Muslim world, in that women were indeed tolerated, and at times even had a firm place, in the *madrasa*.

As Jacobi and Berkey both note, out of all the roles in the field of Islamic scholarship, the transmission of hadiths was most accessible to women for several reasons. In contrast to instruction in the fields of law and theology, the *ijāza* system for hadith did not require intensive tutelage and thus allowed for less contact between teacher and student, which made the field particularly amenable to women.[23] Besides, hadith transmission required mastery of the language and grammar more than expertise in jurisprudential and theological questions – skills that women could acquire even if higher education was inaccessible to them.[24] Apart from the comprehensive anthology by Nadwi, the source material on *muḥaddithāt* is little explored to date and much research is needed to arrive at a more accurate picture of the role of women in the transmission of Islamic scholarship. In particular, it should be of great interest to explain the geographic variation in the phenomenon of women as hadith scholars across the Islamic world, and the intricacies of their participation in formal and informal Islamic education.

Women as Faqīhāt

Apart from transmitting religious knowledge, women could also exercise roles closer to the constitution of religious knowledge, as theologians, muftis, and jurists. As Khaled Abou El Fadl notes, 'in addition to the preservation and transmission of traditions, a careful reading of biographical dictionaries reveals a large number of women who are described as jurists (*faqīhāt*), and who are asserted to have attained a level of competence that qualified them to

---

[21] M. Bencheneb, J. de Somogyi, *al-Dhahabi*, vol. II (EfI), S. 214ff.

[22] On women in religious education during the Mamluk period (1250–1517), see Jonathan Berkey, *The Transmission of Knowledge in Medieval Cairo: A Social History of Islamic Education* (Princeton: Princeton University Press, 1992), 170f. Berkey relates that women were not in a position to become teachers in *madrasas* during the Mamluk time, but often taught men and women outside the formal *madrasas* system. They also often served as founders and benefactors of *madrasas* and functioned as controllers of the endowment, with the authority to appoint teachers and other functionaries (165). Berkey mentions that at least five *madrasas* in Mamluk Cairo were established by women, and probably more in Damascus. See Berkey, 'Women and Islamic Education in the Mamluk Period', 143–157, 144.

[23] Berkey, *The Transmission of Knowledge*, 170f. See also Bulliett, 'Women and the Urban Religious Elite'.

[24] See also the article by Asma Sayeed, 'Muslim Women's Religious Education in Early and Classical Islam', *Religion Compass* V.3 (2011), 94–103. Sayeed also provides an overview of the (quite limited) literature in English on women serving as *muḥaddithāt*, but unfortunately does not review the literature in other languages.

issue fatwas'.[25] An extraordinary example is the Damascene jurist Hujayma bt. Huyayy al-Awtabiyya (d. 701), 'who is said to have taught numerous men, and who enjoyed the confidence of the Caliph 'Abd al-Malik b. Marwan (r. 685–705), and used to meet with him regularly when they would sit together in the back of the Damascus mosque'.[26] The Shafi'i jurist Amina bt. al-Husayn al-Mahamili (d. 987) was 'particularly expert in the law of inheritance. Al-Barqani [*sic*] records that she used to give *fatwas* in the company of Abu Hurayrah.'[27]

The theologian al-Sayyidah Sarah bint al-Shaykh 'Umar ibn Ahmad ibn 'Umar al-Maqdisi of Damascus is said to have lectured on *Sharh Madhhahib Ahl al-Sunna wa-Ma'rifat Shara'i' al-Din* by Ibn Shahin (d. 996) in the early eleventh century. The daughter of Hanafi legal scholar 'Ala' al-Din al-Samarqandi (d. 1144), Fatima, is said to have issued fatwas together with her father. She authored *ijāzas*, wrote numerous works on fiqh and hadith, and led her own *ḥalqa*. She later married the influential Hanafi jurist al-Kashani (d. 1191).[27b]

An example from fourteenth-century Baghdad is Fatima bint 'Abbas ibn Abi al-Fath al-Baghdadiyya al-Hanbaliyya (d. 1333), whom Hafiz ibn Rajab al-Hanbali (d. 1393) described as 'the jurist, scholar, holder of higher *isnads*, the mufti, accurate, of great virtue, knowledgeable in different traditions, the unique one of her time, sought after from every corner'.[28] Among the most brilliant female scholars was 'A'isha bt. 'Abd al-Hadi al-Ba'uniyya (d. 1516), who excelled in Arabic grammar, rhetoric and mysticism, and received a licence to teach law and issue legal opinions (*ijāzat al-tadrīs wa'l-iftā'*). She studied in Cairo and Damascus and gained wide recognition as a jurist.[29]

---

[25] See Abou El Fadl, 'Legal and Jurisprudential Literature', 40.

[26] Ibid

[27] See Nadwi, 'al-Muḥaddithāt: Notes for a Talk', 4. Also Nadwi, *al-Muḥaddithāt, 112.*

[27b] See Willi (Wilhelm) Heffening and Lois Linant de Bellefonds, 'Kashani', in *Encyclopaedia of Islam*, vol. IV, 2nd edn (Leiden: Brill), 690.

[28] See Nadwi, 'al-*Muḥaddithāt*: Notes for a Talk', 4. 29.

[29] Devin J. Stewart, 'Ejāza', in *Encyclopædia Iranica*, Vol. VIII, Fasc. 3 (London: Columbia University, 1982), 273–275, here referring to Najm-al-Dīn Ǧazzī, *al-Kawākeb al-sā'era*, Vol. I (Beirut: al-Maṭba'ah al-Amīrkāniyyah, 1945–1958), 287–292, Beirut. See also Brockelmann, "A'isha', *Encyclopaedia of Islam*, first edn (1913–1936). Brill Online, 2013, Reference, Princeton University, 19 February 2013, http://referenceworks.brillonline.com/entries/encyclopaedia-of-islam-1/aisha-SIM_0478 Others female jurists include the Hanafi Khadija bt. Muhammad al-Juzjani (d. 983); the Hanbali jurist Khadija bt. al-Qayyim al-Baghdadiyya (d. 1299); Amat al-Rahim bt. Muhammad b. Ahmad al-Qastalani (d. 1315); the Hanafi jurist Khadija bt. Muhammad al-Batalyuni (d. 1523); and the Shafi'i jurist Bayy Khatun bt. Ibrahim al-Halabiyya (d. 1535). Women jurists who issued influential responsa include Umm 'Isa bt. Ibrahim al-Harbi (d. 940), the Shafi'i Amina bt. al-Husayn al-Mahamili (d. 987); Sayyida bt. 'Abd al-Ghani al-'Abdari (d. 1249); the Shafi'i Zaynab bt. Makki al-Harrani (d. 1289) of Damascus; Zayn al-'Arab bt. 'Abd Rahman b. 'Umar b. al-Husayn (d. 1304); and the Cairene jurist Hajar bt. Muhammad b. 'Ali b. Abi al-Ta'a (d. 1469). Ibid., and Abou El Fadl, 'Legal and Jurisprudential Literature', extensively based on 'Umar Rida Kahhala, *A'lam al-nisa'* (Beirut: Mu'assasat al-Risala, n.d.).

Women must have been participating in the teaching profession outside of *madrasas* more than may be conceded by contemporary accounts. The twelfth-century Sunni scholar Ibn 'Asakir (d. 1176), for example, notes that he studied under eighty different female scholars.[30] Among the 172 teachers of Taj al-Din 'Abd al-Wahhab al-Subki (d. 1370) were nineteen women. While the Hanbali jurist Ibn Taymiyya (d. 1328) lists relatively few women among his teachers, namely two, the Shafi'i scholar Ibn Hajar al-'Asqalani (d. 1448) provided the names of fifty-three women with whom he studied traditions and al-Sakhawi (d. 1497) notes that he personally received *ijāzas* from sixty-eight women.[31] And, as Berkey notes, 'No less a scholar than Jalal al-Din al-Suyuti (d. 1505) relied heavily on women as his sources for hadith: of the 130 shaikhs of exceptional reliability on whose authority he recited traditions, 33 – more than a quarter of the total – were women.'[32]

Women also often played noteworthy roles as political administrators who greatly influenced the sphere of religious teaching and learning.[33] A case in point is Gawhar Shad Bigum (d. 1457), the female ruler of Herat, on whose orders the Friday Mosque and the *madrasa* of Herat were built, as well as the Gawhar Shad Mosque in Mashhad.[34] Another important episode in this regard occurred in seventeenth-century Aceh, Southeast Asia, when the Sultanate was ruled by a series of female sultans, who, according to Anthony Reid, restored the religious peace by endorsing more lenient policies towards non-Muslim minorities and permitting a greater pluralism of Islamic opinions and interpretations.[35] In nineteenth-century Northern

---

[30] See Nadwi, *Al-Muḥaddithāt.*

[31] See Renate Jacobi, 'Der Gelehrte und die Dichterin. Eine Seelenfreundschaft im mamlukischen Ägypten', in *Studien zur Semitistik und Arabistik. Festschrift für Hartmut Bobzin*, eds Otto Jastrow, Shabo Talay and Herta Hafenrichter (Wiesbaden: Harrassowitz, 2008), 183–203; and Renate Jacobi 'Gelehrte Frauen im islamischen Spätmittelalter', in *Nonne, Königin, Kurtisane: Wissen, Bildung und Gelehrsamkeit von Frauen in der frühen Neuzeit*, eds Michaela Hohkamp and Gabriele Jancke (Königstein: Helmer, 2004), 225–246.

[32] See Berkey, 'Women and Islamic Education', 151. The Shafi'i scholar Ibn Hajar al-'Asqalani (d. 1448) provided the names of fifty-three women with whom, in one way or another, he studied traditions.

[33] On women who functioned as *nazirat* (female controllers), see C. F. Petry, 'A Paradox of Patronage during the Later Mamluk Period', *The Muslim World* LXXIII.3–4 (1983). Ibn Hazm (d. 1064) recounts that the second Sunni caliph, 'Umar, appointed a woman from his tribe, Shifa bint 'Abd Allah al-'Adawiyya, as the market inspector (*muḥtasib*). See Ibn Hazm, *al Muḥalla*, vol. 9 (Beirut: Dār al-Kutub al-'Ilmiyya, 1988), 429–430. The example of the female controller is cited in Ibn Hazm's juridical work in support of his ruling in favour of women being permitted to serve as judges.

[34] Similarly, the wives and daughters of the Safavid Shahs are known to have patronised shrines and places of pilgrimage. Shah-Begi Khanum, also called Tajlu Khanum, the favourite wife of Safavid Shah Isma'il I (r. 1502–1524), as well as her daughter Mahin Banu (1519–1562) are known to have set up endowments in Shirvan, Tabriz, Qazvin, Ray, and Isfahan.

[35] Four female sultans ruled Aceh from 1641 to 1699. 'This intriguing preference [of female sultans], which emulated the earlier practice of neighbouring commercially oriented sultanates in the Maldives and Patani, might be interpreted as a reaction against both tyranny (as under Iskandar Muda) and excessive religious literalism (as under Iskandar Thani and Raniri).' Anthony Reid, 'Aceh', in *Encyclopaedia of Islam* <http://www.ari.nus.edu.sg/docs/ Aceh-project/EI3-1-Reid.pdf>, last accessed 12 April 2011.

Nigeria, Nana Asma'u (1793–1864), a female religious scholar, was put in charge of the educational system in the caliphate of her brother Bello. Being a Qadiriyya Sufi educator, she institutionalised a new form of knowledge transmission (called the *yan-taru*) that allowed for greater participation of women in religious education.[36]

Jurists' Views on Women as Preachers, Legal Scholars and Judges

Apart from transmitting the Islamic tradition and teaching hadith sciences, religious authority might comprise a variety of roles, such as serving as preachers, calling to prayer and leading the prayer, and engaging in legal scholarship as jurists, who might even issue fatwas (*muftis*) or serve as judges in court (*qadis*). A great variety of juristic opinions exists on whether and under what conditions women may exercise these roles, and their justifications sometimes differ sharply even within given schools of jurisprudence (*madhhabs*). Most Sunni and Shi'a *madhhabs* prohibit women from issuing the call to prayer or delivering the *khuṭba* (Friday sermon), as well as from leading men and mixed crowds in prayer, although there are minority schools that do permit it.[37] For instance, Abu Thawr (d. 854) and al-Tabari (d. 923), both of whom founded independent schools of Islamic law, allowed women to lead men in prayer.[38] There is also a minority position in the Hanbali school that allows women to lead men in prayer.[39] Where women pray collectively, the majority opinions in the Shafi'i, Hanbali, and Hanafi schools, as well as the Imami school recommend that a woman lead the prayer.[40]

---

[36] Kathleen McGarvey, *Muslim and Christian Dialogue, the Case of Northern Nigeria* (Oxford: Peter Lang, 2009), 94. See also Beverley B. Mack and Jean Boy, *One Woman's Jihad: Nana Asma'u, Scholar and Scribe* (Bloomington: Indiana University Press, 2000) and their edited volume, *Collected Works of Nana Asma'u, Daughter of Usman 'dan Fodiyo (1793–1864)*, African Historical Sources Series (Michigan: Michigan State University Press, 1997); as well as Jean Boyd, *The Caliph's Sister* (London: Frank Cass & Co., 1988).

[37] Sabiq al-Sayyid, *Fiqh al-Sunna*. 3 vols (Cairo: Maktabat al-Qahira, 1994).

[38] I thank Hossein Modarressi for pointing this out to me. For further reference, see Ibn Rushd, *The Distinguished Jurist's Primer*, vol. 1 (Reading: Garnet Publishing), 161, 1.9.

[39] This is based on the example of Umm Waraqa, who, according to Ibn Sa'd, knew the whole Qur'an and whom the prophet therefore appointed to act as imam. According to this Hanbali minority opinion, 'knowing the Qur'an comes ahead of sex in determining who led a mixed group'. See Christopher Melchert, 'Whether to Keep Women Out of the Mosque: A Survey of Medieval Islamic Law', in *Authority, Privacy and Public Order in Islam. Proceedings of the 22nd Congress of L'Union Européenne des Arabisants et Islamisants*, eds B. Michalak-Pikulska and A. Pikulski (Leuven: Peeters, 2006), 59–69.

[40] For overviews of legal positions regarding women-led prayer, see, for example, Juliane Hammer, 'Performing Gender Justice: The 2005 Woman-led Prayer in New York', *Contemporary Islam* 4.1 (2010), 91–116, as well as Ahmad Elewa and Laura Silvers, 'I *Am* One of the People: A Survey and Analysis of Legal Arguments on Women-Led Prayer in Islam', *Journal of Law and Religion* 26.1 (2010), 141–171. Al-Tusi reports that the Shi'a community unanimously agreed on the desirability of a woman leading women in prayer. Al-Tusi, *Kitab al-Khilaf*, 6 vols (Qum: Mu'assasat al-Nashr al-Islami, 1987–1989), 1:562.

In the realm of the interpretation of religious law, one notices a seeming contradiction in the scholarly views on women as *muftis* (interpreters of the law who may issue *fatwas*) and *qadis* (judges of religious law who issue binding rulings). Most Sunni and Shi'a schools of jurisprudence recognise the eligibility of women to serve as *muftis*, and, interestingly so, not only on issues of particular relevance or interest to women, but on any issue a believer might seek advice on.

By contrast, three of the four dominant Sunni *madhhabs* and most Shi'a schools reject the possibility that women could serve as judges.[41] Most do so on the grounds that women are inferior to men in their ability to reason, while others reject it on sociological grounds: the activity of judging would require women to interact with men that are *haram* to them, and such a situation is of course to be avoided.[42] Yet, as Karen Bauer shows, many of the scholars who reject female judgeship for primarily sociological reasons reveal in other works (for instance, on *tafsīr*) that they also believe in the mental inferiority of women.[43] The two positions apparently often go hand in hand.[44] Virtually all schools put the burden of proof on the position that women can serve as judges, assuming that they cannot.

It is worth noting the exception of the Hanafi school in this context. The Hanafi school, which most Muslims in the world follow today, does permit women to give testimony, and it does allow women to serve as qadis in matters where they can testify.[45] As Bauer clarifies, this is in all cases other than

---

[41] It is worth noting that there are no verses in the Qur'an that explicitly refer to 'maleness' as a prerequisite of interpreting the revelation. However, scholars who oppose women's judgeship often refer to various interpretations of the Qur'anic verses 4:34, 43:18, 33:33, 2:228 to support their arguments. It is mainly by *ijma'* (consensus among jurisprudents) that maleness has been identified as a condition of judgeship. See Sayyid Mas'ud Nuri, *Murur-e Ijmali bar Nazariyeh-e Luzum-e Mard Budan-e Qadi dar Fiqh-e Imami* (n.p., 2011), 1.

[42] A great number of jurists who embrace the idea of female muftis at the same time reject the idea of female judgeship based on women's inferior ability to reason. It is not clear how the two positions can be reconciled: that is, why women's alleged inferior ability to reason would not also limit their ability to serve as muftis. Al-Tabari (below) is the great exception here. Future research will do well in identifying the arguments created to solve the seeming contradiction. Among those who reject female judgeship for chiefly sociological reasons are, for instance, the Shafi'is al-Shirazi (d. 1083) and al-Baghawi (d. *c.* 1122). See Karen Bauer, 'Debates on Women's Status as Judges and Witnesses in Post-Formative Islamic Law', *Journal of the American Oriental Society* 130.1 (2010), 8.

[43] The question on whether women can serve as judges is obviously closely related to the question of whether women's *'aql* is identical to that of men. The Hanafi position, for instance, establishes that women have *'aql* (although their memory is limited) and therefore may serve as judges. According to the Shafi'i position, women are deficient in all types of *'aql* and therefore cannot serve as judges.

[44] Al-Tusi and al-Baghawi are cases in point.

[45] al-Mawardi's 'On Qadis', in *Milestone Documents in World History: Exploring the Primary Sources That Shaped the World*, eds Brian Bonhomme, Cathleen Boivin, and Schlaeger Group (Amenia, NJ: Salem Press, 2010), 437–444.

ḥudūd and *qisās*' (thus, criminal justice).[46] The minority schools of Zahiris and Jariris also supported female judgeship.[47] While most jurists of the Hanbali, Maliki, and Shafi'i schools do not allow for female qadis, in each school dissenting opinions exist among early jurists who do. Among those that do permit female judgeship are the Maliki Ibn al-Qasim (d. 806) as well as the Shafi'i Ibn Abi al-Dam (d. 1244).[48]

While virtually all jurists who permit female judgeship do so for a limited realm of cases, or remain vague on the scope of permitted female judgeship, the mentioned al-Tabari, who initially identified as a Shafi'i and later founded the Jariri school, stands out in the history of Islamic thought for holding that women can judge in all matters.[49] But as Roswitha Badry observes, the fact that women of the first and second generation did generate independent judgments was apparently quickly forgotten or ignored. Later, it became imperative that men certify the judgments of women.[50] Bauer comments 'that despite women's theoretical ability to judge at least in Hanafi lands, I have not found any accounts of a woman acting as a *qadiya* in the Shari'a court'.[51]

Imami jurists in general share the position of the Hanbali, Shafi'i, and Maliki jurists on female judgeship. The requirement of male gender is more often assumed implicitly than explicitly stated.[52] Abdallah Javadi-Amuli (b. 1933), for instance, notes that although Shaykh Mufid (d. *c.* 1022) in his book *al-Muqni'a* lays out as the preconditions for judgeship only *'aql* (mental competence) and in-depth knowledge of the Qur'an and the Sunna, it is clear from his other works that women are considered unfit to serve as judges.[53] Shaykh al-Tusi (d. 1067) in his book *al-Nihāya* affirms similar qualities along with *taqwā* (to be God fearing) while not specifying the

---

[46] For an overview of the different viewpoints of the *madhhabs* on the question of female judgeship, see Bauer, 'Debates on Women's Status'. According to al-Mawardi, they may also not judge where financial affairs are involved.

[47] For instance, the mentioned Zahiri Ibn Hazm (d. 1064) (see footnote 33).

[48] See Bauer, 'Debates on Women's Status', 2–3.

[49] Regarding al-Tabari, see Patricia Crone, *God's Rule, Government and Islam, Six Centuries of Medieval Islamic Political Thought* (New York: Columbia University Press, 2004), 350. Bauer notes that he arrives at this unusual position by drawing an analogy between judging and interpreting the law (that is, serving as a mufti), which was permitted to women without restriction and limitation to women-specific issues.

[50] See also Badry, *Zum Profil weiblicher 'Ulama'*, 16, fn 26.

[51] Bauer, 'Debates on Women's Status', 18. Needless to say, Bauer is referring to the classical period. For female qadis in the modern era, see later sections of this article.

[52] This is the case in *Fiqh al-Rida* attributed to the eighth Shi'a Imam 'Ali ibn Musa al-Rida (d. 817), in Shaykh Saduq's (d. 992) *Muqni' fi al-Fiqh*, Abu al-Salih Halabi's (d. 1055) *Kafi*, in the *al-Muqni'a* by Shaykh Mufid ('Ali 'Abd Allah Muhammad ibn Naman al-Hrethi al-Baghdadi) (d. 1022), in the works of Sayyid Murtada 'Alam al-Huda (d. 1044), in *al-Marasim al-Awwaliya fi al-Ahkam al-Nabawiyya* by Abu 'Ali ibn 'Abd al-'Aziz Daylami, known as 'Salar' (d. 1056), and in Hamzah ibn 'Ali ibn Zuhra's (d. 1189) *Ghunyat al-Nuzu' ila 'Ilm al-Usul wa'l-Furu'*.

[53] Abdallah Javadi-Amuli, *Zan dar āyinah-yi jalāl va jamāl* (Tehran: Markaz-i Nashr-i Farhangi-ye Raja, 1369/1990), 299.

gender of the judge, but elsewhere establishes that women ought to not speak publicly, which renders them unfit for the profession.[54] Muhammad ibn Ahmad ibn Idris (d. 1202), a descendant of al-Tusi's daughter – a religious scholar herself – in his book *al-Sara'ir* suggests that women cannot serve in a public courtroom as 'one must abstain from all things *haram*'.[55] Indeed, most Imami jurists tend to reject female judgeship not because women are intellectually in- or less capable of being judges, but because it would put them in an inappropriate position with regard to men. The reservation most often expressed is hence of sociological nature rather than one assuming mental inferiority.[56]

However, there are voices as early as the seventeenth century that dissent from this *ijma'*. A group of male *mujtahid*s advocated permitting women to serve as judges as long as the witnesses were trustworthy. To these belonged Muqaddas Ardabili (d. 1585) and Shaykh Baha'i (d. 1621). The first proposes that women who have acquired the necessary training in deriving independent reasoning (*ijtihād*) are capable of becoming judges in matters pertaining to women, provided that they are just and satisfy the other agreed requirements: 'There is no prohibition on a woman judging on the basis of women's testimony – for example, hearing two women's testimony –as long as she conforms to the characteristics that are required in a judge.'[57] Parvin Paidar reviews the arguments introduced in *Jami'-i 'Abbasi* by Shaykh Baha'i, which

[54] Here, too, it is clear from other works that al-Tusi does not see a ground to permit women to serve as judges. In *Kitab al-Khilaf* he refers to the well-known hadith from the Sunni tradition: 'If one happens to need something when in prayer, a man would [attract the attention of someone by] say[ing aloud]: Praise to God; saying "Praise to God" [aloud] is for men, and clapping hands is for women; so the Prophet, peace be upon him, forbade women to speak [aloud] in order for their voice not to be heard [by men], out of fear that [a woman's voice] may cause temptation. . .' Al-Tusi, *Kitab al-Khilaf* (Qum: Mu'assasat al-Nashr al-Islami, n.d.), 213–214 [Vol. 6, p. 114], cited in Bauer, 'Debates on Women's Status', 8.

[55] Muhammad ibn Ahmad ibn Idris, *Kitab al-Sara'ir al-Hawi li-Tahrir al-Fatawi,* 2 vols (Qum: Jamā'at al-Mudarrisin, 1989), 2. Cited in Sayyid Mas'ud Nuri, *Murur-e Ijmali,* 1. His wife and daughters attained some prominence as religious scholars and received *ijāzas* from Shaykh al-Tusi. There are some indications that Allameh Helli (d. 1325) had more permissive views on women as judges (and that a number of women in his family were *faqihāt*), but I found no reliable scholarly discussion of the matter.

[56] See Bauer, 'Debates on Women's Status', 7–8.

[57] Aḥmad b. Muḥammad al-Ardabili, *Majma' al-fa'ida wa-l-burhan*, eds Husayn al-Isfahani et al. (Qum: Mu'assasat al-Nashr al-Islāmī, 1993), 12:15, cited in Bauer, 'Debates on Women's Status', 16. It is unclear whether he means that women can only judge over other women, or whether he means they can judge in all cases where they can testify. He justifies his position allowing women to serve as judges with reference to a lack of consensus on the matter. Ardabili, too, studied with the father-in-law of Shaykh Baha'i in Isfahan. Unfortunately, the entry on Ardabili in the *Encyclopaedia Iranica* makes no mention of his extraordinary views on female religious authority.

included that 'women could become judges and pass judicial verdicts on conditions that "the witness is a trusted one"'.[58]

In the past 150 years, a number of Shi'i scholars have written or issued fatwas on the question of female judgeship. Ayatollah Husayn Nuri-Hamidani (b. 1925) regards women's judgeship as admissible only within the framework of family arbitration.[59] Ayatollah Javadi-Amuli is of the opinion that women cannot become judges if one finds definite *ijma'* (consensus) establishing their inadmissability to the profession (which one of course does), or if women's judgeship violates social norms.[60] In particular, the presence of female judges is regarded as inadmissible in contexts where they have contact with the opposite sex.

There are a few contemporary scholars such as Ayatollahs Yusuf Sane'i (b. 1937) and Bujnurdi (b. 1945) who see no difference in the role of male or female judges. In the opinion of Sane'i,

> those well-versed in judicial precedence and who are endowed with justice and other requirements can attain the permit for judges; both *'urf* (custom) and *'aql* (reason) do not distinguish between the role of female and male judges.[61]

Bujnurdi's opinion is that

> women can be judges and that there is no limitation in this regard in Islam. In Islam, the measure of judgeship is justice and not gender. All *hadith* regarding the inability of women to be judges, both in terms of their reasoning and sources are weak. In short, maleness is not one of the conditions of judgeship.[62]

---

[58] Parvin Paidar, *Women and the Political Process in Twentieth-Century Iran* (Cambridge: Cambridge University Press, 1995), 35. One must note that while the first five chapters of *Jami'-i Abbasi* were written by Shaykh Baha'i (Baha' al-Din Mohammad al-Amili), the remaining twenty, including those discussing women's status, were completed by his student Nizam ibn Husayn Savaji (d. after 1629). Like the entry on Ardabili, the entry on Shaykh Baha'i in the *Encyclopaedia Iranica* makes no mention of his extraordinary views on women's judgeship.

[59] Nuri, *Murur-i Ijmali*, 13.

[60] Javadi-Amuli, *Zan dar ayinah-yi jalal va jamal*, 303–304.

[61] Cited in Nuri, *Murur-i Ijmali*, 12. Nuri writes that there are no authoritative hadiths and *akhbar* in the Shi'a tradition that clearly point to the exclusion of women from judgeship. Those hadiths relied on by scholars who support women's exclusion are often critiqued for being weak in their *isnad*. On the distinction between *'aql/nafs* and its implications for arguments about gender in Iran today, see, for instance, Azam Torab, *Performing Islam: Gender and Ritual in Iran* (Leiden: Brill, 2007). '[In contemporary] Iran, *'aql* is generally associated with the realm of order, control and morality, while *nafs* is associated with the realm of disorder, lack of control and passion or desire. The conservative forces construct *'aql* as primarily masculine, associating it more with men and valuing it above *nafs*, which they construct as feminine and associate more with women.' Ibid., 13.

[62] Cited in Shireen Hunter, 'Islamic Reformist Discourse in Iran, Proponents and Prospects', in *Reformist Voices of Islam: Mediating Islam and Modernity*, ed. Shireen Hunter (New York: M. E. Sharpe, 2009), 65.

For sure, the more permissive opinions on female judgeship have not translated into policies. Women serve as full judges in Islamic courts in less than a handful of Muslim countries.[63]

Female Religious Scholars and Educators in Safavid and Qajar Iran

Numerous examples document quite an active involvement of women in the field of Islamic scholarship in modern Iran, often complementing their fathers' and husbands' scholarship, and a few since the seventeenth century have reached the rank of *mujtahid*. In this, women's roles diverge from the earlier example of traditionists: for women in modern Iran are participants in the generation and not only transmission of religious knowledge, including in the fields of theology and jurisprudence. Women educated in the theological disciplines have been able to gain the title of *mollā* and, though rarely, even the rank of *mujtahid*.

Studies of women's education in Iran during the Safavid era (1501–1722) suggest that from the early 1500s, a number of aristocratic women were privately educated in the Qur'anic sciences, among other subjects. As Jasamin Rostami-Kolayi notes,

> Royal women of the court received private training in *Qur'anic* studies, reading, writing, calligraphy, and Persian grammar. Safavid princess Pari Khan Khanum, the daughter of Shah Tahmasp, reportedly mastered Islamic law, jurisprudence, and poetry writing and was a patron to poets.[64]

Female religious scholars of note in the Safavid era were Parikhan Khanum (b. 1548), Durdaneh Nishapuri (d. 1621), Jahan Begum (d. 1659), and Amineh Khwatun Majlesi (d. early 18th c.). Also famous as a renowned poet, the Safavid princess Parikhan Khanum built a *madrasa* (for men and women) in Isfahan for the study of religious sciences, which she then administered. Jahan Begum, apart from being a scientist, wrote parts of a *tafsīr*.[65] Amineh Khwatun Majlesi is said to have contributed to the hadith compendium *Bihar al-Anwar* of her brother Muhammad Baqir Majlisi (d. 1699). She also authored commentaries on philological works, including

---

[63] See Mirjam Künkler, 'The Legal Professions in the Muslim World: Between Social Transformation, Judicial Control, and Feminisation' in Rick Abel, Ole Hammerslev, Hillary Sommerlad, Ulrike Schultz (eds) *Lawyers in 21st-Century Societies*. Vol. II, (Oxford: Hart, forthcoming).

[64] Jasamin Rostami-Kolayi, 'Origins of Iran's Modern Girls' Schools: From Private/National to Public/State', *Journal of Middle East Women's Studies* IV. 3 (fall 2008), 60–61.

[65] See Maria Szuppe, 'The "Jewels of Wonder": Learned Ladies and Princess Politicians in the Provinces of Early Safavid Iran', in *Women in the Medieval Islamic World*, ed. Gavin R. G. Hambly (New York: St. Martin's Press, 1998), 325–47.

the *Alfiyya*, a grammatical treatise of Ibn Malik (d. 1274), and the *Shawāhid* of al-Suyuti.[66]

A number of female religious authorities can be found in the orbit of Shaykh Baha'i, who, as mentioned earlier, held the minority opinion that women could serve as judges. His wife was the daughter of Zayn al-Din 'Ali Minshar 'Amili, the Shaykh al-Islam of Isfahan during the time of Shah Tahmasp (r. 1533–1576). She studied under her father (whose library she inherited) and became a hadith scholar and jurist of note. The daughters of Mulla Sadra (d. 1640), one of the most prominent Shi'i philosophers of the Safavid era and a student of Shaykh Baha'i's, were outstanding religious scholars. Badriyya (d. 1679–1680), also known as Umm Kulthum, studied religious sciences and philosophy with her father. She is reported to have participated in the scholarly discussions actively and eloquently. It is not mentioned that she did this from behind a curtain, as is usually noted in such cases.[67] Another daughter, Zubayda (also known as Sadriyya, d. 1686), was instructed by her father, brother, and husband and specialised in theology, philosophy, and mysticism.

The high appreciation of women's religious education continued during the Qajar dynasty (1796–1925).[68] Rostami-Kolayi suggests that the content of

---

[66] Badry mentions an unspecified 'work of *fiqh*' of hers that was 'promising' but remained incomplete. See Badry, *Zum Profil weiblicher 'Ulama'*, 23. Stewart discusses her entry in Isfahani's biographical dictionary. See Devin J. Stewart, 'Women's Biographies in Islamic Societies: Mirza Abd Allah al-Isfahani's *Riyad al-Ulama*', in *The Rhetoric of Biography: Narrating Lives in Persianate Societies*, ed. Louise Marlowe (Cambridge, MA: Harvard University Press, 2011), 106–139. According to Isfahani, Amina's husband, the great scholar Muhammad 'Ali al-Mazandarani (d. 1675–1676), consulted his wife on how to construe certain phrases in the famous legal text Qawa'id al-aḥkam by Allama al-Hilli (d. 725/1325).

[67] On her and her sisters, see Rajabi *Mashahir-e Zanan-e Irani*, 142, and Hasan al-Amin, *Mustadrakat A'yan al-Shi'a*, vol. III (Beirut: Dar al-Ta'aruf, 1987–1998), 43. At the age of fifteen, Badriyya married her father's student, 'Abd al-Raziq Lahiji (d. 1661), a luminary in the teaching of philosophy. The second sister Zubayda married Mohsen Fayz-e Kashani (d. 1679), one of the most prominent scholars of Safavid Iran. The third sister was Ma'ṣumeh (d. 1681), who married another student, Quṭb-al-Din Muḥammad Nayrizi. See Sajjad Rizvi, 'Mollā Ṣadrā Šīrāzī', in *Encyclopaedia Iranica*, <http://www.iranicaonline.org/articles/molla-sadra-sirazi>.

[68] At the court of Muzaffar al-Din Shah (r. 1896–1907), his mother Shukuh Sultanih employed a female religious instructor (*mulla baji*), Khadijeh Khanum Vaziri, to teach her daughters. Khadijeh Khanum was a companion of Shukuh Sultaneh, a wife of Nasir al-Din Shah (r. 1848–1896). Her daughter, Bibi Khanum Astarabadi-Vaziri (*c.* 1858–1921), wrote a manuscript in 1895/1896, titled *The Faults of Men* (*Ma'ayib al-Rijal*), a satirical response to the popular treatise at the time *On the Disciplining of Women* (*Ta'dib al-Nisa'*) that was widely used to educate girls and women. On Bibi Khanum, see Mehrangiz Mallah and Afsaneh Najmabadi (eds), *Bibi Khanum Astarabadi va Khanum Afzal Vaziri: madar va dukhtari az pishgaman-e ma'arif va huquq-e zanan. Az zaban-e Khanum-e Afzal Vaziri* (Chicago: Negaresh va Negaresh-e Zan, 1996), 65–70. Bibi Khanum Astarabadi founded a girl's school in Tehran named 'Dushizegan' shortly before the constitutional revolution in 1906/1907. Astarabadi was consequently accused of heresy, but successfully resisted the forced closure of her school. Astarabadi's daughters, Afzal Vaziri (1889–1980) and Moluk Vaziri, became teachers at the school and Moluk Vaziri in 1911 established her own school, the Parvarish-e Dushizegan (Girls' Training) School. See also Badry, *Zum Profil weiblicher 'Ulama*, 29.

the instruction for women of the Qajar nobility 'was neither entirely female-specific, nor substantially different from what was taught in *maktab*s (clerically-run elementary schools)'.[69]

Female religious scholars of note in the Qajar era include Nuri Jahan, who in 1809 wrote *Najat al-Muslimat,* a treatise on women's moral conduct; Amineh Ha'eri (d. 1827/28), the daughter of Mulla Baqer Vahid Behbahani (d. *c.* 1792), who is said to have authored the chapter on menstruation in the treatise *Riyad al-Masa'il* of her husband Sayyid 'Ali Tabataba'i (d. 1815); Malekeh Jahan (d. 1868); and Aqa Begum Tabataba'i (d. 1905/6), the mother of Grand Ayatollah Sayyid Husayn Borujerdi (d. 1961).[70]

To date only very few accounts exist of female religious scholars in the Qajar era, as important sources in Persian, Arabic, and Turkish are yet largely untapped.[71] An exception here are the women of the Baraqani family of Qazvin who, as a family deeply involved in the *akhbari-usuli* conflict and the emergence of Babism in the nineteenth century, has received greater scholarly attention.[72] Amineh Qazvini (1787–1852), her mother Fatemeh Qazvini (1756–1844), her two daughters Fatemeh (known later as Qurrat al-'Ayn) and Marziyyeh, as well as other female relatives became renowned Islamic scholars, several of whom did not shy away from public advocacy.

The extraordinary lives of the Baraqani women merit more detailed mention. Amineh Qazvini was the granddaughter of Sayyid Muhammad Mahdi Bahr al-'Ulum (d. 1797), a student of Mulla Baqer Vahid Behbahani (d. *c.* 1792), one of the most prominent teachers in the Atabat (Najaf and Karbala) of all time. Her father, Shaykh Muhammad 'Ali Qazvini, was one the prominent *'ulama* of Qazvin and her mother Fatemeh Qazvini (1756–1844) a noted preacher and scholar herself.[73] In 1804, Amineh

---

[69] Rostami-Kolayi, 'Origins of Iran's Modern Girls' Schools', 60. For analyses of religion and gender in twentieth-century Iran, see, in particular, Paidar, *Women and the Political Process;* Haleh Afshar, *Islam and Feminisms: An Iranian Case Study* (London: Macmillan, 1998); Ziba Mir-Hosseini, *Islam and Gender: The Religious Debate in Contemporary Iran* (Princeton: Princeton University Press, 1999).

[70] See Badry, *Zum Profil weiblicher 'Ulama'*, 24. Malakih Jahan of Shiraz was one of the wives of Mirza Yahya, the half-brother and rival of Baha'ullah, who declared himself the Bab. See Moojan Momen, 'The Cyprus Exiles', in *Baha'i Studies Bulletin* V.3 and VI.1 (June 1991), 84–113. In 1906, she published *Burhan al-Iman*, a book consisting of prayers and recitations praising God.

[71] Among them is Shaykh Zabih Allah Mahallati's *Rayahin al-Shari'ih dar Tarjumih-i Danishmandan-i Banuvan-i Shi'ih* in five volumes (Tehran: Dar al-Kutub al-Islamiyyah, 1954) and *Khayrat-i Hisan* of Muhammad Hasan Khan (I'timad al-Saltanah, d. 1896) (Tehran: 1887–1889).

[72] See, in particular, Abbas Amanat, *Resurrection and Renewal: The Making of the Babi Movement in Iran, 1844–1850* (Ithaca: Cornell University Press, 1989); and Moojan Momen, 'Usuli, Akhbari, Shaykhi, Babi: The Tribulations of a Qazvin Family', *Iranian Studies* XXXVI.3 (September 2003), 317–337. Recent scholarly work has profited from the account of a descendant of the family, 'Abd al-Husayn al-Salihi, *Mawsu'a al-Baraghani fi Fiqh al-Shi'a* (n. p., 1985).

[73] See Rajabi, *Mashahir-i Zanan Irani*, 9–10. Also refer to Murad 'Ali Tavana (for Markaz Umur Musharikat-i Zanan Riyasat Jumhuri), *Zan dar Tarikh-i Mu'asir-i Iran,* vol. I (Tehran: Barg Zaytun, 2001), 195, 327.

married Shaykh Muhammad Salehi Baraqani (1753–1866),[74] one of three brothers from Baraqan who had studied in the Atabat with the prominent *usuli* teachers of the time, including Behbahani, and the couple settled in Qazvin.[75] Muhammad Salehi Baraqani had seven daughters and eight sons, at least one son and two daughters (Qurrat al-'Ayn and Marziyyeh) with Amineh.[76] Amineh began her religious education with her brother 'Abd al-Wahhab Sharif Qazvini (d. 1853), imam of the Masjed-e Shah, and one of the most influential clerics of Qazvin who leaned towards an *akhbari* position. Later, she studied *fiqh* and *usul* with her husband and *hikmat* and *falsafeh* with Shaykh Aqa Hakami (d. 1868) in the women's section of the Salehiyya *madrasa*, which her husband had founded.[77] A great impact on her must have been Mirza Mah-sharaf Khanum (born in the eighteenth century and still alive in the 1810s), an aunt of the Baraqani brothers who after studying in Isfahan and the Atabat, was taken into Fath 'Ali Shah's household (r. 1796–1834) to act as secretary. 'On account of her excellent composition and calligraphy', she is said to have handwritten numerous governmental decrees.[78] Towards the end of her life she taught philosophy and Arabic literature at the Salehiyya, and as such was the instructor of several women of the Baraqani family of the next generation who later distinguished themselves as scholars or popular preachers. It is plausible to assume that the extraordinary phenomenon of so many women from one family - spanning four generations - distinguishing themselves in positions of Islamic learning and leadership owes much to the inspiration from the outstanding example of Mirza Mah-sharaf Khanum.

---

[74] See Momen, 'Usuli, Akhbari, Shaykhi, Babi'; Abbas Amanat, 'Qurrat al-'Ayn: The Remover of the Veil', in *Tahirih in History: Perspectives on Qurrat al-Ayn from East and West. Studies in the Babi and Bahai Religions*, ed. Sabir Afaqi (Los Angeles: Kalimat Press, 2004, 113–158); Isabel Stümpel, 'Tahira Qurrat al-Ain', in *Iran im 19. Jahrhundert und die Entstehung der Baha'i Religion*, eds Christoph Bürgel and Isabel Schayani (Hildesheim: Georg Olms Verlag, 1998), 127–144.

[75] Momen writes that Shaykh Muhammad-Kazim Taleqani (d. 1094/1683) was the first of the family from Taleqan to settle in Qazvin, where he built the Madraseh-ye Navvab, now called the Imam Sadiq Madrasa. See Momen, 'Usuli, Akhbari, Shaykhi, Babi'.

[76] See Momen, 'Usuli, Akhbari, Shaykhi, Babi', 326, who cites al-Salihi, 'Introduction'. The sons were Muhammad (1790–1825), 'Abd al-Wahhab (d. 1877), Hasan (d. 1864), Husayn (d. 1891), Rida (d. 1890), Musa (d. 1880) and Muhammad-'Ali (d. 1897), and possibly a further son, Shaykh Muhammad, Kashif al-Asrar (1824–1877). The daughters were Fatemeh/Qurrat al-'Ayn; Mardhiyyah (*c.* 1817–*c.* 1895), Nargis (1824–1904), Zahra (1824–1902), Fatima (d. 1878), Rubabih (d. 1879) and Khadijah Sultan (d. 1903). The eldest son Muhammad died in 1825/1826 in the aftermath of the first Russo-Persian War.

[77] The Salehiyya, founded in 1817, soon became a centre of learning that attracted students from across Iran and India. Momen writes that as many as 700 students were attending the Salehiyya. Shaykh Muhammad Salih Baraqani's younger brother Mulla 'Ali taught at the Salehiyya, as well as Mulla Saleh's and Amineh's second eldest son, Mirza 'Abd al-Wahhab (d. 1877). One of the most prominent students of the Salehiyya who started his education in Qazvin was Sayyid Muhammad ibn Safdar Husayni, alias Sayyid Jamal al-Din al-Afghani (d. 1897).

[78] See also Badr al-Muluk Bamdad (trans. and ed. F. R. C. Bagley), *From Darkness into Light: Women's Emancipation in Iran* (New York: Exposition Press, 1977), 20.

Another great influence on Amineh was Shaykh Ahmad Ahsa'i (1753–1826), the leading *shaykhi 'alim* of the time, whose classes she frequented during his sojourn in Qazvin. Amineh herself held classes for women in Karbala and Qazvin. She received *ijāzas* from her husband, her brother, and Shaykh Ahmad Ahsa'i,[79] and led her own *ḥalqa* (study circle) in Qazvin and Karbala. Her written works include a long poem (*qasida*) of 480 verses that narrates the events of the massacre at Karbala and a book she wrote with the help of the prominent Hanafi mufti of Baghdad, Abu al-Thana Mahmud Alusi (1802–1854),[80] when she later accompanied her daughter Qurrat al-'Ayn to Baghdad and stayed at his house.[81]

Amineh's daughter, Fatemeh Baraqani (*c.* 1814–1852), better known by her honorary names Qurrat al-'Ayn (Consolation for the Eyes) and Tahereh (the Pure One), presents in many ways an exception to female religious authority in modern Iran, both for her distinction as a scholar and poetess, and the radicalism with which she embraced new teachings.[82] Fatemeh studied Arabic and Persian with her mother, *fiqh, usul, tafsīr,* and hadith with her father as well as with her uncle Mulla Muhammad-Taqi, one of the most fervent *usuli* leaders with strong connections to the court.[83] She studied mysticism with her other uncle, Shaykh Mulla Muhammad-'Ali Baraqani (b. 1761), and her brother, Shaykh Mirza 'Abd al-Wahhab Bararqani Qazvini; and philosophy and gnosis with Mulla Yusuf Hakami (d. 1859) and the mentioned Mulla Aqa Hakami (d. 1868), two cousins of the Baraqani brothers who also taught at the Salehiyya. Because of their expertise in matters of jurisprudence, Qurrat al-'Ayn and her younger sister Marziyyeh were frequently consulted on legal questions by the women of Qazvin.[84] In about

---

[79] Badry, *Zum Profil weiblicher 'Ulama'*, 31. The standards of granting *ijāzas* seem to have been different here from the situation that Berkey describes in Mamluk Egypt, where 'two sisters, for example, received *ijāzas* by virtue of their association with their scholarly brothers'. If this were so in nineteenth-century century Iran, all women of the Baraqani family would have been noted in the relevant dictionaries to have received *ijāzas.*

[80] For more on al-Alusi, see Basheer M. Nafi, 'Abu al-Thana' al-Alusi: An Alim, Ottoman Mufti, and Exegete of the Qur'an', *International Journal of Middle East Studies*, 34 (2002), 465–494.

[81] 'Amineh Khanum Qazvini', in *Aftab*, Wednesday, 13 September 2006 <http:// www.aftab.ir/ lifestyle/view/66357>.

[82] Fatemeh was given the title Qurrat al-'Ayn by the *shaykhi* leader Sayyid Kazim Rashti and was later called Tahirih by Sayyid 'Ali-Muhammad, the Bab. As a child she likely would not have been called Fatemeh, out of deference to her maternal grandmother by the same name who lived in the same household. Her father called her Zarrin-Taj (Crown of Gold) and she is also known as Zakiyyih and Umm Salmah. Momen notes that she probably grew up speaking both Persian and Turkish. He cites an Azeri scholar, Azize Caferzade, who refers to a poem of Qurrat al-'Ayn composed in Turkish. See Momen, 'Usuli, Akhbari, Shaykhi, Babi', 328 n. 64.

[83] Muhammad-Taqi Baraqani was allegedly killed for his persistent denunciation of Babism. He earned the posthumous title of the 'Third (Shi'a) martyr' (*Shahid Thalith*), the first and the second having been medieval theologians in the Lebanon.

[84] Stümpel, *Tahira Qurrat al-Ain,* citing Shaykh Kazim Samandar Qazvini.

1828–1841, Qurrat al-'Ayn moved to Karbala with her husband, Mullah Muhammad (the son of her uncle Muhammad-Taqi Baraqani), where the two continued their studies and had two sons and a daughter.[85]

Karbala was also the place where the teachings of Ahmad Ahsa'i continued to be propagated by one of his most distinguished students, Ahmad Kazim Rashti (1797–1843). A maternal cousin of hers, Mulla Javad Valiyani, introduced Qurrat al-'Ayn to the *shaykhi* writings, which were highly frowned upon in her husband's family. At the height of the *shaykhi-usuli* controversy, Ahsa'i was denounced as *kafir* by Qurrat al-'Ayn's uncle and father-in-law, Muhammad-Taqi Baraqani.[86] Once back in Qazvin, Qurrat al-'Ayn defended the *shaykhi* positions in opposition to her husband and uncle, which eventually led to the couple's separation and Qurrat al-'Ayn's return to her parents' house. At the counsel of the younger brother of her father, Mulla Muhammad-'Ali, himself a *shaykhi*, Qurrat al-'Ayn, together with her daughter, her sister Marziyyeh, and her sister's husband Mulla Muhammad-'Ali Qazvini (another *shaykhi*), travelled once more to Karbala, but Rashti died before her arrival in 1844.[87] She then moved to Sayyid Kazim Rashti's residence where, at the invitation of his widow, she taught his students, both men and women.[88] Influenced by the writings of Sayyid 'Ali-Muhammad from Shiraz (1819–1849) who declared himself the Bab, Qurrat al-'Ayn joined his movement and became the only woman among the Bab's eighteen disciples.[89] Following her acceptance of the Bab, she openly denounced the necessity of Islamic law, in defiance of the Bab's recommended *taqiyya,* and thereafter appeared among Babi believers without the facial veil.[90]

Qurrat al-'Ayn died a martyr to her cause in her mid-thirties, executed in the general wave of Babi persecution of 1852 following the attempt on the life of Nasir al-Din Shah.[91] Until today no female religious authority of Iran

---

[85] The two sons are Isma'il (d. 1306/1888) and Ibrahim (d. 1310/1892), born in Karbala, and the daughter is Zaynab (1253/1837–1333/1914), born in Najaf. According to Ali Al-Wardi, cited in Amanat, *Resurrection and Renewal*, 297, Fatemeh bore a third son in Qazvin, named Ishaq.

[86] His sons, Shaykh Muhammad-Taqi, Shaykh 'Ali-Naqi, and Shaykh 'Abd Allah, in turn studied under the Baraqani brothers at the Salehiyya Madrasa.

[87] Ten days before she arrived, see Rajabi, *Mashahir-i Zanan Irani*, 188.

[88] Men from behind a curtain; see 'Taghir-i Nigah-i Jinsiyati bih Asar-i Sha'iran-i Zan-i Irani', *Zan-i Farda* (2009), <http://zanefarda.ir/1388/12/ تغییرنگاه-جنسیتی-به-آثارشاعران-زن-ایر/>, last accessed 12 April 2011.

[89] Rajabi, *Mashahir-i Zanan Irani*, 187–190.

[90] Contrary to the frequent assertions that she appeared 'unveiled' 'in public', Amanat clarifies with references to Baghdadi that she appeared without the facial veil among believers, but spoke from behind a curtain in gatherings among unbelievers. See Amanat, *Resurrection and Renewal,* 304, n. 55.

[91] See Amanat, *Resurrection and Renewal*, 298. Even though there are no more records of the *ijāzas* she received, it is certain that Sayyid Kazim Rashti regarded her as a *mutjahid.* There are also indications that she received *ijāzas* of *ijtihād* from her father as well as Yusuf Hakami (d. 1276/1859) and Aqa Hakami (d. 1285/1868).

has attained a status comparable to the status that Qurrat al-'Ayn held in Karbala.[92]

Two younger sisters of Qurrat al-'Ayn, Marziyyeh Salehi Baraqani (1817–1895) and her half-sister Rubabeh Salehi Baraqani (d. 1879), also became female religious scholars, although not as distinguished. Like Qurrat al-'Ayn, Marziyyeh is said to have studied Arabic and Persian with their mother; *fiqh, usul, tafsīr*, and hadith with their father and their uncle Mulla Muhammad-Taqi Baraqani (d. 1847), and mysticism with their uncle Shaykh Mulla 'Ali Baraqani and their brother Shaykh Mirza 'Abd al-Wahhab Baraqani Qazvini. Marziyyeh married Mulla Muhammad-'Ali Qazvini, the son of her mother's brother Mulla 'Abd al-Wahhab, the prominent *shaykhi 'alim* of Qazvin. Like Qurrat al-'Ayn, Marziyyeh's husband later became one of the eighteen disciples of the Bab. The couple accompanied Qurrat al-'Ayn to Karbala, where Marziyyeh, too, accepted the Bab.[93] She belonged to the circle of women closest to Qurrat al-'Ayn and was in her own right a learned scholar who taught and issued fatwas in Karbala and later in Qazvin until her death in 1895.

Rubabeh was one of five younger half-sisters to Qurrat al-'Ayn and Marziyyeh, and is said to have enjoyed a similar education. She married the son of Mir Rafi' Taleqani, a prominent physician and scholar of Qazvin, and with him studied in Najaf and Karbala. She later taught women in Karbala and Tehran. On her return to Qazvin, she continued teaching and preaching in the women's section of the Salehiyya *madrasa*. Her written works include a treatise on mysticism, a book on *zakat* and another two on imamate and inheritance (*irth*), respectively. Like her older sisters, Rubabeh is also said to have written poetry in Arabic and Persian.[94] Badry notes that both Marziyyeh and Rubabeh are said to have criticised Nasir al-Din Shah frequently in their sermons after the execution of their sister Qurrat al-'Ayn.[95]

---

[92] According to Stiles Maneck, the bequest of religious writing by Qurrat al-'Ayn encompasses 'a letter written to her cousin Mulla Javad Valiyani; six works are produced in *Zuhur al-Haqq* by Fadil Mazandarani, which includes a letter to Mulla Husayn in Arabic; two public addresses; a letter addressed to the Mufti of Baghdad, Ibn Alusi; an apologetic tract written in defence of the Bab and two letters addressed to the Babis of Isfahan'. Stiles Maneck also notes that 'a centennial volume written by Azali Babis in 1949 and entitled *Qurrat al-'Ayn* provides six other prayers and letters. *Kashfu'l al-Ghita* by Najafi contains a long Arabic treatise. E. G. Browne gives the text and translation of a letter written to Shaykh 'Ali 'Azim in an appendix of *The Tarikh-i-Jadid*.' See Susan Stiles Maneck, 'Tahirih: A Religious Paradigm of Womanhood', *Journal of Baha'i Studies* II.2 (1989), 1–10, here 9 n. 7.

[93] Her husband died in the Babi upheaval at Shaykh Tabarsi. Marziyyeh then married his brother Mirza-Yusuf.

[94] See Rajabi, *Mashahir-i Zanan-i Irani*, 103–104. Also Fa'izih Tavakoli, 'Rubabeh Salehi Baraqani: Banu-i Mujtahid-i Qajar', *Ruzanamyi Sarmayih* 304 (22 October 2006), accessed 25 July 2009. It is not entirely clear whether Tavakoli may be confusing some details of Rubabih's life with that of Marziyyeh. See also *Zanan-i Fadil: Rubabih Salihi va Asiy-i Khanum* (Iranian Institute for Contemporary Historical Studies, Nashriyyih-i Electroniki-yi Zanan, no. 7, n.d.) <http://www.iichs.org/index.asp?id=318&doc_cat=9>, accessed 25 July 2009.

[95] See Badry, *Zum Profil weiblicher 'Ulama'*, 32.

The cousin of Qurrat al-'Ayn, and the sister of her husband, Umm Kulthum Baraqani (d. 1851/1852) is described as a jurisprudent who led her own *ḥalqa* in Qazvin, Tehran, and Karbala.[96] She studied with her great-grandaunt Mirza Mah Sharaf Khanum, then also *fiqh* and *usul* with her father and her uncle, Qurrat al-'Ayn's father. She is said to have authored a *tafsīr* of the Fatiha. The writings of all members of the family are kept in the library of Sayyid Muhammad-Va'iz Rafi'i Qazvini in Qazvin, a male descendant of the Baraqani family.[97]

Women more generally were actively involved in the religious revival movements of the nineteenth century. The wife of the *shaykhi* leader Sayyid Kazim Rashti (d. 1844) allowed Qurrat al-'Ayn to teach Rashti's male and female students in her own house. She also organised the women's league of the Babi movement, called the 'women companions', to which the Baraqani sisters belonged as well as wives of other *shaykhi 'ulama*. Together with other female leaders of the Babi movement, she founded the women's society Anjuman-i Mukhaddarat-i Vatan in 1903.[98]

Female Religious Scholars and Educators in Twentieth-century Iran

The revered mystic and founder of a women's *madrasa* in Isfahan, Nosrat Amin, also known as Hajjiyya Khanom Nosrat Amin Begum (1886–1983), emerged as the leading *mujtahida* in twentieth-century Iran.[99] By the age

[96] Ibid. Also Rajabi, *Mashahir-i Zanan-i Irani*, 18, n. 209. She married Qurrat al-'Ayn's oldest brother, Shaykh 'Abd al-Wahhab Baraqani.

[97] Rajabi mentions a further female scholar from the extended Baraqani family who allegedly reached the *mujtahid* rank, Umm Kulthum Rawjani Qazvini (d. 1902/3), daughter of Shaykh Karim Rawqani. According to Rajabi, she still studied with Qurrat al-'Ayn's father and his brother Mulla Muhammad-Taqi Baraqani. See Rajabi, *Mashahir-i Zanan-i Irani*, 19. She was married to Shaykh Ibrahim Zanjani and had four sons, who also became *'ulama*.

[98] Other women in this circle were Khorshid Begum Khanum (called Shams al-Duha, the wife of Mirza Muhammad-'Ali Nahri), the mother and sister of Mulla Husayn Bushruyeh, the mother of Hadi Nahri, and Rustameh, the first militant female leader in the movement. See, for example, Amanat, *Resurrection and Renewal*, 304ff.

[99] For an in-depth account of Amin, see Maryam Rutner, 'Nosrat Amin (1886/87–1983): A Female Mojtahed', Ph.D. dissertation, New York University, 2020. Also, Mirjam Künkler and Roja Fazaeli in this volume. The main biographies are Nasir Baqiri Bidhindi, *Banu-yi Namunih: Gilva-hayi az Hayat-i Banu-yi Mujtahidih-i Amin Isfahani* (Qum: Daftar-i Tabligat-i Islami-yi Hawzih-i 'Ilmiyyih-i Markaz-i Intisharat, 1382 [2003]); M. 'Amu Khalili, *Kawkab-i Durri: [Sharh-i Ahwal-i Banu-yi Mujtahidih-i Amin* (Tehran: Payam-i 'Adalat, 1379 [2000]), and Nahid Tayyibi, *Zindigani-i Banu-yi Irani: Banu-yi Mujtahidih Nusrat al-Sadat Amin* (Qum: Sabiqun Publishers, 1380 [2001]).

of forty Amin had authored a jurisprudential treatise that earned her high regard among some of the leading *'jurists* of her time and numerous *ijāzas* of *ijtihād*.[100] Amin herself granted *ijāzas* of *ijtihād* and *riwāyat* to her contemporaries including Ayatollah Sayyid Shahab al-Din Mar'ashi-Najafi (d. 1990).[101] Grand Ayatollah Sayyid Husayn Borujerdi (1875–1961) considered Amin on a par with the most important Shi'i jurisprudents of her time.

Amin wrote an impressive array of books both in Persian and Arabic, among them, in Arabic, a collection of legal rules and commentaries written on forty *hadiths* (*al-Arba'in al-Hashimiyya*, 1936) and a compilation of her responses to questions on *fiqh* and *kalam* that were posed to her by scholars in the *ḥawzāt*, *Jami' al-Shatat* (*Collection of Small Pieces*).[102] Amin's most important work in Persian is her principles of *tafsīr* 'Makhzan al-'Irfan dar 'Ulum-i Qur'an' (Sources of Knowing in Sciences of the Qur'an) in fifteen volumes, of which the first appeared in 1956.[103] Apart from the multi-volume *tafsīr*, Amin published at least six books in Persian, of which *Ravesh-e Khoshbakhti va Tawsiyeh beh Khaharan-e Imani* (*The Way to Happiness and Advice for Sisters in Faith*) (1952), became the most popularly known. It was written in response to what she perceived to be cultural ills afflicting the social elite of her time and is directed at a non-expert public readership.[104] Amin also translated into Persian Ahmad ibn Muhammad ibn Miskawayh's (d. 1030) *Tahdhib al-Akhlaq* (*The Refinement of Character*), which was used as a text of instruction in moral philosophy in many universities and *ḥawzāt* until the turn of the twentieth century.

Amin had a great impact on women's religious education when, in 1965, she opened an all-girls Islamic high school (*(Dabirestan-e Dokhtaraneh-ye Amin*), as well as an introductory Islamic studies seminary called Maktab-e Fatima in Isfahan, which provided a unique opportunity for women to

---

[100] The *'ulama* from whom she obtained both *ijāzas* of *ijtihād* and *riwāyat* include Ayatollah Muhammad-Kazim Husayni Shirazi (1873–1947), grand Ayatollah 'Abd al-Karim Ha'eri-Yazdi (1859–1937), both in 1935; as well as Ibrahim Husayni Shirazi Estahbanati (d. 1958), Ayatollah Sayyid Muhammad-'Ali Najafabadi (1877–1939), and Ayatollah Murtada Mazaheri Najafi-Isfahani. In addition, she received an *ijāza* of *riwāyat* from Ayatollah Muhammad-Reza Najafi-Isfahani. See Hamed Abdus, 'Banu Amin, Ulgu-ye Zan Musalman (Lady Amin, the Model of a Muslim Woman)' (The Islamic Revolution Documentation Centre (Markaz-e Asnad-e Inqelab-e Islami), 23 Khordad 1386 [13 June 2007]), <http://www.irdc.ir/article.asp?id=1044> last accessed 12 April 2011.

[101] See Mohsen Sa'idzadeh (written under the name of his wife Mina Yadigar Azadi), 'Ijtihad va Marja'iyyat-i Zanan (Ijtihad and the *Marja'iyyat* of Women)', *Zanan Magazine* VIII (1992), 24. See also Hassan Najafi, 'Ketab Shenasi Banu Amin', *E'temad-e Melli* 946, 10.

[102] Published in Isfahan by al-Matba'ah al-Muhammadiyya in 1344 [1965], but probably available as a manuscript much earlier. The collection of questions and answers is compiled by Hojjatoleslam Morteza Mazaheri, who is also listed as an 'author'.

[103] Published in Isfahan by Chap-e Mohammadi, 1376– [1956–].

[104] Published in Tehran (n.p., 1331 [1952]), 'Bi-Qalam-e Yeki az Banuvan-e Irani' and later Isfahan (Saqafi, 1347 [1968]) under the name 'Yek Banu-ye Irani', also with an introduction by Mostafa Hadavi in Isfahan (Markaz-e Pakhsh, Anjuman-e Himayat az Khanevadeha-ye bi- Sarparast, 1369 [1990]).

complete the first two of three cycles of a typical *ḥawza* education.[105] Amin died four years into the revolution at the age of ninety-seven. Two conferences were held in her memory in 1992 and 1993, in which former students as well as numerous dignitaries participated.[106] During the early years of Sayyid Mohammad Khatami's presidency, a TV series was planned on the Iranian *mujtahida*, which, however, has not been realised to date. The fact that a few Master's theses are now written about her in Iran may indicate a renewed interest in her legacy as a scholar and Islamic educator.[107]

Considering the state's increased support for *ḥawza* education since the 1979 revolution, it is surprisingly difficult to identify leading *mujtahidāt* in contemporary Iran.[108] Although more than a handful carry the title, not a single one is considered on par with the leading voices of theological and jurisprudential dispute today. One of the more prominent female religious scholars in the Islamic Republic is Zohreh Sefati (b. 1948). On her own account, she received her first permission of *riwāyat* in 1996 from Ayatollah 'Ali-Yari Gharavi-Tabrizi. Other *ijāzas* followed by Mohammad-Fazel Lankarani (d. 2007), and by Ayatollah Lotfollah Safi-Golpayegani (b. 1919) who issued her permissions of both *riwāyat* and *ijtihād*.[109] According to Sefati, she herself has given *ijāzas* of *riwāyat* to more than forty male scholars. Among Sefati's more noteworthy teachers was Ayatollah Meshkini (1922–2007)

---

[105] Hamed Abdus, *Banu Amin*, and Muhammad-Taqi Jalili, *Banu Amin*. Several schools were established by Amin's students: a certain 'Khanum Salik' is said to have established Maktab-e al-Zahra in Najaf-Abad. Zahra Mazaheri taught Islamic studies to girls in Qom and is said to have contributed, like Zohreh Sefati, to the establishment of Maktab-e Tawhid, a precursor to Jami'at al-Zahra. See Tayyebi, *Zendegani-e Banu-ye Irani*, 130–132.

[106] *Majmu'ah-i Maqalat va Sukhanrani-ha-yi Avvalin va Duvumin Kungrih-i Buzurgdasht-i Banu-yi Mujtahidih Sayyidih Nusrat Amin (r.h.)* (Qum: Markaz-e Mutali'at va Tahqiqat-e Farhangi, Daftar-e Mutali'at-e Farhangi-e Banuvan, 1374 [1995]).

[107] See Sha'isteh Nadri, Tahqiq dar Zendegi-ye Banu Mujtahedeh Amin va Barrasi Tafsir-e *Makhzan al-'Irfan* (A Research on the Life of Lady Mujtahida Amin and a Study of the *Makhzan al-'Irfan* Exegesis), Azad University of Tehran, defended 1998 under supervision of Mansour Pahlavan; Raziyyeh Maniyya, Ravish Shenasi-e Tafsir-e *Makhzan al-'Irfan-e* Banu-ye Mujtahedeh Amin (The Methodology of the *Makhzan al-'Irfan* Exegesis by Lady Mujtahida Amin), Azad University, Science and Research Branch, n.d.

[108] Mirjam Künkler, "The Bureaucratization of Religious Education in the Islamic Republic of Iran," in *Regulating Religion in Asia: Norms, Modes, and Challenges*, eds. Arif A. Jamal, Jaclyn L. Neo, and Daniel Goh (New York: Cambridge University Press, 2019), 187-206; also Roswitha Badry, 'Überlebens- und Ermächtigungsstrategien von Frauen in der Islamischen Republik Iran', in *Weiblicher Blick – Männerglaube (. . .), Beiträge zur Gender-Perspektive in den Religionen*, ed. Nadine Weibel (Münster: Waxmann Verlag, 2008), 146–162.

[109] For more biographical information on Sefati, see Künkler and Fazaeli in this volume. Following Golpayegani's *ijāza*, Sefati received another permission of *ijtihād* from Ayatollah Muhammad-Hassan Ahmadi-Faqih, her husband. See also Muhammad Bade'i, 'Guftigu ba Faqih Pazhuhandeh Banu Zohreh Sefati' (Interview with the Researcher Jurist, Lady Zohreh Sefati), *Kayhan Farhangi*, 199 (6 April 2003) <http://www.noormags.com/View/Magazine/ViewPages.aspx?numberId=1131&ViewType=1&PageNo=8>, last accessed 7 January 2010. The only biography to date appears to be Fariba Anisi, *Banu Sefati: Zani az Tabar Khorshid* (Markaz-e Umur-e Zanan va Khanevadeh, Nahad Riyasat-e Jomhuri, 1388 [2009]).

who taught her *akhlaq*, *fiqh*, and *usul*.[110] Until their assassinations, she is said to have maintained a strong connection to Ayatollahs Beheshti (d. 1981) and Morteza Motahhari (d. 1979).

Although Sefati is the most visible contemporary female Shi'i authority (she is a member of the Women's Socio-Cultural Council of the Islamic Republic),[111] her status as an Islamic scholar is not comparable to that of Nosrat Amin. In contrast to Amin, Sefati's publications hardly deal with theological and moral matters, but focus on narrow jurisprudential questions concerning 'women's issues'.[112] In 2002, Sefati was asked to brief the Expediency Council regarding a bill revising the marriage age for girls and boys. With recourse to a distinction that Sefati makes between the age of *taklīf* – when one is required to oblige by certain religious regulations such as hijab – and the age of maturity, which allows her to set the marriage age slightly higher than the age of *taklīf* (at thirteen as opposed to nine years), the bill became a law in 2002. Sefati's very conservative interpretations had served the Council well: while the (reformist) parliament at the time had envisioned a much higher legal marriage age, the Expediency Council could justify the regressive measure with which it overturned the parliament's provision with reference to the writings of a female religious scholar.[113]

In the 1970s, a small group of women to which Sefati belonged, sought a *ḥawza* education in Qom and helped establish the city's first all-female seminary, Maktab-e Tawhid.[114] After the 1979 revolution, the seminary was transformed into a state-funded women's *ḥawza*, now called Jami'at al-Zahra, where Sefati used to teach *fiqh* and *tafsīr*.[115]

---

[110] Sefati later married one of her teachers, Ayatollah Muhammad-Hassan Ahmadi-Faqih (d. 2010). She has four daughters.

[111] The Women's Socio-Cultural Council is a subsidiary organisation of the Supreme Council of Cultural Revolution. Its website can be found at <www.womenrc.ir>.

[112] Her publications include *Pazhuhesh-e Fiqh-e Piramun-e Senn-e Taklif* (*A Jurisprudential Inquiry on the Age of Maturity*) (Tehran: Nashr-e Motahhar, 1376 [1997 or 1998]), and *Naw Avara-ha-ye Fiqhi dar Ahkam-e Banuvan* (*New Jurisprudential Rulings on Women*). Another publication is *Ziyarat dar Partu-ye Velayat (Sharhi bar Ziyarat-e Ashura)* (*Pilgrimage Under the Rays of Guardianship*) (Qom: Mojtama'-e 'Ulum-e Dini-ye Hazrat-e Vali-e'Asr, 1376 [1997]).

[113] The bill was passed with the provision that 'marriage of a girl younger than thirteen or a boy younger than fifteen years of age is dependent on the consent of their guardian and also contingent on the court'. Shirin Ebadi, *Huquq-e Zan dar Qavanin-e Jomhuri-ye Islami-ye Iran* (*Women's Rights in the Laws of the Islamic Republic of Iran*) (Tehran: Ganj-e Danesh Publications, 2002). The final version dramatically fell short of both the original draft of the Majles that had raised the marriage age to eighteen for both boys and girls, and the International Convention on the Rights of the Child (CRC), which Iran has signed and ratified.

[114] To this group also belonged Fatemeh Amini and Maryam Behruzi (both mentioned below).

[115] Since Jami'at al-Zahra's curriculum was simplified in 1993/1994 and the course of study changed to a four-year degree, the students' demand for the *dars-e kharej*, the third and highest level of the *ḥawza* education, which Sefati taught, has sharply declined and Sefati has predominantly given private lessons since.

Like other governments in the contemporary Muslim world, the Iranian government has established certain state-funded programmes to meet societal demands for the improved access of women to religious education and the training in religious authority.[116] Nevertheless, despite the fact that educational opportunities for women have expanded dramatically since the 1980s, very few women can be found in the midst of the scholarly religious establishment today. For the twentieth century, beside Nosrat Amin and Zohreh Sefati, we know that the following women received advanced training in the Islamic sciences (the advanced sutuh level, or the dars-e kharej level): Ma'sumeh Izzat al-Shar'i (1891–1951),[117] 'Iffat al-Zaman Amin (1912–1967),[118] Zinat al-Sadat Humayuni (b. 1917),[119] Zahra Mazaheri,[120] Fatemeh Amini (b. 1933),[121] Azam Taleqani (b. 1940),[122] Monireh Gorji (b. 1940s),[123] Maryam

---

[116] For a fascinating ethnographic study of a female preacher in the South of Tehran in the 1990s, see Azam Torab, *Performing Islam: Gender and Ritual in Iran* (Boston: Brill, 2007). 'Mrs Omid has to contend with six other established female preachers, and several less prominent ones, in her neighbourhood. Among them are some younger, theologically trained women, whose loyalties to the state have opened up new prospects for gaining religious leadership, independent of the patronage of older, freelance local preachers such as Mrs Omid. These younger preachers now posed a challenge to the sphere of influence of those who had trained in the traditional way at home.' Ibid., 40. See also Z. Kamalkhani, 'Reconstruction of Islamic Knowledge and Knowing. A Case of Islamic Practices Among Women in Iran', *Women and Islamization*, eds K. Ask and M. Tjomsland (Oxford: Berg Publishers, 1998), 177–193.

[117] Ma'sumeh Izzat al-Shar'i (1891–1951) studied the Qur'an, hadith, Arabic, and Persian literature, taught in schools for several years and in 1916 opened one of Tehran's first girls' schools. See 'A'isha Al-i Ahmad, 'Izzat al-Shar'i' (Iranian Institute for Contemporary Historical Studies, Nashriyye-ye Electroniki-ye Zanan), no. 18, n.d., <http://iichs.org/ index.asp?id=976&doc_cat=9>, last accessed 25 July 2009.

[118] 'Iffat al-Zaman Amin (1912–1967) founded two Islamic schools and wrote the book *Hadith-i Amin*.

[119] Zinat al-Sadat 'Homayuni was Nosrat Amin's most prominent student and received an *ijāza* of *ijtihād* from the latter. She translated Amin's first Arabic work (Arba'in al-Hashimi-yi) into Persian, and is also the author of *Shakhsiyat-e Zan* (Tehran, 1369 [1990]), *Zan mazhar-i khallaqiyat-i Allah* (Tehran: Daftar-i Intisharat-i Islami, 1377 [1998]), and translator of the book *Asrar al-ayat* by Muhammad b. Ibrahim Sadr al-Din Shirazi, *Asrar al-ayat* (Tehran: 'Izz Humayuni, 1984). Zinat al-Sadat Homayuni directed Maktab-e Fatima in Isfahan until 1992. See Tayyebi, *Zendagani*, 124; 'Amu Khalili, *Kawkab-i durri*, 125.

[120] Zahra Mazaheri was another student of Nosrat Amin's. In the 1970s she taught religious studies to girls in Qom, and contributed to the founding of Maktab-e Tawhid. See Tayyebi, *Zendagani*, 124.

[121] See Azadeh Kian-Thiébaut, 'Women's Religious Seminaries in Iran', *ISIM Newsletter* VI (October 2000), 23.

[122] Azam Taleqani, daughter of Ayatollah Taleqani (d. 1979), was an active member of Iran's first post-revolution parliament, but has been banned from running ever since. She was the editor of the women's magazine *Payam-e Hajar* and the president of the women's umbrella organisation *Jame'at-e Zanan-e Enqelab-e Islami* (Association of Islamic Revolutionary Women) set up in 1979. In 1997, she famously registered her candidacy for the Iranian presidency, but was disqualified by the Guardian Council.

[123] Monireh Gorji was the only female member (out of seventy-five members) of the Assembly of Experts of the Constitution in 1979. Gorji's best known publication is *Negaresh-e Qur'an bar Hozur-e Zan dar Tarikh-e Anbiya*. (Tehran: Markaz-e Mutali'at va Tahqiqat-e Masa'il-e Zanan, 1373 [1994]). She used to write for the quarterly journal *Farzaneh*; see <http://www.farzanehjournal.com>. See Shireen Mahdavi, 'Women and the Shii Ulama in Iran', *Middle Eastern Studies* IXX.1 (January 1983), 23–24; also Esfandiari, 'The Majlis and Women's Issues'.

Behruzi (b. 1945–2012),[124] Ma'sumeh Golgiri (b. 1940s),[125] Maryam Mohaqqeq-Damad (b. 1940s),[126] Shahindokht Mawlavardi (b. 1940s),[127] Sedigheh Vasmaghi (b. 1962)[128] and Fariba Alasvand (b. 1967).[129] While most of these women are mentioned in passing as having completed a *ḥawza* education and as having in some capacity played a public role, there are virtually no studies that review their publications and any contributions they may have made to Islamic scholarship. There is also no study to date that has traced the trajectories of Nosrat Amin's students, nor any that reviews the multitude of women's *ḥawza* that now exist in every major town of Iran, no comparison of their curricula, the quality of the education they provide, and the typical career paths of their graduates. Rutner's study in this volume is a first step in this direction. The lacuna is even more surprising given the sharp increase in institutions of religious learning for women in the 1980s and 1990s. The post-revolutionary generation has witnessed a massive governmental campaign in expanding religious training for women and men (it is estimated that 150,000 students presently study in theological seminaries of Iran,

---

124 Maryam Behruzi studied Islamic studies in Qom. She was the co-founder of the Iranian Women's Islamic Association, banned in 1975. In 1978 she was imprisoned and released the following year. As a Member of three parliaments after the 1979 revolution, she participated in women-specific legislative proposals and vehemently criticised discrimination against women in general and female MPs in particular. Until her death, she chaired the largest Islamic Women's Organisation, ami'at-e Zeinab, which extends to eighty-two branches in Tehran and sixty branches in other cities. In the 1990s, the organisation successfully lobbied for legal reform that would grant widows of the Iran–Iraq war custody over their children, which was previously awarded to the deceased man's family. In an act unprecedented in the Islamic Republic, the organisation proposed in 2007 female candidates to the election of the Majles-e Khobregan (Assembly of Experts), a body consisting of religious scholars only. Predictably, the female candidates were rejected by the Guardian Council. oversees eight religious seminaries and Qur"an centers, nominated six female *mujtahids* in 2007 for the historically clerical (and all-male) Assembly of Experts [19]. See Homa Hoodfar and Shadi Sadr, 'Islamic Politics and Women's Quest for Gender Equality in Iran', *Third World Quarterly* 31.6 (2010), 885–903, 896.

125 Like Zohreh Sefati, she hails from Abadan and moved to Qom in the early 1970s. Today she teaches *fiqh* at the *kharej* level at Jami'at al-Zahra.

126 Dr Maryam Mohaqqeq-Damad is a lawyer and instructor at Mufid University and Imam Sadiq University. She is the niece of Sadeq Larijani, the former Head of Judiciary, and of 'Ali Larijani, former Speaker of Parliament.

127 Shahindokht Mawlavardi was head of the Iranian Association for the Protection of Women's Human Rights and Director of International Affairs of President Khatami's Centre for Women's Participation. She is now senior researcher in international law and head of the Islamic Women's Coalition.

128 Sedigheh Vasmaghi is a lawyer and theologian. She has authored the fiqh works *Bāzkhanī-e sharīat* and *Bezāte fiqh* and her book *Woman, Jurisprudence, Islam* has been published in English and German. She has formulated original arguments regarding the process of Qur'anic codification and its consequences for the validity of Qur'anic legal injunctions.

129 Fariba Alasvand is a member of the Scientific Research Committee of The Office for Women's Studies and Research and, like Sefati, a member of the Women's Socio-Cultural Council. She has been teaching since 1990 at Jami'at al-Zahra.

about 50,000 of them female).[130] Compared to the pre-revolutionary situation, the share of girls in the Islamic seminary system has risen exponentially. According to the official website of Jami'at al-Zahra in Qom, now the largest state-run women's seminary, with approximately 12,000 students are currently enrolled and more than 25,000 female students have graduated from Jami'at al-Zahra since its inception in 1985.[131] However, despite the expansive institutional apparatus that the Islamic Republic has erected to promote women's training in religious seminaries, the scholarly fruit is surprisingly difficult to identify. The leading female *'ulama* in Iran today, as few as they are, seem to be products of the pre-revolutionary decentralised seminary culture rather than the massive post-revolutionary apparatus put in place by the state. Indeed, most female *ḥawza* students in contemporary Iran engage in propagation and teaching (in primary and secondary schools) upon graduation, rather than scholarship.[132]

Conclusions

In this article I have sought to highlight the diversity of roles that women have played in the transmission and generation of Islamic knowledge, with a particular focus on modern Iran.

Iran exhibits perhaps the strongest tradition of female religious authority in the modern Middle East, judging from the references of male scholars to their female counterparts, often members of their family. The example of the women from the Baraqani family, some of whom did not only distinguish themselves as renowned preachers and respected scholars, but also as charismatic public leaders, is unsurpassed in modern Iran. In the twentieth century, the example of Nosrat Amin, who emerged a religious authority notably without a distinguished clerical family background, stands out not only for the high level of recognition she enjoyed among the highest-ranking male Shi'i authorities of her time, but also the role she played as an Islamic educator at a time when religious schooling was systematically marginalised by the state. Further, towards the early 1970s, a number of women studied

---

130 Compare http://howzeh-qom.ir. A list of the women's *madrasas* can be found at *Saminih-i Weblog-i Madaris: Hawzih-ha-yi 'Ilmiyyih-i Khaharan* <http://womenhc.com>. A total of 110 seminaries are listed with links to their individual websites. By comparison, Kian-Thiébaut reported that, in 1996, out of 62,731 students in religious seminaries, 9,995 (or 16 per cent) were women. See Kian-Thiébaut, 'Women's Religious Seminaries'.

131 See the official website of Jami'at al-Zahra <http://www.jz.ac.ir/fetr/index.php? option=com_content&view=article&id=161&Itemid=148>, last accessed 13 April 2011.

132 See Fazaeli and Künkler, 'New Opportunities for Old Role Models?'

together with men in the Islamic seminaries in Qom and became sufficiently prominent to establish, with the help and endorsement of eminent grand ayatollahs, their own religious schools and seminaries exclusively instituted for girls and women. We know of at least two successful results of such endeavours, the *Maktab-e Fatima*, established by Nosrat Amin in the late 1960s in Isfahan, and the *Maktab-e Tawhid*, founded in the 1970s in Qom.

The existence of a significant number of female religious authorities in modern Iran has been highlighted to demonstrate that their profound underrepresentation in the literature does not match the empirical phenomenon. One hopes that increasing scholarly attention will be dedicated to examples of female religious authority in the near future, in order to evaluate both the contributiowns women have made to the transmission and production of religious knowledge, as well as the limits of this contribution. For the case of modern Iran, this will mean consulting important biographical dictionaries that are still largely untapped and venturing into little studied archives and private collections of clerical families, as well as expanding on existing oral histories.

A Call for a Comparative Research Agenda

The relevant literature on female religious authority in Islam nearly exclusively consists of case studies that highlight instances of women exercising some form of religious authority in a given context, for instance, hadith transmitters in Mamluk Egypt, female jurists in Safavid and Qajar Iran, *muftiyāt* in nineteenth-century Russia, or *murshidāt* in late twentieth-century Morocco. These accounts are highly informative and offer revealing insights into local forms of religious authority. Hardly any provide diachronic or comparative accounts across different geographies, which would make it easier to evaluate atypical opportunities for women to exercise forms of religious authority, as well as the closure of such opportunities. They usually also do not attempt to assess women's religious authority compared to men's at that time. Yet only a comparative conversation about the variations in female religious authority will facilitate the formulation of hypotheses about the kinds of conditions and developments (theological, jurisprudential, social, economic, political, cultural) which particularly enhanced, promoted, and conversely stifled, the phenomenon of female religious authority in various strands of Islam.

CHAPTER

3

UMM SALAMA: A FEMALE AUTHORITY LEGITIMATING THE AUTHORITIES

Yasmin Amin

The ultimate authority in Shi'i Islam rests with the Imams. Much has been written about what legitimates an Imam and confirms his authority. Considering that the twelve Imams are all male and eleven of them are the progeny of 'Ali and Fatima and therefore by extension the Prophet, Fatima, the most excellent of all females,[1] does not play much of a role, other than being the noble womb that conceived, carried, and gave birth to two of them and established both the line and the link to the Prophet.

According to Tabataba'i, the womb not only is the material unity between individuals of a family, but it also has irrefutable spiritual and physical effects on the individuals.[2] In a tradition by the Prophet, he says to Umm Salama: 'O Umm Salama, the wombs of *ahl al-bayt* are connected to the Merciful One, linked to His throne, so whoever restores the ties of the womb, God restores him, and whoever cuts them, God cuts him off.'[3] In another report by 'Ali, he is quoted as saying: 'When Adam was created, God placed that light in Adam's loins and brought him down to earth. It was carried on the Ark in Noah's loins, then it was thrown into the fire in Abraham's loins. God then transferred it from noble loin to noble womb and from noble womb to noble

---

[1] See, for example, the canonical hadith reports describing the mistresses of the women of Paradise, as well as the four mistresses of all female creatures, as Asiyah, the wife of Pharaoh; Mary, the mother of Jesus; Khadija, the wife of the Prophet; and Fatima his daughter. They are found in the collections of al-Bukhari, al-Tirmidhi, al-Nasa'i, Ibn Hibban, Ibn Abi Shayba, al-Tabarani, Ibn Hanbal, and others.

[2] Muhammad Husayn Tabataba'i, *al-Mizan fi tafsir al-Qur'an*, 20 vols (Qum: Mu'assasat al-Nashr al-Islami, 1981–1982), 4:148.

[3] 'Imad al-Din Abu Ja'far Muhammad b. 'Ali b. Ḥamza al-Tusi, *al-Thaqib fi al-manaqib* (Qum: Mu'assasat Ansariyan, 1991–1992), 61.

loin of all the pure ancestors.'[4] Hence, Fatima's role, even if only as a noble womb, should not be under-estimated, even in a male-dominated hierarchal structure as the Imamate.[5]

Muslim feminists have searched in the Islamic legacy for evidence that supports a more egalitarian reading of the sacred texts. They have also looked for female personalities who played a pivotal and important role in the early Islamic history, establishing the community, to be taken as role models for modern Muslim women. They did that to argue that Islam is not misogynistic, but that the women-unfriendly versions of history are a result of patriarchal readings and practices of which Islam is innocent.[6]

This contribution looks at the role ascribed to a woman in legitimating three of the twelve Imams, most importantly 'Ali. It also looks at how a woman kept the *naṣṣ* (authoritative designation), designating the Imams as the rightful and legitimate authority, safe until they were able to retrieve it to assume their rightful position and enact their authority. The chapter is in three parts and will start by looking at the term *ahl al-bayt* and its interpretations as it shapes the Imamate. This is followed by introducing Umm Salama and the reasons she was particularly revered in Shi'i traditions, as well as her main narrations from the Prophet in support of the *ahl al-bayt* in general and 'Ali in particular and his right to succeed the Prophet and therefore by extension the right of his progeny to the Imamate. Finally, the last part looks at the Imam's authority and the necessity of a *naṣṣ*, designating the Imam as legitimate and Umm Salama's role that earned her the honorific *Ḥāfiẓat al-naṣṣ* ('Keeper of the *naṣṣ*').

Ahl al-bayt

The term *ahl al-bayt* is a term of contention between Sunnis and Shi'is. Historically, as, for example, in pre-Islamic Arabia, the term '*bayt*' signified the ruling family of a tribe.[7] Originally, the term *ahl bayt* or *ahl al-bayt* had nothing to do with the Prophet or his family. In Arabic, linguistically, this term simply means the noble and influential family in the tribe or in a broader sense it referred to the members of any ruling or noble family, Arab or non-Arab alike.[8] Therefore, and in keeping with the accepted usage of the term,

---

4 Abu Ja'far Muhammad b. 'Ali b. al-Husayn Ibn Babawayh al-Qummi, *Kamal al-din wa-tamam al-ni'mah* (Qum: Mu'assasat al-Nashr al-Islami, 1984), 274–279.

5 For more on the 'womb' see Rawand Osman, *Female Personalities in the Qur'an and Sunna: Examining the Major Sources of Imami Shi'i Islam* (New York: Routledge, 2015), 15–18, 33–36.

6 For more details, see the detailed introduction of 'Husniyya's Debate at the Court of Harun al-Rashid: Sectarian Polemics and Female Religious Authority' in this volume.

7 Muqatil b. Sulayman al-Balkhi, *Tafsir Muqatil b. Sulayman* (Cairo: al-Hay'a al-Misriyya al-'Amma li-l-Kitab, 1989), 3:45.

8 Moshe Sharon, *Black Banners from the East: The Establishment of the 'Abbasid State: Incubation of a Revolt* (Leiden: Brill, 1983), 78.

the Umayyads, for example, referred to themselves as *ahl al-bayt*. It has been reported that when al-Hajjaj b. Yusuf al-Thaqafi (d. 714), the famous and infamous governor of Iraq died, 'Umar b. 'Abd al-'Aziz (d. 720) referred to him as 'one of us, *ahl al-bayt*'.[9]

The phrase *ahl al bayt* occurs twice in the Qur'an, once in verse (11:73),[10] referring to the family of Abraham, and again in verse (33:33),[11] referring to Muhammad's family. While most Sunnis extend this term to all the Prophet's relatives and wives, the Shi'is believe it is exclusive to *ahl al-kisā'* and their progeny. *Ahl al-kisā'*, as described in *Ḥadīth al-Kisā'*, are the four who were honoured by being with the Prophet inside his mantle when verse (33:33) was revealed to attest to their divine purification from all imperfections. These four are Fatima, 'Ali, and their two sons, al-Hasan and al-Husayn. The *kisā'* event and the verse connected with it would play an important role in the articulation of the succession of the Imams, as will be demonstrated in the third part. According to Moosa, the *ahl al-kisā'* are 'exalted above the whole community of Islam, and no one in the community is equal to them in position or stature. They are regarded by the Shi'is as the pillars of religion and the stronghold of the Muslim faith. Most significantly, only they, of all Muslims, are by right heirs to the Prophet in leadership of the community.'[12]

Certain traditions concerning the Prophet and 'Ali are relevant to any discussion of the scope of *ahl al-bayt*. Both the Prophet and 'Ali considered Salman al-Farisi, a Persian convert to Islam and a companion of the Prophet who is credited with the idea of digging the trench in 'the Battle of the Trench', to be a member of *ahl al-bayt*. The Prophet is reported to have said: 'Salman is one of us, *ahl al-bayt*.'[13] But Shi'is maintain that the term 'household' or the phrase 'family of the Prophet' refers exclusively to 'Ali, Fatima, and their two sons, because they are the Prophet's relatives in the first degree.

Ḥadīth al-Kisā' is most notably transmitted by Umm Salama, although many different *isnād* chains are recorded. Al-Tabari, for example, records a version of this tradition in his commentary on the Qur'an narrated by Abu Sa'id al-Khudri, according to which the Prophet said that this verse was revealed exclusively for him, 'Ali, Fatima, al-Hasan, and al-Husayn.[14]

---

[9] Ibid., 79.

[10] 'The mercy of God and His blessings are on you, O people of the house, surely He is Praised, Glorious' (Q 11:73).

[11] 'God only desires to keep away the uncleanness from you, O people of the House! and to purify you thoroughly' (Q 33:33).

[12] Matti Moosa, *Extremist Shi'ites: The Ghulat Sects* (Syracuse: Syracuse University Press, 1987), 81.

[13] See Abu al-Faraj 'Abd al-Rahman b. 'Ali b. Muhammad Ibn al-Jawzi, *Sifat al-safwa* (Aleppo: Dar al-Wa'y, 1969), 1:535, 546; Abu 'Abd Allah Muhammad b. 'Ali b. Muhammad Ibn 'Arabi, *al-Futuhat al-Makkiyya* (Cairo: al-Maktaba al-'Arabiyya, 1988), 2:167.

[14] G. Schallenbergh, 'Ibn Taymiya on the *ahl al-bayt*', in *Egypt and Syria in the Fatimid, Ayyubid and Mamluk Eras III: Proceedings of the 6th, 7th, 8th International Colloquium Organized at the Katholieke Universiteit Leuven in May 1997, 1998 and 1999*, eds Jo van Steenbergen and Urbain Vermeulen (Leuven: Peeters, 2001), 413.

Al-Tabari distinguishes between *al-qarāba* (blood-relations) and *ahl al-bayt* in his exegesis of verse (33:33) and argues that the *ahl al-bayt* are the *ahl al-kisā'*. He lists an impressive number of reports on the authority of Umm Salama in particular and also on the authority of Abu Sa'id al-Khudri, 'A'isha, Abu Hurayra, and others. He adds only one report on the authority of 'Ikrima that claims that the verse referred exclusively to the wives of the Prophet.[15]

Abu al-Qasim 'Abd al-Karim al-Qushayri (d. 1072) relates a tradition that when the Prophet was asked 'who are the family of Muhammad', he answered 'they are ever pious Muslim'.[16] Other writers like 'Abd al-Qadir al-Jilani (d. 1166) and and Muhyi al-Din Ibn al-'Arabi (d. 1240) maintain that the term includes the Prophet's wives. 'Abd al-Qadir al-Jilani includes within *ahl al-bayt* not only the wives of the Prophet but other relatives as well such as the Prophet's uncles and their descendants.[17] Al-Jilani divides the family of the Prophet into four categories: 'Ali, Fatima, and their sons al-Hasan and al-Husayn, as the Prophet's relatives of the first degree; the Prophet's wives as those of the second degree; the descendants of al-Hasan and al-Husayn as those of the third degree; and all other relatives as those of the fourth degree.[18] While Muqatil (d. 767) identifies them as the Prophet's wives,[19] Ibn Kathir also mentions the same solitary report by 'Ikrima in his exegesis of verse (33:33) and then goes on to present the same pro-'Alid material amassed by al-Tabari to argue that *ahl al-bayt* includes the Prophet's wives as well as *ahl al-kisā'*.[20] The much later al-Suyuti (d. 1505) interprets the term as exclusively for the Prophet's wives, without mentioning *ahl al-kisā'*.[21]

Stowasser writes that in Shi'i interpretation, as well as in Sufi teachings, the *ahl al-bayt* as mentioned in verse (33:33) refers to the people of the mantle, and especially in Shi'i belief the *ahl al-kisā'*'s descendants are also included. The purification mentioned in (33:33) has thus become understood later to mean that God purified them and their descendants, so that they share in the Prophet's *'iṣma* ('immunity from sin') and hence are *aḥaqq* ('more entitled') to guide and rule the Muslim community. Most of the traditions quoted by classical Qur'an interpreters exclude the Prophet's wives from membership in the *ahl al-bayt*. However, the Sunni interpreters either opine to include the wives together with the Prophet's blood-relatives or

---

[15] Abu Ja'far Muhammad b. Jarir al-Tabari, *Jami' al-bayan 'an ta'wil ay al-Qur'an* (Riyadh: Markaz al-Turath li-l-Barmajiyyat, 2013), 22:5–7.

[16] Moosa, *Extremist Shi'ites*, 78.

[17] The sons of al-'Abbas, who established the Abbasid dynasty in 750 CE.

[18] Moosa, *Extremist Shi'ites*, 78.

[19] al-Balkhi, *Tafsir Muqatil b. Sulayman*, 3:45.

[20] Isma'il b. 'Umar Ibn Kathir, *Tafsir al-Qur'an al-'azim* (Beirut: Dar al-Ma'rifa, 1996), 3:491–494.

[21] Jalal al-Din al-Suyuti,*Tafsir al-Jalalayn* (Beirut: Dar al-Kitab al-'Arabi, 1984), 510.

even state their individual opinion that the term *ahl al-bayt* was directed at the Prophet's wives.[22]

Dabashi states that Muhammad did not have a son. While 'hereditary' refers exclusively to a son following his father, this was not applicable here. However, referring to the more general application of 'kinsmen' and particularly *ahl al-bayt*, then Muhammad can be considered 'Ali's father figure. Muhammad grew up in 'Ali's father's house, 'Ali was his cousin, born ten years before Muhammad's mission and about six years old when he left his own house to live with the Prophet upon his request. Thus, he was raised by the Prophet and later became his son-in-law. Hence, 'Ali was in constant close proximity to the Prophet and as such the recipient of divine grace.[23]

Leaman, however, opines that merit is a criterion for membership in *ahl al-bayt*, who are only the individuals among the Prophet's descendants who also had close affinity in character and spiritual attainment with the Prophet.[24]

For Shi'is, the *ahl al-bayt* are the *ahl al-kisā'*, which also becomes very apparent looking at *Ḥadīth al-kisā'*. Examining 135 Sunni versions and 185 Shi'i versions, all narrated by Umm Salama in various compendia, the most important issue for her in all these different versions is whether or not she was included in the *ahl al-bayt* or not. This is also important because of the implications for the Sunni and Shi'i disputes. For example, her exclusion leaves out the wives of the Prophet and by extension other children of 'Ali by later wives, as well as al-Hasan's children, as will be demonstrated in the third part. It also minimises all the Prophet's wives as less important than Fatima and her two sons, since they did not receive a special Qur'anic blessing.

Ḥadīth al-kisā' is narrated through numerous different chains and by many different transmitters, who all agree that the incident took place in Umm Salama's house. Hence, as an eyewitness, her versions are authoritative as well as popular and used in many hadith compendia. The versions where Umm Salama is included as *ahl al-bayt*, or whether she joined into the *kisā'* (even if only after the Prophet finished his supplication) or only received an affirmation that she is *min ahlihi* (from his *ahl*) are only thirty-three in the 135 Sunni narrations, meaning 24.4 per cent, or almost a quarter on her authority alone.[25] This also means that most of the Sunni versions also exclude her from being a member of *ahl al-bayt*. For example,

---

[22] Barbara Freyer Stowasser, *Women in the Qur'an, Traditions, and Interpretation* (New York: Oxford University Press, 1994), 172–173.

[23] Hamid Dabashi, *Authority in Islam: From the Rise of Muhammad to the Establishment of the Umayyads* (New Brunswick, NJ: Transaction Publishers, 1989), 102.

[24] Oliver Leaman (ed.), *The Qur'an: an Encyclopedia* (Abingdon: Routledge, 2006), 16.

[25] All these versions are discussed at length in Yasmin Amin, *Musnad Umm Salamah and the Factors Affecting Its Evolution* (Leiden: Brill, forthcoming).

in *Musannaf Ibn Abi Shayba* (d. 849) Umm Salama asks: 'What about me?' The Prophet answers: 'you too', whereas in *Musnad Ibn Ḥanbal* (d. 855) she is told that she is one of his wives, a phrasing that excludes the Prophet's wives from the category of *ahl al-bayt* without detracting from their merit. In the *Fada'il al-Sahaba*, also by Ahmad Ibn Hanbal Umm Salama, upon asking whether she also belongs to *ahl al-bayt*, is allowed to join into the *kisā'*, however only after the Prophet had completed his *du'ā'* (supplications). Abu Bishr al-Dulabi (d. 923) in his *al-Kuna wa-l-asma'* records the Prophet's affirmation that she is included in *ahl al-bayt*. The Shi'i versions, on the other hand, never include her, neither among the *ahl al-bayt* nor allow her inside the mantle, even after the supplications have ended. In some versions there is an added commentary casting doubt as to whether she indeed narrated this report and one surprisingly and uncharacteristically even goes as far as accusing her of being self-serving and attempting to raise her own status from being 'just a wife' to being included as a member of *ahl al-bayt* by narrating this. For example, the version narrated by al-Qadi Sayyid Nur Allah Husayni al-Shushtari, known as Qadi Nur Allah or al-Shahid al-Thalith ('the Third Martyr') (d. 1610) in his *al-Sawarim al-muhriqa*.[26]

In Sunni scholarship, the position of *ahl al-bayt* was considerably reduced by including as many acceptable candidates as possible and also to raise the status of the Prophet's wives by conferring the honorific title *ummahāt al-mu'minīn,* in accordance with verse (33:6),[27] on them and highlighting the injunction that nobody was allowed to marry them after the Prophet's death (verse 33:53),[28] as elaborated by al-Zamakhshari (d. 1144).[29] Al-Baydawi, in contrast, highlighted that the Prophet wives' houses are *mahābiṭ al-waḥy* ('locations where revelation descended'), as mentioned in verse (33:34).[30] Therefore, his wives are unique witnesses of God's revelations.[31]

---

[26] Ibid.

[27] 'The Prophet has a greater claim on the faithful than they have on themselves, and his wives are (as) their mothers; and the possessors of relationship have the better claim in the ordinance of God to inheritance, one with respect to another, than (other) believers, and (than) those who have fled (their homes), except that you do some good to your friends; this is written in the Book' (Q 33:6).

[28] 'O you who believe! do not enter the houses of the Prophet unless permission is given to you for a meal, not waiting for its cooking being finished – but when you are invited, enter, and when you have taken the food, then disperse – not seeking to listen to talk; surely this gives the Prophet trouble, but he forbears from you, and God does not forbear from the truth. And when you ask of them any goods, ask of them from behind a curtain; this is purer for your hearts and (for) their hearts; and it does not behove you that you should give trouble to the Apostle of God, nor that you should marry his wives after him ever; surely this is grievous in the sight of God' (Q 33:53).

[29] Mahmud b. 'Umar al-Zamakhshari, *Tafsir al-Kashshaf 'an haqa'iq al-tanzil wa-'uyun al-aqawil fi wujuh al-ta'wil* (Beirut: Dar al-Ma'rifa, 2005).

[30] 'And keep to mind what is recited in your houses of the communications of God and the wisdom; surely God is Knower of subtleties, Aware' (Q 33:34).

[31] 'Abd Allah b. 'Umar al-Baydawi, *Anwar al-tanzil wa-asrar al-ta'wil al-ma'ruf bi tafsir al-Baydawi* (Beirut: Dar Sadir, 1990), 577.

One argument that was used by both Sunni and Shi'i scholars, although to different ends, is the change in the pronoun within the verse. Al-Mazandarani in his *Sharh Usul al-Kafi* uses corroboration from Sunni sources to argue that the purification was only for *ahl al-bayt* and not for the wives. He writes that the majority opinion is that verse (33:33) was revealed only for those pure people. Muslim narrated in his *Sahih* with an *isnād* from 'A'isha that she said: 'The Prophet – peace and blessings be upon him and his family – left one day wearing a black mantle. Al-Hasan b. 'Ali met him, so the Prophet took him into the mantle, then he did the same with al-Husayn, Fatima, and finally 'Ali and then recited verse (33:33).'[32] He continues by quoting al-Qurtubi who opined that the verse indicated that *ahl al-bayt* were honoured by the Prophet because he took them into his mantle. Ibn 'Atiyya said: 'Ibn 'Abbas and 'Ikrima opined that *ahl al-bayt* means the Prophet's wives, however most scholars said that if his wives were meant, then the verb should have been *yuṭahhirakunna* (feminine plural) instead of *yuṭahhirakum* (masculine plural), supplementing this by citing the above-mentioned report by Abu Sa'id al-Khudri.'[33]

In another volume of his book, al-Mazandarani assembles many hadith reports and ties them to a few verses, arguing for the uniqueness and entitlement of *ahl al-bayt* and the exclusion of the Prophet's wives. He quotes several companions who narrated from Abu 'Abd Allah, al-Husayn b. 'Ali, saying about verse (71:28)[34] that it refers to *wilāya* (guardianship) and that whoever accepts the *wilāya* will be allowed to enter into the Prophet's house. As for verse (33:33), he said it addresses the Imams. Al-Mazandarani argues that the shift in pronouns in this section of the verse shows that the wives of the Prophet were excluded, as they were not purified and hence are not infallible. Furthermore, there is no proof that the sections of this verse were revealed at the same time on one occasion and were not added together later, when the Qur'an was collected and written with that particular sequence, as happened with other verses. If it could be proven that the verse was revealed as a whole, then this section still addresses the Imams, even if in the rest of the discourse it addresses the Prophet's wives before and after them. This is by design and has an advantage, namely that God knew that some of the Prophet's wives would commit wrongdoings and injustices towards the Imams and hence they were promised punishment before and after the section. Al-Mazandarani supports his argument by citing a narration by Hammad from Hurayz that he asked Abu 'Abd Allah about

---

[32] Mawla Muhammad Salih al-Mazandarani, *Sharh usul al-Kafi* (Beirut: Dar Ihya' al-Turath al-'Arabi, 2000), 6:113.

[33] Ibid., 113–115.

[34] 'My Lord! Forgive me and my parents and him who enters my house believing, and the believing men and the believing women; and do not increase the unjust in aught but destruction!' (Q 71:28).

verse (33:30),[35] sarcastically asking, 'Who explained that indecency meant carrying a sword and going out to battle?'[36] So, unlike al-Zamakhshari and al-Baydawi, he does not see the merits of the Prophet's wives, but only the merits of *ahl al-bayt*. He then adds another hadith report narrated from Abu 'Abd Allah from his father 'Ali about a section of verse (33:33), 'and do not display your finery like the displaying of the ignorance of yore', explaining that there will be a second *Jāhiliyya*. Al-Mazandarani claims that many exegetes support this opinion and explains that the first *Jāhiliyya* was before Islam and the second one is the *Jāhiliyya* of transgression and wrongdoing, especially towards the Imams. As for the next verse (33:34),[37] he interprets it by saying that it is conceivable that this also means the Imams, 'wisdom' here meaning all religious knowledge, which would enjoin on the Prophet's wives to preserve the rights of the Imams.[38] Finally, he ends this section with a hadith report narrated from Abu Ja'far Muhammad al-Baqir that the purification verse was revealed in Umm Salama's house solely for the Prophet, 'Ali, Fatima, al-Hasan, and al-Husayn, stating that the Prophet had called them and then covered them with his Khaybari mantle and said, 'O God, these are *ahl baytī*, of whom you promised me what you promised!' Then he made supplications to God to purify them and the verse was revealed subsequently. He adds that Umm Salama asked if she was one of them, and the Prophet replied: 'Rejoice O Umm Salama, for you are blessed.' He then quotes Zayd b. 'Ali b. al-Husayn, who said that some ignorant people claim that the Prophet's wives were meant, but the verse uses the masculine plural rather than the feminine plural, which is also used in the following verse. 'Ali b. Ibrahim said that the Prophet's wives were addressed first, and then the *ahl al-bayt*, and then again the Prophet's wives, followed by all Muslims in verse (33:35).[39] He offers the following explanation: perhaps the reason is that those who emulate someone become like him and those who love someone emulate him. [40]

---

[35] [33:30] 'O wives of the prophet! whoever of you commits an open indecency, the punishment shall be increased to her doubly; and this is easy for God' (Q 33:30).

[36] al-Mazandarani, *Sharh usul al-Kafi*, 7:84–85.

[37] 'And keep to mind what is recited in your houses of the communications of God and the wisdom; surely God is Knower of subtleties, Aware' (Q 33:34).

[38] al-Mazandarani, *Sharh usul al-Kafi*, 7:85–86.

[39] 'Surely the men who submit and the women who submit, and the believing men and the believing women, and the obeying men and the obeying women, and the truthful men and the truthful women, and the patient men and the patient women and the humble men and the humble women, and the almsgiving men and the almsgiving women, and the fasting men and the fasting women, and the men who guard their private parts and the women who guard, and the men who remember God much and the women who remember – God has prepared for them forgiveness and a mighty reward' (Q 33:35).

[40] al-Mazandarani, *Sharh usul al-Kafi*, 7:86.

Tabataba'i points out that a similar later supplementation took place for verse (5:3),[41] arguing that the purification verse is isolated and was introduced into *Sūrat al-Aḥzāb* (Chapter 33) on the Prophet's command during the final organisation of the text. To Shi'i opinion the verse did not match in form or content with the surrounding verses. The phrases preceding and following the purification verse are in the plural feminine imperative. The pronominal suffix *-kum* indicates that the wives did not belong to *ahl al-bayt*. Sunni exegetes on the contrary asserted that this pronominal suffix *-kum* allowed the inclusion of *ahl al-kisā'*.[42] Others included Banu Hashim, Banu 'Abd al-Muttalib, and even Quraysh as a whole.[43]

Thus, the same tool of scriptural interpretation served Shi'i counter-arguments. The Shi'i scholars argued, if all the wives were to be rewarded with eternal happiness, there would be no reason in the textual context of the verse to talk about punishment. They added that some of them behaved in a way that could not go unpunished. Al-Mufid stated that God and his Prophet knew already that some of the wives, especially 'A'isha and Hafsa, did not deserve heaven, and this is the reason why grammatically the conditional clause is used in the purification verse.[44]

Shams al-Din Muhammad b. Makki al-'Amili, known as al-Shahid al-Awwal, also quotes Sunni sources to argue for the unique position of the *ahl al-bayt*, saying that al-Tirmidhī narrated a *ḥadīth ḥasan ṣaḥīḥ* (a sound, recommended report) from Umm Salama that the Prophet covered 'Ali, al-Hasan, al-Husayn, and Fatima with his *kisā'* and recited verse (33:33). Umm Salama asked: 'Am I one of them, O Prophet of God?' He said: 'You are *'ala khayr* (blessed).' He also cites *al-Mustadrak* by al-Hakim al-Naysaburi that this conversation took place in Umm Salama's house, where the purification verse was revealed. He added that it is *ṣaḥīḥ* ('sound') according to the conditions of al-Bukhari, even though al-Bukhari did not include it in his collection. He continues, correcting the Sunni position, arguing: 'It is wrong to say that the entire verse is about the women (the Prophet's wives) because

---

[41] 'Forbidden to you is that which dies of itself, and blood, and flesh of swine, and that on which any other name than that of God has been invoked, and the strangled (animal) and that beaten to death, and that killed by a fall and that killed by being smitten with the horn, and that which wild beasts have eaten, except what you slaughter, and what is sacrificed on stones set up (for idols) and that you divide by the arrows; that is a transgression. This day have those who disbelieve despaired of your religion, so fear them not, and fear Me. This day have I perfected for you your religion and completed My favour on you and chosen for you Islam as a religion; but whoever is compelled by hunger, not inclining wilfully to sin, then surely God is Forgiving, Merciful' (Q 5:3).

[42] al-Zamakhshari, *Tafsir al-Kashshaf 'an haqa'iq al-tanzil*, 3:260.

[43] al-Baydawi, *Anwar al-tanzil*, 557.

[44] Abu 'Abd Allah Muhammad b. Muhammad b. al-Nu'man al-'Ukbari al-Baghdadi al-Shaykh al-Mufid, *al-Irshad fi ma'rifat hujaj Allah 'ala al-'ibad* (Beirut: Mu'assasat Al al-Bayt li-Tahqiq al-Turath, 1993), 126.

its start and end are in the feminine plural. The Qur'an changes pronouns frequently.' He then refers to another verse, declaring that it was revealed for them, namely the *Mubāhala* verse (3:62) and concludes that the Prophet explicitly called them my closest kin, which means that nobody else is equal to them in excellence.[45]

As shown, Shi'is frequently support the purification verse and the exclusive position of *ahl al-bayt* by citing verses (3:61–62).[46] The commentators and exegetes call it the *Mubāhala* (the imprecation, or calling down of God's curse on the liar). The revelation of this portion of the Qur'an took place during a meeting between the Prophet and the Christians of Najran. In (631), a Christian delegation of about seventy men went to Medina to debate religious matters with the Prophet, who reprimanded the Christians for believing that Jesus was divine and asked them to embrace Islam, the only 'true' religion of God that considers Jesus a created being like Adam. The debate between the two groups became so heated that the Prophet recited the verse and challenged the Christians to appear the next day for a *Mubāhala* ('curse ordeal'), so that God would determine the truth of their beliefs concerning the divinity of Jesus and call down His curse on the party straying from the truth.[47] The Christians seriously considered the challenge, but when they went the next day, they found him on his way to the appointed place of the *Mubāhala*, wearing a garment made of black wool, carrying his grandchild al-Hasan on his shoulders, and leading his other grandchild al-Husayn by the hand. 'Ali and Fatima were walking behind him. When the Christian leader saw the Prophet with his family, he turned to his men and said that he saw faces whose prayers could move mountains. He implored them not to accept Muhammad's challenge because, if they did, they and their children would certainly perish. Therefore, they rejected the challenge and agreed instead to keep their religion but to pay tribute, including expensive garments, pieces of silver, lances, shields, horses, and camels. They also agreed to place themselves under the *dhimma* (protection) of the Muslims and to extend hospitality for one month to any delegation Muhammad might send to them in the future.[48]

As demonstrated, the term *ahl al-bayt* evolved and acquired specific meanings and was used to include or exclude certain groups and was tied to other verses, both in Sunni as well as in Shi'i circles, for political and ideological

---

[45] al-Shahid al-Awwal Muhammad b. Makki al-Jizzini, *Dhikra al-Shi'a fi ahkam al-Shari'a* (Qum: Mu'assasat Al al-Bayt li-Ihya' al-Turath, 1997), 1:55–56.

[46] 'But whoever disputes with you in this matter after what has come to you of knowledge, then say: Come let us call our sons and your sons and our women and your women and our near people and your near people, then let us be earnest in prayer, and pray for the curse of God on the liars. [3:62] Most surely this is the true explanation, and there is no god but God; and most surely God – He is the Mighty, the Wise' (Q 3:61).

[47] Moosa, *Extremist Shi'ites*, 78.

[48] Ibid., 79.

ends. The Shi'is not only emphasised the *ahl al-bayt* status of 'Ali's descendants, especially the Husaynid branch, but also gave the term a specific and exclusive meaning. Hence the term *ahl al-bayt* for Shi'is acquired a religious connotation and in time lost its original meaning.

Sharon concludes that 'once the term was attached to the person of the Prophet, the road was opened to Shi'i Qur'anic exegesis to establish its origin in the Word of God'.[49] Sharon tried to trace the evolution and to establish at what stage the term had acquired its distinctive and exclusive Shi'i interpretation. He opined that the process that led to the crystallisation of this ideology could be traced to Mukhtar's revolt in (685–687). According to him, 'Mukhtar's usage of the term *ahl al-bayt* in an exclusive 'Alid context grew naturally out of his dedication to revenge the blood of al-Husayn and the blood of his family.' [50] Therefore, he believes that the 'Alid status as the sole representatives of *ahl al-bayt* was accepted in pro-'Alid circles in Iraq in about the year (70/689).[51] In about the year (100/710) the term was already used to refer exclusively to 'Ali's family. By that time, this interpretation was being reinforced by the other major traditions, emphasising 'Ali's exclusive rights to succeed the Prophet, such as *Ḥadīth al-kisā'*, *Ḥadīth Ghadīr Khumm*, *Ḥadīth al-Manzila,* as well as the *Ḥadīth al-Thaqalayn,* and certain versions of *Ḥadīth al-Qārūra,* all narrated by Umm Salama, among other transmitters, which will be discussed in the next section. Even the interpretation of verse (33:33) as referring only to the 'Alid family was already well established, at least in Iraq, by then.[52]

Umm Salama

Umm Salama, one of the Mothers of the Believers, is highly regarded by all Muslims and especially the Shi'is. Shi'i biographical dictionaries mention her virtues and sing her praise, putting her second only to Khadija, the Prophet's first and favourite wife.

For example, al-Shahrawardi mentions that she has numerous narrations and is highly regarded. He introduces her, stating her name Hind bt. Umayya b. al-Mughira, adding her genealogy. He also mentions that her mother was 'Atika bt. 'Abd al-Muttalib, establishing a blood relationship and kinship with both the Prophet and 'Ali. He also mentions her previous marriage to Abu Salama 'Abd Allah b. 'Abd al-Aswad and her children from him - Salama, 'Umar, and Zaynab. He adds that she was the last of the Prophet's wives to die, in the year (682), during the rule of Yazid b. Mu'awiya at the age of eighty-four after al-Husayn was martyred. Al-Shahrawardī

---

[49] Sharon, *Black Banners from the East*, 79.
[50] Ibid., 81.
[51] Ibid., 81–82.
[52] Ibid., 79.

states that she has many narrations enumerating the *faḍā'il* (merits) of the Commander of the Believers and the obligation to follow him, as well as criticism of those who oppose him. She narrated about 'Ali's knowledge and about al-Husayn giving her the soil from Karbala in addition to the soil from the same place given to her by the Prophet for safekeeping. Her narrations include seeing the Prophet in a dream and him telling her of al-Husayn's martyrdom the day he was slain. Al-Shahrawardi reports that she narrated 328 hadith reports. He also highlights her objection to 'A'isha going out to battle and trying to prevent her from going to Basra. He also mentions that when al-Husayn left for Karbala he left her his books and his will that she then gave to 'Ali b. al-Husayn upon his return.[53]

Ibn al-Sabbagh also praises Umm Salama as highly esteemed, and greatly regarded, writing that she is the best of the Prophet's wives after Khadija. Like al-Shahrawardi, he gives her name, her parents' names, establishing the connection to 'Abd al-Muttalib and mentions her first marriage and her children. Unlike al-Shahrawardi, he puts her death in the year (59/678), stating that Abu Hurayra led her funeral prayers and that there is another version claiming that it was her nephew 'Abd Allah b. 'Abd Allah b. Abi Umayya. The author also states that she died when al-Husayn was martyred, which contradicts her dying in (678), as the massacre of Karbala' took place in (61/680), meaning two years later, hence the date offered by al-Shahrawardi seems more plausible.

The sources (both Sunni and Shi'i) disagree about Umm Salama's death date. Some set her death as having occurred in 678,[54] while others claim that it was in 679[55] or 680,[56] and finally some wrote that it occurred in 681.[57] Al-Tabari corroborates this option, stating that al-Haytham b. 'Adi reported that the last of the Prophet's wives to pass away was Umm Salama in the reign of Yazid b. Mu'awiya in 680.[58] From the above it appears that she died in 682 after the massacre of Karbala to enable her to give the books left to her by al-Husayn to his son.

---

[53] Shaykh 'Ali al-Namazi al-Shahrawardi, *Mustadrak Safinat al-Bihar* (Qum: Mu'assasat al-Nashr al-Islami, n.d.), 5:139–140.

[54] Muhammad Ibn Sa'd, *Kitab al-Tabaqat al-kabir*, ed. Eduard Sachau (Leiden: Brill, 1920) 8:96; Ibn Hajar al-'Asqalani, *al-Isaba fi tamyiz al-sahaba* (Beirut: Dar al-Kutub al-'Ilmiyya, 2002), 8:42; Abu Ja'far Muhammad b. Jarir al-Tabari,*Tarikh al-rusul wa-al-muluk* (Beirut: Maktabat Khayyat, 1965), 13:72.

[55] Muhibb al-Din Ahmad b. 'Abd Allah al-Tabari, *al-Simt al-thamin fi manaqib ummahat al-Mu'minin* (Cairo: Maktabat al-Kulliyyat al-Azhariyya, 1982), 147.

[56] Ibn Hajar, *al-Isaba*, 8:242; Ibn Hajar, *Kitāb Tahdhib al-tahdhib* (Cairo: Dar al-Kitab al-Islami, 1909), 12:457; Ibn al-Athir, *Usd al-ghaba fi ma'rifat al-sahaba* (Beirut: Dar al-Kutub al-'Ilmiyyah, 2003), 5:560.

[57] Ibn Hajar, *al-Isaba*, 8:248.

[58] Nur al-Din 'Ali b. Abu Bakr al-Haytami, *Majma' al-zawa'id wa-manba' al-fawa'id*, 10 vols (Beirut: Dar al-Fikr, n.d.), 9:248.

Like al-Shahrawardi, Ibn al-Sabbagh also highlights the narrations enumerating 'Ali's *faḍā'il*, his knowledge, and that she received the soil from Karbala from the Prophet, as well as another sample from al-Husayn. Ibn al-Sabbagh also mentions that she objected to 'A'isha going out to battle and quotes several traditions about what took place between them.[59]

Karim also states her real name and her geneology, however, he suggests a different mother, namely 'Atika bt. 'Amir b. Rabi'a b. Malik b. Judhayma b. 'Alaqa Jadl al-Ta'n b. Firas b. Ghanam b. Malik b. Kinana. He then also mentions her first husband but lists four children instead of three: Salama, 'Umar, Durra, and Zaynab. He states that she was the best of his wives after Khadija bt. Khuwaylid, and was an esteemed immigrant with a great mind, excellent opinions, beauty, and perfection.

Her beauty was also mentioned by al-Kulayni, who reported that she asked permission to go offer her condolences and lament the death of al-Walid b. al-Mughira. He states, 'because of her beauty, she resembled the *jinn*. If she combed out her hair instead of braiding it, it completely covered her body. When she braided it, she tied the ends of her braids to her anklets, so they would not trail behind her in the dirt.'[60]

According to Karim, her loyalty to the Commander of the Faithful and his sons, al-Hasan and al-Husayn, is well known and too obvious to be mentioned. He adds that nobody can do justice to this great woman in a few lines or pages and list all her virtuous qualities and her excellent morals. He even claims that God Almighty attested to her virtues, as did the Prophet and that she spent her entire life as an immigrant defending her faith and principles. He praises her behaviour during her first marriage, saying that she stayed in Abu Salama's, her first husband's, house as a loving wife, not violating any of his wishes, and after his death she was rewarded and honoured by marrying the finest of creations, God's Prophet Muhammad. Unlike the other biographers, he not only mentions that she narrated numerous *ḥadīths,* but that she also taught the people what she learned from his behaviour, impeccable manners, and good nature, by narrating all what she saw him do. He writes extensively about how, after the Prophet's death, she supported his rightful successor, the Commander of the Believers, and defended her Mistress, the Lady of all women, al-Batul Fatima al-Zahra'. He states that she was the trusted confidante of Fatima's sons, al-Hasan and al-Husayn, not sparing any advice and offering it freely to all who usurped the *wilāya* from its rightful designated heirs and violated the Prophet's kin and his family.[61]

---

[59] 'Ali b. Muhammad al-Maliki al-Makki Ibn al-Sabbagh, *al-Fusul al-Muhimma fi ma'rifat al-a'imma* (Qum: Dar al-Hadith, 1977), 1:40–43.

[60] Abu Ja'far Muhammad b. Ya'qub b. Ishaq al-Kulayni, *al-Usul min al-Kafi* (Tehran: Dar al-Kutub al-Islamiyya, 1968–1969), 5:117.

[61] Faris Hassun Karim, *al-Rawd al-nadir fi ma'na hadith al-Ghadir* (Qum: Mu'assasat Amir al-Mu'minin li-l-Tahqiq, 1998–1999), 205–211.

Although Karim includes many traditions as well as anecdotes supporting his claims, and describing Umm Salama, after the Prophet's death, as one of the most vocal defenders of *ahl al-bayt,* particularly Fatima, he does not mention that when Abu Bakr withheld her inheritance of Fadak, Umm Salama spoke out publicly, saying: 'How can this be said to someone like Fatima? She is a *houri* among the living women! How can you claim that the Prophet would forbid any inheritance without telling her of this, when God said in his book in verse (26.214) And warn your nearest relations?" She is the best of women!' As a result of this outburst, Umm Salama did not receive her stipend (pension) for an entire year, according to al-Tabari al-Saghir.[62]

Although Umm Salama narrated many hadith reports covering many different topics and issues, some that were translated and recorded as legal rulings in *fiqh* (jurisprudence) and others that found their way into exegesis or *asbāb al-nuzūl* (occasions of revelation), she was among the favourite authorities quoted on *ahl al-bayt,* by both the Sunnis and the Shi'is.[63] This section will only mention some of her narrations supporting *ahl al-bayt* and their claims to succession.

In the Shi'i compendia, she narrated hundreds of hadith reports, among them several traditions that emphasise 'Ali's and the *ahl al-bayt*'s special status, their right to the succession, and their elevated position. Among these are *Ḥadīth al-Kisā'* (The Mantle of the Prophet), discussed above, with the inclusion of the 'Purification Verse'. She also narrated *Ḥadīth al-Thaqalayn* (The Two Weighty Things). In *Musnad al-Riḍa,* she is listed among the thirty-five Companions who narrated this tradition. Out of all the Companions who narrated this tradition only three were women, the other two being Fatima al-Zahra' and Umm Hani ('Ali's sister).[64] There is also a book devoted to *Ḥadīth* Ghadīr Khumm, which includes several versions narrated on her authority.[65] In his book devoted to *Ḥadīth al-Thaqalayn,* al-'Askari lists several versions of this tradition, among them several different versions by Umm Salama. Two of the versions combine *Ḥadīth al-Thaqalayn* with *Ḥadīth Ghadīr Khumm* about *al-wilāya.*

According to al-'Askari Umm Salama narrated that the Prophet took 'Ali's hand at Ghadīr Khumm and raised it until everyone could see the whiteness of his armpit and said: 'Whoever takes me as his *mawlā* (guardian), 'Ali is his *mawlā*.' Then he added: 'O people, I am leaving you *al-thaqalayn* (two weighty things), God's book and *ahl baytī* (my family) and they will not be separated until they reach the basin.'

---

[62] Abu Ja'far Muhammad b. Jarir b. Rustam al-Tabari al-Saghir, *Dala'il al-Imama* (Qum: Mu'assasat al-Bi'tha, 1992–1993), 124.

[63] Baqi b. Makhlad (d. 889) sets them at 378, while al-Dhahabi (d. 1348) counts 380 and al-Mizzi (d. 1342) only 158 narrations.

[64] Dawud b. Sulayman al-Ghari, *Musnad al-Rida* (Qum: Markaz al-Nashr al-Tabi' li-Maktab al-I'lam al-Islami, 1997–1998), 208–209.

[65] 'Abd al-Husayn Ahmad al-Amin, *al-Ghadīr* (Beirut: Dar al-Kitab al-'Arabi, 1977).

In another version, also ascribed to Umm Salama, there is an addition to the *matn* (textual body) elaborating on how 'Ali and God's book are inseparable, saying: 'this is 'Ali and he is with the Qur'an and the Qur'an is with him, inseparable until they reach the basin', for added confirmation and emphasis.[66] And the basin image recurs in a much shorter version, although it is supplemented by advice to ask 'Ali or the Qur'an about any ambiguous issues. The version reports Umm Salama saying: 'In his last illness before he died and while the room was full of people I heard the Prophet say: "O people, I am about to die . . . and I am leaving you God's book and my family." Then he took 'Ali's hand and said: "This is 'Ali, he is with the Qur'an and the Qur'an is with him, inseparable, until they reach the basin, so ask them about anything you disagree on."'[67]

Umm Salama lived through al-Husayn's entire life, from his birth, through his childhood, adult life, and his death; hence, she has a distinctive and comprehensive perspective, which makes her uniquely suited to narrate traditions about him and about the after-effects of his martyrdom. There are many different versions of *Ḥadīth al-Qārūra* (The Flask).[68] One of the versions preserved in al-Rawandi's *al-Khara'ij wa-al-jara'ih* includes the reference to two soil samples from Karbala, as mentioned by al-Shahrawardi, quoted above. The version takes place when al-Husayn was heading to Iraq; Umm Salama told him not to go as she heard the Prophet say: 'my son al-Husayn will be slain in Iraq.' She said she had soil from there, which the Prophet had given her, kept in a flask. Al-Husayn replied: 'By God I will be killed anyway, even if I do not go to Iraq they will still kill me. If you like I will show you the place where I will die and also my companions' death.' Then he wiped her face with his hands and God allowed her to see everything in a vision. He then gave her some soil from there, which she kept in another flask and he told her: 'if the flasks are flooded with blood then you will know I have been slain.' Umm Salama said that when it was the day of 'Āshūrā' she looked at the two flasks in the afternoon and saw they were flooded with blood and she screamed.[69]

The sources also report that Umm Salama kept the soil from Karbala given to her by the Prophet in a glass flask. She and Fatima al-Sughra, al-Husayn's daughter, who was left behind due to illness, watched the flask daily, anxiously. On the tenth of Muharram, they saw that the soil had

---

[66] Najm al-Din al-Sharif al-Najafi al-'Askari, *Hadith al-thaqalayn* (Najaf: al-Maktaba al-Haydariyya, n.d.), 14–16.

[67] Sayyid Hamid Husayn al-Laknawi al-Naqwi, *Khulasat 'abaqat al-anwar fi imamat al-a'imma al-athar* (Qum: al-Hawza al-'Ilmiyya, 1987–1988), 7:210–211.

[68] For a detailed comparison and analysis of the different versions from both the Sunni and Shi'i corpora see Yasmin Amin, 'Predicting Imam Husayn's Martyrdom in Karbala: The Hermeneutics of Textual Additions in the Evolution of "Ḥadīth al-Qārūra"', in *Lamenting Karbala: Commemoration, Mourning, and Memory* (Leiden: Brill, forthcoming).

[69] Qutb al-Din Abi al-Husayn Sa'id b. Hibat Allah al-Rawandi, *al-Khara'ij wa-l-jara'ih* (Qum: Mu'assasat al-Imam al-Mahdi, 1989).

changed to congealed blood. Both realised that al-Husayn had been slain and mourned him with loud lamentations. It is reported that she cursed the people of Iraq upon hearing the news of al-Husayn's martyrdom in Karbala.[70] In addition, Shahr Ibn Hawshab is said to have visited Umm Salama to offer his condolences for al-Husayn's martyrdom in (61/680).[71] Umm Salama is reported to have been the first person to weep in Medina, in response to al-Husayn's martyrdom.[72]

As for *Ḥadīth al-Manzila*, it is also recorded in several versions and the short version says: the Prophet told Umm Salama: 'O Umm Salama, 'Ali is from me and I am from him, his flesh is of my flesh and his blood is of my blood, and he is to me (*manzila*) like Aaron was to Moses, except that no Prophet will come after me. O Umm Salama, listen and bear witness, this is 'Ali, Master of all Muslims.'[73]

Other important narrations with a distinctly Shi'i flavour are also recorded in the sources, like, for example: it was narrated that the Prophet said: 'I am the city of knowledge and 'Ali its door.' In some other versions of the same tradition there is an addition: 'Whoever wants the city, let him come to the door.'[74] Also with an *isnād* to Umm Salama that she said: 'I heard the Prophet say that 'Ali and his *shī'a* (followers) are the winners on Judgment Day.'[75] Furthermore, Umm Salama said: I heard the Prophet say: the Mahdi is from my clan, from Fatima's progeny. [76] And finally the report that 'Ali was the last person to speak to the Prophet before he died. Umm Salama said: 'By Him by whom I swear, 'Ali was the last one to see the Prophet of God.' The day the Prophet died in 'A'isha's house, the Prophet kept asking: 'Did 'Ali come?' He asked repeatedly. She said: 'We thought he had sent him out for something. 'Ali came and we thought the Prophet wanted something, so we left and sat by the door. I was closest to the door, and I saw 'Ali sit by his left side. The Prophet *nājāhu* (spoke to him privately) and then died. 'Ali was the last person to speak to him.'[77]

---

[70] 'Ali Mashhadi and Nabil Rida 'Alwan, *al-Thaqib fi al-manaqib* (Beirut: Dar al-Zahra', 1991), 9:197.

[71] Abu 'Abd Allah Shams al-Din Muhammad Ibn 'Uthman al-Dhahabi, *Siyar a'lam al-nubala'* (Beirut: Mu'assasat al-Risala, 1982), 2:207.

[72] Ahmad al-Ya'qubi, *Tarikh al-Ya'qubi* (Najaf: Matba'at al-Ghari, 1939–1940), 2:182–183 (# 2536); Muhammad Baqir al-Majlisi, *Bihar al-anwar al-jami'a li-durar akhbar al-a'imma al-athar*, 110 vols (Beirut: Mu'assasat al-Wafa', 1983), 45:228, 230.

[73] Shaykh Hadi al-Najafi, *Mawsu'at ahadith ahl al-bayt* (Beirut: Dar Ihya' al-Turath al-'Arabi, 2002), 11:83.

[74] Shaykh Muhammad 'Ali al-Ansari, *al-Mawsu'a al-fiqhiyya al-muyassara* (Qum: Mu'assassat al-Hadi, 1994–1995), 1:29.

[75] al-Majlisi, *Bihar al-anwar*, 27:143.

[76] Ibid., 51:75–76.

[77] Muhammad b. Sulayman al-Kufi, *Manaqib Amir al-Mu'minin 'Ali b. Abi Talib 'alayhi al-salam* (Qum: Majma' Ihya' al-Thaqafa al-Islamiyya, 1991–1992), 2:87.

These are the most important traditions supporting the *ahl al-bayt* and their claims and rights to succession, although Umm Salama narrates many more about the Prophet's special relationship with 'Ali and numerous others, emphasising his being the designated successor like, for example, the lengthy one recorded by Ibn Babawayh al-Qummi in his *'Ilal al-shara'i'* that combines several shorter ones like parts of the *Ḥadīth Ghadīr Khumm* and parts of *Ḥadīth al-manzila*. The report takes place after the Prophet married Zaynab bt. Jahsh and after the revelation of verse (33:53).[78] According to this report, the Prophet stayed with Zaynab seven days and then went to Umm Salama's house. At about noon 'Ali knocked lightly on the door and the Prophet recognised his knock, while Umm Salama did not. He said to her: 'O Umm Salama, open the door for him.' She said: 'O Prophet of God, who is it who is not aware of what was just revealed about us of God's words. ". . . when you ask of them any goods, ask of them from behind a curtain . . ." who deserves that I open the door to him in my state.' He said to her angrily: 'Whoever obeys the Prophet has obeyed God. Go and open the door, for at the door is a man who is neither a stray, nor indiscreet, nor impatient, he loves God and His Prophet and God and His Prophet love him. He will not come in until you step aside.' Umm Salama got up not knowing who was at the door, but she memorised the words and praise. She went to the door saying: '*Bakh bakh* (praise praise) to the man who loves God and His Prophet and whom God and His Prophet love.' She opened the door and 'Ali held on to its handle until Umm Salama went in and out of sight. Then he opened the door and came in, saluting the Prophet. The Prophet asked: 'Umm Salama, do you know him?' She said: 'yes and welcome to him. This is 'Ali b. Abi Talib.' He replied: 'You spoke the truth Umm Salama, this 'Ali b. Abi Talib, his flesh is of my flesh, and his blood is of my blood, and he is to me like Aaron is to Moses, but there is no prophet after me. Umm Salama, listen and bear witness, this is 'Ali b. Abi Talib, the Commander of the Believers, and the Master of the Muslims, the vessel of my knowledge, and the door that opens to me, he is the executor after me, for the dead of my household and the successor for the living of my community and my brother in this world and in the Hereafter, and he is with me on the highest level. Memorise this Umm Salama and bear witness. He will fight *al-nākithīn* (those who broke their oaths), *al-qāsiṭīn* (the unjust ones) and *al-māriqīn* (those who leave Islam).'[79]

---

[78] 'O you who believe! do not enter the houses of the Prophet unless permission is given to you for a meal, not waiting for its cooking being finished – but when you are invited, enter, and when you have taken the food, then disperse – not seeking to listen to talk; surely this gives the Prophet trouble, but he forbears from you, and God does not forbear from the truth And when you ask of them any goods, ask of them from behind a curtain; this is purer for your hearts and (for) their hearts; and it does not behove you that you should give trouble to the Apostle of God' (Q 33:53).

[79] Abu Ja'far Muhammad b. 'Ali b. al-Husayn Ibn Babawayh al-Qummi, *'Ilal al-shara'i'* (Najaf: al-Maktaba al-Haydariyya, 1966), 1:65–66.

The ending of this tradition is a favourite theme in Shi'i hadith compendia and is repeated combined with various other reports, such as, for example: Umm Salama said that the Prophet told her: 'listen and bear witness that 'Ali is my legatee (*waṣī*) and my *walī* in this world and the Hereafter and that he will fight *al-nākithūn, al-qāsiṭūn* and *al-māriqūn*.'[80] Usually they are followed by a commentary explaining who *al-nākithūn, al-qāsiṭūn,* and *al-māriqūn* are and used to vilify certain groups. For example, in *Ma'ani al-akhbar,* Ibn Babawayh al-Qummi records that the Prophet told Umm Salama, 'O Umm Salama, listen and bear witness that this man, 'Ali b. Abi Talib, is my brother in this life and in the Hereafter. O Umm Salama, listen and bear witness that 'Ali b. Abi Talib is my minister in this life and in the Hereafter. O Umm Salama, listen and bear witness that 'Ali b. Abi Talib will carry my banner in this life and in the Hereafter. O Umm Salama, listen and bear witness that 'Ali b. Abi Talib is my executor and my successor and the protector at the basin. O Umm Salama, listen and bear witness that 'Ali b. Abi Talib is Master of the Muslims and Imam of the pious and the leader and commander of the faithful believers and the slayer of the *al-nākithūn,* al-*qāsiṭūn* and *al-māriqūn*.' Umm Salama asked: 'Who are *al-nākithūn*?' The Prophet replied, 'Those who pledged allegiance to him in Medina and then reneged in Basra.' She asked: 'And who are the *qāsiṭūn*?' He replied: 'Mu'awiya and his people from Syria.' She asked: 'And who are the *māriqūn*?' He said: 'The people of Nahrawan.'[81]

For Shi'is, Umm Salama is also revered for mothering Fatima first and then her children. She is quoted as saying: 'When the Prophet married me, he left it upon me to take care of his daughter . . . I swear by God that she had better conduct than I, and she displayed more knowledge than I in all affairs.'[82]

Sources also detail Umm Salama's role in Fatima and 'Ali's engagement, how she prepared the house for the bridal couple and cooked for the wedding *walīma* (banquet), and then prepared the bride for the wedding. Al-Shaykh al-Tusi (d. 1067) has a lengthy description of the engagement and the wedding with an endearing anecdote that shows the trust shown to Umm Salama. According to al-Tusi, the Prophet said: 'Take my daughter and make her ready in one of the rooms.' Umm Salama asked: 'Which room?' He replied: 'Yours.' He asked his wives to beautify her. Umm Salama asked Fatima: 'Do you have some perfume which you saved for yourself?' Fatima replied: 'Yes.' She got a flask and poured a bit into Umm Salama's palm. Umm Salama said: 'I have never smelled such a beautiful fragrance before in my life', and asked her: 'What is this?' She replied: 'Dihya al-Kalbi

---

[80] Various authors, *Alqab al-Rasul wa-'itratihi*, in *Maktabat ahl al-bayt*, Prod, Noor Software Technologies, Qum, last accessed 18 December 2017.

[81] Abu Ja'far Muhammad b. 'Ali b. al-Husayn Ibn Babawayh al-Qummi, *Ma'ani al-akhbar* (Qum: Intishār Islāmī, 1982), 204.

[82] al-Majlisi, *Bihar al-Anwar*, 43:10.

used to come to see my father and then tell me: "Fatima, bring a pillow for your uncle." I got him the pillows and he sat down. When he got up something fell out from between the folds of his clothes, and he used to ask me to collect it and keep it. 'Ali then asked the Prophet about that and he replied: "This is amber that has fallen from Gabriel's wings."'[83]

The sources also record how 'Ali called for Umm Salama in times of need, when Fatima was delivering her children or when she died, not only because of their close relationship but also because her apartment was to the east of Fatima and 'Ali's quarters.[84] On account of her frail health, Umm Salama also helped Fatima look after al-Hasan and al-Husayn, who frequently played in her house. Sunni and Shi'i sources both show that she had an especially close bond with al-Husayn. Hence, numerous hadith reports that she narrated dealt with *ahl al-bayt*.

Umm Salama is contrasted to 'A'isha on many occasions in order to criticise 'Aʾisha's behaviour, most notably her role in the Battle of the Camel. In lengthy reports and anecdotes, 'A'isha is judged critically, while Umm Salama is praised. Such criticism also serves to highlight 'Ali's status as the rightful successor to the Prophet. An anecdote recorded by al-Sharif al-Murtada in *Rasa'il al-Murtada* narrated that 'Abd Allah b. al-Zubayr was sent by Talha and al-Zubayr to convince 'A'isha to join them, saying: "Uthman was wrongfully killed, and we are afraid that Muhammad's *umma* (community) will be split into fractions. If 'A'isha agrees to come out with us, maybe God will have mercy and preserve the community from splitting apart.' After a lengthy description of how 'Abd Allah b. al-Zubayr approached his aunt and what he said, 'A'isha replies: 'Praise be to God, I was not ordered to go out, and I cannot think of another one of the Mothers of the Believers other than Umm Salama, if she would go then I would go with her.' This is probably a dramatic tool to highlight 'A'ishah's wrong decision and Umm Salama's correct conduct. The anecdote continues that her nephew convinces her to go to Umm Salama to enlist her for their cause. Interestingly, Umm Salama gives her a cold welcome, saying: 'Welcome 'A'isha, by God you have not visited me before, so what is the matter?'[85] After 'A'isha recounts Talha and al-Zubayr's request Umm Salama screamed out for everyone in the house to hear: 'O 'A'isha! Just yesterday you called 'Uthman an infidel and an old fool (*na'thal*) and today you call him the Commander of the Faithful and wrongfully killed? What

---

83 Abu Ja'far Muhammad b. al-Hasan al-Tusi, *al-Amali* (Qum: Dar al-Thaqafa, 1993–1994), 40–43.

84 Muhammad Ilyas 'Abd al-Ghani and 'Umar Muhammad Fallata, *Buyut al-Sahaba hawla al-Masjid al-Nabawi al-Sharif: dirasa 'an al-hujurat al-sharifa wa-al-suffa wa-buyut ba'd al-Sahaba wa-Saqifat Bani Sa'ida wa-al-Baqī'* (Medina: M. I. 'Abd al-Ghanī, 1998), 16.

85 al-Sharif al-Murtada, *Rasa'il al-Murtada,* 4 vols, ed. al-Sayyid Ahmad al-Husayni (Qum: Dar al-Qur'an al-Karim, 1984–1985), 4:66–68.

do you want?' 'A'isha replied: 'Come out with me, maybe God will have mercy on us and heal the community of Muhammad.' Umm Salama countered: 'What do you mean, 'A'isha, to go out with you, when I heard from the Prophet of God what I heard? I implore you by God, who knows your truthfulness, if you mean it. Do you remember on one of your days, I cooked *ḥarīra*[86] in my house and brought it over and the Prophet said: "By God, days and nights will pass and the dogs around the well of Haw'ab in Iraq will bark at one of my wives on an oppressive wrongful quest." The pot fell from my hands, and he raised his head to me and said: "What do you think, Umm Salama?" I said: "O Prophet of God, why wouldn't the pot fall from my hand at what you're saying? What if you believe it to be me?" You then laughed, and he turned to you and asked: "What makes you laugh, you with reddish legs! I think it will be you." Umm Salama continues to list memories that 'A'isha should remember and that all show how 'Ali deserves to succeed the Prophet. Umm Salama said: 'I also implore you to remember the night we were travelling with the Prophet, and he was between me and 'Ali b. Abu Talib talking to us. You steered your camel between him and 'Ali, so he raised his walking stick and touched your camel's face and said: "By God, none of your days is worth one of his, and no one hates him except the hypocrites and liars." Do you remember, O 'A'isha, his illness before he died? Your father came and brought 'Umar with him, while 'Ali was tending to the Prophet's clothes, his shoes, and slippers and mending them behind the house. They asked permission, which was granted and then asked: "O Prophet of God, how are you?" He replied: "I have awoken, praise be to God." They asked: "Is death inevitable?" He said: "It is." They asked: "O Prophet of God, have you appointed anyone to succeed you?" He answered, "My successor is not one of you, but rather the one mending the soles." They left and passed by 'Ali, who was still behind the house mending the soles. You know all that, O 'A'isha, and you will bear witness to God, because you heard it from His Prophet. Then Umm Salama said: "I? Go out against 'Ali after what I heard from the Prophet?" At first it seems that Umm Salama succeeds in convincing 'A'isha to return home and to give up on joining Talha and al-Zubayr. However, the anecdote ends with the statement, "When it was midnight we heard a commotion; 'A'isha had left with them."[87]

According to al-Mayanji, the story ends with 'A'isha showing remorse and regret. It was narrated from 'Aʾisha that she went to see Umm Salama after she returned from the Battle of the Camel. Umm Salama had sworn never to talk to her again for going to war against 'Ali. 'A'isha came in and said: 'Peace be upon you, O Mother of the Believers.' Umm Salama addressed the wall saying: 'O wall, didn't I advise you not to go? Didn't

[86] A soup-like dish made of ghee and flour.
[87] al-Sharif al-Murtada, *Rasa'il al-Murtada*, 4:66–68.

I warn you?' 'A'isha said: 'I seek forgiveness from God and repent to Him. Talk to me, O Mother of the Believers.' Umm Salama repeated: 'O wall, didn't I advise you not to go? Didn't I warn you?' 'A'isha got up and left crying while saying: 'Woe is me for what I have lost.'[88]

The contrast between the co-wives is taken a step further by showing that not only did Umm Salama stay at home, but she nevertheless supported 'Ali by sending her two sons to fight with him, saying: 'If it were appropriate and I could go out with you I would have, instead have my boys, take them, they are charity.'[89]

Umm Salama's behaviour is not only juxtaposed to 'A'isha's but also to others, like, for example, 'Umar. A report is recorded about an Anṣārī woman who had kept the pledge to *ahl al-bayt* and used to visit them often. One day she met 'Umar b. al-Khattab on her way and he asked, 'Old woman, where are you heading?' She replied, 'I am going to Muhammad's *āl* (family/kin) to renew my pledge and to give them their dues.' 'Umar told her, 'Woe to you, today they have no rights over you nor us. They had them during the Prophet's time, but today they do not, so leave.' She left. She met Umm Salama, who asked her: 'What kept you from us?' She told her what had transpired. Umm Salama said: "Umar lied. The rights of *āl* Muhammad still stand and remain an obligation for all Muslims until the Day of Judgment.' The report is followed by a commentary quoting a verse in support of Umm Salama's position. The comment reads: 'This is the right clearly mentioned in God's book' verse (42:23): 'Say: I do not ask of you any reward for it but love for my near relatives.'[90]

The examples cited above indicate that Umm Salama was an enormously popular authority to quote for the rights and special status of *ahl al-bayt*. Her narrations, unlike those of many other female Companions of the Prophet, are found in numerous collections, Sunni and Shi'i alike. Maria Dakake argues that 'Alid women were not active transmitters within the larger Shi'i intellectual circles, but rather had a family legacy passed privately on to their children, most often their daughters. Their limited traditions are usually recorded in exclusively female and family *isnāds* that tend to be rather formulaic in nature. The scarcity of specific women in the *isnād* chains, as well as in the narrative content of Shi'i hadith traditions, suggest that they remained largely outside the sectarian and intellectual circles of the Imams' disciples.[91] Umm Salama's position as a Mother of the Believers and also

[88] 'Ali al-Ahmadi al-Mayanji, *Mawaqif al-Shi'a* (Qum: Mu'assasat al-Nashr al-Islami, 1995–1996), 1:93.

[89] al-Qadi Abu Hanifa al-Nu'man b. Muhammad al-Tamimi, *Sharh al-Akhbar fi fada'il al-a'imma al-athar* (Qum: Mu'assasat al-Nashr al-Islami, n.d.), 2:19.

[90] Mawla Muhammad Salih al-Mazandarani, *Sharh Usul al-Kafi* (Beirut: Dar Ihya' al-Turath al-'Arabi, 2000), 12:172–173.

[91] Maria Massi Dakake, *The Charismatic Community: Shi'ite Identity in Early Islam* (Albany: State University of New York Press, 2007), 244.

her special relationship with the *ahl al-bayt,* makes her uniquely suited to be the link between the Prophet and 'Ali, more so that she was known to be level-headed and intelligent, having advised the Prophet on many politically charged occasions such as the Truce of al-Hudaybiyya, as well as on other occasions during battles and after the conquest of Mecca.

Naṣṣ

According to Kohlberg, the unique position of the Imam is essentially based on two factors: first, he is viewed as a divinely appointed successor to the Prophet and, second, he alone is seen as invested with personal qualities that make him the undisputed leader of all believers.[92]

The same concept was originally phrased by al-Tabari al-Saghir (d. after 1020), the tenth- or eleventh-century Imami theologian who, in his *Dala'il al-Imama,* listed the conditions for the Imamate. The first and most important one is the *naṣṣ,* or explicit textual designation, which he mentions again as a separate condition towards the end of his list. He elaborates saying that the Imamate is a divine, sacred appointment that cannot happen without a designation, either through a divine or a Prophetic *naṣṣ*. He explains that the Prophet does not speak out of his own desires, but that he receives a revelation. The phrasing he uses is identical to verses (53:3–4),[93] even if he does not cite them explicitly. He continues, adding that the Prophet was sent as a mercy for all humankind, alluding to verse (21:107).[94] Therefore, the Prophet would never allow his community to descend into chaos after him or cause disagreements and strife, but would guarantee that justice reign supreme. The Prophet would not want his mission to be either interrupted or terminated after him. Al-Tabari continues, insisting that because the Prophet was faithful to his mission, he therefore left a will. He named his successor explicitly, stating his name on several occasions, in the *mutawātir*[95] hadith report of Ghadir Khumm, which he uttered in the course of the last pilgrimage before his death, in the *wilāya* hadith report on the same occasion, and in the *Ḥadīth al-Manzila,* which was revealed to clarify verse (5:55)[96] and to explain the *manzila.*[97] Righteousness and virtuous upbringing is the second

---

[92] Etan Kohlberg, 'Imam and Community in the Pre-Ghayba Period', 25–53 in *Authority and Political Culture in Shi'ism,* ed. Said Amir Arjomand (Albany: State University of New York Press, 1988), 25.

[93] 'Nor does he speak out of desire' (Q 53:3) and 'It is naught but revelation that is revealed' (Q 53:4).

[94] 'And We have hot sent you but as a mercy to the worlds' (Q 21:107).

[95] 'Successive', meaning that it has been reported numerously by different narrators and through various chains of transmission.

[96] 'Only God is your Ally and His Apostle and those who believe, those who keep up prayers and pay the poor-rate while they bow' (Q 5:55).

[97] Abu Ja'far Muhammad b. Jarir b. Rustam al-Tabari al-Saghir, *Dala'il al-Imama* (Qum: Mu'assasat al-Bi'tha, 1992–1993), 18–19

requirement, as the Imam is the *Qā'im*[98] for the Prophet. Al-Tabari al-Saghir goes on to state that there is no doubt about 'Ali's upbringing, as the Prophet himself brought him up, unlike anyone else of the Companions, and 'Ali always stuck to him like a shadow. He even judges that 'Ali's two sons, who were honoured to be divinely purified in verse (33:33), did not receive the same upbringing as 'Ali. He hastens to add, though, that they were brought up by 'Ali under the supervision of the Prophet.[99] The author elaborates on all the other conditions, such as precedence of knowledge and wisdom,[100] the authentic reports, and traditions because the Imams are *muḥaddathūn* (literally spoken to, meaning divinely inspired), *mufahhamūn* (granted understanding through divine inspiration).[101] Then the author returns to the *naṣṣ* and states in a new condition that the Imam requires a designation by the previous Imam. He then justifies it that just like the Prophet designated 'Ali, the same happened with the twelve Imams. For him, the *naṣṣ* has to be explicit and in accordance with the Prophet's *nuṣūṣ* (plural of *naṣṣ*), such as *Ḥadīth al-Thaqalayn*, the hadith report listing the twelve Imams by name, and other traditions that negate the rights of any other person to claim this position.[102] The author then adds the final two conditions, namely a distinguished lineage and miracles, because just like the prophets were supported by divine miracles so are the Imams.[103]

One of the exclusively Shi'i beliefs is in the existence of supernatural powers in Muhammad's family – powers that had been manifested in him and were transmitted or bestowed on succeeding generations. Watt pointed this out, writing, 'In modern sociological terms this might be described as a belief in the charismatic leader.'[104] Although Watt adds that the actual charismatic leaders – first 'Ali, and then his sons, al-Hasan and al-Husayn, were far from successful in their political activities,[105] success and charisma mean nothing much with regard to the designation of the *naṣṣ*.

---

[98] See Abdulaziz Abdulhussein Sachedina, *Islamic Messianism: The Idea of Mahdi in Twelver Shi'ism* (Albany: State University of New York Press, 1981), 62. Sachedina explains that each Imam is viewed as being the *Qā'im*, who inherits the Prophet's banner, Joseph's shirt, Moses's rod, and Solomon's ring and will once again unfurl the Prophet's banner, which was last raised by 'Ali at the Battle of the Camel. Later, a distinction was made between *al-Qā'im bi'l-Imama* (the one who carries out the duty of the Imamate) that applied to all Imams and *al-Qā'im bi'l-jihād* (the one who carries out the duty of the holy war) in the case of the last Imam, hence, the twelfth Imam is *al-Qā'im* who rises against injustice and is sent by God from among the Prophet's descendants to restore the true faith.

[99] al-Tabari al-Saghir, *Dala'il al-imama*, 20.

[100] Ibid., 21.

[101] Ibid., 24.

[102] Ibid.

[103] Ibid., 25.

[104] W. Montgomery Watt, *Islamic Political Thought* (Edinburgh: Edinburgh University Press, 1968), 119.

[105] Ibid.

Perhaps the first mention of an explicit verbal designation is from a sermon by 'Ali that appears in *Nahj al-Balagha*, known as *al-Khuṭba al-Qāṣi'a*, in which 'Ali recounts of Muhammad:

> I used to follow him like a young camel following its mother's footprints. Every day he would teach me some of his traits and manners, asking me to follow it. Every year he used to go in seclusion to Hira', where I saw him, but no one else did. In those days Islam did not exist in any house except that of the Prophet of God and Khadija, while I was the third. I used to see and watch the effulgence of divine revelation and message, and I breathed in the scent of Prophethood. When the revelation descended on the Prophet of God, I heard the moans of Satan. I asked: 'O Prophet of God, what is this moan?' and he replied: 'This is Satan who has lost all hope of being worshipped. O 'Ali, you see all that I see, and you hear all that I hear, except that you are not a prophet, but you are a minister, and you are surely on the virtuous path.'[106]

A verbal designation might be all an Imam needs, but a physical *naṣṣ* is a powerful symbol. As Dabashi writes, 'The Shi'i organization of authority is further complemented by a system of sacred symbolics that collectively lend legitimacy to its derivative continuity with both the Qur'anic revelation and the Prophet's legacy. In the Quranic references to the particular characteristics of a legitimate leader, two divine attributes, *'ilm* (knowledge) and *qudra* (power) are emphasized as the indication of rightful authority.'[107] Most traditions in the sources tie the *naṣṣ* to these two. One tradition, for example, says that Umm Salama said: 'The Prophet sat with 'Ali in my house, and then called for a goat-skin, upon which 'Ali wrote what the Prophet dictated, even on its margins. Then he gave it to me for safe-keeping without anyone knowing and said: "Whoever comes to you after my demise with such and such sign, give it to him." After the Prophet's death, I waited and then Abu Bakr was appointed to lead the people.' She sent her son 'Umar to attend his first speech saying: 'Go, see what this man does.' He went and sat with the people, and he listened to Abu Bakr's sermon. When Abu Bakr descended from the pulpit, he went home, and so did 'Umar to tell his mother what happened. She waited until 'Umar was appointed to lead the people and then she sent her son again with the same instructions. 'Umar b. al-Khattab also did as Abu Bakr had done before him. Umm Salama waited until 'Uthman was appointed to lead the people and the same sequence of events took place, as in the case of his two predecessors. She waited until 'Ali was appointed to lead the people. She again sent her son to do the same. 'Ali came to the mosque, ascended the pulpit, and then spoke and descended

---

[106] Al-Sharif al-Radi, *Nahj al-balagha: wa-huwa majmu' ma ikhtarahu al-Sharif al-Radi min kalam al-Imam Amir al-Mu'minin 'Ali ibn Abi Talib* (Beirut: Dar al-Ma'rifa, n.d.), 137–160, here pp. 157–158.
[107] Dabashi, *Authority in Islam*, 117.

from the pulpit. When he saw 'Umar, he told him to go and ask for his mother's permission for him to visit her. 'Umar went home and told her what 'Ali had asked, and there he was behind him. She said: 'By God, I know.' 'Ali asked permission to enter and then said: 'Give me the book that the Prophet gave you, with such and such sign.' 'Umar said: 'By God, I saw my mother, get up to a big casket with a smaller one inside. She extracted a book from it and gave it to 'Ali and told me: "My son, follow this man, for by God I have not seen any Imam other than him since the Prophet died."'[108] This tradition is recorded in numerous canonised sources with varying details.[109]

The commentary in various hadith collections makes use of all these traditions to cement the ideology. For example, al-Tabataba'i writes that this hadith report illustrates several points: the first point is that the Prophet did not leave the community without guidance nor without a guiding Imam, but that he designated Imams for the community to explain the divine knowledge, the religious rituals, *sunan*, *ādāb*, manners, what is licit and what is forbidden, wisdom, traditions, and everything that the people might need until Judgement Day, even the correct legal compensation for a scratch. The Prophet did not allow anyone to rule, opine, offer a *fatwā*, or use analogical reasoning (*qiyās*), since no matter lacked a clear divine ruling. However, the Prophet dictated all the rulings and sacred legal injunctions to 'Ali b. Abi Talib and instructed him to write them down, keep them with him, and then give them to the Imams from his progeny. 'Ali wrote them in his own handwriting and gave them to his descendants. The second point is that the Prophet dictated all this knowledge to 'Ali b. Abi Talib exclusively and did not share it with anyone else. He chose that 'Ali should give it to the eleven Imams from his descendants. Therefore, the entire community might derive knowledge of what was licit and what was forbidden according to the sacred law, along with everything else they might need in religious matters after the Prophet's demise, from 'Ali b. Abi Talib and the Imams, because they are the repositories of the Prophet's secret knowledge and the preservers of his religion. The third point is that the book was present and at the disposal of the Imams. Two of the Imams, namely Abu Ja'far Muhammad b. 'Ali b. al-Husayn b. 'Ali b. Abu Talib and his son Abu 'Abd Allah Ja'far b. Muhammad al-Sadiq, showed the book to several of their companions and even to some people of the general public to put them at ease or to present proof and justification for their unique positions and to explain some of their legal pronouncements. The fourth point is that this book was known to the '*āmma* (the public, or the Sunni majority) and the

---

108 Abu al-Hasan 'Ali b. al-Husayn b. Babawayh al-Qummi, *al-Imama wa-l-tabsira min al-hayra* (Qum: Madrasat al-Imam al-Mahdi, 1363), 45.

109 See Muhammad b. al-Husayn b. Farrukh al-Saffar, *Basa'ir al-darajat* (Tehran: Mu'assasat al-A'lami, 1983–1984), 182–188; Abu Sa'd 'Abd al-Karim b. Muhammad al-Sam'ani, *Adab al-imla' wa-l-istimla'* (Beirut: Dar wa-Maktabat al-Hilāl, 1989), 19.

khāṣṣa (the elite, or the Shi'i minority) at the time of these two Imams, for they often quoted it in their answers to questions, saying that this is found in 'Ali's book. The fifth and final point is that what the Imams possess in terms of knowledge of licit and forbidden matters and all other rulings was revealed by the angel Gabriel to the Prophet, and they derived it from him. Therefore, it is prohibited for the community to contradict them and not to follow their opinions and teachings, relying instead on *qiyās* (analogical reasoning) and *ijtihād* (independent judgement). It is well known that the twelve Imams' knowledge originates with the Prophet. This is documented through numerous hadith reports through private and public means of transmissions that have exceeded the norms of *tawātur* and cannot fit into great volumes and volumes. We do not intend to list them here, for these proofs are known and do not need to be mentioned or stated.[110]

In other versions of the same tradition, Umm Salama's preference is noted. When 'Ali came to call on her, she asked: 'What can I do for you?' He replied, 'The book which the Prophet gave to you.' She replied: 'You are its rightful owner,' and then added: 'By God, I wanted it to be you.' When 'Ali received the book, he opened it and said, 'It is new knowledge.'[111] Other versions use particular phrasings to lend more authority to 'Ali and to implicitly undermine the legitimacy of other Caliphs as not being entitled to the title of 'Commander of the Faithful'. For example, the first sentence is changed to have Umm Salama state: 'The Prophet of God gave me a book and told me to hang on to it until I saw the Commander of the Faithful ascend Muhammad's pulpit and then come asking for this book.' This version continues as previously with her son 'Umar attending all the first speeches and then 'Ali claiming the book. This particular version also ties in the two concepts of *'ilm* and *qudra*, for Umm Salama handed him the book and asked: 'What is in it?' 'Ali replied: 'Everything the sons of Adam might need.'[112] In other versions the knowledge is explained further, as Ja'far al-Sadiq narrates that his father Muhammad al-Baqir said: 'In 'Ali's book there is everything anyone needs, even the legal compensation for a scratch.'[113] Its origins are attested in various traditions, which add: "Ali has not left the Shī'a needing anything with regard to what is licit and what is forbidden; we even found the legal indemnity for inflicting a scratch set forth in his book. As soon as you see this book, you know that it was written by *al-awwalīn* ('the ancients'; one could also read this as *al-awwalayn* 'the first two', meaning the Prophet and 'Ali).[114] Yet other versions of the same tradition imply that more than one

---

[110] Sayyid Husayn al-Tabataba'i al-Burujirdi, *Jami' ahadith al-Shi'a* (Qum: al-Matba'a al-'Ilmiyya, 1978–1979), 1:11–12.
[111] al-Saffar, *Basa'ir al-darajat*, 182–188.
[112] Ibid.
[113] Ibid.
[114] Ibid.

book was needed to hold all this particular kind of *'ilm*, even of unseen matters that are not accessible to ordinary human beings. A tradition is narrated by Muhammad al-Baqir in which he states that the Prophet kept dictating to 'Ali, and 'Ali kept writing until the text filled the skin on both sides and its margins. 'There are many such books', he reported; 'if he were to mention them all they could not all be fit in'.[115] Knowledge of the unseen is mentioned explicitly in a narration that does not specify which Imam was asked, but only records Muhammad b. Muslim as saying: 'I asked him [the Imam] about the inheritance of knowledge, what the source of that knowledge was, and whether there was an exegetical work that included all these matters that people discuss, such as marriage, divorce and rituals of devotion.' He replied: "Ali b. Abi Talib wrote down all knowledge of the law and the rituals of devotion and left out nothing, even what is still to come.'[116]

The knowledge is not exclusive to 'Ali but extends to the *ahl al-bayt* among his progeny by Prophetic designation. For example, a tradition records that Abu Ja'far stated: 'The Prophet told 'Ali: "Write down what I dictate to you." 'Ali said: "O Prophet of God, are you afraid of forgetfulness?" He replied: "I am not afraid of forgetfulness, and I have called upon God to protect you and save you from forgetfulness, but write it down for your partners." 'Ali asked: "Who are my partners?" He replied: 'The Imams from your progeny. They will be the salvation of my *umma* (community), and the rain that quenches their thirst. Through them prayers will be answered, calamities averted, and mercy will descend from heaven. This is the first of them." Then he pointed to al-Hasan and then to al-Husayn, saying: "The Imams from your progeny."'[117]

The physical existence of such a *naṣṣ* or such books is also attested to in various traditions. For example, 'Abd al-Malik b. A'yan said: 'Abu Ja'far showed me some books and then asked me why these books were written. I replied: "To hold the most correct clear opinions." He asked me: "And?" I replied: "Knowledge. I heard that your *qā'im* shall rise up one day and will implement what is in these books." He said: "You have spoken the truth."'[118] However, sometimes these physical books seem also to have posed a threat to their rightful owners. Several traditions attest to their being given away for safekeeping. For example, Abu al-Sabah said: 'I told Abu 'Abd Allah that we heard that the Prophet told 'Ali that he was his brother, his companion, his guardian, his *waṣī* and the salvation of the people of his house and his successor for his nation. He also said that he would tell him how things would be after his demise, saying: "'Ali, I have loved for you what I

---

[115] Abu Sa'd 'Abd al-Karim b. Muhammad al-Sam'ani, *Adab al-imla' wa-l-istimla'* (Beirut: Dar wa-Maktabat al-Hilāl, 1989), 19.
[116] al-Saffar, *Basa'ir al-darajat*, 182–188.
[117] Ibid.
[118] Ibid.

have loved for myself, and I hate for you what I hate for myself." Abu 'Abd Allah affirmed this, saying that it was written in 'Ali's book, which he had given away out of fear after the crucifixion of al-Mughira.'[119] This refers to al-Mughira b. Sa'id (or b. Sa'd) who was arrested and executed by Khalid b. 'Abd Allah al-Qasri, the Umayyad governor of Iraq (r. *c.* 724–738) for adherence to the *ghulāt* or extremist Shi'is.[120]

Thus, Umm Salama kept the first *naṣṣ* that designated and legitimated 'Ali as the true Imam and rightful successor through three caliphal reigns until it reached its rightful owner. She also did with his son al-Hasan, as many traditions record. Imam Ja'far al-Sadiq is quoted as saying: 'The books were kept by 'Ali. When he decided to make the journey to Iraq, he entrusted them to Umm Salama, and when he died, she passed them on to Imam al-Hasan.'[121] There are many traditions to that effect, and they are usually collected in the hadith compendia in a chapter titled 'Chapter about the Imams and how the Prophet's books came to them and to the Commander of the Faithful'.[122]

The third Imam who received his *naṣṣ* from Umm Salama is Zayn al-'Abidin b. al-Husayn. Al-Majlisi quotes from *Kitab al-Ghayba* by al-Shaykh al-Tusi that when al-Husayn went to Iraq, he left his will, his book, and other belongings with Umm Salama and instructed her: 'When my eldest son comes to you, give him these.' After al-Husayn was martyred, 'Ali b. al-Husayn came to Umm Salama, and she gave him everything that al-Husayn had left with her.[123] Al-Hurr al-'Amili (d. 1688) adds other symbols to the books and first praises Umm Salama for good conduct and for documenting many traditions, including reports that al-Husayn left his father's books with her, which included the keys of wisdom, the essence of knowledge, the locus of prophethood, and the characteristics of the Imamate. After al-Husayn was slain, his son 'Ali b. al-Husayn came to her, and she delivered them to him.[124] Thus, her title *Ḥāfiẓat al-naṣṣ* ('Keeper of the *naṣṣ*') is well deserved, for she kept safe and handed over the legitimation of three of the twelve Imams.

Interestingly, there is an alternative narrative about al-Husayn and his books. According to this group of accounts, he does not leave them with Umm Salama for safekeeping, despite knowing that he will be martyred in Karbala. According to Imami doctrine, all Imams predicted the place and

---

[119] Ibid.

[120] Andrew Marsham, 'Attitudes to the Use of Fire in Executions in Late Antiquity and Early Islam: The Burning of Heretics and Rebels in Late Umayyad Iraq', 106–127 in *Violence in Islamic Thought: From the Qur'ān to the Mongols*, eds Robert Gleave and István T. Kristó-Nagy (Edinburgh: Edinburgh University Press, 2015), 109–110.

[121] Muhammad b. Ya'qub al-Kulayni, *Usul al-Kafi* (Beirut: Dar al-Kutub al-Islamiyya, 1968–1969), 1:304; Majlisi, *Bihar al-anwar*, 47:18, 19, and 48.

[122] See al-Saffar, *Basa'ir al-darajat*, 182–188.

[123] al-Majlisi, *Bihar al-anwar*, 46:17–20.

[124] Muhammad b. al-Hasan al-Hurr al-'Amili, *Wasa'il al-Shi'a ila tahsil masa'il al-shari'a* (Qum: Mu'assasat Āl al-Bayt li-Ihya' al-Turath, 1993), 30:322.

manner of their own deaths.[125] Al-Kulayni also records a tradition saying that the Imam knows his hour of death.[126] Yet al-Husayn takes his books with him and then hands them over to another female. In most alternative versions, he gives them to his eldest daughter Fatima, although in a few he gives them to his sister Zaynab. According to the recorded tradition, he gave her a wrapped book and a visible will or testament.[127] Al-Majlisi quotes several traditions on the authority of Abu Ja'far Muhammad al-Baqir that state: 'When al-Husayn was about to die, he called his eldest daughter Fatima and gave her a wrapped book and two wills, one open to view (*ẓāhira*) and one hidden (*bāṭina*). Fatima gave 'Ali b. al-Husayn the book, which was later given to his son.'[128]

While it seemed not at all problematic to have females keeping the *naṣṣ* safe and handing it over to the designated Imam when it was their time to receive it, the sources record other traditions in which someone raises an objection to having women in such an authoritative position. Yet these traditions defend that position, not only using Umm Salama's example, who was given the first *naṣṣ* by the Prophet himself, but also other women. For example, al-Majlisi quotes *Ikmal al-Din* by Ibn Babawayh al-Qummi to the effect that Ahmad b. Ibrahim said: 'Hakima bt. Muhammad b. 'Ali al-Rida, the sister of Abu al-Hasan al-'Askari, came to see me, and I asked her: "To whom should the Shi'is turn?" She replied: "To my grandmother, my father's mother." I said: "I should follow someone who has given his will to a woman?" She said: "This follows the example of al-Husayn b. 'Ali, who gave his apparent will to his sister Zaynab bt. 'Ali, for whatever knowledge 'Ali b. al-Husayn possessed was attributed to Zaynab."'[129] This acceptance is also reiterated by al-Shahrawardi, who recorded a report that al-Husayn had left his books with Umm Salama, taking the example of his grandfather, who had left his book with her, containing all eternal knowledge and everything else the community needed except for the timing of Judgement Day, which she then gave to his son 'Ali, Zayn al-'Abidin.[130] Ibn al-Sabbagh also recorded a tradition with a commentary to the same effect.[131]

Concluding Remarks

The interpretation of *ahl al-bayt* in its distinctively and exclusive Shi'i meaning together with the various traditions narrated by Umm Salama have been used to cement Imami Shi'i ideology. For example, al-Mazandarani

125 Kohlberg, 'Imam and Community in the Pre-Ghayba Period', 27.
126 al-Kulayni, *al-Usul min al-Kafi*, 1:258.
127 al-Saffar, *Basa'ir al-darajat*, 182–188.
128 al-Majlisi, *Bihar al-anwar*, 26:35–36.
129 Ibid., 46:7–20.
130 al-Shahrawardi, *Mustadrak Safinat al-Bihar*, 5:139–140.
131 Ibn al-Sabbagh, *al-Fusul al-Muhimma*, 1:40–43.

argues that if the Prophet had been silent and had not explained who his *ahl al-bayt* were, then anyone could have claimed to be included among them. He continues that God Almighty has revealed in his Book a proof of the truthfulness of the Prophet, namely verse (33:33), which was revealed for 'Ali, al-Hasan, al-Husayn, and Fatima, when the Prophet covered them with his mantle (*kisā'*) in Umm Salama's house. He adds a reference to *Ḥadīth al-Thaqalayn*, connecting it to *Ḥadīth al-Kisā'*, reporting that the Prophet made the following supplication: 'O God, every Prophet has a family and *thaqal* ("weighty matter" or "trust") and these are "the people of my house" (*ahl baytī*) and "my weighty matter" (*thaqalī*).' Al-Mazandarani continues, adding that when the Prophet died, 'Ali was the one most worthy, on account of what the Prophet had said about him and how he had always helped people. When 'Ali died, neither Muhammad b. 'Ali, nor al-'Abbas b. 'Ali, nor any other of his children would or could have claimed the succession, because al-Hasan and al-Husayn would have said that God revealed verses about us and hence you should follow us. The Prophet spoke about us, uncleanness was removed from us, and we were purified, but you were not. Hence, after 'Ali died it was al-Hasan who was worthier to be his father's successor, for he was older. After al-Hasan died, his own son could have claimed the succession, but he did not, even though the Qur'an says in verse (8:75): 'and the possessors of relationships are nearer to each other in the ordinance of God; surely God knows all things'. Al-Husayn would then have said that the purification verse was for 'Ali, al-Hasan, and him and not for al-Hasan's sons. When al-Husayn died, none of his household could have claimed the succession, and it therefore went to 'Ali b. al-Husayn, then to his son Muhammad, and so on, each successive Imam being designated by his father.[132]

The same logic was also used in one of the versions of *Ḥadīth al-Qārūra*, as presented by al-Majlisi, in which 'Abd al-Rahman b. Kathir al-Hashimi asked Abu 'Abd Allah: 'Why is it that the descendants of al-Husayn are better regarded than those of al-Hasan, when they were both born the same way and were both purified?' He replied: 'I see that you do not know that Gabriel descended and came to Muhammad before al-Husayn was born and told him that a boy would be born who would be slain by the Muslim community after his demise.' The Prophet replied: 'Gabriel, I do not need this to happen.' Then he spoke to him thrice and then called for 'Ali and told him: 'Gabriel told me that there will be born to you a boy who will be killed by the Muslim community after your demise.' 'Ali replied: 'I do not need this to happen.' Then he spoke to him thrice and said: 'There will be amongst his sons an Imam, and he will inherit the repositories of knowledge.' Then he sent for Fatima and told her that God had given her glad tidings of the birth of a boy, but he will be slain by the Muslim community after his demise. Fatima replied: 'I do not need this to happen.' He spoke to her thrice

132 al-Mazandarani, *Sharh usul al-Kafi*, 6:109–113.

and said: 'There will be amongst his sons an Imam and he will inherit the repositories of knowledge.' She said: 'I accept the will of God.' Then she became pregnant with al-Husayn and carried him for six months and then gave birth. No other infant, who was born after only six months, survived except al-Husayn b. 'Ali and Jesus, son of Mary. Umm Salama looked after him. The Prophet came every day and inserted his tongue into al-Husayn's mouth to suck on, until he was satiated. His flesh grew out of the flesh of the Prophet. He never suckled any milk from Fatima or anyone else, and when verse (46:15)[133] was revealed regarding him and after he attained his maturity at forty years of age, he said, 'O God, instruct me to thank You for Your grace and the blessings You bestowed on me and my father and to do good for You, and may You accept my thanks.' He also asked God to grant him the best of offspring. Had he said the best offspring, then they would all have been Imams, but he qualified it.[134] Thus, all the traditions, as well as the conceptualisation of the *ahl al-bayt* in that particular way, have been combined and have all been utilised to formulate, establish, and strengthen the ideology and conceptualisation of the Imamate.

While the Shi'is rejected the legitimacy of the established Caliphate, they considered 'Ali and his descendants the rightful successors of the Prophet and as such entitled to the Caliphate. They were the divinely inspired and *ma'ṣūm* (infallible) Imams of the community of believers. Divine appointment and divinely sanctioned designation (*naṣṣ*) by the Prophet or the preceding Imam became the distinctive mark of the Shi'i theory of the exclusively male Imamate. The legitimacy of the highest authority in the Shi'i hierarchy was acquired through such explicit designation. While the Imamate was a distinctly male prerogative, the *naṣṣ* granting legitimacy in the case of three of the first Imams – 'Ali b. Abi Talib, al-Hasan b. 'Ali, and 'Ali b. al-Husayn – was delivered to them by a woman, whether Umm Salama, Fatima bt. al-Husayn, or Zaynab bt. 'Ali. In serving this crucial role, the women of *ahl al-bayt*, including the Prophet's wife Umm Salama in particular, come to share in a significant fashion in legitimating the authority of the Imams.

---

[133] 'And We have enjoined on man doing of good to his parents; with trouble did his mother bear him and with trouble did she bring him forth; and the bearing of him and the weaning of him was thirty months; until when he attains his maturity and reaches forty years, he says: My Lord! grant me that I may give thanks for Thy favour which Thou hast bestowed on me and on my parents, and that I may do good which pleases Thee and do good to me in respect of my offspring; surely I turn to Thee, and surely I am of those who submit' (Q 46:15).

[134] al-Majlisi, *Bihar al-anwar*, 23:273 and another expanded version in 24:255.

CHAPTER

4

HEIRESS TO THE PROPHET: FATIMA'S *KHUṬBA* AS AN EARLY CASE OF FEMALE RELIGIOUS AUTHORITY IN ISLAM[1]

Alyssa Gabbay

Introduction

Not long after her father's death, Fatima, daughter of the Prophet Muhammad, covered her head with her veil and left her home, accompanied by a group of her female friends and family members.[2] Walking exactly in the manner of her father, her robes trailing on the ground, she approached the spot where Abu Bakr, the caliph, was seated among a crowd of Emigrants and Helpers.[3] She groaned in sadness, causing those gathered to burst into tears.[4] When their agitation had quieted, she delivered an impassioned sermon that castigated the Muslim community and its leaders on several counts. Satan had duped them, Fatima said, into acting against the teachings of the Prophet, presumably by usurping the caliphate from 'Ali, its proper possessor.[5] Avowedly seeking to avoid sedition, they had fallen into it instead, and were, in effect, stabbing the members of the Prophet's household with sharp daggers.[6] Moreover, by depriving her of a piece of property, Fadak, that she had inherited from her father, Muslims were transgressing the laws

[1] I am grateful to Devin J. Stewart, Mirjam Künkler, Karen Bauer, Raffaele Mauriello, and other participants in 'Of *'Alimas, Muhaddithas*, and *Mujtahidas*: The Past and Present of Female Religious Authority in Shi'i Islam' for their remarks on this paper. Thanks also to Derek Krueger, Eugene Rogers, and Hussien Algudaihi for their input. I am also indebted to Karen Ruffle, whose research on Fatima helped point me in this direction, and with whom I shared many fruitful conversations about the daughter of the Prophet. Any errors are my own.

[2] Abu al-Fadl Ahmad b. Abi Tahir b. Tayfur, *Balaghat al-nisa'*, ed. Ahmad al-Alfi (Qum: Maktaba-yi Baṣīratī, 1942), 32.

[3] Ibn Abi Tahir Tayfur, *Balaghat al-nisa'*, 32–33.

[4] Ibn Abi Tahir Tayfur, *Balaghat al-nisa'*, 33.

[5] Ibn Abi Tahir Tayfur, *Balaghat al-nisa'*, 31–32.

[6] Ibn Abi Tahir Tayfur, *Balaghat al-nisa'*, 32.

of the Qur'an and placing the Book of God behind their backs – a devastating charge indeed.[7]

'Is it in the Book that you should inherit from your fathers, but I should not inherit from my father?' Fatima asked sarcastically. 'You have certainly done a thing unprecedented. So go ahead and take it like a bridled and saddled camel that will meet you on the Day of Gathering.'[8]

The occasion precipitating Fatima's *khuṭba,* as it has become known, was Abu Bakr's decision to deny the Prophet's daughter her claim to Fadak, an ancient oasis town about two or three days' journey from Medina.[9] Inhabited by a colony of Jewish agriculturalists, and producing dates and cereals as well as handicrafts such as woven mats with palm-leaf borders, Fadak had come under Muslim control after a series of expeditions launched by the Prophet beginning in about 627.[10] Frightened by news of his victories, the Jews of Fadak made a pact with the Prophet in which they were allowed to 'remain in Fadak while giving up half their lands and half the produce of the oasis'.[11] This produce was allocated to the Prophet, who gave the revenues of it to needy travellers and to the poor.[12]

After the Prophet's death, and after Abu Bakr had become the first caliph over the protests of those who supported 'Ali, different parties laid claim to Fadak.[13] Fatima argued that it was hers according to the Qur'an inheritance laws.[14] According to some traditions, she said that the Prophet had given it to her as a gift before his death.[15] 'Abbas, a paternal uncle, claimed that it rightly belonged to him as a member of the *'aṣaba,* or the male agnate relatives of the Prophet.[16] Meanwhile, Abu Bakr said that it belonged to the treasury of the Islamic state (*bayt al-māl*) and was to be distributed to the poor and needy.[17] Traditions disputed by Shi'is report that the Prophet had stated that he 'would have no heirs . . . what he left would be *ṣadaqa*' – public property used for charity.[18] Abu Bakr famously quoted the Prophet as saying, '*lā nūrathu, mā taraknāhu ṣadaqa*' – 'No one inherits from us [prophets]; what

---

[7] Ibn Abi Tahir Tayfur, *Balaghat al-nisa'*, 32.

[8] Ibn Abi Tahir Tayfur, *Balaghat al-nisa'*, 32.

[9] L. Veccia Vaglieri, 'Fadak', *EI*².

[10] Veccia Vaglieri, 'Fadak'.

[11] Veccia Vaglieri, 'Fadak'.

[12] Veccia Vaglieri, 'Fadak'.

[13] See Veccia Vaglieri, 'Fadak'; Denise L. Soufi, 'The Image of Fāṭima in Classical Muslim Thought', PhD diss. (Princeton University, 1997), 91–116; Wilferd Madelung, *Succession to Muhammad: A Study of the Early Caliphate* (Cambridge: Cambridge University Press, 1997), 360–363; Abu Ja'far Muhammad b. Jarir al-Tabari, *The History of al-Tabarī*, vol. 9, trans. Ismail K. Poonawala (Albany: State University of New York Press, 1990), 196–197.

[14] Veccia Vaglieri, 'Fadak'.

[15] Soufi, 'Image of Fāṭima', 101–103; 105.

[16] Soufi, 'Image of Fāṭima', 93.

[17] Veccia Vaglieri, 'Fadak'.

[18] Veccia Vaglieri, 'Fadak'; Soufi, 'Image of Fāṭima', 95; Tabari, *History*, 9:196.

we leave is for charity.'[19] In her *khuṭba*, Fatima challenged that assertion, noting that several prophets had designated inheritances for their heirs.[20]

Although Fatima's *khuṭba* addressed the fate of a relatively circumscribed piece of real estate, its effects have rippled widely. Scholars such as al-Irbili (d. 1293), the Shi'i historian and litterateur known for his biographies of the Prophet and the Imams, noted its eloquence.[21] Poets reworked it in stirring elegies.[22] In their treatises on legal matters, prominent Shi'i hadith compilers Ibn Babawayh (d. 991) and Muhammad Baqir al-Majlisi (d. 1699) cited Fatima's sermon to provide explanations for certain laws.[23] In so doing, they recognised the daughter of the Prophet as a model for behaviour and religious knowledge, granting her a status similar, if not precisely equal, to that of the Imams, those men who are considered by Shi'is to be the only legitimate successors of the Prophet Muhammad as religious and political leaders of the Muslim community and who, after his death, bore the function of guiding men and preserving and explaining the Divine Law.[24]

Despite her prevalent image as a meek and mournful housewife, Fatima has emerged in recent scholarship as a figure of religious authority – a woman capable of explaining the tenets of Islam, delivering a legal opinion, and acting as an impeccable model of behaviour for men and women alike.[25] As contemporary scholar Matthew Pierce has observed, many scholars are deploying portraits of a religiously authoritative Fatima to provide 'evidence for the right of contemporary women to assume positions of religious and political authority'.[26] This study advances and elucidates the trend of what Pierce calls a 'resignification of Fāṭima's role in the Shi'i narrative' by showing that scholars depicted Fatima as a religious authority at a date earlier than that which has been widely recognised and by shedding light on how the idea of the feminine became woven into classical Shi'i sources' constructions of authority. [27]

---

[19] Soufi, 'Image of Fāṭima', 95; also Tabari, *History*, 9:196. For a full discussion of the grammatical implications of this statement, see David S. Powers, *Studies in Qur'an and* Hadith*: The Formation of the Islamic Law of Inheritance* (Berkeley: University of California Press, 1986), 123–128, as well as Muhammad Baqir al-Sadr, *Fadak fi al-tarikh*, trans. Abdullah al-Shahin as *Fadak in History* <http://www.shiavault.com/books/fadak-in-history/ last accessed 6 May 2018, 142–151.

[20] Ibn Abi Tahir Tayfur, *Balaghat al-nisa'*, 34.

[21] Soufi, 'Image of Fāṭima', 110. As Soufi notes, in his *Kashf al-ghumma fi ma'rifat al- a'immu*, al-Irbili says of Fatima's *khuṭba* that 'it will embarrass rhetoricians and paralyze eloquent speakers'.

[22] See Soufi, 'Image of Fāṭima', 147.

[23] See Soufi, 'Image of Fāṭima', 111.

[24] Moojan Momen, *An Introduction to Shi`i Islam: The History and Doctrines of Twelver Shi'ism* (New Haven: Yale, 1987), 147.

[25] See, for example, Rawand Osman, *Female Personalities in the Qur'an and Sunna: Examining the Major Sources of Imami Shi'i Islam* (Abingdon, Oxon: Routledge, 2015), 121–125.

[26] Matthew Pierce, 'Remembering Fāṭimah: New Means of Legitimizing Female Authority in Contemporary Shi'i Discourse', in *Women, Leadership, and Mosques: Changes in Contemporary Islamic Authority*, eds Masooda Bano and Hilary Kalmbach (Leiden: Brill, 2012), 346.

[27] Pierce, 'Remembering Fatimah', 346.

Given that Fatima's status is inextricably linked to her relationship to her father, scholars such as Ibn Babawayh and al-Majlisi acknowledge and uphold the concept of bilateral descent - the notion that a daughter may carry on her father's legacy, transmit his bloodline, and inherit his property - to a greater degree than their Sunni counterparts. Here, just like a son, a daughter can inherit both a father's property and his authority. Furthermore, such a stance exerted a positive impact on the legal status of women in Shi'i societies versus Sunni ones, at least on a theoretical basis, and paved the way for women today to occupy roles as religious authorities. Ironically, classical Shi'i scholars probably had no such goal in mind. Their original rationale for including women in the lines of descent and inheritance likely had far more to do with their conviction that Fatima's husband, sons, and other male descendants deserved to occupy the preeminent roles of political and religious authority in the caliphate - the very basis of Shi'ism - than it did with their concerns about gender egalitarianism. Still, unintended consequences are nevertheless consequences.

Fatima, the Imams and Religious Authority

This section addresses how scholars have conceptualised of both political and religious authority in Shi'ism, especially with regard to the Imams, and then will show where Fatima has traditionally fallen on the scale of temporal leadership. As Liyakat Takim has demonstrated in his study, *The Heirs of the Prophet*, Islam in its earliest stages serves as an excellent model of Weber's concept of charismatic authority.[28] Like most charismatic leaders, the Prophet Muhammad was believed to have a special connection with the divine, to be the bearer of 'special extraordinary gifts and feats', and to 'radiate the divine force of charisma'.[29] He was a revolutionary leader who subverted 'social norms, normative traditions, and traditional forms of authority', for he brought a new message that both 'replaced traditional tribal authority with a new ethical-moral structure that negated the old normative order' and entailed the 'abandonment of many pre-Islamic ancestral heroes, customs, and practices'.[30]

In cases of charismatic authority, the death of the founder can give rise to at least two outcomes - both of which can be seen in the history of Islam. The leader's charisma can be 'depersonalised' and 'routinised'; in these cases, it is 'transformed into a charisma of office'.[31] Such was the Sunni vision, in which the Prophet's authority initially transferred to the office of the caliphate and later splintered among several groups.[32] Or it can be inherited

[28] Liyakat N. Takim, *The Heirs of the Prophet: Charisma and Religious Authority in Shi'ite Islam* (Albany: State University of New York Press, 2006), 2–4.

[29] Takim, *Heirs of the Prophet*, 3.

[30] Takim, *Heirs of the Prophet*, 3, 4.

[31] Takim, *Heirs of the Prophet*, 3, 5.

[32] Takim, *Heirs of the Prophet*, 5–7.

by descendants, who may seek to perpetuate their forebear's revolutionary social vision.[33] Such was the case with the Shi'is, who believed that the Prophet's charisma and authority transferred wholly to the Imams.[34] These men, considered the only rightful, legitimate leaders of the Muslim community, included 'Ali (the husband of Fatima and the Prophet's cousin) and 'Ali and Fatima's sons and the Prophet's grandsons, Hasan and Husayn, as well as specific men among their descendants.

The authority of the Shi'i Imams drew on several factors and assumed several guises. As close relatives and, in most cases, direct descendants of the Prophet, they partook in Muhammad's 'peculiar extraordinary traits' and radiated his charisma – a quality that scholars sometimes conceptualised of as a special 'Muhammadan' light that transferred from one imam to his successor.[35] Designated explicitly by his predecessor, each imam received certain scrolls and weapons, which represented his authority and empowered him with *'ilm*, or 'divinely bestowed knowledge'.[36] Because they were the sole people endowed with this knowledge, the Imams were the sole means through which God guided humanity; it was 'through them that God could be worshipped and known'.[37] Often, this guidance manifested in a legal form. Fusing both political and religious authority, the Imam acted 'as both the repository of knowledge and executor of the law'.[38] Even after his death, the Imam continued to have a share in shaping law. As an infallible model for humanity, his sunnah, or behaviour, as enshrined in hadith, formed a basis for creating and interpreting legislation – indeed, he was 'the actual embodiment of the law'.[39] In this manner, he continued to perpetuate the revolutionary ideals instituted by his forebear.

Beyond their status as political and religious leaders in this world, the Imams occupied a special status on a cosmological scale. Viewed as being endowed with preexistence, and sometimes envisioned as 'silhouettes of light revolving around the throne of the Merciful One',[40] they were capable of superhuman feats, among them assuring a place in heaven to believers, for salvation in Shi'ism was conditioned on recognition of and obedience to the Imam.[41]

---

[33] Takim, *Heirs of the Prophet*, 3, 24.

[34] Takim, *Heirs of the Prophet*, 24–26.

[35] Takim, *Heirs of the Prophets*, 26; Soufi, 'Image of Fāṭima', 155–156; Uri Rubin, 'Pre-existence and Light: Aspects of the Concept of Nur Muhammad', *Israel Oriental Studies* 5 (1975), 65, 102; Rubin, 'Nur Muḥammadi'.

[36] Takim, *Heirs of the Prophets*, 26–28.

[37] Takim, *Heirs of the Prophets*, 26.

[38] Takim, *Heirs of the Prophets*, 31–32.

[39] Takim, *Heirs of the Prophets*, 32.

[40] Takim, *Heirs of the Prophets*, 63.

[41] Takim, *Heirs of the Prophets*, 26.

Fatima, the female antecedent of all of the Shi'i Imams with the exception of 'Ali, shared in their extraordinary qualities. Like them, she was traditionally depicted as possessing and transmitting the Muhammadan light – and was sometimes even seen as the origin of it (a concept reflected in one of her most frequent epithets, Fatima al-Zahra' – 'Fatima the Radiant').[42] Like the Imams, she was both physically and spiritually pure and incapable of committing sin.[43] Like the Imams, too, her reach extended beyond that of this world: having enjoyed preexistence, she was envisioned as playing a significant role on the Day of Judgment when, according to some traditions, she would appear as a queen accompanied by angels and houris.[44] There, she would intercede with God on behalf of some who were condemned to hell, saving them from doom on account of their love for the Prophet's family.[45] She would also 'demand justice for the killing of [her son] Husayn', the third Imam who was murdered by the Umayyads (661–750).[46]

Until relatively recently, however, temporal authority – both political and religious – has largely been denied Fatima. In her excellent work about the daughter of the Prophet, contemporary scholar Denise Soufi identifies at least two depictions of Fatima within the classical Shi'i tradition: that of a 'model of female Muslim piety' who was 'known for her patient suffering under the yoke of poverty, her quiet obedience to her husband, and her profound grief at the death of her father', as well as a far less passive role – that of an activist and martyr in the Shi'i cause to claim the caliphate in the struggle for leadership after the death of the Prophet.[47] Soufi graphically illustrates both roles. She notes, for example, accounts of the day of 'the Portico' (*al-Saqīfa*), the meeting at which Abu Bakr was appointed caliph – illegitimately, according to Shi'is – which relate that Fatima tried to block 'Umar and others from entering her house in their quest to force 'Ali to give his oath of allegiance to Abu Bakr.[48] In one particularly polemical version, Fatima bravely confronted a man, 'Umar's servant, Qunfudh, who then whipped and pushed her.[49] The assault led to the miscarriage of her unborn son, Muhassin, and, ultimately, to Fatima's death.[50] Yet despite these accounts, which decisively portray a woman acting on behalf of her beliefs and even suffering martyrdom for them, Soufi suggests that Fatima lacked the trappings of dominion

---

[42] Soufi, 'Image of Fāṭima', 158; Rubin, 'Pre-existence and Light', 102.
[43] Soufi, 'Image of Fāṭima', 152–158.
[44] Rubin, 'Pre-existence and Light', 99–102, Soufi, 'Image of Fāṭima', 181–182.
[45] Soufi, 'Image of Fāṭima', 185–187
[46] Soufi, 'Image of Fāṭima', 187–189.
[47] Soufi, 'Image of Fāṭima', iii, 1.
[48] Soufi, 'Image of Fāṭima', 88.
[49] Soufi, 'Image of Fāṭima', 88–89.
[50] Soufi, 'Image of Fāṭima', 89.

in the temporal realm.[51] Fatima did possess authority among Shi'is as the 'Queen of Women', but this authority would not be 'manifested until the Day of Judgment', when, as noted, she would act as 'avenger for the murder of [her son] Husayn and intercessor for the Shi'a'.[52] Fatima's gender necessitated these restrictions on her authority: as Soufi explains, 'according to the medieval Muslim worldview, women are not allowed to exercise temporal authority'. Therefore, Fatima could not display her 'power in the temporal abode'.[53]

Soufi likewise notes that Fatima 'partakes of the gnostic knowledge of the Prophet and follows his example of piety through prayer and fasting', but, 'unlike the Imams, she rarely displays knowledge of Islamic law, considered to be the purview of men by medieval Muslims'.[54]

Yet, as twentieth- and twenty-first-century Shi'i scholars and activists have striven to loosen restrictions upon female authority – including in the arena of law – they have simultaneously demonstrated greater willingness to attribute temporal authority to Fatima.[55] In 'Remembering Fāṭimah: New Means of Legitimizing Female Authority in Contemporary Shi'i Discourse', Pierce discusses the work of several scholars who have presented or are presenting the 'authoritative model of Fāṭimah as evidence of the right of women to assume positions of religious and political authority', among them 'Ali Shari'ati, Monir Gorgi, Ahmad Azari-Qummi, Jamilah Kadivar, and Javadi Amuli.[56] Several focus on Fatima's role as a revolutionary who, following to some degree Weber's model, perpetuated the social ideals instituted by her father. In his famous essay '*Fāṭima Fāṭima Ast*' ('Fatima is Fatima'), for example, the Iranian sociologist Shari'ati (d. 1977) depicts her as one who would 'bear the responsibility of reflecting within herself the newly created revolutionary values' brought into being by her father.[57] Fatima, he writes,

> became the owner of the values of her father, the inheritor of all the honors of her family. She was the continuation of the chain of great ancestors, the continuation which began with Adam and passed through all of the leaders of freedom and consciousness in the history of mankind.[58]

Similarly, Muhammad Baqir al-Sadr, the prominent Iraqi ayatollah who was executed by the regime of Saddam Husayn in 1980, envisioned the

[51] Soufi, 'Image of Fāṭima', 200–203. See also Pierce, 'Remembering Fāṭimah', 352–353.
[52] Soufi, 'Image of Fāṭima', 200–201.
[53] Soufi, 'Image of Fāṭima', 200–201.
[54] Soufi, 'Image of Fāṭima', 203.
[55] Pierce, 'Remembering Fāṭimah', 352–353.
[56] Pierce, 'Remembering Fāṭimah', 346.
[57] Christopher Paul Clohessy, *Fatima: Daughter of Muhammad* (Piscataway: Gorgias Press, 2013), 216.
[58] Ali Shariati, 'Fāṭima Fāṭima Ast', in *Shariati on Shariati and the Muslim Woman* (USA: ABC International Group, 1996), 159.

daughter of the Prophet as the formidable fomenter of a 'Fatimite revolution', one aimed not only at securing her rightful inheritance, but also at removing those who had usurped the leadership of the Muslim community and installing its rightful ruler – that is, her husband 'Ali. As he writes, it was a revolution 'by which Fatima wanted to pluck out the cornerstone [upon] which history was built after the day of the Saqeefa'.[59] As Rachel Feder notes, Sadr's portrait of Fatima diverges sharply from the typical depictions of an incessantly weeping, weak woman whose sadness paralyses her. Rather, her tears galvanise her to anger and action: 'in Sadr's version it is her grief that procures her inspiration to embark upon revolutionary action. Sadr's Fatima is emotionally and mentally stable; her thoughts are lucid and determined, and she is in a suitable condition to undertake decisive action'.[60]

Other scholars focus on Fatima's role as an impeccable model for humankind. Arguing that Fatima was 'not only infallible (*ma'ṣūma*) but also absolutely infallible (*ma'ṣūma muṭlaqa*)', the senior cleric Javadi Amuli maintains that 'her sunnah is just as authoritative as 'Ali's'.[61] This reasoning, as Pierce observes, both supports the argument that 'the use of Fāṭimah as a role model is grounded in the *sharī'ah*', and implies that 'the potential for women's authority is no less than men's'.[62]

Interestingly, however, Fatima did appear as a temporal religious authority even in the classical sources and showed herself as a legal authority to a degree greater than perhaps she has been given credit for. This idea emerges in the manner that these sources make use of her *khuṭba*. The significance is very great, for it adds more ammunition to the case for female authority in Shi'ism.

Fatima's *Khuṭba*

In *Fihrist kutub al-Shi'a*, al-Shaykh al-Tusi (d. 1067) attributes a work titled al-*Khuṭba al-zahrā'* – 'The Brilliant Oration' – to the eighth-century Shi'i historian Abu Mikhnaf (Lut b. Yahya b. Sa'id al-Kufi, d. 773–774). It is clear from al-Tusi's presentation that *al-zahrā'* is a description of the oration and not a reference to Fatimah. Instead, the text was evidently one of the many orations attributed to 'Ali b. Abi Talib.[63] One suspects that this title, *al-Khuṭba al-zahrā'*, may have inspired the creation of an oration attributed to Fatima,

---

[59] Sadr, *Fadak fi al-tarīkh*, 58.

[60] Rachel Kantz Feder, 'Fatima's Revolutionary Image in *Fadak fi al-Tarikh* (1955): The Inception of Muhammad al-Sadr's Activism', *British Journal of Middle Eastern Studies* 41.1 (2014), 86–87.

[61] Amuli, cited in Pierce, 'Remembering Fāṭimah', 357.

[62] Pierce, 'Remembering Fāṭimah', 357.

[63] Muhammad b. al-Hasan al-Tusi, *Fihrist kutub al-Shi'a*, ed. 'Abd al-'Aziz al-Tabataba'i (Qum: Maktabat al-Muhaqqiq al-Tabataba'i, 1999), 381–382.

Khuṭbat al-Zahrā'. The *khuṭba* of Fatima, 'the Radiant One', while it is likely not historically authentic, dates from the ninth century at the latest. While several sources present versions of Fatima's *khuṭba*,[64] the earliest is that contained in the work by the Baghdadi litterateur Ibn Abi Tahir Tayfur's (d. 893) anthology *Balaghat al-nisa'* (The Eloquent Statements of Women).[65] Ibn Abi Tahir Tayfur's account actually comprises two versions, which differ somewhat in their *isnād*s and content; most later sources cite the second version, which, according to a notation within it, is intended to include the first.[66] In the first, shorter version, after arriving at the gathering of Abu Bakr, the Emigrants and Helpers, Fatima begins her speech by praising God and remembering the abject state in which the Arabs lived before the coming of the Prophet.[67] She reminds her audience of how the Prophet defeated polytheism and the 'Arab wolves and the rebellious of the People of the Book'.[68] She exalts 'Ali as the defender of the faith and notes that after the Prophet's death, the Muslims have returned to their evil ways.[69] She criticises them for their usurping of the caliphate and of Fadak, and warns them that an evil day awaits them.[70] She concludes by mournfully addressing her father's tomb, an act provoking great weeping among those gathered.[71]

In the second version, Fatima likewise begins by praising God, elaborating at greater length upon His attributes.[72] God sent Muhammad, she says, 'as a fulfillment of His mandate, a means of implementing His decree'.[73] She informs the crowd that they are 'the servants of God, appointed to enforce His commands and prohibitions, the bearers of His religion and revelation, entrusted by God to keep yourselves virtuous, His messengers to the nations'.[74] She observes that following the Qur'an leads to salvation, for it contains God's 'brilliant proofs, His explicit commands, His warning prohibitions, His manifest signs, His sufficient statements, His recommended virtues, His granted dispensations, and His recorded laws'.[75] Fatima then presents the major edicts and principles of Islam and provides reasons for

---

[64] These include the *Sharh al-akhbar fi fada'il al-a'imma al-athar* of Abu Hanifa b. Muhammad al-Tamimi al-Qadi al-Nu'man (d. 974); *Al-Saqifa wa-Fadak* by Abu Bakr Ahmad b. 'Abd al-'Aziz al-Basri al-Jawhari (d. 935); and *Dala'il al-imama* by Muhammad b. Jarir b. Rustam al-Tabari al-Shi'i (d. eleventh century). See Soufi, 'Image of Fāṭima', 109 n. 130.

[65] Soufi, 'Image of Fāṭima', 106. See Appendix for a translation. For more on Ibn Abi Tahir Tayfur, see Toorawa, *Ibn Abi Tahir Tayfur and Arabic Writerly Culture*.

[66] Ibn Abi Tahir Tayfur, *Balaghat al-nisa'*, 34; see also Soufi, 'Image of Fāṭima', 107.

[67] Ibn Abi Tahir Tayfur, *Balaghat al-nisa'*, 30–31.

[68] Ibn Abi Tahir Tayfur, *Balaghat al-nisa'*, 31.

[69] Ibn Abi Tahir Tayfur, *Balaghat al-nisa'*, 31–32.

[70] Ibn Abi Tahir Tayfur, *Balaghat al-nisa'*, 32.

[71] Ibn Abi Tahir Tayfur, *Balaghat al-nisa'*, 32.

[72] Ibn Abi Tahir Tayfur, *Balaghat al-nisa'*, 33.

[73] Ibn Abi Tahir Tayfur, *Balaghat al-nisa'*, 33.

[74] Ibn Abi Tahir Tayfur, *Balaghat al-nisa'*, 33.

[75] Ibn Abi Tahir Tayfur, *Balaghat al-nisa'*, 33–34.

them, including fasting, prayer, and pilgrimage – a matter that will be discussed later in this study. Fatima then turns her attention to the injustice that has been perpetrated against her. She notes the Qur'anic verses that support leaving an inheritance to close relatives, including daughters, and points to others to dispute the idea that prophets do not leave inheritances.[76] For example, she invokes Qur'an 27:16, 'Solomon inherited David' and Qur'an 19:5–6, in which Zacharia calls upon God, saying, 'so give me from yourself an heir who will inherit me and inherit from the family of Jacob'.[77]

Fatima then declares:

> You claim that I have no right and no inheritance from my father, and that there is no blood relationship between us! . . . 'Then is it the judgment of the time of ignorance they desire? But who is better than God in judgment for a people who are certain [in faith]'? [Q 5:50]. Am I to be unjustly vanquished with regard to my inheritance?[78]

Fatima spends the remainder of the *khuṭba* directing severe criticism at the Emigrants and Ansar who had betrayed her and the Prophet. She concludes, ominously, 'God is a witness of what you do and "those who have wronged are going to know to what [kind of] return they will be returned" [Q 26:227]. I am the daughter of a warner, with news of a severe punishment. So, do as you will – and indeed, we will do as we will. Wait; indeed, we are waiting.'[79]

Although inheritance of property was the ostensible reason for the *khuṭba*, the speech served many different, interrelated functions. In claiming to inherit Fadak, Fatima also claimed her right to a less quantifiable substance from the Prophet: religious authority for herself and her family. The *khuṭba* both made this argument and, as will be seen, has been used by scholars to make it.

How the *Khuṭba* Appears in the Sources

How historically accurate are the classical accounts of Fatima's *khuṭba*? In her discussion of Fadak, Soufi sees no reason to doubt that a dispute over the property itself occurred, observing:

> It is probable, indeed natural, that Fāṭima asked for her inheritance from her father, as she was the Prophet's principal heir and stood to inherit at least one-half of his estate. If she had believed Fadak, the *ṣadaqa*, and Khaybar to be the Prophet's private property, she would have asked for them as part of her inheritance. That she and the Prophet's paternal uncle, 'Abbās, did so, is implied in the argument over possession of these properties

[76] Ibn Abi Tahir Tayfur, *Balaghat al-nisa'*, 34–35.
[77] Ibn Abi Tahir Tayfur, *Balaghat al-nisa'*, 34.
[78] Ibn Abi Tahir Tayfur, *Balaghat al-nisa'*, 34–35.
[79] Ibn Abi Tahir Tayfur, *Balaghat al-nisa'*, 36.

> that occurred between 'Ali and 'Abbās during 'Umar's reign. According to third/ninth-century Sunni sources, the two men were arguing over the Prophet's property which he obtained in accordance with Qur'an 59:6–7 (i.e., Fadak and the *ṣadaqa* . . .).[80]

Assuming that Fatima did lay claim to the property, did she deliver a *khuṭba* at her father's mosque, and, if so, how closely did it resemble the *khuṭba* we read today? After all, Ibn Abi Tahir Tayfur's *Balaghat al-nisa'* – although we lack an exact date for its composition – was most certainly written more than two centuries after the actual events were supposed to have occurred. Ibn Abi Tahir Tayfur himself acknowledged doubts surrounding its authenticity. He had mentioned to a contemporary 'Alid, Abu al-Husayn Zayd b. 'Ali b. al-Husayn b. 'Ali b. Abi Talib,[81] that certain people were claiming that Fatima's *khuṭba* was contrived by Abu al-'Ayna', the well-known Baghdadi litterateur Abu 'Abd Allah Muhammad b. al-Qasim b. Khallad al-Basri, who was a contemporary of Ibn Abi Tahir Tayfur and died in 896. Zayd naturally denied this and said that the *khuṭba* had been transmitted among the descendants of Abu Talib and among learned Shi'is before Abu al-'Ayna''s grandfather was born.[82]

Given the different versions that appear, the likelihood exists that scholars inaccurately transmitted at least some parts of Fatima's *khuṭba* or even fabricated some portions. For example, as will be seen, the part of the sermon cited by Ibn Babawayh (d. 991) differs in wording from that of Ibn Abi Tahir Tayfur. Versions cited by al-Jawhari (d. 935) and al-Tabari al-Shi'i (d. eleventh century) also differ slightly from each other and from that of Ibn Abi Tahir Tayfur, primarily in the responses given by Abu Bakr to the sermon.[83] The poem Fatima addresses to her father also varies in length and wording among different authors, as well as in attribution.[84] These differences, as well as the different *isnād*s cited by each author, produce the image of a text with a complex history – or, rather, of multiple texts with multiple antecedents. Yet the purport of the sermon remains the same in each. It is beyond the scope of this article to probe more deeply into the accuracy and origins of the *khuṭba*. What is of relevance to this study is the fact that medieval and contemporary scholars incorporated parts of the *khuṭba* into their legal treatises and discussions, thus placing Fatima on a level similar to, if

---

[80] Soufi, 'Image of Fāṭima', 93. See also Madelung, *Succession to Muhammad*, 62–64.

[81] The text implies that this is Zayd the son of Zayn al-'Abidin, the fourth Imam of the Twelver Shi'is, but this is a chronological impossibility, because Zayd died in 740, and the conversation must have taken place in the second half of the ninth century.

[82] See Soufi, 'Image of Fāṭima', 106–107. For more on Abu al-'Ayna', see Toorawa, *Ibn Abi Tahir Tayfur and Arabic Writerly Culture*, 112–117.

[83] See Soufi, 'Image of Fāṭima', 109–110.

[84] See, for example, al-Tabari al-Shi'i, *Dala'il al-imama*, 35; Ibn Abi Tahir Tayfur, *Balaghat al-nisa'*, 32; also, Soufi, 'Image of Fāṭima', 108, n. 128, for how the poem appears in other sources.

not exactly equal to, that of the Imams. The following paragraphs present three examples of the jurisprudential uses to which scholars put the *khuṭba.*

Ibn Babawayh (al-Shaykh al-Saduq)

An illustrative example of the legal treatment of Fatima's *khuṭba* is that of Ibn Babawayh, known in the Twelver Shi'i learned tradition as al-Shaykh al-Saduq (d. 991). Ibn Babawayh is, of course, one of the 'three Muhammads' who authored the monumental 'Four Books', the collections that form the Shi'i hadith canon.[85] Ibn Babawayh's contribution to these collections consisted of *Man la yahduruhu al-faqih*, or '[The Book for] The One Who Does Not Have a Jurist Present'. However, Ibn Babawayh also wrote many other works, among them *'Ilal al-shara'i'*, which, as its title indicates, provides justification or reasons for divine ordinances in the form of hadith. Like other Shi'i hadith collections, this text treats the Imams as a source of sunna in addition to the Prophet – and, it accords a similar status to Fatima. That is, it cites Fatima not merely as a transmitter of hadith about the Prophet, but as a model, herself, for behaviour.

The section citing Fatima falls in what is arguably the most important part of the book – a chapter called *'Ilal al-shara'i' wa-usul al-islam*, or 'The Causes of Laws and Ordinances, and the Fundamentals of Islam', which explains such acts of devotion as prayer, charity, and fasting during the month of Ramadan. (Other parts of the book address a dizzying array of subjects, including, to name but a few examples, 'Why One Person Will Remain in Heaven Forever, and Another Person in Hell'; 'Why the Hand of a Poor Man or Laborer is Not Cut Off If He Steals'; 'Why the Prophet Named 'Ali 'Abu Turab' [Father of Dust]'; and 'Why Winter and Summer Exist'.[86]) Section one of the chapter cites 'Ali. Sections two, three, and four cite Fatima's *khuṭba.*

In none of these sections does Ibn Babawayh appear to be referring to Ibn Abi Tahir Tayfur's version of the *khuṭba.* Section two, the longest, provides the following *isnād*: Zaynab bt. 'Ali → Ahmad b. Muhammad b. Jabir → Isma'il b. Mahran → Ahmad b. Abi 'Abd Allah al-Barqi → 'Ali b. al-Husayn al-Sa'd al-'Abdi → Muhammad b. Musa b. al-Mutawakkil, which differs significantly from that of Ibn Abi Tahir Tayfur's text, with the exception of Zaynab, the original transmitter.[87] Moreover, there are small but potentially significant differences in the text, which cites the portion of the *khuṭba* in which Fatima speaks of the benefits of following the Qur'an the manner in which it elucidates God's purpose, and specifies the meaning of God's

---

[85] For more on Ibn Babawayh, see Momen, *Introduction to Shi`i Islam*, 78.

[86] Abu Ja'far Muhammad b. 'Ali al-Saduq Ibn Babawayh, *'Ilal al-shara'i'* (Najaf: Al-Maṭba'a al-Ḥaydariyya, 1970), 523, 535, 155, 247.

[87] Ibn Babawayh, *'Ilal al-shara'i'*, 248.

edicts. For example, the order in which some of the phrases appear differs slightly. Moreover, Ibn Babawayh's version includes some topics that do not appear in Ibn Abi Tahir Tayfur's text, including jihad, avoiding the unjustified consumption of orphans' wealth, kindness to parents, maintaining relations with kin, and fair rulings, while omitting mention of the reason for the prohibition of alcohol. On the whole, however, the texts are similar enough to admit close kinship. The following is a translation of the parts explaining the meaning of God's edicts:

> God ordained faith as a purification for you from polytheism, prayer as an elevation from arrogance, alms as a source of prosperity, fasting as a confirmation of sincerity, pilgrimage as an establishment of religion, justice as a harmony of the hearts. Obeying us brings order to the nation and our leadership is a safeguard from disunity.
>
> Jihad brings honor to Islam, patience is the best means for obtaining rewards, enjoining good is for the welfare of the public, kindness to parents is a safeguard from God's wrath. Maintaining relations with kin increases your numbers, and the law of retribution reduces bloodshed. Fulfilling vows is a way toward forgiveness, fairness [in business dealings] with weights and measures eliminates injustice, avoiding slander is a barrier from damnation. Abandoning theft brings about integrity, banning the unjustified consumption of orphans' wealth is a protection from injustice, and fair rulings bring happiness to the community. God, the exalted, prohibited polytheism so that one can be devoted to Him only. 'So fear God as He should be feared' [Q 3:102] in that which He has commanded you to do and that which He has forbidden.[88]

As she does in the version of the *khuṭba* cited by Ibn Abi Tahir Tayfur, Fatima here confirms and explains the laws and principles of Islam – including prayer, charity, fasting, pilgrimage, fairness, fulfilment of vows, and avoiding theft and polytheism – and the reasons behind them. The *khuṭba* is, as Gorgi and Ebtekar note, 'more than a discourse in defense of her personal rights to inheritance. It provides a strong philosophical and logical background on the foundations of Islamic religion and thought.'[89] Ibn Babawayh's use of Fatima's *khuṭba* thus stands as an example of how a classical Shi'i hadith scholar depicted the daughter of the Prophet as a figure of temporal authority.

---

[88] Ibn Babawayh, *'Ilal al-shara'i'*, 248–249. With some modifications, I have mostly cited the translation of the *khuṭbah* by Monir Gorgi.

[89] Monir Gorgi and Massoumeh Ebtekar, 'The Life and Status of Fatima Zahra: A Woman's Image of Excellence', *Farzaneh Journal of Women's Studies and Research in Iran and Muslim Countries* (1997), 67. See also Karen Ruffle, 'May You Learn from Their Model: The Exemplary Father–Daughter Relationship of Muhammad and Fatima in South Asian Shi'ism', *The Journal of Persianate Studies* 4.1 (2011), 25–27; Osman, *Female Personalities*, 123.

Al-Majlisi

Several centuries later, in Safavid Iran, the eminent Shi'i scholar Muhammad Baqir al-Majlisi (d. 1699) – sometimes known as one of the three 'modern Muhammads'[90] – likewise cites Fatima's *khuṭba* in his 'monumental hadith encyclopedia *Bihar al-anwar* in which he rearranged the entire corpus of Twelver Shi'ite traditions'.[91] Like Ibn Babawayh, al-Majlisi draws on the text to elucidate the reasons for God's implementation of certain laws. Although he does not offer an *isnād*, it appears likely that he derived the text from Ibn Babawayh's *'Ilal al-shara'i'*, since the wording is nearly identical.[92]

For example, in a section on upholding the ties of kinship (*ṣilat al-raḥm*), he writes: 'Fatima (may the blessings of God be upon her) in her *khuṭba* said: God enjoined upholding the ties of kinship [as a means of increasing your numbers].'[93] In a chapter on slander and obscene language, he writes: 'Fatima (may the blessings of God be upon her) in her *khuṭba* said: God enjoined refraining from slander as a barrier from damnation.'[94] In a chapter on the benefits of prayer and the penalty of abandoning it, he writes: 'Fatima (may the blessings of God be upon her) in her *khuṭba* said, 'God enjoined prayer as a means of avoiding arrogance.'[95] Finally, in a section on the benefits of fasting during the month of Ramadan, al-Majlisi writes: 'Fatima (may the blessings of God be upon her) in her *khuṭba* about Fadak said, "God enjoined fasting as a means of confirming sincerity."'[96] Again, Fatima herself appears here as a model for behaviour. She is not merely transmitting hadith – she herself is a source of hadith. In this sense she occupies a status similar to that of the Imams: a temporal religious authority.

Inheritance

Finally, Fatima's *khuṭba* exhibits striking parallels with Shi'i laws of inheritance, and in some cases exerted an influence upon the shaping of those laws. A quick summary of how Sunni and Shi'i laws treat heirs – admittedly, one of the most complex subjects in Islamic law – will set the stage for this discussion. As many scholars have observed, what chiefly distinguishes Sunni laws of inheritance from Shi'i is the place of prominence given by the

---

[90] Momen, *An Introduction to Shi`i Islam,* 174.

[91] Rainer Brunner, 'Majlesi, Moḥammad-Bāqer', *Encyclopaedia Iranica* <http://www.iranicaonline.org/articles/majlesi-mohammad-baqer>, last accessed 6 May 2016. For more on al-Majlisi and the 'modern Muhammads', see Momen, *Introduction to Shi`i Islam,* 114–117, 174.

[92] In fact, the critical edition cites Ibn Babawayh. See, for example, Muhammad Baqir b. Muhammad Taqi Al-Majlisi, *Bihar al-anwar* (Tehran: Al-Maktaba al-Islāmiyya, 1956), 79:111 n. 5.

[93] Al-Majlisi, *Bihar al-anwar,* 74:94.

[94] Al-Majlisi, *Bihar al-anwar,* 79:111.

[95] Al-Majlisi, *Bihar al-anwar,* 82:209.

[96] Al-Majlisi, *Bihar al-anwar,* 96:368.

former to a category of heirs known as the *'aṣaba*, or male agnate relatives of the deceased, in addition to the heirs to whom the Qur'an allots set shares, the *ahl al-farā'iḍ*.[97] This distinction makes itself felt most severely in cases in which a man leaves only daughters and no sons.

To elaborate: in Sunni law, after all of the shares delegated by the Qur'an have been distributed, the remainder goes first to the *'aṣaba*, relatives of the male line. In Twelver Shi'i law, however, after the distribution of the property to the Qur'an heirs, both male and female relatives, from male and female lines, maintain the right to inherit.[98] Moreover, in Sunni law, 'collateral' male relatives – such as the grandfather of the deceased, or an even more distant male relative – may reduce a daughter's share in the inheritance. In Sunni law, if the deceased leaves only a daughter and no sons, for example, the daughter only receives a daughter's share, and the rest goes to agnates. In Shi'i law, the entire inheritance may be hers. As Takim writes, 'under Sunni law, a single surviving daughter was limited to a maximum of half of the inheritance no matter how distant the next eligible male-line relative was. By excluding the agnates, Shi'i law gave the same daughter the whole inheritance.'[99] Ja'far al-Sadiq, the sixth Shi'i Imam, voiced Shi'i defiance of the male agnate relatives in his reported remark, 'Dust in the jaws of the *'aṣaba*.'[100]

Some Shi'i scholars cite the case of Fatima and Fadak to justify gender-egalitarian statutes. In his discussion of inheritance laws, for example, the Isma'ili jurist al-Qadi al-Nu'man (d. 974) cited several Imams who stated that an only daughter should exclude any agnates from inheritance, writing, 'It is not as our opponents say to those who are in similar circumstances as Fatima . . . They wish to deny the right of Fatima in the inheritance of the Messenger of God.'[101] Indeed, in his interpretation of Fatima's *khuṭba*, al-Qadi al-Nu'man 'linked the inheritance issue to that of the succession of the Imamate and concluded that Fatima had acted as a witness (*ḥujja*, lit. "proof") to her contemporaries'.[102] The term *ḥujja*, 'proof', is especially suggestive of religious authority because it is applied frequently to the Imams,

---

[97] See *Encyclopedia of Women and Islamic Cultures*, 'Law: The Four Sunnī Schools of Family Law', 444–445; and 'Law: Other Schools of Family Law', 2:448–449. (Henceforth abbreviated as *EWIC*.)

[98] Adele Ferdows, 'The Status and Rights of Women in Ithna 'Ashari Shi'i Islam', in *Women and the Family in Iran*, ed. Asghar Fathi (Leiden: Brill, 1985), 25; also see Wilferd Madelung, 'Shi'i Attitudes toward Women as Reflected in Fiqh', in *Society and the Sexes in Medieval Islam*, ed. Afaf L. Marso (Maibu: Undena, 1979), 74.

[99] See *EWIC*, 'Law: Other Schools of Family Law', 2:448. See also Keddie, who writes, 'In Shi'i law daughters without brothers inherited everything, whereas in Sunni law they generally got no more than half.' Nikki R. Keddie, *Women in the Middle East: Past and Present* (Princeton: Princeton University Press, 2007), 210.

[100] Cited in Noel J. Coulson, *A History of Islamic Law* (Edinburgh: Edinburgh University Press, 1964), 113.

[101] Al-Qadi al-Nu'man, *Da'a'im al-Islam*, 2:361.

[102] Cortese and Calderini, *Women and the Fatimids*, 10.

who are considered God's 'proofs' to humankind.[103] Thus, even in a medieval setting, Fatima's words were seen as authoritative in a legal sense and contributed to better inheritance conditions for women.

Today, of course, when gender egalitarianism is a more prominent and popular issue, the feminist implications of Fatima's hagiography and the Shi'i inheritance scheme occupy the foreground of debates over succession to a much greater extent than previously. Shi'i polemicists who vigorously defend Fatima's claim to Fadak often structure their arguments around female inheritance, or at least prominently highlight that issue. In a tract on Fadak, for example, the author of the blog 'Shi'a Pen', Sayed Hassan Bukhari, writes that according to the laws of the Qur'an a daughter inherits from her father, and that denying her this right is a violation of the Qur'an.[104] The author also invokes the pre-Islamic era, in which females did not inherit but rather were seen as 'chattel'. Islam, Bukhari writes, 'put an end to this discriminatory practice, and Abu Bakr resurrected it by denying Sayyida Fatima (as) her inheritance rights'.[105] Bukhari openly portrays Fatima as a religious authority in this matter, writing:

> May the Peace and Blessings be upon Muhammad and Al-e Muhammad. We thank Hadhrat Fatima Al- Zahra (as) for removing the layers of darkness from our eyes and the obstacles from our path and for spreading the light for us in darkness, by going and speaking against such actions which were contradictory to the Holy Qur'an and Sunnah.[106]

Once more, here in a contemporary setting, we see the deliberate means by which Shi'i commentators incorporate a woman into their configurations of authority.

The Question of Descent from Daughters

As suggested in the previous section, bilateral descent, or descent from both male and female lines, underlies how scholars have cited and deployed the *khuṭba*. Bilateral descent implies that a daughter as well as a son can inherit a father's characteristics as well as his property. She can also perpetuate his bloodline and act as his successor. Such a concept was by no means unanimously accepted in medieval Islamic societies, where patrilineal tendencies continued to hold sway (as they did and do in most societies). Even if some classical jurists asserted that both men and women contributed equally to conception, more popularly people regarded women as 'incubators', or as

---

[103] See Mohammad-Ali Amir-Moezzi, *Le Preuve de Dieu: La mystique shi'ites à travers l'oeuvre de Kulaynî IXe-Xe siècle* (Paris: Les Éditions du Cerf, 2018).

[104] <http://www.shiapen.com/comprehensive/fadak/inheritance-rules-in-quran.html>; also, Sayed 'Ali Imam, telephone conversation with author, 25 February 2016.

[105] See <http://www.shiapen.com/comprehensive/fadak/inheritance-rules-in-quran.html>.

[106] See <http://www.shiapen.com/comprehensive/fadak/conclusion.html>.

supplying the 'material substance for the child' while the men supply the seed containing the child's essence.[107] Thus, the Persian historian Rashid al-Din (d. 1318), in denying that Hasan and Husayn are the prophet's descendants, cited an Arab poet: 'Our sons are the sons of our sons, [but] the sons of our daughters are the sons of distant men' (or 'strangers unrelated').[108]

Accompanying this notion is another one common to patrilineal societies, which holds that a daughter cannot really show forth her father's qualities. Nor can she inherit, for any property or money bequeathed to her would slip from the hands of the birth family. Rather, she herself is property that can be handed on to another. As Simone de Beauvoir writes of patriarchal regimes in general,

> If she were an inheritor, she would to an excessive degree transmit the wealth of her family to that of her husband; so she is carefully excluded from the succession. But inversely, because she owns nothing, woman does not enjoy the dignity of being a person; she herself forms part of the patrimony of a man: first of her father, then of her husband.[109]

Of course, even if they manifested some aspects of them, few Sunni societies adhered fully to this stark patrilineal model. Daughters could and did inherit, after all, and sometimes they succeeded their fathers to positions of power.[110] But patrilineal schemes often figured (and continue to figure) prominently in laws and customs involving inheritance and nationality.[111]

On a theoretical basis at least, Shi'ism, with Fatima as a model, gives greater credence to the notion that a daughter can carry on her father's bloodline, show forth his attributes, and inherit his property. Largely on account of Fatima's status as mother of Hasan and Husayn, theoretical Shi'ism embraces and promotes the concept of bilateral descent, with all of its implications for inheritance and successorship. Sayyidship, for example, can be passed down by an only daughter. In the *khuṭba*, as has been seen, Fatima implicitly puts herself on the same level as a son with regard to inheritance, and points to the Qur'an for support, saying, 'Is it in the Book that you should inherit from your fathers, but I should not inherit from my father? You have certainly done a thing unprecedented.' Likewise, she cites the Prophet saying, 'Man is

---

[107] See Carol Delaney, 'The Meaning of Paternity and the Virgin Birth Debate', *Man* 21.3 (1986), 495, in which she examines ideas about procreation among Muslims villagers in Turkey.

[108] Hamed Fayazi, 'Rashid al-Din's Interpretation of Surat al-Kawthar', *The Muslim World* 102 (April 2012), 286. See also p. 293 for the poem in Arabic.

[109] Simone de Beauvoir, *The Second Sex*, trans. H. M. Parshley (New York: Knopf, 1952), 93.

[110] Among the many examples available, see special issue of *The Journal of Persianate Studies* 4.1 (2011), eds Gabbay and Clancy-Smith; and Maya Shatzmiller, *Her Day in Court: Women's Property Rights in Fifteenth-Century Granada* (Cambridge, MA: Harvard University Press, 2007).

[111] See, for example, *EWIC*, 'Inheritance: Contemporary Practices', 2:300; and 'Kinship, Descent Systems', 2:330–334; and 'Kinship, Descent Systems and State', 2:335–343; and 'Kinship and State', 2:347–357.

preserved through his children' – a clear indication that she perpetuates his lineage.[112] Repeatedly emphasising that she is the daughter of the Prophet, Fatima implies that this kinship tie cloaks her with prophet-like authority – 'I am the daughter of a warner, with news of a severe punishment' – and, indeed, that she functions as his heir both in terms of inheritance and succession.[113] By citing Qur'an 27:16, for example, 'Solomon inherited [or succeeded] David', Fatima may be suggesting that she 'succeeds' the Prophet by inheriting some of his spiritual insight and authority.[114] Shi'i thought, in alignment with these statements, presents a more egalitarian vision of women's status in society, indicating that women can carry on their father's lineage and inherit both his property and authority.

I would like to qualify any possible rosiness of the portrait I have painted here of women's status in Shi'i societies by injecting a few notes of cynicism or realism. First, it would be inaccurate, I think, to suggest that Shi'i societies, on the grounds of recognition of bilateral descent, have afforded women far more opportunities for equality than Sunni ones. As scholar of Shi'ism Moojan Momen observes, 'In theory, Shi'ism has a more favorable attitude towards women than Sunni Islam. These favorable differences are largely annulled, however, by some specific Shi'ite practices as well as the social realities of women's lives in Shi'ite communities.'[115] To give but a few examples, even though the law may be on their side, Shi'i women are often deprived of their inheritances or pressured into renouncing them, just as Sunni women are.[116] Shi'i jurists generally forbade women from becoming judges, basing their arguments on reports in the canonical hadith collections by scholars such as Ibn Babawayh.[117] Despite his evident admiration for Fatima, al-Majlisi, along with other Safavid 'ulama', envisioned restricted roles for women: he proposed that women belonged in the privacy of the *andarūn* ('harem') and that the best wife was 'one who bore many children, was chaste, dear to her relatives, humble in front of her husband, made herself up only for him, and obeyed only him'.[118] Moreover, many contemporary scholars have pointed out that an idealisation of Fatima can actually

[112] Ibn Abi Tahir Tayfur, *Balāghāt al-nisā'*, 36.
[113] Ibn Abi Tahir Tayfur, *Balāghāt al-nisā'*, 36.
[114] In one commentary on the Qur'an, the translator and editor glosses 27:16 thus: 'The point is that Solomon not only inherited his father's kingdom but his spiritual insight and the prophetic office.' See Abdullah Yusuf Ali (trans.), *The Holy Qur'an* (Brentwood: Amana, 1983), 981 n. 3,254.
[115] Moojan Momen, 'Women in Shi'ism', *Encyclopaedia Iranica* <http://www.iranicaonline.org/articles/women-shiism>, last accessed 6 May 2016.
[116] See *EWIC*, 'Inheritance: Contemporary Practice', 2:302–303.
[117] Robert Gleave, '"She Should Not Raise Her Voice When Amongst Men": Imāmī Arguments Against (and for) Women Judges' (paper presented at 'Of *'Alimahs, Muhaddithahs*, and *Mujtahidas*: The Past and Present of Female Religious Authority in Shi'i Islam', Princeton University, 6–8 March 2014).
[118] Kathryn Babayan, 'The "Aqa'id al-Nisa'": A Glimpse at Safavid Women inn ocal Isfahani Culture', in *Women in the Medieval Islamic World: Power, Patronage and* Piet, ed. Gavin Hambly (New York: St Martin's Press, 1998), 369–370.

lead to greater oppression for women, who are doomed to labour under the image of a perfect woman whose standards they can never meet.[119] Clearly, recognising a high status for Fatima does not automatically translate into better legal rights for women.[120]

Second, as implied earlier, political reasons likely played a large role in the construction of Fatima and in the development of more favourable laws for women in Shi'ism, rather than any intrinsic Shi'i acknowledgement of female merit. Shi'is, convinced that Hasan, Husayn, and their descendants were the rightful successors to the Prophet, needed to acknowledge that Fatima occupied an exalted position, and thus perforce needed to incorporate 'the feminine' - particularly, daughters and mothers - into their ideas of lineage and of religious hierarchy. Naturally, they needed to recognise bilateral descent.[121] Even the emphasis placed on Fatima's right to Fadak derives - as many scholars have observed - from the larger matter it symbolises: the caliphate.[122] Granting Fadak to Fatima would likely have proven the thin edge of the wedge that served to compel the claim of political succession based on family ties.[123] The rights of daughters to inherit only later came to play a large part in the Fadak debate and in Shi'i criticisms of Sunni practices. Indeed, although historians normally (and justifiably) try to avoid speculation, it is interesting to ponder whether Shi'i scholars and polemicists would have fought so vigorously for female inheritance rights had the Prophet's offspring born the name 'Fadl' rather than 'Fatima'.

---

119 See, for example, Soufi, 'Image of Fāṭima', 204.

120 Although Fatima was not, naturally, regarded as a goddess in Shi'i societies (despite Henri Corbin's tendency to associate her with pre-Islamic female deities), one can still see an echo of Eller's argument here that goddesses 'may be strongly, if ambivalently, distinguished from human women, and the differences between the two repeatedly emphasized: that is, goddesses "accentuate what womanhood is *not*"' as often as they reflect a culture's notion of what women are . . . There is simply no one-to-one relationship between goddess worship and high status for women', Cynthia Eller, *The Myth of Matriarchal Prehistory: Why an Invented Past Won't Give Women a Future* (Boston: Beacon Press, 2000), 104.

121 Soufi, 'Image of Fāṭima', 152. It is interesting to note that a similar acknowledgement and idealisation of women necessarily became part of the Sunni political picture. Abu Bakr gained prestige and legitimacy through his daughter's marriage to the Prophet; thus, just as Shi'is affirm that the Prophet most loved Fatima and 'Ali, Sunnis say that Abu Bakr and 'A'isha were his best beloved. As Spellberg notes, 'while political power was determined by primarily patrilineal demonstrations, the connective foundations of Islamic political structure were enhanced by distinctly feminine familial bonds'. See Denise A. Spellberg, *Politics, Gender and the Islamic Past: The Legacy of Aisha Bint Abi Bakr* (New York: Columbia University Press, 1996), 28, 33, 34, 103.

122 Sadr writes, 'Fadak was a symbolic meaning, representing a great notion and not that seized piece of land in the Hijaz'; the drive to recover it represented the quest 'to regain a stolen throne, a lost crown and a great glory and to revive the inverted umma'. See Sadr, *Fadak fi al-tarikh*, 58.

123 As Poonawala notes the 'claim of inheritance based on family ties would have opened the door widely to [their] right to the succession'. See Tabari, *History*, 9:196 n. 1,356. See also Soufi, 'Image of Fāṭima', 104–105.

Nevertheless, one is struck by the stature the sources accord to Fatima. Ibn Babawayh and al-Majlisi cite Fatima's words on legal matters with the respect bestowed upon one who is the direct offspring of the Prophet and a religious authority in her own right. As mentioned earlier, this trend has gained momentum in the post-modern era. Muhammad Baqir al-Sadr, the prominent Iraqi Shi'i ayatollah mentioned earlier, adduced Fatima's *khuṭba* to support his argument about the proper succession to Muhammad. Al-Sadr attributed to Fatima a clearer understanding of the attempt among interlopers to seize the caliphate than that of 'Ali himself, writing,

> [W]e have to note that Fatima (s) was the first – if her husband was not the first – to declare the partisan nature of the ruling party. She accused them of political plotting, then she was followed, in this thought, by some of her contemporaries like Imam 'Ali (s) and Mu'awiya b. Abi Sufyan.[124]

He likewise wrote,

> How wonderful you were, O daughter of the Prophet, when you took the mask off the bitter truth and predicted for your father's *umma* a terrible future, in whose skies red clouds would glimmer – How shall I put it? [Rather], rivers would overflow with blood and be filled with skulls! You reproached the 'good' ancestors for their deeds by saying, 'Unquestionably into sedition they have fallen, and indeed, Hell will encompass the disbelievers' [Q 9:49].[125]

To Fatima, then, is attributed the divine foreknowledge of the fate of the ummah and an infallible sense of how the caliphate should be structured.

Shi'i researcher and blog author Sayed Hassan Bukhari even extrapolates Fatima's words about Fadak to create an analogy between her deprivation of that property and 'Ali's deprivation of the caliphate, noting:

> And through her actions it became clearer to us that, if the property of the Holy Prophet (s) could be confiscated, if the most beloved to the Holy Prophet, Hadhrat Fatima al-Zahra (as), could be deprived of her rights, by the Companions of the Holy Prophet (saww) then surely it is reasonable to accept that Imam Ali (as) too was deprived of his Leadership in Islam.[126]

Fatima's words thus form the basis for 'Ali's claim to the caliphate. 'Ali's quest finds validation in his wife's statements – an unusual case indeed, in which a female's words appear to weigh more than a male's.

---

[124] Sadr, *Fadak fi al-tarikh*, 124–125. I have made some changes to the translation for the sake of clarity.

[125] Sadr, *Fadak fi al-tarikh*, 126.

[126] See <http://www.shiapen.com/comprehensive/fadak/conclusion.html>.

Conclusion

It is upon these foundations that contemporary scholars in Iran, Iraq, and elsewhere are building the case to see Fatima as a religious authority – and to invest other women with authority as well. Mehdi Mehrizi, a prominent Shi'i cleric in Qom, cited Fatima's arguments about Fadak as described in *Kitāb al-Kāfi* by al-Kulayni (d. 941), another of the major canonical collections of Shi'i hadith, to support the idea that a woman's testimony is equal to that of a man. (Often, jurists have cited Qur'an verses such as 2:282 to say that a woman's testimony is worth half that of a man's.) As he noted, Fatima 'went to Abu Bakr and said that Fadak is ours. She went, not 'Ali, and said that Fadak is ours, and Abu Bakr judged in favor of Fatima [according to this version of the event].' He concluded, 'If Fatima did not believe, and Abu Bakr did not believe, that the testimony of women was worth that of half of a man' – why should people today accept that precept?[127]

Alongside these depictions, it is interesting to note that, as Künkler and Fazaeli have observed, 'Iran exhibits a strong tradition of female religious authority in the Middle East.'[128] Did Fatima provide a precedent for this phenomenon in Iran, where these voices seem to be especially strong? Or did pre-existing inclinations to see women as religious and temporal authorities help shape depictions of Fatima? Given that female rulership was not unknown during pre-Islamic times, the latter may be possible.[129] In any event, it is fascinating to watch the Fatima of the *khuṭba* take her place beside the Fatima of the home.

---

[127] Mehdi Mehrizi, Ḥujjat al-Islam wa al-Muslimīn, Personal interview by Karen Bauer, Qom, Iran, 9 June 2011.

[128] Mirjam Künkler and Roja Fazaeli, 'The Life of Two *Mujtahidahs*: Female Religious Authority in 20th Century Iran', in *Women, Leadership, and Mosques: Changes in Contemporary Islamic Authority*, eds Masooda Bano and Hilary Kalmbach (Leiden: Brill, 2012), 154.

[129] See, for example, Alyssa Gabbay, '"In Reality a Man": Sultan Iltutmish, His Daughter, Raziya, and Gender Ambiguity in Thirteenth Century Northern India', *The Journal of Persianate Studies* 4.1 (2011), 50–51.

APPENDIX

THE SPEECH OF FATIMA THE DAUGHTER OF THE MESSENGER OF GOD (PEACE BE UPON HIM) WHEN ABU BAKR DENIED HER FADAK[1]

Abu al-Fadl said, 'I mentioned to Abu al-Husayn Zayd b. 'Ali b. al-Husayn b. 'Ali b. Abi Talib (God's blessings be upon them) the speech of Fatima (peace be upon her) when Abu Bakr denied her Fadak. I said to him, "Certain people claim that it was contrived and that it is actually the composition of Abu al-'Ayna'." He responded, "I have seen the learned descendants of Abu Talib reporting it from their fathers and teaching it to their sons, and certainly my father passed this same text to me from my grandfather with an *isnād* to Fatima – peace be upon her. Shi'i scholars also transmitted it and studied it before Abu al-'Ayna''s *grandfather* was born! Al-Hasan b. 'Alwan reported it from 'Atiyya al-'Awfi, who heard 'Abd Allah b. al-Hasan citing it from his father." Then Abu al-Husayn asked, "Why do they deny Fatima's speech, while they report a much stranger speech of 'A'isha upon the occasion of her father's [that is, Abu Bakr's] death? If it were not for their hatred of us, the *Ahl al-Bayt*, they would recognise its truth." Then he mentioned the incident when Abu Bakr – may God's blessing be upon him – determined to deny the inheritance of Fadak to Fatima, daughter of the Prophet – peace be upon him. When Fatima was informed of that denial, she wrapped her veil around her head and came, with a group of friends and family members stepping on the tails of her dress, walking exactly in the manner of the Messenger of God – peace be upon him – until she reached Abu Bakr sitting among a crowd of the Emigrants and the Helpers. A cloth partition was then hung up between them. She moaned in such a manner that it caused the public to burst into tears and the assembly to break into

[1] From Ibn Abi Tahir Tayfur's *Balaghat al-Nisa'*, trans. Hussien Algudaihi and Alyssa Gabbay; adapted partly from 'The Sermon of Fatima Zahra (AS)', by Monir Gorgi.

disorder. She waited until their cries quieted and their agitation had calmed, and then she began her speech, praising God and asking for blessings upon the messenger of God, whereupon the people again began weeping. She waited until they had stopped, then resumed her speech,

> **There has certainly come to you a Messenger from among yourselves. Grievous to him is what you suffer; he is concerned for you and is kind and merciful to the believers** (Q 9:128). If you know who I am talking about, then you will find him to be my father and not your fathers, who made a pact of brotherhood with my cousin and not with any of your men. He announced warnings and openly conveyed the message. He was firm in dealing with the polytheists, striking and silencing them. He destroyed the idols and defeated their heroes until they were crushed and fled, so that darkness turned into light and the plain truth was proclaimed. The leader of faith spoke out, and the whining of the devils was silenced. You were teetering on the brink of a pit of fire, the way a drop of water teeters on the lips, like prey for the greedy, like a hot ember in the hands of one in haste, like the ground waiting for people to tread on it. You used to drink from stagnant, brackish pools and eat leaves, powerless and always in fear that those around you would abduct you. But God then rescued you through His Messenger – peace be upon him – after a long struggle, after being surrounded by beasts of men, Arab wolves, and the rebellious ones among the People of the Book. Whenever they stoked the fires of war, he extinguished them. Whenever the horns of misguidance sprouted forth or a gap opened up for the polytheists' disobedience, he would unleash upon them his brother ['Ali], who would not return until he had trampled their heads with the soles of his feet and extinguished their flames with his sword. 'Ali exhausted himself and strove purely for God's satisfaction, was close to the Messenger of God, and a master among God's devoted ones, while you were living in comfort and luxury, safe and secure. When God chose for His prophet the abode of His prophets [that is, death], your attributes of hypocrisy became apparent, and the covering garment of the religion was abandoned. The silent one from among the misguided spoke out; the dormant one came to the forefront; the stallion camel of the wrongdoers brayed and strode into your courtyards. The Devil thrust his head out from his place of hiding and called out to you. He found you responsive to his call and ready to fall for his deceptions. He provoked you and found you easily swayed; he incited you and found you quick to anger. You branded camels that were not your own, and you approached watering places that did not belong to you. You did all this while the era of the Prophet was still near, grief for his loss was immense, and the wound had not yet healed. You did this only[2] because you claimed that you wanted to avoid sedition. **Unquestionably, they have fallen into sedition, and indeed, Hell will encompass the disbelievers** (Q 9:49). How dare you? **So how are you deluded?** (Q 6:95). For God's book is still with you, its warnings are clear, and its commands obvious. Are you willing to turn your back on it? Or do you wish to rule according to something else? What an evil exchange this would be for wrongdoers! **Whoever desires other than**

---

[2] Reading *innamā*; the text reports that another copy has *badāri* in place of *innamā*.

> **Islam as religion – never will it be accepted from him, and he, in the Hereafter, will be among the losers** (Q 3:85). You would not have accomplished this [taking Fadak] without previously taking over the succession. So, you are sipping the foam and secretly conspiring. Yet we tolerate what you have done, which is like being stabbed with sharp daggers. Moreover, now you claim that there is no inheritance for us. Is it the laws of the time of ignorance that you desire? **But who is better than God in judgment for a people who are certain [in faith]?** (Q 5:50). O Emigrants, should I be deprived of my inheritance? Is it in the Book that you should inherit from your fathers, but I should not inherit from my father? You have certainly done a thing unprecedented. So, go ahead and take it, like a bridled and saddled camel that will meet you on the Day of Gathering. Certainly, God is the best judge, Muhammad is the claimant, and the appointed date is the Day of Resurrection. At that time the wrongdoers will lose, and **For every happening is a finality; and you are going to know** (Q 6:67).

Then she turned to the Prophet's tomb and said:

> After your death, tragic incidents have occurred
> If you were here, there would be no need for speeches
> When we lost you, it was as though the earth had lost its rain
> Your people have failed; witness them and do not be absent.

He said: "We have never ever seen a greater number of people weeping."'

[Second version]

[Abu al-Fadl continued], 'An Egyptian named Ja'far b. Muhammad whom I met in al-Rafiqa reported to me that his father had said, "Musa b. 'Isa told us that 'Abd Allah b. Yunus said that Ja'far al-Ahmar reported that Zayd b. 'Ali – may God have mercy upon him – reported from his aunt Zaynab – may God be pleased with her – that she said [that when] Fatima – may God pleased with her – learned that Abu Bakr had decided to take Fadak from her, she donned her veil and went out with a group of her women friends and family members, the hem of her dress trailing behind her, walking exactly in the manner of the Messenger of God – peace be upon him – until she reached Abu Bakr sitting among a crowd of the Emigrants and the Helpers. She moaned once, causing the public to burst into tears. When their agitation had quieted, she [began by praising God]. Then they installed a curtain as a partition. Then she said,

> Praise be to God for His blessings. Thanks be to Him for all that He has revealed and all that He has provided from His bounty. Thanks be to Him for His plentiful blessings and the perfect gifts He has continuously provided. Their number is too large to count, too vast to measure, and beyond comprehension. God is worthy of praise for His blessings, and He will double our rewards if we ask for them. I bear witness that there is no god but God – a creed the meaning of He has rendered sincere devotion; the attainment of which He has instilled in mankind's hearts; and with the comprehension of

which He has illuminated the minds of mankind. He cannot be perceived with eyes, and He is beyond imagination. He created things *ex nihilo*, without following a previous model. He did not create them out of need, nor did He shape them for any benefit save to establish His power, to lead His creatures to worship Him, and to reinforce His call. Then He created reward for obedience to Him and punishment for disobedience to Him in order to deter His creatures from His wrath and to urge them to His paradise.

I bear witness that my father, Muhammad, is His servant and messenger. God selected him as a prophet before creating him, chose him before appointing him, and named him before sending him, at a time when creatures were concealed in the unseen, submerged in horrible fear, and bound to nothingness. God, the exalted, has knowledge of future incidents and their results. God, the exalted, sent him as a fulfilment of His mandate, a means of implementing His decree. The Prophet found the nations divided in their faiths, devoted to their fires, worshipping their idols, denying God despite knowing Him. Thus, God, the exalted, illuminated their darkness with Muhammad – peace be upon him – removed the mysteries from their hearts, and cleared the gloom from their vision. Then God, in His mercy, took the Prophet, fully willing, from the burden of this world. He is now in comfort, surrounded by the righteous angels, celebrating with the powerful King, in the satisfaction of the merciful Lord. The blessings of God be upon Muhammad, the Prophet of mercy, the one entrusted with the revelation, the chosen one, the best from among His creatures, and the one who pleases Him. May the peace and blessings of God be upon him."

"Speaking to the crowd, she continued,

Now then, you are the servants of God, appointed to enforce His commands and prohibitions, the bearers of His religion and revelation, entrusted by God to keep yourselves virtuous, His messengers to the nations. You have alleged that you have a share [in my inheritance]. Did God grant you a special covenant in your favor, leaving us as a remnant and making us successors to you? We have God's Book, the evidence of which is clear, the verses of which reveal our rights, and the proofs of which are manifest. Hearing its words leads to eternal life, following it leads to God's satisfaction, and heeding it grants salvation. It contains God's brilliant proofs, His explicit commands, His warning prohibitions, His manifest signs, His sufficient statements, His recommended virtues, His granted dispensations, and His recorded laws. God ordained faith as a purification for you from polytheism, prayer as an elevation from arrogance, fasting as a confirmation of sincerity, alms as a source of prosperity, pilgrimage as an establishment of religion, justice as a harmony of the hearts. Obedience to us brings order to the nation, and our leadership safeguards it from disunity. Loving us empowers Islam, and patience is the best means for earning reward. The law of retribution reduces bloodshed. The fulfilment of vows is a way toward forgiveness, fairness with weights and measures eliminates injustice, the prohibition of alcohol prevents you from committing sins, the avoidance of slander is a barrier from damnation, and the abandonment of theft brings about integrity. God, the exalted, prohibited polytheism so that one can be devoted to Him only. So **fear God as He should be feared and die**

> **not, except in submission to Him** (Q 3:102). Obey God in that which He has commanded you to do and that which He has forbidden, for **only those fear God, from among His servants, who have knowledge** (Q 35:28)."

"Then she said: ""O people, I am Fatima, and my father is Muhammad – peace be upon him. I repeat what I said at the beginning: **There has certainly come to you a Messenger from among yourselves** (Q 9:128)."" Then he recited the speech in a form similar to what Zayd b. ʻAli – peace be upon him – reported from his father. Then she said in continuation of her speech,

> Is it for the belongings of Mohammad that you have abandoned the book of God? God, the exalted, stated, **Solomon inherited David** (Q 27:16), and God, the exalted, stated in the story of John, the son of Zachariah, **So give me from yourself an heir who will inherit me and inherit from the family of Jacob. And make him, my Lord, pleasing to You** (Q 19:5–16). God also said, **And those of [blood] relationship are more entitled [to inheritance] in the decree of God than the [other] believers** (Q 33:6); He said, **God instructs you concerning your children: for the male, what is equal to the share of two females** (Q 4:11); and He said, **One of you if he leaves wealth [is that he should make] a bequest for the parents and near relatives according to what is acceptable – a duty upon the righteous** (Q 2:180). And you claim I have no right and no inheritance from my father, and that there is no blood relationship between us! Are you so special that God specified a verse for you from which he excluded my father – peace be upon him? Or are you saying that my father and I are of two distinct faiths, so we do not inherit from each other? Are not my father and I of one faith? Or perhaps you think you are more knowledgeable of the specifics and generalities of the Quran than the Prophet – peace be upon him? **Then is it the judgment of the time of ignorance they desire? But who is better than God in judgment for a people who are certain** (Q 5:50). Am I to be unjustly vanquished with regard to my inheritance? **And those who have wronged are going to know to what kind of return they will be returned** (Q 26:227).

"He mentioned that after she had finished addressing Abu Bakr and the Emigrants she turned to the gathering of the Helpers and said,

> You are the remaining supporters of the faith, and you are the fortresses that embraced Islam. What is this weakness in defending my right? Has not the messenger of God – peace be upon him – said [that] man is preserved through his children? How quickly have you acted against him, and how soon have you plotted against us! Do you say that Muhammad – peace be upon him – has died? Surely this is a great misfortune; its anguish is endless; it is a wide and gaping wound that cannot be healed. The earth has become dark in his absence, and the most favoured of God have become depressed by this disaster. Mountains succumbed, hopes were extinguished, and sanctity was dishonoured at the time of his death – peace be upon him. The Book of God which was revealed in your courtyards in your evenings and your mornings declared this to us. It was called and recited into your ears. Yet before this, the same thing befell previous prophets and messengers of God: **Muhammad is nought but a messenger, before whom other messengers have passed away.**

> **So if he was to die or be killed, would you turn back on your heels to unbelief? And he who turns back on his heels will never harm God at all; but God will reward the grateful** (Q 3:144).
>
> O sons of Qayla![3] Will my inheritance from my father be denied while you look on? You are implicated in this affair! You are hesitant to support me although you are numerous and possess weapons and power and property. And this while you are brave and were chosen by God to protect His religion, the supporters of His messenger and the people of Islam, the cream of the crop that God selected to defend the people of the prophet's household. You fought the Arabs, challenged the nations, and confronted the ignorant. You were obedient to us until the powerful wheel of Islam defeated its opponents, the results of our struggle were realized, the arrogance of polytheism was brought to its knees, the flames of war were extinguished, the turbulence of chaos quieted, and the order of faith was established. So why, after enlightenment, have you become confused? Why, after being so brave, have you turned away? And why, after working openly, have you concealed yourselves for a group that has regressed? Do you fear them? **But God has a greater right that you should fear Him, if you are truly believers** (Q 9:13). I think you have favoured the comfortable life and chosen luxury, so you drifted from the religion. You rejected that which you have understood and spit out that which you have ingested. **If you should disbelieve, you and whoever is on the earth entirely – indeed, God is free of need and praiseworthy** (Q 14:8). Surely, I have said all I have said fully aware that you intend to forsake me and knowing the betrayal you harbour in your hearts. It is but an overflowing of the soul, the venting of fury, an unburdening of the chest, and a presentation of proof. So keep [the caliphate] with a rejection of Islam, lacking legitimacy, with everlasting shame, marked with the wrath of God and forever disgraced. It is chained to the **fire of God, [eternally] fueled, which mounts directed at the hearts** (Q 104:6–7). God is a witness of what you do, and **[t]hose who have wronged are going to know to what [kind of] return they will be returned** (Q 26:227). I am the daughter of a warner with news of a severe punishment. So, do as you will – and indeed, we will do as we will. Wait; indeed, we are waiting."

Abu al-Fadl said: 'A group of people mentioned that Abu al-'Ayna' claimed he had composed this speech. However, some people transmitted it and believed that it was Fatima's speech; and we recorded it despite what it contains [that is, statements critical of the Companions].'

[3] The ancestor of the Aws and Khazraj tribes.

CHAPTER

5

FEMALE AUTHORITY IN THE TIMES OF THE SHI'I IMAMS

Liyakat Takim

Shi'i discourse on women has focused on prominent figures like Fatima, the daughter of the Prophet, and Zaynab bt. 'Ali, his granddaughter. Because of their spirituality and piety, they are highly revered in Shi'i circles.[1] Rather than elaborating on the traditions that they narrate, Shi'i profiles of Fatima and Zaynab are limited to comments on their opposition to oppression and defiance of the Umayyad caliphate. Scholars such as Abdulaziz Sachedina, Hossein Modarressi, and Liyakat Takim have studied the male companions of the Imams and the authority that they wielded.[2] Apart from Asma Sayeed's and Devin Stewart's recent articles, there has been little academic discussion of women in Shi'i biographical literature.[3] This chapter will examine the contributions of pre-occultation Shi'i women who appear in medieval Shi'i biographical texts. It will also discuss modern accounts of these female figures and their contributions as elaborated in Nahleh Naeeni's recent work *Shi'ah Women Transmitters of Hadith*, which, although it contains a wealth of information, provides distinctly hagiographical accounts of the women it

---

[1] See Christopher Paul Clohessy, *Fatima: Daughter of Muhammad* (Piscataway: Gorgias Press, 2013); Zahra (1997).

[2] Abdulaziz Sachedina, *The Prolegomena to the Qur'an* (Oxford: Oxford University Press, 1988); Hossein Modarressi, *Tradition and Survival: A Bibliographical Survey of Early Shi'ite Literature* (Oxford: Oneworld, 2003); Liyakat Takim, *The Heirs of the Prophet: Charisma and Religious Authority in Shi'ite Islam* (Albany: State University of New York Press, 2006).

[3] Devin J. Stewart, 'Women's Biographies in Islamic Societies: Mirza 'Abd Allah al-Isfahani's *Riyad al-'Ulama*", in *Rhetoric of Biography: Narrating Lives in Persianate Societies*, ed. Louise Marlow (Boston: Ilex Foundation, 2011); Asma Sayeed, 'Women in Imami Biographical Collections', in *Law and Tradition in Classical Islamic Thought: Studies in Honor of Professor Hossein Modarressi*, eds Michael Cook, Najam Haider, Intisar Rabb and Asma Sayeed (New York: Palgrave, 2013).

profiles.[4] Where appropriate, mention will also be made of *Tanqih al-Maqal* by 'Abd Allah al-Mamaqani (d. 1933) and other related modern literature.[5]

The female companions of the Imams will be discussed from various perspectives, and it will be shown that the sources depict them as figures who transmitted the teachings of the Imams and performed a myriad of different functions on their behalf. By deciphering salient characteristics of their contributions, this study argues that these women played broader roles apart from transmitting religious knowledge. Some women are described as scholars in their own right. Others are portrayed as influential religious figures who were trustees of the Imams and had access to secrets that helped shape Shi'i beliefs and practices.

Because the extant biographical texts were compiled more than 200 years after the events, my discussion is based largely on what the sources narrate rather than attempting to confirm the historicity of their activities. It is important to remember that, due to the tendentious nature of the sources, it is impossible to verify the accuracy of the stories the texts narrate. Stated differently, we cannot establish, with absolute certainty, the actual conditions that existed in seventh- and eighth-century Shi'ism. Hence, the historical accounts and figures to be discussed should be seen as plausible rather than actual narratives of the female figures in the pre-occultation era.

Early Shi'ism and the Delegation of the Imams' Authority

As I have discussed elsewhere, a corollary to the Shi'i belief in the authority of the Imam is that, as inheritors of the Prophet's comprehensive authority, the Imams are to provide authoritative guidance to their followers at all times.[6] The view that the teachings of the Imams must be disseminated to the community even under the most inimical conditions precipitated the need for the agency of the disciples of the Imams, the *rijāl*.[7]

The Imams appointed their close disciples as their representatives in various parts of the Shi'i world. 'This agency was an important landmark in Shi'i intellectual history insofar as it signified a transition from the centralised, universal authority of the Imams to a more structured and regionalised office of the *rijāl*.'[8] Prominent companions of the Imams like Zurara b. A'yan (d. 767), Burayd b. Mu'awiyah (n.d.), and Muhammad b. Muslim (d. 767)

---

[4] Nahleh Gharavi Naeeni, *Shi'ah Women Transmitters of Hadith: A Collection of Biographies of the Women Who Have Transmitted Traditions*, trans. Gail Babst (Qum: Ansariyan, 2011).

[5] 'Abd Allah al-Mamaqani, *Tanqih al-Maqal*, 3 vols (Tehran: n.p., n.d.).

[6] Takim, *The Heirs of the Prophet*.

[7] The term *rijal*, literally 'men', is a technical term used in Twelver Shi'i tradition to refer to those prominent male personages who are seen as having been closely associated with the Imams.

symbolised the growing authority of the disciples, who, in places like Kufa and Qum, had assumed leadership of the Shi'i community.

In addition, the *rijāl* themselves emerged as authoritative figures, not only because they were trained and designated by the Imams, but also because they offered their personal interpretations of the teachings of the Imams. The *rijāl* asserted this authority by expressing themselves in their various activities and roles, furnishing them, in the process, with the ability to exemplify and articulate normative Shi'i beliefs and practices. They consolidated their position within the community and gradually controlled the judicial and other financial affairs. Later, Shi'i biographical texts further enhanced the authority of the *rijāl* through various forms of textual and interpretive enterprises.[9]

Women in the Early Twelver Shi'i Biographical Works

Four of the five earliest extant Twelver Shi'i biographical works contain entries for women. *Ikhtiyar Ma'rifat al-Rijal* is Abu Ja'far Muhammad b. al-Hasan al-Tusi's (d. 1067) abridgement of the earlier *Ma'rifat al-Rijal* of Abu 'Amir Muhammad b. 'Umar al-Kashshi (d. 978). Four female associates of the Imams are mentioned in this work. Women are also mentioned briefly in Ahmad b. Muhammad b. Khalid al-Barqi's (d. 887) *Kitāb al-Rijal* and Ahmad b. 'Ali al-Najashi's (d. 1058) biographical work, also titled *Kitab al-Rijal*. In fact, al- Najashi's *Kitab al-Rijal* mentions only two women out of the 1270 disciples he profiles. Al-Tusi's *Kitab al-Rijal* is in the form of a *ṭabaqāt* work (book of classes) in which he chronologically lists the disciples of the Imams and who they related traditions from. As he authenticates only a few of the disciples mentioned in this work, the value of al-Tusi's *Kitab al-Rijal* has been limited.[10] He lists a total of sixty-three women who narrated from the Prophet and the Imams. Apart from mentioning their names and the Imams from whom they reported, al-Tusi gives very little information about these women.[11] In contrast to these works, the only early biographical work that does not mention women is al-Tusi's *Fihrist Kutub al-Shi'a*. As I will indicate, besides the biographical literature, the contributions of these women is also discussed in Shi'i hadith, juridical, and devotional texts.

---

8 Takim, *The Heirs of the Prophet*, 80–81.

9 Ibid. chapters four and five. Even though there were a number of female companions of the Imams, my book focused exclusively on the male disciples. This work will try to fill the lacuna on the study of the female companions of the Imams.

10 Asaf Muhsini, *Buhuth fi 'Ilm al-Rijal* (Qum: n.p., 1983), 119.

11 Muhammad b. Ja'far al-Tusi, *Kitab al-Rijal* (Najaf: al-Matba'a al-Haydariyya, 1961).

Female Figures in Ayatullah al-Khu'i's Mu'jam al-Rijāl al-Hadith

Besides these early biographical works, I also examine some modern biographical works. These works are important as they summarise and synthesise the previous biographical profiles on Shi'i women in the early period and, at times, authenticate or indicate reservations regarding them. The modern works are also crucial in comprehending women's contribution because they cite reports from hadith, devotional, and other genre of literature. In the process, they discuss a wider ambit of the women's activities within the Shi'i community.

A prominent modern scholar of the *rijāl* literature, Ayatullah Abu al-Qasim al-Khu'i (d. 1992), was recognised by many Shi'i scholars as the most important Shi'i jurist of his time.[12] He is reported to have composed more than fifty titles in various fields. Al-Khu'i's twenty-three-volume biographical text known as *Mu'jam Rijal al-Hadith* is devoted primarily to Shi'i transmitters of hadith from the Prophet and Imams. In this work, al-Khu'i cites narrations from various Shi'i hadith and *rijāl* works and also highlights the *ruwāt* (transmitters) who appear in *isnād*s under different names. Under each transmitter, al-Khu'i also discusses the transmitter's connection and interaction with the Imams and explains any anomalies that may exist. Sections of the last volume are devoted to female figures. This portion includes hadith transmitters and other women associated with the Imams.

In this monumental text, al-Khu'i profiles 15,706 companions of the Imams; of these, only 134 are women. Even when he mentions them, he provides very few details about the women he profiles. This is not surprising, given the fact that transmitting oral traditions was primarily the domain of men and because normative culture and custom determined that women and their lives not be discussed in public.

Certain themes emerge from al-Khu'i's profile of female figures. Frequently, al-Khu'i merely states that a woman was a companion of the Prophet (*min aṣḥāb al-Rasūl*) or of an Imam without elaborating. In most instances, they are mentioned without any indication as to their role in the wider public sphere, that is, who they were, what their contribution was, how they influenced the biographical literature, what kind of authority they wielded, and what roles they played in society. Furthermore, unlike the case of their male counterparts, regarding whom more details on their interaction with the Imams and contribution to the cause of the Imams are cited, there is no such discussion for the female reporters.

As a matter of fact, al-Khu'i does not profile some women who are discussed in other modern biographical works like those of al-Mamaqani's *Tanqih al-Maqal* or Muhsin Amin's *A'yan al-Shi'a*. Few of the women profiled in al-Khu'i's work are authenticated. In all probability, since women

---

[12] For a biography of al-Khu'i, see Sachedina, *The Prolegomena to the Qur'an,* 3–22.

did not feature in the public domain, there is little information that would lead to their authentication. More emphasis is laid on the sources of their narration, the Imams with whom they associated, or the transmitters who narrated from them. In his *Tanqih al-Maqal*, 'Abd Allah al-Mamaqani, another important modern *rijāl* scholar, also authenticates very few women. Instead, he often states that since a female figure transmitted a tradition from an Imam or was from within the Imam's family, she must have been a Shi'i and hence should be considered reliable.[13] However, compared to other biographical works, al-Mamaqani's text provides a more nuanced understanding of Shi'i female religious participation. There is more discussion of women's association with the Imams, hadith transmission, and their contribution to the Shi'i cause. The work of al-Mamaqani exemplifies an interpretive process in which a text impacts the present by idealising the past. He engages in a text-based hermeneutical enterprise, on occasion extending the profile of some women beyond the intent of earlier scholars, such as al-Tusi, al-Najashi, and al-Kashshi.[14]

Shi'i Women in the Early *Rijāl* Works

Study of the ninth-, tenth-, and eleventh-century biographical works of al-Barqi, al-Kashshi, al-Tusi, and al-Najashi reveals that in the pre-occultation period, when the Imams were able to provide direct guidance to their community, the dispersion of religious authority was restricted to the close male disciples of the Imams.[15] Social and cultural norms in early and classical Muslim societies dictated that interaction between the sexes be limited. As Devin Stewart has noted, 'features such as the absence of full names of women (and references to them only in terms of their relations to male scholars, for example, sister of X or mother of Y), were, in all probability, due to the need to shield women from public attention.'[16]

Regarding the contributions of women in the transmission of traditions, it should be noted that Shi'i women reported traditions from practically all the Imams. Starting with the first Imam, 'Ali b. Abi Ṭalib (d. 661), female Shi'is transmitted various genres of traditions up to at least the time of the tenth Imam, 'Ali al-Hadi (d. 868). Since the eleventh Imam, al-Hasan al-'Askari (d. 874), spent much of his time in exile in Samarra', very few Shi'is, men or women, reported traditions from him.

Female transmitters report from the sixth Imam, Ja'far al-Sadiq (d. 765), more than they do from any other Imam. This is because most hadith on

---

[13] For the case of Umm Farwa, the mother of Ja'far al-Sadiq, see al-Mamaqani, *Tanqih al-Maqal*, 3:73.
[14] Takim, *The Heirs*, 177–178.
[15] For a discussion of the contribution of the disciples of the Imams see Takim, *Heirs of the Prophet*, chapter four.
[16] Sayeed, 'Women in Imami Biographical Collections', 86.

Shi'i legal questions can be traced to the times of the fifth and sixth Imams. It should also be noted that the female *ruwāt* (transmitters) in Shi'i biographical literature narrated traditions on various topics. Contrary to what one might expect, they did not restrict their reports on legal and ritual issues that affect women in particular, such as the laws regarding menstruation or the clothing that women should wear in public or when praying. Shi'i female hadith transmitters reported on subjects ranging from matters of purity to the merits of the soil of Karbala, the Imamate, and Shi'i devotional exercises. Thus, for example, the aunt of Muhammad b. Ziyad, a disciple of al-Sadiq, reports on the merits and curative powers of the dust of Karbala, where al-Husayn (d. 680) is buried.[17]

As chiliastic ideas became more widespread among the Shi'is during and after the time of the fifth Imam, the female transmitters also narrated traditions that pertained to eschatology. Some women reported traditions on pivotal issues like the belief in al-Mahdi (b. 870), the twelfth Shi'i Imam. Umm Hani al-Thaqafiyya, who transmitted traditions from the fifth Imam, Muhammad al-Baqir (d. 733–737), appears in traditions that interpret verse Q 81:16 to prophesy the birth and appearance of the twelfth Imam, who is considered by Shi'is to be the Messiah (al-Mahdi). There is a discrepancy in the traditions she reports, since some traditions foretell the birth of the Imam in 870 CE, whereas others state that he will be born at the end of time. Regardless of this discrepancy and the authenticity of the traditions, the appearance of Umm Hani in the traditions indicates the pivotal role that women are reported to have played in the transmission of various genres of traditions.[18]

That the female transmitters narrated traditions on many topics can be discerned from the fact that a narrator named Asma' is reported to have transmitted traditions from the Prophet on supplications that help avert calamities, disasters, and fear.[19] Women also report hadith that influence and shape Shi'i acts of devotion. For example, Habiba (also known as Umm Dawud) narrated a tradition regarding Shi'i devotional exercises from al-Sadiq. This is a famous supplication that is recommended to be recited in the month of Rajab. Apparently, the Imam taught it to her when her son was imprisoned by the Abbasid Caliph al-Mansur (d. 775). It is meant to be recited when one seeks God's assistance for victory, relief from suffering, and prosperity.[20]

---

[17] See Ja'far b. Muhammad Ibn Qawlawayh, *Kamil al-Ziyarat* (Najaf: al-Matba'a al-Mubaraka al-Murtadawiyya, 1938): chapter ninety-four, *hadith* #4; Abu al-Qasim al-Khu'i, *Mu'jam Rijal al-Hadith* (Beirut: Dar al-Zahra, 1983), 23:224–225.

[18] Muhammad b. Ya'qub al-Kulayni, *al-Kafi fi 'Ilm al-Din* (Tehran: Daftar Farhang Ahl al-Bayt, n.d.), 1:276; Muhammad b. 'Ali b. al-Husayn al-Saduq, *Kamal al-Din wa-Tamam al-Ni'ma* (Qum: Mu'assasat al-Nashr al-Islami, 1985), 1:33; Naeeni, *Shi'ah Women Transmitters of Hadith*, 133; al-Khu'i, *Mu'jam Rijal al-Hadith*, 23:181.

[19] al-Khu'i, *Mu'jam Rijal al-Hadith*, 23:170

[20] On Umm Dawud see also Muhsin al-Amin, *A'yan al-Shi'a* (Beirut: Dar al-Ta'aruf, 1951), 3:476; Naeeni, *Shi'ah Women Transmitters of Hadith*, 87–88.

In many instances, Shi'i women heard traditions from the Imams and then transmitted them to male transmitters. In this fashion, they became important intermediaries between the Imams and their male disciples. Since they formed an important link in the chain of transmission, women became authoritative figures in that the legacy of the Imams is both preserved and transmitted through them. For example, Umm Ishaq bt. Sulayman narrated hadith from al-Sadiq. Her son, al-'Abbas b. al-Walid, reports traditions from her.[21] Similarly, Umm Salama narrates from al-Sadiq, and her son Muhammad b. Muhajir narrates from her. Umm Salama transmitted a tradition on the method and recitation of the invocation of *takbīr* – the statement that God is great – in the funeral prayer (*ṣalāt al-mayyit*). Interestingly, the same tradition is reported from her both in al-Kulayni's *al-Kafi* and in al-Tusi's *Tahdhib al-Ahkam*.[22] Umm Hani al-Thaqafiyya heard traditions from Muhammad al-Baqir and then narrated them to Muhammad b. Ishaq and Asid b. Tha'laba.[23] There are many other examples of women acting as intermediaries between the Imams and their male associates.

The status of a female transmitter is measured not only by what she relates but also by the authority figure from whom she transmits traditions and the figures who narrate from her. Muhammad b. Abi 'Umayr, a prominent figure in Shi'i hadith literature and a companion of the seventh Imam, narrated hadith from Umm Salama.[24] In such examples, we find that women and men appear in the same *isnād* and often narrate from each other.

Another important figure was Fatima bt. Harun b. Musa Al Furat. A distinctive feature of her profile is that Harun b. Musa al-Tall-'Ukbari (d. 995–996) relates from her. Al-Tall-'Ukbari was a teacher of al-Tusi and Ja'far b. Muhammad al-Qawlawayh (d. 978) and reports from many other figures, including the famous Shi'i biographer al-Kashshi.[25] Many other transmitters reported from him. Al-Tall-'Ukbari's eminent status can be discerned from the fact that he transmitted all the *uṣūl* works that were available to him[26] and that even al-Najashi, the famous Shi'i biographer, would visit him.[27] Thus, for Al-Tall-'Ukbari to narrate traditions from Fatima Al Furat indicates her important status as a hadith transmitter.

---

[21] al-Khu'i, *Mu'jam Rijal al-Hadith,* 23:173.

[22] al-Khu'i, *Mu'jam Rijal al-Hadith,* 23:177; See also Naeeni, *Shi'ah Women Transmitters of Hadith,* 98–99, where al-Mamaqani and Muhsin al-Amin are quoted as declaring that she was trustworthy.

[23] al-Khu'i, *Mu'jam Rijal al-Hadith,* 23:181.

[24] Naeeni, *Shi'ah Women Transmitters of Hadith,* 97; al-Mamaqani, *Tanqih al-Maqal,* 3:73.

[25] Asaf Muhsini, *Buhuth fi 'Ilm al-Rijal* (Qum: n.p., 1983), 58.

[26] The term *aṣl*, literally 'source', designates a notebook that comprises traditions heard directly from the Imams. A *kitāb*, in contrast, may include hadith reports from the Imams but is transmitted through an intermediary. There is much controversy within the Shi'i ranks on the merit of the *uṣūl* works. However, the authors of the *uṣūl* works enjoy a higher status than other authors, since their collections are seen as reflecting the Imams' exact sayings. See Etan Kohlberg, Al-Usul al-Arba'u Mi'a', *Jerusalam Studies in Arabic and Islam* 10 (1987), 128–166.

[27] al-Najashi, *Kitab al-Rijal,* 308.

Women's contribution as transmitters of Shi'i hadith can be properly assessed within the wider context of providing authoritative guidance to the community. Hadith was an indispensable vehicle through which the teachings of the Imams could be disseminated. Moreover, it has to be remembered that the Shi'i legal tradition was interwoven with the hadith literature. Thus, the female transmitters were disseminating the various genres of teachings of the Imams through the hadith they narrated.

By reporting various genres of traditions, the women, like their male counterparts, protected Shi'i beliefs against the impingement of extraneous beliefs and practices. The inherent motive for the traditions – especially those pertaining to the Imamate – was to characterise the origins of the community as divinely sanctioned. The emergence of Shi'i hadith at this point in Shi'i history was also crucial in that it helped crystallise and propagate the distinct doctrinal positions that the Shi'is had espoused. More significantly, the proliferation of Shi'i hadith at this point asserted the community's independence from Sunni hadith and Sunni legal and theological schools. The women profiled played an important role in the transmission and preservation of the Imams' teachings.[28]

Although the women reported hadith in different fields, they, unlike their male counterparts, were not specialists in the law or theology. Female disciples of the Imams were not trained in jurisprudence by the Imams, nor did they narrate thousands of traditions from them. Disciples like Muhammad b. Muslim al-Thaqafi (d. 767), in contrast, had heard thousands of traditions. Hisham b. al-Hakam (d. 807) was an accomplished theologian. Thus, it is correct to say that the female associates were not considered to be trained traditionists or theologians in the Shi'i community.

Bearers of the Imams' Secrets

Many traditions cited in Shi'i biographical works indicate that the Imams would often share spiritual secrets with some of their male disciples. For example, in a tradition that accentuates the close relationship between Ja'far al-Sadiq and Mu'alla b. Khunays, the Imam is quoted as warning him as follows: 'Conceal our secrets, for whoever conceals our secrets, God creates a light between his eyes and gives him strength among the people.'[29] 'These secretive teachings can often be difficult to handle; only those whose hearts have been purified can accept them.'[30]

---

[28] See the discussion on the significance of hadith in disseminating the Imams' traditions in Takim, *The Heirs*, 118–119.

[29] Muhammad b. Ibrahim al-Nu'mani, *Kitab al-Ghayba* (Tehran: Maktabat al-Saduq, n.d.), 38; Ahmad b. Muhammad b. Khalid al-Barqi, *Kitab al-Mahasin* (Najaf: Matba'a al-Haydariyya, 1964), 201.

[30] Muhammad b. al-Hasan al-Saffar, *Basa'ir al-Darajat fi Fada'il Al Muhammad* (Qum: Maktabat Ayat Allah al-Mar'ashi, 1983), 21, 23.

Like their male disciples, the Imams reportedly shared some of their secrets with their female associates. Umm Sa'id al-Ahmasiyya was the recipient of some of Ja'far al-Sadiq's secrets. According to some traditions, Ja'far al-Sadiq said that due to her elevated status, she will rise with the Mahdi when he reappears.[31] Umm Sa'id is quoted several times by Ibn Qawlawayh, especially in traditions that extol the merits of visiting Karbala.[32] Her importance in transmitting Shi'i hadith can be deciphered from the fact that some prominent companions of Ja'far al-Sadiq like Muhammad b. Abi 'Umayr, Yunus b. Ya'qub, Abu Dawud al-Mustaraq, and al-Husayn al-Ahmasi narrated hadith from her.[33]

Another female confidant of the Imams was Umm Aslam, whose exact name is unknown. She is one of three female companions each known as 'the owner of the pebble'. Apart from a tradition that al-Kulayni narrates concerning her, nothing is known about her biography or date of death. Al-Kulayni's tradition suggests that she was alive during the time of fourth Imam, Zayn al-'Abidin, in about the years 713–714, and that she died before he did. Umm Aslam was among the companions and transmitters of traditions from the Prophet, 'Ali, al-Hasan, al-Husayn, and Zayn al-'Abidin and had met all of them. She was reportedly entrusted with the secrets of the Imamate.[34] On the basis of this report, al-Mamaqani claims, 'At the very least, we can conclude from this tradition that Umm al-Aslam was a follower of the Imamiyya group and that the Prophet's family accorded her a special status.'[35]

Umm Aslam also reported the famous pebble tradition, a tradition that is important because it establishes the identity of the first four Imams who would succeed the Prophet: 'Ali b. Abi Talib, Hasan, Husayn, and Zayn al-'Abidin. Al-Kulayni narrates from Ja'far b. Zayd b. Musa that he related from his ancestors that they said:

> "One day Umm Aslam was in the home of Umm Salama and saw the Prophet there. She asked, 'May my father and mother be sacrificed for you, O Messenger of God – I have studied books and know that each Prophet had a successor. Moses had a deputy during his lifetime and a successor after his death. Jesus, too, had a successor. So who is your successor, O Messenger of God?' The Prophet answered, 'O Umm Aslam, my deputy during my lifetime and my successor after my death are one and the same person. O Umm

[31] Naeeni, *Shi'ah Women Transmitters of Hadith*, 89.

[32] Ibn al-Qawlawayh, *Kamil al-Ziyarat*, 158–159.

[33] al-Khu'i, *Mu'jam Rijal al-Hadith*, 23:177.

[34] Naeeni, *Shi'ah Women Transmitters of Hadith*, 59. The authority of an Imam is substantiated by the scrolls and weapons of the Prophet that the Imam reportedly inherited. The weapons and the armour of the Prophet are decisive in establishing the authority of an Imam for these are among the signs (*'alāmāt*) that can establish the identity of the true Imam. The weapons can only fit a divinely designated Imam. Imams are also believed to possess certain scrolls that are transmitted to the succeeding Imam. See Takim, *Heirs of the Prophet*, chapter one.

[35] Mamaqani, *Tanqih al-Maqal*, 3:70.

> Aslam, he who does as I do now is my deputy and successor.' Then he picked up a pebble from the ground and rubbed it with his finger until it turned into powder. He then imprinted it with his ring, and said, 'He who does what I did just now is my deputy during my life and my successor after my death.'"
>
> Umm Aslam recounted, 'I left the Prophet's house and went to see the Commander of the Faithful ('Ali b. Abi Talib). I asked him, "May my father and mother be sacrificed for you. Are you the deputy and successor of the Messenger of God?" He answered, "Yes, O Umm Aslam." Then, he picked up a pebble from the ground and rubbed it with his finger until it became just like flour. He imprinted it with his ring, and said, "He who does what I did now is my successor." I went to see (his son) al-Hasan, who was then a youth. I said to him, "O my master! Are you the successor of your father?" He answered, "Yes, O Umm Aslam," and he picked up a pebble and did the same things the other two had done. I left him and went to see al-Husayn, and verily I had the impression that he was very young. I asked him, "May my father and my mother be sacrificed for you – Are you the successor of your brother?" He said, "Yes, O Umm Aslam. Give me a pebble." Then, he did as the others had done. Umm Aslam lived long enough to see 'Ali b. al-Husayn after his father was martyred. Upon his return (from Karbala), she asked him, "Are you the successor of your father?" He answered, "Yes," then he did as the others had done. May God bless them all.'[36]

Besides establishing claims regarding the Imams, such reports perform the polemical function of nullifying the claims advanced by rival contenders to the Imamate. They also confirm the extent of confusion regarding succession that existed, even for the close disciples of the Imams, and the challenges that the Shi'is encountered in ascertaining the identity of an Imam's successor. By her recognition and acknowledgement of an Imam, Umm Aslam was identifying and proclaiming the Imam of the time and, at the same time, refuting claims made by rival contenders. In the process, she, along with other female figures, was promulgating and perpetuating the central belief in the doctrine of the Imamate. Moreover, the Imam's expression of trust in her by confiding to her the identity of his successor is an important indication of the prestige enjoyed by the female associates of the Imams.

Whether true or contrived, the hadith report indicates not only that Umm Aslam reported from the Prophet and the Imams but also, more importantly, that she had witnessed and reported some of their miraculous powers, thereby raising her status as an associate of the Imams. The tradition bestows great authority on her as one who was able to establish and identify the successors of several Imams. It also shows the confidence that the Imams had placed in her since, because of political vicissitudes, the Imams would divulge the identity of their successor to only a few close disciples. In many ways, this tradition elevates the status of Umm Aslam to the same level as some of the prominent male disciples of the Imams.

---

[36] Naeeni, *Shi'ah Women Transmitters of Hadith*, 59–60; al-Kulayni, *al-Kafi*, 1:355.

A tradition that is similar to this is reported regarding Hababa al-Walibiyya. She is reported to have met the first eight Imams and witnessed the sealing of a pebble by all of them. It is also reported that even though she was almost 113 years old when she met the fourth Imam, Zayn al-'Abidin, her youth was restored by a miracle performed by the Imam.[37] Apparently, she transmitted written instructions from every Imam to his successor until the time of the eighth Imam, 'Ali al-Rida, when she passed away.[38] When she complained to al-Husayn of her leprosy, the Imam was able to cure her.[39] The report is particularly favourable to Hababa, since it indicates that she benefited from the Imam's extraordinary powers. Anecdotes such as these evince not only the miraculous powers of the Imams but also the close connection that women like Umm Aslam and Hababa al-Walibiyya are alleged to have had with the Imams. Their reputation and status were enhanced in reports that indicate that they were the beneficiaries of the miraculous powers of the Imams.

For Shi'i biographers, such miraculous anecdotes are important to cite as they provide proof of the Imams' extraordinary abilities and their authority. The traditions on the miracles of the Imams are also important to cite as they undermine the claims of false claimants to the Imamate. Such anecdotes indicate that, although they were fewer in number, the female disciples of the Imams performed many functions that were undertaken by their male counterparts. These include reporting hadith, identifying the true successor of an Imam, and reporting polemical traditions regarding the Imamate.

The miracle reports narrated by female figures accentuate the Imams' miraculous abilities. Shi'i hadith and biographical texts indicate that, in comparison to the female disciples, the male counterparts were more than passive beneficiaries of the extraordinary knowledge and miraculous abilities of the Imams. Some male disciples reportedly claimed to have acquired the extraordinary knowledge and abilities of the Imams, enabling them to perform feats that could be matched or surpassed only by the Imams.

In his introductory reports, al-Kashshi cites traditions not only on the Imams' esoteric knowledge (*'ilm*), but also on the acquisition of this category of *'ilm* by their loyal companions. By exhibiting their loyalty to the Imams, the *rijāl* could not only acquire their esoteric knowledge but also further appropriate those elements that would invest extraordinary powers in them.[40] According to al-Kashshi, through knowledge acquired from the Imams, Maytham al-Tammar, a companion of 'Ali, could predict future

---

[37] al-Kulayni, *al-Kafi*, 1:346; al-Saduq, *'Uyun Akhbar al-Rida*, 2:536.

[38] al-Saduq, *'Uyun Akhbar al-Rida*, 2:537; Muhammad b. 'Ali Ibn Shahrashub, *Manaqib Al Abi Talib*, 3 vols (Najaf: al-Matba'a al-Haydariyya, 1956), 1:257; Maria Dakake, *The Charismatic Community: Shi'ite Identity in Early Islam* (Albany: State University of New York Press, 2007), 222.

[39] Muhammad b. 'Umar al-Kashshi, *Ikhtiyar Ma'rifat al-Rijal*, ed. al-Mustafawi (Mashhad: Danishgah-i Mashhad, 1969), 115.

[40] On details of these see Takim, *The Heirs*, chapter three, 92–94.

events,[41] a feat that was later matched by Muhammad b. Sinan (d. 835), a disciple of the tenth imam.[42] 'Ali b. Abi Ṭalib had reportedly dictated the *'ilm al-balāyā wa'l-manāyā* (esoteric knowledge of future trials and deaths) to Rushayd al-Hujri.[43] In addition, he taught Salman al-Farisi (d. 644–647) the greatest name of God, which enabled him to partake in the Imams' esoteric knowledge. On account of his supernatural knowledge, Salman could even foretell the unfolding of the events of the Battle of Karbala in minute detail.[44] Al-Baqir is reported as saying that, just like 'Ali, Salman al-Farisi was also a *muḥaddath*, in other words, that he could hear but not see angels.[45]

Jabir b. Yazid al-Ju'fi (d. 745), a companion of the fifth Imam, is also reported to have been endowed with the ability to perform miracles. He is reported to have received esoteric truths from al-Baqir, secrets that he apparently found difficult to conceal.[46] The Sunni hadith expert Abu Ja'far al-'Uqayli al-Makki (d. 933–934) reports in his biographical work that Jabir was also empowered to predict future events. Other reports suggest that al-Baqir had made Jabir consume a special elixir (*qa'b jayshanī*), a drink that helped him memorise 40,000 traditions.[47] Anecdotes such as these indicate that although the male and female associates shared many traits, the biographical texts accentuate the male companions' ability to perform extraordinary feats.

The Female Members of the Imams' Families

Female members of the Imams' families also played crucial roles during the pre-occultation era. This is because the Imams would relate some of their statements and confide secrets and testaments to female members of their families. Thus, the wives, sisters, aunts, and daughters of the Imams form important links in transmitting their legacy. For example, Fatima, also called Umm Farwa, was the mother of Ja'far al- Sadiq. She was also the granddaughter of Abu Bakr and is buried beside her son in Medina. Known for her piety and faith, she transmitted traditions from Ja'far al-Sadiq. According to the historian 'Ali b. al-Husayn al-Mas'udi (d. 956), Umm Farwa was a very pious woman who transmitted traditions from the fourth Imam, Zayn

41 al-Kashshi, *Ikhtiyar Ma'rifat al-Rijal*, 78–79.
42 al-Kashshi, *Ikhtiyar Ma'rifat al-Rijal*, 581–582.
43 al-Saffar, *Basa'ir al-Darajat*, 264–266.
44 al-Kashshi, *Ikhtiyar Ma'rifat al-Rijal*, 20.
45 al-Kashshi, *Ikhtiyar Ma'rifat al-Rijal*, 12. Salman is also depicted as freely conversing with the angel of death. Al-Kashshi, *Ikhtiyar Ma'rifat al-Rijal*, 52.
46 Arzina Lalani, *Early Shi'i Thought: The Teachings of Imam Muhammad al-Baqir* (London: I. B. Tauris, 2000), 108.
47 Muhammad b. 'Amr al-'Uqayli, *Kitab al-Du'afa' al-Kabir* (Beirut: Dar al-Kutub al-'Ilmiyya 1984), 1:194. Takim, *The Heirs*, 94.

al-'Abidin.[48] She also transmitted traditions from her husband, Muhammad al-Baqir, the fifth Imam. Some reports suggest that Ja'far al-Sadiq related traditions from his mother.[49] Another prominent female transmitter was Umm Salama, a sister of Ja'far al-Sadiq. She related many traditions from him and, according to al-Mamaqani, was trustworthy.[50] Similarly, Sa'ida was a devout slave girl who was freed by al-Sadiq. Besides narrating al-Sadiq's teachings, she reportedly had in her possession the *waṣiyya* (will and testament) of the Prophet.[51]

The female members of the Imams' families perform another important function. Besides reporting the traditions of the Imams and their miraculous prowess, they also report the birth of an Imam, something to which male members did not have direct access. Hakima, the daughter of al-Kazim, is reported to have transmitted traditions from her brother, 'Ali al-Rida (d. 818). More importantly, she witnessed and reported traditions on the birth of her nephew, the ninth Imam, Muhammad al-Taqi al-Jawad (d. 835) at a time when many Shi'is doubted if al-Rida had a son. Through her accounts of the birth of the ninth Imam, she was able to put the Shi'is' minds at rest.[52] Undoubtedly, one of the most important female figures in Shi'i hadith literature was Hakima, the daughter of the ninth Imam. Her importance lies in her narration of the birth of the twelfth Imam. As a matter of fact, she is one of the few people to provide an eyewitness account of his birth.[53] Her testimony enabled Shi'is to dispel doubts regarding the birth and existence of the Imam.

Another woman present at the birth of the twelfth Imam was Mariya. Even though very little is known about her, she is said to have narrated traditions from the twelfth Imam. According to the Shi'i jurist al-Saduq (Ibn Babawayh al-Qummi, d. 991), she said, 'The wrongdoers claim that the existence of the proof of God is irrational. If I am allowed to speak, their doubts will be removed.'[54] Another important female figure was Samana al-Munaqrash al-Maghribi. She was a slave girl who was bought by the ninth Imam and subsequently gave birth to the tenth Imam. Known for her piety and virtue, Samana is reported to have fasted most of the time and transmitted traditions from the Imams.[55]

---

[48] 'Ali b. Husayn al-Mas'udi, *Ithbat al-Wasiyya* (Najaf: al-Matba'a al-Haydariyya, n.d.), 152.

[49] al-Kulayni, *al-Kafi*, 1:472.

[50] al-Mamaqani, *Tanqih al-Maqal*, 3:82.

[51] al-Kashshi, *Ikhtiyar Ma'rifat al-Rijal*, 366; Sayeed, 'Women in Imami Biographical Collections', 81.

[52] Muhammad al-Baqir al-Majlisi, *Bihar al-Anwar al-Jami'a li-durar Akhbar al-A'imma al-Athar*, 110 vols (Beirut: Dar Ihya' al-Turath al-'Arabi, 1983), 48:316; al-Mamaqani, *Tanqih al-Maqal*, 3:76.

[53] Muhammad b. Muhammad b. al-Nu'man al-Mufid, *Kitab al-Irshad*, trans. I. K. A. Howard (London: Balagha & Muhammadi Trust, 1981), 530–531; al-Khu'i, *Mu'jam Rijal al-Hadith*, 23:187.

[54] al-Saduq, *'Uyun Akhbar al-Rida*, 2:430.

[55] al-Majlisi, *Bihar al-Anwar*, 5:114–115.

Female members of the Imams' families were also bearers and transmitters of *waṣāyā,* formal testimonies and transmissions of authority from one Imam to the next. The *waṣāyā* were entrusted to women since they were the safest and most reliable mode of transmission. This is because access to women's chambers was restricted to those men who were closely related to them. Umm Ahmad (d. 806) was the mother of Ahmad b. Musa b. Ja'far and one of the wives of al-Kazim (d. 799). According to a tradition cited by Naeeni, 'The Imam left the trusts of the Imamate with her and told her, "Whoever comes to you at any time and asks you for these trusts, know that I have attained martyrdom and that this person is my successor after me. He is the Imam whom you and all the people must obey." After the death of al-Kazim, al-Rida came to Umm Ahmad and asked her for the trust. She asked him: "Was your father martyred?" He answered, "Yes. I am returning from his funeral right now. So, give me the trust my father left with you when he left for Baghdad, because I am his successor and the Imam of all jinns and human beings." Umm Ahmad rent her collar in grief, then gave the trust over to him and swore her allegiance to him as the next Imam.'[56]

The significant role that female associates of the Imams played is also seen in the fact that al-Kazim is reported to have entrusted his testament to Umm Ahmad. She was one of the executors of his will.[57] Such anecdotes indicate that women were more than passive transmitters of hadith. They performed multiple roles, including transmitting the trusts of the Imamate and acting as executors of the Imams' wills. Such anecdotes also suggest that as bearers and transmitters of *waṣāyā* the female disciples often performed functions that their male counterparts could not.

Another woman, Umm Khalid, is reported to have been a very eloquent speaker. Her entry in the biographical works describes a meeting between her and Ja'far al-Sadiq. In this meeting, she asked al-Sadiq about the reliability of Kuthayr al-Nawwa' who had espoused the beliefs of a heretical sect. In response, the Imam condemned him for his heresy. Umm Khalid is also identified as a supporter of Zayd b. 'Ali (d. 740). It is reported that her hand was amputated because of her support for Zayd's revolt against the Umayyads in Kufa.[58]

Like the *rijāl,* some of the Imams' female companions composed books during the times of the Imams that subsequent scholars read and reported from. Al-Najashi mentions a book that 'Ulayya bt. 'Ali b. al-Husayn, a daughter of the fourth Imam, had composed.[59] She also reports traditions from

---

[56] al-Majlisi, *Bihar al-Anwar,* 48:307; al-Mas'udi, *Ithbat al-wasiyya,* 166; Naeeni, *Shi'ah Women Transmitters of Hadith,* 57.

[57] al-Saduq, *'Uyun Akhbar al-Rida,* 1:42; al-Khu'i, *Mu'jam Rijal al-Hadith,* 23:172.

[58] al-Kashshi, *Ikhtiyar Ma'rifat al-Rijal,* 208–9; al-Khu'i, *Mu'jam Rijal al-Hadith,* 23:176.

[59] al-Najashi, *Kitab al-Rijal,* 215.

the fourth Imam. Zurara b. A'yan (d. 767), a prominent hadith transmitter, reports traditions from her.[60] Similarly, Kulthum bt. Salim is reported to have transmitted a book from al-Rida.[61] Al-Najashi states that both 'Ulayya and Kulthum had texts from which they narrated. Although much fewer in numbers, these women are important since they transmit more than a few traditions; in fact, some recorded and transmitted a whole book.

Shi'i women also played roles as members of important families. Umm Aswad was among the descendants of the famous A'yan family and the first person among her clan to accept Shi'ism. Within her family, she, having been informed by Abu Khalid al-Kabuli, was among the first who recognised the authority of the Imam al-Kazim. She was a sister of the aforementioned Zurarah, and it is also reported that she was the one who closed Zurara's eyes after his death. A scholar in her own right, she is also reported to have transmitted traditions from Ja'far al-Sadiq.[62]

A study of Shi'i biographical, hadith, and devotional works indicate that the Imams engaged directly with their female associates. These texts also attest to the wide range of activities in which the women were involved, ranging from the transmission of the Imams' teachings to preserving the scrolls and testaments of the Imamate. Although the female disciples performed many of the functions that their male counterparts did, their roles were more circumscribed. The Imams, for example, did not delegate their authority to their female associates nor were the Shi'is told to refer to them when they needed religious guidance. In addition, social and cultural norms dictated that the women could not perform many of the functions that male companions of the Imams did. They could not engage in disputations with male adversaries, nor did they possess the legal expertise of the *rijāl*. Gender restrictions barred them from other fields. They could not, for example, act as arbiters (*ḥukkām*) in the community, nor could they handle its finances in the absence of the Imams. Unlike their male counterparts, the female associates of the Imams were barred from the judiciary.

Conclusion

Biographical narratives are important because they construct a normative and canonical reading of the historical lives of the women profiled. The authority of the women in Shi'i biographical literature is premised on the various roles they performed in the Shi'i community. The evidence from

---

60 al-Khu'i, *Mu'jam Rijal al-Hadith*, 23:195.

61 al-Khu'i, *Mu'jam Rijal al-Hadith*, 23:199.

62 Abu Ghalib al-Zurari, *Risala fi Al A'yan*, ed. Muhammad Rida al-Husayni (Qum: Maktabat al-I'lam al-Islami, 1989), 231; Naeeni, *Shi'ah Women Transmitters of Hadith*, 61.

early and classical Imam biographical works, although sparse, provides a more nuanced understanding of the development of Shi'i women's religious participation than was heretofore available through consultation only of hagiographical and devotional literature.

This chapter has focused on a domain that has been largely neglected by Western scholars in their studies on pre-ghayba Shi'ism. It has demonstrated that besides the male companions of the Imams, women played important roles in the dissemination of the Imams' teachings in the Shi'i community. They also performed a myriad of other functions that the male disciples could not. In performing these functions, the female disciples of the Imams complemented rather than competed with the male disciples of the Imams.

CHAPTER

6

'SHE SHOULD NOT RAISE HER VOICE WHEN AMONG MEN': IMĀMĪ ARGUMENTS AGAINST (AND FOR) WOMEN JUDGES[1]

Robert Gleave

That the appointment of a woman as a judge is a controversial point in the Islamic legal tradition is clear from the discussion in books of Muslim jurisprudence (*fiqh*). The contours of the debate have been discussed within the context of both the qualities of a judge and the position of women more generally in Islamic legal discussions.[2] Most Muslim legal schools do not permit women to be judges – or to put it technically, they specify 'maleness' (*dhukūra*) among the qualities of a judge (*ṣifāt al-qāḍī*). Their arguments include those arguments based on rational considerations and supposedly 'clear' texts of revelation. Among the so-called rational considerations are the assessments that women are deficient in their rational faculty (*'aql*), judgement (*ra'y*), and religion (*dīn*). These supposed facts provide reasons why women cannot act as judges. There are also sayings attributed to the Prophet Muhammad that support these widespread 'facts'. Among the texts are the Quranic verse (Q 4:34) – 'Men have authority over women because God made the one superior to the other' – and the statement attributed to the Prophet Muhammad, 'No nation prospers when they appoint a woman.' These revelatory statements are interpreted to mean that women cannot be in any position of authority over men – and since a judge is always one who has authority

[1] The research for this chapter was partially funded by the ERC Project 'Law, Authority and Learning in Imami Shi'ite Islam' (695245).

[2] Among the literature that discusses the role and validity of women judges, primarily in the contemporary context, there is: M. Kunkler and D. Kloos, 'Studying Female Islamic Authority: From Top-Down to Bottom-Up Modes of Certification', *Asian Studies Review* 40.4 (2016), 479–490; Monique C. Cardinal, 'Why Aren't Women Sharīʿa Court Judges? The Case of Syria', *Islamic Law and Society* 17.2 (2010), 185–214; and, more recently, Nadia Sonneveld and Monika Lindbekk (eds), *Women Judges in the Muslim World: A Comparative Study of Discourse and Practice* (Leiden: Brill, 2017).

over the disputing parties in a case, women cannot be judges. The arguments here, both revelatory and rational, are general concerning women in positions of authority; they are not specific to women being judges. That these are not specific arguments has led some scholars to argue that the prohibition on women being judges does not have a specific piece of evidence – and, on the justifiable presumption that things are permitted until they are demonstrated to be prohibited, women can be judges, at least in some areas of the law. The schools line up as follows:[3]

(a) The overwhelming majority of Mālikīs, Shāfiʿīs, Ḥanbalīs, Ibāḍīs, Imāmī Shīʿīs, and Zaydī Shīʿīs prohibit women assuming the position of being a judge.
(b) The overwhelming majority of Ḥanafīs permit women being judges in matters where they can act as witnesses, because, for them, if one can be a witness in a case, one must also be able to act as a judge. This means that for certain aspects of criminal law ('crimes against God', *ḥudūd*, and homicide and personal damage, *qiṣāṣ*), a female judge is not permitted.
(c) Ibn Jarīr al-Ṭabarī (d. 310/923) (whose school of law, if it ever existed in significant numbers, died out soon after his death) and the Ẓāhirīs (or more precisely, Ibn Ḥazm (d.456/1064), the only Ẓāhiri for whom we have extensive legal texts) allow women to be judges without restrictions (*muṭlaqan*). Ṭabarī argued that if a woman can gain knowledge of the law to give personal opinions (*fatwā*), she can also be a judge; Ibn Ḥazm argues that there are no texts that explicitly forbid a woman being a judge, and there are plenty of texts that indicate that she can have limited authority in some areas of society.

In each of the major schools (the four Sunni schools to survive into the later medieval period, the Ibāḍī and the Imāmī and Zaydī Shīʿī schools) also had those who dissented from the school's prevalent position, adopting the arguments of the Ḥanafis, Ṭabarī, and Ibn Ḥazm (usually without crediting them as such). My principal concern in this paper is to investigate whether there is a distinctive Shīʿī dynamic to the discussions around the permissibility of women acting as judges. That is, are there elements of the legal discussions concerning the permissibility of women judges that are distinctively Shīʿī? My primary interest is not so much the position of women generally in Shīʿī law, but rather the development of Shīʿī legal arguments

---

[3] See Karen Bauer, 'Debates on Women's Status as Judges and Witnesses in Post-Formative Islamic Law', *Journal of the American Oriental Society* 130.1 (2010), 1–2, for a summary of the early views on women's judgeship across the schools. To her sources can be added the Zaydī position, as reported in Aḥmad b. Yaḥyā Ibn al-Murtaḍā, *al-Baḥr al-Zakhkhār*, vol. 5 (San'a: Dār al-Ḥikma al-Yamāniyya, 1988), 118–119.

concerning the question of whether a woman can act as a judge and issue a valid legal ruling.

It is worth examining the manner in which the Imāmī Shīʿī prohibition on women judges is presented in the early Shīʿī legal texts, and dissecting in detail the argumentation therein. The Shīʿī jurists, when it suits their purpose, will cite selected reports from the Imāmī hadith collections; at times they may not cite the reports explicitly but will echo the reports' sentiments (or rather their reading of the sentiments). The reports considered decisive are ones that explicitly mention women becoming judges. These we can call reports of *direct reference*. The most common form of such reports is a list of legal duties that women are not required to perform (and, perhaps, it is not 'proper' or even 'valid' for them to perform).[4] There are a number of such reports related from more than one Imam.

A report in Ibn Bābawayh's *Man lā yaḥḍuruhu al-faqīh* quotes from a *waṣiyya* of the Prophet to ʿAlī. The list begins with Friday Prayer (*laysa ʿalā al-nisāʾ jumʿa* – 'it is not incumbent upon women to carry out Friday Prayer'), and running through congregational prayer, announcing the call to prayer (*adhān*). Among these items is 'being appointed to the position of judge' (*tawallī al-qaḍāʾ*[5]).

> [The Prophet] said: O ʿAlī, it is not [obligatory/appropriate for] women to [be involved in] Friday prayer, congregational prayer, the call to prayer, the rising up [for prayer], visiting the sick, follow in a funerary procession, rush between Ṣafā and Marwā, kiss the [Black] Stone, shave the head [while on Hajj], take up judgeship (*tawallī* or *tuwallā al-qaḍāʾ*), act as a counsellor, perform the ritual sacrifice (unless it is absolutely necessary), perform the *talbiya* prayer out loud, to stay with a grave, hear a sermon, take on her own guardianship in marriage, leave her husband's house without his permission.[6]

A similar list can be found in Ibn Bābawayh's *al-Khiṣāl*, cited from Imām Muḥammad al-Bāqir:

> Muḥammad b. ʿAlī al-Bāqir said, 'It is not [obligatory/appropriate for] women to [be involved in] the call to prayer, the *iqāma* [the call to prayer immediately before prayer commences], Friday prayer, congregational prayer, visiting the sick, follow in a funerary procession, perform the *talbiya* prayer out loud, rush

[4] The Arabic phrase used here is *laysa ʿalā al-nisāʾ*, which can be translated as 'it is not incumbent upon women'. It is not an unambiguous phrase here – as it could be translated 'it is not for women to' (that is, 'it is not proper for them').

[5] It could possibly be transliterated *tuwallā al-qaḍāʾ*. The difference is not major – it is not appropriate for her to 'be appointed for judgeship' would be an accurate translation – although it could be argued that *tuwallā* implicitly means she 'adopts' the position of judge, while *tawallī* gives the impression of her being 'appointed'.

[6] Muḥammad b. ʿAlī Ibn Bābawayh, *Man lā yaḥḍuruhu al-faqīh*, vol. 4 (Qum: Manshūrāt-e Nashr-e Islāmī, n.d.), 263 #821.

> between Ṣafā and Marwa, kiss the [black stone], enter the Ka'ba, shave the head [while on hajj] – and they should only cut the hair of women – take up a judgeship (*wa-lā tuwallā al-mar'a al-qaḍā'*).[7]

Other Shīʿī reports relate the question of women taking the position of judge to the myth of Eve. Al-Shaykh al-Mufīd in his *al-Ikhtiṣāṣ* cites a report:

> The Prophet was asked about Adam, whether he was created from Eve or Eve created from him. He said, 'Eve was created from Adam. If it were the case that Adam was created from Eve, then divorce (*ṭalāq*) would be in hands of women, and not in the hands of men.' He said, 'Was she created from all of him, or only from a part of him?' and [the Prophet] replied, 'No, from part of him. If Eve was created from all of him, then judging (*al-qaḍā'*) would have been permitted for women, just as it has been for men.'[8]

The famous 'delegation' reports might be seen as directly indicating that a woman cannot be appointed as a judge – although they are less explicit that these 'list' reports. In the 'delegation' reports, Imam Ja'far al-Ṣādiq is asked to whom the community should turn to decide disputes, and he replies that you should look to a 'man' (*rajul*) who relates hadith and knows *ḥalāl* and *ḥarām*; he is a 'a *qāḍī*' over you. It might be said (as it is by some, to which we shall return below) that the Imam specifying that you should look to a man (*rajul*) means you cannot look to a woman. Others argue that this is a debatable exegetical manoeuvre.

There are, of course, other pieces of revelatory evidence that address women's position in society generally, and imply an inferior status, and that are cited as such by later jurists. These are, one could say, *indirect references*, in the sense that their relevance requires greater exegetical work on the part of the commentator or jurist. They do not directly mention judgeship, and therefore an argument needs to be made (either from a general category to a specific, or on an a fortiori basis) that judgeship is implicitly referred to in the reports. The Quranic *qawwāmūn* verse (Q 4:34) is cited as proof that women should not have any authority (judgeship included) over men. This is a common use of the Quranic verse between the Sunnis and the Shīʿa. There is also the much-cited report of the Prophet: 'No nation prospers when they appoint a woman.'[9] Similarly, there is a report attributed to Imam al-Ṣādiq (found in much later sources), citing God's words when he rejects Adam and Eve from paradise: 'and I will make not one of you [f. pl.; that is, women] an arbiter (*ḥākim* – or perhaps simply a judge) and not will I send from amongst you any prophet'.[10] Given the difference between a *ḥākim* and a *qāḍī*, there

---

[7] Muhammad b. 'Alī Ibn Bābawayh, *al-Khiṣāl* (Qum: Mu'assasat al-Nashr al-Islami, 1403), 585, #12.
[8] al-Shaykh al-Mufīd, *al-Ikhtiṣāṣ* (Beirut: Dār al-Mufīd, 1414 [1993]), 50.
[9] On this famous hadith, see the analysis of Mohammad Fadel, 'Is Historicism a Viable Strategy for Islamic Law Reform? The Case of "Never Shall a Folk Prosper Who Have Appointed a Woman to Rule Them",' *Islamic Law and Society* 18.2 (2011), 131–176.
[10] Mīrzā Ḥusayn al-Nūrī, *Mustadrak al-Wasā'il*, vol. 14 (Qum: Mu'assasat Āl al-Bayt, 1408 [1988]), 287, #16732.

might be a case for making this an indirect reference to the legitimacy of women taking up the position of judge. The position of judge would not be appropriate for such a category of person, so the argument goes. There are others that describe, in general terms, what a woman should not do (mix with men, raise her voice, have authority over men, and so on) that are taken by jurists to imply that women cannot be judges, since a judge is required to do these things. It is normally easier for a jurist to argue with direct (rather than indirect) reference reports. On the other hand, direct reference reports pose a greater exegetical challenge to those wishing to argue against the direct reference; this can be contrasted with indirect reference reports, where a claim of irrelevance is much easier to establish.

Reports such as these do not necessarily determine the positions taken in works of jurisprudence since not all scholars agree that these reports (that are not widely transmitted) have probative force. Nevertheless, the presence of a number of reports, both of direct and indirect reference, do make it easier for an Imāmī Shīʿī jurist to argue for the inadmissibility of women judges.

If we turn to the legal argumentation, perhaps the first proper discussion is found in al-Tusi's *al-Khilāf*:

> It is not permitted for a woman to be a judge in any section of the law. Al-Shāfiʿī affirms this. Abū Ḥanīfa says that it is permitted for her to be a judge in those areas she is able to be a witness – which is all the law except the prescribed and retributive criminal rules (*ḥudūd* and *qiṣāṣ*). Ibn Jarīr [al-Ṭabarī] says that it is permitted for her to be a judge in all areas where a man can be a judge because she is one of the people who can exercise independent legal judgement (*ijtihād*).
>
> Our reasoning here is that that permitting [women to be judges] requires evidence because acting as a judge is itself a matter of a legal regulation. Whoever says, 'She is worthy of it' needs legal evidence.
>
> It is reported from the Prophet that he said, 'No nation prospers when they appoint a woman.' And he said, 'They [male] place them [feminine] last because God has placed them [feminine] last.'
>
> Anyone who permits her to take up the role of being a judge has placed her before them and made a man inferior to her.
>
> [The Prophet] said, 'If something [disruptive] happens to someone during prayer, then let him shout out '*subḥān allāh*' ['praise be to God']'. Shouting *subḥān allāh* is for men, and clapping (*taṣfīq*) is for women.'[11] So the Prophet forbade her from speaking so that he does not hear her voice through fear of [him] being tempted (*iftitān*) by her. Hence, forbidding her from taking up the position of judge, which requires her to speak and other things, is preferable.[12]

[11] This most likely refers to something that requires the person to alert the other members of the congregation – a danger perhaps or something similar. Bauer refers to this passage in 'Debates', 8–9. This is a citation of a Prophetic report (also found in Sunni collections) rather than al-Tusi himself speaking, and the use of *subḥān allāh* or clapping appears to be a way in which one can alert other worshippers that something has happened to endanger the validity of the prayer or the well-being of the worshippers.

[12] Muhammad b. Hasan al-Tusi, *al-Khilāf*, vol. 6 (Qum: al-Mu'assasat al-Nashr al-Islāmi, 1407), 213.

In understanding the arguments expressed here, it is worth remembering the generic features of al-Tusi's *al-Khilāf*. As its name suggests it is a book of juristic differences, and the primary parties are the four Sunni legal schools, together with various other Sunni jurists, and all of these are compared and contrasted with Imāmī Shīʿī legal opinion. Argumentation for the Shīʿī position is, quite often, expressed in terms that might have purchase with the Sunni opponents. They may not always express internal Shīʿī argumentation, but arguments for the Shīʿī doctrine that might work for Sunni jurists – because the work is intended as a polemic against Sunni legal opinions. It undoubtedly draws on Sunni works of 'legal differences' (*khilāf*) that had, by al-Tusi's time, become a popular legal genre.

It is with this in mind that we read the section on 'our reasoning' (*dalīlunā*), which concludes nearly every example of legal difference in the work. In this section, we see that the three reports cited are ones that are not found in Shīʿī hadith collections (including those of al-Tusi):

[1] 'No nation prospers when they appoint a woman.'
[2] 'They [male] place them [feminine] last because God has placed them [feminine] last.'
[3] 'Prophet forbade her from speaking so that he does not hear her voice through fear of [him] being tempted (*iftitān*) by her.'

It should also be noted that they are all indirect (or non-explicit) evidence for the illegitimacy of women's judgeship. Because the reports are only indirectly related to the question of women's judgeship, they are made to establish general rules that bar women from many areas of public life, and the reasoning can be expressing syllogisms:

[1] Judges have to be appointed; no nation prospers when they appoint a woman; therefore, do not appoint a woman as judge.
[2] Judges have to be raised above the general people; women cannot be raised above men; therefore, do not appoint a woman as judge.
[3] Judges have to raise their voices above the general people; women cannot raise their voices above men; therefore, do not appoint a woman as judge.

The first needs no gloss (that is, the reasoning from hadith to ruling is deemed so obvious it requires no explanation). The second does, in al-Tusi's view, require minimal gloss (that is, appointing a woman as a judge raises her above a man, and this hadith rejects this). The third requires a lengthier explanation: the report concerns stopping a prayer in order to attend to a need that has suddenly arisen. Al-Tusi is citing a report found in Sunni collections, among which is *Musnad* of Ahmad Ibn Hanbal where instead of the phrase '*man fātahu shay'un fī al-ṣalāh*' ('If something escapes someone during prayer'), the Aḥmad report reads *man nābahu shay'un fī al-ṣalāh* ('if something unfortunately happens to someone during prayer').[13] In these circumstances, men should shout out the phrase *subḥān allāh* (praise be to God, *tasbīḥ*); women should clap. From this al-Tusi deduces that women should not speak in front of men even at the point where they may be a serious incident occurring that endangers at least the validity of the prayer (and perhaps more). The women should not raise their voice because it might 'tempt' the men, and since being a judge requires women to speak in front of men, it is therefore impossible for a woman to be a judge without her, at the same time, transgressing another element of the law (namely the command for her to keep silent in front of men). These all seem what might be called 'legal technicalities' that bar a woman from being a judge. They are based on extraneous factors (and one could argue, factors that are not something the women can do anything to remedy). They do not commit al-Tusi to any position on women being deficient in reason or religion, but instead indicate that it is simply a matter of requirements laid down by the law that prevent a woman from being a judge.

This, it seems to me, is not a particularly convincing argument - or at least it is not so difficult to present a counter-argument to this legal reasoning. First, the report is specific (it relates to how to stop a congregational prayer in an emergency). Second, women are not prohibited from speaking in the presence of men in all circumstances. Third, al-Tusi's argument that it is because of a fear of temptation that the women must clap is pure supposition. It is, perhaps, because of these potential objections, that al-Tusi does not declare that the report proves that women taking up judgeship is illegitimate. He states, instead that it is more appropriate (*awlā*) that they do not. While not wishing to argue against al-Tusi here, the fact that he deems these the appropriate arguments to present in his *al-Khilāf* tell us more about what he thinks will work with the intended audience of *al-Khilāf* (namely, non-Imāmī jurists), rather than the internal Shīʿī case for the illegitimacy of women judges. There were more convincing texts, more explicit texts available to al-Tusi, but they are from Shīʿī Imams and through Shīʿī *isnāds*. He does not cite them, because they would not work with his audience. So instead he cites texts, acceptable for his audience, and he attempts to make them into evidence for the view of the Imāmīs and Shāfiʿīs (and others not mentioned), against the views of the Ḥanafīs and al-Tabari.

At least, though, there is argumentation here; al-Tusi presents sources and a process (however rudimentary) of legal reasoning. In other Imāmī

---

[13] Ahmad b. Hanbal, *al-Musnad*, vol. 5 (Beirut: Dār al-Fikr, 1991), 330; some variants, such as that in Muslim's *Ṣaḥīḥ*, are more explicit saying *man nābat'hu nā'ibatun fī al-ṣalāh* ('if a misfortune befalls someone during prayer'). Muslim, *al-Ṣaḥīḥ*, vol. 1 (Beirut: Dār al-Kutub al-'Ilmiyya, 1994), 316.

legal texts, contemporary with al-Ṭūṣī or a little later, there are merely lists of criteria that a judge must have, among which is 'being male' (*dhukūra*). The exclusion of women is sometimes mentioned explicitly, usually explaining that she is not to be linked with or contracted (*in'iqād*) to being a judge. Among the list are the usual suspects: being adult, free, of good moral record (*kamāl al-'adl*), being literate, having sight, unimpaired rational faculties (*kamāl al-'aql*), having knowledge (*'ilm* – by which is meant being knowledgeable about the law), and a deep awareness of *fiqh*. Maleness (*dhukūra*) is regularly mentioned in the list, and usually these qualities are seen as prerequisites (*yushtaraṭu fīhi*). Occasionally, the requirement to be male is given a gloss in the *fiqh* texts: 'she is not to be contracted as a judge in any circumstance';[14] 'neither a child . . . nor a woman should be contracted as a judge';[15] a judge must be male and not female without exception.[16] It could be argued (and has been by more reform-minded scholars) that maleness is cited alongside reason, knowledge, insight, and the like (*'aql, 'ilm, fiqh 'an baṣīra*), which means that women are quite capable of fulfilling all these criteria. That is, women are not, essentially, deficient in *'aql* or *'ilm*, otherwise there would be no need to specify this additional quality of maleness.

The *fiqh* work that perhaps has attracted more commentaries than any other in the Imāmī tradition, the *Sharā'i' al-islam* of al-Muhaqqiq al-Hilli, is carefully phrased:

> A woman should not be contracted to be a judge even if she fulfills all the conditions/qualities (*sharā'iṭ*).[17]

Does this mean that being a man is not one of the conditions/qualities of being a judge? It is merely that only a man can practically fulfil the requirements? The subclause 'even if she fulfils the conditions' (*wa-in istakmalat al-sharā'iṭ*), found in the *Sharā'i'*, [18] is repeated in other works. Sometimes, in order to make it quite clear that maleness is actually one of the conditions,

---

[14] Ibn al-Barraj, *al-Muhadhdhab*, vol. 2 (Qum: al-Mu'assasat al-Nashr al-Islami, 1406), 599.

[15] Muḥammad b. Makkī al-'Āmilī al-Shahīd al-Awwal, *Al-Durūs al-shar'iyya fī fiqh al-imāmiyya*, vol. 2 (Qum: Mu'assasat al-Nashr al-Islami, 1419Sh), 70.

[16] Zayn al-Dīn al-'Āmilī al-Shahīd al-Thānī, *al-Rawḍa al-Bahiyya fī sharḥ al-Lum'a al-Dimashqiyya*, vol. 3 (Qum: Amīr, 1410), 70. Al-Shahīd al-Thānī is here commenting on the passage in al-Shahīd al-Awwal's *al-Lum'a* where he says that a judge must be 'sound [of reason], knowledgeable, fitting to give fatwas, male, literate and sighted, except for the judge who is involved in arbitration'. The exception is vague, and it could mean that all of these qualities are not necessary for the arbitration judge. Al-Shahīd al-Thānī argues that the exception only applies to the condition of being sighted, 'and an exception [from the condition of maleness] for a judge for arbitration (*taḥkīm*) [in cases of is unlikely, though it is possible (*wa-in kān muḥtamilan*)]'.

[17] Al-Muḥaqqiq al-Hilli, *Sharā'i' al-islām*, vol. 4 (Qum: Amīr, 1409 AH), 860.

[18] Some lists, most notably that found in the *Tabṣirat al-Muta'allimīn* of al-'Allama al-Hilli, do not even mention the condition of maleness – leaving open the possibility that al-'Allāma did not think it a pre-requisite of being a valid judge that he is male. Al-'Allama al-Hilli, *Tabṣirat al-Muta'allimīn fī aḥkām al-dīn* (Tehran: Intishārāt-e Faqīh, 1368Sh).

the phrase is changed to 'if she fulfils the rest of the conditions' (*wa-in jama'at bāqī al-sharā'iṭ*).[19] This is supplemented by other glosses on the 'conditions list' item for maleness made by subsequent authors of works of jurisprudence. Al-Shahid al-Awwal (d. 786/1384), for example, says the judge should have all the qualities of the mufti (and a woman can be a mufti); although he goes to on to add that the judge must, in addition to being qualified to give fatwas, be male, and literate, and sighted.[20] Another example is that a woman cannot be a judge because, according to Fayd al-Kashani (d. 1091/1680), it is not appropriate for her to mix with men and raise her voice among them (*raf' al-ṣawt baynahum*).[21]

It is not the essential inability of women to fulfil the prerequisites of being a judge that are being hinted at here. Women are, by implication (so it is claimed by some), able to fulfil the conditions of being a judge. It is simply that the social (and perhaps legal) restrictions on her mixing with men and raising her voice among them prevent her taking up the position. Women judges are theoretically possible, but practically impossible. In this sense, it is similar to the implicit reasoning in some legal texts concerning the acceptance of women's testimony, mentioned by Mohammed Fadel.[22] The inclusion of the criterion of maleness could mean that women can fulfil all the other criteria of being a judge (reason, good morals, knowledge of the law); it would simply contravene other aspects of the law if they were to be appointed to the role. It might be suggested, as mentioned above, that even in al-Tusi's *al-Khilāf*, it is not women's essential inadequacies that prevent them being judges. Instead, it is men who cannot cope with her having authority over them (being 'placed before' them), and tempting them with her 'talking' – it is the idealised relationship of the sexes in the juristic literature that prevent her from being a judge, rather than any inherent female deficiency.

The only comprehensive dissenting voice in the pre-classical Imāmī tradition is, as far as I can tell, Ahmad b. Muhammad al-Muqaddas al-Ardabili (d. 993/1585). He includes a carefully worded passage in his commentary on al-'Allama al-Hilli's *Irshād al-Adhhān*. Al-'Allama lists the qualities of a judge, and includes in the list, without comment, 'maleness'. Al-Ardabili comments thus:

> As for maleness being a condition [of being a judge], then this is clear in those areas where it is not permitted for a woman to give orders/take leadership/have authority (*lam yajuz li-l-mar'a fihi amr*). In other areas, though, we know of no clear indicator, though it is the dominant school opinion (*mashhūr*). If there had been a consensus of the jurists (*ijmā'*), then there would be no dis-

[19] This is more notably found in the much commented *fiqh* text, al-'Allama al-Hilli, *Qawā'id al-aḥkām*, vol. 3 (Qum: Mu'assasat al-Nashr al-Islami, 1419Sh), 421.

[20] Al-Shahid al-Awwal, *al-Lum'a al-Dimashqiyya* (Qum: al-Quds, 1411), 79.

[21] Kashani, *Mafātīḥ al-sharā'i'*, vol. 3 (Qum: Khayyam, 1401), 246.

[22] Fadel, 'Is Historicism a Viable Strategy for Islamic Law Reform?'

> cussion. However, if [there is] no [*ijmā'*], then the total prohibition [on women being judges] is a matter of dispute. There is no bar on [a woman] making a judgment on the basis of women's testimony, having heard their testimony – from two women, for example, on a matter – providing she can be described as having the qualities [that qualify her to give] rulings (*ittiṣāfihā bi-sharā'iṭ al-ḥukm*).[23]

Al-Ardabili, is regarded generally as a bit of a maverick in the Imāmī legal tradition; he located himself outside of the Safavid heartlands, basing himself in Najaf, and refused a request to work for the Safavids.[24] He indicates that a woman, with the requisite qualities (*sharā'iṭ*), might be able to act as a judge in those areas where she is permitted to have judicial authority, because (he argues) we already accept that she can act as a witness.[25] It is not equality, that is for sure, but it is an acceptance that there might be a counter-argument to the total prohibition on women judges. Most pertinently, maleness should not be seen as a precondition of judgeship, but as a secondary, practical qualification for most cases – that is, it is a case-specific rule rather than an absolute requirement.

In the nineteenth century, Imāmī legal works became much more discursive, with new approaches and discussions explored by various authors. A possible reason for this growth in the sophistication of legal argument is a new-found freedom: the restriction of the period of dominance of the hadith-based Akhbārī school.[26] On the question of whether maleness is a precondition for a judge, one sees the development of the argument quite clearly. The discussion becomes more precise, more detailed, and more nuanced. The debate continued over whether maleness was a prerequisite for being a judge with jurists taking both positions (or variations on them). Even for those who took the view that there was no theoretical bar to a woman being a judge, there remained a practical bar on women judges as it would be impractical.

There are hints that the absolute prohibition on women judges begins to be undermined. For example, Mirza Qummi (d. 1231/1815) in his *Ghanā'im al-ayyām*[27] argues that the conditionality of maleness is established only by

---

[23] Although it is possible that *sharā'iṭ al-ḥakam* should be read here – she has the qualities of a male arbiter. Ardabīlī, *Majma' al-fā'ida*, vol. 12 (Qum: Mu'assasat al-Nashr al-Islami, 1414), 15.

[24] Wilferd Madelung, 'Shi'i Attitudes Toward Women as Reflected in "fiqh",' in *Society and the Sexes in Medieval Islam*, ed. Afaf Lutfi al-Sayyid-Marsot (Malibu: Undena Publications, 1979), 69–79.

[25] (Or perhaps as an arbiter – *ḥakam*) in cases where she hears the testimony of two women. Indeed, I would argue that the *ḥakam* reading becomes more likely since the thrust of his argument appears to be that since he accepts women as arbiters *in those areas that they are permitted to adopt this role*, there is a good (but not decisive) argument for accepting them as judges also *in those areas that they are permitted to adopt this role*.

[26] See R. Gleave, *Scripturalist Islam* (Leiden: Brill, 2007).

[27] Al-Mirza al-Qummi, *Ghanā'im al-ayyām* (Qum: Maktab al-I'lam al-Islami, 1417), 643.

consensus (*ijmā'*) and not by a revelatory text (*dalīl*). It cannot be proven through women being unable to speak before men, or being forgetful (given that speaking before claimants, and having a good memory are essential qualities of a judge). These (negative) qualities are not found in all women (that is, some women can speak and can remember) and are therefore not essential to womenkind. Hence, for Qummi, there is some ambiguity or problematic element (*ishkāl*) in any absolute prohibition on women judges, since this view is only able to be proven through consensus, and rulings established through an alleged consensus are, theoretically, more open to dispute and challenge. Al-Naraqi (d.1245/1829) in his *Mustanad al-Shī'a* argues that the conditionality of maleness may well be proven by consensus, but it is not consensus on an issue for which there is no text; rather it is consensus on the understanding of an extant text. This is probably a reaction to Qummi's position, as al-Naraqi says that 'some of them have tried to problematise the condition of [being a man], but this is weak'.[28] When the Imam says, in the famous delegation hadiths referenced above, that he has to appoint a 'man' (*rajul*) to be judge, he is, by implication, excluding a woman from being a judge; this implication is, in itself, not decisive. However, there has been a consensus that the implication is valid – and this, it appears, reduces the problematic nature of the consensus supposedly identified by al-Qummi. By this stage, the argumentation has become more focused on the dissection of the exclusively Imāmī texts, and there is no pressing need, as there was for al-Tusi in his *al-Khilāf*, to refer to reports found outside of the Imāmī tradition.

In the more recent past, the debate over whether women can be judges has continued; the majority position remains that this is not possible – in principle or for practical reasons. In the writings of Husayn Al-Muntaziri, (d. 2009) on the political institution of the 'Guardianship of the Jurist' (*wilāyat al-faqīh*), he links the role of the jurist who has the right of the guardianship of the community (*wilāya*) to the established position of the judge. The qualities of a judge are, by transference, also the qualities of the jurist (*faqīh*), he argues, among which is 'being male'. Al-Al-Muntaziri, though, is aware that this is controversial, and so, after mentioning this requirement in his famous work *Dirāsāt fī wilāyat al-faqīh,* embarks on a general description of the position of women in Islam. His explanation of the inability of a woman to be a judge, and hence the *faqīh,* is based on the inherent difference between men and women (*tafāwut al-rajul wa-l-mar'a*). Women are more focused on the home, while men are more prone to go out and earn a living. Women are more apt to care for the upbringing of children, while men are breadwinners. Some argue that justice (*al-'adl*) requires equality between men and women. However, true justice does not require equal treatment for all people in a particular class. To ask someone to do

---

[28] Muḥammad Mahdī al-Narāqī, *Mustanad al-Shī'a,* vol. 17 (Qum: Sitara, 1419), 35.

something that is beyond their abilities, or something to which they are not suited merely because one asks that of another person, is not just or fair. Hence, expecting women, whose natural disposition is not to adopt guardianship over others, to be a judge, or the *faqīh*, would actually be an unjust and unfair act. This, al-Muntaziri states, is not to insult the nobleness of women; it is simply to identify the appropriate level of natural aptitude regarding the delegation of authority (*innamā yurād ri'āyat al-tanāsub al-ṭabī'ī fī tafwīḍ al-mas'ūliyya*).[29] Generally speaking, though, al-Muntaziri is not convinced of the revelatory arguments (the citations from the Qur'an, the saying of the Prophet and Imams, and the claim of consensus) by past jurists. All of these are open to dispute and legitimate objections, he says. Instead, he believes the most convincing evidence that women should be neither judges nor the supreme juristic authority and power (*faqīh*) is history and reason. He explores the views of others (non-Shī'ī jurists) on the issue, and commenting on the Hanbali jurist Ibn Qudama's (d. 620/1223) statement, 'If it were to be permitted [for a woman to be a judge], then history would not be empty of this [phenomenon]', he writes:

> This is an accurate statement on the topic. The Umayyads and the Abbasids ruled over the community for more than 600 years, and they were devoted and infatuated with women and slave girls. The influence of their women, daughters and sisters is well-known; that people of superiority and knowledge were found amongst them. But they mostly put in charge people who were not suitable, even their slaves – and with all of this, one does not hear of them ever appointing a woman to have power to be a judge. From this, it is known that the people have an aversion to this; [appointing women to be judges] was unheard of amongst them, as it would impossible for the rulers to go against [the people] in this matter.[30]

One might debate the claim that there have been no female judges during the Umayyad and Abbasid periods, but al-Muntaziri's use of this historical argument is interesting. Clearly, he is making the implicit claim that some form of community custom has legal probative value – that is not a common argument of Shī'ī thinkers generally (for whom, the practice of government in Muslim history can hardly be a model for how the community should be ruled).

After examining all the reports and revelatory material, al-Muntaziri concludes that the citations establish generally that women should not be given authority in the area of judgeship. However, reports are always open to interpretation and doubt as to their provenance. Hence, he argues, there is a further argument for those who doubt the message of the reports

---

[29] Husayn al-Muntaziri, *Dirāsāt fī wilāyat al-faqīh wa-fiqh al-dawla al-Islāmiyya*, vol. 1 (Qum: Manshūrāt al-Markaz al-'Ālamī, 1408), 345.
[30] Al-Muntaziri, *Dirāsāt*, vol. 1, 338.

– the system of legal presumptions that allow a Shī'ī jurist to give an opinion when the evidence is uncertain (these are known as the procedural principles – *al-uṣūl al-'amaliyya*):

> And so on and so on, with different reports in different chapters. Some of these are known to be generally certain, in addition to some which are of sound transmission. After considering them all together, [the reports] indicate, undeniably, that it is not appropriate for her like [namely, women] to have power, including being a judge, given the natural disposition of women and their duty to be hidden and covered. So it is obvious that the matter is clear, and there is no reason to cast doubt on it.
>
> Given that even the slightest doubt is sufficient [to reconsider the matter], the fundamental presumption in things (*al-aṣl*) is that no one has power over another; and there is no general or unrestricted statement which establishes that women should be included [in those who have power].[31]

Here, then, the argument is that the natural order of things is that one person does not have power over another – that is, that each person is free from oversight and guardianship. In order to impose legal oversight (*wilāya, qaḍā'* – that is, one person having power over another), clear legal evidence is required. There is clear legal evidence that God has allowed there to be judges who take legal authority over others, and there is clear evidence that those judges are permitted to be men. What is missing, according to al-Muntaziri, is clear legal evidence that these judges can also be women. In the absence of such evidence, the fundamental presumption (*aṣl*) remains, and women are not permitted to have legal authority over others.

There has been few dissenting voices among the major Shī'ī scholars from the view that women cannot be judges, although there are few lesser known scholars who are exploring the arguments in favour of women judges. Al-Muntaziri's argument from the *aṣl*, though, has been the subject of some criticism. One such implicit criticism came from Ayatallah 'Abd al-Karim Musawi al-Ardabili (d. 2016), like al-Muntaziri a onetime friend of Ayatallah Khomeini, and similarly deeply involved in the post-revolutionary government of Iran. Al-Ardabili was head of the Iranian judiciary and head of Iran's supreme court, and it was this experience that led him to write an extensive work on the working of the judiciary in Islamic law, known as *Fiqh al-Qaḍā'* ('The Jurisprudence of Judging'). In the section detailing the qualities of a judge, he discusses the disputed quality of 'maleness', arguing strongly against the presumption that a judge must be male, and criticising the interpretations of the revelatory texts of those who bar women from being judges. He particularly points out the weakness of

---

31 Al-Muntaziri, *Dirāsāt*, vol.1, 360.

the argument from 'the fundamental presumption' (*al-aṣl* – the basis for al-Muntaziri's argument):

> And one of the things which diminishes the declaration [of those who oppose women judges] is this: that [they argue] it is a requirement of the *aṣl* that she not undertake the position of being a judge.
>
> However, there is nothing in the [evidence related to the] topic which constitutes a general or unqualified indicator upon which to base a permission to be a judge, nor is there anything which indicates that taking up such an appointment applies generally to men and women. So in order to exclude women from [the people generally] we need an indicator which will bring specification into consideration and go against this logical presumption. In such circumstances, we must refer to the procedural presumptions to investigate the issue. If there is no fundamental presumption here, or if we dispute what it is, then it is more likely that [a woman is] permitted to be a judge in those areas where the subject matter permits women to be so.[32]

The reasoning is wrapped up in Shīʿī juristic jargon, but the argument he appears to be making is as follows: there is nothing in the evidence that also establishes the position of a judge that establishes that these statements are general (applying to both men and women) or specific (applying to men alone). The revelatory evidence is insufficiently clear to establish this. When revelatory evidence is unclear in this way, the justified rational presumption is that the statements are not exclusive to men, but cover all people, both male and female. Therefore, although the evidence is not decisive either way, the logical presumption is that both men and women are permitted to be judges. Anyone who wishes to argue otherwise needs to bring explicit and indubitable evidence that women have been excluded from the taking up the role of judge. Such evidence does not exist, and therefore the presumption is they are permitted.

Al-Ardabili's permission for women judges, though, remains a minority opinion. One of the preeminent comprehensive works of *fiqh*, the *Fiqh al-Ṣādiq* of the Iranian cleric Muhammad Sadiq al-Ruhani (b. 1926) runs to forty-one volumes in its most recent edition, and presents itself as a commentary on al-ʿAllama's *Tabṣirat al-Mutaʿallimīn*. As mentioned above, this work is one of the few to neglect to mention that maleness is a condition of being a judge. Ruhani puts this down to a slip, declaring that this definitively (*qaṭʿan*) needs to be discussed. The reason being that there are jurists within the Shīʿa who are arguing that women can be judges. This gives Ruhani the prompt to break out of the *fiqh* genre and embark on an uncharacteristically passionate invective against the deterioration of morals in the Muslim world:

---

[32] al-Sayyid ʿAbd al-Karīm al-Mūsawī al-Ardabīlī, *Fiqh al-Qaḍāʾ*, 2 vols (Qum: Maktabat Amīr al-Muʾminīn, 1987), 1:89.

> However, in these times of ours, women have been given the oversight of public affairs, and been awarded important positions in the judiciary, and as representatives and ministers and the like. They have been made equal with men in all matters, even including divorce and the like. Even more distressing than this are the claims of those in charge of the affairs of those countries that all of this is in line with the assessments of the law, because, Islam decrees that women and men are equal in all societal matters. They think that the veil (*ḥijāb*) is not part of religion, and just as a man is able to look at other men, so it should be permitted for him to look at women – et cetera, et cetera with all the things they say and do. Corruption is thereby brought into society in ways one cannot mention – we ask God to make the Master of His Order (may God hasten His holy appearance) be manifest and protect the Muslims from the hand of their useless intrusions into the minds of the Muslims; and may He save them from the meddling of this Fifth Column, and may He bring about the destruction of anyone who is seduced into these frivolities in the land of the Muslims.[33]

Those who argue for women to be judges are, he says, a Fifth Column for the foreigners (non-Muslims); they are responsible for the degradation or morals in the Muslim world, and Ruhani prays for the speedy return of the Twelfth Imam to restore the proper order of things.

Conclusions

That the argument over the validity of women judges continues is not only a sign of the vibrant tradition of Shīʿī jurisprudence, but also strong feelings the question evokes among some jurists. For Ruhani this is not a matter simply of juristic preference for one view over another. The question has become fundamental to the moral state of the Muslim community.

Nevertheless, there is much in the Shīʿī legal discussions (quite separate from the reports of the Imams' sayings) that indicate that the question of whether or not women have the potential to gain the qualities in order to be a judge is settled early on. The jurists recognised that women have the ability to fulfil all the requirements of being a judge aside from the requirement of maleness. Women can have complete rational faculties and understanding, knowledge sufficient to issue fatwas, and gain the rank of *mujtahida*. If they could not, then there would be no need to name the qualification of 'maleness' (*dhukūra*) alongside reason and knowledge. This is rationalised in purely practical ways – a woman cannot mix with men, and she cannot speak out over them or be raised above them in terms of authority. These are rules taken from elsewhere in the *fiqh* that make women judges an impossibility for many pre-modern writers; but they are not objections

---

[33] Muḥammad Ṣādiq al-Rūḥānī, *Fiqh al-Ṣādiq*, vol. 38 (Qum: al-Ghadīr, 2010), 30. The title ('The Jurisprudence of a Truthful One') could be read as a pun both on his name and the title of Imam Jaʿfar.

to women being judges because of any deficiency in intelligence or ability. In the modern works, the bar on women judges continues (in the main), but is justified in other ways (such as the natural disposition of women to be focused on the family and home).

There is recognition by many in the tradition (Al-Muqaddas al-Ardabili, Mirza Qummi, al-Musawi al-Ardabili, and even al-Muntaziri) that the revelatory evidence is not decisive, and other arguments are triggered when such evidence is unclear. The supposed consensus is undermined and questioned, and any agreement can be viewed having much reduced probative force.

To return to the question of whether there is anything distinctive about the Shīʿī debates here: first, one can say that the debate for much of the medieval period and up to the present day, focuses on Shīʿī revelatory material (reports of the Imams and the consensus of the Imāmī jurists). Inevitably, there are certain specific Shīʿī elements relating to those materials. But there are additional elements that are Shīʿī specific. One relevant issue could be that any judge in Shīʿī jurisprudence is not appointed by the ruler of the times (the Sultan), but in reality is working for the hidden Imam. Just as the Imam appoints his successor from among his male relatives through a process of designation, so only men can be designated as judges. The judge is acting for the Imam, as his representative, and this can only properly be done by someone who shares – even in a lesser manner – his characteristics (knowledge, moral probity, reason and so forth). Characteristics such as legitimate birth and maleness are unchangeable (at least in the presumptions of jurisprudence) in the individual, and therefore create non-negotiable barriers to being appointed. It is not so much about being rational or learned – but about being an appropriate representative for the hidden Imam. This point is never appealed to explicitly, but could (along, of course, with straightforward misogyny and patriarchy) explain the resistance to women judges within the tradition. To demonstrate this more fully would require a more detailed exposition of the sources, but it remains a possible explanation.

The refusal, in works of jurisprudence at least, to countenance the notion that women are deficient and to put forward that as the reason for their inability to act as judges (as one finds more regularly in Sunni works of jurisprudence) also needs some form of explanation. One possibility is that this reflects the importance of women's juridical participation in the Shīʿī tradition. One can think of various examples, particularly the famous Fadak affair (where property of the Prophet was denied to Fatima by Abū Bakr) and Fatima's importance as a legal actor within it. Again, the affair is never the subject of explicit reference in works of jurisprudence (one would not expect it to be, given the generic constraints), but such stories provide precedents that can inform that arguments have life within a tradition, and that are rejected.

The Imāmī Shīʿī discussions over the legitimacy of women judges, particularly from the nineteenth century to the present, share some material with cognate Sunni discussions. Nonetheless, the Shīʿī position on women judges is not so different from their Sunni counterparts. It is not always, then, the conclusions reached that creates the characteristic expression of a tradition, but rather the distinctiveness of the Shīʿī juristic discussions lies in the singular forms of argumentation (emerging as they do from the community's idea of its history) that underpin those conclusions.

CHAPTER

7

HUSNIYYA'S DEBATE AT THE COURT OF HARUN AL-RASHID: SECTARIAN POLEMICS AND FEMALE RELIGIOUS AUTHORITY

Devin J. Stewart

Feminist movements around the world have aimed at the betterment of the lot of women through concerted action, whether political, social, or intellectual, and they exhibit certain regularities and shared features across different cultures, while at the same time drawing on indigenous forms and institutions in idiosyncratic fashions. One of the outstanding regularities, especially in the initial stages of a feminist movement, is the attempt to render women historically visible – to conduct a historical survey, searching out, selecting, gathering, and amassing evidence that women of the past actually played significant roles in political, intellectual, or cultural history, and were not simply anonymous spectators to a drama played out entirely by men. A second and related regularity is the explicit presentation of particular women of the past as models for emulation in order to inspire contemporary women to pursue education and careers, and to become politically and intellectually active.

In an excellent study, Marilyn Booth has highlighted the pivotal role biographical writing played in Egyptian feminism during the late nineteenth century and early twentieth. By presenting exemplary women, Western and Eastern, Muslim and Christian, women writers aimed to provide their peers with models who would inspire them to acquire an education and to become active as teachers and writers. Many of these biographies appeared as short sketches in a newly popular form of publication, the women's magazine, but they also figured in works like *al-Durr al-manthur fi tabaqat rabbat al-khudur* ('Scattered Pearls, on the Generations of the Mistresses of Seclusion'), by Zaynab Fawwaz (1860–1914), a work that Booth analyses perceptively.[1] *Al-Durr al-manthur* fits in and draws on the conventions of a traditional genre

[1] Marilyn Booth, *'May Her Likes Be Multiplied': Biography and Gender Politics in Egypt* (Berkeley: University of California Press, 2001).

of Arabo-Islamic writing, the biographical dictionary, termed either *ṭabaqāt* ('classes' or 'generations') or *tarājim* ('biographical entries'), and shares with other members in the genre the function of highlighting exemplarity. For the gender politics of the time, it was crucial to present young women with models to impress upon them the opportunities they had to change their lives, above all through literacy and education. Exposure to exemplary women of the past, including women from their own region and cultural background, who had become learned, who had written and taught, and who had made their opinions known to the public served to expand the horizons of the possible for contemporary women.

While there are undoubtedly major differences between the context of Egypt in the nineteenth century and the contexts of the pre-modern Islamic world, notably the influence of the colonial powers of Britain and France and exposure to Western European cultural production and feminist discourse, one may ask whether the function of female exemplarity existed before the nineteenth century. The biographical dictionary was a popular genre in the Islamic world, from the ninth century until modern times; the presentation of exemplary lives represented a persistent and central strategy of such works, and many pre-modern biographical dictionaries (but certainly not all) indeed included women, beginning with one of the very first examples of the genre, *al-Tabaqat al-kubra* ('The Major Book of Classes') by Ibn Sa'd (d. 845), which is devoted to the Companions of the Prophet, both male and female. Another outstanding example is *al-Daw' al-lami' li-ahl al-qarn al-tasi'* ('The Shining Light, on the People of the Ninth Century') by Muhammad b. 'Abd al-Rahman al-Sakhawi (d. 1497), which devotes the entire twelfth volume of the twelve-volume work, 168 pages in all, to women's biographies.[2] Who was the intended audience of such works? Did it include women? In what ways were the women presented as examples, and how did the authors suppose that these portrayals would be received? Were males supposed to have their attitudes and practices changed through exposure? Would women be exposed to some of the material through male intermediaries, or would some women be able to gain access directly? Many of these questions are difficult to answer because doing so requires extensive information about the circulation and use of books in the pre-modern Islamic world that is not easily retrieved. In an earlier study analysing women's biographies in the *c.* 1694–1695 work *Riyad al-'ulama' wa-hiyad al-fudala'* ('Gardens of the Scholars and Pools of the Learned') by Mirza 'Abd Allah al-Isfahani (d. 1717–1727), my attention was drawn to the fictional figure of Husniyya, who began as a character in a forged, fictional debate on the topic of Sunni–Shi'i polemics set at the court of the Abbasid Caliph Harun al-Rashid but made her way into the

[2] Ruth Roded, *Women in Islamic Biographical Collections: From Ibn Sa'd to Who's Who* (Boulder: Lynne Rienner, 1994).

Twelver Shi'i biographical tradition.[3] The following remarks attempt to answer some of these questions through an examination of this fascinating text from sixteenth-century Iran that portrays Husniyya as an exemplary learned woman, one who potentially serves as a model for female education.

Husniyya is a prominent figure of female religious authority in the Twelver Shi'i tradition, a slave-girl who supposedly bested in debate the leading Sunni scholars of her day at the court of Caliph Harun al-Rashid (r. 786–809). According to the introduction to the debate, she belonged to an Imami Shi'i merchant but served in the house of the Shi'i Imam Ja'far al-Sadiq (d. 765), acquiring prodigious learning through study under the Imam and his relatives. Several decades after the death of Ja'far al-Sadiq, her master lost his fortune and ended up penniless. Husniyya suggested that he sell her to the Caliph for 100,000 dinars. She instructed her master that, when the Caliph asked why her price was so high, he should reveal the fact that she was so learned that she could defeat the most prominent scholars of the realm in debate. The master did as she instructed, and Harun agreed to arrange the debate. After a suitable delay, the debate was held, and Husniyya won a resounding victory recognised by the Caliph and his Vizier Yahya al-Barmaki (d. 806), vindicating Shi'i doctrinal positions in law and theology against leading Sunni authorities and convincing a large part of the audience of the truth of Shi'ism. As a result, hundreds of scholars converted to Shi'i Islam. The Caliph was so impressed that he paid Husniyya's owner, as a reward, 100,000 dinars, the price he had initially demanded, without, however, purchasing Husniyya. Husniyya was a highly literate and articulate woman, learned enough not merely to be counted among the scholars but actually to surpass her male counterparts. She thus embodied religious authority, based primarily on superior training in theology and law, as well as superior knowledge of the interpretation of the Qur'an, hadith, and the early history of the Islamic community that she had gained through privileged access to the Imam Ja'far al-Sadiq. It was this knowledge that enabled her to prove the veracity of Imami Shi'i doctrine even when faced by a biased and stubbornly oppositional Sunni audience.

Scholarship on Husniyya's Debate to Date

The text of Husniyya's debate, popular in Iran for centuries, first became known in the West when Sir John Malcolm (1769–1833), of the East India Company, included a paraphrase of it in his *History of Persia*, published in

[3] Devin J. Stewart, 'Women's Biographies in Islamic Societies: Mirza 'Abd Allah al-Iṣfahani's *Riyad al-'Ulama*", in *The Rhetoric of Biography: Narrating Lives in Persianate Societies*, ed. Louise Marlowe, *The Rhetoric of Biography: Narrating Lives in Persianate Societies* (Cambridge, MA: Harvard University Press, 2011), 106–139, esp. 131–132.

London in 1815.[4] Having come across the text during his stays in Iran in 1799–1801, 1808, and 1810–1812,[5] he describes the work as 'a small tract, called Hussunneah, by one of their most learned divines', and the most popular anti-Sunni polemical treatise among Shi'ites.[6] Malcolm gives the main character's name as Hussunneah, reading Hasaniyya rather than Husniyya; this is clear from the fact that he renders the common male given name Hasan as Hussun throughout his work. He gives the author's name at one point as Shaikh Abool Futtovah and at another as Shaikh Abool Futtoyah of Rhe.[7] The correct form is Abu al-Futuh al-Razi, a well-known Shi'i scholar of the thirteenth century CE, but the form Malcolm intended to represent is not entirely clear. Later European scholars rendered this as Abu al-Futuwwah.[8] Concerning the provenance of the book, Malcolm reports the following:

> The Persian author of the book says, that when he was returning from Mecca he stopped at Damascus, and obtained from a Syud of Syria the manuscript he has translated. The probability is, that the book was first written in Persian; and it is ascribed to Shaikh Abool Futtoyah of Rhe, a very eminent and zealous Sheah divine.[9]

Malcolm thus doubts the claim that the work was the Persian translation of an Arabic original: it was probably originally composed in Persian. He also seems to find the attribution to Abu al-Futuh al-Razi suspect, and he refers to the man who claims to be the translator as 'the Persian author of the book'.

Already by the turn of the twentieth century, it had been recognised that the story of Husniyya was related to that of the slave-girl Tawaddud in *The 1001 Nights*, and was thus an interesting parallel to the Spanish work *La Doncela Teodor* (The Maiden Teodor), whose connection to the story of Tawaddud had been established decades earlier.[10] (The story of Tawaddud will be summarised below.) As far as I have been able to determine, the first Western investigator to notice the connection between Husniyya and

---

[4] Sir John Malcolm, *History of Persia, from the Most Early Period to the Present Time: Containing an Account of the Religion, Government, Usages, and Character of the Inhabitants of that Kingdom*, 2 vols (London: John Murray and Longman and Co., 1815), 2:253–262.

[5] On Malcolm, see John William Kaye, *The Life and Correspondence of Major-General Sir John Malcolm, K.C.B.*, 2 vols (London: Smith and Elder, 1856); A. K. S. Lambton, 'Major-General Sir John Malcolm (1769–1833) and *The History of Persia*', *Iran* 33 (1995), 97–109.

[6] Sir John Malcolm, *History of Persia*, 2:253.

[7] Sir John Malcolm, *History of Persia*, 2:253 n. y., 262.

[8] Josef Horovitz, 'Die Entstehung von *Tausendundeine Nacht*', *The Review of Nations* 4 (April 1927), 104.

[9] Sir John Malcolm, *History of Persia*, 2:261–262.

[10] Victor Chauvin, *Bibliographie des ouvrages arabes ou relatifs aux arabes publiés dans l'Europe chrétienne de 1810 à 1885*, vol. 7 (Liège: H. Vaillant-Carmanne, 1903), 117–119. For more on the Spanish adaptation, see Isidro J. Rivera and Donna M. Rogers, *Historia de la Donzella Teodor: Edition and Study* (New York: Global Publications, 2000).

Tawaddud was the Belgian Orientalist Victor Chauvin (1844–1913). In 1899, he published a short piece on Tawaddud in which he stated that a version of *The 1001 Nights* story had appeared in Sir John Malcolm's *History of Persia*, which he had read in the French translation. The frame of the Persian story told by Malcolm, he explained, clearly derived from the story of Tawaddud, but the focus of the debate was quite different and entailed the heroine proving the superiority of the Shi'i sect. Chauvin did not name the heroine of the Persian story in his short description.[11] In 1903, Chauvin mentioned the French translation of Malcolm's *History of Persia* in the entry on Tawaddud in his bibliography of European scholarship on *The 1001 Nights*, also on the grounds that, like the *Doncela Teodor*, the account of Hasaniyyah (*sic*) was based on that of Tawaddud.[12] In 1927, Josef Horovitz described the story of Hasaniyyah (*sic*) as a reworked, Shi'i version of the Tawaddud story.[13] In 1937, Albert Wesselski wrote a substantial article on the three accounts, arguing that all derived from Byzantine models, picking up on a comment by Horovitz that pointed to a story translated from Greek about 'The Philosopher and the Slave Girl Qitar', which Ibn al-Nadim (d. 380/990) had mentioned in the *Fihrist*.[14] Chauvin had already pointed out that the story of Tawaddud was parallel and perhaps related to that of Saint Catherine of Alexandria, who, according to legend, had emerged victorious from a debate with fifty scholars at the court of the Emperor Maximian (286–305 CE) or Maxentius (306–312 CE). He suggests that both the Tawaddud story and the text of Husniyya may derive from them through an earlier Shi'i polemical text.[15]

Later in the twentieth century, Iranian scholars became aware of the connection of the story of Husniyya with that of Tawaddud in *The 1001 Nights*. Yusuf Ünal has pointed out that the Ottoman author Ahmet Feyzi (1839–1909) already mentioned the Tawaddud story in his Turkish refutation of the *Husniyya* debate, *Fayḍ-i rabbānī*, which he completed during the reign of

---

[11] Victor Chauvin, *Tawaddoude ou la docte esclave* (Liège: Charles Gothier, 1899), esp. 3. This short piece of three pages was published as a separate pamphlet, but it was also published in the journal *Le Mouvement* in the same year.

[12] Chauvin, *Bibliographie des ouvrages arabes*, 7:118, writes, 'Malcolm, Histoire de la Perse, 1821, 4, 70–85,' which corresponds to the story of Hasaniya (Husniyya) in the fourth volume of the French translation.

[13] Josef Horovitz, 'Die Entstehung von *Tausendundeine Nacht*', *The Review of Nations* 4 (April 1927), 85–111. He comments on the story of Tawaddud on pp. 103–104 and mentions the story of Husniyya on p. 104; Horovitz, 'The Origin of the Arabian Nights', *Islamic Culture* 1 (1927), 36–57, esp. 52. [This is essentially an English translation of the German article above.] The story of Husniyya is not mentioned in Horovitz's other publications. Horovitz, 'Tawaddud', *Zeitschrift der Deutschen Morgenländischen Gesellschaft* 57 (1903), 173–174; Horovitz, 'Tawaddud', *EI*[1], vol. 8 (Leiden: Brill, 1936), 702.

[14] Albert Wesselski, 'Die gelehrten Sklavinnen des Islams und ihre Byzantinischen Vorbilder', *Archiv orientalni* 9 (1937), 353–378, esp. 358–362; Horovitz, 'Entstehung', 103.

[15] He also suggests a possible connection with the legend of the female philosopher, Hypatia of Alexandria (*c.* 370–415 CE). Chauvin, *Tawaddoude ou la docte esclave*, 2.

Sultan Abdul Hamid II (r. 1876–1909). He did not state directly that the story of Husniyya was adapted from that of Tawaddud, but he juxtaposed the two texts, arguing that the Shi'i debate was an obvious forgery, while the other text was authentic and showed the superior learning of Sunnis.[16] Iranian scholars had access to the complete original text of Husniyya's debate, and not just the summary of Sir John Malcolm, and they were also able to consult the biographical dictionary *Riyad al-'ulama' wa-hiyad al-fudala'* of Mirza 'Abd Allah al-Isfahani, which will be discussed below. They thus referred properly to Husniyya – al-Isfahani gives the vowelling explicitly in *Riyad al-'ulama'* – and to Abu al-Futuh, and they were aware that Abu al-Futuh was the famous twelfth-century Shi'i commentator on the Qur'an Abu al-Futuh al-Razi. Moreover, they were able to identify the text as a forgery from sixteenth-century Safavid Iran.

In 1960, Muḥammad Taqī Dānishpazhūh pointed out the connection to the story of Tawaddud in his description of manuscripts of Husniyya's debate in the collection of Tehran University.[17] 'Alī Riḍā Dhakāwatī Qaragözlü wrote a piece on *Dāstān-i Ḥusniyya* ('The Tale of Husniyya') in his collection of short essays on scores of works in literature and the Islamic religious sciences, published in 1961.[18] In this essay, he states directly that the author of the work was Ibrāhīm b. Walī Astarābādī (fl. 16th c.), who lived during the reign of Shah Tahmasb and claimed to have translated Husniyya's debate into Persian from an Arabic text by Abu al-Futuh al-Razi.[19] Qaragözlü points out that the popularity of the text was based in part on the style, which was simple and more authentically Persian than many translations of religious texts during the Safavid period, which were so heavily Arabic in word order and sentence structure as to be barely recognisable as Persian.[20] He also connects Husniyya's debate with *Risāla-yi Yūḥannā*, another forged Shi'i, anti-Sunni polemical text also attributed to Abu al-Futuh al-Razi, in which a Christian investigates the Islam sects and finds Twelver Shi'ism superior to Sunni Islam. In his view, the attribution of both to Abu al-Futuh al-Razi should be rejected.[21] He discusses the debt of Husniyya's debate to the story of Tawaddud and the similarity of the frame in general, despite the differences in detail.[22] The topics of debate, a wide spectrum of sciences in the case of Tawaddud, were reduced to the religious sciences alone in the account of Husniyya, reflecting in his assessment a cultural difference between the

---

[16] Ünal, *More than Mere Polemic*, 125–126.

[17] Muhammad Taqi Danishpazhuh, *'Fihrist-i nuskha-a-yi khaṭṭi-yi kitabkhana-i danishkada-i adabiyyat'*, *Majalla-i Danishkada-i adabiyyat-i Tihran* 1 (1960), 3–526, esp. 208–210.

[18] 'Ali Rida Dhakawati Qaragözlü, *Majara dar majara: sayr-i 'aql va-naql dar panzdah qarn-i hijri* (Tehrān: Intisharat-i Haqiqat, 1961), 443–455.

[19] Dhakawati Qaragözlü, *Majara dar majara*, 444–445.

[20] Dhakawati Qaragözlü, *Majara dar majara*, 445.

[21] Dhakawati Qaragözlü, *Majara dar majara*, 446.

[22] Dhakawati Qaragözlü, *Majara dar majara*, 447–453.

time of the Caliph Harun al-Rashid and that of Shah Tahmasb.[23] Qaragözlü points out that in both texts Harun is a fictional character and does not correspond to the actual, historical Harun. He asks how Harun could have shown favour to Shiʿis, when the seventh Imam, Musa al-Kazim, died in the caliph's prison, and he quotes the Shiʿi poet Diʿbil b. ʿAlī al-Khuzāʿī (d. 246/860–861), who commented on the irony that the town of Ṭūs is the site of both the grave of the worst of men, the Abbasid caliph Harun, and that of the best of men, the eighth Shiʿi Imam, ʿAlī al-Riḍā.[24]

Margaret R. Parker mentions the debate of Husniyya briefly in the course of her 1996 work on the Spanish *Doncella Teodor*. She calls attention to the fact that the story of Husniyya is clearly related to the Tawaddud story, along with the Spanish Doncella Teodor, a Brazilian Portuguese version of the latter, and Maya versions of the story in several of the prophetic books termed *Chilam Balaam*. Drawing on the article of Wesselski, she proposes that the chronology of versions of the story might be Qīṭār, Catherine of Alexandria, Husniyya, Tūdūr (the Arabic version found in Spain), Tawaddud, and then Doncella Teodor.[25]

Three recent studies have addressed the debate of Husniyya as a polemical text. Murat Han Aksoy's 2010 master's thesis stressed the role of Husniyya's debate in setting a lasting, popular frame for Shiʿi–Sunni polemics.[26] The most comprehensive discussion of the debate of Husniyya to date is the 2016 master's thesis of Yusuf Ünal, which analyses the text as a product of polemical discourses in sixteenth-century Iran. Refuting the view of Parker, he argues that the text of Husniyya's debate was certainly posterior to the story of Tawaddud, for it was authored in the sixteenth century and falsely attributed to the sixth-/twelfth-century scholar Abu al-Futuh al-Razi. In addition to examining the polemical content of the debate, he discusses the adaptation of the story of Husniyya from the story of Tawaddud in *The 1001 Nights* in some detail. He also shows that Husniyya acquired a biography in Twelver Shiʿi works beginning in the late seventeenth century and even a physical existence in the form of a shrine in northeastern Iran. Finally, the thesis examines subsequent polemical literature surrounding the text in nineteenth- and twentieth-century Iran, Ottoman Anatolia, and India, showing that the debate of Husniyya played a central role in

---

[23] Dhakawati Qaragözlü, *Majara dar majara*, 449–450. It should be recognised that the original story of Tawaddud could not have been written during the time of Harun al-Rashid, but must have been written several centuries later, and so cannot reflect the cultural scene of that period directly.

[24] Dhakawati Qaragözlü, *Majara dar majara*, 451–452.

[25] Margaret R. Parker, *The Story of a Story across Cultures: The Case of the Doncella Teodor* (London: Tamesis, 1996), 17–18. Parker mischaracterises Wesselski's statement slightly. He does not state that Husniyya is necessarily earlier than Tawaddud, but that both Tawaddud and Husniyya derive from a Shiʿi polemical text that resembles Husniyya's debate.

[26] Murat Han Aksoy, *Şii paradigmanın oluşum sürecinde Hüsniye'nin yeri ve önemi* (Husniyya's Place and Importance in the Process of Formation of the Shiʿite Paradigm), Master's Thesis, Çukurova Üniversitesi, 2010.

establishing the parameters of sectarian debate and confessional identity in these societies.[27]

In 2017, Rosemary Stanfield-Johnson published a substantial study on the text of Husniyya's debate, 'From *One Thousand Nights* to Safavid Iran: A Persian *Tawaddud*'. In it, she examines the textual and ideological relationship between Husniyya's story and that of Tawaddud in *The 1001 Nights* as well as the appearance of Husniyya in Shi'i biographical dictionaries. She also discusses the textual history of the work from the sixteenth to the nineteenth century on the basis of manuscripts from the Salar Jung Library in Hyderabad, the Shāhchirāgh Library in Shiraz, and the British Museum in London. She concludes, tentatively, that the text came into being at some point between 958/1551 and 1070/1655 and that later writers added an introduction describing the translator's access to the original Arabic text and dedicating the work to Shah Tahmasb. In her view, Muhammad Baqir al-Majlisi may have added the introduction or played some role in shaping the text as it is preserved in later manuscripts.[28]

Scholars to date have thus correctly identified the story of Tawaddud from *The 1001 Nights* as the model for the Shi'i polemical debate of Husniyya, and they have brought out many important aspects of the transformation of the one story into the other. In the present study, I intend to focus on the text's portrayal of Husniyya as a female figure of Shi'i religious authority, and, while I agree on the whole with many of the interpretations of these earlier studies, I revise a number of points they have made and add points of detail.

Comparison with the Story of the Slave-girl Tawaddud in *The 1001 Nights*

The debate of Husniyya is a clever adaptation of a story from *The 1001 Nights*, as Chauvin pointed out in 1899 and as 'Alī Riḍā Dhakāwatī Qaragözlü, Yusuf Ünal, and Rosemary Stanfield-Johnson have explained in greater detail.[29] The story in *The 1001 Nights*, which occurs from night 437 until 462 and is called by Richard F. Burton 'The Tale of Abu al-Husn and his Slave-Girl', is quite similar to the account of Husniyya's debate in general outline. A man squanders the wealth he has inherited from his father through dissolute living and becomes destitute. In order to remedy the situation, his slave-girl Tawaddud, whom he has inherited from his father, suggests that he offer her for sale to the Caliph Harun al-Rashid

[27] Yusuf Ünal, *More than Mere Polemic: The Adventure of the Risālah-i Ḥusniyah in the Safavid, Ottoman and Indian Lands*, Master's Thesis, Boğaziçi University, 2016.

[28] Rosemary Stanfield-Johnson, 'From *One Thousand and One Nights* to Safavid Iran: A Persian Tawaddud', *Der Islam* 94.1 (2017), 158–191.

[29] Wesselski, 'Die gelehrten Sklavinnen des Islams und ihre Byzantinischen Vorbilder', 358–362; Ünal, *More than Mere Polemic*, 37–45.

for 10,000 dinars. When he does so, the Caliph asks why he is demanding such a high price. Tawaddud's master informs him that it is on account of her prodigious learning, which is so impressive that she excels the leading scholars of the age. Following her suggestion, a debate is arranged. Tawaddud ends up besting her many opponents, scholars in law, the Qur'an astronomy, medicine, music, and even chess and backgammon, taking the robes of each scholar she defeats as a prize. At the end, she has earned the respect and praise of the Caliph. He pays 100,000 dinars for Tawaddud, but when he allows her to make any request of him that she desires, she asks to be returned to her master. Harun complies with her request, and in addition gives her a prize of 5,000 dinars, grants her master a 1,000-dinar monthly stipend, and makes him one of his boon companions.[30]

Scholars have disagreed over the place and date of the origin of Tawaddud. Enno Littmann expressed the view that the story must have originated in Baghdad – apparently because of the setting – at a time when the figure of al-Nazzam, who appears as Tawaddud's principal opponent in the debate, was still remembered. Littmann suggests that the story must have been reworked in Egypt on account of its mention of Coptic months, but he does not set a date.[31] André Miquel estimates that the story was composed in Iraq by the end of the twelfth century CE. He views the setting as entirely Iraqi and argues against an Egyptian origin on the grounds that the Coptic months were well known outside of Egypt. He calls attention to two pieces of evidence: that the backgammon player, after losing, goes off muttering in 'Frankish' (*ifranjiyya*), which suggests a date after the establishment of the Crusader states of Outremer at the very end of the eleventh century, and the mention of cotton cultivation, which dates to the late twelfth century. He explains that the author may have 'tipped his hat' to Egypt because of Saladin's leading role in the anti-Crusade.[32] My own view is that the story was composed in Egypt roughly in the thirteenth century. The Iraqi elements may be due either to an effort to imitate other stories of *The 1001 Nights*, or to the influence of a yet earlier account that has been adapted. The story's lack of reference to al-Nazzam's adherence to Mu'tazili theology, or to Mu'tazilism at all, suggests to me a late and non-Iraqi origin. The fact that the Coptic months of Kiyahk, Barmudah, Misra, Hatur, and Amshir appear in the debate over astronomy indeed suggests that the story was composed in Egypt.[33] Miquel's counter-argument is not convincing, and other aspects

[30] *The Book of the Thousand Nights and a Night, A Plain and Literal Translation of the Arabian Nights Entertainments*, translated and annotated by Richard F. Burton (New York: The Heritage Press, 1934), 1,772–1,821.

[31] Enno Littmann, *Die Erzählungen aus den Tausendundein Nächten*, 6 vols (Frankfurt am Main: Insel-Verlag, 1966), 6:726–727.

[32] André Miquel, *Sept contes des Mille et Une Nuits* (Paris: Sindbad, 1981), 35–36.

[33] *The 1001 Nights*, Burton translation, 1,809.

of the text also point to Egypt. Tawaddud, in the course of a discussion of the almanac and astrological predictions, refers to preservation of the populace of Egypt and Syria from the depredations of the Sultan.[34] This statement suggests that Syria and Egypt are both under the rule of a single sultan, and that Syria, mentioned second, is subordinate to Egypt. The compiler writes from the viewpoint of an Egyptian. During the Fatimid (969–1171) and the Ayyubid (1171–1250) periods, the titles most often used would have been caliph and king, suggesting an origin in the Mamluk period (1250–1517). In addition, the story suggests that the most prominent Islamic legal school is the Shafi'i, because Tawaddud mentions the authority of al-Shafi'i with regard to the correct manner of performing ablutions and the prayer for the two Festival days.[35] The dominance of the Shafi'i *madhhab* was not established in Egypt until after the fall of the Fatimids and the advent of Ayyubid rule in 1171. The portrayal of the 'Frankish' character of the backgammon player also fits better in Egypt, which witnessed direct and intense contact with the Franks, than in Iraq. I therefore conclude that the story of Tawaddud was composed in Egypt and estimate that its composition took place at about the thirteenth century.

The elements that are the same in the two stories are the following. The master is induced to sell the slave-girl, at her suggestion, because he has lost his wealth. The slave-girl is extremely learned and clever. The slave-girl is sold to the Caliph Harun al-Rashid, and her price is 100,000 dinars.[36] The debate occurs at Harun al-Rashid's court. Both accounts feature, in addition to the Caliph, his famous Vizier Yahya b. Khalid al-Barmaki (d. 806). Both accounts mention the presence at the debate of the leading scholars of Baghdad at the time. Both accounts stress the presence of a peculiar prop: a golden seat or stool. The leader of the opposing group of scholars is a prominent scholar named Ibrahim, who is summoned from Basra. These last two details in particular are striking. If one were to fabricate, in the sixteenth century, the record of a polemical debate that took place in front of Harun al-Rashid, one would not likely portray one of the main parties in the debate as arriving from Basra. After all, Baghdad was viewed not only as the political capital but also as the intellectual capital of the Islamic world. The fact

---

[34] *The 1001 Nights*, Burton translation, 1,810.

[35] *The 1001 Nights*, Burton translation, 1,781, 1,783.

[36] There is a discrepancy regarding the price of the slave-girl in the text of the Tawaddud story. She tells her master to set her price initially at 10,000 dinars (p. 1,775), but, at the end, Harun al-Rashid pays 100,000 dinars as her price (p. 1,821). It is possible that one or the other figure is a copyist's error, but perhaps the discrepancy is intended, since it shows that Harun meant to pay ten times Tawaddud's asking price. Stanfield-Johnson reports that whereas Tawaddud's price is 10,000 dinars, Husniyya's price is 100,000 dinars; the difference may be meant to signal Husniyya's superior merit. Stanfield-Johnson, 'A Persian Tawaddud', 189. This is probably not intended; the value of 100,000 dinars in the tale of Husniyya derived directly from the story of Tawaddud.

that the name is Ibrahim in both cases makes it even more unlikely that the similarities could be the result of coincidence.

There are a number of differences between the two stories that reflect the ways in which the story has been adapted in order to render it a Shi'i, anti-Sunni polemic. The name of the slave-girl, the main protagonist of the account, was changed, perhaps because *Tawaddud* 'Affection' sounded too light-hearted, or too reminiscent of seductive singing and performing slave-girls for a religious polemic. It is possible that the forger's choice of the name *Ḥusniyya* was influenced by the name *Abū al-Ḥusn* in the original story of Tawaddud. Alternatively, her name might be a portmanteau word of sorts based on *ḥusn al-niyya* 'good intentions'. The choice of name may also have been influenced by a number of cognate terms that occur in the text. Beauty (*ḥusn*) is emphasised immediately when she is introduced: 'She was also unparalleled in beauty (*ḥusn*) and loveliness, and her name was *Ḥusniyya*.'[37] Another connection is with excellence or the ability to gain approval, because at several points in the debate, the text reports that the audience applauded Husniyya's presentation and 'found her excellent' (*taḥsīn-i Ḥusniyya mīkardand, taḥsīn-i vey nemūd, Ḥusniyya-rā . . . taḥsīn nemūdand*).[38]

In the Husniyya debate, her Shi'i owner is not named, whereas Abu al-Husn appears prominently in the story of Tawaddud as the name of the original master's son, who became her master upon his father's death. The original, anonymous master in the story of Tawaddud and the sole master in the story of Husniyya are both merchants. In the Tawaddud story, she becomes the property of her owner's son, and the original master did not lose his wealth. Instead, the son squandered the wealth he had inherited from his father, a typical occurrence in *The 1001 Nights*. The story of Husniyya features neither son nor inheritance, and the cause of the master's near bankruptcy is not explained in detail.[39]

Tawaddud debates her opponents on many topics, meant to represent all the sciences and also some other skills. Ibrahim b. Sayyar al-Nazzam, the famous Mu'tazili theologian, acts as the leader of the scholars, and he brings along with him a retinue of scholars who are experts in many fields. Tawaddud meets nine opponents who are specialists, only one of whom is named: the first a jurist (pp. 1,777–1,789), the second an expert on the Qur'an (pp. 1,789–1,797), the third a physician (pp. 1,797–1,805), the fourth an astronomer (pp. 1,805–1,811), the fifth a philosopher (pp. 1,811–1,813), the sixth a theologian (pp. 1,813–1,818), the seventh a chess-player (pp. 1,818–1,820), the eighth a backgammon player (p. 1,820), and the ninth a musician who plays the lute and sings (p. 1,820). The sixth scholar, the theologian (*mutakallim*), is Ibrahim b. Sayyar, who is able to discourse on all arts and sciences (p. 1,813);

[37] Abu al-Futuh al-Razi, *Mukalama-yi Husniyya*, ed. Muhammad Rida Zad-hush (Abadan, Iran: Porsesh, 2010), 23.
[38] *Mukalama-yi Husniyya*, 60, 142, 162.
[39] Ünal, *More than Mere Polemic*, 42.

his appearance is the climax of the battle of wits, for he is supposed to be superior in intelligence to all the others.

In Husniyya's case, only three opponents are described, and she debates her opponents only on topics that are related in some fashion to Islamic religious doctrine and Sunni–Shi'i polemics. The leading scholar, who debates her last, is named Ibrahim b. Khalid. The other figures are the prominent Hanafi jurist, Abu Yusuf (d. 798), and the eponymous founder of the Shafi'i legal school, Muhammad b. Idris al-Shafi'i (d. 820).[40] While the story of Tawaddud shows that a woman could best the leading scholars in all fields, the debate of Husniyya proves the superiority of Shi'i Islam. The expert knowledge of Husniyya is associated primarily with that of the Imam Ja'far al-Sadiq, and, to a lesser extent, with unnamed sons or descendants of the Imam and other scholars in his entourage.[41] Her learning is also limited, for the most part, to the fields of the religious sciences.[42] In contrast, *The 1001 Nights'* text does not reveal the source of Tawaddud's extensive and profound learning or the means by which she acquired it. Tawaddud takes the robes of each scholar she defeats in debate to mark her victory, while Husniyya does not.

The leader of the scholars in the story of Tawaddud is the famous Mu'tazili theologian al-Nazzam (d. 835–845). He is introduced as Ibrahim b. Sayyar al-Nazzam explicitly, when Harun al-Rashid summons him from Basra, and it is widely known that al-Nazzam was born and resided in Basra, the first centre of Mu'tazili learning.[43] Burton gives his name as 'Ibrahim bin Siyyár the prosodist' (p. 1,777) – apparently interpreting *al-Naẓẓām* as a reference to *naẓm* 'poetry' when it refers instead to the craft by which he earned a living in his youth, fashioning amulets that were threaded on a string (*niẓām*). *The 1001 Nights* text does not explain that al-Nazzam was a Mu'tazili theologian, identifying him instead as a philosopher and theologian (*mutakallim*), but Burton renders the latter designation 'rhetorician', on account of the association of the term with its cognate, *kalām* 'speech'. Al-Nazzam is evidently supposed to represent the pinnacle of erudition in the sciences; he is the most intelligent scholar with the broadest accomplishments. He was probably chosen for this role in the narrative because of his reputation for brilliance, and perhaps because it would not have been seemly to show the embarrassment of some other revered figure of Sunni tradition. The forensic skill of al-Nazzam in addition to his other learning is confirmed by historical sources. He was acclaimed for having debated the adherents of various religions and doctrines, including the Christian Job of Edessa (Ayyub al-Ruhawi), the Jew

[40] Ünal, *More than Mere Polemic*, 43.
[41] Ünal, *More than Mere Polemic*, 43.
[42] Ünal, *More than Mere Polemic*, 44.
[43] Stanfield-Johnson refers to him as the *qāḍī* of Baghdad. Perhaps this results from a confusion with the Hanafi jurist Abu Yusuf, who was the judge of Baghdad. Stanfield-Johnson, 'A Persian Tawaddud', 162.

Manassah b. Salih, dualists, and proponents of the eternity of the world (*dahriyya*). It was also widely known that he had come to the Abbasid court in Baghdad during the period in which Tawaddud's story is set. He is supposed to have refuted Aristotle in the presence of Ja'far b. Yahya al-Barmaki (d. 803) during the reign of Harun al-Rashid, and he visited the court of al-Ma'mun after 819 CE.[44] The anonymous author of the story of Tawaddud therefore seems to have selected al-Nazzam as a major character in part because of his particular historical accomplishments, but he elides al-Nazzam's adherence to Mu'tazili theology, something that suggests that the text was written at a point after the eleventh century, when Mu'tazili theology had been marginalised and to a certain extent forgotten.

In Husniyya's debate, the name of the foremost opponent has been changed from Ibrahim b. Sayyar to Ibrahim b. Khalid.[45] His entrance into the story is a bit different. He is not summoned immediately from Basra by Harun al-Rashid, as is al-Nazzam in the Tawaddud story, along with a large entourage of other scholars. Rather, he is summoned only when the scholars in Baghdad, represented by Abu Yusuf and al-Shafi'i, prove ineffective in debate against Husniyya, and Harun angrily intervenes. Ibrahim b. Khalid is identified in addition in some passages of the text as *al-'Awnī* or *al-'Awfī*. Murat Han Aksoy calls him 'an imaginary figure'.[46] The Ottoman author Ishak Efendi (d. 1892) states, 'Since a scholar and jurist with a name that resembles Ibrahim b. Khalid from the region of Basra is not to be found in any history or book, no doubt or error remains that the above-mentioned name, appearing as it does among boldfaced lies, came into being out of imaginary fantasies.'[47] Yusuf Ünal argues that the point behind the change in name is to stress the scholar's Sunni – as opposed to Mu'tazili – identity.[48] In the account of Husniyya's debate, this scholar is supposed to represent a hardened, obstinate *nāṣibī*, a fervent anti-Shi'i and enemy of the Prophet's family and of the Shi'is.

However, the transformation of this character was not carried out consistently, because later on in the account his name is given as Ibrahim Nazzam.[49] Dhakawati Qaragözlü noted the oddity that the name of the main opponent in Husniyya's debate appears sometimes as Ibrahim Nazzam and sometimes as Ibrahim b. Khalid 'Awni, but a number of scholars seem to have overlooked the latter name and focused exclusively on al-Nazzam.[50] Sir John Malcolm renders it in one passage as 'Ibrahim Nizam of Bussorah'.[51] In

---

[44] Josef Van Ess, 'Abu Esḥaq Nazzam', *Encyclopaedia Iranica* 1, 275–280.
[45] Ünal, *More than Mere Polemic*, 43–44.
[46] Murat Han Aksoy, *Şii Paradigmanın Oluşum Sürecinde "Hüsniye'nin Yeri Önemi*, 9.
[47] Harputlu İshak Efendi, *Tezkiye-i Ehl-i Beyt* (Istanbul: İstanbul Üniversitesi Nadir Eserler Kütüphanesi, 1878) (Manuscript No. T 2182), 4b.
[48] Ünal, *More than Mere Polemic*, 43–44.
[49] *Mukalama-yi Husniyya*, 84.
[50] Dhakawati Qaragözlü, *Majara dar majara*, 450.
[51] Sir John Malcolm, *History of Persia*, 2:255, 256, 261.

a biographical entry devoted to al-Nazzam in *Rawdat al-jannat*, the Twelver Shi'i biographer Muhammad Baqir al-Khwansari (d. 1895) tells of the role that al-Nazzam played as the chief opponent in the story of Husniyya.[52] Agha Buzurg al-Tihrani reports that in the text Husniyya was supposed to be debating the famous theologian al-Nazzam.[53] The appearance of the name Nazzam in Husniyya's debate leaves no doubt that the text is actually based on the story of Tawaddud, but it creates some questions regarding the intentions of the author of Husniyya's debate regarding this character. It is possible that the historical theologian al-Nazzam actually debated Shi'i scholars of his time: the text of a disputation between al-Nazzam and al-Hisham b. al-Hakam about eternal residence in paradise has been transmitted by al-Shaykh al-Tusi (d. 1067).[54]

Al-Shāfi'ī's name is mentioned in both debates, but he is one of the main questioners in Husniyya's debate, while he is only cited in passing as an authority in Tawaddud's account. Tawaddud mentions his views regarding ablutions and the technicalities of daily prayer, which suggests that she herself follows the Shafi'i legal school.[55] The character of Abu Yusuf appears only in the story of Husniyya and has no counterpart in the Tawaddud story.

The story of Husniyya features an important supporting character who has no counterpart in the story of Tawaddud. Harun al-Rashid, the text states, has a cousin (*ibn 'amm*) who is himself a Shi'i, or is at least sympathetic to Shi'is. His attraction to Shi'ism is described as an open secret, but Harun loves this particular cousin so much that he cannot refuse him anything. The name of the cousin is given as Khalid b. 'Isa. (This character will be discussed below.) No such character appears in the story of Tawaddud.

Another point of difference has to do with the golden seat that figures in the debate. In *The 1001 Nights*, the Caliph has Tawaddud sit on a golden seat during the debate as a mark of his consideration for her, having been swayed by her great beauty and elegance, while in the story of Husniyya's debate, Ibrahim b. Khalid sits on the golden seat, which serves as a symbol of his arrogance and false pride. Husniyya sits on the floor, opposite her opponent, exhibiting pious and proper humility.

In *The 1001 Nights* version, Tawaddud praises the Companions of the Prophet, while Husniyya explains their negative characteristics and moral failings and ends up cursing them explicitly.[56] When she does so, only the intercession of the Caliph and his Vizier Yahya al-Barmaki prevents the

---

[52] Muhammad Baqir al-Khwansari, *Rawdat al-Jannat fi ahwal al-'ulama' wa'l-sadat*, 8 vols (Qum: Isma'iliyan, 1970–1971), 1:151–153.

[53] Agha Buzurg al-Tihrani, *Tabaqat A'lam al-Shi'a*, vol. 7: *Ihya' al-dathir min al-qarn al-'ashir* (Beirut: Dar Ihya' al-Turath al-'Arabi, 2009), 2.

[54] 'Abd Allah al-Hasan, *al-Munazarat fi al-'aqa'id wa'l-ahkam*, 2 vols (Qum: Sharikat al-Mustafa li-Ihya' al-Turath, 2007), 1:99–101.

[55] *The Book of the Thousand Nights and a Night*, 1,779, 1,783.

[56] Ünal, *More than Mere Polemic*, 44.

audience from doing violence to her. There are no such attacks in the story of Tawaddud. It is she, rather, who shows some initial aggression, by insisting that her opponents doff their robes when they lose. In the course of Husniyya's debate, 400 Sunni scholars, members of the audience, are convinced of the truth of Shi'i Islam and convert. There is no such conversion in the course of Tawaddud's debate.[57]

One crucial overlap between the two texts is a question from the opposing scholar both to Tawaddud and to Husniyya about the relative merits of 'Alī – the cousin, son-in-law, and rightful heir of the Prophet according to the Shi'is – and al-'Abbās, the uncle of the Prophet and the forefather of the Abbasid Caliphs.[58] In both cases, the opponent is attempting to get her into trouble with the Caliph, for if she expresses preference for 'Alī, then she will be implying that the Abbasid Caliphs do not have a legitimate claim to the Caliphate, directly insulting the patron of the debate. In this scene in the story of Tawaddud, al-Nazzam asks,

> 'Tell me which is more excellent, Ali or Abbas?' Now she knew that, in propounding this question, Ibrahim was laying a trap for her, for if she said, 'Ali is more excellent than Abbas,' she would lack excuse with the Caliph for undervaluing his ancestors, so she bowed her head a while, now reddening, then paling, and lastly said, 'Thou asked me of two excellent men, each having his own excellence . . .' When the Caliph Harun al-Rashid heard her, he stood up and said, 'Thou hast spoken well, by the Lord of the Ka'abah, O Tawaddud!'[59]

It is perhaps this question in the Tawaddud account, which is directly related to Shi'i claims concerning the right of 'Alī to lead the Muslim community, that inspired the author of Husniyya's debate to write the Shi'i polemical version of the Tawaddud's story. Chauvin remarked as much already in 1899: '*Ce qui a pu donner à l'auteur persan l'idée de faire de Tawaddoude le champion des chiites, c'est un passage du conte des Mille et une nuits, où la jeune fille (qui est du rite orthodoxe chaféite), affirme qu'Ali et Abbas ont, chacun, leurs mérites.*'[60] Wesselski also discusses this shared element of the two debates, and it forms the focus of Stanfield-Johnson's discussion of the two debates' ideological messages.[61]

On the basis of this question, Albert Wesselski argues that Tawaddud was a Shi'i and that her tactful answer to this question was a performance of *taqiyya*, or dissimulation. According to him, her references to Shafi'i legal opinions adopted a typical form of Shi'i dissimulation, since Shi'is often

---

[57] Ünal, *More than Mere Polemic*, 45.

[58] *Mukalama-yi Husniyya*, 39.

[59] *The Book of the Thousand Nights and a Night*, 1,817.

[60] Chauvin, 'Tawaddoude ou la docte esclave', 3.

[61] Wesselski, 'Die gelehrten Sklavinnen', 361; Stanfield-Johnson, 'A Persian Tawaddud', 164–165, 182–189.

claim adherence to the Shafi ʻi legal school when trying to pass as Sunni Muslims.[62] He even suggested that the story of Tawaddud was based on an earlier Shiʻi polemic, perhaps not the Husniyya debate itself, but a text that was similar in ideological content and a precursor of Husniyya's debate.[63] This is reading too much into the text in addition to getting the historical relationship wrong. Stanfield-Johnson correctly stresses Tawaddud's Sunnism.[64] Just prior to this question, Tawaddud presents a common Sunni view regarding the conversions of Abu Bakr and ʻAli to Islam: she argues that the first male convert was actually Abu Bakr. Even though ʻAli adopted Islam very early on, his conversion does not give him precedence because he was still a boy, and Abu Bakr was the first adult male Muslim. This is actually an explicit rejection of the Shiʻi interpretation, which stresses ʻAli's overall precedence and superiority to Abu Bakr.[65] The Tawaddud story must be the earlier of the two, and it does not derive from an anti-Sunni polemic.

Tawaddud follows the Shafiʻi legal school and is not a Shiʻi. One does not have to be a Shiʻi to believe that ʻAli b. Abi Talib was superior to the Abbasid caliphs' ancestor, al-ʻAbbas, since the standard Sunni doctrine became that the best of men, after the Prophet, were the Rightly-Guided caliphs Abu Bakr (632–634), ʻUmar b. al-Khattab (634–644), ʻUthman b. ʻAffan (644–656), and ʻAli b. Abi Talib (656–661), in that order. All other Companions of the Prophet were considered inferior to them, so Tawaddud, even as a Sunni, would have had to state that al-ʻAbbas was inferior to ʻAli if she were forced to answer explicitly.

While Stanfield-Johnson correctly rejects the suggestion that Tawaddud was a Shiʻi, she proposes the unlikely view that the shared ideological element of the two stories is a critique of Muʻtazili doctrine.[66] As pointed out above, it is not even clear that Husniyya's main opponent is identical with al-Nazzam, and Husniyya's debate actually refers to the Sunni scholars in attendance as Ashʻaris. In addition, neither account shows an awareness of al-Nazzam's adherence to Muʻtazili theology or an understanding of the specifics of Muʻtazili doctrine, something that is an important indication of the late composition of the Tawaddud story. Some Muʻtazilis adopted the view that ʻAli was superior to the Prophet's other Companions and that Abu

---

62 Wesselski, 'Die gelehrten Sklavinnen', 361. On the Twelver Shiʻi performance of dissimulation by claiming allegiance to the Shafiʻi legal school, see Devin J. Stewart, *Islamic Legal Orthodoxy: Twelver Shiite Responses to the Sunni Legal System* (Salt Lake City: Utah University Press, 1998), 61–109; Stewart, 'Husayn b. ʻAbd al-Samad al-ʻAmili's Treatise for Sultan Suleiman and the Shiʻi-Shafiʻi Legal Tradition', *Islamic Law and Society* 4 (1997), 156–199; Stewart, 'A Case of Twelver Shiite *Taqiyyah* in 16th-Century Damascus: Claimed Adherence to the Shafiʻi Legal School', *Rivista degli Studi Orientali* (2016), 11–27.

63 Wesselski, 'Die gelehrten Sklavinnen', 362; Ünal, *More than Mere Polemic*, 41.

64 Stanfield-Johnson, 'A Persian Tawaddud', 183–184.

65 Stanfield-Johnson, 'A Persian Tawaddud', 185.

66 Stanfield-Johnson, 'A Persian Tawaddud', 185.

Bakr was *mafḍūl* 'surpassed in excellence', although still a legitimate caliph, but it is difficult to detect a concern with Mu'tazili doctrine in the text.

Husniyya's debate thus takes on a new aspect that was not found in Tawaddud's debate, since this text is a forged anti-Sunni polemic, in the tradition of other Shi'i texts, such as Radi al-Din 'Ali b. Musa Ibn Tawus's (d. 1266) *al-Tara'if fi ma'rifat madhhab al-tawa'if,* which features a similar fictional character, a Christian named 'Abd al-Mahmud who discovers the religious truth of Shi'i doctrine. The character of Tawaddud in part draws on of the figure of the witty and accomplished Abbasid slave-girl, a standard character not only in *The 1001 Nights* but also in Abbasid history and letters. After all, a slave-girl such as Khayzuran could end up the wife of the Caliph al-Mahdi (r. 775–785), mother of both the Caliph al-Hadi (r. 785–786) and the Caliph Harun al-Rashid, and a powerful figure in Abbasid court politics. However, the typical intelligent slave woman's accomplishments were focused on secular topics, including poetry, song, music – especially playing the lute – and matters of love and sex, the latter usually implied rather than discussed directly.[67] The story of Tawaddud expands these accomplishments to learning in general, while the story of Husniyya focuses on the religious sciences. The story of Tawaddud makes a statement about female intelligence in general, while the story of Husniyya makes a statement about female religious authority, in addition to the truth of Shi'ism.

The Date and Circumstances of the Forgery

The introduction to Husniyya's debate presents the text as the Persian translation of an Arabic work by the well-known Shi'i scholar Abu al-Futuh Jamal al-Din Husayn b. 'Ali b. Muhammad al-Khuza'i al-Razi, who lived in the late eleventh century and twelfth. Abu al-Futuh was born *c.* 1087. His family, who traced their pedigree back to the Arab tribe of Khuza'a, had lived in Nishapur for many generations, but Abu al-Futuh's direct ancestors had settled in Rayy, where he was raised and where he studied and taught. Little is known of his activities during his lifetime, but he was evidently a preacher and professor with a special interest in Qur'anic commentary. He was the teacher of Muntajib al-Din Ibn Babawayh (d. *c.* 1189) and Ibn Shahrashub (d. 1192), both authors of Shi'i biographical texts that have survived. His death date is not known, but a *terminus post quem* of 1157 is established by an *ijāza* he wrote: Mirza 'Abd Allah al-Afandi al-Isfahani saw a copy of the first quarter of Abu

[67] See Abu 'Uthman 'Amr b. Bahr al-Jahiz, *The Epistle on Singing Girls of Jāḥiẓ,* trans. A. F. L. Beeston (Warminster: Aris Phillips Ltd, 1980); Julia Bray, 'Men, Women, and Slaves in 'Abbasid Society', 121–146 in *Gender in the Early Medieval World: East and West, 300–900,* eds Leslie Brubaker and Julia M. H. Smith (Cambridge: Cambridge University Press, 2004); Fuad Matthew Caswell, *The Slave Girls of Baghdad* (London: I. B. Tauris, 2011).

al-Futuh's *tafsīr* in Isfahan, on the back of which the author had penned an *ijāza* to one of his students in 552 AH.[68] Abu al-Futuh is known primarily for this Persian commentary on the Qur'an, *Rawd al-jinan wa-rawh al-janan* ('Meadows among Gardens, and Repose of the Heart'), which is extant and has been published.[69] He also authored *Ruh al-ahbab wa-rawh al-albab fi Sharh al-Shihab* ('The Soul of Loved Ones and Repose of Minds, A Commentary on *The Shooting Star*'), a commentary on a collection of sayings of the Prophet Muhammad by the Shafi'i author and supporter of the Fatimids al-Qadi al-Quda'i (d. 1062). *Sharh al-Shihab* is at least partially extant in two manuscripts in Iran but has not been published.[70] Both works were used by Muhammad Baqir al-Majlisi as sources for his monumental encyclopædia of Shi'ism, *Bihar al-anwar*. Abu al-Futuh died and was buried in Rayy, near the tomb of the Imam-zadah 'Abd al-'Azim, despite later sources' claim that his tomb is in Isfahan. Muhsin al-Amin suggests that the latter is actually the tomb of Abu al-Futuh As'ad al-Bajali, who died there in 1203–1204.[71]

Several works have been falsely attributed to Abu al-Futuh al-Razi. The anti-Sunni polemical treatises *Risala-yi Husniyya* and the *Risala-yi Yuhanna* are both attributed to Abu al-Futuh al-Razi, but he is unlikely to be the author of either, since they are not mentioned in sources before the seventeenth century. A third false attribution to Abu al-Futuh al-Razi is that of *Tabsirat al-'awamm*, a well-known Shi'i anthology.[72] Scholars have argued about the correct author a great deal; it was evident that the work

[68] Mirza 'Abd Allah al-Isfahani, *Riyad al-'ulama' wa-hiyad al-fudala'*, 6 vols, ed. al-Sayyid Ahmad al-Husayni (Qum: Maktabat Ayat Allah al-Mar'ashi al-'Amma, 1981), 2:157.

[69] Abu al-Futuh al-Razi, *Rawd al-jinan wa-rawh al-janan fi tafsir al-Qur'an*, 20 vols, eds Muhammad Ja'far Yahaqqi and Muhammad Mahdi Nasih (Mashhad: Intisharat-i Astan-i Quds-i Radawi, 1998); 'Askar Huquqi, *Tahqiq dar Tafsir-i Abu al-Futuh Razi* (Tehran: Danishgah-i Tihran, 1967); Travis Zadeh, *The Vernacular Qur'an: Translation and the Rise of Persian Exegesis* (Oxford: Oxford University Press, 2012), 448–456 .

[70] Mss. Tehran, Danishgah-i Tihran 127 and 1727. Mustafa Dirayati, *Fihristwara: Dastnivisht-ha-yi Iran*, 12 vols (Tehran: Kitabkhana, Muza, va-Markaz-i Asnad-i Majlis-i Shura-yi Islami, 2010), 5:921.

[71] On Abu al-Futuh al-Razi, see Ibn Shahrashub, *Ma'alim al-'ulama'*, ed. 'Abbas Iqbal (Tehran: Fardin, 1934), 128; Muntajib al-Din 'Ali b. Babawayh al-Razi, *al-Fihrist*, ed. Sayyid Jalal al-Din Muhaddith Urmawi (Qum: Kitabkhanah-yi 'Umumi-yi Ayat Allah Mar'ashi Najafi, 1987), 48; Nur Allah Shushtari, *Majalis al-mu'minin*, 2 vols, eds Sayyid Ahmad et al. (Tehran: Kitab-furushi-yi Islami, 1975), 1:489–490; al-Hurr al-'Amili, *Amal al-amil fi 'ulama' Jabal 'Amil*, 2 vols, ed. al-Sayyid Ahmad al-Husayni (Baghdad: Maktabat al-Andalus, 1,065–1,066), 2:99–100, 356; Mirza 'Abd Allah al-Isfahani, *Riyad al-'ulama'*, 2:156–63; Muhammad Baqir al-Khwansari, *Rawdat al-jannat*, 2:314–317; Muhsin al-Amin, *A'yan al-shi'a*, 10 vols, ed. Hasan al-Amin (Beirut: Dar al-Ta'aruf, 1984), 6:124–126; Mirza Muhammad 'Ali Mudarris, *Rayhanat al-adab fi tarajim al-ma'rufin bi'l-kunya wa'l-laqab*, 8 vols (Tehran: Kitab-furushi-yi Khayyam, 1995), 4:226–227; Henri Massé, 'Abu al-Futuh al-Razi', *EI*^{2} (1960), 1:120; M. J. McDermott, 'Abo 'l-Fotuh Razi', *Encyclopaedia Iranica* (2001), 1: 292; Robert M. Gleave, 'Abu l-Futuh al-Razi', *Encyclopaedia of Islam, Three*, consulted online 19 September 2017, first published 2007.

[72] Mirza 'Abd Allah al-Isfahani, *Riyad al-'ulama'*, 2:159.

was written several generations after the time of Abu al-Futuh al-Razi.[73] It has now been established, on the basis of an Arabic translation of the work that is extant in manuscript but has not been published, that *Tabsirat al-'awamm* was authored by Jamal al-Din Muhammad b. al-Husayn b. Hasan al-Razi al-Abi (fl. 13th c.). He completed the work on 22 May 1233 in Shiraz.[74] Sources from the twelfth until the seventeenth century do not report any of these titles in presenting Abu al-Futuh's bibliography. The first work that discusses these works in connection with Abu al-Futuh al-Razi is *Riyad al-'ulama'*.

The supposed translator, Ibrahim Wali al-Din al-Astarabadi (fl. 16th c.), is not well known. No entry devoted to him appears in the biographical dictionaries *Amal al-amil, Riyad al-'ulama'*, or *Rawdat al-Jannat*. It is not until the twentieth-century works of Muhsin al-Amin (d. 1952) and Agha Buzurg al-Tihrani (d. 1970), *A'yan al-shi'a* and *Tabaqat a'lam al-shi'a*, that one finds biographical notices devoted to him. Muhsin al-Amin states that Abu al-Futuh al-Razi collected the debate and that al-Astarabadi translated it.[75] Agha Buzurg tells the story of *Risala-yi Husniyya*, drawing on *Riyad al-'ulama'* and manuscripts of Husniyya's debate. He gives the name of the translator as Ibrahim b. Wali Allāh al-Astarabadi, adding that some manuscripts add to his name al-Mir Diya' al-Din. He reports that the debate is fictional (*khayāliyya*), that the opponent is the Mu'tazili theologian al-Nazzam, and that, according to al-Isfahani, Abu al-Futuh al-Razi wrote the debate and attributed it to Husniyya.[76]

Some evidence suggests that Ibrahim al-Astarabadi was a real scholar of sixteenth-century Safavid Iran and not a fictional character. In the entry on Abu al-Futuh al-Razi, Mirza 'Abd Allah al-Isfahani states that he has devoted an entry to Ibrahim al-Astarabadi under the letter *alif* in *Riyad al-'ulama'*, but no such entry appears in the published work.[77] There is little reason to doubt, however, that al-Isfahani had some information about this scholar and indeed had written a biographical notice.[78] Another piece of evidence is the attribution of the name Gurgin – the name of a heroic figure in the *Shahnameh* who is a companion of Rustam – to al-Astarabadi, for this name does not appear in the text and must ultimately derive from independent evidence, unless some confusion occurred.[79] As Yusuf Ünal has pointed

[73] Agha Buzurg, *al-Dhari'a*, 3:319–320.

[74] See Hasan Ansari, 463–476 in Hasan Ansari (ed.), *Barrasi-ha-yi Tarikhi.*

[75] Muhsin al-Amin, *A'yan al-shi'a*, 2:110.

[76] Agha Buzurg, *Ihya' al-dathir*, 1–2.

[77] Mirza 'Abd Allah al-Isfahani, *Riyad al-'ulama'*, 2:159; Stanfield-Johnson, 'A Persian Tawaddud', 168.

[78] It is worth mentioning that *Riyad al-'ulama'* includes other dead-end cross-references that suggest that parts of the original manuscript have been lost or overlooked in the preparation of the published edition. For example, the published work includes no entry on the famous thirteenth-century scholar Radi al-Din Ibn Tawus.

[79] Muhsin al-Amin, *A'yan al-Shi'a*, 2:110; Agha Buzurg, *Iḥya' al-dathir fi 'ulama' al-qarn al-'ashir*, 1–2.

out, several works by Ibrahim al-Astarabadi are extant in manuscript in Iran, although the titles reported do not reveal much of their contents: *al-Adab wa'l-sunan, Ahadith,* and *Akhbar*.[80] Examination of these works may provide a fuller and more detailed picture of his life and work, but, in any case, their existence confirms that he was an active scholar in the Safavid period.

In the introduction to *Risala-yi Husniyya,* Ibrahim al-Astarabadi reports that he translated an original Arabic work by Abu al-Futuh al-Razi that he was shown by Shi'i Sayyids in Damascus when he stopped on the way back from performing the pilgrimage to Mecca. He states that he went to perform the pilgrimage in 1551, so this must have been early in the next year, 1552.[81] Recognising the text's importance, he decided to translate it into Persian for the benefit of readers in Safavid territory who were not accomplished in Arabic, and he dedicated his translation to Shah Tahmasb (1524–1576).[82] However, authors of Shi'i biographical works have rightly expressed scepticism about the attribution to Abu al-Futuh al-Razi.[83] Agha Buzurg al-Tihrani explains that Husniyya is an adopted name or pseudonym (*ism musta'ār*) used to present the doctrinal polemic. He compares the account to polemical works in which the authors made use of fictional names, including *Kitab al-Tara'if* by Radi al-Din Ibn Tawus (d. 1274–1275), in which an anti-Sunni polemic is voiced by a Christian character named 'Abd al-Mahmud, and *'Ayn al-'ibrah fi ghabn al-'itrah,* by Radi al-Din's brother Jamal al-Din Ahmad Ibn Tawus (d. 1274–1275), written under the pseudonym 'Abd Allah b. Isma'il, similarly a Christian or Jewish character who voices the author's opinions.[84] He also compares it to *Hikayat al-Jazira al-Khadra'* ('The Story of the Green Island'), a text about the Twelfth Imam living on a remote island that is attributed by Fadl b. Yahya al-Tibi (fl. 1299–1300) to a certain Zayn al-Din 'Ali b. Fadil al-Mazandarani, as well as to general

---

[80] Respectively, Dirayati, *Fihristwara,* 1:63 (Mashhad, Astan-i Quds-i Radawi, 16824), 1:302 (Tehran, Danishgah-i Tihran, 938.1), 1:409 (Mashhad, Astan-i Quds-i Radawi, 8397). See also *Mawsu'at mu'allifi al-Imamiyya,* 8 vols (Qum: Majma' al-Fikr al-Islami, 2000), 1:444; Ünal, *More Than Mere Polemic,* 34.

[81] It was typical for pilgrims coming from Iran and points further East to join the pilgrimage caravan from Damascus, since the pilgrimage caravan from Baghdad was defunct. If al-Astarābādī performed the pilgrimage in December 1551, then he would have first reached Damascus by October 1551 in order to join the pilgrimage caravan for that year, and he would have returned to Damascus with the pilgrimage in February 1552. His statement suggests that he came across the work when he was returning to Iran through Damascus rather than when he was on his way to perform the pilgrimage.

[82] The dedication to Shah Tahmasb is missing in the printed version of the text. It is preserved in the manuscript of the British Library, Oriental MSS, Egerton 1020, fols 3v–7v.

[83] Al-Khwansari, *Rawdat al-Jannat,* 2:309; Muhsin al-Amin, *A'yan al-Shi'a,* 6:126; Agha Buzurg, *Ihya' al-dathir,* 1–2.

[84] These works are both extant and published. See Radi al-Din 'Ali Ibn Tawus, *al-Tara'if fi ma'rifat al-madhahib wa'l-tawa'if,* 2 vols (Qum: Matba'at al-Khayyam, 1980); Jamal al-Din Ahmad Ibn Tawus, *'Ayn al-'ibra fi ghabn al-'itra* (Qum: Dar al-Shihab, n.d.); Etan Kohlberg, "Ali ibn Musa Ibn Tawus and His Polemic against Sunnism', *Religionsgespräche im Mittelalter,* eds Bernard Lewis and Friedrich Niewöhner (Wiesbaden: Harrassowitz, 1992, 325–350.

allegorical works such as Ibn Tufayl's (d. 1185) *Hayy b. Yaqzan* ('Alive Son of Awake') and Ibn 'Arabi's (d. 1240) *'Anqa' Mughrib* ('Fabulous Gryphon').[85]

There are many hints that the attribution to Abu al-Futuh al-Razi does not hold water. The text purports to describe historical events in Baghdad from the reign of Harun al-Rashid in the late eighth century or early ninth, but it includes no indication of al-Razi's sources, despite the fact that he lived more than three centuries later and could not have acquired this information directly. Abu al-Futuh al-Razi's famous work, his Qur'anic commentary *Rawd al-jinan wa-rawh al-janan* ('Meadows among Gardens, and Repose of the Heart'), is written in Persian, yet al-Astarabadi claims that al-Razi wrote the original debate of Husniyya in Arabic. No such Arabic text has been found, and lists of Abu al-Futuh al-Razi's works in biographical literature do not mention Husniyya's debate until the end of the seventeenth century.[86] The text reports that Harun al-Rashid became sympathetic to Shi'is, when there is no historical evidence that he was favourably disposed to them towards the end of his reign.[87] There are other indications, some linguistic, that the Persian text was not translated from Arabic, but was composed originally in Persian. For example, the term *madhhab* is used frequently in the text to mean 'religion' in a way what would not have been idiomatic in Arabic.[88]

Husniyya's debate – like the story of Tawaddud – includes a number of anachronisms, indicating that it could not have originated during the reign of Harun al-Rashid in the late eighth century CE. The text asserts that many scholars attending the debate were Ash'aris.[89] Given that Abu al-Hasan al-Ash'ari (d. 936) was active a century after the reign of Harun al-Rashid, this is a chronological impossibility. The text refers to the Imams' numbering twelve,[90] but the debate is set during the life of the eighth Imam, 'Ali al-Rida (d. 818), when the number of Twelve Imams had not yet been established. Husniyya states that she was bought for a few *Nāṣirī* dirhams, when the Abbasid Caliph for whom they were named, *al-Nāṣir* li-Din Allah, reigned from 1180 to 1225 CE, four centuries after the reign of Harun al-Rashid, and decades after the death of the supposed source of the debate text, Abu al-Futuh al-Razi.

The fact that the tale of Husniyya's debate is a forgery suggests that the author of the text was not Abu al-Futuh al-Razi at all, but rather Ibrahim al-Astarabadi, the self-proclaimed translator.[91] In my view, the date al-Astarabadi mentioned in the introduction is probably correct, or at least very

---

[85] Agha Buzurg al-Tihrani, *Ihya' al-dathir*, 2. On the last work, see Gerald T. Elmore, *Islamic Sainthood in the Fullness of Time: Ibn al-'Arabi's Book of the Fabulous Gryphon* (Leiden: Brill, 1999).
[86] Ünal, *More than Mere Polemic*, 33.
[87] Ünal, *More than Mere Polemic*.
[88] *Mukalama-yi Husniyya*, 25, 26.
[89] *Mukalama-yi Husniyya*, 83–84.
[90] *Mukalama-yi Husniyya*, 91.
[91] Qaragözlü, *Majara*, 444–445; Ünal, *More than Mere Polemic*, 32–34.

close to the date of his creation of the text: he presumably wrote the work in 1551 or shortly thereafter, since he mentioned performing the pilgrimage to Mecca in that year. He must have attributed the original debate to Abu al-Futuh al-Razi in order to grant it historical legitimacy and a venerable Shi'i pedigree. It may have seemed easier to do this with al-Razi rather than with scholars such as al-Shaykh al-Mufid and al-Shaykh al-Tusi, whose biographical details and bibliographies were too well known to make such an attribution plausible.

Rosemary Stanfield-Johnson remains circumspect in her discussion of the manuscript tradition, concluding only that the work was composed at some point from 1551, the date cited in the introductions to some versions, to *c.* 1655, the tentative dating of the earliest extant manuscript of the work.[92] Some versions of the work do not include the dedication to Shah Tahmasb, and Stanfield-Johnson supposes that later copyists added a fake dedication in order to establish the provenance of the 'translation' in the sixteenth century, corroborating al-Astarabadi's claim that he became aware of the original work on his trip to perform the pilgrimage in 1551.[93] It seems reasonable to me to credit al-Astarabadi's account of the 'translation' of Husniyya with regard to his pilgrimage trip and its date. The dedication to Shah Tahmasb is likely original. A later copyist may have removed the dedication subsequently, perhaps because it was seen to distract from the doctrinal content or because it was seen as off-putting to contemporary rulers or readers who did not have a high opinion of the Safavids for some reason.

Stanfield-Johnson also points out a connection of Husniyya's debate with the late Safavid scholar and prolific author Muhammad Baqir al-Majlisi (d. 1699). She notes that *Risala-yi Husniyya* was published in Iran in 1870–1871 along with al-Majlisi's work *Hilyat al-muttaqin* ('Ornament of the God-Fearing') and that Sa'id Nafisi (d. 1966) called al-Majlisi one of the translators of Husniyya.[94] She leaves the question open as to whether al-Majlisi was somehow involved with redacting the Husniyya text.[95] Yusuf Ünal has already explained that Nafisi's claim was simply wrong. There would have been no need to translate Husniyya's debate into Persian, because the 'translation' of al-Astarabadi was already widespread. Mirza 'Abd Allah al-Isfahani, who was al-Majlisi's student and would have known his work in detail, did not mention anything about al-Majlisi in connection with Husniyya's debate. Al-Majlisi does not mention Husniyya in *Hilyat al-muttaqin*.[96] The two works were published in one volume because they were both accessible works, in Persian, on Shi'i doctrine, suitable for

[92] Stanfield-Johnson, 'A Persian Tawaddud,' 190–191.
[93] Stanfield-Johnson, 'A Persian Tawaddud,' 174–176.
[94] Stanfield-Johnson, 'A Persian Tawaddud,' 179–180.
[95] Stanfield-Johnson, 'A Persian Tawaddud,' 179–181.
[96] Ünal, *More than Mere Polemic*, 61–62.

a wide reading public in Iran. It appears that the association of *Risala-yi Husniyya* with al-Majlisi derives entirely from the fact that the two works were published together. There is no reason to suppose that al-Majlisi had anything to do with the textual tradition of *Risala-yi Husniyya*, and the supposed connection only dates from the late nineteenth century.

Reading between the lines of al-Astarabadi's introduction suggests that he may in fact have come across the story of Tawaddud in a version of *The 1001 Nights* in Damascus while on his way to perform the pilgrimage, and that this inspired him to compose Husniyya's debate.

Summary of the Debate

The debate has two strands. One strand consists of straight polemics, which clearly draw on earlier polemical texts and resemble closely the discourse found in theological treatises, treatises on the Imamate, and other texts that defend Shi'i doctrines. The second strand consists of the dramatic story, which highlights the actions, thoughts, and emotions of the characters involved. The story of Husniyya is appealing as a text in large part because the author succeeds in interweaving both strands, the polemics and the drama, as Yusuf Ünal has pointed out, stressing in particular the humorous, graphic, and exaggerated descriptions of the embarrassment of Husniyya's opponents, Abu Yusuf, al-Shafi'i, and especially Ibrahim b. Khalid, when they are repeatedly silenced and defeated in debate.[97] The following presents a summary of the dramatic elements of the story.

When Husniyya's master loses his wealth, he complains to Husniyya and asks her to figure out a way out of the predicament. She owes him something, he reminds her, because he has brought her up and seen to her training. She suggests that he offer her for sale to Harun al-Rashid for 100,000 dinars. When the Caliph enquires as to why her price is set so high, he should reveal that she is very learned. The master is reluctant, because he does not want to lose her to the Caliph, whom he describes as a tyrant. She reassures him, saying that the blessings of love for the Prophet's family are on their side; no one will be able to separate her from him.

They first go to the house of the Vizier, Yahya b. Khalid al-Barmaki. The master proposes to sell Husniyya to the caliph, and when Yahya sees her, he agrees to arrange an interview. The master meets the caliph at court, and the interview proceeds as Husniyya had predicted. Harun asks why Husniyya's price is so high, and the master explains that she is extremely learned and will be able to beat the leading scholars of the realm in debate. Husniyya enters, blessing the caliph and reciting praise poetry for him. Harun, impressed by her beauty and demeanour, asks her about her religion, and she confesses that it is Shi'i Islam. She requests that the

[97] Ünal, *More than Mere Polemic*, 53–55.

Caliph summon the scholars to question her, if her faith is going to be a matter of discussion. Harun al-Rashid agrees, and he and Yahya have a side conversation in which they plan to execute Husniyya as a heretic in the most gruesome manner when she loses the debate.

On the day of the debate, all the scholars of Baghdad are assembled, along with the officials of the state and the rulers of far-off lands visiting Harun's court. The leading representative of the scholars of Baghdad is the Chief Judge Abu Yusuf, the well-known disciple of Abu Hanifa. Al-Shafi'i is also in attendance, and the narrator reveals that Abu Yusuf and al-Shafi'i are sworn enemies. When the debate begins, Husniyya does not hide her adherence to Shi'ism. She does extremely well in the initial phase of the debate, easily responding to the scholars' questions and defending her views through citation of Qur'anic verses and other proofs. Harun grows angry at the incompetence of Abu Yusuf and al-Shafi'i and decides to adopt another approach. He sends a swift messenger to Basra to retrieve the most learned scholar of the age, Ibrahim b. Khalid 'Awfi, who is reported to teach an audience of 400 scholars in his lectures. The continuation of the debate is delayed until Ibrahim arrives from Basra.

When Ibrahim arrives, Harun assembles the scholars of Baghdad once again, along with the state officials and the rulers of far-off lands. He has Ibrahim sit on a golden seat to speak. When Husniyya enters, she sits across from Ibrahim on the floor. Ibrahim remonstrates when he realises that this assembly has been arranged for him to debate with a woman. He considers this beneath his stature and complains of being subjected to ridicule in this manner. Harun al-Rashid explains the situation and asks him to proceed. Ibrahim asks Husniyya a series of eighty-three questions, of which only the last three are recorded in the text, and Husniyya is able to answer all of them convincingly. While doing so, she accuses Ibrahim of harbouring enmity for 'Ali b. Abi Talib and being a stubborn opponent of the family of the Prophet.[98]

After answering all of these questions, Husniyya requests her turn to interrogate Ibrahim.[99] She asks a series of questions about the identity of the rightful heir of the Prophet, the source of evil acts, predestination, and other theological topics. Eventually, Ibrahim is unable to answer, and the Vizier Yahya al-Barmaki upbraids him for his inability.[100] Husniyya continues, proving that 'the saved sect' (*al-firqa al-nājiya*) is that of the devotees of the family of the Prophet, and proving that 'Ali was closer to the Prophet than was Abu Bakr. At this point, Harun is impressed by her defence of 'Ali's status, proving the Imamate of his 'cousin'. He tells Yahya as an aside that if she 'followed our way' (*bar ṭarīq-i mā būd*), that is, if she were a Sunni, he

[98] *Mukalama-yi Husniyya*, 28, 37.
[99] *Mukalama-yi Husniyya*, 41.
[100] *Mukalama-yi Husniyya*, 61.

would stop at nothing to marry her. Yahya responds that, in any case, she deserves to be honoured and treated generously.[101] Harun soon orders that a tray of gold coins be brought and poured over her head.[102]

For one section of the debate, Husniyya turns to Abu Yusuf and al-Shafi'i to address and critique them for some of the reprehensible opinions found in the Hanafi and Shafi'i legal schools. She berates Abu Yusuf for considering it permissible to perform the ritual prayer in Persian, reciting, for example, when one is supposed to recite a surah or Qur'anic passage, *do derakht-e sabz* – 'two green trees' – a reference to the term *al-mudhāmmatān*, which occurs in *Sūrat al-Raḥmān* (Q 55:64). She also denounces him for considering it lawful to eat rabbit meat, play chess, engage in various types of gambling, drink boiled wine, and follow a sinner in prayer; for ruling that tanned dogskin is ritually pure; and for forbidding temporary marriage (*mut'a*). She denounces both the Hanafis and the Shafi'is for using analogy as a principle of legal hermeneutics, and she denigrates al-Shafi'i for the opinions that a pregnancy may last four years and that one may marry one's own illegitimate daughter. She even suggests that al-Shafi'i declared a four-year pregnancy possible in order to prescind the ruling that he himself was a bastard. This infuriates al-Shafi'i, who is so irate that he can barely breathe.[103]

Then Husniyya announces that such reprehensible and obviously incorrect opinions had become widespread during the caliphates of Abu Bakr and 'Umar, and she described these two caliphs as unbelievers in blunt terms: *shaykheyn-e fājereyn-e fāseqeyn-e ṭāghiyeyn-e bāghiyeyn-e kāfereyn-e mal'ūneyn-e mardūdeyn-e makhdhūleyn* – '"the two old men," – debauched and sinful, brutal and tyrannical, miscreant and cursed, rejected and forsaken'.[104] At this point the scholars of Baghdad all raise a tremendous hue and cry. Al-Shafi'i, enraged, picks up a pen-case (*dawāt*) and tries to pelt Husniyya with it. Harun intervenes. Laughing, he addresses the fulminating jurist, 'O Shafi'i! She is a slave girl, and we have pardoned her in advance for everything she says and does. Of what use is it to kill her, if you cannot prove her wrong with the Qur'an and the *hadith* of the Messenger?'[105]

Husniyya then resumes her debate with Ibrahim. In this section, she calls on Abu Yusuf several times to support her interpretations of the incidents of Ghadir Khumm – when the Prophet, on the way back from the Farewell Pilgrimage, gave a speech declaring the special relationship between himself and 'Ali – and the *Mubāhala*, when the Prophet performed a mutual curse ordeal, gathering Fatima, 'Ali, Hasan and Husayn under his cloak, against the representatives of the Christian delegation from Najran.[106] Both incidents

[101] *Mukalama-yi Husniyya*, 81.
[102] *Mukalama-yi Husniyya*, 83.
[103] *Mukalama-yi Husniyya*, 91–94.
[104] *Mukalama-yi Husniyya*, 95.
[105] *Mukalama-yi Husniyya*, 95.
[106] *Mukalama-yi Husniyya*, 104–105.

show 'Ali's closeness to the Prophet and suggest that he should have been the leader of the Muslim community after the Prophet's death. She also presents a lengthy justification of the licitness of *mut'a* marriage, in which she argues that it was banned by 'Umar in one of his many heretical decisions.[107] Harun al-Rashid is so impressed by Husniyya's argument, which includes prominent citations of the words of his ancestor, 'Abd Allah b. 'Abbas, that he declared *mut'a* legal in his realm, and it became widespread later in his reign.[108]

An important supporting character in the story is a cousin of the Caliph named Khalid b. 'Isa, who is an open supporter of the family of the Prophet and apparently a Shi'i. Harun loved him dearly and never refused his requests, despite his proclivity towards Shi'ism. At one point, when Husniyya stumps Ibrahim on an issue related to Fatima's inheritance of land at Fadak, Khalid takes a handful of dirhams and pours them over her head.[109] Such a character does not appear in the story of Tawaddud. Al-Astarabadi may have modelled him on the Qur'an figure of 'the believer from Pharaoh's family' (*rajul mu'min min āl Fir'awn*) who, although belonging to the dynastic family of Pharaoh, has secretly adopted the faith of the oppressed Hebrews. In the course of a confrontation between Moses and Pharaoh, he intervenes and stands up for Moses, giving a speech supporting him when Pharaoh threatens to have him killed (Q 40:22–54). Harun did have a cousin named 'Isa: 'Isa b. Ja'far b. al-Mansur, who was appointed governor of Oman but was captured, imprisoned, and killed by rebels *c.* 800. His marriage to Fatima bt. al-Husayn b. Zayd b. 'Ali probably indicates some 'Alid sympathy, although that does not necessarily imply adherence to Shi'ism. Another possible relative of Harun is 'Isa b. Musa b. Muhammad b. 'Ali, who also married a female descendant of Husayn, Fatima bt. 'Abd Allah b. Ja'far b. Muhammad b. 'Ali b. al-Husayn b. 'Ali b. Abi Talib. The character of Khalid b. 'Isa would ostensibly be modelled on the son of one of these two members of the Abbasid family, perhaps more likely the son of 'Isa b. Ja'far b. Mansur, but I have not been able to find any mention of such a son in the sources.[110]

Husniyya proves that Abu Bakr and 'Umar both committed mortal sins because they mistreated Fatima, especially with regard to her inheritance. Fatima was angry with them when she died, and a Prophetic hadith states, 'Fatima is a part of me. Whoever wrongs her, has wronged me, and whoever wrongs me, has wronged God.'[111] Since Abu Bakr and 'Umar wronged Fatima, they wronged God, and consequently they are unbelievers. Muslims ought to curse them because of the dictates of the Qur'an verse, 'Those who wrong God and His Messenger – may God curse them in this world and

---

[107] *Mukalama-yi Husniyya*, 129–137.
[108] *Mukalama-yi Husniyya*, 136–137.
[109] *Mukalama-yi Husniyya*, 142.
[110] I thank my colleague Asad Aḥmad for information on these figures.
[111] Al-Bukhari, *al-Sahih, Kitab Fada'il al-Sahaba, Bab Manaqib Fatima*, 1.

the next!' (Q 33:57). Therefore, Husniyya states explicitly that Abu Bakr and 'Umar were tyrants and unbelievers who should be cursed.[112]

When Husniyya curses Abu Bakr and 'Umar openly, Ibrahim b Khalid, Abu Yusuf, al-Shafi'i, and the other scholars get up and attack her, trying to kill her.[113] She defends herself as best she can: 'She also, to the extent of her power, sought to defend herself. She grabbed Ibrahim's beard in her hand and would not let go.' Yahya al-Barmaki points out to the Caliph that this is a shameful act on the scholars' part: 'You sit today in the place of the Messenger of God. A slave girl has proved wrong all of the scholars of the age and shown them to be incapable of answering her, and they, out of oppression and aggression, are attempting to harm and kill her in your very assembly!' Harun al-Rashid's cousin comes to Husniyya's rescue, fending off the attackers with his sword. They, including Ibrahim b. Khalid, back off and sit down. Harun then berates them, and Ibrahim in particular:

> Have you no shame before God?! All of you who are present consider yourselves the most learned and educated scholars of the age, but at the question of a slave girl you prove to be incapable and confused. You have become the laughing stock of both the elite and the common people, yet even so, you are not ashamed to try to kill or harm her?![114]

After the attack, Husniyya is not deterred but rather continues intrepidly. She first berates the assembly: 'You stubborn, wretched opponents! You enemies of the family of the Messenger!' She accuses them of leading the believers astray, treating charlatans as great scholars, and forging hadith reports as evidence. They have relied on such unreliable and disreputable figures as 'A'isha, Anas b. Malik, Abu Hurayra, 'Amr b. al-'As, and Mu'awiya, 'each one of whom was among the worst people of his age!' She taunts Ibrahim, asking what proofs he has of the excellent character of al-Siddiq (Abu Bakr) and al-Faruq ('Umar). What justification does he have for the murder of Husayn? Then she recounts the martyrdom of Imam Husayn at the Battle of Karbala, and everyone in the assembly weeps. At that point, Harun has exquisite robes brought as a gift for her.[115]

Husniyya then relates a few last topics. She discusses 'Ali's role in delivering *Sūrat Barā'a* (Q 9) to the pagan Meccans, a task the Prophet would assign to no other, and the mission of Usama, that Abu Bakr and 'Umar were ordered to join but ended up abandoning because, aware that the Prophet was sick and might die, they wanted to be in a position to take advantage of the opportunity. Ibrahim and the other scholars of Baghdad

---

[112] *Mukalama-yi Husniyya*, 151.
[113] Reading *Abū Yūsuf va-Shāfi'ī* for *Abū Ayyūb Shāfi'ī* in the text. *Mukalama-yi Husniyya*, 151–152. The text reads *Abū Yūsuf* in *Risala-yi Husniyya*, MS Egerton 1020, fol. 158r.
[114] *Mukalama-yi Husniyya*, 152.
[115] *Mukalama-yi Husniyya*, 158.

are unable to answer her questions and hang their heads out of shame. Husniyya delivers her final statement:

> Praise and gratitude be to God that during the reign of the Caliph, I, a weak wretch, revealed openly and without fear or terror everything that came to my mind about the merits and excellent qualities of the people of the house of the Messenger - may God bless him and his family - and the unbelief, heresy, oppression, and opposition of their enemies. I silenced the enemies of the faith with proof and evidence, when none of the devotees of the Family has gained the success that I, a weak slave woman has gained during this reign.[116]

Yahya al-Barmaki responds, 'You have not been remiss in anything, and you have established the truth of your religion', confirming her victory in the debate.[117] All of those present bless Husniyya and praise her. Thus ends the debate. A total of 400 of those present converted to Shi'ism that very day, and Harun al-Rashīd ceased to harass Sayyids and Shi'is in his realm from that time on. Harun's nephew and other supporters of the family of the Prophet showered Husniyya with gifts. Harun gave Husniyya another set of exquisite robes, but he whispered to her that she should leave Baghdad because her life would be in danger. Ibrahim came down from his golden seat and left the assembly along with Abu Yusuf and al-Shafi'i, all put to shame, their reputations ruined. The crowds, including Harun's Shi'i cousin, mocked them as they left. Husniyya and her master left Baghdad with a large group and travelled to Medina. They served the Imam al-Rida - peace be upon him - and the rest of the Sayyids of the People of the House - peace be upon them.[118]

Husniyya's Life and Education

Husniyya's life is discussed at several points in the text, and these passages provide the sketch of a life story that is not found in the parallel account of Tawaddud's debate. The character of Husniyya is introduced as follows in the opening frame-tale of the debate:

> It has been transmitted that the leader of the world, the consummate scholar of the age, the confluence of meanings, the Second Teacher,[119] who both knew God and was learned through God, Master Abu al-Futuh Razi Makki - may God have mercy on him - reported that during the caliphate and reign of Harun al-Rashid lived a man who was a very wealthy merchant and among the best-known inhabitants of Baghdad. He was widely reputed for his love

---

[116] *Mukalama-yi Husniyya*, 161.
[117] *Mukalama-yi Husniyya*, 161–162.
[118] *Mukalama-yi Husniyya*, 162.
[119] He is called 'the second teacher' in order to indicate his high rank as a scholar. 'The First Teacher' (*al-mu'allim al-awwal*) was Aristotle.

> of the family of the chaste and good ones,[120] and he was in continual contact with the Imam Ja'far, son of Muhammad[121] - may God bless him and his family - and fulfilled the duties of servitude towards him. After the martyrdom of that Presence[122] through the oppression of the enemies of the faith,[123] he lost all his wealth and worldly possessions, and poverty and want became his lot. He had nothing left but a slave girl whom he had bought when she was five years old. He had sent her to the Qur'an school, she had frequented the venerable sanctuary of the Imam Ja'far al-Sadiq - peace be upon him - for ten years, and she had busied herself with studying the religious sciences and the varieties of certain knowledge for nearly twenty years. She was also unparalleled in beauty and loveliness, and her name was Husniyya.[124]

The opening frame indicates that the master bought Husniyya when she was five. She spent ten years in the service of the Imam Ja'far al-Sadiq, and she continued studying the religious sciences for nearly twenty years. The period of twenty years is evidently meant to correspond with the actual historical dates involved. Ja'far al-Sadiq died on 14 December 765, and the reign of Harun al-Rashid lasted from 786 until 809 CE. From the death of al-Sadiq to the beginning of Harun's reign, 14 September 786, is a difference of just under twenty-one years. Since the Judge Abu Yusuf is one of the characters present at the debate, it presumably would have occurred before his death in 798, that is, between 786 and 798 CE. In the manuscript, the narrative refers to the death of Musa al-Kazim, which, as mentioned, would place the date of the debate near 799.

---

[120] Meaning *ahl al-bayt*, the descendants of the Prophet.

[121] That is, Ja'far al-Sadiq, the sixth Imam of the Twelver Shi'is, son of Muḥammad al-Bāqir, the fifth Imam.

[122] Pers. *Ḥaḍrat*, 'presence', an honorific title for the Imam: 'his majesty, his lordship'. Shi'ite sources claim that the Abbasid Caliph al-Mansur (r. 754–775) had Ja'far al-Sadiq poisoned in 765. The MS copy states that the bankruptcy of Husniyya's master occurred after the martyrdom of Musa al-Kazim (d. 799), and not Ja'far al-Sadiq, and also states that anti-Shi'i elements urged Harun to kill Musa and other *sayyids*, against his better judgement. MS Egerton 1020, fol. 8r–v. This makes sense chronologically, because Musa died during Harun al-Rashid's reign. However, if Abu Yusuf was present, the debate should have taken place before his death date, 798, which would have been several years before Musa al-Kazim died. If one ignores Abu Yusuf, the debate would have to have taken place between 799 and 803 CE. It thus appears that al-Astarabadi, the forger of the debate, was not very careful about chronology, including Abu Yusuf in the debate but suggesting that it took place after the death of Musa al-Kazim, during the Imamate of 'Ali al-Rida.

[123] Malcolm writes, 'a merchant of Bagdad, when reduced to poverty on account of his religious persuasion'. Malcolm, *History of Persia*, 253. Stanfield-Johnson writes that the wealthy Shi'i merchant 'has been rendered impoverished and subject to the sectarian animosity of al-Rashid'. Stanfield-Johnson, 'A Persian Tawaddud', 162. They and Ünal (*More than Mere Polemic*, 34, 42) have understood the text as stating that the merchant became impoverished as a consequence of oppression by unnamed Sunnis. However, I believe that the oppression of the Sunnis is cited in the text as the cause of the martyrdom of Ja'far al-Sadiq in particular. The cause of the merchant's bankruptcy is not specified, and he is not reported to have been subject to oppression.

[124] *Mukalama-yi Husniyya*, 23.

In the middle of the debate there is a pause after Husniyya has stumped Ibrahim b. Khalid, her adversary, and the audience is moved to feel devotion for *ahl al-bayt*. At this point, the text provides another sketch of her biography.

> Then Harun commanded that they bring a tray of gold coins, and they poured them over the head of Husniyya. All the officials of the state and the prominent men of the provinces who were in attendance at that assembly declared Husniyya excellent. The searing brand of love for *ahl al-bayt* had been imprinted on the foreheads of most of the sultans of that age who had come from the corners of the earth and were present in the caliphal capital, and the truth of the religion of *ahl al-bayt* had been proved to them. Seeing that the members of the Abbasid dynastic family dominated the assembly, they were unable to show their newly adopted doctrine. As one they blessed Husniyya, and everyone expressed amazement at her eloquence. Most of the Ash'arī scholars had bent their heads out of shame, and Ibrahim Nazzam was sitting, ashamed, on the golden seat, when Husniyya said, 'Ibrahim! Today you are the most learned and accomplished of the scholars of this age, and I am a slave girl of no consideration, whom they captured among the disbelievers and took prisoner. My master bought me for a few Nāṣirī dirhams.[125] He taught me the auspicious creed of the adherents to Islam, and I gained the honor of entering the religion, acquiring knowledge of the One God of necessary existence. When the eyes of my understanding opened, I came to know my Prophet and my Imam. I now have several nagging doubts in my mind about which I will ask you. You should remove these problems for me from my mind through the determination of truth and establishment of certainty, and not through violence and ordeal, that I might be obliged to praise you as much as possible, and that, after today, I might spend my time in study with you as my teacher.[126]

This passage reveals that Husniyya had been captured as a young child and taken prisoner. Her master then had bought her for a modest price – in contrast to her current value. He taught her the Islamic creed, and she became a Muslim, learning the basics of Shi'i Islamic doctrine, including recognition of God, the Prophet, and the Shi'i Imam of the age.

Husniyya provides a more detailed account of her education after she has stumped Ibrahim again in debate and when the Caliph, Harun al-Rashid, expresses astonishment at her erudition:

> When Harun saw Ibrahim in this state, he turned to Husniyya and asked, 'Husniyya! From where did you acquire such learning?'
>
> Husniyya answered, 'This should not remain concealed. When I reached the age of five years,[127] my master sent me to the venerable sanctuary of my

---

[125] Reading *Nāṣirī* for *Nāṣira* in the text. *Nāṣirī* dinars were named after the Abbasid Caliph al-Nasir li-Din Allah (r. 1180–1225); this is one of several anachronisms in the text. The text of the MS also appears to read *nāṣira*, or perhaps *tājira*, but another word that looks like *q-l-b* is written below it. MS British Museum, Oriental, Egerton 1020, fol. 82r.

[126] *Mukalama-yi Husniyya*, 83–84.

[127] This statement is slightly different from the previous passage, in which Husniyya reports that she was captured and enslaved at the age of five years.

Lord the Imam Ja'far al-Sadiq – peace be upon him – that I might serve in attendance at that lofty threshold and learn the stipulations of ritual purity and the rules governing the rites of devotion. Because I spent a considerable time engaged in service in that venerable sanctuary and thereby became acquainted with the ways of ritual purity, piety, prayer, and fasting, I continually practised them, until seven years of my life had gone by. One day, when his Presence entered the venerable sanctuary and requested water for ablutions, it so happened that the person who was designated to serve his person was not there. So I immediately ran, and, taking up the vessel of water, brought it to his Presence. When the blessed gaze of his Presence fell on me, he asked me, "Who are you?"

I replied, "I am the assistant of So-and-So, and it has been some time that I have been engaged in service in this venerable sanctuary."

He inquired, "Do you perform your prayers?"

I replied, "Yes, O master."

He asked, "Do you know the proper manner of ablutions and ritual purity?"

"Yes," I replied.

For every question he posed, I responded with an appropriate answer. His Presence was overcome with wonder. He inquired about my circumstances from the dedicated servants of the blessed and lofty threshold, and they explained my circumstances to him. He sent someone to retrieve my master, and my master arrived.

The Imam stated, "This slave girl is very intelligent. Sell her to me."

My master responded, "O son of the Messenger of God! May my life be your ransom a thousand times over. Please let my slave girl attend you; I, too, am one of your slaves and servants."

From that very day, the burden of serving the person of his Presence was assigned to me. When the signs of the attainment of the age of reason appeared in me, he continually taught me. Sometimes, with regard to his Presence, I was unable to show the necessary hardiness, so I studied the sciences in attendance on his sons and disciples, each one of whom was a king in the council of eloquence and a moon in the firmament of the sciences. Thus it transpired that through the blessings and attention of that Presence, the ability to study became established in me. I mainly read from the books of *tafsir* and *hadith*. From that holy Presence, I learned the true answers regarding questions that the scholars of Islam are incapable of solving. I exerted such effort and devoted attention to such an extent that today, in the assembly of the caliph of the age, I have proved the truth of my own sect to friend and foe, and I have not been bested in debate.'[128]

---

[128] *Mukalama-yi Husniyya*, 123–124. The text of the last sentence reads: *va-tā ghāyat ejtehād-o ehtemām kardam keh emrūz dar majles-i khalīfe-ye zaman ḥaqīqat-e mazhab-e khod-rā bar muvāfeq-o mokhālef sābet kardam va-munqaṭe' nashodam* ('I *exerted effort* and paid attention to such an extent that today, in the assembly of the caliph of the age, I have proved the truth of my own sect to friend and foe, and I have not been bested in debate'). The use of the word *ijtihād* ('effort') here led Stanfield-Johnson to suppose that Husniyya was being represented as having attained *ijtihād* and to translate, 'and that was how I achieved the height of *ijtihād* and diligence'. While Husniyya is certainly portrayed as having reached a high level of learning, there is no direct indication that she is a *mujtahida*. Stanfield-Johnson, 'A Persian Tawaddud', 164, 188–189.

The Imam took special notice of Husniyya when she was just seven, and she began acting as his personal servant at that point. He started teaching her at some later point, when she reached the age of reason. She studied with him and also with his sons and disciples, who, it is implied, were able to explain things to her in a simpler fashion. These passages stress several aspects of Husniyya's life: her status as a slave-girl, her direct contact with the Imam Ja'far al-Sadiq and his household, and her education. Education was a central component of her life, and she continued to acquire knowledge after Ja'far al-Sadiq died. She studied with descendants and disciples of the Imam, but it is also suggested that she had developed the ability to study and assimilate knowledge on her own. In particular, she read widely in the fields of *tafsir* and *hadith.*

Husniyya in the Biographical Tradition

In *The History of Hamadhan*, Abu Shuja' Shirawayh b. Shahradar (d. 1115) reports that the renowned litterateur Badi' al-Zaman al-Hamadhani (d. 1008) had two teachers, writing, 'Ahmad b. al-Husayn b. Yahya b. Sa'id b. Bishr, Abu al-Fadl, known by the epithet "the Wonder of the Age" (*Badī' al-Zamān*), transmitted from Abu al-Husayn Ahmad b. Faris b. Zakariyya' and 'Isa b. Hisham al-Akhbari.'[129] The former scholar, Ahmad b. Faris (d. 1005), was an expert lexicographer and author of several grammatical works and *al-Sahibi fi fiqh al-lugha*, dedicated to the minister al-Sahib Ibn 'Abbad (d. 995). He had taught Badi' al-Zaman in his youth, presumably in his native town of Hamadhān. The latter scholar, 'Isa b. Hisham al-Akhbari, in all likelihood never existed. Rather, Shirawayh created a historical existence for the fictional character 'Isa b. Hisham, the narrator of Badi' al-Zaman's best-known literary work, the *Maqamat*. Since each episode in al-Hamadhani's *Maqamat* opens with the phrase "Isa b. Hisham narrated to us' (*ḥaddathanā 'Īsā bnu Hishām*), this figure was understood to have been al-Hamadhani's direct teacher. His identification as an *akhbārī*, meaning a 'historian' or 'collector of reports', similarly derives from the verb of transmission *ḥaddathanā* that appears in those opening phrases, on account of its association with oral reports. Shirawayh also assumed that 'Isa b. Hisham was a native of Hamadhan, like al-Hamadhani himself and al-Hamadhani's other teacher, Ahmad b. Faris. A similar process occurred with the protagonist of al-Hariri's (d. 1122) *Maqamat*, Abu Zayd al-Saruji. According to commentators, Abu Zayd was a native of Serug who fled to Basra when his town in what is now southeastern Turkey – Turkish Suruç – was conquered by the Crusaders and his daughter was taken captive. Al-Hariri supposedly came across him begging in the mosque of the Bani Haram quarter of

129 Yaqut al-Hamawi, *Mu'jam al-udaba'*, 20 vols (Beirut: Dar Ihya' al-Turath al-'Arabi, 1988), 2:161–162.

Basra.[130] This personage is described as a real, historical figure who inspired al-Hariri to write the *Maqamat*, but it seems more likely that his historical existence as well was concocted from passages in al-Hariri's *magnum opus*. Such transformations of fictional characters into historical personalities are not infrequent in the pre-modern literatures of the Islamic world, in part because most literary vignettes were presented as historical anecdotes. The learned slave-girl Husniyya, heroine of this forged, anti-Sunni polemic, provides yet another example of a fictional character who, through the reception of the original text, gained a historical reality.

Yusuf Ünal and Rosemary Stanfield-Johnson have already discussed the transformation of Husniyya into a historical figure and a Persian at the same time.[131] Mirza 'Abd Allah al-Isfahani (d. after 1717) accorded her a biographical notice in his biographical dictionary devoted to scholars of the Twelver Shi'i tradition, *Riyad al-'ulama' wa-hiyad al-fudala'* ('Gardens of the Scholars and Pools of the Learned'), which he completed *c.* 1694–1695. He included the notice on Husniyya in the section devoted to women scholars, which appears in the last volume of the work.[132] As far as investigation to date reveals, this was the first time that Husniyya appeared in a Shi'i biographical work. In earlier biographical works such as *Ma'alim al-'ulama'* by Ibn Shahrashub (d. 1192), the *Fihrist* of Ibn Muntajib al-Din (d. after 1179–1180), and *Khulasat al-aqwal* by al-'Allama al-Hilli (d. 1325), no entry is devoted to her. This is of course to be expected, since the story of Husniyya was likely authored by Ibrahim al-Astarabadi in the sixteenth century. However, *Amal al-amil*, a Shi'i biographical work completed in 1686 by Muhammad al-Hurr al-'Amili (d. 1688), also omits mention of Husniyya. Mirza 'Abd Allah's entry on her reads as follows.

Husniyya

> She was a slave girl who had been taken captive and had adopted Islam during the time of Harun al-Rashid. She was learned in the literary arts and the religious sciences, and an exacting scholar who had insight into *hadith* reports. The Persian treatise compiled by Master Abu al-Futuh al-Razi, the author of the famous Persian commentary on the Qur'an, which treats the story of her debate over the Imamate in the assembly of Harun al-Rashid, is famous. In this treatise, the very high level of learning and the most exalted standing of Husniyya is evident, to such a degree that it crosses the mind that this treatise, which was recorded by the above-mentioned Master Abu al-Futuh, was authored and set down by him, but that he attributed it to Husniyya in order to make the doctrines of the Sunnis look bad, and thereby to vituperate against

[130] Ahmad b. al-Mu'min al-Qaysi al-Sharishi, *Sharh Maqamat al-Hariri al-Basri*, 4 vols, ed. Sidqi Muhammad Jamil (Cairo: Dar al-Fikr), 1:23. See also Charles Dumas, *Héros des Maqâmât de Ḥariri: Abou Zéïd de Saroudj* (Algiers: Adolphe Jourdain, 1917).

[131] Ünal, *More than Mere Polemic*, 55–59; Stanfield-Johnson, 'A Persian Tawaddud', 165–171.

[132] Mirza 'Abd Allah al-Isfahani, *Riyad al-'Ulama'*, 5:403–410.

> the scandal of their creed, as his peer Ibn Tawus, the author of *al-Iqbal*, did in the well-known work *Kitab al-Tara'if*, for he said in it, 'I am a man of the people of the Pact,' and debated and argued with the proponents of the four *madhhab*s until he had presented perfectly convincing arguments against them and proved the doctrines of the Shi'is and then stated that he converted to Islam. This situation has confused a group of learned men, even the great stallions among the scholars, on account of their lack of knowledge about this, and they have reckoned that *Kitab al-Tara'if* was written by 'Abd al-Mahmud the Protected Christian (*Dhimmī*), when Ibn Tawus is actually the one who introduced the book through him as a device of concealment (*tawriya*). But God knows best the true nature of things. This has been explained above in their biographical notices.[133]

In this biographical notice, Mirza 'Abd Allah does not mention the alleged translator, Ibrahim al-Astarabadi, at all, but rather treats Abu al-Futuh al-Razi as the author of the text. He also states that the work was originally composed in Persian despite the fact that al-Astarabadi presents the text as the translation of an Arabic original, perhaps because he assumed that Abu al-Futuh wrote consistently in Persian. In the course of the entry, he voices the view that Abu al-Futuh al-Razi concocted the literary fiction of Husniyya for polemical purposes, just as Radi al-Din Ibn Tawus devised the character 'Abd al-Mahmud the Dhimmī for polemical purposes in *al-Tara'if*. In creating a biographical entry for Husniyya, Mirza 'Abd Allah, despite his suspicions, is creating an independent existence for her. He also ends his discussion with the statement, 'But God knows best the true nature of things', leaving the question of the reality of her existence open to some degree.

Mirza 'Abd Allah also refers to Husniyya in his biographical notice on Abu al-Futuh al-Razi. There, he discusses the treatise on Ḥusniyya in conjunction with another treatise, *Risala-yi Yuhanna*, which presents a pro-Shi'i, anti-Sunni polemic in the voice of a Christian named Yuhanna, adding that the attribution of both treatises to Abu al-Futuh al-Razi is not proved.[134] The contents of the two entries show particular differences.

> Among his writings also is *Risala-yi Yuhanna*, in Persian, according to what is attributed to him. It is a well-known, elegant, and excellent treatise which asserts that the four legal schools are invalid and that the Ja'farī legal school, by which I mean the Imami *madhhab*, is correct. In it, he presented the discussion on the tongue of Yuhanna the Dhimmī, a Christian Evangelist, portraying

---

133 Mirza 'Abd Allah al-Isfahani, *Riyad al-'ulama'*, 5:406–407; Devin J. Stewart, 'Women's Biographies in Islamic Societies', 131–132. By 'their biographical notices', he means those of Abu al-Futuh al-Razi and Radi al-Din Ibn Tawus, but while the published edition of *Riyad al-'ulama'* includes an entry on Abu al-Futuh al-Razi, it does not include an entry on Radi al-Din Ibn Tawus; it seems to have been lost.

134 Mirza 'Abd Allah al-Isfahani, *Riyad al-'ulama'*, 2:156–163.

> him as someone who had been an unbeliever but then adopted Islam, examined [Islamic doctrine] and investigated the various sects, choosing the Imami sect, after the manner of *al-Tara'if* by Ibn Tawus, on the Imamate, inasmuch as [Ibn Tawus] spoke on the tongue of 'Abd al-Hamid the Protected Christian (*Dhimmī*).
>
> He also wrote, according to what has been attributed to him, *al-Risala al-Husniyyah* – with an *u-* vowel following the dot-less *Ḥ* [that is, not *j* or *kh*], with no vowel following the dot-less *S* [that is, not *sh*], then *N*, followed by geminated *Y* with two dots below, and ending with *H* [that is, *ḤuSNiYYaH*]. This is also a valuable, excellent, and famous treatise. It had been in Arabic but a certain [scholar] translated it into Persian, on the issue of the Imamate. He put it on the tongue of a slave girl whose name was Husniyya. She had been an unbeliever, but then converted to Islam, and she spoke in the presence of Harun al-Rashid concerning the doctrine of the Shi'a and the invalidity of the doctrine of the Sunnis. It also has excellent benefits, but the attribution of the two treatises to him has not been proved. It was stated earlier, in the chapter on [names beginning with] *alif*, in the entry on the Master Ibrahim al-Astarabadi, that this treatise is sometimes attributed to him, but its translator was the Master Ibrahim who has just been mentioned, and the Master Abu al-Futuh is responsible for originating the treatise. It is also possible that this account was transmitted by Master Abu al-Futuh, and not by [al-Astarabadi], as is suggested by the beginning of that treatise, so take note.[135]

The contents of this entry differ from those of the entry on Husniyya in several respects. For one thing, Mirza 'Abd Allah mentions Ibrahim al-Astarabadi prominently here, introducing him as the translator of the text and referring to a biographical notice he devoted to that scholar earlier in *Riyad al-'ulama'*, in the chapter on names beginning with *alif* – that is, along with other figures named 'Ibrahim'. The entry on Husniyya ignored al-Astarabadi altogether. There, Mirza 'Abd Allah stated that the treatise was written by Abu al-Futuh in Persian, but here he informs readers that the original was in Arabic. There, he seemed to voice no doubt that Abu al-Futuh was the author of the treatise. Here, he admits that the attribution to Abu al-Futuh is not entirely solidly established. In addition, he suggests that there may be some confusion in the transmission history of the text, and that Abu al-Futuh may not have authored the work, but instead transmitted the text from a yet earlier, and unknown, author.

In any case, with the publication of *Riyad al-'ulama'*, Husniyya may be said to have entered the annals of Shi'i scholars and gained a historical reality outside the debate text itself. This existence would grow in ensuing centuries. As Yusuf Ünal points out, she has made her way into modern, standard Shi'i reference works as a great female scholar.[136] The inclusion of

[135] Mirza 'Abd Allah al-Isfahani, *Riyad al-'ulama'*, 2:158–159.
[136] Ünal, *More than Mere Polemic*, 55–59.

Husniyya in the biographical tradition renders her similar to other women scholars whose accomplishments are mentioned in such texts, equating her authority, however extraordinary or unusual, with theirs, and thus allowing her to serve, like them, as a model for other aspiring women scholars.

Muhammad Baqir al-Khwansari (d. 1895) mentions Husniyya twice in his biographical dictionary of Sunni and Shi'i scholars, *Rawdat al-jannat.* He devotes an entry neither to Husniyya nor to Ibrahim b. Wali Allah al-Astarabadi, but in the entry on Abu al-Futuh al-Razi, he briefly mentions Mirza 'Abd Allah's attribution of *Risala-yi Yuhanna, Risala-yi Husniyya,* and *Tabsirat al-'awamm* to al-Razi, and he agrees with him that the attribution of the first two is likely correct, although the third is not.[137] He provides a more substantial discussion of Husniyya in the entry on Ibrahim b. Sayyar al-Nazzam,[138] explaining that he played the role of the chief opponent in Husniyya's debate.

> However, it is apparent from *al-Risala al-Husniyya*[139] attributed to Abu al-Futuh al-Razi, author of the *Qur'ānic Commentary,* as the author of *Riyad al-'ulama'* mentioned, that this Nazzam was an Ash'ari[140] and that he believed that the acts of created beings are created by Exalted God; that evil, unbelief, disobedience and sin occur through the decree and power of God, even though they are not in accord with His desire; and that the Qur'an is preeternal. He had authored two hundred volumes, in every science, which were famous among the inhabitants of Egypt, Syria, and Basra. He lived in Basra, and was a contemporary of Harun al-Rashid, who summoned him to Baghdad in order to debate the slave girl named al-Husniyya[141] who had been raised in the house of our Master al-Sadiq – peace be upon him. She debated him in the presence of al-Rashid and his vizier Yahya b. Khalid al-Barmaki, and she debated al-Shafi'i and Abu Yusuf, the judge in Baghdad as well, and she defeated al-Nazzam and all of them in various questions. Al-Nazzam had first asked her eighty questions, which she answered in the presence of the Caliph, then she asked him questions which he was unable to answer. It is related therein that she asked him, alluding indirectly, 'Why is it that the Shi'is do not declare the meat of a menstruating rabbit or of puppies licit?[142] Why have they not considered that tanning renders dog skin and all other inherently impure materials pure? Why do they not consider cooked wine permissible, and chess and all other types of gambling, such as horse-racing and the

[137] Muhammad Baqir al-Khwansari, *Rawdat al-jannat fi ahwal al-'ulama' wa'l-sadat,* 8 vols (Qum: Isma'iliyan, 1970–1971), 2:317.
[138] al-Khwansari, *Rawdat al-jannat,* 1:151–153.
[139] *Al-Ḥusayniyya* in the text.
[140] It has been mentioned above that this is an anachronism in addition to being wrong on doctrinal grounds, since al-Nazzam was one of the chief representatives of the Mu'tazili school of theology.
[141] The text reads *al-Ḥusniyya,* with the definite article.
[142] Stanfield-Johnson, 'A Persian Tawaddud', 168 has 'a bleeding small dog'.

> *ṭanbūr*,[143] forbidden? Why do they prohibit sodomy? Why do they refuse to follow sinners in prayer, limiting themselves to prayer leaders endowed with probity, and why don't they accept the opinion of even one sinner? . . .' and so on, to the end of what she enumerated, as it appears in *Riyad al-'ulama'*.[144]

Stanfield-Johnson already called attention to this biographical entry and the reference therein to Husniyya's debate, making several important observations but also misinterpreting some points of detail having to do with al-Nazzam in particular.[145] Al-Khwansari, in an odd, ahistorical statement, voices the view that on account of his radical opinions, al-Nazzam among Sunni theologians is *parallel to* the Akhbaris among the Shi'is.[146] Stanfield-Johnson, pointing out that the term Akhbari does not appear in the text of *Husniyya*, interprets this as a claim on al-Khwansari's part that al-Nazzam was contemporary with, and an ally of, the Akhbaris, writing, 'He accuses al-Nazzam of being in league with the Akhbari Shi'is.' Al-Nazzam was merely similar to the Akhbaris, in al-Khwansari, on account of his heretical views. She also states that al-Khwansari referred to 'the translation of Mawla Amin Astarabadi' and did not provide a biography of al-Astarabadi.[147] This implies that al-Khwansari may have been referring to Ibrahim al-Astarabadi, the supposed translator of Husniyya, to whom he did not devote an entry in *Rawdat al-jannat*. However, al-Khwansari is referring here to a different figure altogether. After comparing al-Nazzam to the Akhbaris, he provides a cross-reference, informing the reader that he has described the heretical opinions of the Akhbaris in 'the biographical notice' (*tarjama*) – not 'translation' – of Muhammad Amin al-Astarabadi (d. 1626–1627), the famous founder of the Akhbari movement in the seventeenth century. Al-Khwansari provides a substantial biographical notice on Muhammad Amin al-Astarabadi in *Rawdat al-jannat*, and in it includes a detailed discussion of their distinctive opinions.[148]

Al-Khwansari presents here a substantial summary of the debate of Husniyya, including details that could not have come from independent historical sources, such as the incorrect statement that al-Nazzam was an Ash'ari. For this reason, Stanfield-Johnson deduces that he must have had a

[143] There is a problem in the text, which refers to *al-miḍmār* and *al-ṭanbūr* as types of gambling: *wa-sā'ir anwā' al-qumār min al-miḍmār wa'l-ṭanbūr wa-ghayrihimā*. Al-Khwansari, *Rawdat al-jannat*, 1:153. *Al-miḍmar* means 'racetrack', but *al-ṭanbūr* designates a variety of stringed instruments that generally resemble a lute but have a long, thin neck and a smaller, pear-shaped body. The corresponding passage in the published text of Husniyya, despite the fact that the rest of it matches al-Khwansari's Arabic translation quite closely, omits these terms, reading, *va-jamī'-i shuqūq-i qumār-rā ḥarām dānand* ('and they consider forbidden all varieties of gambling'). *Mukalama-yi Husniyya*, 94. *Al-miḍmār* may be an error for *al-mizmār*, 'wood-pipe'.

[144] al-Khwansari, *Rawdat al-Jannat*, 1:153.

[145] Stanfield-Johnson, 'A Persian Tawaddud', 168.

[146] al-Khwansari, *Rawdat al-Jannat*, 1:151.

[147] Stanfield-Johnson, 'A Persian Tawaddud', 168, 168 n. 28.

[148] al-Khwansari, *Rawdat al-Jannat*, 1:151; 1:120–139.

copy of the debate at his disposal, although he does not give any information about it.[149] However, al-Khwansari states twice explicitly that his source of information is *Riyad al-'ulama'*. The reason one would conclude that the information came directly from a copy of the debate is that the list of legal rulings in al-Khwansari's summary does not appear in the published edition of *Riyad al-'ulama'*. It is possible, though, that al-Khwansari had access to a manuscript copy of *Riyad al-'ulama'* that differed from that on which the modern edition was based. In particular, his copy of *Riyad al-'ulama'* may have included the entry on Ibrahim al-Astarabadi that Mirza 'Abd Allah states that he wrote, as we have seen above, but that is nowhere to be found in the published text.

The most striking feature of al-Khwansari's summary is that it treats Husniyya as a historical figure. Despite his references to *Riyad al-'ulama'* and despite the statement that *al-Risala al-Husniyya* is attributed to Abu al-Futuh al-Razi, the remaining elements of the passage do not cast doubt on the information related. The writing suggests that he accepts the treatise's narrative as historical, factual information about both al-Nazzam and Husniyya herself. As Stanfield-Johnson aptly puts it, al-Khwansari's account gives one the impression that he 'has ignored the distinction between history and fiction'.[150] Even more than in *Riyad al-'ulama'*, Husniyya has become a historical figure in *Rawdat al-jannat*. Al-Khwansari seems to have removed most of the elements that raised questions about the veracity of the work in the writing of Mirza 'Abd Allah al-Isfahani, but it is just possible that the missing entry on Ibrahim al-Astarabadi did in fact present a less sceptical assessment of the veracity of the treatise than that which occurred in *Riyad al-'ulama'*.

Several twentieth-century biographers are more circumspect. In *A'yan al-Shi'a*, Muhsin al-Amin mentions Husniyya's debate twice. Following Mirza 'Abd Allah al-Isfahani, he includes *Risala-yi Yuhanna*, *Risala-yi Husniyya*, and *Tabsirat al-'awamm* in his list of Abu al-Futuh al-Razi's works, but nevertheless points out that the attribution of *Risala-yi Husniyya* to al-Razi has not been definitively established. Also drawing on one of Mirza 'Abd Allah's remarks, he writes, 'It is probable (*yuḥtamalu*) that this treatise has been transmitted on the authority of Abu al-Futuh and not that it is one of the texts he authored.'[151] In the biographical notice he devotes to Ibrahim b. Wali Allah al-Astarabadi, al-Amin describes Husniyya's debate and quotes the introduction to the treatise, in which al-Astarabadi explains how he found the treatise and translated it. Al-Amin then suggests that Husniyya is a fictional character created by Abu al-Futuh al-Razi, who wrote the treatise on the model of Radi al-Din Ibn Tawus's work *al-Tara'if*, and he refers readers to his explanation of this in 'the biographical notice on

---

[149] Stanfield-Johnson, 'A Persian Tawaddud', 168.
[150] Stanfield-Johnson, 'A Persian Tawaddud', 168.
[151] Muhsin al-Amin, *A'yan al-Shi'a*, 6:126.

the supposed Husniyya' (*tarjamat Ḥusniyya al-maz'ūma*).[152] Unfortunately, there appears to be no biographical notice on Husniyya in the published text of *A'yan al-shi'a*.

Agha Buzurg mentions Husniyya in three entries in his voluminous catalogue of Shi'i works, all referring to the text of Husniyya's debate but under three different titles: *Tarjamat al-Husniyya*, *al-Husniyya*, and *al-Munazara ma'a Ibrahim b. Sayyar*.[153] In all three he reports that the work is by Ibrahim al-Astarabadi, but two of them omit mention of the supposed author Abu al-Futuh al-Razi.[154] Only the entry on Husniyya mentions that the treatise is attributed to Abu al-Futuh al-Razi.[155] Agha Buzurg also mentions Husniyya again in his entry on Ibrahim al-Astarabadi in his biographical work on Shi'i scholars of the tenth century, *Ihya' al-dathir min al-qarn al-'ashir*, one volume of his large work *Tabaqat a'lam al-Shi'a*. In that entry he accepts the interpretation that the text was a fictional account authored by Abu al-Futuh al-Razi.[156] He does not address the character of Husniyya herself in any detail.

Husniyya also appears in the eight-volume Persian biographical dictionary *Rayhanat al-adab*, first published from 1948 to 1955 by Muhammad 'Ali Mudarris. The work is a general biographical dictionary focusing on Shi'i scholars of all periods, especially those who are known by a patronymic (*kunya*) or epithet (*laqab*). The entry on Husniyya includes the following statement:

> Husniyya: a captured slave girl who accepted Islam in the time of Harun al-Rashid. She was a learned, erudite, and meticulous woman, who had considerable insight into religious traditions and reports. The Persian treatise of Abu al-Futuh Razi about a debate that Husniyya had in the assembly of Harun on the issue of the Imamate is famous and has been printed in Iran. It provides convincing proof of Husniyya's extreme erudition and tremendous learning.[157]

Mudarris then goes on to report Mirza 'Abd Allah al-Isfahani's view that Abu al-Futuh wrote the debate himself. However, his initial presentation of Husniyya, which stresses her tremendous learning, does not suggest that she is a fictional character. An abridged version of this notice appears in 'Umar Rida Kahhala's biographical dictionary of women of the Arab and Muslim

---

152 Muhsin al-Amin, *A'yan al-Shi'a*, 2:110.

153 Agha Buzurg al-Tihrani, *al-Dhari'a ila tasanif al-Shi'a*, 25 vols (Beirut: Dar al-Adwa', 1983), 4:97; 7:20; 22:302–303.

154 Agha Buzurg al-Tihrani, *al-Dhari'a ila tasanif al-Shi'a*, 4:97; 22:302–303.

155 Agha Buzurg al-Tihrani, *al-Dhari'a ila tasanif al-Shi'a*, 7:20.

156 Agha Buzurg, *Ihya' al-dathir*, 1–2.

157 Muhammad 'Ali Mudarris, *Rayhanat al-adab fi tarajim al-ma'rufin bi-l-kunya wa-l-laqab*, 8 vols (Tehran: Chapkhana-yi Haydari, 1995), 2:45.

world, *A'lam al-nisa'*.[158] A more detailed notice on Husniyya appears in the similarly titled work *A'lam al-nisa' al-mu'minat*, drawing on *Riyad al-'ulama'*, *Rawdat al-jannat*, *A'yan al-Shi'a*, and *al-Dhari'a ila tasanif al-Shi'a*.[159] Yusuf Ünal has pointed out that Husniyya appears in modern Iranian reference works devoted to famous Muslim women, and that she has been rendered a tangible historical character and, specifically, a Persian. Muhammad Hasan Rajabi includes Husniyya in his work devoted to famous women of Iran and the Persophone world, describing her as a famously eloquent, learned Iranian woman.[160]

The text of the debate does not specify her ethnicity or even her native region – just reporting that she was an unbeliever, for, in order to be validly enslaved according to Islamic law, she must have been an unbeliever living outside the territory under Islamic rule. At the end of the debate, Husniyya and her master are reported to have left Baghdad and travelled to Medina to serve the Imam al-Rida and other *sayyids* of *ahl al-bayt*.[161] Both the explicit reference to non-Arab origins and the reference to service to 'Ali al-Rida would have allowed later readers to connect Husniyya with Persian background and the shrine of the Eighth Imam, in Mashhad. In fact, Husniyya came to have her own shrine, of Bibi ('the Lady') Husniyya, in the town of Torbat-i Haydariyya, 154 km south of Mashhad.[162] It is not clear at what date this shrine was established.

Husniyya's Learning and Religious Authority

Debate served a number of purposes in the pre-modern Islamic world. First, it was a method for the training of scholars who hoped to enter the ranks of the learned. Second, it was a forensic tool to determine the truth or falsehood of individual doctrines. Theologians needed to be skilled in defending orthodox doctrines and in defeating heretical ones. It was a collective obligation for the Muslim community to train scholars who could perform this task successfully. Debate was thus the main process by which religious and scientific truths became established. Third, the process of repeated debates established a relational hierarchy among individuals in the scholarly community. Just as official matches determine the ranks of modern boxers, wrestlers, or tennis players, public debates in the pre-modern Islamic world determined

---

158 'Umar Rida Kahhala, *A'lam al-nisa' fi 'alamay al-'Arab wa'l-Islam*, 5 vols (Beirut: Mu'assasat al-Risalah, 1984), 1:264.

159 Muhammad al-Hassun and Umm 'Ali Mashkur, *A'lam al-Nisa' al-mu'minat* (Tehran: Intisharat-i Uswah, 1990–1991), 300–302.

160 Muhammad Hasan Rajabi, *Mashahir-i zanan-i irani va-parsi-guy az aghaz ta mashruta* (Tehran: Intisharat-i Surush, 1995), 75–76; Ünal, *More than Mere Polemic*, 60.

161 *Mukalama-yi Husniyya*, 162.

162 Ünal, *More than Mere Polemic*, 58–59.

the relative ranks of jurists, theologians, and other scholars. In *The 1001 Nights*, this is made explicitly clear when al-Nazzam announces at the end of the debate, referring to Tawaddud: 'I call all who are present in the assembly to witness that she is more learned *than I and every other learned man*.'[163] The fact that she had defeated him, the highest-ranking scholar, meant that she was more accomplished than all other scholars. Similarly, Husniyya's victory is not merely a singular event. It proves that she is the most learned scholar in the realm, for the same reason.

This particular debate suggests that religious authority in Shi'ism, in this case and in many others, is tied directly to anti-Sunni polemics. This goes along with the idea that the chief task of theologians is to defend orthodox doctrine from heresy, and it accords with Sunni theologians' view of themselves as the most important defenders of the faith. Shi'i tradition is replete with accounts of debates of the foremost authorities with various representatives of Sunni doctrine, including Sunni Caliphs and famous scholars such as Abu Hanifa.[164] Husniyya is proved to be an outstanding religious authority within Shi'ism because she is able to champion Shi'i views against their most constant, critical, and formidable opponents.

Husniyya is at the bottom of the social hierarchy, being both a woman and a slave. This status is represented in blunt terms in the Islamic law of compensation (*diya*): the life of a free man is worth 100 camels, a free woman fifty camels, a male slave fifty camels, and a female slave twenty-five camels. She also comes originally from a community of unbelievers, and her immediate ancestors were unbelievers. In a society where pedigree counts, and in this text is emphasised by constant reference to the descendants of the Prophet, Husniyya occupies the lowest rank as well. Yet, despite these social handicaps, her value is set at 100,000 gold dinars, a far cry from her initial price of a few dinars. The contrast is striking, and meant to indicate that a person's true status may be quite the opposite of her apparent place in mundane society. This is a theory of the underdog and the downtrodden, suggesting that real values may be hidden. It is also a vindication of education, for it was dedicated study that changed her value so radically.

Husniyya's low status serves to embarrass her Sunni opponents. On a number of occasions, she taunts Ibrahim, asking him how he, who is held to be the most learned scholar of the age, cannot answer the questions of a humble slave-girl! The debate is all the more effective because her opponents and those who attend the assembly cannot treat her as an equal. It would be

---

163 *The Thousand and One Nights*, 1,818; my emphasis.

164 Al-Shaykh 'Abd Allah al-Hasan (ed.), *Munazarat fi al-imama*, 4 vols (Qum: Sharikat Dar al-Mustafa li-Ihya' al-Turath, 2007); Al-Shaykh 'Abd Allah al-Hasan (ed.), *Munazarat fi al-'aqa'id wa'l-ahkam*.

unseemly for them to attack such a weak and vulnerable person, and when they set out to do just that, it shows their base and cowardly nature. The use of someone of lower status as a spokeswoman for Shi'i doctrine is a type of protest against oppression – the truth wins the day despite the significant societal disadvantages of those who uphold it. Her humility prevails over Ibrahim b. Khalid's arrogance, and he, Abu Yusuf, and al-Shafi'i are put to shame. This is a metonymy for the position of Shi'is and Sunnis in Islamic history. The weak, humble, and downtrodden minority will eventually prevail over the arrogant and tyrannical majority.

While Husniyya shows proper humility, she is not meek, subservient, or reticent. From the beginning of the story, she eschews *taqiyya* and confesses her belief in Imami Shi'ism openly. She presents Shi'i doctrines candidly and forcefully, and she does not try to conceal or pass over certain views in silence, including doctrines that often cause trouble for Shi'is in Sunni societies, particularly those having to do with the status of the Prophet's Companions. She confronts her opponents head-on, and at several points the text stresses that she has no fear. This reminds the audience of portrayals of the bravery of Shi'i martyrs and of the demeanour of Zaynab in accounts of her confrontation with the Umayyad Caliph Yazid after the tragedy of Karbala.

The debate holds up a woman as a religious authority. Husniyya is an authority not only for a small number of people or only for other women. Rather, she is superior to the leading scholars of the Islamic empire, and she is the leading representative of Twelver Shi'i Islam in its confrontation with the dominant Sunni ideology. She did not attain this position of authority by heredity, for her ancestry is the lowliest, since she was the member of a community of unbelievers conquered outside the Islamic Empire. Rather, she attains it through learning, and it is her native ability – her reason and her mental agility – that called the Imam Ja'far al-Sadiq's attention to her in the first place. Husniyya is able to win the debate because of her epistemological superiority, which comes from her privileged access to the Imam.[165] However, the Imam is not just a conduit of holy power or charisma that he bestows on her. The Imam teaches her in the ordinary manner, and she is his student. This brings up an important point about the Imam. The Imam is defined here as a scholar – an exceptional scholar, first among all the scholars of Islamdom, but nevertheless a scholar in the ordinary sense. He imparts his learning as other teachers would, and his learning fits into the standard religious sciences and the characteristic divisions of the sciences. Husniyya also has indirect access to him through his sons and disciples. The 'sons' might include the later Imams, Musa al-Kazim (d. 789) and 'Ali al-Rida (d. 818), as well

[165] This point is made by Ünal, *More than Mere Polemic*, 43.

as other relatives. Both the Imams and the disciples are portrayed as teachers of exoteric knowledge. The text even makes the point that their instruction developed Husniyya's own capacity to acquire and assimilate knowledge. Through them, she gained the ability to be an autodidact, and she continued to study after Ja'far died. Her authority is based clearly on education in the religious sciences, and not on charisma, esoteric instruction, or inspiration.

In Shi'ism in general, it is often held that the Imam is the sole religious authority. What, then, is the status of Husniyya? At the time of the debate, she would have been living during the time of the Eighth Imam, 'Ali al-Rida. However, the Imams after Ja'far al-Sadiq are only mentioned in passing in the text. Husniyya is the star of the debate, and she is the authority. The text was actually written in the sixteenth century, long after the Greater Occultation, at a time when strong justifications had been accepted for the religious authority of the Twelver jurists in the absence of the Imam, such as the theory of *al-niyāba al-'āmma* – 'general deputyship' – espoused by 'Ali b. 'Abd al-'Al al-Karaki (d. 1534) and Zayn al-Din al-'Amili (d. 1558). One might argue that the portrayal is thus simply anachronistic. In addition, though, it reflects a theory that subordinate religious authorities are possible; they are dependent on and derive from the authority of the Imam. Husniyya's religious authority as a scholar derives from and exists under the aegis of the Imam's authority, which grants it legitimacy. Liyakat Takim has made an argument for this type of authority on the part of the Imam's companions and disciples.[166] Even though the tradition refers to them as *rijāl* – 'men' – ironically, it is clear that the category includes women companions as well. For example, al-Tusi's *Rijal*, which attempts to give a comprehensive list of the companions of each Imam, includes a sub-section, at the end of each section devoted to a particular Imam, labelled *bāb al-nisā'* – 'the chapter on women'.[167] Liyakat Takim has written on the religious authority exercised by women during the time of the Imams.[168]

A survey of al-Tusi's *Rijal* reveals that some of the twelve Imams had considerable numbers of female companions, and that some of them were slaves who must have worked in the Imam's household. The term 'companion' implies not merely acquaintance or interaction, but also that the person in question transmitted reports to others outside the Imam's circle. The number of female companions varies widely, as does the total number of companions of either sex.

---

[166] Liyakat Takim, *The Heirs of the Prophet: Charisma and Religious Authority in Shi'ite Islam* (Albany: State University of New York Press, 2006).

[167] Al-Tusi, *al-Rijal*, ed. Jawad al-Qayyumi al-Isfahani (Qum: Mu'assasat al-Nashr al-Islami, 2009), passim.

[168] See Liyakat Takim's contribution to this volume.

Female Companions of the Imams in al-Tusi's *Rijal*

'Ali b. Abi Talib	3 female companions (p. 89, nos. 915–917)
Hasan	1 female companion (p. 96, no. 958)
Husayn	1 female companion (p. 106, no. 1,057)
Zayn al-'Abidin	1 female companion (p. 120, no. 1,228)
Muhammad al-Baqir	2 female companions (p. 151, nos. 1,695–1696)
Ja'far al-Sadiq	13 female companions (pp. 327–328, nos. 4,909–4921)
Musa al-Kazim	1 female companion (p. 347, no. 5,194)
'Ali al-Rida	no female companions
Muhammad al-Jawad	2 female companions (p. 380, nos. 5,628–5629)
'Ali al-Naqi	1 female companion (p. 394, no. 5,814)
Hasan al-'Askari	no female companions

Of the female companions of the Imam Ja'far al-Sadiq in particular, a number were slaves. One of Ja'far al-Sadiq's companions, Jawhara, is referred to as his *jāriya* 'slave girl' (no. 4,918). Two others, Salima and al-Mughira, are referred to as his *mawlāt*, 'client' or 'freedwoman' (nos. 4,910, 4,913). While one may become a client through adoption or other means, the term suggests that they were slaves of Ja'far al-Sadiq whom he subsequently freed. Yet another is an *umm walad* – a slave woman who bore a master's child – of the Imam's relative Ja'far b. Abi Talib. The reason behind inclusion of these women as companions of the Imam is not to call attention to the mere fact of their contact with the Imam, but also to suggest that they played some role in the transmission of knowledge from the Imams to other members of the Shi'i community.

Other sources reveal yet another female companion of Ja'far al-Sadiq who was a slave-woman: Sa'ida, another *mawlāt* or freedwoman of the Imam.[169] She may be identical with a Sa'ida whom al-Tusi lists as one of Musa al-Kazim's companions in his *Rijal*, without providing any additional information.[170] Asma Sayeed has called attention to Sa'ida in her study of women in Shi'i biographical collections, pointing out that privileged access to the Imam enabled her to become learned in religion and a figure of religious authority.[171] Stanfield-Johnson points out that this historical figure, attached to the household of Ja'far al-Sadiq and possessed of learning, is similar to the fictional character of Husniyya.[172] Two reports in the early Shi'i text

[169] Al-Saffar, *Basa'ir al-darajat*, 2 vols (Qum: Mu'assasat al-Imam al-Mahdi, n.d.), 1:318, 340; al-Tusi, *Ikhtiyar ma'rifat al-rijal* (Qum, 2006), 308.
[170] Al-Tusi, *al-Rijāl*, 347, no. 5194.
[171] Asma Sayeed, 'Women in Imāmī Biographical Collections', in *Law and Tradition in Classical Islamic Thought*, eds Michael Cook et al. (New York: Palgrave Macmillan, 2013), 81–98, at 81.
[172] Stanfield-Johnson, 'A Persian Tawaddud', 191.

Basa'ir al-darajat, by Muhammad b. al-Hasan b. Farrukh al-Saffar al-Qummi (d. 902–903) depict a scene – apparently the same one, but at different lengths and slightly different terms – in which Ja'far al-Sadiq scolds Sa'ida for not carrying out her duties properly. The longer and more detailed of the two accounts may be translated as follows:

> Muhammad b. 'Abd al-Jabbar related to us, on the authority of Abu al-Qasim 'Abd al-Rahman b. Hammad, on the authority of Muhammad b. Sahl, on the authority of Ibrahim b. Abi al-Bilad, from 'Isa b. 'Abd Allah b. Muhammad b. 'Umar b. 'Ali – may peace be upon him – from his mother Umm al-Husayn bt. 'Abd Allah b. Muhammad b. 'Ali b. al-Husayn – peace be upon him – who said: 'While I was sitting at the house of my paternal uncle Ja'far b. Muhammad, he called Sa'ida – a slave girl (*jāriya*) who belonged to him, and who held a favored status with him (*wa-kānat lahu bi-manzila*) – and she brought him a cloth bag. He examined his seal upon it, then broke the seal and looked inside the bag. Then he raised his head to her and berated her harshly.' [Umm al-Husayn] said: 'I remonstrated, "May I be your ransom! How can you do this? I have never seen you raise your voice to anyone at all, so how could you do so to Sa'ida?" He responded, "My dear daughter, do you know what she has done?! This is the banner of the Messenger of God – may God bless him and grant him peace – 'the Eagle.' She neglected it so that it was eaten by vermin." Then he took out a black cloth, shook off the dust, and placed it on his eyes. Then he gave it to me, and I put it on my eyes and my face. Then he took out a purse containing gold coins, the amount of two hundred dinars, and said, "My father gave these from the money he got for selling [the land at] al-'Amudan, for a disaster that will occur in Medina from which only those who are at a distance of three miles away will escape. For it he sold [the land at] al-Tibah. By God, my father did not live to see it, and by God, I don't know whether I will live to see it." Then he brought out another purse, smaller than the first, and said, "This he paid also, for a disaster that will strike Medina, from which only those who are at a distance of a mile away will escape. For this he sold [the land at] al-'Urayd. By God, my father did not live to see it, and by God, I do not know whether or not I will live to see it."'[173]

In this text, the Imam scolded Sa'ida for not properly storing a relic of the Prophet Muhammad, his banner 'the Eagle'. Through her surprised reaction, the Imam's niece, Umm al-Husayn, reveals that Sa'ida had a special status with the Imam – that is, that he had a special fondness or consideration for her. The account does not explain why she enjoyed this status, but the context suggests that she was the custodian of priceless relics of *ahl al-bayt*, something that suggests that she was privy to secrets of the Imam that were not available to others.

---

[173] Al-Saffar, *Basa'ir al-darajat*, 1:340. A different version of the account is given at 1:318.

Another portrayal of Sa'ida is provided by a text that has been discussed by Asma Sayeed. Transmitted by al-Kashshi (fl. 4th/10th c.) and preserved in al-Tusi's abridgement of al-Kashshi's work, *Ikhtiyar ma'rifat al-rijal*, the biographical entry on Sa'ida reads as follows:

> Sa'ida the freedwoman of Ja'far – peace be upon him Muhammad b. Mas'ud [al-'Ayyashi] said that 'Ali b. al-Hasan [al-Faddal al-Kufi] had related to him, that Muhammad [b. al-Hasan] b. al-Walid had related to him, on the authority of al-'Abbas b. Hilal [al-Shami], that Abu al-Hasan al-Rida – peace be upon him – stated that Sa'ida the freedwoman of Ja'far – peace be upon him – was among the learned, for she knew everything she had heard from Abu 'Abd Allah [Ja'far, the Imam] – peace be upon him. And that she had in her possession the testament of the Messenger of God – may God bless him and keep him safe. And that Ja'far said to her, 'I beseech God, who made you known to me in this world, to marry me to you in Paradise.' And that she lived near the house of Ja'far – peace be upon him – and was never seen in the [Prophet's] Mosque but that she was saluting the Prophet – may God bless him and keep him safe – going out to Mecca, or returning from Mecca. He also stated that her last words were, 'We have accepted recompense, and we have become safe from punishment.'[174]

This account assigns to Sa'ida an extremely exalted status, portraying the Imam Ja'far al-Sadiq praying to God to make her his wife in Paradise. As in the account from *Basa'ir al-darajat*, she is associated with rare and secret relics of the Prophet – here the document of the Prophet's will and testament.[175] However, in this case, there is no suggestion here that she has not carried out her duties correctly. It states explicitly that she was learned – *min ahl al-faḍl* – and it is revealed that this is due to her knowing all the pronouncements of the Imam that she had heard.

The account that al-Kashshi provides may derive from an earlier biographical work. The account exhibits parataxis, a number of phrases introduced by *dhakara anna* – 'he stated that' – and followed by . . . and that (*wa-anna*) . . . and that . . . and that . . .,[176] without maintaining parallelism between the phrases. This suggests that the passage has been abridged from a significantly longer account and that significant material that perhaps wove the individual statements into a more coherent narrative has been removed. It is likely as well that this passage was not transmitted as an isolated hadith

[174] Al-Tusi, *Ikhtiyar Ma'rifat al-rijal*, 308.

[175] Asma Sayeed and Stanfield-Johnson understand the text to be claiming that Sa'īda transmitted the Prophet's *waṣiyya* as an oral report, but I believe that the intended meaning of the text is that she had the original historical document in her possession. Sayeed, 'Women in Imāmī Biographical Collections', 81; Stanfield-Johnson, 'A Persian Tawaddud',191.

[176] The modern editors have vowelled the text *dhakara anna . . . wa-inna . . . wa-inna . . . wa-inna . . . wa-inna*, which is incorrect; since the statements are all parallel and dependent on *dhakara*, they should read *wa-anna* instead.

report but was part of an authored book. In fact, it may have been cited in several books by figures in the *isnād*. 'Ali b. al-Hasan b. 'Ali b. al-Faddal, a scholar of the late ninth century and son of a prominent Shi'i scholar and transmitter, is known to have authored a biographical work titled *Kitab al-Rijal*.[177] Al-'Ayyashi, the last transmitter in the *isnād*, may have quoted the notice on Sa'ida in his biographical work *Ma'rifat al-naqilin*, a title listed by Ibn al-Nadim (d. 990) in his bibliography in the *Fihrist*.[178]

Sa'ida's example suggests that the basic premise of Husniyya's debate, that a slave-girl may have become learned through contact with the Imam, was considered within the realm of possibility by al-Kashshi, by his sources, and by many later readers. It is still possible that Sa'ida did not exist, but was a character created for the purposes of the texts cited above. Nevertheless, it seems clear that some of the Imams had contact with their own female slaves or female slaves of their acquaintances, and that some of those female slaves came to be considered their companions, which implied not only mere contact but also the transmission of knowledge. Stanfield-Johnson suggests that the account of Sa'ida may have served as an inspiration for the story of that other learned slave-girl, Tawaddud.[179] Given that Shi'i biographical literature was not widely circulated among Sunnis in pre-modern times, the possibility seems farfetched. However, since Ibrahim al-Astarabadi was clearly steeped in Twelver Shi'i religious texts, he was likely to have known of Sa'ida, or other slave-girls mentioned in historical sources as having served the Imams, and such knowledge may have influenced him in the composition of Husniyya's debate. But, if this were the case, why didn't al-Astarabadi name the main character Sa'ida instead? The answer would seem to be obvious: Sa'ida was a slave of the Imam himself, while the Tawaddud story frame requires the slave to be owned by an impoverished merchant who is driven to sell her, and one could not portray the Imam in such a fashion. The slave-girl must be owned by a different master.

The content of the debate provides a portrayal of Husniyya's religious authority. Both Murat Han Aksoy and Yusuf Ünal have explained that the content of Husniyya's debate draws on and maps out the contours of Shi'i anti-Sunni polemics in general. A number of Shi'i writers, including Mirza 'Abd Allah al-Isfahani, describe the debate as focusing on the Imamate alone, recognising the dominant topic but nevertheless omitting significant parts of the debate.[180] Aksoy argues that the debate covers two categories: theology and law. In his assessment, the theological topics include the following: the Imamate, Prophecy, the Status of the

---

177 Al-Najashi, *Kitab al-Rijal* (Qum: Mu'assasat al-Nashr al-Islami, 1997–1998), 257–259.

178 Ibn al-Nadim, *Kitab al-Fihrist*, 2 vols, 2nd edn, ed. Ayman Fu'ad Sayyid (London: al-Furqan Foundation, 2014), 1:685.

179 Stanfield-Johnson, 'A Persian Tawaddud', 191.

180 Mirza 'Abd Allah al-Isfahani, *Riyad al-'ulama'*, 2:159; Agha Buzurg, *al-Dhari'a ila tasanif al-Shi'a*, 4:97; 7:20.

Qur'an, divine determinism, predestination, the identity of 'the saved sect' (*al-firqa al-nājiya*), the status of *ahl al-bayt*, and the beatific vision of God. The legal topics include inheritance and *mut'a* or fixed-duration marriage.[181] This is an adequate and more specific description, but it is still incomplete. Ünal describes the debate as involving two main topics, the Imamate and theology, leaving out the law.[182] I suggest a division of the topics of debate into four rubrics: 1) the Imamate, 2) early Islamic history, 3) theology, and 4) law. All of these sciences are portrayed as important for the scholar who aspires to religious authority, and it is understood that the sciences that are important for sectarian polemics against Sunnis are exactly those that are important for religious authority.

At several points, the text of the debate refers to the evidence or proof texts on which Husniyya's texts are based. These include Qur'anic verses, commentaries on the Qur'an, hadith reports, and accounts of early Islamic history. Husniyya relates that she mainly read *tafsir* and hadith, which implies that the interpretation of the Qur'an and hadith are the main areas of expertise through which one gains religious authority. In the debate, Husniyya makes the point that most verses of the Qur'an can be correctly understood through the statements of the Prophet and the members of his family, meaning the Imams.[183]

The emphasis among these topics is decidedly on the Imamate and theology. The Imamate is obviously a central question in Shi'ism and the main topic of Shi'i–Sunni polemics in general. The topic of the Imamate came to be recognised as an important sub-topic within Islamic theology early on; this is emphasised in the *Maqalat al-Islamiyyin* of al-Ash'ari (d. 936), an influential heresiography that begins with a chapter on the Imamate. Writing in the ninth century, al-Jahiz described the theologians as 'sniffers out of heresy', and theologians have in general been presented as the defendants of Islam against doctrinal heresy and heretical movements. It is this defensive function that appears to be most operative in the debate of Husniyya. She defends Shi'i doctrinal positions and champions the Shi'is' views; this is the chief manifestation of her religious authority. The leading opponent in the debate, Ibrahim b. Khalid, is portrayed primarily as a theologian.

Law, however, is not ignored; it appears secondarily. In the Husniyya debate, the Hanafi and Shafi'i Sunni legal schools are represented by two jurists in particular, Abu Yusuf, the famous student of Abu Hanifa and chief judge at the Abbasid capital, as well as Muhammad b. Idris al-Shafi'i. Abu Hanifa cannot appear in the debate because he died before the reign of Harun al-Rashid. It is noteworthy that the story does not refer to any representative of the Maliki or Hanbali legal schools, or even to any members of those legal schools. As Ünal has pointed out, this would seem to reflect

[181] Murat Han Aksoy, *Şii Paradigmanın Oluşum Sürecinde 'Hüsniye' nin Yeri Önemi*, 34–66.
[182] Ünal, *More than Mere Polemic*, 46–53.
[183] *Mukālama-i Husniyya*, 64.

the social situation in Iran just before Ibrahim al-Astarabadi was writing, and not the situation in Iraq in earlier centuries, because the Hanafi and the Shafi'i were the two most important schools of law in Iran before the Safavids' conversion of the populace to Shi'ism; he has suggested that the reason behind the inclusion of Abu Yusuf and al-Shafi'i in the debate was the intent to critique the two most prevalent Sunni legal traditions in Iran.[184] The debate suggests that the legal *madhhab* is understood to be part of the parameters of the determination of orthodoxy, even though the text focuses on theological more than legal issues. Certainly, Husniyya's references to the legal rulings of Abu Hanifa and al-Shafi'i and her denouncement of their individual legal rulings not just as erroneous but as preposterous and outrageous are intended to detract from the reputation of Sunni legal scholarship in contrast to that of the Shi'is. Ja'far al-Sadiq appears so prominently at least in part because the foundation of the Twelver Shi'i legal *madhhab* was attributed to him by the jurists of later centuries. One thus may see in the prominence of Ja'far in the text a reflection of his representation of the legal school of the Twelvers, but his teaching, while important, is accompanied by that of the later Imams.

The specific sources of these polemical sections have not been identified. One suspects that the majority of the discussion of the Imamate and theological topics derives from, or is inspired by, standard works such as al-Tabrisi's *al-Ihtijaj*, Ibn Tawus's *Kitab al-Tara'if,* or al-'Allama al-Hilli's *Nahj al-sidq*. The material that treats the rulings of the Hanafi and Shafi'i legal schools in detail probably derives from a different text or set of texts, including Shafi'i critiques of Hanafi law and Hanafi critiques of Shafi'i law. The debate also refers to a debate between the wise fool Buhlul and Abu Hanifa that is known from other sources.[185]

Husniyya is also helped in the debate by blessings. Before the debate, she tells her master that he should not worry about her: 'O master, do not fear, because, as long as I am alive, through the blessings of love for the People of the House of the Messenger . . . no one will be able to separate me from you.'[186] She adds, 'O master, do not consider it too much that, on account of the blessing of the Presence of the Messenger and the People of his House . . . I will not be defeated or silenced.'[187] When Husniyya explains how she was educated, she states, 'Thus it transpired that through the blessings and attention of that Presence, the ability to study became established in me.'[188] Her performance is mainly a matter of learning, but she gives credit to blessings as well, suggesting that while individual effort is crucial, grace also plays a significant role.

---

[184] Ünal, *More than Mere Polemic*, 44.
[185] *Munazarat fi al-'aqa'id wa'l-ahkam*, 1:61–62.
[186] *Mukalama-yi Husniyya*, 24.
[187] *Mukalama-yi Husniyya*, 24.
[188] *Mukalama-yi Husniyya*, 123–124.

Husniyya provides one example of the extension of the Holy Family, the descendants of the Prophet revered by Shi'is, who include the five 'People of the Cloak' – the Prophet, 'Ali, Fatima, Hasan, and Husayn – or 'the Fourteen Immaculate Ones' – the twelve Imams plus Muhammad and Fatima. Minor characters who are not related by blood may nevertheless become attached to the Holy Family by virtue of their close contact with and devotion to its members. For example, 'Ali's slave, Qanbar, and Fatima's slave, Fidda, both become important figures in the Holy family on account of their loyal service. They represent the devotees of the Prophet's family who though they are not genetically related to the Imams, do not have ties of marriage with the family, and do not even come from Arab stock, can nevertheless be considered members of the Holy Family. Similarly, Husniyya is attached to Ja'far al-Sadiq's household and becomes part of the Holy Family by extension. She thus serves as a model for Shi'i women believers who are Persian, Indian, Turkic, or at least non-Arab, allowing them to identify with an exemplary figure who is closely connected with the Imams.

Scholars have discussed the establishment of women's religious authority through top-down processes versus bottom-up processes. There is some expectation that, given the restrictions placed on women by patriarchal structures, women will be more likely to gain recognition through bottom-up processes than through top-down processes.[189] It is clear in this case, that Husniyya has gained recognition through a top-down process, since her religious learning was provided and sanctioned first by the Imam himself and by his sons and students, and later by the Abbasid Caliph Harun al-Rashid.

Perhaps the most striking feature of the story is its assumption that a woman can not only become educated but even attain an outstanding rank among the educated. The text does not express surprise that a woman can become learned. Rather, it expresses surprise that a slave woman from a lowly background can do so. The text does not refer directly to other women in society, so it is difficult to make a definitive statement about female learning in general. Perhaps the author thought that it would have been easier for women of higher social standing to acquire an excellent education. Alternatively, perhaps the point is that Husniyya's slave status allowed her to mix more freely with men who were not her direct relatives, so it would have been more difficult for free women to acquire an education. It is known from other biographies of female scholars that they often gained access to learning through male relatives, usually fathers or brothers, who were scholars. The master–servant relationship may be viewed as another avenue through which a female might gain learning.

Husniyya became the Imam's personal servant, although not his slave, because her master declined to sell her to the Imam. The text, however, does

---

[189] David Kloos and Mirjam Künkler, 'Studying Female Islamic Authority: From Top-Down to Bottom-Up Modes of Certification', *Asian Studies Review* 40.4 (2016), 479–490.

not hint at there being any problem either with her serving him or with her studying – apparently in private – with him. Nor does it hint at there being any difficulties with her studying with his sons and disciples. Overall, the text appears to be unconcerned with or unconscious of the segregation of the sexes in the realm of education. There is no indication of any problem or impropriety arising from Husniyya's interaction with men. This is perhaps an indication that, in the author's view, certain girls are naturally intelligent and precocious, and that it is indeed appropriate for such girls to be educated, even if that means having extensive contact with men. One may even detect an assumption that their intelligence will keep them within the bounds of proper behaviour despite the lack of gender segregation. The elements of the story that are presented as remarkable are the tremendous degree of Husniyya's intelligence and the special degree of learning of her primary teacher.

Even if Husniyya is recognised as a fictional character, she still serves as a model for ordinary Shi'i women. She is endowed with extraordinary intelligence, but it is not miraculous or divine intelligence. She enjoys the privilege of having had the Imam Ja'far al-Sadiq as her teacher, but he teaches her in the ordinary manner. At one point in the debate, she cites a hadith report that she relates directly from Ja'far, which he related from his grandfather Zayn al-'Abidin, from al-Husayn, from 'Ali, about a statement that the Prophet had made to Salman al-Farisi.[190] This shows that she had studied hadith with him in the ordinary manner. The fact that she, who was a lowly slave, could acquire great learning should indicate to other Twelver Shi'i women that they, too, could aspire to great learning and become authority figures. Such things did not occur as a matter of course, but they were both allowed and possible. Husniyya's status as a scholar of Qur'an, hadith, *tafsir*, theology, and law imply that these specific fields were open to women and that women could master them, even to a level that rivalled and surpassed that of their male peers.

The genre of the biographical dictionary, including *Riyad al-'ulama'*, performs both an exemplary function and an authoritative function. Marilyn Booth has discussed the connection between biographies and exemplarity in connection with nineteenth- and twentieth-century works that focus on women's biographies.[191] In addition, such works put forth complex and sustained arguments for the authority of the particular class whose accomplishments they recorded: grammarians, hadith experts, Shafi'i jurists, Mu'tazili theologians, commentators on the Qur'an, and so on. The genre also serves

---

[190] *Mukalama-yi Husniyya*, 89.

[191] Booth, *'May Her Likes Be Multiplied'*; Marilyn Booth, *Classes of Ladies of Cloistered Spaces: Writing Feminist History through Biography in Fin-de-siècle Egypt* (Edinburgh: Edinburgh University Press, 2015).

to define the relational hierarchy that exists within the group, determining the relative ranks of individual scholars. The mere fact that Mirza 'Abd Allah al-Isfahani includes Husniyya in his section on women's biographies indicates that he regards her as an authority, just as he regards as authorities the male figures in his work who contributed to the scholarly tradition of Twelver Shi'ism. In addition, the fact that she, and not some other senior Shi'i scholar, debates the leading scholars of the Sunnis suggests that her relative rank is very high, above that of her male colleagues. She represents the entire Twelver sect against its opponents.

The emphasis on law and theology in Husniyya's debate stands in marked contrast to the relatively widespread attention in pre-modern texts to women scholars who were involved in the transmission of hadith. Such women experts in hadith have been subject of considerable scholarly attention to date.[192] One might see this as part of a general difference between Sunni and Shi'i learned culture; Asma Sayeed has argued that the tendency among women scholars towards accomplishment in law as opposed to hadith increased in the Safavid and modern periods,[193] although it is perhaps early in the development of this field of enquiry to make such sweeping generalisations, and one must admit the existence of certain Sunni women who were trained jurists. Certainly, Shi'i women transmitters of hadith have been studied.[194] For many centuries of Islamic history, hadith did not play, in Twelver Shi'i circles, as prominent a role as it did in Sunni circles. An examination of Sunni biographical dictionaries that mention women, such as 'Abd al-Rahman al-Sakhawi's (d. 1497) *al-Daw' al-lami' li-ahl al-qarn al-tasi'* ('The Shining Light, on the People of the Ninth Century'), reveals that the vast majority had some involvement in hadith transmission, whereas only a few of the women scholars who are mentioned in *Riyad al-'ulama'* of Mirza 'Abd Allah al-Isfahani had significant involvement in that field. In contrast,

---

[192] Jonathan Berkey, 'Women and Islamic Education in the Mamluk Period', in *Women in Middle Eastern History: Shifting Boundaries in Sex and Gender*, eds Nikkie Keddie and Beth Baron (New Haven: Yale University Press, 1991), 143–157; Jonathan Berkey, *Transmission of Knowledge in Medieval Cairo: A Social History of Islamic Education* (Princeton: Princeton University Press, 1992); Ruth Roded, *Women in Islamic Biographical Collections: From Ibn Sa'd to Who's Who* (Boulder: Lynne Rienner Publishers, 1994); I. Schneider, 'Gelehrte Frauen des 5./11. Bis 7./13. Jh. nach dem biographischen Werk des Dahabi (st. 748/1347)', in *Philosophy and Arts in the Islamic World: Proceedings of the 18th Congress of L'Union Européenne des Arabisants et Islamisants held at the Katholieke Universiteit Leuven, 3–9 September 1996*, eds U. Vermeulen and Daniel de Smet (Leuven: Peeters, 1997), 107–21; Mohammad Akram Nadwi, *al-Muhaddithat: The Women Scholars of Islam* (London: Interface, 2007); Asma Sayeed, *Women and the Transmission of Religious Knowledge in Islam* (Cambridge: Cambridge University Press, 2013).

[193] Devin J. Stewart, ' Women's Biographies in Islamic Societies', 121; Asma Sayeed, 'Women in Imāmī Biographical Collections'.

[194] Nahleh Gharavi Naeeni, *Shi'ah Women Transmitters of Hadith: A Collection of Biographies of the Women who Have Transmitted Traditions*, trans. Gail Babst (Qum: Ansariyan, 2011); Sayeed, 'Women in Imami Biographical Collections'.

the topics of law and theology stand out as crucial sciences on which religious authority is based. The contributions of women scholars to the field of law have received much less attention in secondary scholarship.[195] A handful of studies have come forth: Mona Hassan has discussed the contributions of 'Amra bint 'Abd al-Rahman (d. 724).[196] Emil Homerin has studied the prominent female jurist and scholar of mysticism 'A'isha al-Ba'uniyya (d. 1517).[197] Beverly Mack and Jean Boyd have studied the scholarship of the Nigerian Nana Asma'u (1793–1864), daughter of the Sokoto Caliph Usman dan Fodio, who wrote poetry in Hausa, Fulfulde, and Arabic on history, Islamic doctrine, and other topics.[198] Mirjam Künkler and Roja Fazaeli have written about accomplished Shi'i women jurists, *mujtahidas*, in twentieth-century Iran.[199]

Another striking feature of the text is the absence of other women. No signs of female networks of learning appear. One might also expect that a female figure would serve primarily as an authority for other females, something that frequently appears in pre-modern and modern discussions of female learning in the Islamic sciences, but that is not the case here.[200] A prominent example is that of al-Shahid al-Awwal's daughter Fatima, who is supposed to have answered legal questions of women having to do with 'women's' issues. Husniyya studied exclusively under male teachers, the Imam, his descendants, and his disciples. One imagines that his disciples could possibly have included women, but there is no explicit mention of female disciples in the text. In the debate itself, Husniyya is surrounded by an entirely male audience, whether the Caliph, his officials, her master, or the Sunni scholars in attendance. There is no indication that Husniyya learned from women, studied along with learned women peers, or taught other women. Also missing is any indication that Husniyya was an author or wrote any treatises or commentaries on Islamic religious texts.[201]

In examining women's authority in modern religious contexts, scholars have noted the important features of state intervention, male invitation,

---

[195] Khaled Abou El Fadl, 'Legal and Jurisprudential Literature: 9th to 15th Century', *Encyclopedia of Women and Islamic Cultures* (Leiden: Brill, 2012).

[196] Mona F. Hassan, 'Relations, Narrations, and Judgments: The Scholarly Networks and Contributions of an Early Female Muslim Jurist', *Islamic Law and Society* 22.4 (2015), 323–351.

[197] 'A'isha al-Ba'uniyya, *The Principles of Sufism*, ed. and trans. Th. Emil Homerin (New York: New York University Press, 2014).

[198] Beverly B. Mack and Jean Boyd, *One Woman's Jihad: Nana Asma'u, Scholar and Scribe* (Bloomington: Indiana University Press, 2000).

[199] Mirjam Künkler and Roja Fazaeli, 'The Life of Two *Mujtahidah*s: Female Religious Authority in 20th-Century Iran', in *Women, Leadership and Mosques: Contemporary Islamic Authority*, eds Masooda Bano and Hilary Kalmbach (Leiden: Brill, 2011), 127–160.

[200] Cf. Kloos and Künkler, 'Studying Female Islamic Authority', 486.

[201] Künkler and Fazaeili, 'The Life of Two Mujtahidahs', 129.

and female initiative,[202] and one may identify all three in the portrayal of niyya here. The Caliph Harun al-Rashid and his Vizier Yahya al-Barmaki play an important role in the text because they ratify Husniyya's victory in addition to guaranteeing her safety, which allowed her to expound Shi'i doctrines freely. Both Ja'far al-Sadiq and Harun al-Rashid represent the state in some sense, because the Shi'i Imam is the legitimate ruler of the Muslim Community.

Male facilitation is certainly important in Husniyya's story. Her master provided for her education, and he makes a point of insisting on this. He taught her the Islamic creed and the fundamentals of belief. He introduced her to the household of Ja'far al-Sadiq. The Imam Ja'far al-Ṣādiq noticed her and took it upon himself to teach her. Other descendants and disciples of the Imam, presumably male, also taught her.

Husniyya assumes an active role throughout the story. Her initiative to undertake her fellow servant's job despite her young age was what began her relationship with Ja'far al-Sadiq. Even in her initial meeting with the Imam, her boldness is evident when she does not shy away from the Imam's questions but answers in a forthright manner. The Imam then took an interest in her education, but her description of her education indicates that she continued to read and study on her own long after her formal education with the Imam, presumably on account of his passing away. She devises the plan to save her master from bankruptcy and poverty – in fact, he begs her to come up with a way out of his predicament, depending on her intelligence and ability. Husniyya gains a resounding victory in the debate, showing ingenuity not only in answering questions but also in interrogating her opponents. Her active role is perhaps nowhere more evident than in her forceful defence of herself against physical attack, when she grabs hold of Ibrahim b. Khalid's beard and will not let go – a dramatic and striking image. Her attainment of religious authority is thus portrayed to a significant extent as due to her own initiative and a product of individual dynamism.

By a complex process, the fictional heroine of a story from *The 1001 Nights* was transformed into a female figure of Twelver Shi'i religious authority. In sixteenth-century Safavid Iran, Ibrahim al-Astarabadi drew on the story of Tawaddud and on Shi'i polemical texts to create a dramatic debate in which Husniyya defended Shi'i doctrine against the leading Sunni scholars of her age, including the Hanafi judge Abu Yusuf, the famous jurist al-Shafi'i, and the fanatical anti-Shi'i Ibrahim b. Khalid al-'Awfi, modelled in part on the famous Mu'tazili theologian al-Nazzam. The debate celebrates her tremendous learning in the religious sciences of theology and law in particular and her wide reading of hadith and Qur'anic commentary, as well as her native

[202] Kloos and Künkler, 'Studying Female Islamic Authority', 487.

intelligence and boldness. Subsequently, Husniyya entered Shi'i biographical works, along with other female scholars, and she even acquired a physical presence at her shrine in the town of Torbat-i Haydariyya in Khurasan. Husniyya serves a model for Twelver Shi'i women aspiring to religious learning and authority, her example indicating that social station and non-Arab lineage are not a barrier to education, that intelligent girls ought to be encouraged to seek an extensive religious education, and that female initiative and bold action produce positive, and even socially acceptable, results. The figure of Husniyya has grown more and more tangible since the sixteenth century, making her an even more concrete inspiration for Twelver Shi'i women seeking religious authority.

CHAPTER

8

LAYLI AS QUEEN OF HEAVEN BY MUHAMMADI OF HERAT, *C.* 1565

Michael Barry

Master Muhammadi and Sixteenth-century Safavid Painting

Last of the great masters of Herat and himself one of the very finest painters of the Safavid mid-sixteenth century, the artist who invariably signed his name as Muhammadi-yi Harawi, 'Muhammadi of Herat', pondered several of the loveliest creations of his towering predecessor, Bihzad, also of Herat (1465–1535), and just as lovingly recreated their prototypes.

Bihzad was the most revered of all Eastern Islamic manuscript illuminators, first as the towering artist of the late fifteenth-century Sunni Timurid kingdom of Herat, then as the consecrated master painter of the early sixteenth-century Safavid régime. After Bihzad's native city of Herat was annexed to the Safavid Empire of Iran in 1510 AD, the new Shi'ite authorities were keen to adopt fully as their own the incomparable cultural legacy of the fallen Timurid capital. Bihzad himself converted to Shi'ism and in 1522 AD was appointed by Shah Isma'il to be the Safavid Empire's *shaykh* of the guild of all the realm's craftsmen of the book. In the teeth of supposed Islamic prohibition of figurative arts, the language of Shah Isma'il's royal edict proclaimed Bihzad to be 'the mirroring manifestation of the rare subtleties of figures', *maẓ'har-i nawādir-i ṣuwar.*

This starkly Neoplatonic wording, in fact penned by the learned royal scribe Khwandamir of Herat in Shah Isma'il's service, implied that Bihzad's saintly mind mirrored the archetypal images or 'abiding essences' (*a'yān thābita*) in the mind of God, mental configurations akin to Plato's Ideas through which God was believed to have created visible forms (*ṣūra,* plural *ṣuwar*).

Bihzad as Shaykh of the Order (*ḥirfeh*) of all Safavid artists of the book was thus regarded by the edict's language as a visionary seer akin to the most inspired poets who, in their day, were regarded as having also peered into the invisible world – in the manner of, say, a Nizami or a Hafiz respectively styled by their civilisation 'Mirror of the Unseen World' (*Āyineh-yi Ghayb*) and 'Tongue of the Unseen World' (*Lisān-ul-Ghayb*). That is, like these poets, Bihzad was considered capable of visibly reproducing these holy images with stylus and brush on paper, for his disciples to learn and trace in turn.

After Bihzad's death in 1535, succession to Mastership of the Order passed to his grand-nephew Muzaffar 'Ali, reflecting royal Safavid hopes that the *himmat-i Bihzadi* or 'Bihzadian holy zeal' might be transmitted, as in any Sufi Order, in the family line. But when Muzaffar 'Ali died in 1576, only the artist Sadiqi Beg, no blood relation to the founding master, was deemed possessed of sufficient talent to perpetuate the tradition of 'Bihzadian holy zeal' – as Sadiqi Beg tells us himself in a preface to his Persian-language treatise on 'The Canon of Figures' (*Qānūn-uṣ-Ṣuwar*.) Still, the second generation of Safavid artists laboured diligently under Muzaffar 'Ali's Grand Mastership to hone Bihzad's models reverently in the royal workshop. These artists included the talented Muhammadi.

No mere imitator, however, Muhammadi recreated Bihzad's prototypes with a sensitive brush, fresh iconic elaborations, and profound allegorical insights, much in the manner that successive Persian-language poets also harped on well-known themes: Amir Khusro and Jami, for example, taking up Nizami's love-stories anew – or for that matter, the way Classical Greek tragedians tirelessly rehearsed the same subjects, or modern authors repeatedly draw on Shakespeare.

Figure 8.1 'Seated Princess', by Muhammadi, probably Herat, *c.* 1565; Soudavar Collection, Art and History Collection; Freer and Sackler Galleries, Washington, DC, LTS1995.2.171 – repr. in A. Soudavar, *Art of the Persian Courts*, no. 92, p. 237, and M. Barry et al., *The Canticle of the Birds*, p. 143.

One of Muhammadi's most striking variants upon an ultimately Bihzadian model appears upon the cover of this book.

Muhammadi's so-called 'Seated Princess', dated *c*. 1565, was designed as an isolated album page for the delight of one of the Safavid princes, possibly Sultan-Ibrahim, nephew to the reigning Shah Tahmasp and governor of the Khurasan territories now divided between Iran (Mashhad) and Afghanistan (Herat).

Bought by the renowned A. Soudavar collection, Muhammadi's picture is now preserved in Washington, DC's Freer–Sackler Galleries. Muhammadi's immediate model, in fact, is a very similar album page by Mirza 'Ali of Tabriz dated *c*. 1540, now in the Harvard Art Museums, displaying identical pose and attire, albeit drawn in reverse with other colours, and lacking the telltale symbolic arch-like frame deliberately added in Muhammadi's version.

Figure 8.2 'Seated Princess', by Mirza 'Ali, Tabriz, *c*. 1540; Harvard Art Museums/Arthur M. Sackler Museum, Gift of John Goelet, formerly in the collection of Louis J. Cartier. © President and Fellows of Harvard College.

Like contemporary workshops in Renaissance Italy, fifteenth- and sixteenth-century royal libraries in Tabriz, Shiraz, Herat, and Mashhad often exchanged designs through 'pounced' copies: that is, outlines of a motif were pricked with tiny needle holes in a page sent as a gift or sample; once this 'pounced' page was received, fine charcoal dust was allowed to dribble through the holes to form a shadowy outline on the sheet of paper beneath, which the copyist then retraced with a stylus – reversing the original direction at will.

Muhammadi in Khurasan obviously reworked such a model derived from Mirza 'Ali's design in Tabriz, because such a design was regarded as fraught with cultural significance, to be repeated and elaborated for his own princely patron.

Lying beyond these Ladies by Muhammadi and Mirza 'Ali, however, lurked a Bihzadian archetype, as we shall see.

The twin Ladies by these two eminent painters may appear to us as elegant as early twentieth-century Parisian coquettes or silent film stars, but they not only testify to the extreme stylish refinement of Safavid figurative art at its mid-sixteenth-century zenith. These mysterious princesses beckon us across five centuries arrayed in ornaments steeped in the symbolic code of their own age: a code perhaps baffling to modern viewers, but crystalline to contemporaries of Mirza 'Ali and Muhammadi.

The precise visual codes of Timurid then Safavid painting, transmitted from masters to disciples in the discipline of the royal workshops that produced these illuminated manuscripts or composed albums of individual pictures for an elite audience of kings and princes, were largely lost to memory with the fall of the Safavid dynasty and dispersal of its library staff after 1722 CE.

Early twentieth-century rediscovery of 'Persian miniatures' by enthusiastic European collectors stressed formal and decorative qualities alone: bright and shadowless primary colour combinations, bold geometric patterns, delight in flat surface ornament and refusal of linear perspective and other aspects of post-Renaissance European illusionism that, to be sure, influenced Matisse hence all modern art ever since the French master admired the first exhibition in Paris of Eastern Islamic art in 1903, another in Munich in 1910, and a fresh one in Paris in 1912.

But Europe's purely aesthetic approach to Persian painting ignored its original cultural and literary context – dealers like Georges Demotte in Paris just before World War I even snipped pictures right out of their manuscripts to sell them more profitably piecemeal – leaving this art to hang largely mute and stripped of its initial symbolic significance, as it were, upon our modern Western museum walls, in Europe then in North America, for the rest of the twentieth century.

In fact, fifteenth- and sixteenth-century Timurid and Safavid artists played with literary cues as intricate as the wording in verses by the Persian-language poets that these painters so closely illustrated: verses upon which these deeply literate painters offered their own highly significant pictorial glosses, intimately to accompany the pertinent text with their images for erudite princely readers who leafed through these illuminated manuscripts or individual album pages.

In Bihzad's Shadow: Master Muhammadi's 'Seated Princess' within the Niche of Prayer

Like Mirza 'Ali's Seated Princess of *c.* 1540, Muhammadi's Lady of *c.* 1565 sports an identical lapis lazuli-tinted *tāj* or crown, circled with a band of gold wrought into a fantastic Chinese-style finial, albeit topped in Muhammadi's picture by an aigrette or *sar-pēch,* both adornments clearly denoting a royal princess or even Queen.

In both paintings she also coquettishly dangles a kerchief or *mandīl* from her right sleeve. This apparently frivolous detail actually betokens her royalty as much as her crown and egret.

In Timurid then Safavid art, only princely characters may clutch, dangle, or tuck into their belt such a strip of cloth denoting royal rank, derived in Islamic court etiquette ever since 'Abbasid times from the *mappa* or imperial kerchief once brandished by Byzantine emperors as a sign of sovereign power. (Eastern Roman rulers ceremoniously tossed this *mappa* into the arena to start the chariot races.) Successors to the Byzantines, the Ottoman sultans are always seen gripping such a symbolic kerchief in their portraits enthroned in splendour: but so do Safavid shahs, Uzbek emirs, and Mughal emperors – and the Ladies here.

Yet the spectacle that these Ladies contemplate is intensely private. Each Lady inclines her lovely head to regard a sprig of narcissi, a flower known to medieval Persianate literati as the *abhar-ul-'āshiqīn* or 'narcissus of lovers', here delicately pinched between the long, tapering aristocratic fingers of her left hand.

Dark lovelocks or *zulf* further heighten the brilliant complexion of her face seen as silvery pale as the moon's – while her eyebrows meet over her nose in twin arches that medieval Persian-language poets often liked to compare upon a lady's brow to the niche of prayer in a mosque or *miḥrāb:* the face of the Belovèd providing, as it were, the true focus for Her lover's spiritual love and mystical contemplation.

Indeed, Muhammadi's Lady sits within the arch of a *miḥrāb,* inviting Her viewers to contemplate Her as the radiant manifestation of the Divine. Muhammadi's purposely added *miḥrāb* highlights the motif's symbolism.

Immediate artistic models for Muhammadi's striking depiction of the Lady as sitting within a *miḥrāb* were furnished by traditional fifteenth-century representations of the Lady Layla, or *Layli* in Persian and Turkish pronunciation, a feminine figure regularly portrayed in Timûrid art as sitting in the niche of prayer of a mosque, becoming the focus of Her lover Majnun's meditation.

Such images were normally illustrations to the eminent Azerbaijani-Persian poet Nizami's romance of *Layli and Majnun* (written in 1188 CE), for

Figure 8.3 'Layli and Majnun in School', illustration to Nizami's *Khamseh* by Bihzad and Qasim 'Ali, Herat, 1494; British Library, London, Or. 6810, folio 106 verso; repr. in Basil Gray, *Persian Painting*, p. 123. © The British Library Board.

his scene where the beautiful girl Layli is first beheld by her future lover Qays when they are both young children in school. A gust of wind accidentally blows off Layli's face-cloth, revealing her lovely face. Struck with passion as if he had just beheld a brief glimpse of the Divine, Qays will become the 'Majnun', that is, 'the mad one for love', when Layli's clan will deny him wedlock with her.

Timurid art throughout the fifteenth century depicted this scene as if the primary school were sheltered within a mosque – indeed usually the case in that age – with a schoolmaster teaching pupils, young Qays with stylus and inkwell preparing to write his first poem in Layli's praise, and Layli herself strategically placed within the *miḥrāb*.

A particularly outstanding example of such a Lady-in-the-Mihrab is offered by an illustration to a sumptuous royal Timurid manuscript of Nizami's five narrative poems copied in Herat in 1494 CE (now British Library Or. 6810), with illuminations by all three leading artists in the city then labouring in the same workshop: Mirak Naqqash and his two disciples, Qasim 'Ali and the great Bihzad himself.

The specific image of Layli sitting in the mosque's niche of prayer is attributed to all three artists. Qasim 'Ali signed the picture between two columns of text, but a later hand in the lower margin inscribed the name of Mirak, and a still later scrawl by the Mughal Emperor Jahangir himself (r. 1605–1627), who came to own this manuscript in seventeenth-century India, unhesitatingly attributed the painting to 'Bihzad'. Possibly all three artists collaborated on the picture, then a common royal workshop practice – although modern scholarship retains mainly Bihzad's name.[1]

In what we can conventionally call at any rate the Bihzadian prototype, the 'schoolmaster' teaches not only the pupils, but us his readers, for he is an idealised representation of the poet Nizami himself configured as the guiding Active Intelligence, an originally Aristotelian concept allegorised ever since Avicenna's eleventh-century philosophical fable *Ḥayy ibn Yaqẓān* as a wise old man decked with all the majesty but none of the infirmities of age: an archetypal figure of initiation repeated, in precisely this same guise and pose, in a number of Timurid manuscripts (for example, the Oxford Bodleian *Kulliyyāt* of Nawa'i dated 1486 and the Egyptian National Library *Bustān* of Sa'di from 1488).

What the wise old poet teaches us is this – according to Nizami's verses framed within the image itself:

این پرده دریده شد ز هر سوی وآن راز شنیده شد به هر کوی
زین قصه که محکم آیتی بوَد در هر دهنی حکایتی بود
کردند به هم بسی مدارا تا راز نگردد آشکارا
بند سر نافه گر چه خشک است بوی خرش او گوای مشک است
بادی که ز عاشقی خبر داشت برقع ز جمال خویش بر داشت

The curtain was torn away on every side, / The secret was heard in every lane, /
Sure sign of the story appeared, / The tale of it ran on all lips. /
No matter how much they warned one another / That their secret not appear, /
However baked shut the seal upon a pod, / A whiff of its musk will arise: /
The very wind, aware of such a Love, / Removed the Veil from over Her Beauty.

The Bihzadian image dramatises the precise moment of the veil slipping away from Layli's countenance as a central mystical metaphor for the apparition of the Divine in a holy manifestation unto the eyes of the loving soul, with the face of the Beloved considered a true mirror of the Divine. In Nizami's day, the Arabised Neoplatonic term for Greek *epiphania* (as in the word used by

---

[1] Basil Gray, *Persian Painting* (Geneva: Éditions Skira, 1961); Michael Barry, *Figurative Art in Medieval Islam and the Riddle of Bihzâd of Herât (1465–1535)* (Paris: Flammarion and New York: Rizzoli, 2004–2005). [With exhaustive bibliography referring to studies by C. Adle, S. Canby, B. Gray, S. Melikian-Chirvani, B. Robinson, A. Soudavar, P. Soucek, S. C. Welch and others.]

Christian Arab translators to signify the Divine 'Manifestation' upon Mount Tabor in the Gospels) was *al-tajallī*, the 'effulgence' of the Divine.

This notion of *tajallī* or Epiphany– as reflected upon a human countenance – became an absolutely central concept in the mystical metaphysics of Sufism, for example, in the works of the influential Spanish-Arab thinker Ibn 'Arabi (1165–1240 CE), who moved and taught throughout the Near East and whose teachings ultimately spread throughout almost the entire Islamic world. Nizami did not live long enough to discover Ibn 'Arabi's writings himself, but already by the end of the twelfth century very similar Neoplatonising pantheistic ideas pervaded all intellectual Muslim circles from Seville to Lahore, with stress on the notion of the Divine mirrored upon a human face.

After the middle of the thirteenth century, erudite readers of Persian invariably understood Nizami's poetry in light of Ibn 'Arabi's concepts: for example, the two most celebrated Persian-language versions of the Layli and Majnun story by Nizami's successor poets, Amir Khusro of Delhi in the fourteenth century, then by Jami of Herat in the fifteenth, blended the visions of both the Spanish-Arab thinker, and the Azerbaijani poet. Manuscript illuminators of the Timurid court at Herat in turn took into account both poetic versions by Amir Khusro and Jami also when illustrating Nizami's own rendition of the tale, as making up the whole canonical tradition of *Laylī-o Majnūn*. Turkish-language renditions in the fifteenth and sixteenth centuries by Nawa'i and Fuzuli further attest to the tale's widespread popularity.

This is because the very tale of Layli and Majnun, with its account of frustrated love, pinched a highly sensitive cultural nerve. In all traditional Islamic urban society from Spain to India, segregation of the sexes after puberty and rigidly enforced arranged marriages between clans and the consequent sexual frustration were so severe that the first glimpse of his promised bride by a young man often only occurred on the wedding night. Women's seclusion heightened the sheer sense of mystery that cloaked the whole female world in the eyes of young men exasperated by desire. Thus, the revelation of a woman's face easily turned into the civilisation's symbol for the first glimpse of the Divine vouched unto the male ascetic, finally deserving to see the Divine after a long trial of emotional suffering.

On the climactic wedding-night, a bridegroom lifted his bride's veil at last to discover her face framed by night-dark tresses, an experience emotionally so intense for many young males that it furnished the civilisation with a favourite metaphor for the mystical perception itself: the *Kashf al-Maḥjūb* or 'unveiling what is veiled'. Fittingly, the first Persian-language treatise on Sufism, by Hujwiri writing in eleventh-century Lahore, was entitled with the wedding term: *Kashf al-Maḥjūb*.

In the Bihzadian illustration, young Qays dips his stylus into the inkwell to pen his first poem in Layli's praise, while the Tree of Life growing up from beside the Fount of Life (corresponding here to the ablution well of the mosque) rises over the saintly lover like a protective canopy. This tree is always depicted in Bihzad's workshop as a plane-tree flamboyant in motley autumn foliage in accordance with Ibn 'Arabi's treatise on the *Shajarat al-Kawn* or 'Tree of Life' ('on beholding the Perfect Man, the Cosmic Tree leaned forth lovingly and trembled in all the multiplicity of its colours', *mālat ilayhi wa-htazzat bi-kathrati l-alwān*).

Layli for her part sits in the *miḥrāb*, perfectly designated in the image not only by its arch, but by the explicit Qur'anic quotation running in *thuluth* calligraphy directly above it: *wa-huwa qā'im-un yuṣallī fī l-miḥrāb,* 'and upright was he, praying towards the mihrab' (3:40). Qays is understood as properly directing his contemplation towards Layli's suddenly unveiled face as if a worshipper before the *miḥrāb,* because he recognises that her countenance has become the *tajallī,* the mirrored effulgence of the Divine: whose radiance will lead his heart to final union with the Divine. Nizami's poetry in turn says so as explicitly as the image's design:

ای کعبهٔ من جمال رویت   محراب من آستان کویت

The beauty of thy face becomes my Ka'ba,
The threshold of the path to thee becomes my Mihrāb.

Just as Master Muhammadi in the 1560s closely meditated and produced a magnificent variation on one of Bihzad's illustrations, 'The Saint and the Ploughman', to the great 1486 manuscript of 'Attar's *Manṭiq-uṭ Ṭayr* or 'Canticle of the Birds' then preserved in the Safavid dynastic shrine at Ardabil (this original is now in the Metropolitan Museum of Art of New York City; Muhammadi's variant is in the Louvre Museum in Paris), so the artist provided his own twist to Mirza 'Ali's early 'Seated Princess' by adding the arch of the *miḥrāb* – in reference to the Bihzadian illumination for the Layli and Majnun story.

Not that Mirza 'Ali in 1540 had not provided his own understanding of Layli. In Mirza 'Ali's version of the 'Princess', the Lady in fact wears red – just as in the Bihzâdian painting, Layli wears red. This colour hints to the profound grasp by artists of the Timurid and Safavid age of the subtlest of Nizami's meanings. At the end of his tale, Nizami describes Majnun calling out in anguish over Layli's tomb: *ay Dizh-Bānū-yi man,* 'oh my Lady of the Castle!' – in allusion to Nizami's own tale of the Lady of the Red Castle in the *Haft Paykar* or 'Seven Icons' (finally completed in 1197), who wears red and whose lovers must wear red to signify their own readiness to pour out their hearts' blood to woo her, since She symbolises the Divine hidden behind the magic brazen ramparts of the Castle of the Other World; in other words She is the Queen of Heaven.

Just so, in *Laylī-o Majnūn,* the Lover will only unite with his Beloved – the Queen of Heaven – in the Other World.

Muhammadi thus makes clear the identity of his 'Princess' in his own interpretation of the archetype. Just as in Mirza 'Ali's model, his Lady wears the crown and dangles the kerchief of a Queen – for she is Layli as Queen of Heaven, seated in a *miḥrāb* as in the model offered by Bihzad's School.

A Play on Flowers and a Play of Words on Eyes

The Lady in the versions by both Mirza 'Ali and Muhammadi contemplates narcissi – another telltale detail.

The narcissus or *nargis*, also called the *abhar-ul-'āshiqīn* or 'narcissus of lovers' (as in the title of a mystical treatise by the early thirteenth-century Sufi master Rozbihan-i Baqli of Shiraz), in medieval Persian poetry and painting is a common metaphor for the human eye.

In a word, the Lady in both paintings contemplates Herself: for since these narcissi are symbols of human eyes, She sees Herself through the eyes of Her lovers.

Is the Lady then not only a mirrored manifestation of the Divine, but Herself the Divine?

According to the Sufi teachings of the Andalusian master Ibn 'Arabi and his literary disciples from Spain to India, human eyes are the very eyes through which the Divine looks upon the Divine.

In the opening lines to the opening chapter of Ibn 'Arabi's most influential masterpiece 'The Gemstones of Wisdom' or rather 'Bezels of Wisdom' (*Fuṣūṣ al-Ḥikam*), penned in Damascus in 1220 CE and endlessly glossed by succeeding generations of Eastern Muslim scholars including Shi'ite thinkers well into the Safavid period, Spanish Islam's most eminent mystical genius wrote words that the paintings by Mirza 'Ali then Muhammadi then render as a daring pictorial conceit.

Ibn 'Arabi describes creation of the visible world as the wish of an unseen God to look upon God as if in a mirror. But the universe looms into view as a cloudy, unfocused mirror, because this non-human universe has no consciousness of self, still less consciousness of God. God therefore creates the human being because only the human mind, through consciousness of both itself and of its Creator, can clearly mirror God to God. The human mind – if of course kept saintly, pure, and aware – becomes a polished mirror of God.

Yet in Ibn 'Arabi's recondite mystical word-play, God is at once an Essence, *'ayn,* a Fount, *'ayn,* yet also an Eye, *'ayn*: since one and the same Arabic noun can mean all three.

But in one of the boldest of his many audacious spiritual metaphors, the Andalusian master affirms that no eye can see itself except in a mirror: hence God's need to create the human eye to look upon God's own Eye – and thus upon God's own creative Fount, hence upon God's own Essence.

Moreover, the Permanent Archetypes of the world's visible forms that abide in the mind of God are also 'eyes': the abstract founts and invisible essences of all the manifest forms of the universe also correspond to God's 'most beautiful names' but can also be called the *a'yān thābita* or 'abiding eyes' / 'abiding founts'/ 'abiding essences' – and these further Divine Eyes also need their own visible forms, as it were, to mirror themselves back to themselves.

In a spiritual pun, Ibn 'Arabi alludes to a common Arabic expression for the pupil in the eye: *insān al-'ayn* – 'the man-in-the-eye'.

In Ibn 'Arabi's vivid, almost hallucinatory visualisation of powerful images that goes far to explain his attraction for poets and painters, the little round black hole in the human eye is the vector of exchanged sight between the human creature and its Divine Creator.

Ibn 'Arabi further compares this 'man-in-the-eye' to the gem in a ring encircled by its bezel: like the human mind that is God's mirror, the 'man-in-the-eye', then, is the seal of the universe – for only the human mind's vision, once created, mirrors and so can comprehend God's universe.

In Ibn 'Arabi's own dense wording:[2]

لما شاء الحقّ سبحانه من حيث أسماؤه الحسنى التي لا يبلغها الاحصاء أن يرى أعيانها - وإن شئتَ أن يرى عينه في كونٍ
ويظهر سرّه إليه : فإن رؤية الشيء نفسه بنفسه ما هي مثل رؤيته نَفْسَه –جامعٍ يحصر الأمر كلّه لكونه متصفاً بالوجود
فيأمرِ آخرِيكون له كالمرآة : فإنه يظهرُ له نفسه في صورة

When the Most Praised Reality, in so far as It is qualified by Its most beautiful names whose number might not even be counted,
wished then to look upon Its own Eyes (or Founts, or Essences)
– and if you wish, this would be as much as to say that It wished to look upon Its own Eye (Fount, Essence)
within a comprehensive being that should encompass the entire universe
(in so far as this being's own sheer being might be qualified by its sheer existence) –
and thereby manifest unto this being Its own Secret:
for the vision of a thing unto itself is not like the vision it enjoys through something else, as in a mirror –
then indeed did It manifest Itself, unto this extant being, as a configured Image.

Ibn 'Arabi deliberately uses a rather sexless word for God (authorised by the Qur'an): *al-Ḥaqq*, 'The Reality'.

His noun for 'figure', 'shape' or 'icon', *sura,* can refer to two things: either the vast visible universe or macrocosm, or the universe concentrated in the figure of Man as mirrored in Man's spiritual awareness: as in a microcosm.

The Image that Ibn 'Arabi's Reality conjures up, before the clouded mass of the universe as it looms into existence, is the human figure itself newly wrought by the Divine, as expressed through the writer's allusion to the famous story of the creation of Adam into whom God breathed the living spirit of intelligence, the *rūḥ* or 'holy breath'.

'Adam' in Ibn 'Arabi's writings signifies, of course, the prototypical human being himself or *Insān Kāmil*, 'the Perfect Human'. The polished mirror that is Adam's mind reflects, through the visible form of Adam's

[2] Ibn 'Arabi, *Fusūs al-Hikam* (Bezels of Wisdom) (Cairo: 'Afîfî, 1946), 48–49.

own person or *sūra*, the abiding and refulgent manifestation (or *tajallī*) of the invisible Divine, *al-fayḍ al-tajallī ad-dā'im*:

الفيض التجلّي الدائم

Ibn 'Arabi adds:

فانقضى الأمرُ جلاء مرآة العالم ـفكان آدم عينَ جلاء تلك المرآة و روح تلك الصورة

'And the Reality commanded that the universe's mirror be polished – and Adam became the very Eye and Essence in the polishing of that mirror, and also the Breath of Intelligence within that universe's vast visible form.'[3]

Eve as Queen of Heaven

Throughout his opening chapter on 'Adam', and again in his concluding chapter on the Prophet Muhammad, Ibn 'Arabi alludes to the story told in sûra 2: 32–34 of the Qur'an. The Reality creates the form of Adam, and commands that the angels bow down in reverence before Adam. Only one creature in heaven refuses to do so, the Devil, on grounds that God had first commanded that worship should be addressed to God alone. God in wrath casts the Devil out of heaven.

Sufi meditation on the spiritual paradox of this story – why should God punish the Devil for observing God's own first command? – tried hard to crack the adamantine contradiction apparently lodged in the story's heart. Bold solutions offered by al-Hallaj in tenth-century Baghdad, by 'Ayn-ul-Quzat of Hamadan in the twelfth century, and finally by Rozbihan-i Baqli of Shiraz and Spain's Ibn 'Arabi at the turn of the twelfth and thirteenth centuries, resolved the Devil's riddle in a manner whereby rigorous philosophical logic finally overcame orthodox objections, at least throughout the age of Sufism's triumph in Islamic civilisation: roughly from the middle of the twelfth century CE until the rise of literalist Wahhabism in the middle of the eighteenth. In the fifteenth- and sixteenth-century golden age of Islamic painting in the Tîmûrid and Safavid domains, however, the following Sufi interpretation, broadly consonant with Ibn 'Arabi's thought, widely prevailed.

The Reality, synonymous with infinity, is impossible for the human mind to grasp, and of course impossible for the human eye to see. But just as in mathematics, where infinity is impossible to encompass yet designated by a symbol, the endless sequence of numerals nevertheless makes itself at least partly accessible to the human mind and visibly manifest through numerical symbols: invisible infinity, in other words, does make itself visible – through visible signs.

Just so, the all-pervading Reality, or infinity, made itself manifest through the visible universe.

---

[3] Ibn 'Arabi, *Fuṣūṣ al-Ḥikam*, 49.

This universe, however, remained imperfect, because it was devoid of awareness of itself.

The Reality therefore manifested Itself more perfectly in the Prototypical Human or *Insān Kāmil,* 'the Perfect Man': because endowed with the spirit of intelligence, gifted with language, crowned with the capacity to articulate thought – a fraction of the universe, yet both aware of itself and of the surrounding universe.

Human awareness is thus the eye through which the Reality looks upon the Reality – or to paraphrase Ibn 'Arabi's depth of meditation in the words of modern astrophysics: the human mind is the consciousness that the universe has of itself.

Just as numerals manifest and thus 'mirror' infinity, and thus are not *other* than infinity, so Adam as a symbol is not *other* than God, but the mirror or *tajallī* of God.

The Devil, according to al-Hallaj, 'Ayn-ul-Quzat, Rozbihan, and Ibn 'Arabi, failed to grasp that Adam was not *other* than God, but God's necessary and visible reflection.

According to Ibn 'Arabi's understanding, the angels metaphorically represent attributes of the human mind, called upon therefore to bow down before the totality represented by 'Adam'.

Al-Hallaj and 'Ayn-ul-Quzat, to be sure, saw spiritual heroism, even if mistaken heroism, in the Devil's refusal to bow, an admirable martyrdom in trying to uphold God's apparent command even against God and a superb willingness to endure the consequent wrath of God – even though Rozbihân and Ibn 'Arabi for their part mostly dismiss the Devil as a mere unconscious mirroring of God's aspect of Wrath.

What is truly interesting in terms of art is that the human figure, which the Devil thus refused to recognise as the mirroring *tajallī* of the Divine, could be not only male, but even female, in Islamic literature and painting of the twelfth to eighteenth centuries.

In his closing chapter on the Prophet Muhammad, Ibn 'Arabi stresses the dignity of the female. The Prophet himself, he writes, loved three things above all: women (a female word), perfume (a masculine word in Arabic), and prayer (a feminine) – and contrary to the usage of Arabic grammar where the masculine normally predominates, he notes, the sentence in which the Prophet says this is conjugated in the feminine mode; Eve moulded of the rib of Adam means that woman is part of man; man's love for woman is necessary awareness of his own completeness; wedded love between man and woman gives the closest idea of the ecstasy of mystical union; the matter or matrix of the universe is itself a grammatically feminine concept (*mādda*).

Even the ultimate Reality of the Divine, according to Ibn 'Arabi, is an Arabic feminine: the 'Essence' or *Dhāt.* Like the Prophet's words on women (female), perfume (male), and prayer (female), in that order, so the human male stands between the female Essence that gives him birth, and the female human that issues from him in an inalterable trinity.

What the angels were called upon to worship in perfect human form, therefore, could thus be perceived as Man and Woman together, since Woman includes Man, indissolubly linked. Thus, Ibn 'Arabi:[4]

ولم تكن الشهادة إلا في مادّة – فشهود الحقّ في النساء أعظم الشهود
وأكمله–وأعظم الوصلة النكاح و هو نظير التوجّه الإهى

There is no possibility of witnessing existence except through its manifestation in visible matter – and to witness the Divine Reality in women is the greatest and most perfect manner of witness: and the greatest form of union is wedlock, and this is similar to the Divine Union itself.

Safavid artists of the sixteenth century sought to render such a mystical vision of the Male–Female union through the visual vocabulary most practically available to them.

Figure 8.4 'The Angels Bow Before Adam and Eve': illustration to a *Fāl-Nāmeh* or 'Book of Omens' for Shah Tahmasp, Qazvin, *c.* 1560; Arthur M. Sackler Gallery, Washington, DC, S1986.254 – repr. in Barry et al., *The Canticle of the Birds*, p. 139.

[4] 'Arabi, *Fusūs al-Hikam*, 217.

One of the anonymous painters of a royal Safavid *Fāl-Nāmeh* or 'Book of Omens' (now in Washington, DC 's Freer Gallery), sumptuously produced in the decade of the 1560s, hence immediately contemporary to the works of Muhammadi, represents Adam and Eve together, richly arrayed and both enthroned as King and Queen of Heaven. The heads of both human figures are surrounded with a flaming halo betokening their saintly *tajalliyāt* or epiphanies.[5] *Both* mirror the Divine.

Adam alone here clutches the kerchief or *mandīl* of royalty (as God's viceroy or *khalīfa* on earth), but the Queen arrestingly appears in almost exactly the same crown and pose as her sisters in the paintings by Mirza 'Ali and Muhammadi: her right hand hides in the long sleeve of her caftan, the fingers of her left delicately pinch an invisible object, as it were – as if the narcissi of Layli. This 'Eve' clearly reflects some workshop archetype on which both Mirza 'Ali and Muhammadi drew: with these two other artists supplying flowers for her to pinch.

The image also limpidly translates Ibn 'Arabi's vision. The angels bow before the Perfect Human: not just before Adam, but before Adam and Eve, Male and Female, enthroned together. Only the turbaned Devil above, with darkened countenance, tugs his white beard in metaphysical perplexity. The artist even caricatures the Devil as an orthodox literalist *mullā* rigidly adhering to the surface letter of the Law, because incapable of sounding mystical depths and the hidden meanings of Scripture, poetry, and art.

The painting confirms the Queen of Heaven motif: the Lady named 'Eve' or 'Layli', whose countenance mirrors the Divine, in Timurid and Safavid art can Herself signify the Divine Unveiled – in a feminine aspect.

Sufi literature from the twelfth century onwards make this feminisation of the Divine Epiphany as crystalline as spiritual symbolism can bear. Ibn 'Arabi's *Tarjumān al-Ashwāq* or 'Interpreter of Desires' addresses verses to God evoked in openly feminine grammatical forms. 'Attar's Shaykh San'an in 'The Canticle of the Birds' is led to higher spiritual awareness through his love for the Christian Princess who draws aside the 'veil' or *burqu'* of her dark lovelocks that hid her radiant countenance. Nizami's characters 'Farhad' and 'Khusrow' signify two successive stages of the loving male soul, one denied and the other vouchsafed union with the Divine Beloved configured as Queen Shirin – just as Majnun aspires to be united with the Lady Layli in the Other World: herself compared to the sometimes terrifying Red Princess of the Other World's Brazen Castle whose male lovers lay down their lives for Her sake save for one solitary soul who can finally

---

[5] The halo or *farr* denoting a good and saintly ruler derives originally, in world art, from a pre-Islamic Persian mark of royalty, subsequently borrowed by the religious iconography of both Christianity in the West, and Buddhism in the East, where the Chinese modified its originally circular shape into a flame-like radiance – reborrowed in this form by the Muslim artists in the wake of the thirteenth-century Mongol invasions.

answer Her riddles.[6] When poets like Hafiz refer to themselves as a humble 'Farhad' or 'Majnun', they blatantly imply that their Beloved can, indeed, be perceived as a feminine.

This is why modern Western translations of medieval Persian poetry – with its admittedly ambiguous genders – that systematically render the Beloved by a masculine, sometimes stray wide off the mark. The temperament of the individual mystic plays a role, of course: the page-boy Ayaz focusing his contemplation upon Sultan Mahmud, in the poetry of 'Attar, while the verses of Nizami stress an exclusively female Beloved, reveal the same obvious contrast to be found in the Christian West between the writings of, say, a Saint John of the Cross who describes his feminine soul yearning for Jesus 'who wounds me gently in the side', and a Dante who follows his Lady Beatrix into the Other World.

Still, W. H. Whinfield's otherwise remarkably accurate rendition (London 1880) of the fourteenth-century Persian 'Rosebower of Mystery' or *Gulshan-i Rāz* by the Sufi Mahmud-i Shabistari of Tabriz, so carefully glossed by Muhammad ibn Yahya Lâhiji at the end of the Tîmurid and into the early Safavid age, obviously errs in turning the poet's focus unrelentingly towards a Divine addressed strictly as male. Shabistari's imagery plays rather on the mystery of the female: she removes the veil of Her dark lovelocks – symbolising the night or pre-eternal Darkness of non-Manifestation in which the Divinity hides in Her Majesty's Wrath (*qahr, jalāl*)– to display, unto Her lover, the cheek of Her shining countenance in the spiritual Manifestation, *tajallī,* of Her Mercy's Lovely Grace (*luṭf, jamāl*). Timurid and Safavid painting highlights the same spiritual paradox in which Sufi-minded literature delighted, as it were in the teeth of an otherwise fiercely patriarchal civilisation: teasingly and boldly reversing traditional gender roles, better to jolt conventional and merely superficial orthodox devotees into profounder religious meditation.

Thus Sufi authors by the turn of the twelfth and thirteenth centuries, whether in Arabic or in Persian and from Ibn 'Arabi in Spain to Nizami in Azerbaijan, are seen audaciously exalting a female figure as one who provides ethical guidance to her male lover, who teaches him deeper spiritual truths, and who discloses her hitherto veiled countenance unto him as a mirrored manifestation of the Divine. Ibn 'Arabi first says how proud he is to have learned Sufism from an aged female mystic in his native Spain whom he regards as his true mother, then registers the full shock of an ennobling Neoplatonic love in Mecca upon beholding the loveliness – illuminated by dazzling intelligence – of the daughter of his Persian hosts, the Lady Nizam bint Rustam: his own guiding Lady Beatrix. Meanwhile his exact contempo-

---

[6] Nizami's late twelfth-century 'Tale of the Red Princess' in the *Haft Paykar*, a blood-soaked dramatisation of the Divine manifested as a Lady of Wrath, through a later Persian prose version translated by François Pétis de la Croix in Constantinople in 1712, and in turn adapted for the theatre by Gozzi (1762), then Schiller (1801), became the ultimate source for Puccini's 1924 opera *Turandot* = Turan-Dukht, 'The Lady of Turan'.

rary Nizami describes in romances of spiritualised courtly love how Queen Shirin instructs her King Khusrow to grow and mature into a wiser ruler; how the seven brides of King Bahram enlighten their own royal spouse with seven tales of spiritual initiation; how Majnun is vouchsafed a glimpse of the Divine through contemplation of his Lady Layli.

Persian painting only attained the technical sophistication and sheer aesthetic refinement needed to illustrate Ibn 'Arabi's concepts and Nizami's and 'Attar's tales roughly a full hundred years after these authors lived: truly beginning to flower in the fourteenth century, with manuscript illuminations in Herat, Tabriz, Qazwin and Isfahan at last reaching a zenith of artistic accomplishment in the later fifteenth through the sixteenth and well into the seventeenth centuries (much as Italian painting only succeeded in the Quattrocento and Cinquecento to rival those heights of creativity earlier reached in Trecento literary masterpieces by Dante, Petrarch, or Boccaccio).

Still, a Sufi mystic like Shabistari can be seen to write in his Persian verses, in the early fourteenth century, exactly what Muhammadi paints. I quote in conclusion Shabistari's Persian original followed by Whinfield's translation – only with slight modification such as the *He* turned into *Her,* and Muhammadi's art at once looms into view (verses 717–727 and 743–751):

Question XIII
What means the mystic by those expressions of his?
What does he indicate by 'eye' and 'lip'?
What seeks he by 'cheek', 'curl', 'down', and 'freckle?'
He, to wit, who is in 'stations' and 'states?'
Answer XIII
Whatsoever is seen in this visible world,
Is as a reflection from the sun of that world.
The world is as curl, down, freckle and brow,
For everything in its own place is beautiful.
The epiphany is now in beauty, now in majesty,
Cheek and curl are the similitudes of those verities.
The attributes of 'The Truth' are mercy and wrath,
Cheek and curl of fair ones are types of these two.
When these words are heard by the sensual ear,
At first they denote objects of sense.
The spiritual world is infinite,
How can finite worlds attain to it?
How can the mysteries beheld in ecstatic vision
Be interpreted by spoken words?
When mystics treat of these mysteries,
They interpret them by types
For objects of sense are as shadows of that world,
And this world is as an infant, and that as the nurse.
. . .
See what proceeds from the eye and the lip,
Consider their attributes in this place.

From Her eye proceed languishing and intoxication,
From Her ruby lip the essence of being.
Because of Her eye all hearts are burning,
Her ruby lip is healing to the sick heart.
Because of Her eye hearts are drunken and aching,
By Her ruby lip all souls are clothed.
Though the world is not regarded by Her eye,[7]
Her lip ever and anon shows compassion.
Sometimes with humanity She charms our hearts,
Sometimes She grants help to the helpless.
By smiles She gives life to man water and clay,
By a breath She kindles the heavens into a flame.

سؤال

چو خواهد مرد معنی ز آن عبارت   که دارد سوی چشم و لب اشارت
چه جوید از رخ و زلف و خط و خال   کس کاندر مقاماتست و احوال

جواب

هر آن چیزی که در عالم عیانست   چو عکسی ز آفتاب آن جهانست
جهان چون زلف و خط و خال وابروست که   هر چیزی بجای خویش نیکوست
تجلّی که جمال و که جلالست   رخ و زلف آن معانی را مثالست
صفات حقّ تعالی لطف و قهر ست   خ و زلف زآن دو بهر ست
چو محسوس آمد این الفاظ مسموع   نخست از بهر محسوسند موضوع
ندارد عالم معنی نهایت   کجا بیند مر او را لفظ و غایت
هر آن معنی که شد بر ذوق پیدا   کجا تعبیر لفظی باید او را
چو اهلِ دل کند تفسیر معنی   بمانندی کند تعبیر معنی
که محسوسات از آن عالم چو سایه است   که این چون طفل و آن مانند دایه است

(...)

نگر کز چشم شاهد چیست پیدا   رعایت کن لوازم را بدانجا
ز چشمش خواست بیماری و مستی   ز لعلش گشت پیدا عین هستی
ز چشم او همه دلها جگر خوار   لب لعلش شفای جان بیمار
ز چشم اوست دلها مست و مخمور   ز لعل اوست جانها جمله مستور
بچشمش گرچه عالم در نیاید   لبش هر ساعتی لطفی نماید
دمی از مردمی دلها نوازد   دمی بیچارگان را چاره سازد
بشوخی جان دهد در آب و در خاک   بدم دادن زند آتش بر افلاک

[7] *Ba-chashm-ash gar-chih ʿālam dar nayāyad* here more probably mystically means : 'even though the whole visible world could not fill Her Eye/Essence . .' This refers to the pre-eternal Darkness of Her Majesty in which all virtual things are contained; then Her lip, uttering the creative Word of Grace, causes this visible world to become manifest – yet many secrets nevertheless still remain hidden in the abyssal depth of Her Divine Essence.

CHAPTER

9

PRINCESSES, PATRONAGE AND THE PRODUCTION OF KNOWLEDGE IN SAFAVID IRAN*

Yusuf Ünal

Introduction

Under Safavid rule (1501–1722), early modern Iran experienced major religious, political, and cultural changes animated by the conversion process from Sunni to Shi'i Islam. The adoption of Shi'ism as the faith of the Safavid ruling elite and the realm and the promotion of Persian through state-sponsored translation projects from Arabic engendered congruence between the faith and the land.[1] Various aspects of the new confessional development and conversion in Safavid Iran have been explored by a host of studies over the past decades.[2] One of the most under-studied aspects of this phenomenon, however, is the active role that Safavid royal women played in this shift of religious discourse and in the formation of a new confessional identity. Although scholarship on Iranian women has made great strides over the last few decades,[3] the participation of Safavid royal women in court politics and their patronage of art and architecture have dominated the field. The primary objective of the present study is to explore Safavid royal women's contribution to the propagation of Shi'ism and the production of knowledge in the medium of the Persian language

---

[1] Tijana Krstic, *Contested Conversions to Islam: Narratives of Religious Change in the Early Modern Ottoman Empire* (Stanford: Stanford University Press, 2011), 14, 97; Rudi Matthee, *Persia in Crisis: Safavid Decline and the Fall of Isfahan* (London, I. B. Tauris, 2011), 15.

[2] For a bibliographical summary, see Andrew J. Newman, *Safavids: Oxford Bibliographies Online Research Guide* (Oxford: Oxford University Press, 2013).

[3] Maria Szuppe, 'La participation des femmes de la famille royale à l'exercice du pouvoir en Iran safavide au XVIe siècle (Première Partie)', *Studia Iranica* 23.2 (1994), 211–258; Szuppe, 'La participation des femmes de la famille royale à l'exercice du pouvoir en Iran safavide au XVIe siècle (Seconde Partie)', *Studia Iranica* 24.1 (1995), 61–109; Szuppe, 'The "Jewels of Wonder": Learned Ladies and Princess Politics in the Provinces of Early Safavid Iran', in *Women in the*

through patronage of religious scholars and the production of works in many fields related to Shiʿi heritage, including theology, prayer, Prophetic tradition, Qur'anic studies, language, and dynastic history. The present study examines texts that were dedicated to the Safavid princesses. Thirteen such works have been identified through extensive research in the Shiʿi bio-biographical works and major manuscript catalogues. With few exceptions, these works are still in manuscript in various libraries of Iran; with one exception, all were written in Persian. Five different Safavid princesses who lived during different periods and phases of Safavid rule and who had different personal characteristics and marital status commissioned these texts.

This study begins with an exploration of the life and career of Mahin Banu, known as Shahzada Sultanum (1519–1562), and eight works commissioned by her about Arabic grammar, Shiʿi doctrine, the Qur'an, and history. She was followed by two of her nieces, Pari Khan Khanum II (1548–1578) and Zaynab Begum (d. 1640), daughters of Shah Tahmasb, who sponsored a Safavid chronicle and a collection of hadith respectively. Next, it introduces two daughters of Shah ʿAbbas I (r. 1587–1629), Shahzada Begum and Aqa Khan Begum, and the works sponsored by them about Shiʿi prayers, rituals, and supplications. Three such works are identified, one commissioned by Shahzada Begum and two by Aqa Khan Begum.

The Study of Safavid Royal Women

Previous studies have deepened our understanding of the Safavid women, especially with regard to their role in court politics and their patronage of

Medieval Islamic World, ed. Gavin R. G. Hambly (New York: Palgrave, 1998), 325–348; Szuppe, 'Status, Knowledge, and Politics: Women in Sixteenth-Century Safavid Iran', in *Women in Iran; From the Rise of Islam to 1800*, eds Guity Nashat and Lois Beck (Urbana and Chicago: University of Illinois Press, 2003), 140–169; Kathryn Babayan, 'The 'Aqa'id al-Nisa': A Glimpse at Safavid Women in Local Isfahani Culture', in *Women in the Medieval Islamic World*, ed. Hambly, 358–359; Shohreh Golsorkhi, 'Pari Khan Khanum: A Masterful Safavid Princess', *Iranian Studies* 28 (1995), 143–156; Fariba Zarinebaf-Shahr, 'Economic Activities of Safavid Women in the Shrine-City of Ardabil', *Iranian Studies* 31 (1998), 247–261; Kishwar Rizvi, 'Gendered Patronage: Women and Benevolence During the Early Safavid Empire', in *Women, Patronage, and Self-Representation in Islamic Societies*, ed. D. F. Ruggles (Albany: State University of New York Press, 2000), 123–153; Banafshah Hijazi, *Daʿifah: barrasi-i jaygah-i zan-i Irani dar ʿasr-i Safawi* (Tehran: Qasida-sara, 2002); ʿAbbas-Quli Ghaffari-fard, *Zan dar tarikh-nigari-yi Safawiyya* (Tehran: Mu'assasa-yi Intisharat-i Amir Kabir, 2005–2006); ʿAbd al-Majid Shuja', *Zan, siyasat va-haram-sara dar ʿasr-i Safawiyya* (Sabzavar: Intisharat-i Umid-i Mihr, 2005–2006); Nazak Birjandifar, 'Royal Women and Politics in Safavid Iran', Master's Thesis, McGill University, 2006; Rudi Matthee, 'From the Battlefield to the Harem: Did Women's Seclusion Increase from Early to Late Safavid Times?', in *New Perspectives on Safavid Iran*, ed. Colin P. Mitchell (London: Routledge, 2011), 97–121; Kioumars Ghereghlou, 'Zaynab Begum', *Encyclopædia Iranica*, online edition, 2016 <http://www.iranicaonline.org/articles/zaynab-begum>.

art and architecture. The most comprehensive work to date on royal women of the early Safavid period is that of Maria Szuppe, whose long article in French was published in two parts in 1994 and 1995. Later, abridged versions of these articles were published in English.[4] Szuppe's study deals with the lives and political careers of the early Safavid princesses of the sixteenth century. Although she made brief inroads into the education of the Safavid princesses and their cultural activities, the patronage relationship between the early Safavid princesses and Safavid scholars fell outside the purview of her study.[5] Moreover, Szuppe maintained that, in the sixteenth century, 'the women of the Safavid elites were more visible and more socially active than in the later period, when they exercised their political power from behind harem walls'. She attributed the political activism, independence, and visibility of the Safavid princess to their Turco-Mongol ancestry and the religio-cultural ambiance informed by Central Asian, pagan mores, syncretic faith, and relatively free heterodoxy. According to this view, the more the Safavids became detached from Central Asian tribal mores and latitudinarian religious outlook, the more the influence of orthodox Shi'i Islam crept into gender politics and led to strict gender segregation, marginalising women behind walls and veils. This linearising approach, detecting a development from 'tolerant' and 'high-spirited' culture to oppressive orthodoxy, was also adopted by Kathryn Babayan and Shireen Mahdavi, who argued that female participation in public life was curtailed and confronted by the Safavid policies designed under the nefarious influence of dominant clerics such as Muhammad Baqir al-Majlisi.[6] According to Mahdavi, one of the outcomes of the seclusion of women, especially affluent urban women, was their contribution to the enrichment of Iranian cuisine, since they enjoyed enough time and leisure at home.[7]

The emphasis on the tribal, eclectic, and Turko-Mongol roots of early Safavid society in the context of the royal women's political activism and independence has been questioned by several studies. Kishwar Rizvi's 2000 chapter on gendered patronage in the early Safavid Empire suggested that Szuppe's explanation of the royal women's political activism and influence with the nomadic mores and Turko-Mongol tradition is

[4] Szuppe, 'La participation (Première Partie)', 211–258; Szuppe, 'La participation (Seconde Partie)', 61–109.

[5] She mentions several titles of books commissioned by Mahin Banu and 'Abdi Beg Shirazi's chronicle, which was dedicated to Pari Khan Khanum. Szuppe, 'La participation des femmes (Seconde Partie)', 244.

[6] Babayan, 'The 'Aqa'id al-Nisa'', 358–359; Shireen Mahdavi, 'Muhammad Baqir Majlisi, Family Values and the Safavids', in *Safavid Iran and Her Neighbors*, ed. Michel Mazzaoui (Salt Lake City: University of Utah Press, 1998), 81–100, esp. 81–89.

[7] Shireen Mahdavi, 'Women, Shi'ism and Cuisine in Iran', in *Women, Religion and Culture in Iran*, eds S. Ansari and V. Martin (London: Routledge, 2001), 10–26.

incomplete, because it does not take into consideration the influence of Islam. Rizvi states:

> To assume that Safavid women were aberrations within the social structure of Islam is to present a monodimensional aspect of both the religion and of them. In addition, the nomadic Mongol customs of the thirteenth century cannot adequately explain the choices that defined society in the sixteenth century, of which the Turkmen elite were an integral component.[8]

Rizvi rightly stresses that the early Safavid women 'reinterpreted and made use of the dominant forms of religious expression, whether it was made publicly visible in the architecture of the shrines they visited or remained less visible in the form of their pious, charitable activities'.[9] Nazak Birjandifar's 2006 master's thesis echoes Rizvi's critique, characterising Szuppe's focus on the role of Turkish nomadic traditions as 'an oversimplified view of the very complex cultural setting of the Safavid empire, which consisted of Islamic, Turko-Mongol, and Iranian traditions'.[10] Birjandifar highlights that the education that the early Safavid royal women received – which included the Islamic religious sciences of Islamic law and Qur'anic studies – and the inheritance rights they enjoyed – which was stipulated and protected by the sacred law – facilitated their elevated status in court politics and their financial independence.[11] Furthermore, although Birjandifar's study is primarily concerned with the political careers of the two early Safavid royal women, Pari Khan Khanum and Mahd-i 'Ulya, the wife of Shah Muhammad Khudabanda (r. 1578–1587), it also mentions briefly Pari Khan Khanum's cultural and literary patronage. She comments on Pari Khan's interest in poetry and her patronage of Muhtashim Kashani (1528–1588), the court poet of the time, arguing that 'women's patronage of literature and the arts widened the scope of their social influence and gave them direct access to leading scholars and learned men of their time'.[12] Drawing on new textual evidence, the present study corroborates the views of Rizvi and Birjandifar as regards the role of religious discourse in the formation and display of the princesses' authority and influence. Ten of the thirteen commissioned works discussed in this study were patronised by the early Safavid princesses, eight by Mahin Banu and two by Pari Khan Khanum and Zaynab Begum. Seven of these ten works had to do with Shi'i doctrine and other religious fields. This brief statistic, revealing the preferences and inclinations of the early Safavid princesses, supports the view that the Safavid royal women used, shaped, and propagated Shi'i religious discourse and projected their power and authority through their patronage.

---

[8] Rizvi, 'Gendered Patronage', 124.
[9] Rizvi, 'Gendered Patronage', 125.
[10] Birjandifar, 'Royal Women and Politics', 3–4.
[11] Birjandifar, 'Royal Women and Politics', 32–33, 38.
[12] Birjandifar, 'Royal Women and Politics', 98.

Mention should also be made of Rudi Matthee's critical review in 2015 of the scholarship on Safavid women. Matthee rightly points out that the term Safavid women has been used as an overarching category that overlooks the social standings, classes, and backgrounds of the women discussed, whereas Safavid women encompassed different subcategories, such as royal, elite, urban, rural, rich, and poor. Matthee argues that female participation in public life and the question as to whether they veiled or not depended on their social and economic status rather than on the period during which they lived. He posits, 'The main and enduring dichotomy, it seems, was less between the early and later period than between elite women and "ordinary" women, between Muslim and non-Muslim ones, and between the urban and rural worlds, respectively.'[13]

The present study also contributes to a growing literature on the role of royal women in shifting confessional identity and discourse beyond the context of Safavid Iran in the early modern world. Studies on the roles of royal women in Reformation Europe appear in the edited volume *Fürstinnen und Konfession: Beiträge hochadliger Frauen zur Religionspolitik und Bekenntnisbildung*, which examines the roles of various princesses of Reformation Europe in theological education and confession formation. The book demonstrates that during the Reformation a far-reaching entanglement of territorial politics and confessional identity formation became visible, bringing spiritual and secular powers of all emerging denominations into close proximity. This entanglement resulted in the territorialisation of the confessional division or the overlap between a territory and a confession. European royal women and particularly princess emerged as key actors in the promotion of the confessional doctrines in their own territories through their patronage of clergy to produce devotional and doctrinal texts in vernacular translations for the edification of a mixed audience of elite and ordinary readers.[14] Other studies on the subject have underscored the commitment of the royal women of Reformation Europe to propagating the faith and purifying the realm by fighting against the 'pernicious' heretical beliefs.[15] As Pernille Arenfeldt puts it, apart from being steadfast patrons of the church and clergy, royal women were also defenders of God's word, alerted their husbands and brother to threats of heresy

---

[13] Matthee, 'From the Battlefield to the Harem', 97–120, 111.

[14] Daniel Gehrt, *Fürstinnen und Konfession: Beiträge hochadliger Frauen zur Religionspolitik und Bekenntnisbildung* (Göttingen: Vandenhoeck & Ruprecht, 2015), 7–15.

[15] Margaret P. Hannay and Mark P. Moraned (eds), *Silent but for the Word: Tudor Women as Patrons, Translators and Writers of Religious Work* (Ohio: Kent State University Press, 1986); Melissa Franklin-Harkrider, *Women, Reform and Community in Early Modern England: Katherine Willoughby, Duchess of Suffolk, and Lincolnshire's Godly Aristocracy, 1519–1580* (Woodbridge: Boydell Press, 2008); Katherine Gill, 'Women and the Production of Religious Literature in the Vernacular, 1300–1500', in *Creative Women in Medieval and Early Modern Italy: A Religious and Artistic Renaissance*, eds E. Ann Matter and John Coakley (Philadelphia: University of Pennsylvania Press, 1994), 64–104.

and fought together with the (male) rulers against the infidels.[16] Pernille also points out that 'in the didactic treatises and panegyric literature, the sixteenth-century Protestant theologians consistently presented the female consort as a Kirchenmutter, a Hausmutter, and a Landesmutter (a mother of the church, a mistress of the house, and a mother of the territory and its population)'.[17] The latter detail indicates that the religious texts sponsored by European royal women not only contributed to promotion of the faith but also to projection of their image and authority, just like the works patronised by the Safavid princesses.

Patronage, Conversion and Vernacularisation

Patronage is one of the tools with which authority was exercised and reconfirmed.[18] According to André Lefevere, there are three main components of patronage; (i) an ideological component, which acts as a constraint on the choice and development of both form and subject matter; (ii) an economic component – the patron ensures that writers and rewriters are able to make a living; and (iii) a social component – acceptance of patronage implies integration into a certain support group and its lifestyle.[19] These three components help us understand the elements of the Safavid court patronage. The frequently invoked pronouncement, 'the adoption of Shi'i Islam as an official religion' by the Safavids, for the most part boiled down to the patronage of Shi'i scholars, works, and institutions, and the de-patronage of Sunni scholars and their works, along with any other religious group or inclination that fell outside the parameters of the state-sponsored faith. Safavid court patronage provided a significant incentive for scholars of the time to operate within the recognised religious framework if they wanted to receive royal favour, status, or rank. Otherwise, they risked persecution, harsh economic conditions, or low status. Sunni scholars who lived in Safavid Iran were led to choose one of the following course of actions; (i) seeking royal Safavid patronage by converting to Shi'i Islam or concealing their Sunni identity; (ii) seeking patronage outside the Safavid court by migrating to a Sunni realm where they could receive the favor of Sunni patrons, especially the Ottoman and Mughal rulers; or (iii) living a life with modest financial means or inferior social standing.

Among the scholars patronised by the Safavid princesses were several scholars who descended from prominent Sunni families. Royal patronage

---

[16] Pernille Arenfeldt, 'Gendered Patronage and Confessionalization: Anna of Saxony as a "Mother of the Church"', *Renæssanceforum* 4 (2008), 1–26.

[17] Arenfeldt, 'Gendered Patronage and Confessionalization', 6.

[18] Wolfgang Reinhard, *Freunde und Kreaturen: 'Verflechtung' als Konzept zur Erforschung historischer Führungsgruppen: römische Oligarchie um 1600* (Munich: Ernst Vögel, 1979), cited in Arenfeldt, 'Gendered Patronage and Confessionalizaiton', 3.

[19] André Lefevere, *Translation, Rewriting, and the Manipulation of Literary Fame* (New York: Routledge, 2017), 13–14.

must have been an important impetus behind their conversion to Shi'i Islam and the Safavid cause. Overall, royal patronage was instrumental in shaping religious orientations within Shi'i Islam throughout the Safavid period.

As Lefevere points out, patronage affects form as well as subject matter. Sponsorship by Safavid princesses of Persian-language works rather than Arabic indicates their preference for the vernacular for the presentation of the content to a broader audience. The promotion of Persian scholarship by the Safavid princesses should be situated in a larger collective, long-term, and sustained translation movement supported by the entire royal family, Safavid dignitaries, high-ranking administrators, and the Shi'i clergy. The translation movement intersected with proselytisation and preaching as complementary enterprises amid the Safavid conversion process. Therefore, one can say that conversion engendered large translation projects, while widely disseminated translated texts encouraged further conversion.[20] Consequently, a huge body of Shi'i religious texts - legal, theological, traditional, and polemical - was translated into Persian, and hence religious knowledge was rendered more accessible to ordinary people in the realm.[21]

Certain material conditions, such as international trade and royal monopoly for the export of luxury goods like silk and carpet as well as revenues from agriculture and state lands, prepared the background against which court patronage could take place and flourish. The unification of the eastern and western halves of the Iranian plateau under a relatively centralised political entity contributed to the enhancement of financial conditions during the Safavid period.[22] Enjoying great financial wealth and independence, Safavid princesses channelled some of their income to patronage activities and looked out for the welfare of their clients and beneficiaries. Limited economic resources of the royal family rendered the competition for royal patronage among the scholars of the realm fierce. A significant way in which scholars could attract royal favour or undermine rivals was to compose works dedicated to members of the royal family.[23] The asymmetrical

[20] For the relationship between conversion and translation, see Ronit Ricci, *Islam Translated: Literature, Conversion, and the Arabic Cosmopolis of South and Southeast Asia* (Chicago: University of Chicago Press, 2011), 12–31; Travis Zadeh, *The Vernacular Qur'an: Translation and the Rise of Persian Exegesis* (Oxford: Oxford University Press, 2012), 29, Gill, 'Women and the Production of Religious Literature', 64.

[21] M. T. Danishpazhuh, 'Yak parda az zandagani-yi Shah Tahmasb-i Safawi', *Majalla-yi danishkada-yi adabiyat wa-'ulum-i insani-yi Mashhad* 7.4 (1972), 975–982; Muhammad Rida Husayni, 'Nahdat-i tarjuma-i bih farsi dar 'asr-i Safawi', *Mutala'at-i Tarjuma* 45 (2014), 31–45; Muhsin Naji Nasrabadi, 'Sayr-i tarjuma dar Iran wa-mu'arrifi-yi kitab-ha-yi farisi-yi chap-shuda', *Ayina-i Pazhuhish* 68 (2001), 104–11.

[22] Willem M. Floor, *The Economy of Safavid Persia* (Wiesbaden: Reichert, 2000); Rudi Matthee, *The Politics of Trade in Safavid Iran: Silk for Silver, 1600–1730* (Cambridge: Cambridge University Press, 1999), 1–15.

[23] Devin J. Stewart, 'Polemics and Patronage in Safavid Iran: The Debate on Friday Prayer during the Reign of Shah Tahmasb', *Bulletin of the School of Oriental and African Studies* 72.3 (2009), 427–428.

relationship between the patron and the client, however, does not imply that only the client was in a dependent position. If anything, the patron also was dependent on her client to fashion her royal image, project her power and authority, and boost the legitimacy of her political participation and active roles. Moreover, patrons counted on their clients to bring the literary system in line with their own ideology. Therefore, their relationship was founded on mutual dependence and reciprocity.[24]

Lastly, some of the preface authors stated clearly that their works were undertaken at the request of a Safavid princess, 'whose noble order cannot be disobeyed', while others dedicated their works to Safavid princesses without referring to such an order. One may question whether a dedication alone is enough to suggest that the author was an active client or recipient of the patronage of the dedicatee. Diana Tyson maintains that, even though 'dedication alone is not sufficient to prove active patronage', it does indicate 'that the person must have been interested in letters and in the subject of the work, and this goes at least some way towards indicating that he (or she) may have actually commissioned the work or encouraged its writing'.[25] Concurring with Tyson's argument, the present study views the dedicatory remarks and eulogies of the dedicatee as an index of an active patronage relationship between the author and the Safavid princess. Otherwise, it would be hard to explain why a Safavid author, without any royal order, would have dedicated almost all his works to the same Safavid princess and introduced himself as a royal and devout servant of her court, had he not been an active recipient of her patronage.[26]

The Anatomy of the Preface

Persian *Dībācha,* or the Arabicised form *dībāja,* originally referred to the gold embroidered fringe on a luxurious robe and by extension the countenance of the beloved. It came to be used, however, as a technical term for the preface, preamble, or introduction to a work, which, in particularly valuable texts, was often gilded or embellished with painting or other materials.[27] Preface writing, already a well-established practice before the rise of the

---

[24] Lefevere, *Translation, Rewriting, and the Manipulation,* 15–16; Arenfeldt, 'Gendered Patronage and Confessionalization', 3.

[25] Diana B. Tyson, 'Patronage of French Vernacular History Writers in the Twelfth and Thirteenth Centuries', *Romania* 100.398 (1979), 180–222, esp. 184–185; June Hall McCash, 'The Cultural Patronage of Medieval Women: An Overview', in *The Cultural Patronage of Medieval Women,* ed. June Hall McCash (Athens: The University of Georgia Press, 1996), 1–50, esp. 2.

[26] A prominent example is the 'Aziz Allah b. 'Inayat Allah al-Husayni al-Ardabili al-Khalkhali, who dedicated at least three works to Mahin Banu Sultanum.

[27] Tahir Üzgör, 'Dîbâce', *TDV İslâm Ansiklopedisi* (Istanbul: TDV Yayinlari, 1994), 9:277–278.

Safavids, drew on a stock of standard tropes and metaphors.[28] Our knowledge of Safavid prefaces and the ways in which they reflect the ideological transformation in Safavid Iran is limited. Sholeh Quinn's 1996 essay on the prefaces of Safavid chronicles and David Roxburg's 2000 book on Safavid album prefaces examined their general structure and functions and maintained that they were informed by the political and religious climate and were the primary sites where the author displayed his political allegiances through his eulogy for the patron.[29] Quinn shows that the preface was composed of three main structural elements: (i) a religious prologue, (ii) information about the author, and (iii) information about the work. These main sections also included subsections. The second section usually included the author's 'statement of intent' in which he described why he wrote the work. In this section the author sometimes cited a particular event or acknowledged the request of a patron as a motive for the composition of the work. The third section generally consisted of a table of contents, varying in descriptive detail, in which the author outlined the rest of his work.

The structure outlined by Quinn for the prefaces of Safavid chronicles is quite similar to those of the works commissioned by the Safavid princesses. Despite the conventional nature of the prefaces, it is clear that the authors customised traditional metaphors and tropes for their sponsors. The use of particular honorific titles, the frequent invocation of women of Islamic salvation history, and the quotation of Qur'anic passages in praise of certain Safavid princesses indicate that the prefaces were tailored in accordance with the personality, role, and status of the patrons to whom the prefaces were dedicated.

Last but not least, apart from their role in the formation and circulation of the royal image of the princesses and reinforcement of their religio-political authority, the prefaces were also instrumental in establishing the authority and popularity of the authors themselves. Even though the authors' statements about themselves are brief and enveloped in the expressions of humility and self-deprecation, their names usually appear in the same passage in which the royal names were invoked. They projected themselves as well-wishing and devout servants of the royal family in a display of loyalty and an effort to strengthen their ties with the patrons and to secure their favour.

---

28 On the preface in Arabic literature, see Peter Heinz Otto Freimark, 'Das Vorwort als literarische Form in der arabischen Literatur', doctoral dissertation, Westfälischen Wilhelms-Universität, Münster, 1967. On the function of prefaces outside the Islamic world, see Kevin Dunn, *Pretexts of Authority: The Rhetoric of Authorship in the Renaissance Preface* (California: Stanford University Press, 1994); Jeanine Hurley, 'Authoring Audiences: Rhetorical Strategies in Eighteenth-century Prefaces', PhD dissertation, University of Maryland, 2003.

29 Sholeh A. Quinn, 'The Historiography of Safavid Prefaces', in *Safavid Persia: The History and Politics of an Islamic Society*, ed. Charles Melville (London and New York, I. B. Tauris, 1996), 1–25; David J. Roxburgh, *Prefacing the Image: The Writing of Art History in Sixteenth-century Iran* (Leiden: Brill, 2001).

Mahin Banu Shahzada Sultanum (1519–1562): 'Patron of the Scholars and the Learned'

Mahin Banu, known as Shahzada Sultanum, was a daughter born in 1519 to Shah Isma'il I and Tajlu Khanum. She was full sister of Shah Tahmasb and came of age during his reign.[30] Although the Safavid chronicles and other historical accounts are notorious for their paucity of information about Safavid royal women, *Khulasat al-Tawarikh* preserves a relatively detailed account of Mahin Banu that makes it possible to establish the contours of her religio-political life. From this and other available accounts emerge several components of a powerful image of the princess. First, she was a shrewd and influential political figure who wielded immense power in the political arena during Shah Tahmasb's rule as a confidant and counsellor in the inner circle of the Shah's court. Second, her royal image figured a carefully crafted religious persona, a lady betrothed to Imam Mahdi and bearing a host of religious attributes such as the Second Mary, the Fatima of the Time, the Bilqis of the Age, the Khadija of the Period, the Second Hagar, and so on, as well as many other honorific titles with religious and political colourings. Finally, she was a generous patron who played a major role in the formation of the religious landscape and production of Shi'i knowledge as a munificent benefactor of scholars and charitable.[31]

Mahin Banu served as the quintessential role model for succeeding female members of the Safavid dynasty, both admired and emulated.[32] Despite her significance, Mahin Banu has been given short shrift in the modern literature on Safavid royal women, which has focused on the political careers of Shah Tahmasb's daughter Pari Khan Khanum II and Mahd-i 'Ulya (d. 1579), the wife of Muhammad Khudabanda (r. 1578–1587).[33] Important exceptions to this are Maria Szuppe's seminal articles in French and Hani Khafipour's doctoral dissertation, which devotes a relatively lengthy discussion to Mahin

---

[30] Qadi Ahmad, Ahmad b. Husayn Munshi Qummi, *Khulasat al-tawarikh,* 2 vols, ed. Ihsan Ishraqi (Tehran: Intisharat-i Danishgah-i Tehran, 2004), 1:429–430; Hasan Beg Rumlu, *Ahsan al-tawarikh,* ed. 'Abd al-Husayn Navvali (Tehran: Intisharat-i Babak, 1978), 182; Hani Khafipour, *The Foundation of the Safavid State: Fealty, Patronage, and Ideals of Authority (1501–1576)*, doctoral dissertation, University of Chicago, Chicago, 2013; Szuppe, 'The Jewels of Wonder,' 329–330; Szuppe, 'Status, Knowledge, and Politics', 144; Shuja', *Zan, siyasat, wa-haram-sara,* 117–121.

[31] Qumi, *Khulusat al-tawarikh,* 430–431; Sharaf Khan Bidlisi, *Sharafnamah: Tarikh-i mufassil-i kurdistan,* ed. V. V. Zernof, 2 vols (Tehran: Asatir, 1957–1958), 2:217–218; Szuppe, 'Status, Knowledge, and Politics', 152–156.

[32] Iskandar Beg Munshi noted that Pari Khan Khanum aspired to attain such a position that 'she would have greater influence in matters of state than Tahmasb's sister, Shahzadah Sultanum'. Iskandar Beg Munshi, *The History of Shah Abbas the Great,* trans. Roger Savory, 2 vols (Boulder: Westview, 1978), 1:298; Szuppe, 'Status, Knowledge, and Politics', 156–157; Szuppe, 'Status, Knowledge, and Politics', 156–157.

[33] Nazak Birjandifar's thesis 'Royal Women and Politics in Safavid Iran' mentions Mahin Banu only in passing and discusses almost exclusively the life and careers of Pari Khan Khanum and Mahd-i 'Ulya.

Banu's political influence at the court of Shah Tahmasb. However, neither of these studies explored Mahin Banu's patronage of the production of Shi'i religious knowledge in a Persian medium.[34] Moreover, Khafipour's portrayal of Mahin Banu misses several crucial elements of her multi-faceted character.[35] Although the contemporary sources, the chronicler Qummi and the traveller Membré, provide significant details concerning Mahin Banu's projection of a public religious image heavily coloured by messianic underpinnings, these details fall outside of Khafipour's narrative about Mahin Banu. As Qummi reports, 'all matters of state and finance were to be contingent upon her evaluation, and he would not act without her consultation, discretion, and knowledge' (*bī-mashvarat va-ṣalāḥ va-āgāhī-yi ū*).[36] Mahin Banu evidently enjoyed strong ties with her brother and held considerable sway over the court and decision-making processes. Yet, in the lines preceding this praise of her political might and power, Qummi extols Mahin Banu's piety and virtue:

> Shahzada Sultanum, whose noble name was Mahin Banu, was the youngest daughter of paradise-dwelling Shah [Isma'il]. Since the traces of self-discipline, asceticism, purity, probity, and chastity were manifested in her face [and] character, the Alexander-like Shah [Tahmasb], her noble full brother, agreed to be under her command and vowed (*nadhr*) her majesty to the Noble Imam, Lord of the Age, Vicegerent of the Merciful [that is, Imam Mahdi]. Because she was learned and wise, he rendered all matters of state and finance contingent upon her approval and did not act without her consultation, discretion, and knowledge. He accorded her the status of the queen of the age and the lady of the time.[37]

Explicit in this quotation is the messianic aspect of her image. As an embodiment of chastity, probity, and piety, Mahin Banu was betrothed to the awaited Imam by her brother. A contemporary source, Michele Membré, corroborates Qummi's remarks regarding Tahmasb's designation of his sister as the fiancée of the Hidden Imam. A Venetian envoy, Membré travelled to the court of Shah Tahmasb in 1540 in order to propose an alliance between the Safavids and Christian powers of the Mediterranean against their common enemy, the Ottomans. In the course of his description of the Shah's court, Membré records his remarks about the Shah's sister:

> The King has a sister in his house whom he does not want to marry off, because, he says, he is keeping her to be the wife of the Mahdi. This Mahdi is a descendant of 'Ali and Muhammad; and he says he keeps her on the grounds that he is the court and the true place of Muhammad. Likewise, he has a white

---

[34] Maria Szuppe only mentions in passing several works commissioned by Mahin Banu. See Szuppe, 'La Participation des femmes (première partie)', 244.
[35] Khafipour, 'The Foundation of the Safavid State', 84–85.
[36] Khafipour, 'The Foundation of the Safavid State', 163.
[37] Qummi, *Khulasat al-tawarikh,* 430.

> horse, as well, which he keeps for the said Mahdi, with a saddle cloth of crimson velvet and silver shoes, and sometimes pure gold ones. No one rides this horse, and they always place it in front of all of his other horses.[38]

Membré's observation captures the messianic expectations and ethos of the time, which were deeply embedded in the court culture and formed part of the royal image. This messianic representation of the princess as the fiancée of the Hidden Imam was not a solitary manifestation of prevailing messianic ideology of the era. On the contrary, a host of contemporary sources demonstrate that Shah Tahmabs was portrayed as a deputy of the Hidden Imam, or his reign was construed a prelude to the governance of the awaited Hidden Imam. His rule presaged the Parousia of the Mahdi; he was the Last Emperor before the Imam's reign of justice before the end of the world.[39] Mahin Banu's representation as Imam's future wife was in line with this religious milieu, in which the messianic expectations and beliefs were so pervasive on both popular and scholarly levels. Messianic beliefs continued to be constituent elements of the dynastic discourse, legitimation, and projection of the royal image, and they coexisted with the intensifying Shi'i doctrinal and legal discourse. The confluence of messianic and legal-doctrinal discourses started to emerge from the beginning of Shah Isma'il's conquests.[40] The projection of Mahin Banu's image with messianic underpinnings and her patronage of the production of the Shi'i doctrine are merely one aspect of the confluence of messianic and legal-doctrinal discourses.

What were Mahin Banu's roles in the state's affairs, the projection of dynastic power and legitimacy, and the production of religious knowledge? What factors were responsible for the emergence of such a powerful political and religious figure? A significant ingredient of her accomplishments and rise to prominence was the education and training that she received.

---

[38] Michele Membré, *Mission to the Lord Sophy of Persia (1539–1542)*, trans. A. H. Morton (Cambridge: E. J. W. Gibb Memorial Trust, 1999), 25–26.

[39] This outlook is epitomised in *Risala dar-sharh-i hadith-i dawlatuna fi akhir al-zaman*, an eschatological treatise written by an anonymous author during the reign of Shah Tahmasb. The treatise expounded on a hadith attributed to Ja'far al-Sadiq, 'Every nation has its governance, and our governance is in the end-times.' The treatise argues that this hadith prophesied the advent of the Safavid dynasty as a prelude to the awaited reign of the Hidden Imam and that the phrase *ākhir al-zamān* is a chronogram for the coronation of Shah Tahmasb. Rasul Ja'fariyan, *Mahdiyan-i durughin: bih zamima-yi sih risala: Risala dar sharh-i hadith-i dawlatuna fi akhir al-zaman; Risala-yi mubashshara-iy shahiyya; Risala-yi al-huda Sayyid Muhammad Nūrbakhsh* (Tehran: 'Ilm, 2012–2013). This treatise was not a solitary example of this messianic discourse and expectation. See the *Risala-yi mubashshara-yi shahiyya* (*c.* 1550s), in which Pir Ghulam 'Ali Tusi Sharif predicted that the second coming of Mahdi would take place in 963 AH (1555–1556 CE). Rasul Ja'fariyan, 'Risala-yi mubashshara-yi shahiyya', *Payam-i Baharistan* 2.16 (1391), 1,033–1060; Kioumars Ghereghlou, 'Chronicling a Dynasty on the Make: New Light on the Early Safavids in Ḥayātī Tabrīzī's *Tārīkh* (961/1554)', *Journal of the American Oriental Society* 137.4 (2017), 805–832, here, 809–810; Ghereghlou, 'Chronicling a Dynasty', 809–810.

[40] Shah Ismail's patronage of Muhaqqiq al-Karaki is an important indication of this development.

As Maria Szuppe has stressed, advanced education equipped princesses with mastery of intellectual tools matching those of their brothers and husbands.[41] Particularly the religious education a princess received brought her within the proximity of the prominent scholars of the time, prior to her relationship with scholars through patronage. At times, her pupil–mentor relationship evolved into a patron–client relationship, as the prefaces of the dedicated works reveal.

As Qummi noted, 'Mahin Banu always committed herself to learning and acquiring knowledge.'[42] He also provided important details about the sorts of knowledge she sought and the mentors with whom she studied: 'initially she concentrated her focus on Arabic morphology and syntax, and Hakim Nur al-Din Kashi dedicated a Persian translation of *al-Kafiya* to her'.'[43] Qummi does not elaborate, but Iskandar Beg Munshi reports that Kashi was a prominent physician in the court of Shah Tahmasb.[44] Drawing on Qummi's passage, Maria Szuppe noted that Mahin Banu was 'taught of the rules of grammar and the Persian language by Nur al-Din Kashi'.[45] Nazak Birjandifar supposes that *al-Kafiya* was the translation of the first *sura* of the Qur'an, *al-Fatiha,* quoting the definition of *kafiya* from Dihkhuda's famous dictionary.[46] First, *al-Kafiya* was a well-known work on Arabic syntax by Ibn al-Hajib (d. 1249). Second, extant copies of *al-Kafiya* show that it was translated into Persian by Abu al-Fath Husayni at the request of Mahin Banu. Neither Shi'i bibliographical works nor the modern Persian manuscript catalogues record any translation of *al-Kafiya* by Hakim Nur al-Din Kashi.

Qummi gives a bit more detail about Mahin Banu's Arabic studies, stating, 'She deemed that these sciences [that is, Arabic syntax and morphology] would deliver no otherworldly rewards. Therefore, she turned her attention to recitation of the Qur'an and began studying the science of Qur'anic recitation.'[47] Mahin Banu then looked for a prominent teacher with whom to study. Qummi writes, 'Mahin Banu summoned Mawlana 'Imad al-Din 'Ali Qari Astarabadi, who was in holy Mashhad at that time, and studied with him the science of Qur'anic recitation in order to have perfect command of God's Word.'[48] A prolific scholar, 'Imad al-Din al-Qari also assisted her with the distribution of her charities.[49] He authored a work on the method

[41] Szuppe, 'La Participation des femmes (seconde partie)', 76–77; Szuppe, 'Status, Knowledge, and Politics', 148.

[42] Qummi, *Khulasat al-tawarikh,* 430.

[43] Qummi, *Khulasat al-tawarikh,* 430.

[44] Iskandar Beg Munshi, *The History of Shah Abbas the Great,* 2 vols, trans. Roger M. Savory (Boulder: Westview Press, 1978), 1:263.

[45] Szuppe, 'La Participation des femmes (première partie)'; Szuppe, 'Status, Knowledge, and Politics', 150.

[46] Nazak Birjandifar, 'Royal Women and Politics', 34, 34 n. 101.

[47] Qummi, *Khulasat al-tawarikh,* 430. Cf. Birjandifar, 'Royal Women and Politics', 34.

[48] Qummi, *Khulasat al-tawarikh,* 430.

[49] Munshi, *History of Shah Abbas the Great,* 1:240; Afandi, *Riyad al-'ulama',* 4:100.

of recitation of the Qur'an and dedicated it to her. Their relationship was thus both that of mentor and pupil one and that of a client and patron. He remained among her close associates until she passed away, and he even led her funeral procession.

Mahin Banu also studied with Dust Muhammad, an accomplished calligrapher, manuscript illuminator, and painter of the time. She excelled in calligraphy, and specimens of her handwriting survive until the present day.[50] She must also have been attracted to Shi'i doctrine, devotional literature, and history, considering that she was dedicated a host of works in these subjects, probably reflecting her interests. Her training also included physical activities such as horse riding and archery, which enabled her to accompany Shah Tahmasp on horseback during hunting expeditions.[51]

According to Qummi, every day, as soon as she finished addressing the needs of the Muslims and seeing to the welfare of the Shi'is and believers, Mahin Banu retired to worship, study, and observe the required daily prayers.[52] Since she was the counsellor of the shah and her approval and advice were sought for court decisions, administrative and financial affairs must have been part of her daily routine. She also played a significant role in major political and diplomatic affairs. For instance, in 1544 she acted as an intermediary between Shah Tahmasb and the Mughal Emperor Humayun (r. 1530–1543 and 1545–1556). She managed to convince the shah to support Humayun in his eventually successful bid to reclaim the throne of India. Moreover, she supported her favourite nephew Ibrahim Mirza and helped him to achieve better official positions, including the governorship of Mashhad.[53] Mahin Banu also exchanged official letters with Hurrem Sultan, the favourite wife of Ottoman Sultan Suleyman (r. 1520–1566). A letter from Mahin Banu informed Hurrem that the carpets had been sent in honour of the completion of Suleiman's mosque and assured her that all the people of Iran prayed for Suleiman and the continuation of his sultanate. The letter then lauded the recent treaty between the two states, the Treaty of Amasya, which had been signed in 1555.[54]

Mahin Banu also enjoyed a considerable fortune and financial independence, which accounted for her legacy and facilitated her patronage activities. Qummi's biographical notices shed significant light on her patronage power. 'Each year,' Qummi wrote, 'through the medium of Mawlana 'Imad al-Din al-Qari, she distributed generous donations, so much that it was impossible to

---

[50] Szuppe, 'The Jewels of Wonder', 329–330; Andrew J. Newman, *Safavid Iran: Rebirth of a Persian Empire* (London: I. B. Tauris, 2008), 3.

[51] Szuppe, 'Status, Knowledge, and Politics', 151.

[52] Qummi, *Khulasat al-tawarikh*, 430.

[53] Szuppe, 'La Participation des femmes (première partie)', 245; Szuppe, 'La participation des femmes (seconde partie)', 77; Rizwi, 'Gendered Patronage', 128; Birjandifar, 'Royal Women and Politics', 45.

[54] Leslie P. Peirce, *The Imperial Harem: Women and Sovereignty in the Ottoman Empire* (Oxford: Oxford University Press, 1993), 221; Szuppe, 'Status, Knowledge, and Politics', 154.

keep track of them, to people in Karbala, Najaf, among the *sayyids* in Medina the Honorable and in other sanctuary cities, and among the Arabs of Jabal 'Amil and Jaza'ir.' Some of the sources of her income included lucrative estates and properties in Shirvan, Arasbar,[55] Tabriz, Qazvin, Savejbulagh,[56] Shahryar, Ray, Isfahan, and Garmrud[57] of Astarabad, the revenues of which were consecrated to the Fourteen Infallible Ones. From these revenues, she established an endowment for the welfare of women, which aided the marriages of orphan girls. She also made generous donations and sent ornaments to holy sites in Iran, mainly to the shrine of Imam Rida in Mashhad, where she made a pilgrimage in 1549, accompanied by Shah-Quli, minister of Shah Tahmasb.[58] On her deathbed, 'she vowed some of her jewellery, precious possessions, and china to the Lord of the Age and Vicegerent of God; other possessions were sent to holy shrine of the Eighth Imam, Imam Rida, in Mashhad'. Mahin Banu also donated a number of manuscripts to the shrine of Mashhad. The list of the extant copies of the donated works reveals that most treated Shi'i doctrine and devotion.[59] The list included some of the works that she had sponsored. The donation of these texts to one of the most revered religious sites must have increased their circulation and popularity. Mahin Banu was evidently concerned both with the production of knowledge through commissioning works by contemporary scholars and with the establishment of a textual community to facilitate their circulation. One of the donated works bears the deed of the princess, which records the terms of use of the works:

> This book has been consecrated to the Sublime Threshold and the Sacred Garden of Rida – May peace be upon Him. The Noble Majesty, the One Whose Status is on par with that of Bilqis, the Khadija of the Age, Honor of the World, Sultanum the Safavid royal woman, the endower of the present book, stipulated that students may study this book provided that they keep it in their home no longer than a week and that they not sell it to anyone, purchase it from anyone, or donate it to anyone else. May the curse of God, the angels, and the people be upon whoever breaches these stipulations.[60]

---

[55] Today's Arazbar, a village and municipality in the Aghjabadi region of Azerbaijan.

[56] Bulagh a village in Taraznahid Rural District, in the Central District of Saveh County, Markazi Province, Iran.

[57] Garm Rud is a village in Kolijan Rostaq-i Olya Rural District, Kolijan Rostaq District, Sari County, Mazandaran Province, Iran.

[58] Qummi, *Khulasat al-tawarikh*, 430–432. Rizvi, 'Gendered Patronage', 128.

[59] Abd al-Hamid Mawlawi identifies thirteen extant manuscripts donated by Sultanum in the Mashhad Astan-i Quds-i Radawi Library. Mawlawi claimed that there were three royal women called Sultanum in the early Safavid period: the wife of Shah Isma'il I, the wife of Shah Tahmasb, and the daughter of Shah Ismail I. In his view, the wife of Shah Tahmasb donated the manuscripts, but he does not offer any evidence to support this claim. In my opinion, the endower of these manuscripts was Mahin Banu Sultanum, daughter of Shah Isma'il and sister of Shah Tahmasb. Some of the prefaces of the donated works identify the donor unambiguously as Shahzada Mahin Banu Sultanum. Abd al-Hamid Mawlawi, 'Sultanum', *Mutala'at-i Islami* 4 (1351), 241–261, at 244–246.

[60] Mawlawi, 'Sultanum', 243–244.

Clearly these stipulations were intended to ensure that the works remained in the service of the public by prohibiting it from being sold or purchased and that more students could make use of it by limiting its loan period to a week for a student.

Lastly, Qummi lauded the munificence and magnanimity of the princess, stating, 'She spent all her blessed time attending to scholars, the learned, the poor, and Safavid subjects equally, and nobody, whether Persians or Turks, junior or senior, closer or farther, obedient or rebellious, was shorn of the boundless munificence and limitless patronage of that wonder of the time.'[61] The following section presents some of the scholars who received the princess's patronage and dedicated works to her.

Tarjuma wa-sharh-i I'tiqadat-i Saduq *(Translation of and Commentary on* The Creeds, *by al-Saduq) by Abu al-Fath al-Husayni*[62]

Al-I'tiqadat (The Creeds) or *I'tiqadat al-Imamiyya* (The Creeds of the Imamis) is an early Shi'i doctrinal work attributed to Abu Ja'far Ibn Babawayh al-Qummi (*c.* 919–991), known as al-Saduq.[63] It presents the doctrines of the Imami sect, listing and explaining the articles of faith in thirty-four chapters.[64] Ibn Babawayh was the most eminent traditionist and jurist of the school of Qum and the author of one of the four canonical hadith works of the Twelver Shi'is. He is considered a prominent scholar and authority.[65]

This work was translated into Persian at the request of Mahin Banu Sultanum by Abu al-Fath Husayni Sharifi (d. 1568–1569), an eminent scholar of the reign of Shah Tahmasb. The earliest biographical notice about him appears in *Ahsan al-tawarikh,* in which Hasan Beg Rumlu writes,

> This year [976], too, Mawlana Amir Abu al-Fath, a Sayyid, died suddenly at Ardabil. He was pupil of Mawlana 'Isam al-Din, and he studied in Transoxiana, and settled at Ardabil. Among his works are: Commentaries on the *Kubra;* on the Morals of Discussion; on the *Tahdhib* on Logic; on the Treasury of Knowledge; on The Elements of Jurisprudence; on a Discussion of the Absolute Unknown; on the *Matali';* also, a tract on the eleventh chapter of the Persian Commentary on the Qur'anic Commands.[66]

---

[61] Qummi, *Khulasat al-tawarikh*, 430–432; Khafipour, 'The Foundation of the Safavid State', 165–167.

[62] Abu al-Fath al-Husayni, *Tarjuma wa-sharh-i i'tiqadat-i Saduq* (Tehran: Kitab'khana-i Majlis-i Shura-yi Milli, MS 10176, 962/1554–1555).

[63] Agha Buzurg al-Tihrani, *al-Dhari'a ila tasanif al-shi'a,* 25 vols (Qum: Isma'iliyan, 1987), 2:226. Also, see 'Introduction' in *Tarjuma-i i'tiqadat-i Saykh Saduq,* with a commentary by Muhammad b. Muhammad Mufid, translated by Muhammad 'Ali b. Muhammad Hasani (Tehran: 'Ilmiyya-yi Islamiyya, 1371), 1–11.

[64] It was translated into English by A. A. Fyzee as *A Shi'i Creed* (Oxford: Oxford University Press, 1942).

[65] Martin McDermott, 'Ebn Babawayh (2)', *Encyclopædia Iranica,* 8/1, 2–4; an updated version is available online at <http://www.iranicaonline.org/articles/ebn-babawayh-2>, last accessed 10 January 2018.

[66] Hasan Beg Rumlu, *A Chronicle of the Early Safawis: Being the Ahsanu't-tawarikh of Hasan-i-Rūmlū,* trans. Charles Norman Seddon (Baroda: Oriental Institute, 1931), 192.

In *Riyad al-'ulama'*, Mirza 'Abd Allah Afandi records his biographical notice under the name al-Amir Abu al-Fath b. al-Amir al-Makhdum al-Husayni al-Qazvini al-'Arabshahi and introduces him as follows:

> Learned scholar, theologian, traditionist, expert on jurisprudence, Qur'an commentator, Abu al-Fath was a descendant of al-Sayyid al-Sharif al-Jurjani. He was claimed to be the son of Mirza Makhdum al-Sharif al-Sunni, notice! He was a prominent figure at the court of Shah Tahmasb. Among his works is a well-known commentary on the verses concerning legal rulings in the Qur'an in Persian, which was given the title of *Tafsir-i shahi* (The Royal Qur'an Commentary) and commissioned by the Shah [Tahmasb].[67]

Moreover, Mirza 'Abd Allah Afandi notes several other books that belong to Abu al-Fath and reiterates his foregoing claim that Abu al-Fath's father was Mirza Makhdum, stating, 'The father of this man was Mirza Makhdum al-Sharifi, the Sunni, who is renowned for his *Nawaqid al-rawafid*.'[68] However, Wali Allah Ishraqi and Thiqat al-Islam al-Tabrizi countered Mirza 'Abd Allah's claim and suggested that Mirza Makhdum al-Sharifi was not his father, because Abu Fath lived during the reigns of Shah Isma'il I and Shah Tahmasb, whereas his alleged father was an outspoken Sunni scholar of a later period and supporter of anti-Shi'i policies during the reign of Shah Isma'il II (r. 1576–1577). Moreover, Wali Allah Ishraqi maintained that Abu al-Fath's father was a famous Shi'i scholar of the reign of Shah Isma'il I named al-Sayyid Muhammad 'Ali and known as Mirza Makhdum b. Shams al-Din al-Sayyid Muhammad b. Mir Sayyid Sharif al-Jurjani. Mirza 'Abd Allah Afandi and other biographical sources confused this Shi'i scholar with the Sunni Mirza Makhdum al-Sharifi because of the resemblance of their names.[69] That said, as E. Glassen noted, Abu al-Fath probably shared the same lineage with Mirza Makhdum al-Sharifi the Sunni, as they both were descendants of a famous Sunni scholar, al-Sayyid al-Sharif al-Jurjani (d. 1413). Moreover, Glassen also suggested that Abu al-Fath embraced Shi'i Islam when he settled in Ardabil after having studied with Sunni scholars in Transoxiana. It is hard to ascertain whether he was born to a Shi'i parents or converted to Shi'i Islam after he settled in Ardabil, as Glassen claimed, but it is certain that his writings in Persian on Shi'i doctrine, jurisprudence, and Qur'anic commentary contributed to the spread of Twelver Shi'ism in the early Safavid period.[70] As the title of his commentary, *Tafsir-i shahi* ('The Royal Qur'an Commentary'),

---

[67] Mirza 'Abd Allah Afandi al-Isfahani, *Riyad al-'ulama' wa-hiyad al-fudala'*, 6 vols, ed. al-Sayyid Ahmad al-Husayni (Qum: Maktabat Ayat Allah al-Mar'ashi al-'Amma, 1981).

[68] Afandi, *Riyad al-'ulama'*, 5:486–487.

[69] Thiqat al-Islam 'Ali b. Musa al-Tabrizi, *Mir'at al-kutub*, eds Muhammad 'Ali Ha'iri and 'Ali Sadrayi Khuyi, 7 vols (Qum, Iran: Kitabkhana-i 'Umumi-yi Hadrat Ayat Allah 'Uzma Mar'ashi, 1414/1993–1994), 5:208–212; Wali Allah Ishraqi, 'Introduction', in *Tafsir-i shahi aw ayat al-ahkam* by Abu al-Fath b. Makhdum al-Husayni, ed. Wali Allah Ishraqi, 2 vols (Tehran: Nowid, 1363/1984–1985), 1:13.

[70] E. Glassen, 'Abu'l-Fath Hosayni', *Encyclopædia Iranica*, I/3, 285; an updated version is available online at <http://www.iranicaonline.org/articles/abul-fath-sarafi-sarifi-hosayni-arabsahi-b>, last accessed 13 January 2018.

indicates, it was composed at the request of Shah Tahmasb. This Persian commentary reflected a larger tendency of the time to compose commentaries in Persian. As Ahmad Amiri suggested, commentaries on the legal rulings of the Qur'an reached new heights at that time, thanks to the efforts of the early Safavids in the compilation of legal rulings.[71]

Abu al-Fath also translated *al-Kafiya,* an Arabic grammar by Ibn al-Hajib, into Persian at the request of Mahin Banu (discussed below) and wrote a host of commentaries in several fields. As the list of Abu al-Fath's works indicates, he was conversant with several fields in the Islamic sciences.[72] He enjoyed close ties with the Safavid court and authored most of his works for Shah Tahmasb and Mahin Banu. He was also commissioned by Shah Tahmasb to compose a new recension of *Safwat al-safa* by Ibn Bazzaz. In the preface to his composition, Abu al-Fath explained why he undertook a new composition, remarking, 'It existed in his time only in versions corrupted as a result of dissimulation or falsification by Sunnite antagonists', and he incorporated the genealogy of the Safavids going back to Musa al-Kazim in his recension.[73] As mentioned above, the genealogy had already been forged prior to Abu al-Fath's recension in 1533, but he could have been commissioned to make this hagiographical work more accessible and the forged genealogy more popular.

In the preface to his translation of *al-I'tiqādāt*, after an encomium to God, the Prophet, and the Imams, Abu al-Fath introduces the author of the source text, Ibn Babawayh, as the master of *mujtahid*s, the reliable scholar of Prophetic tradition, the eminent and outstanding jurist of the saved sect, the Imamis. Then, he states that his translation was penned in response to a noble order that had to be obeyed from Mahin Banu Sultanum. He extols the religious virtues and worldly grandeur of the princess with a number of honorific titles. For instance, he lauds her might and power as 'the King of Kings', 'the Favorite One under the Oversight of God', 'the Sun in the Heaven of Glory and Majesty', 'the Precious Full Moon in the Firmament of Virtue and Generosity', and 'the Moonfaced one of the Palace of Justice and Welfare of Her Subjects' among other epithets.[74] Couched in rhetorical flourishes are references to her generosity, justice, political influence, and power, characteristics that were consonant with her political career and power at the court and her generous patronage and charity.

The honorific titles with religious connotations used in the preface are revealing with regard to the projection of her religious image and the religious authority accorded to her. Abu al-Fath praises her as 'the Shining Venus of the

---

[71] Ahmad Amiri, 'Tahlilī bar rawand-i tafsir-nawisi-yi fiqhi dar dawra-yi safawi', *Sahifa-yi mubin* 40 (1386/2007), 45–57.

[72] Dirayati lists eighteen works under the name of Abu al-Fath Makhdum Jurjani, see Mustafa Dirayati, *Fihristwara: Dastnivisht-ha-yi Iran*, 12 vols (Mashhad: Mu'assasa-yi Pazhuhish-i al-Jawad, n.d.), 11:318–319.

[73] Glassen, 'Abu'l-Fath Hosayni', 285.

[74] Abu al-Fath al-Husayni, *Tarjuma wa-sharh-i I'tiqadat-i Saduq*, 1b–2b.

Progeny of Fatima the Radiant One', and 'Great Lady of the Descendants of Khadija the Great' in line with the Safavid claim being the descendants of *ahl al-bayt*. He also praised the princess as 'the Patron (*murabbī*) of the Ja'fari Sect and the religion of Twelver Shi'ism' and 'the Fortifier (*muqawwī*) of the Law of Muhammad and 'Ali', which are unambiguous references to her role in promotion of the Shi'i doctrine and law as well as in the protection of the Shi'i scholars of the time. Then, the honorific titles were concluded with a prayer with which Abu al-Fath asked God to perpetuate the reign of the princess until the advent of the Hidden Imam. Finally, the author introduces himself as Abu al-Fath al-Husayni and states that the primary objective of his undertaking is to present the Persian translation of the Shi'i doctrines and articles of the faith, which were substantiated and explained with the commentary of the Qur'anic verses and interpretation of the prophetic traditions.[75]

The translation of *al-I'tiqadat*, a compact treatise that presents the basic theological doctrines on the unity and attributes of God, predestination, free volition and human action, death, fate after death, prophets, imams, infallibility, dissimulation, and so forth, was well suited to the context in which proselytisation and conversion brought about the demand for doctrinal works in Persian. Moreover, owing to its significance, translations of *al-I'tiqadat* were rendered by other Safavid scholars as well.[76] Apart from this doctrinal treatise, Abu al-Fath also dedicated his Persian translation of an Arabic grammar book to the same princess.

Tarjuma wa-sharh-i Kafiya-i Ibn-i Hajib *(Translation and Commentary of* al-Kafiya *[The Sufficient] of Ibn al-Hajib) by Abu al-Fath al-Husayni*[77]

Al-Kafiya is a well-known work on Arabic syntax. Its author, Jamal al-Din Abu 'Amr 'Uthman b. Abu Bakr, known as Ibn al-Hajib, was a native Egyptian who died in 1249 in Alexandria. Ibn al-Hajib earned a reputation as a Maliki jurist, but he is primarily known as a grammarian thanks to *al-Kafiya* and its companion volume on morphology, *al-Shafiya*, which have been widely used in Arab and Muslim countries, as the large number of extant commentaries indicates. Both have been printed in many editions.[78]

---

[75] Abu al-Fath al-Husayni, *Tarjuma wa-sharh-i i'tiqadat-i Saduq*, 1b–2b.

[76] For instance, one of the well-known translations was rendered by a contemporaneous Safavid scholar, Abu al-Hasan 'Ali b. Hasan Zawara'i, a prolific author and prominent student of Muhaqqiq al-Karaki, who gave his translation the title of *Wasilat al-najat dar tarjuma-yi i'tiqadat-i Shayk Saduq*. See Afandi, *Riyad al-'ulama'*, 3:395; Muhammad Baqir al-Khwansari, *Rawdat al-jannat fi ahwal al-'ulama' wa'l-sadat*, 8 vols (Beirut: al-Dar al-Islamiyya, 1991), 4:376–377; Rula J. Abisaab, *Converting Persia: Religion and Power in the Safavid Empire* (London and New York: I. B. Tauris, 2004), 28.

[77] Abu al-Fath al-Husayni, *Tarjuma wa-sharh-i kafiya-i B. Hajib* (Tehran: Kitab'khana-i Majlis-i Shura-yi Milli, MS 1250, 10176/2, 962/1554–1555).

[78] H. Fleisch, 'Ibn al-Hadjib' in EI^2, eds P. Bearman, Th. Bianquis, C. E. Bosworth, E. van Donzel, W. P. Heinrichs; Brockelmann, *GAL*, SI: 531–537.

At the beginning of the preface to his translation, Abu al-Fath al-Husayni introduced the source text as valuable treatise, which is 'sufficient (*kafiya*, punning on the title of the work) for the science of Arabic syntax and cures the disease of ignorance'. He states that 'the work has been arranged to include significant interpretations of construction of some example sentences while avoiding prolixity and hyperbole'. Unlike his translation of *al-I'tiqadat*, which was commissioned by the royal order, in his translation of *al-Kafiya*, Abu al-Fath states that his translation attracted the attention of Mahin Banu, as he was in the process of translating it. Moreover, he expresses his hope that his 'incoherent translation may become the object of the attention of the Princess of all Mankind' and 'through the favorable consideration of the Queen of the Age, which is as effective as alchemy, that she may deliver complete benefit to the students, so that the divine rewards for doing so may be connected with the annals of the blessed deeds of her Highness'. From this statement, one infers that, rather than by a direct royal commission, the translation of this famous grammar book might have been undertaken by Abu al-Fath of his own accord, but later it somehow attracted the attention of the princess, and therefore he dedicated his translation to her in order to receive her favour.[79]

The honorific titles that Abu al-Fath used in the preface to his translation reflect the proximity of the princess to the scholars of the time and her support for them. He praises her as the 'Manifestation of Divine Favors', 'Patron (*murabbī*) of the Scholars and the Learned', and 'Fortifier of the Righteous and the Pious'. He also extols the noble genealogy of Mahin Banu, calling her 'the Essence of the Family of the Prophet and Progeny of the Dynasty of 'Ali', 'Brightly Burning Candle in the Palace of Nobility (*siyādat*) and Felicity', and 'Shining Full Moon in the Heavens of Impeccability and Purity'. Furthermore, Abu Fath glorifies her as 'Khadija of the Time' and 'Bilqis of the Age' by evoking the memories of these emblematic historical female figures. Khadija was the first wife of the Prophet and mother of Fatima, wife of 'Ali. She was known for her unwavering support for the Prophet as well as for her richness, generosity, and charitable deeds for the poor and the new converts in the nascent Islamic community.[80] By comparing Mahin Banu to Khadija, Abu Fath highlights the princess's generosity, patronage, and her commitment to religion. Moreover, the representation of the princess's piety through Khadija was complemented with her comparison with Bilqis, the feminine epitome of grandeur and political might. Abu al-Fath considers Mahin Banu's fortune and political power comparable with those of Bilqis and praises her

[79] Perhaps Qummi's above-discussed remarks about Hakim's translation of *al-Kafiya* can be taken in this light, as they might have meant to say that Hakim presented Abu al-Fath's translation to the attention of Mahin Banu rather than that he himself undertook the translation.

[80] Nabia Abbott, 'Women and the State in Early Islam', *Journal of Near Eastern Studies* 1.1 (1942), 106–126.

as the 'Queen of the Kings'. His eulogy is followed by a prayer with which he asked God to perpetuate her imperial majesty and prosperity until the rise of the Mahdi's governance.[81]

Mahin Banu's support for the Persian translation of an Arabic grammar text attests to her full-fledged commitment to the Persianisation of knowledge in general. The fact that *al-Kafiya* was written by a Sunni scholar neither precluded Abu al-Fath from undertaking the translation of the text nor Mahin Banu from supporting such a project in a setting in which confessional awareness intensified. Although the priority of the Safavid royal family and scholarly circles was producing and reproducing Shi'i knowledge in Persian, the practice of transferring knowledge from Sunni scholarship continued throughout the Safavid period, predominantly but not exclusively in technical fields such as linguistics, medicine, zoology, and philosophy.[82] The Persian translation of *al-Kafiya* must have contributed to its popularity and wide circulation in Safavid Iran, as the abundant number of extant manuscript copies have indicated. Moreover, it became one of text books and components of the religious education in the Safavid higher institutions.[83]

Arkan al-iman *(The Pillars of the Faith)* (c. *1557) by al-Mawla Abu al-Hasan al-Sharif b. Ahmad Abiwardi al-Kashani (d. 1559)*[84]

Arkan al-iman is a work of dogmatic theology and Shi'i doctrine. Abu al-Hasan b. Ahmad al-Abiwardi authored this treatise at the request of Mahin Banu Sultanum and completed it in February 1557.[85] Although Abu al-Hasan has been unnoticed, and his works have hitherto remained untapped by modern researchers, he was by no means an obscure figure in his own time, neither were his works devoid of significance. Several Safavid chronicles and biographical works provide some information concerning his career. Hasan Beg Rumlu notes the date of Abiwardi's death in *Ahsan al-tawarikh,* along with some remarks about his scholarly merits and career, couched in glowing terms. In fact, Rumlu had studied *Sharh*

[81] Abu al-Fath al-Husayni, *Tarjuma wa-sharh-i Kafiya-yi Ibn Hajib*, 2b–3a.

[82] Muhammad Rida Husayni, 'Nahdat-i tarjumah-i bah farisi dar 'asr-i Safawi', *Mutala'at-i Tarjuma* 45 (1393/2014), 31–45; 'Abd al-Husayn Adharang, *Tarikh-i tarjuma dar Iran : az dawran-i bastan ta payan-i 'asr-i Qajar* (Tehran: Qaqnūs, 2015).

[83] Attesting to its circulation as a textbook in the Safavid colleges, Ni'mat Allah Jazairi's (d. 1701), a scholar of the later Safavid period, recalls the memories of his days in a college in Isfahan in his autobiography and tells that he memorised *al-Kafiya* by moonlight and later wrote a commentary on it. Devin J. Stewart, 'The Humor of the Scholars: The Autobiography of Ni'mat Allah al-Jaza'iri (d. 1112/1701)', *Iranian Studies* 22.4 (1989), 47–81, here 56–57, 60, 63–64.

[84] al-Mawla Abu al-Hasan al-Sharif b. Ahmad Abiwardi/Bawirdi al-Kashani, *Arkan al-iman*, Tehran: Kitab-khana-i Majlis-i Shura-yi Milli, MS 5627, fols 1b–2b.

[85] Afandi, *Riyad al-'ulama'*, 5:435–437.

al-Tajrid, a commentary on a Nasir al-Din al-Tusi's work *al-Tajrid fi 'ilm al-kalam* by 'Ali Qushji (d. 1474), with Abiwardi.[86] His biographical notice reads as follows:

> Mawlana Abu al-Hasan, son of Mawlana Ahmad Bawardi. He was an accomplished and high-souled man, unrivalled in his keenness of intellect. He died on Sunday the twenty-sixth of Ramadan. Among his works are: *Ithbat al-wajib; Rawdat al-jinan,* on philosophy; a tract on logic; a commentary on Nasir al-Din's *Fara'id,* on the law of succession; a text titled the *Shawariq* on scholastic theology; and a note on metaphysics. The author read a commentary on the *Tajrid* under this great man.[87]

Qummi's account of Abiwardi enables us to elaborate on Rumlu's brief notice. In his *Khulasat al-tawarikh,* Qummi states:

> In the same year [966 AH = 1559 CE] the master of the age, Mawlana Abu al-Hasan son of Mawlana Ahmad Bawardi, who was well-versed in the revealed sciences, scholastic theology, philosophy, mathematics, and astronomy and unrivalled among his peers, with such an acute mind and sharp wit that nobody among the prominent scholars of the time was capable of engaging a scholarly debate with him, left the abode of delusion for the abode of repose on 26 Ramadan 966 [12 July 1559], at the bloom of his youth, the age of thirty. Among his works are a Persian treatise about the proof of the Necessary Being (*Ithbat al-wajib*), dedicated to Shahzada Sultanum, an Arabic treatise on the same subject, dedicated to Khan Mirza; *Rawdat al-jinan,* on philosophy; a treatise on logic; a commentary on *Fara'id* of Khwaja Nasir al-Din Muhammad al-Tusi; and the *Shawariq,* on scholastic theology. According to a reliable scholar, he had such a retentive memory that he was preoccupied with revising the books of the transmitters of the Prophetic tradition (*kutub al-rijal*) and *hadith* works, as well as with the composition of *Tahdhib-i ahadith,* which included seventy thousand couplets and was undertaken by himself alone. By reviewing all the *hadith* collections and their chains of the transmitters, he committed them to memory and was capable of recording them without the help of a single copyist. Mawlana spent most of his time in Kashan, the abode of faith, with Khan Mirza, the son of Ma'sum Beg Safawi, who was the deputy of the Shah and possessor of fiefs in Kashan.[88]

This passage reveals that Abiwardi was a prominent and prolific scholar – *Fihristwara* enumerates nineteen books attributed to him[89] – who stood out among his peers and managed to secure a place in the orbit of the princess's

[86] İhsan Fazlıoğlu, 'Qushji: Abu al-Qasim 'Ala' al-Din 'Ali b. Muhammad Qushçi-zade', *The Biographical Encyclopedia of Astronomers* (New York: Springer, 2007), 946–948; İhsan Fazlıoğlu, 'Osmanlı Düşünce Geleneğinde 'Siyasi Metin' Olarak Kelâm Kitapları', *Türkiye Araştırmaları Literatür Dergisi* 1/2 (2003), 379–398.

[87] Rumlu, *Ahsan al-tawarikh,* 179.

[88] Qummi *Khulasat al-tawarikh,* 404.

[89] Dirayati, *Fihristwara,* 11:96–97.

patronage and that of the Shah's deputy in Kashan. Whereas he dedicated his Arabic work to Khan Mirza, he was requested to author a work on the same subject in Persian, which suggests that Mahin Banu commissioned works mostly, if not exclusively, in Persian. Her concern for spreading knowledge in Persian must have been a point to reckon with for those who wished to attract the princess's patronage.

Mirza 'Abd Allah Afandi also devotes a notice to Abiwardi in *Riyad al-ulama'*:

> Known as Abu al-Hasan al-Kashi, he was an eminent master, learned man, scholar, jurisconsult, and a prominent figure of the reign of Shah Tahmasb. He authored fine works, including a book on the dogmatic theology titled *Rawd al-jinan* ('The Meadow of the Paradise'). Another well-known work of his, with useful insights, which I saw in Isfahan, Herat, Dehkhwareqan,[90] and elsewhere was *Sharh Risalat al-fara'id* of Nasir al-Din al-Tusi ('Commentary on the Treatise Concerning the Division of Estates'). Equally famous was his lengthy treatise, *Ithbat al-wajib wa-sifatih* ('Proof of the Necessary Being and His Attributes'), which he completed in Sabzavar on 15 Rabi' al-Awwal 963 (7 February 1556) and that I came across in Ardabil, Herat, and elsewhere. Moreover, he completed his Persian treatise on the doctrine, commissioned by one of the daughters of Shah Tahmasb, in late Rabi' al-Awwal 964 (February 1557). I stumbled upon a copy of this treatise in Herat. Note that he introduced himself as Abu al-Hasan al-Sharif in this excellent treatise – take note! He also authored a short Persian treatise concerning the fines of blood money and its legal rulings at the request of the king of the time (Shah Tahmasb), which I saw in Farah. Furthermore, he wrote another treatise with the title *al-Husna fi hikmat al-tabi'a*[91] ('The Most Beautiful Treatise, on the Philosophy of Physics'), which is an abbreviated version of abovementioned *Rawd al-jinan*, and I came across it in Farah as well. He made it clear that he was a Shi'i in the preface of the abovementioned *Rawd al-jinan* and his other works. It is inferred from the commentary of Amir Fakhr al-Din al-Sammaki[92] on the subject of the proof of Necessary Being and from the book *Rawd al-jinan* that the foregoing Amir Fakhr al-Din al-Sammaki was a coeval of Abu al-Hasan or lived very close to the latter's generation. In his commentary, al-Sammaki rebutted the work of Abiwardi extensively. Take note of this! Both this scholar (that is, Abu al-Hasan) and Mirza Jan al-Sunni, mentioned in the biographical notice of al-Amir Ghiyath al-Din Mansur, appropriated Ghiyath al-Din's views on many subjects and plagiarised from his books.

[90] Today's Adharshahr in eastern Azerbaijan.

[91] It was recorded in *Fihristwara* as *al-Husna fi al-qawa'id al-tabi'a*. Dirayati, *Fihristwara*, 11:96–97.

[92] 'On the night of Monday, the ninth day of Dhu al-Qa'dah [984] [28 January 1577] Mawlana Amir Fakhr al-Din Sammaki died. He was pupil of Amir Ghiyath al-Din Mansur of Shiraz. He wrote notes on theological subjects, and a commentary on the *Tajrid*.' Rumlu, *Ahsan al-tawarikh*, 209.

After these remarks, Mirza 'Abd Allah Afandi quotes Rumlu's account completely and concludes with the following note:

> It is clear that the father of Abu al-Hasan, al-Mawla Ahmad al-Abiwardi, had several commentaries on books about logic such as *al-Shamsiyya* and *Sharh al-Matali'*. Although Abu al-Hasan was originally from Abiward, he resided in Kashan, and therefore he was called al-Kashi. Do not let this confuse you. His father, too, was an Imami scholar. Note that.[93]

This passage demonstrates that Abiwardi received the favour of Shah Tahmasb, Mahin Banu, and the shah's deputy in Kashan, Khan Mirza, for his various works. It also indicates that some of Abiwardi's writings engendered some responses from other prominent scholars of the time, such as Fakhr al-Din Sammaki, who was a pupil of Ghiyath al-Din Manṣur Shirazi and enjoyed close relationship with Shah Tahmasb and a great popularity.[94] Abiwardi himself also engaged some scholarly discussion with some prominent scholars of the time.[95] Moreover, it is interesting to note that Afandi made special mention of Abiwardi's pronouncement of his Shi'i identity and of his father's Shi'i background. Part of the reason for this detail might have been the fact that in the early Safavid period especially Persian aristocratic families and scholars with Sunnite origin 'were believed to have carried into Safavid times no more than a veneer of dissimulating Shi'ism'. For instance, the Dashtaki family, a member of whose was the aforementioned Ghiyath al-Din al-Mansur, was one of these families.[96] Therefore, Mirza 'Abd Allah could have meant to avert any suspicion that would have been cast on Abiwardi's adherence to Shi'ism. In fact, as far as *Arkan al-iman* is concerned, Abiwardi seems a vociferous opponent of Sunni Islam with his espousal of cursing and insulting the first three caliphs as a religious requirement.

Arkan al-Iman is composed of five parts (*faṣl*), and each part includes several chapters (*maqṣid*). Oneness of God and His attributes, Divine Justice, Prophecy, Imamate, and the Hereafter form the five parts of the work, a structure that follows those of Ibn Babawayh's *al-I'tiqadat* or more closely *Tajrid al-i'tiqadat* of Nasir al-Din al-Tusi (d. 1274). Compared to *al-I'tiqadat* and *Tajrid,* however, *Arkan al-iman* devotes a lengthier discussion to the part of Imamate, in which he addresses the necessity of Imams, their infallibility, and God's grace that entails God to provide humankind with guidance through sending apostles and imams. Particularly, in the fourth and fifth chapters of this part, respectively, *Dar ithbat-i butlan-i khilafat wa-ru'asa-yi arbab-i nifaq* ('Proving the Invalidity of the Caliphate and Leaders

---

[93] Afandi, *Riyad al-'ulama'*, 5:435–437.
[94] Munshi, *History of Shah Abbas,* 1:233.
[95] Qummi, *Khulasat al-tawarikh,*
[96] Abisaab, *Converting Persia,* 18.

of the People of Hypocrisy') and *Dar ithbat-i an ki in mala'in-i gumrah 'alayhim la'natu Allahi abadan mustahiqq-i la'n wa-'adhab-i ilahi hastand wa-tabarra az ishan bar kaffa-yi mukallafan wajib wa-lazim ast* ('Proving That These Deviated Accursed Ones [Caliphs] – God's curses be upon all of them – Deserve Eternal Divine Retribution and That Dissociation from Them is Incumbent upon all Those Who are in Possession of Their Mental Faculties'), Abiwardi advocates that 'Ali b. Talib was divinely nominated heir of the Prophet, whose right was usurped by the first three caliphs, although he was the most virtuous of all after the Prophet among the Muslim community. Therefore, he charged those who followed the first three caliphs with apostasy and compared them to the nation of Moses who went astray and worshipped a golden calf in the absence of Moses, when he went up to Mount Sinai to have an audience with God. Moreover, he compared the caliphs and subsequent Sunni dynasties and leaders to al-Samiri ('the Samaritan') who was believed to have made an idol calf out of gold and to the pharaohs of Egypt, as tyrant leaders who deviated the majority from the true path of God. Abiwardi also considered dissociation from and cursing the caliphs as a religious imperative. After enumerating 'felonies' of the caliphs and presenting some pieces of evidence about the Imamate, Abiwardi stated that the crimes and felonies of the first three caliphs are abundant and proofs regarding 'Ali's designation as an heir are too many, but lest the details of this subject bore Her Excellency, Mahin Banu, he cut the discourse short. However, he also added that should a noble order be issued by the princess for him to author a treatise addressing this subject in detail, he would accordingly undertake such an honourable task.[97]

In his preface to *Arkan al-iman,* Abiwardi states that he – 'this dust of the road of the wayfarers of the sublime religion, Abu al-Hasan Sharif' – always harboured an intention to write a treatise on the doctrines of the faith and the essentials of the correct religion as an act of devotion and obedience to divine commands. However, he was delayed in materialising this intention by the obstacles of time, until he received 'a noble decree from behind the veil of honour and impeccability, and from beyond the heaven-like-curtain of the royalty and nobility', commissioning him to author a work on this subject. 'Since this royal order can never be disobeyed, he fastened the belt of obedience around the waist of his will and undertook this noble task.' Moreover, Abiwardi hailed his patron as the 'Refuge of the Learned' and eulogised her as 'the Mary of the Age', 'the Khadija of the Time', 'the Bilqis of the Period', 'the Second Hagar', and 'the Beloved of Fatima', in order to stress her chastity, magnanimity, grandeur, and religious devotion.[98]

---

[97] Abiwardi, *Arkan al-iman,* fols 8a–13a.
[98] Abiwardi, *Arkan al-iman,* fols 1b–2b.

Tafsir-i kalima-yi tahlil *by Sayyid 'Aziz Allah b. 'Inayat Allah Husayni Ardabili Khalkhali*

This short treatise is a commentary on the expression of God's unity, which represents the foundation of the faith and one's confession in Islam. Sayyid 'Aziz Allah Ardabili Khalkhali dedicated the work to Mahin Banu Sultanum in 1555–1556. One manuscript copy is extant in the Astan-i Quds-i Radawi Library in Mashhad, and an edition was published by the Institute of Islamic Studies at Astan-i Quds-i Radawi.[99] In their introduction, the editors note that the declaration of God's oneness has long been the subject of theological and exegetical attention. 'Ayn al-Qudat Hamadani (d. 1131), 'Abd al-Rahman Jami (d. 1492), and Jalal al-Din al-Dawwani (d. 1502) were only a few among those scholars who wrote on the subject.[100] 'Aziz Allah Ardabili's treatise built on prior works in this tradition, quoting frequently from linguists and Qur'anic commentators such as al-Dawwani, Sibawayh (d. 796), al-Zamakhshari (d. 1144), and al-Qadi al-Baydawi (d. 1286).[101]

A brief biographical notice under the heading *Sayyid 'Aziz Allah Husayni Mudarris-i Maqbara-i Shaykh Safi dar Ardabil* in *Riyad al-'ulama'* casts some light on his life and scholarly career.

> He was a learned scholar and theologian of the reign of Shah Tahmasb. For his biographical account one should check the chronicles. Among his works was his brief commentary on one of the works of Shaykh Tusi about *usul al-din* (fundamental theology), a copy of which I came across in Ardabil. This commentary was written in Persian and dedicated to Shah Tahmasb. 'Aziz Allah must have been originally from Ardabil.[102]

He reports that 'Aziz Allah was one of the scholars who taught at the madrasa in the shrine complex of Shaykh Safi, the eponymous ancestor of the Safavid dynasty, in Ardabil –'Aziz Allah's native region. Moreover, Afandi cites only one work belonging to 'Aziz Allah and claims that it is a commentary written in Persian on a doctrinal work by Abu Ja'far al-Tusi (d. 1067) and dedicated to Shah Tahmasb. Later Shi'i bio-bibliographical sources supply a bit more detail about 'Aziz Allah's works. Aqa Buzurg Tihrani notes that 'Aziz Allah wrote his commentary on Tusi's work entitled *Muqaddimat al-kalam* in 1559–1560 and dedicated it to Shahzada Mahin Banu Sultanum, rather than to Shah Tahmasb. 'Aziz Allah wrote *Tafsir-i kalima-i tahlil* for the same princess in 1555–56, as indicated by a manuscript in the Quds-i Radawi Library.[103] However, as the Quds-i Radawi Library's catalogue and

---

[99] 'Aziz Allah Husayni, *Tafsir-i kalima-i tahlil/tahliliyya* in *Majmu'a-yi rasa'il-i khatti-yi farsi,* ed. Bunyad-i Pazhuhish-ha-yi Islami Astan-i Quds-i Radawi, 12 vols (Tehran: Bahruz, 1989), 1:46–59.

[100] 'Aziz Allah Husayni, *Tafsir-i kalima-yi tahlil,* 46.

[101] 'Aziz Allah Husayni, *Tafsir-i kalima-yi tahlil,* 50, 51, 53.

[102] Afandi, *Riyad al-'ulama',* 3:314.

[103] Tihrani, *Tabaqat a'lam al-shi'a: Ihya al-dathir min al-qarn al-ashir,* 17 vols (Beirut: Dar Ihya' al-Turath al-Arabi, 2009), 7:139

Mustafa Dirayati's catalogue of Persian manuscripts indicate, 'Aziz Allah's commentary was written in Arabic, not in Persian, and was dedicated to the princess Mahin Banu.[104] In addition to *Tafsir-i kalima-i tahlil* and *Sharh usul al-din* or *Muqaddimat al-kalam,* the collection that contains the manuscripts donated by Shahzada Mahin Banu Sultanum at the Quds-i Radawi Library includes another short treatise attributed to 'Aziz Allah Husayni entitled *Sharh-i tasbihat-i arba'ah.* This is a treatise on doctrine with a dedication to Shahzada Mahin Banu.[105] In Mustafa Dirayati's catalogue, however, three works have been registered under the name of 'Aziz Allah b. 'Inayat Allah Husayni Khalkhali, namely, *Tafsir-i kalima-yi tahliliyya, Sharh usul al-din,* and *Tarjuma-yi risala-yi wajiza.*[106] Although Dirayati's list does not include *Sharh-i tasbihat-i arba'a* among 'Aziz Allah's works, it turns up *Tarjuma-i risala-i wajiza,* which other sources failed to mention. According to Dirayati's list, the only extant copy of the *Tarjuma-i risala-i wajiza* has been sitting at the National Library of Iran.[107] As the preface of this work indicates, *Tarjumah-i risala-i wajiza* is a translation of a famous book by Muhammad b. Makki al-'Amili, known as Shahid al-Awwal (d. 1384), namely, *al-Alfiyya fi fiqh al-salat al-yawmiyya.*[108] There is no preface or dedication by 'Aziz Allah, so it seems that he preferred to keep al-Shahid al-Awwal's original preface.[109] However, the colophon of text indicates that its translation was completed by ''Aziz Allah b. 'Inayat Allah Husayni' in February 1547.[110]

Thus, four extant works are attributed to 'Aziz Allah:

1. *Tafsir-i kalima-yi tahlil* (*c.* 963/1555–1556) in Persian, dedicated to Mahin Banu.
2. *Sharh usul al-din* or *Muqaddimat al-kalam* (*c.* 967/1559–1560) in Arabic, dedicated to Mahin Banu.
3. *Sharh-i tasbihat-i arba'a* (undated) in Persian, dedicated to Mahin Banu.
4. *Tarjuma-i risala-i wajiza* (*c.* February 1547) in Persian without dedication or translator's preface.

'Aziz Allah must have authored these works while he was teaching at the *madrasa* in the shrine of Shaykh Safi, a significant religious complex and

[104] For the preface and colophon of *Sharh-i usul al-din* see http://digital.aqr.ir/newindex.aspx?pid=13&GID=35148&ID=39581. Dirayati, *Fihristwara,* 6:443.

[105] 'Aziz Allah Husayni, *Sharh-i tasbihat arba'a,* Mashhad, Saziman-i Kitabkhana-ha, Muzah-ha wa-Markaz-i Asnad-i Astan-i Quds, MS 3372; Ali Sadra-yi Khuyi, *Fihrist-i nuskha-ha-yi khatti hadith wa-'ulum-i hadith-i shi'a,* 12 vols (Qum, Iran: Mu'assasa-yi 'Ilmiyi Farhangi-yi Dar al-Hadith, Sazman-i Chap wa-Nashir, 1963–1964), 9: 311.

[106] Dirayati, *Fihristwara,* 11:403.

[107] Dirayati, *Fihristwara,* 5:839.

[108] 'Aziz Allah b. 'Inayat Allah Husayni, *Tarjuma-yi risala-i wajiza* (Tehran: Sazman-i Asnad wa-Kitabkhana-i Milli-yi Jumhuri-yi Islami-yi Iran), MS 1955/1, February 1547, fol. 14a.

[109] 'Aziz Allah, *Tarjuma-yi risala-yi wajiza,* 1b–2a.

[110] 'Aziz Allah, *Tarjuma-yi risala-yi wajiza,* 137b–138a.

dynastic site that was expanded under the first two Safavid rulers. Mahin Banu, a prominent sponsor of these new construction projects, was strongly committed to the upkeep of the shrine, as Hayati Tabrizi reports in his recently discovered chronicle, which dates from *c.* 1554.[111] Her patronage of 'Aziz Allah, who dedicated three of his four extant works to Mahin Banu Sultanum, indicates that she was not only concerned with architectural patronage of the complex but also with the production of religious knowledge and advancement of scholarship in this growing educational institution of the shrine. In my opinion, this detail is significant given that little is known about the instructors and teachers of this institution because of the reticence of the contemporary sources and dearth of modern research. Although Maryam Moazzen's recent monograph expanded our knowledge about the higher education in Safavid Iran, the examination of the *madrasa* in the shrine of Ardabil and those who held teaching positions there in the sixteenth century fell outside the purview of her study, for she has concentrated on Shi'i higher learning in the late Safavid period.[112] Kishwar Rizvi, in contrast, provides significant insights into the shrine's architectural structure and its growing prominence in the decades preceding to the Safavids and after their rise to power. She has demonstrated that 'what had initially been a modest Sufi lodge, consisting of Shaykh's residence and retreat, had developed by the seventeenth century into a vast complex, with halls for initiation ceremonies and scriptural studies, as well as a magnificent library'. As a part of this development and structural expansion, in the middle of the sixteenth century a *madrasa* and a *dar al-hadith* (Hall for hadith study) were built at the shrine of Shayk Safi in order to codify the newly introduced Shi'i laws.[113] Moreover, Rizvi maintained that the *dar al-hadith* could be viewed as the manifestation of the policies of bringing ulama from Arab lands to propagate the Shi'i doctrine, as an example mentioning Mir Sayyid Husayn Mujtahid 'Amili, who held the office of *mudarris* and *shaykh al-islam* in Ardabil where he set about establishing the *shari'a*.[114] However, the royal patronage of local Persian scholars like 'Aziz Allah indicates that royal support and patronage were not exclusive to 'Amili émigré scholars during the formation of this educational institution. Persian scholars under royal patronage contributed to production of knowledge and propagation of the faith as well. In return of this royal favour, 'Aziz Allah expressed his gratitude and stated several times that the composition of doctrinal works was the most important and noblest service that a royal servant at the threshold of the government could offer.

---

[111] Ghereghlou, 'Chronicling a Dynasty', 813.

[112] Maryam Moazzen, *Formation of a Religious Landscape: Shi'i Higher Learning in Safavid Iran* (Leiden: Brill, 2018).

[113] Kishwar Rizvi, *The Safavid Dynastic Shrine: Architecture, Religion and Power in Early Modern Iran* (London: I. B. Tauris, 2011), 5–8.

[114] Rizvi, *The Safavid Dynastic Shrine*, 83.

'Aziz Allah begins by praising God and the Prophet in the preface to his *Tafsir-i kalima-yi tahlil*, then he glorifies the Family of the Prophet and the twelve infallible Imams as the 'bearers of the secrets of the revelation and revealers of esoteric aspects of the unity of God (*tawhid*) and its profession'. He views the creedal statement (*kalima-yi tawhid*) not only as the foundation of one's faith and confession but also an evidence of the twelve infallible Imams. His couplet reads,

> Those Imams are the leaders of the path of perception
> Pioneers of the highway of certainty
> Like the twelve mansions of the celestial sphere
> Their number is [equal to the letters of] *la ilaha illa Allah*.[115]

After the encomiums of praise for God, the Prophet, and the Imams, 'Aziz Allah goes on to state that he wrote this brief treatise in order to explain the meanings of the profession of God's oneness and to attract the favour and attention of the princess. He seeks to 'remove the veil from the bashful faces of the dames of meanings and the beauties of the truth with the feeble fingers of his thoughts and makes this presentation a means by which he appeals to Her Holiness, the Prosperous and Esteemed Princess, the Precious Pearl'. Moreover, he extolls the worldly grandeur and spiritual eminence of Mahin Banu. He glorifies her as 'the Queen of Kings and Sultans', 'Owner of the Necks [that is, Master] of All Mankind', and 'Adorner of the Throne of Royalty'. Praising her generosity and munificence, 'Aziz Allah writes, 'Her excellency is embellished by the ranks of dignity and generosity', 'The sun of her grace, like the grace of the Sun, shines over the world', and 'the clouds of her shadow, like the shadows of the clouds, cast their shade on the heads of both great and small'. Furthermore, like other preface authors, 'Aziz Allah stressed the privileged and exalted spiritual status of Mahin Banu and invoked the Qur'anic verse in which God addressed the Virgin Mary and announced her chosen status, above that of all other women. In this connection, he stated, 'Her excellency is an embodiment of the verse, "Truly God has chosen you and purified you, and has chosen you above the women of the worlds" (Q 3:42).' Her God-chosen status was coupled with an extraordinary spiritual power through which 'she could see the mysteries of the perceptible world by peering through the veil of the unseen with Her own eyes, and unravel the knots of complicated problems from the tangled string of the people's hope with the fingers of knowledge and intelligence'. 'Aziz Allah remarks, 'The surroundings of her palace are as sacred as the precinct around the holy city in reverence,' drawing an analogy between the harem and the sacred precinct of the Ka'ba in Mecca.

---

[115] *Ān imāmān-i rāh-burda-yi bīn/ pīshwāyān-i shāhrāh-i yaqīn; Hamchu burj-i falak-i dawāzdah māh/ 'adad-i lā ilāha illā 'llāh.'* The number of the letters of the creedal statement equals twelve: La (2) ilaha (3) illa (3) Allah (4).

'Aziz Allah's eulogy of the princess in his prefatory section was punctuated and concluded with blessings. He asked God to 'eternalize the shadow of her kingship (*salṭanat*) and munificence for as long as the heavens continue to be studded with the ornament of stars'. He expresses the hope, 'May God – be He exalted and praised –make her existence and magnanimity a continuous means through which welfare and order among her subjects are delivered and established. In return for her noble service, may He reward her – "And as for that which benefits mankind, it remains on the earth" (Q 13:17).' Finally, he said, 'It is to be hoped that this beautiful chaste lady, adorned with her blessed attributes, make a better appearance to the sight of the discerning examiners, and be protected and guarded from the sight of the squint-eyed fault-finders, whose vision was afflicted by the pannus of ignorance and recalcitrance.'[116]

In short, 'Aziz Allah's interpretation of the creedal statement as evidence for the Imamate was consonant with the doctrinal orientation of the Safavid dynasty. With this presentation he curried the favour of Mahin Banu, the prominent sponsor of the shrine complex where he served as a professor. He attributed to the princess notable religious authority and endowed her with a privileged status and superior spiritual capacity. 'Aziz Allah's remarks reveal the preface's function in forming the patron's image and endorsing her authority. After praising the princess's religious attributes and exalted status, 'Aziz Allah expresses his hope that the princess would make a better appearance in the sight of her subjects, revealing that one purpose behind the preface was to convey an ideal image of his patron.

Tarjuma/Sharh-i tasbihat-i arba'a *(n.d.) by 'Aziz Allah b. 'Inayat Allah Husayni*[117]

In this brief treatise, 'Aziz Allah expounds on four expressions: *Subhan Allah* ('Glory be to God'), *al-hamdu li-llah* ('Praise be to God'), *La ilaha illa Allah* ('There is No Deity but God'), and *Allahu akbar* ('God is Great') and suggests that they form the basis of the five pillars of Islamic doctrine: *tawhid* (Oneness of God), *'adl* (justice), *nubuwwa* (prophecy), *imama* (imamate), and *ma'ad* (the hereafter). He states that it is incumbent upon all believers to learn the meanings of these expressions to attain perfect faith.[118] Although it is not certain whether the word *sharh* or commentary in the title meant a commentary on a prior work or just an explanation of the four expressions, the short treatise may have been written as a commentary on a very brief treatise

---

[116] 'Aziz Allah Husayni, *Tafsir-i kalima-yi tahlil*, 48–50.

[117] 'Aziz Allah b. 'Inayat Allah Husayni, *Sharh-i tasbihat-i arba'a* (Mashhad: Kitabkhana-yi Astan Quds-i Radawi), MS 3372. Although 'Aziz Allah's treatise has been recorded under the title *Sharh-i tasbihat-i arba'a* on the title page of the manuscript, he introduces it in his preface as a translation of the four expressions, *Tarjuma-yi tasbihat-i arba'a*.

[118] 'Aziz Allah, *Sharh-i tasbihat-i arba'a*, 1b–12a.

on the same subject, *al-Baqiyat al-salihat* ('The Enduring Good Deeds') by al-Shahid al-Awwal (d. 1384).[119] 'Aziz Allah's Persian commentary may represent the continuation of the scholarly interest in Shahid al-Awwal's short treatise, including 'Ali b. Muhammad Nabati Bayadi 'Amili (d. 1472–1473), during the early Safavid period.[120]

'Aziz Allah's preface to *Tarjuma/Sharh-i tasbihat-i arba'a* also begins by glorifying God and the Prophet, followed by praise of the Prophet's Family and the infallible Imams. In his eulogy of the Imams, 'Aziz Allah states,

> Sincere and pure blessings are due to His noble family and descendants, each one of whom is a world-illuminating sun in the twelve stations of the zodiac of glory and election/chosenness and an ark of salvation for those who are in perplexity and drowned in the sea of turmoil. The evidence attesting to the truth of this claim is [the hadith of] 'Certainly my Family are like Noah's Ark; whoever embarks on it will be saved, and whoever turns away from it will perish.'

Following the encomium and glorification of God, the Prophet, and the Twelve Imams, 'Aziz Allah begins his statement of intent: 'The best gift and noblest present that true devotees (*mukhliṣān-i bilā ishtibāh*) and well-wishing loyal servants (*khādimān-i dawlat-khwāh*) may offer for the sublime service of the glorious threshold of those modestly concealed in the abode of infallibility and purity and those sovereigns of the assembly of modesty and chastity are rare jewels and glowing pearls of the creeds of the faith.' Therefore, he said, he rendered the Persian translation of a gift to the exalted court of Princess Mahin Banu, 'the Ornament of the Women of the Paradise', 'the Khadija of the Age', and 'the One whose glory is on par with that of Bilqis'. Lastly, he prayed for the perpetuity and prosperity of the reign of the princess, 'May the shadow of her protection and munificence over the believers be prolonged until the Day of Judgment', and wished that his present to the princess might be accepted by her.[121]

For the audience, the opening blessing at the beginning of the preface is the first site that reveals the Shi'i persuasion of the author, since it includes praises for the twelve Imams and some other references to the Imamate. Moreover, the present preface also serves the author for projecting himself as a loyal, well-wishing, and benevolent servant of the Safavid princess with his commitment to propagating the faith. This display of loyalty and devotion must have sought to elicit the favour of the princess and reinforce the bond between the author himself and his patron. However indirect they might be or shrouded with self-deprecating expressions, the author's statements about

---

[119] Muhammad b. Makki al-Shahid al-Awwal, *Arba' rasa'il kalamiyya* (Qum, Iran: Bustan-i Kitab-i Qum, 2002), 233–236.

[120] 'Ali b. Muhammad Nabati 'Amili, *al-Kalimat al-nafi'at fi sharh al-baqiyat al-salihat,* in Muhammad b. Makki, *Arba'a rasā'il kalamiyya*, 237–289.

[121] 'Aziz Allah, *Sharh-i tasbihat-i arba'a,* fols 1b–2a.

himself in the preface must have also served the enhancement of the status and standing of the author in the sight of his patron or audience in general.

Sharh-i usul al-din-i Shaykh Tusi (c. 1559–1560) *by 'Aziz Allah b. 'Inayat Allah Husayni*[122]

In his bibliographical dictionary, *al-Dhari'a ila tasanif al-shi'a,* Aqa Buzurg Tehrani, provides a brief summary of this text under the title of *al-Masa'il al-kalamiyya,* and notes that it consists of thirty-three brief explanations of theological issues such as the Proof of the Necessary Being (God), Prophecy, Imamate, the Hereafter, and so on. It seems that this short treatise, attributed to al-Shaykh al-Tusi, has a structure similar to Ibn Babawayh's and Nasir al-Din's above-mentioned works on Shi'i doctrine. Moreover, Aqa Buzurg Tihrani asserts that 'Aziz Allah wrote a Persian commentary on this work and dedicated to Shah Tahmasb.[123] However, as Hajj Sayyid Muhammad 'Ali Rawdati has discussed in his article, the only extant copy available at the Quds-i Radawi library was written in Arabic rather than Persian and dedicated to Princess Mahin Banu.[124]

In the preface to his brief commentary, 'Aziz Allah uses very similar phraseology to that of *Sharh-i tasbihat-i arba'a,* stating, 'The best gifts in the service of the women of purity and chastity of the sublime threshold are the pearls and shining gems of the faith.' As a gift to 'the Khadija of the Age' and 'the Fatima of the Time', he wrote his commentary on 'one of the works of the chief of the jurists of the Sacred Law, Abu Ja'far Muhammad al-Tusi, which was very brief, in order to expand on its noble content'.[125]

Mufrada-yi 'Asim or Usul-i qira'at-i 'Asim *by 'Imad al-Din al-Sharif al-Astarabadi al-Qari (Mir Kalan) (fl. 16th c.)*[126]

Mufrada-yi 'Asim, also known as *Usul-i qira'at-i 'Asim* introduces the principles of reading of the Qur'an according to the famous reader, 'Asim of Kufa (d. 745).[127] It was written by 'Imad al-Din al-Sharif al-Astarabadi al-Qari (fl. 16th c.) by the commission of Princess Mahin Banu. The author does provide the year of the completion of the treatise either in the preface or in the colophon, but he refers to one of his well-known works, *Tuhfa-yi shahiyya,*

---

122 'Aziz Allah, *Sharh-i usul al-din-i Shaykh Tusi,* Mashhad, Astan-i Quds-i Radawi, MS 194 (1559–1560).

123 Tihrani, al-*Dhari'a ila tasanif al-shi'a,* 20:364.

124 Hajj Sayyid Muhammad 'Ali Rawdati, *Du risala-yi kalami az Shaykh Tusi,* see <http://tusi.kateban.com/post/2344>, last accessed 15 January 2018; Dirayati, *Fihristwarah,* 6:443.

125 'Aziz Allah, *Sharh-i usul al-din,* fols 1b–2a.

126 'Imad al-Din al-Sharif al-Astarabadi al-Qari, *Mufrada-i 'Asim/Usul-i qira'at-i 'Asim* (Tehran: Kitab'khana-yi Majlis-i Shura-yi Milli, MS 4070/1 (17th–18th c.)).

127 Rudi Paret, 'Ḳira'a', *Encyclopaedia of Islam,* vol. V (Khe-Mahi), new edition, ed. Clifford Edmund Bosworth (Leiden: Brill, 1986), 127–129.

completed *c.* 1549–1550 and dedicated to Shah Tahmasb,[128] elsewhere in the treatise.[129] It was therefore completed sometime from 1550 to 1562, the death date of Mahin Banu.

Apart from Mahin Banu's patronage, 'Imad al-Din received Shah Tahmasb's favour and patronage too, considering that he was commissioned by the shah to write some works for him and the contemporary sources pointed to their close relationship. Iskandar Beg Munshi wrote in his chronicle:

> 'Imad al-Din, born in Astarabad, was an expert in the arts of Qur'anic recitation and wrote both detailed works and brief manuals on the subject. During the reign of Shah Tahmasb, he was one of the theologians regarded with favor by the Shah. He was always ready to press the claims of the learned, poor, and deserving, and he was respected by high and low alike. The class of Qur'an readers benefited particularly from his efforts.[130]

Munshi's notice indicates that 'Imad al-Din enjoyed close ties with the royal family and played a considerable part in bringing the concerns and needs of the scholars of the time to the attention of the royal family and in shaping their decisions in terms of distributing their patronage among the scholars and other beneficiaries. From Munshi's notes, it can also be inferred that scholars of the knowledge of the Qur'an (*'ilm al-Qur'an)* must have enjoyed more privileged and advantageous status thanks to 'Imad al-Din. In other words, 'Imad al-Din seems to have created his own circle of patronage by favouring people from the field of Qur'anic studies to other scholars of different disciplines, while he himself was still in the circle of Mahin Banu's and Shah Tahmasb's patronage and protection.

In addition to Qummi and Munshi, Afandi provides a relatively more detailed and lengthier notice in his bio-bibliographical dictionary about the works of 'Imad al-Din al-Qari. Considering that little is known about this scholar in modern scholarship, Afandi's notice is worth quoting entirely, which reads as follows:

> Learned, erudite, jurisprudent, traditionist, Qur'an reciter, pious theologian. He was one of the scholars and eminent figures of the reign of Shah Tahmasb. Author of a number of works, particularly in the science of the Qur'an, including a treatise in Persian titled *Tuhfa-yi shahiyya* (The Royal Gift), which contains excellent observations. He wrote it for Shah Tahmasb. I saw a copy of it in Astarabad, copied by the famous al-Sayyid al-Amir Sharaf al-Din 'Ali al-Shulistani in 1586–87, probably in his youth. He also wrote, *Ithbat al-wajib* and a short treatise concerning the principles of the reading of Ibn Kathir (*Qira'at Ibn Kathir)* according to the transmissions of Abu al-Hasan al-Buzzi (d. 864) and Abu 'Amr Qunbul (d. 904–5) with the method of

---

[128] Dirayati, *Fihristwara,* 2:962.

[129] al-Astarabadi al-Qari, *Mufrada-yi 'Asim,* fol. 5b.

[130] Munshi, *History of Shah Abbas,* 247.

al-Shatibi (d. 1194), a copy of which I came across in the province of Amul, Mazandaran. He has another treatise on the reading of Nafi' (d. 785) according to the transmissions of Abu Musa Qalun (d. 834–35) and Abu Sa'id Warsh (d. 812–13). Moreover, he wrote a brief treatise regarding the principles of the reading of Abu 'Amr (d. 770) according to the transmissions of al-Duri and al-Susi (d. 874) with the method of al-Shatibi (d. 1194), upon a copy of which I stumbled in the same province (Amul). Also, he has a Persian treatise concerning the reading of 'Asim (*Qira'at 'Asim)* with the method al-Shatibi, including an introduction, three chapters, and a conclusion. He authored this treatise with the commission of the Shah's wife or his daughter. Another treatise of his deals with the reading of Ibn Kathir (d. 738) (*Qira'at Ibn Kathir)* according to the transmissions of al-Buzzi and Qunbul with the method of Shatibi and Taysir, a copy of which I saw in the same province (Amul) and it could have been the same as the above-mentioned one. Also among his works are the Persian translation of *al-Ihtijaj* of al-Shaykh al-Tabrisi and a commentary on *Nahj al-balagha* of al-Sayyid al-Radi. Note that these last two works were attributed to al-Mawla 'Imad al-Din, whereas most of the above-mentioned works were attributed to al-Mawla 'Imad al-Din 'Ali b. 'Ali al-Sharif al-Qari of Astarabad by birth and of Mazandaran by residence. Some of his works were recorded under the name of 'Imad al-Din 'Ali b. 'Imad al-Din 'Ali al-Astarabadi, while others under the name of al-Mawla 'Imad al-Din of Astarabad by birth and of Mazandaran by residence, as well as under the name of al-Mawla 'Imad al-Mazanadarani al-Kalbari. It is obvious that all these names refer to the same person.[131]

Both works that Mirza 'Abd Allah Afandi describes here and other works attributed to 'Imad al-Din[132] show that the majority of his works relate to the seven or ten canonical readings of the Qur'an.[133] The variant readings of the Qur'an were limited to seven by Ibn Mujahid (d. 936) and ten by Ibn al-Jazari (d. 1429). Later on it became a mainstream Muslim view that the seven and ten readings of the Qur'an were canonical and divine, because they were *mutawātira,* that is, transmitted from the Prophet and his Companions to later generations through multiple concurrent transmissions, as Shady Hekmat Nasser has discussed. The main justification for the existence of seven variant readings was the 'mysterious' Prophetic tradition of the *sab'at aḥruf* ('the seven modes of recitation'), which suggested that Qur'an was revealed with different modes of reading, so that variant readings are possible and legitimate. However, a great degree of vagueness surrounds the intended

[131] Afandi, *Riyad al-'ulama'*, 4:154–155.

[132] Dirayati records twenty-three works attributed to 'Imad al-Din Dirayati. *Fihristwara,* 11:614. Dirayati lists 'Imad al-Din's works under the name 'Ali b. 'Ali Sharif Astarabadi (d. 10th c.).

[133] The seven canonical readers according to Ibn Mujahid are Nafi' (d. 785), Ibn Kathir (d. 738), Abu 'Amr b. al-'Ala' (d. 860), Ibn 'Amir (d. 736), 'Asim (d. 745), Hamzah (d. 773), and al-Kisa'i (d. 804). According to al-Jazari, Abu Ja'far Yazid b. al-Qa'qa' (d. 747), Ibn Muhaysin (d. 740), al-A'mash (d. 765), Ya'qub al-Hadrami (d. 821), al- Hasan al-Basri (d.728), and several others were as famous and credible as the seven readers.

meaning of *ḥarf* in this Prophetic tradition.[134] Nasser has suggested that the majority of Shi'is rejected the notion of variant readings of the Qur'an and considered the mainstream Sunni's view regarding seven and ten canonical readings of the Qur'an as proof of the general Shi'i conviction that Qur'an was tampered with and falsified by the third caliph, 'Uthman (r. 644–656).[135] Therefore, Nasser maintained, 'Not believing in the *tawātur* of the eponymous readings is only a natural result of the general beliefs of the Shi'a; since the Qur'an is falsied and altered, there is actually no point in adopting any system of reading.'[136] Consequently, according to Nasser, the Shi'a never developed a sophisticated discipline of *qirā'āt* as did the Sunnis. He also maintained, 'The Shi'is nowadays read the Qur'an according to the reading of 'Asim in the recension of his student Hafs. This is probably justified by the fact that the *isnād* of this canonical reading goes back to 'Ali b. Abi Talib.'[137]

Although the majority of the Shi'a rejected variant readings, as Nasser has pointed out, several Shi'i authorities permitted use of the seven readings. Nasser writes, 'Al-Tusi states that the norm among the Shi'a is that the Qur'an must have been revealed according to one *ḥarf* and one reading only; however, they agreed to recite it according to the Readings of the *qurrā'*. The same position is expressed by al-Hilli, al-Khu'i, and al-Khumayni.'[138] The favourable views in studying different readings of the Qur'an expressed by prominent pre-Safavid scholars could have provided a basis on which 'Imad al-Din established his scholarship in the early Safavid period. In his major works, such as *Tuhfa-yi shahi* or *Mufrada-yi 'Asim,* 'Imad al-Din does not discuss whether the existence of variant readings is justifiable or the view of Shi'i scholars on the subject. Rather, he states in both treatises that, after the doctrines of faith, knowledge of the Qur'anic readings (*qirā'āt)* and proper recitation of the Qur'an (*tajwīd*) is the noblest field of all the Islamic sciences. It is incumbent upon everybody to strive to learn the proper recitation of the Qur'an because it is required for the performance of one's daily prayers.[139] Moreover, 'Imad al-Din introduces a full chain of transmitters to the reading of 'Asim, starting with his teacher, Sayyid Hasan al-Husayni al-Astarabadi, known as al-Sayyid al-Maghribi, and going back to 'Ali b. Abi Talib.[140]

Although some Shi'i authorities had already endorsed the usage of the variant readings of the Qur'an and 'Imad al-Din received royal commission and patronage to author some of his works on the same subject, his works

---

[134] Shady Nasser, *The Transmission of the Variant Readings of the Qur'an: The Problem of Tawatur and the Emergence of Shawadhdh* (Leiden: Brill, 2012), 5–33.

[135] Nasser, *The Transmission of the Variant Readings of the Qur'an*, 32–33.

[136] Nasser, *The Transmission of the Variant Readings of the Qur'an*, 114.

[137] Nasser, *The Transmission of the Variant Readings of the Qur'an*, 33.

[138] Nasser, *The Transmission of the Variant Readings of the Qur'an*, 114.

[139] 'Imad al-Din al-Sharif al-Astarabadi al-Qari, *Tuhfa-yi shahi,* Tehran, Kitab-khana-yi Majlis-i Shura-yi Milli, MS 12255, fols 9b–10b.

[140] 'Imad al-Din, *Mufrada-yi 'asim,* fols 4b–5b.

might have caused some eyebrows to be raised among those who rejected the variant readings and held that Qur'an was falsified by the caliphs. Moreover, his considerable influence in the court, which he used in favour of those who specialised in the reading and reciting the Qur'an could have engendered discontent among the scholars from different fields, who scrambled for the patronage of the royal family. The biographical dictionaries do not mention such a rivalry between him and other scholars of the time or any negative reaction to his writings for that matter, but the silence of the contemporary sources does not mean that such discontent with 'Imad al-Din's elevated position at the court of Shah Tahmasb and Princess Mahin Banu never occurred. The latter point gains more significance and pertinence if we consider it in the light of the composition of another contemporary religious narrative, *Hikaya-yi jazira-yi khadra* ('The Story of the Green Island'), which contained antagonistic opinions against the different readings of the Qur'an.

The Story of the Green Island appeared in a treatise entitled *Risala-i ithbat al-ghayba wa-kashf al-hayra* ('Proof of Occultation and Removal of Confusion'), also known as *Iqbal-nama,* by Mir Shams al-Din Asadullah Mar'ashi Shushtari (d. 1555–1556), who dedicated it to Shah Tahmasb. Shushtari was a prominent student of Muhaqqiq al-Karaki (d. 1534) and became *ṣadr* of Shah Tahmasb in 1536–1537, replacing Mir Mu'izz al-Din Muhammad Isfahani, both of whom had been nominated by al-Karaki, and remained in this position until his death.[141] The Story of the Green Island narrates an intriguing journey of a certain Shams al-Din Mazandarani to the Green Island, where the Twelfth Imam and his companions were believed to be living. According to the story, Mazandarani studied with a Sunni scholar the science of the Qur'an and seven different readings before he peregrinated to the utopian Green Island. Once he arrived there, he found an elective community under the guidance of the Mahdi through his descendant and deputy in charge, Shaykh Shams al-Din. Mazandarani decided to study the sciences of the Qur'an with Shams al-Din and asked his permission to attend his study circle. Once the permission was granted, Mazandarani started studying the recitation of the Qur'an. During his recitation of the Qur'an, he mentioned the different readings of certain verses according to Sunni scholars such as Kisa'i, 'Asim, Hamzah, and Abu 'Amr. However, the names brought up incited the anger of Shams al-Din, who snapped at al-Mazandarani and said:

> We do not recognize these people! But we believe without doubt that the Qur'an was revealed on seven letters (*bar haft ḥarf*). After the Prophet performed his farewell pilgrimage, Gabriel came down to him and said, 'O Muhammad! God commissioned me to recite the Quran with you from the beginning to the end so that I could correct you, should any disagreement arise between our recitations.

[141] Abisaab, *Converting Persia,* 19–20.

Gabriel and the Prophet recited the Qur'an and the event was attended by a host of his Companions, such as 'Ali, Hasan, Husayn, Ubayy b. Ka'b, 'Abd Allah b. Mas'ud, and other Companions like 'Uthman b. 'Affan, the head of the hypocrites, were present during the recitation. Whenever a disagreement arose during the recitation, Gabriel provided the correct recitation and 'Ali b. Abi Talib noted the confirmed and corrected recitation. Let it be known that although 'Uthman, curse be upon him, was also present in this gathering and listened to the recitation, since he was accursed and irreligious, the recitation of the Qur'an had no influence or effect on his soul. On the contrary, his disbelief and hypocrisy deepened. By the same token, most of the scribes of the revelation became apostates after the demise of the Prophet, and their closeness and testimony to the revelation and conference with the Prophet had no effect on them, because of their disbelief, hypocrisy, and disease in their hearts. To this effect, God says, 'In their hearts is disease, so God has increased their disease; and for them is a painful punishment because they habitually used to lie.'[142]

The dialogue featured in this fictitious narrative is of significance because of several reasons. In the first place, it suggests that although the variant readings of the Qur'an had existed during the life of the prophet, different readings were removed with Gabriel's intervention and instruction during the last Ramadan that the Prophet observed before his death. However, although many Companions were present in this gathering, most of them did not hold on to the reading that was confirmed by Gabriel. In the second place, expressed by the deputy of Imam Mahdi, this position was attributed an aura of certainty and was obviously at odds with the scholarship of 'Imad al-Din, whose scholarship for the most part was devoted to the study of the variant readings of the Qur'an. Therefore, one can say that this fictitious scene of the narrative in which Mazandarani was reprimanded for his preoccupation with the seven canonical readings of the Qur'an could have been devised against 'Imad al-Din to undermine the legitimacy of his scholarship and thereby tarnish Imad al-Din's fame and influence at the court. That said, regardless of whether the foregoing dialogue in the story was developed out of discontent with 'Imad al-Din's scholarship and influence, the existence of the dialogue in a popular narrative of the time clearly indicates that different convictions concerning the variant readings of the Qur'an coexisted at least during the early Safavid period.

In the preface of his treatise, he begins with the praises of God, the Prophet, and His Family. Then, he introduces himself as 'this miserable and humble man with many shortcomings, wanderer of the desert of confusion who is lost in the valley of ignorance, needy of the forgiveness of God who leads aright, 'Imad al-Din 'Ali al-Sharif al-Qari al-Astarabadi'. 'Imad al-Din

---

142 Mir Shams al-Din Asadullah Mar'ashi Shushtari, *Iqbalnamah,* Tehran University Library, MS. 656, fols 38a–39b.

moves on to state that he was commissioned by a royal decree that one cannot disobey, issued by the 'Descendant of Musa Kazim [the seventh Imam] and the Safavid dynasty', 'Manifestation of the Divine Favors and Purveyor of the Splendor of Kingship', 'the Bilqis of the Age', and 'the Khadija of the Time'. These honorific titles are followed by others and a short poem in which 'Imad al-Din eulogised the princess:

> That master whom God has addressed
> Lady of the two worlds, Mary of Bilqis Excellency
> Oh, you under the weight of whose generosity the neck of the sky has sagged
> And because of the waves of your munificence the ocean has been scared to death
> Comparing to the swiftness of your resolution, lightning would look calm and still
> Comparing to the speed of your patience, mountains would seem moving in rush
> In the garden if the breeze tells about your grace
> In the ocean if the cloud talks about your words
> The silver chest of jasmine becomes dirt out of desire
> And the cheeks of imperial pearl turn red out of shame.[143]

The praise of the princess, expressed in poetical and rhetorical terms, stresses her generosity, political deftness and resolution, grandeur and modesty at the same time. Mahin Banu's religious and worldly merits are epitomised in his apt description of the princess as Mary of Bilqis-like Excellency (*Maryam-i Bilqis-janab*). Mary as an epitome of chastity and divinity and Bilqis as an emblematic figure of political might and grandeur are not arbitrary choices on the part of the author, who was enthusiastic in the projection of Mahin Banu's religious and political power as a prominent beneficiary of her patronage.

Tarikh *(1554) by Qasim Beg Hayati Tabrizi*

The *History* of Hayati Tabrizi was an early Safavid chronicle that had long been thought lost. A recent study by Kioumars Ghereghlou has revealed that this chronicle was bound together with large portions of volume three of Ghiyath al-Din Khwandamir's (d. 1536) *Tarikh-i Habib al-siyar fi akhbar-i afrad-i bashar* and catalogued erroneously as *Tarikh-i Shah Isma'il*, an anonymous seventeenth-century history of Shah Isma'il.[144] Hayati Tabrizi's work gave an account of both the pre-dynastic and the dynastic phase of Safavid history, shedding some fresh light on the early years of the nascent Safavid state. In particular, it provided details about the Safavid shrine complex in

---

[143] Imad al-Din, *Mufrada-yi 'asim*, fols 2b–3a.
[144] Kioumars Ghereghlou, 'Chronicling a Dynasty'.

Ardabil, new edifices added to the complex in the first half of the sixteenth century, and the superintendents of the shrine. The author dedicated the chronicle to Mahin Banu Sultanum, even though it was commissioned by Shah Tahmasb.[145]

Little is known about Hayati Tabrizi. When he wrote the preface to the chronicle, in the spring of 1554, Hayati was a senior bureaucrat and enjoyed close ties with Shah Tahmasb, Mahin Banu, and other female members of the royal family. The chronicle was informed by the messianic outlook and discourse of the time: the author hailed Shah Tahmasb as 'the deputy of the Mahdi' and drew on Hurufi and esoteric interpretations throughout his work. Ghereghlou compares Hayati Tabrizi's discourse and messianic tendencies with those of a contemporary, 'Ali Tusi, who prophesied the advent of the Imam in 963 AH (1555–1556) in a treatise dedicated to Shah Tahmasb, *Mubashshara-yi shahiyya.*[146] Hayati Tabriz wrote his dedication two years before the expected Parousia and offered it the Princess Mahin Banu, who was considered the fiancée of the awaited Imam and remained unmarried until her death.

In his ornate and poetic preface, Hayati Tabrizi showers Princess Mahin Banu with praises by using many honorific titles and evoking some Qur'anic and historical references. He begins by calling her the 'Star of the Religion and Fortune (*dawlat*)'. The remaining epithets extol her exalted status in these two domains, faith-religion and fortune-state. He glorifies the princess as 'the Shadow of God', 'the Shadow of God's Grace', 'the Splendor of the Crown and the Exalter of the Throne', and 'the Shining Light of Eternal Prosperity', referring both to here divine sanction and her worldly power. Like the preface authors addressed above, Hayati Tabrizi recalls the legacy of the Queen of Sheba, Bilqis, a female epitome of magnificence and pomp. He is the loyal subject of Mahin Banu, 'who has become the second Bilqis in dignity from the beginning of time and who has been endowed by God with the kingdom of Solomon until the end of time.'

Citing Qur'anic verses referring to Mary, Hayati Tabrizi suggests that God elected Mahin Banu and made her superior to all other women. She is 'one whose pure thought is "Indeed God has chosen you and purified you and chosen you above the women of the worlds" (Q 3:42), and whose admirable manners are "distinguished in this world and the Hereafter and among those close to God" (Q 3:45)'. Mahin Banu is comparable to Mary; her exalted status is granted and sanctioned by God. The author thus accords her extraordinary spiritual status and religious authority. He describes her as being endowed with exceptional intelligence and profound understanding: 'Her brilliant nature is aware of the mysteries of

---

[145] Ghereghlou, 'Chronicling a Dynasty', 810.

[146] Ghereghlou,'Chronicling a Dynasty', 809–810. See also Rasul Ja'fariyan, 'Risala-yi mubashshara-yi shahiyya dar ithbat-i Mahdi dar sal-i 963', *Payam-i Baharistan* 16 (1391), 1,033–1057.

the sciences and wisdom, and her discerning mind is cognisant of what is seen and known.' He also praises her efforts in commanding right and promoting the faith with unwavering perseverance and patience, again citing the Qur'an: 'Her glory is the cypress of the garden of "Arise and warn!"' (Q 74:2) and 'Her edifice is the flower of the rose-garden of "So be patient"' (Q 76:24). In their original context, these verses are instructions to the Prophet Muhammad, entrusting him with the task of spreading the word of God in then pagan society and urging him to endure any hostility on the part of the pagans in the process of his propagation of the new faith. As a descendant of the Prophet and recipient of the uninterrupted guidance of the infallible Imams, Mahin Banu was entrusted with an analogous mission, the propagation of the 'true faith', Shi'ism, in the Safavid realm, which was predominantly Sunni and surrounded by the hostile Sunni states of the Uzbeks and the Ottomans.

Pari Khan Khanum II (1548–1578)

Pari Khan Khanum was a daughter of Shah Tahmasb from a Circassian mother. Of all the Safavid princess and other royal women, Pari Khan Khanum has attracted the most scholarly attention to date. Several factors may account for her privileged status in the modern historiography of women in the Safavid period.[147] First, she represents one of the clearest examples of the exercise of political authority and influence on the part of a Safavid princess in state affairs. She acted as a confidant and regent of the Shah and played major roles in the successions of two consecutive monarchs of the Safavid dynasty. Second, her life and career were relatively well documented by contemporary Safavid chroniclers and foreign travellers, in comparison with those of other Safavid royal women.[148]

Earlier studies of Pari Khan Khanum focused on her position as an influential counsellor and confidant at the court of her father, Shah Tahmasb. The death of her aunt Mahin Banu, who left a legacy of political and administrative activity, in 1562, when Pari Khan Khanum was at the age of fourteen, enabled the latter to rise to prominence at court. Her power reached its apogee late in the reign of her ailing father. Following the death of Shah Tahmasb she reined in court politics and secured the enthronement of her brother, Isma'il Mirza, as Shah Isma'il II. She hoped that her brother would appreciate her efforts to

---

[147] Golsorkhi, 'Pari Khan Khanum', 143–156; Szuppe, 'La Participation I', 219–244; Szuppe, 'La Participation I', 72–74; Szuppe, 'Jewels of Wonder', 325–348; Szuppe, 'Status, Knowledge, and Politics', 144; Nazak, 'Royal Women and Politics', esp. 49–77, 102–107; Rizvi, 'Gendered Patronage', 126–128.

[148] Munshi's *Tarikh-i 'alam-ara-yi Shah 'Abbasi* and Qummi's *Khulasat al-tawarikh* furnish detailed accounts of Pari Khan Khanum. For other contemporary sources, see Golsorkhi, 'Pari Khan Khanum', 143–1,156.

facilitate his liberation from prison and his rise to the throne and enable her to hold sway over the court. Much to her disappointment, however, Isma'il II strove to curtail his sister's ambitions and to restrict her role in political affairs. Before long, however, Isma'il II's reign came to a premature close, and with it his policy to scale back anti-Sunni rhetoric by discontinuing cursing rituals against the symbols of Sunni Islam. Shah Isma'il II's sudden death led to the emergence of Pari Khan Khanum once again as a power-broker who played a major role in determining the next ruler. She backed her purblind half-brother Muhammad Khudabanda, hoping that his physical deficiencies would facilitate her dominance at court. Although she managed to get her candidate enthroned, her aspirations to attain a dominant position were again thwarted by the new monarch's equally ambitious and politically shrewd wife, Mahd-i 'Ulya, who managed to annihilate her rival. In 1578, soon after the accession of Muhammad Khudabanda to the throne, Pari Khan Khanum was strangled at the command of the monarch. She was only thirty at the time.[149]

Like Mahin Banu, Pari Khan remained celibate throughout her life, and according to a seventeenth-century Safavid chronicle she was 'tied [by marriage] to the hidden Imam'.[150] Her royal pedigree, financial independence, education, political acumen, and celibacy enabled Pari Khan Khanum to stand out above her rivals as a masterful actor in the political arena until her fall.[151] Although the sources do not describe Pari Khan Khanum's education in any detail, the letter that she sent to Isma'il II provides significant hints about her training in religious studies. Under house arrest and accused of adultery and of conspiracy against Isma'il II, Pari Khan Khanum wrote the letter to defend herself and her dignity. She addressed her brother directly, reproaching him, 'I have studied the books of the law all my life, and I have memorized most of the Qur'anic exegeses, so why should I be labeled like this?'[152] Her expression of affront also revealed that she had received training in the religious sciences of law and *tafsir* in particular and must have had access to teachers in these fields.

The sources do not reveal the identity of these teachers or scholars whom Pari Khan Khanum may have sponsored. She showed interest in poetry and literature, and she reportedly entered into a poetic contest

[149] On the policies of Shah Ismail II, see Shohreh Golsorkhi, 'Ismail II and Mirza Makhdum Sharifi: An Interlude in Safavid history', *International Journal of Middle East Studies* 26.3 (1994), 477–488; Rosemary Stanfield Johnson, 'Sunni Survival in Safavid Iran: Anti-Sunni Activities during the Reign of Tahmasp I', *Iranian Studies* 27.1–4 (1994), 123–133.

[150] Pari Khan Khanum II was betrothed to her paternal cousin, Badi' al-Zaman Mirza b. Bahram Mirza, but they never got married. She remained unmarried until she was executed. See, Szuppe, 'La Participation I', 219. For her association with the Hidden Imam, see Quzani, *Afdal al-tawarikh* [volume II], fol. 274b.

[151] Szuppe, 'Status, Knowledge, and Politics', 144; Szuppe, 'Jewels of Wonder', 331; Rizvi, 'Gendered Patronage', 128.

[152] Birjandifar, 'Royal Women and Politics', 34, 102–107.

with the renowned court poet Muhtashim Kashani (1528–1588). Kashani wrote several poems in honour of Pari Khan Khanum, extolling her political might by comparing her power with that of the Queen of Sheba: 'Pari Khan, who is the king of the angels and of mankind; Even Bilqis learned kingship from her!'[153] The sources do not allow one to elaborate on the princess's patronage relations with the scholars of the time or her contribution to the production of Shi'i knowledge. She is reported to have founded a *madrasa* that was named after her, but the *madrasa* could not stand the test of time and vanished without leaving any architectural trace or textual evidence regarding its operation.[154] No work directly commissioned by Pari Khan Khanum has come to light, contrary to the claims of some modern researchers.[155] Nonetheless, prince Sulayman Mirza, one of the sons of Shah Tahmasb, commissioned a certain 'Abd 'Ali b. Mahmud Khadim Jabalqi (fl. 16th c.) to translate and comment on al-Shahid al-Awwal's *Alfiyya* in Pari Khan Khanum's honour.[156]

Besides, in his famous Safavid chronicle, *Takmilat al-akhbar*, 'Abdi Beg Shirazi (d. 1581), who completed his work in 1570, dedicated his work to Pari Khan Khanum in a section where he chronicled the developments of the year of 1548. He recorded, 'Two victories were granted from the realm of the unseen (*'ālam-i ghayb*) to the Shah, the supporter of the faith': the first was the 'felicitous birth . . . of the Princess of the World and Its Inhabitants' . . . 'Mistress of the Modest Women of the Time', 'in whose name this work was written with well-wishes for her life and fortune'. She is 'the Noble Majesty,

---

[153] Birjandifar, 'Royal Women and Politics', 53; Siddiqa Jamali and Muhammad Husayn Karami, 'Zan-sitayi dar shi'r-i farisi: barrasi wa-tahlil-i sitayish-i mamduhan-i zan dar qasayid-i madhi,' *Shi'r-pazhuhi* 31 (1396), 121–1,144, at 127, 131, 138–139.

[154] Muslih al-Din Mahdawi, *Isfahan-i dar al-'ilm al-sharq: madaris-i dini-yi Isfahan* (Isfahan: Sazman-i Farhangi Tafrihi Shahrdari-yi Isfahan, 1967), 87; Abu al-Qasim Rafi'i-i Mihrabadi, *Athar-i milli-yi Isfahan* (Tehran, 1974), 29; Maryam Moazzen, *Formation of a Religious Landscape*, 39.

[155] For instance, Golsorkhi claimed that 'contemporary scholars wrote numerous treatises, both in her honor and in her name. She read these treatises and bestowed rewards on their authors.' However, in the footnote she stated, 'Shirazi's *Takmilat* seems to be the only extant treatise dedicated to Pari Khan Khanum.' Golsorkhi, 'Pari Khan Khanum', 147, 147 n.16. Rosemary Stanfield-Johnson echoed Said Amir Arjomand, who quoted from Danishpazhuh, stating that 'the shah and his powerful daughter Pari Khan Khanum patronized a large translation project that would popularize Shi'ite religious writings'. In the article to which Stanfield-Johnson and Arjomand referred, Danishpazhuh refers to only one work sponsored by Sulayman Mirza in honour of Pari Khan Khanum. Rosemary Stanfield-Johnson, 'The Tabarra'iyan and the Early Safavids', *Iranian Studies* 37.1 (2004), 47–71, esp. 69; Said Amir Arjomand, 'Religion and Statecraft in Pre-Modem Iran', *Iranian Studies* 27.1–4 (1994), 7.

[156] Muhamad Rida Nasiri, *Athar-i afarinan*, 6 vols (Tehran: Anjuman-i Athar wa-Mafakhir-i Farhangi, 1384/2006), 2:180; M. T. Danishpazhuh, 'Yak parda az zandagani-yi Shah Tahmasb-i Safawi', *Majalla-yi danishkada-yi adabiyyat va-'ulum-i insani-yi Mashhad* 7.4 (1972), 915–997, esp. 980. Dirayati, *Fihristwara*, 2:124, 11:449. In the manuscript at the Quds-i Radawi Library, which Danishpazhuh cited in his article. However, there is no preface or dedication to Pari Khan Khanum. See 'Abd 'Ali b. Mahmud Khadim Jabalqi, *Sharh-i Alfiyya*, Mashhad, Quds-i Radawi Library, MS 2484.

the Honor of the World, and Fatima of the Age, Pari Khan Khanum – may God cause the shadow of the cradle of her rule over the head of people to be everlasting'. The second development was the retreat of the Ottoman army from Tabriz to Anatolia 'on the occasion of the arrival of this auspicious and felicitous newborn'.[157]

'Abdi Beg's dedication must have written at a time when Pari Khan Khanum featured as an unrivalled female actor at the court of Tahmasb. In presenting his chronicle to Shah Tahmasb, 'Abdi Beg may also have wished to curry the princess's favour. The dedication reveals how elevated the position and authority of the princess was perceived to be by the contemporary elite. 'Abdi Beg attributes a divine aura to the birth of the princess whose coming facilitated triumph against the Ottomans and acknowledges her political authority and rule (*salṭanat*). By comparing her to Fatima, he also highlights her privileged religious status as a descendant of the Prophet.

Zaynab Begum (d. 31 May 1640)

Zaynab Begum was the fourth daughter of Shah Tahmasb from a Georgian concubine mother named Huri Khan Khanum.[158] She was raised under the tutelage of Shah-quli Beg Shamlu.[159] Like Mahin Banu Sultanum and Pari Khan Khanum, Zaynab Begum remained unmarried throughout her life. Although she was betrothed to the governor of Khorasan, 'Ali Quli Khan Shamlu in 1576–1577, the marriage was never consummated because of the unexpected death of the latter a few months later.[160] Zaynab Begum continued to live in the royal harem in Qazvin. As Kioumars Ghereghlou has pointed out, by the end of the reign of Shah Tahmasb, Zaynab Begum was considered a fiancée of the Hidden Imam.[161] As in the cases of Mahin Banu and Pari Khan Khanum, the celibacy of Zaynab Begum was one factor that accounted for her rise to prominence as a masterful female actor whose power surpassed those of other female actors of the royal household. She successfully supported the succession of Prince 'Abbas Mirza (later Shah 'Abbas) in the succession struggles that arose in Qazvin during the closing years of the reign of Muhammad Khudabanda, who died in 1587.[162]

---

[157] 'Abdi Beg Shirazi Navidi, *Takmilat al-akhbar*, ed. 'Abd al-Husayn Nava'i (Tehran: Nashr-i Nay, 1369/1990), 99; Tahrani, *al-Dhari'a*, 4:410.

[158] Hasan b. Murtada Husayni Astarabadi, *Tarikh-i sultani: Az Shaykh Safi ta Shah Safi*, ed. Ihsan Ishraqi (Tehran: Intisharat-i 'Ilmi 1987), 56. The most substantial study of Zaynab Begum to date is Kioumars Ghereghlou's entry 'Zaynab Begum,' *Encyclopædia Iranica*, online edition, 2016, <http://www.iranicaonline.org/articles/zaynab-begum>, last accessed 10 January 2018. See Fazli Beg Khuzani Isfahani, *A Chronicle of the Reign of Shah 'Abbas*, eds Kioumars Ghereghlou and Charles Melville (Cambridge: Gibb Memorial Trust, 2015).

[159] Astarabadi, *Tarikh-i sultani*, 56; Ghereghlou, 'Zaynab Begum'.

[160] Szuppe, 'La participation des femmes I', 219; Ghereghlou, 'Zaynab Begum'.

[161] Ghereghlou, 'Zaynab Begum'.

[162] Ghereghlou, 'Zaynab Begum'.

After the accession of Shah 'Abbas, Zaynab Begum served as confidant and counsellor to the Shah, who is said to have valued his aunt's advice above anyone else's. She oversaw the upbringing of Shah 'Abbas's sons in the royal harem. She exercised so much influence in court politics that local governors and military chiefs often asked her to intervene on their behalf with the shah.[163] Zaynab Begum administrated the affairs of the crown sector of the Safavid bureaucracy, and in 1592–1593, she was made the *khāṣṣa* governor of Kashan, holding this position until 1613–1614, when she was disgraced, stripped of all her posts, and banished to Qazvin.[164] For this post two bureaucrats acted as her deputies in Kashan. She was also assisted by Mirza Lutf Allah Shirazi, who served as the vizier of the princess, in addition to his service as a grand vizier at the court of Shah 'Abbas.

Like her female predecessors, Zaynab Begum accompanied the Shah on military campaigns and played a decisive advisory role. When Ottoman forces advanced on Azerbaijan, they posed a grave threat to the Safavids, but since they outnumbered the Safavid troops, Shah 'Abbas was reluctant to enter into a military engagement. At this critical juncture, Shah 'Abbas sought the advice of his aunt, and Zaynab Begum scolded him for hesitating and urged him to fight. Following her advice, on 6 November 1605 Shah 'Abbas fought the Ottomans in the battle of Sufiyan, which turned out to be one of his greatest military victories. When the Ottomans were faced with disaster, the Ottoman queen mother sent a letter to Zaynab Begum through Gulchahra, an intermediary who was the wife of a Georgian king held prisoner in Istanbul, promising her that if she was successful, her husband would be freed. The intent of the letter was to get Zaynab Begum to convince the Shah to conclude a peace treaty. The choice of a Georgian queen for this mission – ultimately unsuccessful – was a well-calculated move on part of the Ottomans, given that Zaynab Begum's mother was Georgian. However, the Ottoman enterprise failed to strike a peace with the Safavids. All these developments attest to the privileged status of Zaynab Begum in state affairs and her influence on the most powerful ruler of the Safavid dynasty, Shah 'Abbas I.[165]

---

[163] Szuppe, 'La participation des femmes II', 68; Matthee, *Persia in Crisis*, 203, Ghereghlou, 'Zaynab Begum'.

[164] Khuzani Isfahani, *A Chronicle of the Reign of Shah 'Abbas*, 120, 294, 465–466, cited in Ghereghlou, 'Zaynab Begum'.

[165] Ghaffari-fard, *Zan dar tarikh'nigari-yi safawiyya*, 33–34; Anthoine Di Gouvea, *Relation des Grandes Guerres et Victoires Obtenues par Le Roy de Perse Chah 'Abbas contre Les Empereurs de Turquie Mahomet Et Achmet son Fils En Suite du Voyage de Quelques Religieux de l'Ordre des Hermites de S. Augustin envoyez en Perse par le Roy Catholique Dom Philippe Second Roy de Portugal* (Rouen, 1646), 286, cited in David Blow, *Shah Abbas: The Ruthless King Who Became an Iranian Legend* (London: I. B. Tauris, 2014), 81–82, 173. Zaynab Begum also accompanied Shah 'Abbas I on his famous pilgrimage to Mashhad. See Charles Melville, 'Shah Abbas and the Pilgrimage to Mashhad', in *Safavid Persia*, ed. Charles Melville (London: I. B. Tauris, 1996), 191–229.

Zaynab Begum's power and influence in the court continued unabated during the initial reign of Shah Safi (r. 1629–1642). She once again played a key role in the royal succession, convincing the Shah on his deathbed to designate Sam Mirza (later Shah Ṣafi) his heir-apparent in January 1629. When the Shah died, the news of his death was not broken to people at the discretion (*ba-maṣlaḥat*) of Zaynab Begum for the fear that it would cause social unrest or insurrection. Zaynab Begum, in collaboration with allies at court, especially Zaynal Khan Shamlu, gathered signatures from the grandees of the empire, endorsing Safi's candidacy. These efforts bore fruit; Sam Mirza was crowned as Shah Safi, and Zaynab Begum retained her prominent status in the royal household. However, before long she was expelled from the palace when many Safavid princes were killed and most of 'Abbas I's grandsons were blinded by order of the Shah.[166]

The stellar political career of this formidable princess was coupled with her charitable activities that shaped the landscape of the realm. Zaynab Begum funded the construction of many caravanserais, hospitals, roads, and bridges.[167] She is reported to have spent a total of 100,000 *tumans* for her charitable projects.[168] The large revenues of the affluent villages of Yazd that she owned and the poll tax that she was allowed to collect from the Zoroastrian community in Yazd enabled her to finance extensive patronage activities.[169] She also contributed to the production of Shi'i religious knowledge through the patronage of Shi'i scholars. 'Ali al-'Amili (d.1692), an 'Amili scholar who had settled in Isfahan, reports the following example of Zaynab Begum's behaviour in his anthology *al-Durr al-manthur,* which he included his autobiography:

> One strange occurrence which befell me was that when I decided to travel from Isfahan to the holy city of Mecca, I secretly sold some books I had brought with me, without letting it be known. The next day, a eunuch named Khwaja Iltifat came to see me. He was a servant of Zaynab Begum, the daughter of Shah Tahmasb, may God have mercy on them both. He said, 'I want you to tell me whether you have sold any of your books recently.' I replied, 'Tell me why you ask, so that I might then answer you.' He explained, 'The Begum sent for

[166] Muhammad Ma'sum Isfahani, *Khulasat al-siyar*, ed. Iraj Afshar (Tehran: Mu'assasah-yi Pishgam, 1989), 33–37; Ghereghlou, 'Zaynab Begum'; Ghaffari-fard, *Zan dar tarikh'nigari-yi safawiyya,* 38; Susan Babaie et al., *Slaves of the Shah: New Elites of Safavid Iran* (London: I. B. Tauris, 2004), 34–38, 42–43; Kathryn Babayan, *Mystics, Monarchs, and Messiahs: Cultural Landscapes of Early Modern Iran* (Cambridge, MA: Harvard University Press, 2003); Matthee, *Persia in Crisis,* 203; Wali-quli b. Dawud-quli Shamlu, *Qisas al-khaqani,* 2 vols (Tehran: Vizarat-i Farhang-i Irshad-i Islami, 2005), 1:212; Abisaab, *Converting Persia,* 101; Newman, *Safavid Iran,* 74.

[167] Rizwi, 'Gendered Patronage', 129; Ghaffari-fard, *Zan dar tarikh'nigari-yi safawiyya,* 54; Hijazi, *Da'ifa,* 314; Birjandifar, 'Royal Women and Politics', 33.

[168] Ghaffari-fard, *Zan dar tarikh'nigari-yi safawiyya,* 54.

[169] Khuzani Isfahani, *A Chronicle of the Reign of Shah Abbas,* 300, cited in Ghereghlou, 'Zaynab Begum'; Kioumars Ghereghlou, 'On the Margins of Minority Life: Zoroastrians and the State in Safavid Iran', *Bulletin of the School of Oriental and African Studies* 80.1 (2017), 45–71, esp. 17–18.

me just now, and when I went to her she asked, "Is there in this city a man named Shaykh 'Ali, a descendant of the Shaykh Zayn al-Din?" "Yes," I said. She continued, "Last night I saw Shah 'Abbas in a dream, making a statement to this effect: "We used to invite this man's ancestors to come to Iran, but they refused. Now that he has come, he reaches such a state that he must sell his books while you are present?!" When I heard this, I informed him what had happened, namely, that I had sold the books without letting it be known.'[170]

Although one may construe this account as an indication of the financial straits 'Amili jurists faced during the seventeenth century, as Rula Abisaab has suggested,[171] it also shows Zaynab Begum's commitment to the welfare of the learned under her aegis.

Ahadith-i qudsiyya *by Muhammad Yazdi (fl. 17th c.)*

Zaynad Begum also patronised scholarly works. It is reported that the first Imam, 'Ali b. Abi Talib, translated and related forty chapters or passages from the Old Testament in Hebrew; Ibn 'Abbas allegedly transmitted the work, and it circulated widely. Known as *al-Ahadith al-qudsiyya* or *al-Saha'if al-arba'un, Chihil Sahifa,* or *Arba'un sura,* this anthology was initially in circulation in Arabic.[172] It was translated to Persian by a certain Muhammad Yazdi at the request of Zaynab Begum, as the preface of the extant text indicates. Unfortunately, Shi'i bio-biographical works furnish little information about Muhammad Yazdi's life, career, or relationship with the princess. He must have originally hailed from Yazd, the province where Zaynab Begum possessed her revenue-producing properties, and one assumes that her connections with Yazd may have played a role in her patronage of him.

The date when the translation was completed is unknown. The extant manuscript only includes the date of the copy, 1674–1675, three decades after the death of the princess. The library catalogue maintains that this work was sponsored by another woman of the Safavid period, Zaynab Begum Ardistani, wife of the physician Hakim al-Mulk[173] and founder of Madrasa-yi Nimaward,

---

[170] This translation is quoted from Devin J. Stewart's unpublished paper on the autobiography of 'Ali al-'Amili. I would like to thank Prof. Stewart for kindly sharing the draft of this paper with me. For the original account, see 'Ali b. Muhammad Shaykh 'Ali Kabir, *al-Durr al-manthur min al-ma'thur wa-ghayr al-ma'thur,* 2 vols (Qum: Maktabat Ayat Allah al-'Uzma al-Mar'ashi al-Najafi, 1978–1979), 2:242.

[171] Abisaab, *Converting Persia,* 101–102.

[172] Tihrani, *al-Dhari'a,* 1:278–279, 15:8; 'Ali Sadra-yi Khu'i, *Fihrist-i nuskha-a-yi khatti-yi hadith wa-'ulum-i hadith-i shi'a,* 12 vols (Qum: Mu'assasa-i 'Ilmi-yi Farhangi-yi Dar al-Hadith, 1963–1964), 7:47, 69.

[173] His full name is Amir Muhammad Mahdi b. Mir Aqa Beg b. Mir Yahya b. Amir Hasan Sayyid Ruhullah b. Sayyid Radi Tabataba'i Ardistani. For more information about his life and patronage activities, see 'Iffat Khushnudi, 'Mu'arrafi-yi Hakim al-Mulk Ardistani wa-mawqufat-i ishan', *Waqf-i Mirath-i Jawidan* 91–92 (1974–1975), 205–236.

which was built during the reign of Shah Husayn.[174] This is certainly a misattribution. First, in the preface to his translation, Muhammad Yazdi introduces Zaynab Begum as the 'Princess of the World and Its Inhabitants' (*Shahzāda-yi 'ālam wa-'ālamiyān*), along with a host of honorific titles.[175] Zaynab Begum Ardistani did not belong to the royal family,[176] but was the a daughter of a *sayyid* known as *Shaykh al-Islam* Amir Muhammad Ardistani.[177] Second, the endowment deed of Madrasa-yi Nimaward introduces the endower as Zaynab Begum Ardistani but does not use the title *shahzada* or other royal epithets, instead citing titles that extoll her chastity, munificence, and modesty.[178] It is safe to conclude that the translation was commissioned by Zaynab Begum, the aunt of Shah 'Abbas I.

---

[174] Several confusions surround Zaynab Begum Ardistani and her *madrasa*. First, Maryam Moazzen, in her recent publication on Safavid higher education, mentions Madrasa-yi Nimaward but mistakenly introduces its founder as 'Zinat Begum', while the sources refer to her as 'Zaynab Begum'. Moazzen claims that Zinat Begum founded two *madrasas*, Madrasa-yi Kasa Garan and Madrasah-yi Nimavard, but most Persian sources report that Zaynab Begum sponsored Madrasa-yi Nimavard and that her husband Hakim al-Mulk patronised Madrasa-yi Kasa Garan. See Moazzen, *Formation of a Religious Landscape*, 50–51. Hakim al-Mulk travelled to Mughal India with Zaynab Begum. When he cured the daughter of the Mughal Emperor Aurangzeb (r. 1658–1707) after other physicians had failed, the emperor rewarded him by showering him with gold coins. Hakim al-Mulk and Zaynab Begum returned to Isfahan with their fortune and built the two *madrasas*. See Khushnudi, 'Mu'arrafi-yi Hakim al-Mulk Ardistani', 205–236; Khushnudi, 'Mu'arrafi-yi Zaynab Begum wa-madrasa-yi wa-masjid-i mawqufat-i way', *Waqf-i Mirath-i Jawidan* 87 (1373–1374), 105–124; Nuzhat Ahmadi, 'Waqf'nama'ha-yi banuwan dar dawra-yi Safawi', *Waqf-i Mirath-i Jawidan* 19–20 (1957–1958), 98–103; Lutfallah Hunarfar, *Ganjinah-yi athar-i tarikhi-yi Isfahan* (Isfahan: Kitab-furushi-yi Saqafi, 1971), 652–666, 679–681; Heinz Gaube and Eugen Wirth, *Der Bazar von Isfahan* (Wiesbaden: Reichert, 1978), 213, 242; Hasan b. 'Ali b. Mahmud Jabiri Ansari, *Tarikh-i Isfahan wa-Rayy* (Isfahan: Majalla-i Hirad, 1943), 307; Abu al-Qasim Rafi'i Mihrabadi, *Athar-i milli-yi Isfahan* (Tehran: Chap-khanah-yi Ittihad, 1974), 504–505.

[175] Muhammad Yazdi, *Tarjumat al-ahadith-i qudsiyya*, fol. 2a.

[176] Although the title of 'Begum' was used mainly by royal women, it was not exclusive to them. Some female descendants of scholarly and elite families used the same title as well. One of the daughters of Muhammad Taqi al-Majlisi was known as Amina Begum. See Muhsin al-Amin, *A'yan al-shi'a*, 10 vols, ed. Hasan al-Amin (Beirut: Dar al-Ta'aruf li'l-Matbu'at, 1984), 5:95; Muhammad Muhsin Ha'iri, *Tarajim a'lam al-nisa'*, 2 vols (Beirut: Mu'assasat al-'Ilmi li'l-Matbu'at, n.d.), 1:206–207; Afandi, *Riyad al-'ulama'*, 5:407; Dhabih Allah Mahallati, *Rayahin al-shari'a dar tarjuma-yi danishmandan-i banuan-i shi'a*, 6 vols (Tehran: Dar al-Kitab al-Islamiyah, 1989), 3:329; Nasiri, *Athar-afarinan*, 1:74. Another Amina Begum was the daughter of the famous jurist Aqa Muhammad Baqir Wahid Bihbihani. See Muhammad Rida Nasiri, *Athar-afarinan*, 6 vols, eds Husayn Muhaddith-zada et al. (Tehran: Anjuman-i Athar wa-Mafakhir-i Farhangi, 2006), 1:74. Ghaffari-fard mistakenly introduces Amina Begum as the daughter of Muhammad Baqir Majlisi, when she was his sister. Ghaffari-fard, *Zan dar tarikh'nigari-yi safawiyya*, 53.

[177] Muhammad Husayn Rayyahi, 'Mawqufat-i mandagar-i banuwan az isfahan-i dawr-i Safawi', *Waqf-i Mirath-i Jawidan* 71 (1970), 143–168, 155; Nasiri, *Athar-afarinan*, 3:178; Mahallati, *Rayahin al-shari'a*, 4:303.

[178] Khushnudi, 'Mu'arrafi-yi Zaynab Begum', 114.

In the preface, Muhammad Yazdi states that he undertook the translation in response to a request of the princess, 'whose command cannot be disobeyed and whose order cannot be opposed'. The honorifics he invokes regarding her patronage power and munificent are consistent with Zaynab Begum's career. He praises the princess as 'the Refuge of all Mankind', 'Patron of the Elite and the Common', 'Refuge for the Scholars and the Pious', and 'Shelter for the Poor and the Wretched'. He also praises Zaynab Begum's sublime political and religious status. For instance, he hails her as 'the Princess of the World', and 'the Shadow of God on the Two Worlds', a title with strong religio-political connotations used for male rulers in the Islamicate world. He also stressed her noble genealogy and praised her as 'Progeny of the Household of the Master of the Messengers' and 'Descendant of the Family of the Best Successors [of the Prophet]', titles that were in harmony with the Safavid claim to descent from the Prophet and the seventh Imam. He described her as 'the Impeccable one of the World and Faith' and 'Honour of the World'. Yazdi's preface conforms to the pattern of the prefaces discussed above, presenting Zaynab Begum as analogous to famous historical female characters and describing here as 'the Second Mary', 'the One Whose Position is on a Par with that of Bilqis', and 'the Khadija of the Age'. Finally, he concludes his praise of the princess with a blessing following her name: 'may God make Her shadow over the heads of the believers last till the Day of Judgment'.

Yazdi's eulogy is followed by a brief introduction of the work and the author. He states, 'This treatise, full of benefits and eloquent admonitions, including a selection of forty chapters from the words of the *Torah* that God addressed to Moses son of Amram – peace be upon Him – has been translated into Persian by this humblest servant and the sincerest supplicant, Muhammad Yazdi.' He closes his prefaces with the following plea: 'It is hoped that this translation will be honored by approval of her consideration, which is as effective as alchemy.'[179]

Shahzada or Fakhr al-Nisa' Begum (fl. 17th c.), Daughter of Shah 'Abbas I

Shahzada Begum was one of the six daughters of Shah 'Abbas I. The years of her birth and death are not recorded by the Safavid chronicles. However, Shamlu records that she died during the reign of her father, that is, before 1629.[180] Like her five sisters, she was married to a prominent Persian *sayyid* and administrator-cleric, Mirza Muhsin Radawi, caretaker (*mutawallī*) of the shrine of Imam Rida in Mashhad, and from this marriage she had two

[179] See Muhammad Yazdi, *Tarjuma-yi ahadith-i qudsiyya*, fols 1b–2b.

[180] Shamlu, *Qisas al-khaqani*, 1:205.

sons, Mirza Abu al-Qasim and Mirza Muhammad.[181] After the death of Shah 'Abbas I, however, his successor Shah Safi first blinded her sons and then executed them in 1632–1633, just as he did with Shah 'Abbas's other grandchildren. According to some Shi'i sources, Shahzada Begum had another son, Mirza Abu Salih, who later married Maryam Begum, the daughter of Shah Safi I, and assumed the post of *ṣadr al-mamālik* under Shah 'Abbas II (r. 1642–1666). He also built a *madrasa* at the Mashhad shrine, Madrasa-yi Salihiyya or Madrasa-yi Nawwab, in 1675–1676.[182]

The marriage of Shahzada Begum and her sisters to prominent Persian *sayyid*s and scholars represented a significant shift in the practice of royal marriage and reproduction. As Kathryn Babayan notes, until the days of Shah 'Abbas I, royal marriages occurred between the royal women and the Qizilbash elite, but 'with 'Abbas I's reforms, royal marriage with *sayyid* religious notables became the mode'. Unlike the Ottomans, who married their sisters and daughters to royal slaves, Safavid women were married to the elite to forge and cement alliances and consolidate their dynastic authority and power until the late sixteenth century. In other words, "Abbas I's strategy of marriage alliances with *sayyid* notables was one way of linking the fate of the crown (*tāj*) with that of the turban (*'imāma*).""[183] However, three years after Shah 'Abbas I's death, Shah Safi had forty women of the harem and all of 'Abbas's grandsons born to his daughters blinded or killed lest they aspire to overcome the Safavid successor to the throne, in an attempt to establish a clear father-to-son succession system.[184]

al-Tuhfa al-nawwabiyya wa-l-hidaya al-ukhrawiyya *(Noble Gift and Guidance for the Hereafter) by Muhammad Ja'far, known as Abu al-Muẓaffar al-Husayni*

The preface of a Persian work with a dedication to Shahzada Begum breaks the silence about her and projects an image of a generous patron, as well as

[181] Five of Shah 'Abbas 's six daughters were married to members of prominent *sayyid* families and *'ulama'*. Shahzada Begum was married to Mirza Muhsin Radawi (the *mutawalli* of the shrine of Imam Rida); Aqa Begum to Sultan al-'Ulama'; Hawwa Begum to Mirza Rida Shahristani (*ṣadr*) and after his death to Mirza Rafi' al-Din Muhammad (*ṣadr*); Shahr-Banu Begum to Mir 'Abd al-'Azim (Darugha of Isfahan); Malik-i Nisa' Begum to Mirza Jalal Shahristani (the *mutawallī* of the shrine of Imam Rida); Zubaydah Begum to 'Isa Khan Qurchi-bashi (the *wakīl al-salṭanah*). See Shamlu, *Qisas al-khaqani,* 1:205; Nasr Allah Falsafi, *Zindigani-yi Shah 'Abbas-i Awwal,* 3 vols (Tehran: Chap-i Kaywan, 1955), 2:198–203; Babayan, *Mystics, Monarchs, and Messiahs,* 400–401 n. 86.

[182] Tihrani, *Tabaqat a'lam al-shi'a: al-qarn al-hadi 'ashar,* 6 vols, ed. 'Ali Taqi Munzawi (Qum: Mu'assasa-yi Isma'iliyan, 1413 [1992–1993]), 5:283; Tihrani, *al-Dhari'ah,* 8:234–235; al-Amin, *A'yan al-shi'a,* 6:362; Mirza Muhammad Baqir al-Radawi, *Shajara-yi tayyiba dar ansab-i silsila-yi sadat-i 'alawiyya-yi radawiyya* (Tehran: Chapkhana-yi Haydari, 1352 [1973]), 232–235; Newman, *Safavid Iran,* 225 n.37.

[183] Babayan, *Mystics, Monarchs, and Messiahs,* 382; David Blow, *Shah 'Abbas,* 186.

[184] Shamlu, *Qisas al-khaqani,* 1:212; Abisaab, *Converting Persia,* 101; Newman, *Safavid Iran,* 74.

a pious and exalted female figure. Abu al-Muzaffar Muhammad Ja'far al-Husayni translated *Miftah al-falah* ('The Key to Being Saved'), a collection of prayers by Baha' al-Din Muhammad al-'Amili (d. 1031/1621) into Persian, adding three additional chapters. He titled the work *al-Tuhfa al-nawwabiyya wa-l-hidaya al-ukhrawiyya* ('Noble Gift and Guidance for the Hereafter') and dedicated it to Shahzada Begum. The only extant copy of *al-Tuhfa al-nawwabiyya* is located at the library of Sipahsalar *madrasa,* also known as Kitabkhanah-yi 'Ali Shahid Mutahhari.[185] The colophon of this manuscript indicates that it was copied by a calligrapher named Muhammad Husayn al-Isfahani in 1675–1676. The date of composition of this work is not given in this copy, but it apparently must have been completed during the lifetime of Shahzada Begum. If Shamlu's information regarding Shahzada's death is accurate, then it must have been written by 1629, the year of Shah 'Abbas I's death.

In his preface, the author introduces himself as 'Muhammad Ja'far, known as Abu al-Muzaffar al-Husayni'. There is no notice on this figure in the biographical dictionaries or chronicles from the Safavid era. Some modern Shi'i sources introduce the work in question very briefly without providing details about the author. Aqa Buzurg al-Tihrani introduces *al-Tuhfa al-nawwabiyya* in his short bibliographical entry and claims that 'Abu al-Muzaffar al-Husayni authored this work for Nawwab Shazada Begum, a princess of the Safavid dynasty who built Madrasa-yi Shahzada-ha in Isfahan'.[186] Tihran comes up with a new claim about the dedicatee of the work: that Shahzada Begum was the builder of the Madrasa-yi Shahzada-ha in Isfahan. However, this two-storey residential *madrasa,* known as Madrasa-yi Shahzada-ha, was built by Shahr-Banu, daughter of Shah Sultan Husayn (r. 1694–1722).[187] Given that when the *al-Tuhfa al-nawwabiyya* was copied in 1675–1676, Shahr-Banu was not even born, Princess Shahr-Banu could not have sponsored this work. Tihrani must have been confused by the name Shahzada Begum. A modern source corrects Tihrani's mistake without mentioning his name. In *Athar-i afarinan,* Muhammad Rida Nasiri introduces *al-Tuhfa al-nawwabiyya,* stating that it was dedicated to 'Shahzadah Begum, one of the daughters of Shah 'Abbas I and a woman philanthropist with great love for and interest in knowledge'.[188]

---

[185] Muhammad Ja'far, known as Abu al-Muzaffar al-Husayni, *al-Tuhfa al-nawwabiyya wa'l-hidaya al-ukhrawiyya,* Tehran, Kitab-khanah-yi 'Ali Shahid Mutahhari, MS 2130 (1675–1676); Dirayati, *Fihristwara,* 2:1011.

[186] Tihrani, *al-Dhari'a,* 3:478–479; Tihrani, *Musannafat-i shi'a: tarjumah wa-talkhis,* 4 vols (Mashhad: Astan-i Quds-i Radawi, Bunyad-i Paszhuhash-i Islami, 2003), 1:571; 2:55; Tihrani, *Tabaqat a'lam al-shi'ah,* 5:112. Also see Ali Sadra-yi Khu'i, *Fihristagan-i nuskha-ha-yi khatti-yi hadith wa-'ulum-i hadith-i shi'a,* 12 vols (Qum: Mu'assasa-i 'Ilmi-yi Farhang-i Dar al-Hadith, 2003), 8:446.

[187] Mihrabadi, *Athar-i milli-yi Isfahan,* 39; Jabiri Ansari, *Tarikh-i Isfahan wa-Rayy,* 308; Stephen P. Blake, *Half the World: The Social Architecture of Safavid Isfahan, 1590–1722* (Costa Mesa: Mazda, 1999), 167; Moazzen, *Formation of a Religious Landscape,* 66.

[188] Nasiri, *Athar-i afarinan,* 3:290.

The first six chapters of *al-Tuhfa al-nawwabiyya* translate *Miftah al-falah*, but Muhammad Ja'far does not refer to the latter's author, Baha' al-Din 'Amili, who was a prominent polymath and *shaykh al-islam* of the Safavid capital, Isfahan.[189] As Devin Stewart has suggested, *Miftah al-falah* was one of Baha' al-Din's most popular works intended for a wide audience.[190] Written on about 27 June 1606 in Ganjeh, at the royal camp in Azerbaijan, *Miftah al-falah* has served as a manual of prayers structuring one's day according to certain prayers and worship. In his preface, Baha' al-Din states that he wrote this work at the request of believing brethren, explaining what every believer should know for their prayers during the day and night and presenting the required, recommended, and commended deeds and acts of devotion.[191] The story has it that Mu'izz al-Din, the judge of Isfahan, was instructed in a dream by one of the Imams to copy a book called *Miftah al-falah* and to follow the instructions contained therein. The next morning, he asked the scholars of Isfahan about the book, but they averred that they had never heard of a work by that title. When Baha al-Din returned from Azerbaijan, he informed Mu'izz al-Din that he had just completed a book of prayers and had given it the title *Miftah al-falah* but had not revealed it to anyone. Baha' al-Din wept upon hearing Mu'izz al-Din's dream, which he understood to be a great omen, and Mu'izz al-Din was the first to copy the book.[192] This story, giving the *Miftah al-falah* a holy aura, indicates that it was well received and that copies began to proliferate soon after its composition. Persian translations of *Miftah al-falah* along with its Persian commentaries increased the popularity of *Miftah* among the Persian speakers.[193] *Al-Tuhfa al-nawwabiyya*, completed during the reign of Shah 'Abbas I, must have been one of the earliest translations of *Miftah al-falah*, if Shamlu's record of Shahzada Begum's death date is accurate. Muhammad Ja'far supplemented Baha' al-Din's manual by adding three more chapters to the work that focused on prayers for various

[189] Devin J. Stewart, 'A Biographical Notice on Baha' al-Din al-'Amili (d. 1030/1621)', *Journal of the American Oriental Society* (1991), 563–571.

[190] Stewart reports that this work was written in Persian, but Baha' al-Dīn originally wrote it in Arabic, and then a number of scholars translated it into Persian. Devin J. Stewart, 'Baha' al-Din Muhammad al-'Amili (1547–1621)', pp. 27–48 in *Dictionary of Literary Biography: Arabic Literary Culture, 1350–1850*, eds Joseph E. Lowry and Devin J. Stewart (Wiesbaden: Harrassowitz, 2009), 41. For the list of the translations of and commentaries on *Miftah al-falah*, see Muhsin Naji Nasrabadi, *Kitab-shinasi-yi Shaykh Bahai* (Mashhad: Astan-i Quds-i Radawi, Bunyad-i Pazhuhash-ha-yi Islami, 2009), 527–558; Tihrani, *al-Dhari'a*, 4:136–137.

[191] Baha' al-Din Muhammad al-'Amili, *Miftah al-falah fi 'amal al-yawm wa'l-layla min al-wajibat wa'l-mustahabbat* (Beirut: Mu'assasat al-A'lamī, 1980), 2.

[192] Abbas Qummi, *Safinat al-Bihar wa-madinat al-hikam wa'l-athar ma'a tatbiq al-nusus al-warida fiha 'ala bihar al-anwar*, 8 vols (Qum: Uswa, n.d.), 7:326; Stewart, 'Baha' al-Din Muhammad al-'Amili (1547–1621)', 41.

[193] Among the most popular translations of *Miftah al-falah* was that of Aqa Jamal al-Din Muhammad b. Husayn Khwansari (d.1713–1714), which he completed for Shah Sulayman. See Nasrabadi, *Kitab-shinasi-yi Shaykh Baha'i*, 547. The most notable commentary on it was by Sultan al-'Ulama'. Nasrabadi, *Kitab-shinasi-yi Shaykh Baha'i*, 555.

occasions and holy days throughout the year as well as prayers and rules of etiquette for travelling, regarding daily prayers. With these additions, Muhammad Ja'far provided devout Shi'is with a comprehensive schedule allowing them to structure their entire day and year by observing a set of prayers and rules of etiquette.

In the preface to his work, Muhammad Ja'far stated that he received generous patronage from the princess, just as his forefathers had enjoyed ample graces and constant benevolence of the sublime palace and lofty threshold of the Safavid dynasty. He adds that he 'has benefitted from the education of the high sun (i.e., Shahzada Begum); the guide to the paths of pious deeds, obedience, and worship; the teacher of the etiquette of prayer, and the preacher of devotion'. As a motivation behind his undertaking, Muhammad Ja'far states that his translation was intended to make the content of the work accessible to common people so that they could reap benefit from it for the welfare of their afterlife. In other words, he considers his composition as a public service, apart from a service to the princess in return for her generosity. The honorific titles he applies to the princess paint a powerful female royal figure and a generous patron: 'the Queen of the World', 'Bearer of Divine Benefit for all Mankind', 'Illuminating Candle of 'Ali's Harem', 'the *Ka'ba* for the Supplications of Powerful Kings and Rulers', 'the Princess Whose Threshold of Majesty is the Throne of Governance and Kingdom of Prosperous Rulers and Kings', 'the Large Tree of the Garden of the Shadow of God', 'Descendant of the Safavids', 'Honour of all Creation', and so on. In praise of her generosity, Muhammad Ja'far states, 'The clouds of her generosity and munificence are continuously pouring, and the sky of her magnanimity and affection is always raining' and, 'The surface of the earth is eclipsed by the vastness of a portion of her table of feasting and grace.' Furthermore, he extolls her religious virtues and piety by stating that 'she observes all the acts of obedience and worship, performs the required and recommended prayers thoroughly, and follows through what is commanded and forbidden diligently'. Finally, he calls Shahzada Begum the 'Possessor of Fatima's Character and Mary's Nature' as well as 'Rabi'a of the Safavid dynasty'. These three historical figures were renowned for their modesty, asceticism, and piety. Among them, although the names of Fatima and Mary are commonly used as honorific titles in the prefaces in question and other Shi'i sources to extoll the religious virtues of the Safavid royal women, the name of Rabi'a was used only for Shahzada Begum and for her sister Khan Aqa Begum, as will be discussed below.

Muhammad Ja'far's preface portrays a royal female figure with considerable political influence and a generous patron with utmost piety and devotion who sponsored scholars of the time and promoted religious knowledge in Persian. As a member of the royal family and wife of the *mutawallī* of Mashhad, Shahzada Begum must have possessed considerable wealth that enabled her to sponsor the scholars at the orbit of her patronage or to finance some other charitable activities. Moreover, from the metaphorical expression of 'the *Ka'ba* for the Supplications of Powerful Kings and Rulers' one could surmise that the princess could have played some intermediary role between the central royal court and the rulers and administrators in her proximity. Such a role would be hardly surprising considering that political intermediary or intercession in favour of some rulers and prominent figures was a common practice that featured in the political careers of many Safavid royal women.

Khan Aqa Begum, Daughter of Shah 'Abbas I

Khan Aqa Begum was also one of the six daughters of Shah 'Abbas I. Like her sisters, Aqa Begum was also married to a prominent Persian scholar, Mir 'Ala' al-Din Husayn, known as Khalifa Sultan and Sultan al-'Ulama' (d. 1654). This marriage, which dates to 27 November 1608, produced four children, who shared the fate of other grandchildren of Shah 'Abbas I, being blinded by order of Shah Safi.[194] Her marriage to Khalifa Sultan occurred after the shift in matrimonial policy mentioned above, aimed to buttress the legitimacy of the Shah. Serving as a vizier from 1624 to 1632 under the reigns of Shah 'Abbas and Shah Safi, Khalifa Sultan grew up as a *sayyid* in Isfahan, but his family originated in Mazandaran. Moreover, through his mother Khalifa Sultan was also related to Shah 'Abbas's own Mar'ashi *sayyid* mother, Khayr al-Nisa', and his father served as a *ṣadr* during the reign of Shah Tahmasb.[195] As a distinguished student of Baha' al-Din al-'Amili, Khalifa Sultan was accomplished in several fields, including philosophy, theology, medicine, and mathematics. He played a major part in shaping the religious policies of his time. As Rula J. Abisaab has pointed out, 'Khalifa Sultan was keen on making public knowledge his onslaught on all signs of religious "deviance" and "immorality", ranging from brothels to certain forms of entertainment'. According to Abisaab, 'Khalifa Sultan's social standing and political influence marked the demise of the once prominent émigré jurists'; he emerged as a spokesman for the propertied and pedigreed Persian clerical elite.[196]

Although the contemporary Safavid chronicles provided detailed biographical notices on Khalifa Sultan, they are almost entirely silent about the life and career of his wife, Aqa Begum. Nevertheless, texts she commissioned provide some hints regarding the princess's life, showing that she was active in making religious knowledge available to the public in Persian form through her generous patronage of scholars. According to the Shi'i

---

[194] Nasr Allah Falsafi, *Zindigani-yi Shah 'Abbas-i Awwal,* 2:200–201; Muhsin al-Amin, *A'yan al-shi'a,* 6:164–167, 6:303, 9:252; Hijazi, *Da'ifah,*129; Newman, *Safavid Iran,* 54; Babayan, *Mystics, Monarchs, and Messiahs,* 401 n. 86.

[195] Munshi, *The History of Shah Abbas,* 2:1,234–235; al-Amin, *A'yan al-shi'a,* 6:164–167; Newman, *Safavid Iran,* 54; Abisaab, *Converting Persia,* 100–101.

[196] Abisaab, *Converting Persia,* 101.

biographical dictionaries and catalogues, Aqa Begum commissioned the translation of two religious works: *al-Iqbal bi'l-a'mal al-hasana fima yu'mal fi'l-sana,* by Radi al-Din b. Tawus (1193–1266) on prayers for various occasions, and *Anis al-'abidin* (or *zahidin)* (Companion for Worshippers [or Ascetics]), on supplications and prayers by Muhammad b. Muhammad al-Tabib, an early Safavid scholar. The translation of these prayer manuals enabled ordinary believers to observe their devotional rituals and prayers in a language they could comprehend and to design their entire year by committing themselves to a certain set of prayers and supplications slated for different occasions. These manuals were intended to deepen the spiritual discipline and devotional commitment of common people and designed for frequent consultation throughout a year. Their prefaces bearing dedications to the princess served as a prominent venue in which common people encountered royal imagery.

Tarjuma-yi al-Iqbal bi'l-a'mal al-hasana fima yu'mal fi'l-sana *of Radi al-Din 'Ali b. Musa Ibn Tawus, anonymous*[197]

In Karbala on 22 July 1252, Radi al-Din b. Tawus completed *al-Iqbal bi'l-a'mal,* one of the most comprehensive Shi'i prayer collections.[198] Ibn Tawus spent most of his life in Hilla and Baghdad in Iraq. He was in Bagdad when the city was captured by the Mongols in 1258, after which he was appointed marshall (*naqīb*) of the 'Alids by Hülegü. Ibn Tawus expressed his gratitude to the Mongol ruler in *al-Iqbal,* giving an eschatological twist to the Mongol invasion in his *al-Iqbal* by asserting that a report related that Imam Ja'far al-Sadiq foretold the destruction of the 'Abbasid empire and presaged that the Muslim community would be ruled by a just and honest person from the *ahl al-bayt,* who would in turn be succeeded by Imam Mahdi.[199]

In his works Ibn Tawus stressed the performance of supererogatory prayers and other acts of devotion, visiting the shrines of the Imams, and observing the Shi'i holy days, and *al-Iqbal* was no exception. The work has three volumes. The first volume includes thirty-seven chapters on the holy month of Ramadan and its virtues, instructions for observing each day of the month, as well as prayers and instructions for *'Īd al-Fiṭr* (the Feast of Breaking the

---

[197] *Tarjuma-yi al-Iqbal bi'l-a'mal al-hasana fima yu'mal fi'l-sana* by anonymous translators, Qum, Mar'ashi Library, MS. 1344 (December 1678); Dirayati, *Fihristwarah,* 2:76–77. I was unable to examine the preface of this translation directly.

[198] Radi al-Din 'Ali b. Musa Ibn Tawus, *al-Iqbal bi'l-a'mal al-hasana fima yu'mal fi'l-sana,* ed. Jawad Isfahani, 3 vols (Qum: Maktab al-I'lam al-Islami, 1416); Tihrani, *al-Dhari'a,* 2:263–264; Etan Kohlberg, *A Medieval Muslim Scholar at Work: Ibn Tawus and His Library* (Leiden/New York: Brill, 1992), 37–39.

[199] On Ibn Tawus, see Kohlberg, *A Medieval Muslim Scholar at Work,* 3–23.

Fast). The second volume, with nine chapters, addresses the virtues of the months of Shawwal, Dhu al-Qa'da, Dhu al-Hijja (including instructions and supplications specific to the pilgrimage), *'Īd al-Aḍḥā* (the Feast of Sacrifice), *'Īd al-Ghadīr* (the exclusively Shi'i holy day commemorating the occasion when the Prophet Muhammad appointed 'Ali his successor) along with its virtues and supplications for the occasion, the commemoration of the *Mubāhala* (curse ordeal), celebrated by Shi'is on the twenty-fourth of Dhu al-Hijja,[200] as well as supplications and prayers for the rest of the same month. The third volume includes nine chapters, in which are addressed the virtues of and prayers for the remaining months of the year. In short, *al-Iqbal* forms a comprehensive Shi'i prayer manual for the entire year.[201]

The preface of the Persian translation of *al-Iqbal* reports that it was undertaken by 'a group of prominent scholars and distinguished learned men with high credibility and utmost reliability' at the request of Khan Aqa Begum. Presumably on account of the work's size, the translation was entrusted to a group of translators - unnamed - rather than to an individual. The preface introduces *al-Iqbal* as 'the most comprehensive work on supplications and prayers' written by 'a great master and foremost of the Muslim nation', Sayyid Radi al-Din b. Tawus, praising him as 'the most honorable, learned, erudite, credible, ascetic, pious, pure, and virtuous man'. The preface explains, 'the explanations of the supplications and exposition of the prayers were written in Arabic, and the majority of people were unable to comprehend and live through its teachings, and hence deprived of its divine blessings and rewards'. Therefore, Princess Khan Aqa Begum entrusted the task of translating it into Persian to a group of scholars of her time. This statement reveals that translation was considered a service to the community, rendering devotional writings accessible to the common people for their spiritual welfare. As sponsor of the translation, Khan Aqa Begum was praised as 'the Refuge of all Mankind', 'the Possessor of Bilqis's Grandeur', 'Owner of the Character of Rabi'a and Zahra' (i.e., Fatima)', 'Exemplar of all the World and Its Inhabitants', and 'Princess of the World and Its Dwellers'. These honorific titles also project a pious female image by comparing the princess to Fatima and Rabi'a, suggesting that she shares their spiritual character holy status, thus according her a great deal of religious authority. Like her sister Shahzada Begum, Princess Khan Aqa Begum was also compared to the female mystic saint, Rabi'a al-'Adawiyya. Perhaps the nature of the translated work or the personality of the patron accounted for this honorific title. Ibn Tawus was recognised as having mystical proclivities and as having been the recipient

---

[200] Moojan Momen, *An Introduction to Shi'i Islam: The History and Doctrines of Twelver Shi'ism* (New Haven: Yale University Press, 1985), 13–14.
[201] Jawad Isfahani, 'Introduction', in Ibn Tawus, *al-Iqbal bi'l-a'mal*, 7–22.

of miracles (*karamat*).[202] In accordance with this description, the preface of the Iqbal's translation introduced him as the most ascetic (*azhad)* of Shi'i scholars. Muhammad Baqir al-Majlisi, discussing a prayer of al-Husayn for the day of *'Arafa* (the ninth of Dhu al-Hijja), asserts that it includes Sufi expressions that are uncharacteristic of the Imam's prayers and that do not appear in Ibn Tawus's other books.[203] The exaltation of the princess as the possessor of Rabi'a's virtues is fitting in a work by a scholar with mystical tendencies who stresses devotional commitment, spiritual discipline, and persistent supplication. The princess was also portrayed as a pious patron who maintained her community's spiritual welfare by introducing them an exemplary spiritual model and by blazing a trail in pious deeds in accordance with the Prophetic tradition. 'The one who innovates a good innovation [in Islam] has its reward and a reward similar to those who follow him until the Day of Reckoning.'

The preface introduces the princess as the daughter of the 'heaven-dwelling' Shah 'Abbas, whose name is followed by the blessing, 'may His grave be fragrant, and may Paradise be His abode', indicating that the translation was completed after the death of Shah 'Abbas in 1629. It reminds the audience that the great benefits and blessings of this book have been delivered to them by 'the Beloved of the World and all Mankind', stating, 'It is therefore incumbent upon everyone who derives benefit from this work to give thanks to the princess, to commemorate this great dame by reciting *Surat al-Fatiha,* and to wish from God goodness and felicity for her in this world and in the hereafter.'

Tarjuma-yi Anis al-'abidin *or* Anis al-zahidin

Anis al-'abidin or *Anis al-zahidin,* an Arabic work on supplications, was written by Muhammad b. Muhammad al-Tabib, a scholar of the early Safavid period.[204] Little information about him exists, but two books are attributed to him in Persian manuscript catalogues, including *Anis al-'abidin*. The translation of this work into Persian increased its popularity and circulation.[205] *Anis al-'abidin* consists of an introduction in three parts on rules regarding supplication and the supplicant and ten chapters on supplications and prayers for different occasions.[206] Al-Tabib cites Ibn Tawus's book on supplications and prayers titled *Kitab al-Sa'adat*[207] and quotes extensively from the famous book of Shi'i supplications, *al-Sahifa al-sajjadiyya.*[208]

---

[202] Kohlberg, *A Medieval Muslim Scholar at Work,* 14.
[203] Kohlberg, *A Medieval Muslim Scholar at Work,* 38.
[204] Hasan al-Sadr, *Takmilat amal al-amil,* 6 vols, ed. Husayn-'Ali Mahfuz (Beirut: Dar al-Muwarrikh al-Arabi, 2008), 5:95; Tihrani, *al-Dhari'a,* 2:460; Amin, *al-Shi'a fi masarihim al-tarikhi* (Qum: Mu'assasa-yi Da'irat-i Ma'arif al-Fiqh al-Islami, 2005–2006), 551.
[205] Dirayati cites two titles under the name of Muhammad b. Muhammad al-Tabib, *Anis al-'abidin* and *Sharh al-qanuncha.* Dirayati, *Fihristwara,* 11:701; 6:910; 2:277.
[206] See Tihrani, *al-Dhari'a,* 2:460–461.
[207] Kohlberg, *A Medieval Muslim Scholar at Work,* 54.
[208] Tihrani, *al-Dhari'a,* 2:460.

Like *al-Iqbal, Anis al-'abidin* is voluminous work on supplications (431 folios).[209] Its size probably convinced Aqa Begum to commission a collective translation for the sake of speedy completion. The completed work reveals the proximity between the princess and the prominent scholars of the time, who received the benefaction of the princess. In return, they crafted a powerful, munificent, and pious image of her evident in the prefaces of these popular works, while contemporary chronicles remained silent about this important female royal figure.

Conclusion

Royal princesses were at the forefront of the production of religious knowledge in Safavid Iran. They played a substantial role in shifting the religious discourse and the formation of a new confessional identity in early modern Safavid Iran through their promotion of Shi'ism and the propagation of the faith. They enjoyed immense power and influence in the court politics and also were recognised as significant religious authorities. Among the underlying factors accounting for their religious authority were their sacred genealogy, religious education, patronage of religious knowledge, and support for scholars of the religious sciences.

This study has examined thirteen works bearing dedications to five different Safavid princesses. With one exception, these texts were written in Persian, an obvious indication of an interest in and rigorous support for the proliferation of knowledge in the vernacular. Eight works were sponsored by Mahin Banu Sultanum, a formidable princess of the early Safavid period, and most of these focused on Shi'i doctrine. Her patronage of the religious texts in Persian demonstrates a concerted effort to make religious knowledge more accessible to a wider audience and popularise the Shi'i theological doctrine in early Safavid society. All of the scholars sponsored by Mahin Banu were Persians, whose contribution to the formation of the Shi'i community and advancement of scholarship in the early Safavid period has been poorly studied partly because of the skewed focus of the modern scholarship on the Arab immigrant scholars in Safavid Iran. One of the contributions of this study is to throw some light on the lives and careers of these scholars, drawing on Shi'i biographical works.

Mahin Banu's model was followed by her nieces, Pari Khan Khanum and Zaynab Begum, daughters of Shah Tahmasb, who were also active participants in court politics and sponsors of the Shi'i scholars. These three masterful women represent a triplet of celibate lives and influential political careers.

---

[209] I have consulted one of the extant manuscript copies in Arabic in the Mar'ashi library in Najaf, which houses several copies of the work. Muhammad b. Muhammad al-Tabib, *Anis al-'abidin*, Qum, Kitabkhana-i Ayat Allah Mar'ashi, MS no. 1322 (1660–1661). For the other copies, see Dirayati, *Fihristwara*, 2:277–278.

Two daughters of Shah 'Abbas I, Shahzada Begum and Khan Aqa Begum, were active in the seventeenth century and sponsored several Persian collections of prayers and supplications. Unlike their three predecessors, these two princesses were married off to two prominent Persian administrative clerics and probably enjoyed a lesser degree of political power in comparison to the celibate princesses of the early Safavid period. Unfortunately, Safavid sources are too reticent about them to enable historians to reconstruct the contours of their lives and careers. The prefaces of the works they sponsored, which extol them for their diligence in observing their prayers and for their commitment to spiritual purification of their community, are probably the only places in which the specifics of their personalities come through. The preface authors invoked the memory of the famous mystic Rabi'a al-'Adawiyya, comparing the spiritual ranks of the princesses to hers. The invocation of Rabi'a was exclusive to the eulogies of Shahzada Begum and Khan Aqa Begum among the princesses discussed here. The personal piety of the princesses and the content of the commissioned works, which focused on spiritual purification, persistence in supplication, and the observance of prayers, must have prompted the authors to call them 'the Rabi'a of the Age'.

The elements of image-making deployed by the preface authors for the projection of the princesses' religious and political authority were manifold and multi-faceted. The preface authors extolled their female patrons with a panoply of honorifics with both religious and political colourings, such as 'Princess of the World and Mankind', 'the Shadow of God', 'the Manifestation of Divine Grace', 'Promulgator (*murawwij*) of the Rulings of the Sacred Law', 'Patron (*murabbī*) of Scholars and the Learned', 'Fortifier (*muqawwī*) of the Righteous and the Pious', 'Patron of the Ja'fari Sect and the Religion of Twelver Shi'ism'.[210] These titles convey an image of a female figure who enjoyed a considerable degree of political and religious authority, as well as a commitment to promoting the faith, promulgating state-sponsored knowledge, and protecting the scholars.

In addition, the Safavid princesses were compared to several revered female historical characters, such as Mary (the mother of Jesus), Hagar (the wife of Abraham and mother of Ishmael), Bilqis (the Queen of Sheba), Khadija (the first wife of the Prophet Muhammad), Fatima (the daughter of the Prophet, wife of Ali, and mother of the Imams), and the famous mystic Rabi'a al-'Adawiyya. The Safavid princesses were glorified as embodiments of these religious characters in their own historical period, called 'the Mary of the Time' or 'the Fatima of the Age'. Equally significant is that the Qur'anic verse in which God addressed Mary, 'O Mary, indeed God has chosen you and purified you and chosen you above the women of the worlds' (Q 3:42), was frequently invoked by the preface authors in order to attribute

[210] See Appendix II for the honorific titles used for the Safavid princesses.

a similar, God-chosen status of the Safavid princesses. The Safavid princesses were thus portrayed as a religio-historic continuation of a series of the divinely elected women who were held to be superior to all other women. The princesses were conferred an exalted status above all other contemporary women because they were 'the essence and fruits of the family of the Prophet and the Infallible Imams'.[211] Comparison with the Queen of Sheba served to reinforce the political legitimacy of the princesses, since she set the precedent for female sovereignty and grandeur in Islamic discourse. The Qur'an mentions Bilqis as a pagan but an able ruler and does not take issue with her sovereignty. As Charis Waddy points out, 'The fault found with her is not that she rules, but that her faith is false.' She continues, 'No objection is raised to her position and authority as a woman.' Therefore, 'Women who became rulers in the Muslim world were always compared with her.'[212]

The Safavids claimed descent from the seventh Imam, Musa al-Kazim, and the Safavid monarchs were viewed as the deputies of the Hidden Imam. Moreover, their rule was considered as a prelude to that of the Hidden Imam, whose Parousia was believed to be imminent. Three of the Safavid princesses discussed here, Mahin Banu (1519–1562), known as Shahzada Sultanum – daughter of Shah Isma'il I (r. 1501–1524) and full sister of Shah Tahmasb (r. 1524–1576) – Pari Khan Khanum (d. 985/1578) – daughter of Shah Tahmasb – and Zaynab Begum (d. 1050/1640) – daughter of Shah Tahmasb – were designated as the fiancées of the Hidden Imam in Safavid chronicles and foreign travellers' accounts.[213] These three princesses had significant characteristics in common. They all remained unmarried throughout their life. Part of the reason behind their political influence and prominence had to do with their voluntary celibacy and association with the Hidden Imam. Spouseless, they were able to remain at the centre of power instead of being married off to contemporary notables, which would

---

[211] The claim that the Safavid princesses were descendants of the Prophet's Family and the Infallible Imams appeared in most of the prefaces examined in the present study.

[212] Charis Waddy, *Women in Muslim History* (London: Longman, 1980), 33. Bilqis made a distinctive appearance in Shi'i tradition. Amina Inloes has discussed the Shi'i recension of the story of Bilqis, which is devised to demonstrate the supremacy of 'Ali. The sword of 'Ali, Dhu al-Fiqar, was sent down from the heaven at the time of Adam and passed down from prophet to prophet until it came into the possession of Bilqis, who presented it to Solomon. See Amina Inloes, 'The Queen of Sheba in Shi'a Hadith', *Journal of Shi'a Islamic Studies* 5.4 (2012), 423–440.

[213] For Mahin Banu's designation as the Mahdi's fiancée, see Qummi, *Khulasat al-tawarikh*, 1:430; Membré, *Mission to the Lord Sophy of Persia*, 25–26. Qummi calls Mahin Banu *nadhr-i hadrat-i imam al-himam sahib al-'asr wa-l-zaman...* Fadli Beg Quzani Isfahani, *Afdal al-tawarikh* [volume II] (London: British Library, MS Or. 4678, 17th century), 274b quoted from Ghereghlou, 'Zaynab Begum', writes, *Zaynab Begum ki nadhr-i sahib-i zaman ast* 'Zaynab Begum, who is betrothed to the Owner of the Age'. Quzani says of Pari Khan Khanum, *dar habala-yi sahib al-amr bud* – 'she was tied to by marriage the Hidden Imam'. I would like to express my gratitude to Kioumars Ghereghlou for making the unpublished volume of Quzani's chronicle available to me.

have required them to relinquish some of their power and leverage under the dominance of their husbands. Informed by the messianic beliefs and expectations of the time, the designation of the princesses as the fiancées of the Hidden Imam must have been made to boost their religious and political authority and ward off any concerted attempt to undermine or question their positions as bachelor female actors in early Safavid society.

The religious education that Safavid princesses received in various Islamic sciences such as Arabic, Islamic law, and the Qur'an rendered them conversant with religious scholarship. Through this education, they had direct access to eminent scholars of the time. Their connection with the clerical establishment, however, was not limited to a mentor–pupil relationship. Some of the Safavid princesses, like the daughters of Shah 'Abbas addressed here, were also instrumental in forming marriage bonds between the royal family and notable families of Persian scholars, reinforcing the ties between the Safavid dynasty and the local Persian elites and thereby buttressing the legitimacy of the ruling family.

Patronage relationships between the Safavid princesses and religious scholars were efficient means of projecting the princesses' religious authority. The prefaces of the works dedicated to them served as significant venues in which the image of the princesses was crafted and circulated. They princesses were accorded a high degree of religious authority by the preface authors through eulogies that abound with honorific titles, portraying them as promulgators of the faith, refuges for the scholars, and paragons of piety, devotion, and religious commitment. The public personas of the princesses were modelled after a host of historic female figures highly revered in Islamic tradition, such as Mary, Bilqis, Fatima, Khadija, and Rabi'a al-'Adawiyya. As contemporary incarnations of their historical precursors, the Safavid princesses were introduced and extolled by their clients as God's privileged and chosen servants who were endowed with spiritual excellence and superiority.

Prefaces to dedicated works are useful sites for analysis of the Safavid dynasty's patronage networks and investigation of the ways in which imperial discourse and royal images were crafted. Future research on the many unexamined Safavid prefaces promises to decipher Safavid religious idiom and reconstruct the relationship between royal patrons and the scholars under their aegis.

CHAPTER

10

THE LIVES OF TWO *MUJTAHIDĀT*: FEMALE RELIGIOUS AUTHORITY IN TWENTIETH-CENTURY IRAN

Mirjam Künkler and Roja Fazaeli

A nascent stream of scholarship has brought to light the quite significant involvement of women in the transmission of hadith, especially from the tenth to the sixteenth centuries CE. Jonathan Berkey, Renate Jacobi, Mohammad Akram Nadwi, Richard Bulliet and Asma Sayeed have documented why within Islamic scholarship the field of hadith transmission was particularly amenable to women, especially when compared to theology and law.[1] By contrast, the role of women in the generation rather than transmission of Islamic knowledge is yet little documented. Although numerous references to individual examples of female theologians, and at times even Islamic jurists, exist, their lives and works have hardly been the subject of scholarly inquiry. In the case of modern Iran, we know of more than 100 women, mostly daughters and wives of influential scholars, who made a name for themselves in fields of Islamic learning, among them dozens who attained a level of learning comparable to that of *mujtahids*.

We thank Brill Publishers for the permission to re-print this chapter in slightly edited form from Masooda Bano and Hilary Kalmbach (eds), *Women, Leadership and Mosques: Changes in Contemporary Islamic Authority* (Brill, 2012), 127–160. Following the EUP house style, diacritics have been omitted in personal names, except for 'ayn and hamza.

[1] See Jonathan Berkey, 'Women and Islamic Education in the Mamluk Period', in *Women in Middle Eastern History*, eds Nikkie Keddie and Beth Baron (New Haven: Yale University Press, 1 991), 143–157, at 144; Renate Jacobi, 'Gelehrte Frauen im islamischen Spätmittelalter', in *Nonne, Königin, Kurtisane: Wissen, Bildung und Gelehrsamkeit von Frauen in der frühen Neuzeit*, eds Michaela Hohkamp and Gabriele Jancke (Königstein: Ulrike Helmer Verlag, 2004), 225–246; Muhammad Akram Nadwi, *Al-Muhaddithat: The Women Scholars in Islam* (Oxford and London: Interface Pub-lications, 2007); Richard W. Bulliet, 'Women and the Urban Religious Elite in the Pre-Mongol Persian', in Women *in Iran, From the Rise of Islam to 1800*, eds Guity Neshat and Lois Beck (Champaign: University of Illinois Press, 2003), 68–79; Asma Sayeed, 'Muslim Women's Religious Education in Early and Classical Islam', *Religion Compass* V.3 (2011), 94–103.

Yet their presence in the contemporary literature is limited to brief references to their names and origins. Analyses of their works and contributions to Islamic knowledge, as well as the limits thereof, are still wanting.

The present chapter introduces two Iranian female *mujtahidāt*, Nosrat Amin (1886–1983) and Zohreh Sefati (1948–), who represent like few other contemporaries the status of female religious authority in twentieth-century Iran, divided by the important cesura of the 1979 revolution. Nosrat Amin is one of the most influential *Shi'i* female religious authorities of modern times, who in her own right granted men *ijāzas* of *ijtihād* and *riwāya*.[2] Zohreh Sefati is the most prominent female religious authority of the Islamic Republic and was a long-time member of the Women's Social and Cultural Council (*Shura-ye Farhangi-ye va Ejtema'i-ye Zanān*), where she headed the committee on *fiqh* and law. Both women's work was strongly influenced by the socio-political environment in and against which they defined themselves. Nosrat Amin experienced Iran's Constitutional Revolution of 1906 in her early twenties, Zohreh Sefati the 1979 Revolution in her early thirties. While Amin underwent her formative period as an Islamic scholar at a time when *madrasas* were gradually being replaced by secular state schools and religious courts by the apparatus of a modern state judiciary, Sefati experienced the reversal of some of these reforms when the 1979 Revolution sought to Islamicise the entire legal system and expand the status of religious learning.

A comparison of the two women's lives and works illustrates the extent to which political circumstances have shaped the opportunities for women to aspire to and acquire religious authority. The theoretical framework employed by Masooda Bano and Hilary Kalmbach, distinguishing between female initiative, male invitation, and state intervention as factors facilitating female religious authority, help our understanding of the career paths these female scholars chose.[3] In the case of both women, their own initiative was key to propel them to the knowledge and scholarship they produced. Male agency played a role in so far as it was Amin's father who

---

[2] For a detailed discussion of the concept of *ijāza*, see, Devin J. Stewart, '*Ejāza*', in *Encyclopædia Iranica*, Vol. VIII, Fasc. 3 (London: Columbia University, 1982), 273–275.

[3] *Women, Leadership and Mosques: Changes in Contemporary Islamic Authority*, eds Masooda Bano and Hilary Kalmbach (Brill, 2012), 31–36.

supported her intellectual interests and financed her studies even after she was married. For Sefati, it was male invitation that allowed her to be considered a candidate for the Socio-Cultural Council to which she was eventually appointed. Even though membership in this council did not elevate her access to and engagement with scholarship, it did endow her with a degree of institutional authority that helped the dissemination of her works, and the media's disposition towards interviewing her on matters of public interest. The state, by contrast, despite its strong regulation of religion and of education both before and after the 1979 revolution, played a surprisingly small role in facilitating the scholarly achievements of the two women. It was not state schools or state-funded higher education that furthered these women in their paths. When Amin opened a girls' *maktab* in the 1960s, this was diametrically opposed to the educational policies of the Shah's White Revolution. If anything, she defined herself against the contemporary educational project of the state. When the Islamic Republic opened the first women's *ḥawza* (Jāmi'at al-Zahrā') in the mid-1980s, Zuhrah Sefati initially joined it as an instructor at the highest level of learning (*dars-e khārej*), but left the *ḥawza* later when she felt a state-initiated curriculum reform had transformed the institution from one of scholarship to one of propagation training. Today, she still offers private lessons. State intervention then in both cases, across the reign of Mohammad Reza Shah and the Islamic Republic, rather obstructed than facilitated women's theological training. It can be said that both women owe their achievement primarily to their own initiative, not male invitation and not state intervention, although male invitation was often a facilitator.

A Note on Sources

An examination of female religious scholars in Iran and their status in the field of religious learning entails certain challenges. The scholars' main writings are available in less than five North American and European libraries, and secondary sources are extremely rare. Only few biographies (*zendeginämeh*) of Amin and Sefati exist in Persian.[4] The present research relies on primary documents,

[4] The three main biographies of Nosrat Amin are Naser Baqeri Bed'hindi, *Bānū-yi nimūnah: gilwahāyī az ḥayāt-i bānū-yi mujtahida Amīn Iṣfahānī* (Qum: Daftar-i Tablīghat-i Islāmī-yi Ḥawzah-yi 'ilmiyya-yi Qom, Markaz-i Intishārāt, 1382 [2003], Marjan 'Amu Khalili, *Kawkab-i durrī: [sharḥ-i aḥvāl-i bānū-ye mujtahida Amīn]* (Tehran: Payām-e 'Adālat, 1379 [2000]), and Nahid Tayyebi, *Zindagānī-yi Bānū-yi Īrānī: Bānū-yi mujtahida Nuṣrat al-Sādāt Amīn* (Qum: Sābiqūn Publishers, 1380 [2001]). Tayyebi's text seems at times to glorify Amin, perhaps because Tayyebi wrote under the supervision of Zinat al-Sadat 'Alaviyya Homayuni (b. 1917), Amin's most prominent female student who later administered the school Amin established in the mid-1960s in Isfahan. The relationship of the other two biographers to their subject is not known. There is a *yādnāmeh* that Tayibbi cites, but rather than an autobiographical memoir, it is a booklet published in preparation of the two conferences held in honour of Amin in 1992 and 1993. (On the conferences, see note 10.) The booklet includes reprints of several of the

such as the *tafsīr* of Amin and other writings of the two women, published interviews with the two, as well as scholarly commentaries on Amin's and Sefati's writings, and discussions of the two *mujtahidāt* in Iranian women's magazines and other media. This material has appeared in Persian, French, Spanish, Italian, English, and German. Until Maryam Rutner's 2020 dissertation on Amin, not a single doctoral dissertation or other scholarly monographs appear to have been written on the works of these women, or for that matter on other female religious scholars in twentieth-century Iran.[5] Fortunately, Sefati has given a number of interviews to the Iranian press and international media that indicate some of her political and theological positions. Amin's life has been the subject of three biographies as well as several short biographical entries.[6] Several of Amin's writings (such as her *tafsīr Makhzan al-'Irfān* and her later mystical works) and two of Sefatī's books are available in a few university libraries in Europe and North America.[7] Amin's earlier more sophisticated legal works, by contrast, seem to be available only at Princeton, Harvard, and SOAS University of London (School of Oriental and African Studies). Secondary literature in languages other than Persian mentions either scholar only in passing and hardly ever dedicates more than one or two sentences to their works and socio-political impact.[8] Despite the outstanding position she acquired as the leading *mujtahida* of twentieth-century Iran, Amin's work is

---

ijāzas that Amin received and issued. See *Yādnāmah-i bānū-yi mujtahida Nuṣrat al-Sādāt Amīn: mashhūr bi Bānū-yi Īrāni* (Isfahan: Vizārat-i Farhang wa Irshād-i Islāmī; Markaz-i Muṭāla'āt-i wa Tahqīqāt-i Farhangī, 1371 [1992]). The one biography of Sefati we are aware of is: Fariba Anisi, *Banu Sefati Zan-i az Tabar-i Khurshīd,* Markaz-i Umūr-i Zanān wa Khānivādah, Nahād Riāsat-i Jumhūrī, 1388 (2009).

5 See Maryam Rutner, *Nosrat Amin (1886/87–1983): A Female Mojtahed,* Ph.D. dissertation, New York University, 2020. Two MA dissertations we are aware of are Shaistah Nazri, *Taḥqīq dar Zindagī-yi Bānū mujtahida Amīn wa Barresī Tafsīr Makhzan al-'Irfān* (A Research on the Life of Lady Mujtahida Amin and A Study of Tafsīr-e Makhzan al-'Irfān), Azad University of Tehran, defended 1998 under supervision of Mansur Pahlavan; and Raziyya Mania, *Ravish-shinasi Tafsīr-i Makhzan al-'Irfān Bānū-yi Mutjtahidah Amīn* (The methodology of the Tafsīr Makhzan al-'Irfān by Lady Mutjtahidah Amīn), Islamic Azad University, Science and Research Branch, no date. We have not had access to the two theses.

6 The short biographical entries can be found in Hajji Mulla 'Ali Wa'iz Khiyabani Tabrizi, *Tarikh-i 'ulama-yi mu'asirin* (Tehran: Matba'ah Islamiyya, 1366 [1947] (also 2003)), 311–325; Puran Farrukh'zad, *Dānishnāmah-i zanān-i farhangsāz-i Irān wa jahān: zan az katībah tā tārīkh (Tehran: Intishārā*-i Zaryāb, 1378 [1999]); Fakhri Qavimi, *Kārnāmah-'i Zanān-i mash'hur-i Īrān dar 'ilm, ādab, siyāsat, maz'hab, hunar, tā lim wa tartib az qabl az islām tā 'asr-i hazir* (Tehran: Vizārat-i Āmūzish wa Parvarish, 1352 [1973]); Muhammad Hasan Rajabi, *Mashāhīr-i Zanān-i Īrānī wa Pārsī'gūyi: az Āghāz tā Mashrūtah* (Tehran: Surūsh, 1995); Dhabihallah Mahallati, *Rayāḥīn al-sharī'ah dar tarjumah-i dānishmandān-i bānūwān-i shī'ah* (Tehran: Dār al-Kutub al-Islamiyya, 1374 [1954]); and Aḥmad Bihishtī, *Zanān-e nāmdar dar Qur'ān, Ḥadīth wa Tārīkh,* vol. I (Tehran: Sazman-i Tablīghat-i Islāmī, 1989), 122–126.

7 Zohreh Sefati, *Ziyārat dar partaw-i vilāyat: sharhī bar ziyārat-i 'Āshūrā* (Qom: Mujtama'-i 'Ulūm-i Dīnī-i Hazrat-i Valī-i 'Asr, 1376 [1997]) and *Pazhūhishī fiqhī pīrāmūn-i sinn-i taklīf* (Tehran: Nashr-i Mutahhar, 1376 [1997 or 1998]).

8 The only exceptions with regard to Nosrat Amin here are Roswitha Badry, 'Zum Profil weiblicher "Ulama" in Iran: Neue Rollenmodelle für "islamische Feministinnen"?', *Die Welt des Islams* XL.1 (March 2000), 7–40 (Sefati finds no mention in Badry's article) and Maryam Rutner, 'Religious Authority, Gendered Recognition, and Instrumentalization of Nusrat Amin in Life and after Death', *Journal of Middle East Women's Studies* 11 (2015), 24–41.

not widely known and referenced.[9] The few engagements with her scholarly work that do exist in Persian are more of political than scholarly nature.[10]

The present chapter offers only brief overviews of the two scholars' biographical data, some theological and political positions they have held, and how they have shaped their environment by virtue of these as well as their public role. Much work is needed to place the scholars' lives and works in their historical context and to illuminate how their works interact with the discourses and socio-political circumstances of their time, to what extent they reflect or challenge predominant religious interpretations, and how far the scholars intellectually venture onto new ground. It is our hope that the introduction provided in this chapter will incite such future work, and illuminate through informed scholarship how they initiated and shaped developments in female religious authority of twentieth-century Iran.

Nosrat Amin (1886–1983): From the *Maktab Khaneh to Maktab-e Fatima*

Nosrat Amin, also known as *Hajjiyyeh Khanom Nosrat Amin Begum*, was born in Isfahan in 1886.[11] Apart from distinguishing herself in the fields of hadith and *fiqh*, she was also a revered mystic and writer on ethics.[12]

---

[9] Her work is catalogued in Western libraries under a myriad of different names and references that can make searching for her works an ordeal. As noted below, she is sometimes referred to as simply 'Banoo/Banu Amin', 'Lady Amin', 'Banoo/Banu (Amin) Isfahani/ Esfahani', 'Banoo/ Banu Irani', or 'Nosrat/Nuṣrat Khanom/Khanum'.

[10] Characteristically, the book that seems to be very closely associated with her 'work' is a translation she published of Ahmad ibn Mohammad ibn Miskawayh's (d. 1030) *Tahdhīb al-Akhlāq* ('The Refinement of Character') towards the end of her life. Even the volume that brings together the contributions to two conferences that were held in Amin's honour in Tehran in 1992 and 1993 is substantively very thin. Few speakers seem to have read any of her works carefully. Interestingly enough, "Ali Larijani, parliamentary speaker since 2008, belongs to those who seem to have concerned themselves more deeply with her work. In particular, he discusses the very last book she published, written in Arabic: *al-Nafaḥāt al-Raḥmāniyya fī al-Vāridāt al-Qalbiyya*. See *Majmū'ah-'i maqālāt wa sukhanrānīhā-yi avvalīn wa duvumīn Kungrih-'i Buzurgdāsht-i Bānū-yi Mujtahida Sayyidah Nuṣrat Amīn (rah)* (Qum: Markaz-i Mutala'at va-Tahqiqat-i Farhangi, Daftar-i Mutala'at-i Farhangi-ye Banuwan, 1995).

[11] Most library catalogues indicate her birth year at 1890 or 1891, although her biographies name 1886.

[12] Her most detailed biographies are noted above in footnote 4. Magazine articles that shed light on the portrayal of Nosrat Amin in the Islamic Republic include 'Panjumīn Namāyishgāh-i Qur'ān-i Karīm: jilwī'ī arzishmand az ḥuḍūr-i bānūwān-i qadīm-i Qur'ān', *Zan-i Ruz* (No. 1641: 8–11, 25 January 1998); and 'Bānū Amīn: Bāyad az Qishr-i Khānum-hā, 'Ālim wa Mujtahid Tarbiyat Shawad', *Zan-i Ruz,* (No. 1372: 6–11, 15 August 1992), as well as the conference publication (see Mu'avanat-i Farhangī, *Majmū'ah-'i maqālāt*). The conference publication includes papers by Mohammad Khatami (then Minister of Culture and Islamic Guidance and later President of Iran), "Ali Larijani (later parliamentary speaker), Zohreh Sefati, and others. At the fifth Qur'an exhibition in Tehran in 1998, an entire separate room was dedicated to Amin's writings and Qur'an commentary. Of note is also the TV series planned in 2004 (but to date not realised) on the 'sole woman jurisprudent'. The serial had been approved in 2000 under the Khatami presidency, and would consist of thirteen episodes of 30 minutes' duration each.

Amin's religious education began in a local Isfahani *maktab khaneh (Qur'an* school) where she studied the Qur'an and Persian literature. Amin married at the age of fifteen and continued her studies in the Islamic sciences *fiqh* (jurisprudence), *uṣūl al-fiqh* (principles of jurisprudence), and Arabic, *hikmat* (metaphysics) and *falsafa* (philosophy).[13] Her main teacher at that time was Ayatollah Mir Sayyid 'Ali Najafabadi (1869–1943), who, it is said, taught Amin private classes in her own house.[14] Even after her marriage, it was her father, an Isfahani merchant, rather than her husband, who financed her religious education.

Nuṣrat Amin's first work *al-Arba'īn al-Hāshimiyya* was published in the late 1930s and found much acclaim, particularly in Najaf.[15] Shortly thereafter, some of the leading contemporary *'ulamā'* began to post questions to Nosrat Amin in order to probe her knowledge in the various fields of religious learning and her familiarity with the sources. These questions and her responses were later published in the book *Jāmi' al-Shatāt*. Her teachers and interlocutors included Ayatollahs Mohammad Kazem Yazdi (1832–1919), Ibrahim Hosayni Shirazi Estehbanati (1880–1959), Mohammad Reza Najafi-Isfahani (1846–1943), Abdolkarim Qomi, Mohammad Qasem Shirazi (1873–1948), and Grand Ayatollah Abdolkarim Ha'eri Yazdi (1859–1937), the founder of the Qom seminaries. After mastering the various

---

[13] Rasul Tudih Zarih, *Bānū Amīn: Her Life, On the Occasion of the Anniversary of the Death of Mujtahida of the World of Islam, Haji-ye Lady Amin Known as Banu-ye Irani*, Pāygāh-i Iṭṭilā''rasānī-i Ḥawzah-hā-yi 'Ilmiyya-yi Khawharān, 1999, <http://www.hawzah.net/hawzah/Magazines/MagArt.aspx?MagazineNumberID=4015&id=22611>, accessed 8 August 2008. Amin's husband was her cousin Haj Mirza (also known as Moin al-Tujjar). Her father is known by the name of Hajji Sayyid Mohammad 'Ali Amin al-Tujjar. His sister Hashemiyya al-Tujjar is said to have been a *mujtahida* herself who received *ijtihād* certifications in *fiqh* and *uṣūl*. Further, Nosrat Amin seems to have had a niece, Iffat al-Zaman Amin (1912–1967 or 1977), also known as Iftikhar al-Tujjar, who received an *ijāza* of *riwāya* in Najaf from Ayatollah Mahmud Hashemi Shahrudi, who served as the Head of Judiciary of the Islamic Republic of Iran 1999–2009. Nosrat Amin was the wife of the brother of Iffat al-Zaman's father, Sayyid Ahmad Amin.

[14] 'Bānū-yi 'Ilm wa Taqwá', *Payām-e Zan*, No. 5, July–August 1992 (Murdād 1371), 34. See also Sayyid Morteza Abtahi, 'Bi Munāsibat-I Salgard-i dar Gudhashtī Bānū Mujtahida Amin', *E'temād-e Mellī*, newspaper, No. 926, 27 Khordād 1388 (17 June 2009), 10. Abtahi writes that Amin began her seminary studies with Shaykh 'Abdulqasem Zufre'i (1844– 1933), Husayn Nizam al-Din Kuchi, Sayyid 'Abdolqasem Dehkhordi (1856–1935), and Mirza Aqa Shirazi (1877–1956). This is partially mirrored in Rajabi who states that she reached the *muqaddima* (introductory) level with 'Abdulqasem Zufre'i. See Rajabi, *Mashahir-i zanan-i Irani*, 23.

[15] The following website credits Amin's aunt Hashemiyya al-Tujjar with a work by the same title. We wonder whether it is possible that Hashemiyya al-Tujjar began the work that her niece later completed. See: <http://pr.alzahra.ac.ir/artist-women/333-1389-07-04-11-38-23>, accessed 30 March 2011.

inquiries, she obtained endorsements by an array of senior scholars and became widely recognised as an authoritative *mujtahida* among *Shi'i 'ulamā'*.[16]

By the 1930s, Ayatollah Mohammad Kazim Hosayni Shirazi (1873–1947) and Grand Ayatollah Abdolkarim Ha'eri Yazdi had both granted her *ijāzas* of *ijtihād* and *riwāya*.[17] Allameh Mohammad Taqi Ja'fari (1924/1925–1998) would go so far as to rank Amin among the very few exceptional *Shi'i* scholars:

> Having read the written works of this lady, I can say without any doubt that she should be named as one of the greatest *Shi'i* scholars. Her scientific/scholarly methods are not only fully comparable to the works of other prominent scholars but given her attainment of highest levels of spiritual authority, she should be counted as one of the outstanding scholars.[18]

Grand Ayatollah Sayyid Hosayn Borujerdi (1875–1961) is said to have held her in highest regard and considered her on par with the leading Shi'i scholars of her time. Allameh Muohammad Hosayn Tabataba'i (1904–1981) and Ayatollah Morteza Motahhari (1920–1979) are recounted as some of her revered visitors, and the contemporary Ayatollah Yusuf Sane'i (b. 1937) would go so far as to rank Amin as one of the most accomplished Shi'i scholars of the twentieth century.[19] Despite these laudatory evaluations, it is difficult to ascertain the extent to which these scholars really engaged with her work. References to her writings that reveal deep familiarity with her work are wanting throughout the literature.

---

[16] Such endorsements would usually take the form of an authorisation to represent the interpretations of an established religious authority (the author of the *ijāza*). For example, Ayatollah Mohammad Reza Najafi-Isfahani stated, 'I permit to this learned and noble Sayyidah, follower of the Holy Lady Fatima al-Zahra' (S.A.) to narrate from my side whatever I accept from the books of *hadith, fiqh, tafsīr* and *ad'iya*.' Quoted in Hamid 'Abdus, *'Bānū Amīn, Ālgū-i Zan Musalmān'* (The Islamic Revolution Documentation Centre) (Markaz-i Asnad-i Inghilāb-e Islāmī), 23 Khurdād 1386 [13 June 2007]), <http://www.irdc.ir/article.asp?id=1044>.

[17] Other *'ulamā'* from whom she obtained both *ijāzas* of *ijtihād* and *riwāya* include Ibrahim Hosayni Shirazi Estehbanati (d. 1958), Ayatollahs Sayyid Mohammad 'Ali Najafabadi (1877–1939), and Morteza Mazaheri Najafi-Isfahani. In addition, she received an *ijāza* of *riwāya* from Ayatollah Mohammad Reza Najafi-Isfahani. In the biographies by Tayyebi and Baqeri Bed'hindi as well as in the *yādnāmeh*, several *ijāzas* are printed, including those by Ayatollahs Mohammad Reza Najafi-Isfahani (1846–1943), Qasem Shirazi, Estehbanati, and Morteza Mazaheri Najafi-Isfahani.

[18] Mohammad Taqi Jalili, *Bānū Amīn*, article from the series *Shakhṣīyati-hā-yi Ḥawzavi* (Markaz-i Mudīrīat-i Ḥawzahā-yi 'ilmiyya-yi Khawharān) (Centre for the Management of Women's Seminaries), 1999, <http://www.kowsarnoor.net/index.php?action=article&cat=113&id=646&artlang=fa>.

[19] See Ziba Mir-Hosseini, *Islam and Gender. The Religious Debate in Contemporary Iran* (Princeton: Princeton University Press, 1999), 160.

Amin herself granted *ijāzas* of *ijtihād* and *riwāya* to her contemporaries,[20] including *ijāzas* of *riwāya* to Ayatollah Sayyid Shahab al-Din Mar'ashi-Najafi (d. 1990), and to Zinah al-Sadat Homayuni (b. 1917), her most prominent female student who translated her first Arabic work (*Arba'īn al-Hāshimiyya*) into Persian.[21]

In 1965, Amin opened an all-girls Islamic high school (Dabirestan-e Dokhtarāneh-ye Amin) in Isfahan as well as an introductory Islamic seminary exclusively for women, called *Maktab-e Fatima*.[22] This was the first such institution on Iranian soil, and as such perhaps in the Shi'i world.[23] In the *maktab*, which counted between 600 and 1,000 attendees, students were trained in Persian, Arabic, *fiqh*, *hikmat*, *'irfān*, *tafsīr*, *uṣūl*, *falsafa*, *mantiq*, and English. Students attended classes for three hours in the afternoon and could reach the end of the *muqaddima* (preliminaries) cycle of a *ḥawza* education.[24] This presented a unique opportunity for women – who

---

[20] That women used to grant *ijāzas*, and used to do so for both men and women, was also common in medieval Islam. Goldziher writes, for instance, of 'the learned Zaynab bint al-Sha'ri (d. 617) [1220–1221 CE] of Nisabur . . . whose *ijāza* in turn was sought after by men like Ibn Khallikan'. . . . And 'in Egypt learned women gave *ijāzāt* to people listening to their lectures right up to the Ottoman conquest. Amongst the learned members of the Zuhayra family there is a woman Umm al-Khayr whose *ijāza* is asked for in 938 [1531–1532 CE] by a visitor to Mecca'. Ignaz Goldziher, 'Women in Ḥadīth Literature', in *Muslim Studies*, vol. II (Chicago: Aldine Publications Co., 1966), 366–368.

[21] See Mohsen Saidzadeh (written under the name of his wife Mina Yadigar Azadi), 'Ijtihād wa Marja'īyat-i Zanān' (Ijtihād and Marja'īyat of Women), *Zanan Magazine* (No. 8: 24, 1992). See also Hasan Najafi, 'Kitāb Shināsī Bānū Amīn', *E'temād-e Mellī* (No. 946, 10), and Sayyid Morteza Abtahi, *Bi Munāsibat-i Sālgard-i*. M. J. Fischer claims (perhaps based on Rajabi) that Nosrat Amin was granted an *ijāza* by Ayatollah Mar'ashi-Najafi rather than the other way around. However, all her biographies and other sources indicate that Amin granted an *ijāza* of *riwāya* to Mar'ashi-Najafī. See Michael M. J. Fischer, *Iran: from Religious Dispute to Revolution* (Cambridge, MA and London: Harvard University Press, 1980), 250. As students who received their *ijāzas from Amin*, Rutner also lists hojjatoleslam Zuhayr al-Husun, Sayyid 'Abbas Hosayni Kashani, Sayyid Mohammad 'Ali Ghazi Tabataba'i, Sayyid Mohammad 'Ali Ruzati, Shaykh 'Abdolhosein Amini, Shaykh 'Abdallah Sabiyati, and Sayyid Muslih al-Din Mahdavi. Rutner, *The Changing Authority*.

[22] Hamid 'Abdus, *Bānū Amīn*, and Muhammad Taqi Jalili, *Bānū Amīn*. Amin also founded a mosque, the Fatima Khanom Mosque, located not far from her tomb at the *Takht-e Fūlād*.

[23] We know of women's sections in the *ḥawza* (as opposed to female-only *ḥawzāt*) at least since the early nineteenth century, such as the prestigious women's section of the Ṣālehīyya seminary in Qazvin, and later the women's section of grand Ayatollah Shari'at-Madari's *ḥawza Dār al-Tablīgh* in Qom.

[24] A typical *ḥawza* education comprises three levels of about four years' duration each. The first is the level of *muqaddima* (preliminaries), broadly equivalent to secular secondary school. Here students learn grammar, syntax, rhetoric, and logic. The second cycle, *suṭūḥ* (surfaces of the texts), comprises an intermediate phase and an upper phase. Students learn the deductive methodology of jurisprudence and the principles of juridical understanding, *uṣūl al-fiqh*. The second level is broadly equivalent to undergraduate university studies. *Dars-i khārij* is the third cycle ('graduate' or 'outside study'), comparable to doctoral studies. Students are trained through chiefly discursive means and debate. At the end of this cycle, students should obtain from one or several scholars the certification (*ijāza*) that they

otherwise hardly had access to a *ḥawza* education – and as such probably laid a ground stone for the women's *maktab*s that were set up a decade later in Qom and then in other cities of Iran, and later around the Shi'i world.[25] From the beginning until 1992, *Maktab-e Fatima* was directed by Amin's student Zinah al-Sadat Homayuni.[26] Some of Amin's students later became teachers in the *maktab*; others opened their own schools.[27]

Both the high school and the *maktab* carried particular importance as they were set up at a time when the Shah had established in 1963 the so-called 'Literacy Corps' (*Sepaye Dānesh*) and in 1970 the 'Religious Corps' (*Sepahe Din*) whose long-term goal was not only to extend literacy across the country, but also to replace *madrasas* and theological seminaries as important centres of learning by state-run secular high schools and Islamic Studies programmes in the universities.[28] At the same time, it was nearly impossible for women to gain access to sophisticated training in Islamic sciences in the traditional *ḥawza*. The fact that Amin decided to establish the *maktab* and the all-girls high school at this time indicated her political independence, as well as her determination to ensure continuation of the tradition of female religious scholarship in Iran in the face of a secularising state.[29] Both institutions seem to have been exclusively funded by Amin, perhaps from her deceased husband's fortune.[30]

---

are able to engage in *ijtihād*. Yet many students graduate as *muhassil* (literally student/learner, someone trained in reproducing existing arguments) rather than *mujtahid* (someone trained to engage in *ijtihād*, and generate novel theoretical arguments). For an overview of a classical *ḥawza* education, see Michael M. J. Fischer, *Iran: From Religious Dispute to Revolution* (Cambridge, MA: Harvard University Press, 1980), 63, 247–248; and Roy P. Mottahedeh, 'Traditional Shi'ite Education in Qom', in *Philosophers on Education: Historical Perspectives*, ed. Amélie Oksenberg Rorty (London: Routledge, 1998), 451–457.

[25] See Roja Fazaeli and Mirjam Künkler, *New Opportunities for Old Role Models? Training Female 'ulamā' in* Jāmi'at al-Zahrā'. Paper presented at the workshop *Clerical Authority in Shi'ite Islam: Knowledge and Authority in the Ḥawza*, held at the University of Exeter, 9 December 2009.

[26] Beside translating one of Amin's works, Homayuni is also the author of *Shakhṣīyat-i Zan* (The Personality Features of Woman), Tehran, 1369 [1990], *Zan mazhar-i khallāqīyat-i Allāh*, Tehran, Daftar-i Intishārāt-i Islāmī, 1377 [1998], further a translation of the book *Asrar al-ayat* by Muḥammad ibn Ibrāhīm adr al-Din Ṣ Shīrāzī, Tehran, 1984. When Homayuni retired in 1992, Hasan Imami, a relative of hers, took over the directorship. See Nahid Tayyebi, *Zindagani-i Banu-ye Irani: Banu-ye Mujtahida Nusrat al-Sadat Amin* (Qum: Sabiqun Publishers, 1380 [2001]), 124; Marjan 'Amu Khalili, *Kawkab-i durri: sharh-i ahwal-i banu-yi mujtahida Amiin* (Tehran: Payām-i 'Adālat, 1379 [2000]), 125.

[27] See Tayyebi, *Zindagānī*, 130f.

[28] George W. Baswell, 'Civil Religion in Contemporary Iran', *Journal of Church and State* 21 (1979), 223–246.

[29] For instance, in Najafabad and Qom. Tayyibi notes that Amin's student Zahra Mazaheri taught religious studies to girls in Qom, 'where [later] Maktab-e *Tawḥīd* was founded', the predecessor of Jāmi'at al-Zahrā'. For details, see Fazaeli and Künkler, *New Opportunities*.

[30] See *Yādnāmeh-ye bānū-ye mujtahida Nuṣrat al-Sādāt Amīn: mashhur bi Bānū-yi Īrāni* (Isfahan: Markaz-i Muṭāla'āt-i wa-Tahqīqāt-i Farhangī, Tahqiqat-i Farhangi, 1992). Moreover, the all-girls

Amin's scholarly career was accompanied by personal hardship. During her lifetime, she lost seven of her eight children, mainly due to illness, and outlived her husband by nearly thirty years.[31] She died four years after the 1979 revolution at the age of ninety-seven and her grave at the ancient cemetery of Isfahan, *Takht-e Fulād*, continues to be a site of pilgrimage.

Nosrat Amin's Writings

Amin distinguished herself by numerous works in theology, mysticism, ethics, and poetry and proved by example that women can advance their education and levels of theological qualifications to reach a level of theological (though not sociological or institutional) authority equal to men.[32]

Amin wrote works both in Persian and Arabic. Her first work was the mentioned *al-Arba'īn al-Hāshimiyya,* a collection of legal rules and commentaries written in Arabic on forty hadith, which she completed in 1936 at the age of fifty.[33] *Al-Arba'īn al-Hāshimiyya* was later translated into Persian by her student Zinah al-Sadat Homayuni.[34] A second work published in Arabic was *Jāmi' al-shatāt* ('Collection of Scattered Pieces'), the mentioned compilation of her responses to questions on *fiqh* and *kalām* posed by scholars of the *ḥawza.*[35] It was on the basis of these two books that Amin received her first *ijāzas* of *ijtihād* in the 1930s. The third book Amin published in Arabic is

high school presented an important alternative to the state-run coeducational schools and withdrew from those parents reluctant to let their daughters study in the company of men any justification to deny their girls access to education. Rutner in 'The Changing Authority of a Female Religious Scholar in Iran' writes that due to lack of female teachers for the high school, 'only Persian literature was taught at the beginning. Later, male teachers were hired to cover other fields.' Rutner bases this on the introduction to the Persian translation (conducted by Homayuni) of Amin's *Al-Arba'īn al-Hāshimiyya*, p. 1, which we have not seen.

[31] Only her son Sayyid Muḥammad 'Alī Mu'īn Amīn survived her. See <http://www.iqna.ir/fa/news_detail.php?ProdID=252803> and <http://www.magiran.com/npview.asp?id=1384159>. He and his wife, Furūgh al-Sādāt, took care of the house after Amīn's husband passed away.

[32] We understand sociological authority here in the sense of social perceptions towards a female religious leader. Even if Amin may have compelled sceptics due to her theological expertise, sociologically that expertise was limited due to her identity as a woman. With institutional authority we refer to authority due to the networks and discourses that one is part of. As a woman, she lacked the institutional access to *'ulamā'* networks and opportunities to engage in frequent discussions with her male colleagues.

[33] Published in Iran by al-'Alawiya al-Amnīya, 1959 or 1960, and in Damascus by Dār al-Fikr, 1978.

[34] The Persian translation was published as *Tarjumeh-ye Arba'īn al-al-Hāshimiyya* (Tehran: Hudá, 1365 [1986]).

[35] Published in Isfahan by al-Matba 'a al-Mohammadiyya in 1344 [1965], but probably available as a manuscript much earlier. The collection of questions and answers was probably compiled by Ayatollah Morteza Mazaheri Najafi-Isfahani, who granted Amin an *ijāza* of *riwāya* and is also listed as an 'author'.

Al-Nafaḥāt al-Raḥmāniyya fī al-Wāridāt al-Qalbiyya,[36] which is predominantly a work of mysticism. Apparently, it was only translated into Persian in 2009.

Amin's first publication in Persian was *Sayr wa-Soluk dar Ravesh-e Awliyā'ye Allāh* ('The Spiritual Journey of God's Saints'), published in 1944, in which she describes paths towards spiritual fulfilment.[37] Notably, the book was first published under a man's name, Mohammad 'Ali Amin Nosrat, at a time when Amin was already known in some circles as a *mujtahida*. Perhaps she had chosen a pseudonym in deference of her husband.[38] Indeed, none of the works published during her lifetime appear under her name, but usually under the authorship of 'yek banu-ye Irani' ('an Iranian lady').[39]

Her second book published in Persian was a translation of Ahmad ibn Muhammad ibn Miskawayh's (d. 1030) *Tahdhīb al-Akhlāq* ('The Refinement of Character') from Arabic. It was first published in 1949 under the title *Akhlāq wa-rāhī sa'ādāt: Iqtibās az ṭahārat al-Irāqī Ibn Miskawayh*,[40] and is used as a text of instruction in moral philosophy until today in many universities and *ḥawza*. Several of our interviewees associated Nosrat Amin's name most closely with this book (and it seems to be a book frequently possessed by female and male *ḥawza* students), without necessarily realising that it is a work of translation.[41]

Her next book, *Ravesh-e Khoshbakhtī va Tawsiyya bi Khwāharān-e Imāni* ('The Way to Happiness and Advice for Sisters in Faith'), published in 1952, was written in response to what she perceived to be the cultural ills of the societal elite of the time.[42] It is her only work directed at a popular and predominantly female audience.

---

[36] Re-printed in Isfahan: Intishārāt Gulbahār, 1376 [1997], but probably first published in 1369 AH/1329 AP [1950], and finished, according to Tayyebi (p. 92) in 1940. It is not clear whether *al-Nafaḥāt* was an ongoing work or whether it was completed by 1940. A Persian translation appeared in 2009: Mehdi Eftekhar (trans.), *Nasim-hā-yi Mihrabānī: al-Nafaḥāt al-Raḥmāniyya fī al-Wāridāt al-Qalbiyya, Tarjama wa-Sharh* [Translation and Commentary] (Qum: Nashr-i Ayat-i Ishraq, 2009). Tayyebi mentions an Iraqi journalist who came to visit Amin in 1950. According to Tayyebi the story of his meeting with Amin was published as a preface in a later edition of *al-Nafaḥāt*.

[37] Published in Tehran by Chāpkhānah-i Islāmī, 1323 [1944].

[38] Sources also indicate that Amin's husband was unaware of her scholarship and was indeed surprised when he learned she had been awarded certifications of *ijtihād*.

[39] Similar patterns can be observed with regard to the work of other female religious authorities, such as 'A'isha 'Abd al-Rahman of Egypt (b. 1913). The Egyptian female Qur'an scholar published as 'Bint al-Shāṭi'' in consideration of her conservative father, it is said, who would not have approved of a public presence, including publications, by a female member of the family.

[40] Published in Isfahan: Thaqafī, 1328 [1949] 'bi-qalam-i yakī az bānūwān-i Īrānī'; later also published in Tehran: Nahḍat-i Zanān-i Musalmān, 1360 (1981). Beside her translation it contains her commentaries and explanations on the text. In 1990, a new translation appeared, which may have replaced her translation in the *ḥawza* of Iran.

[41] These interviews are held in conjunction with our research on women's *ḥawza*.

[42] Published in Tehran, 1331 [1952] 'bi-qalam-i yakī az bānūwān-i Īrānī' and later Isfahan: Thaqafī, 1347 [1968] under the name 'Yek bānū-yi rānī', also with an introduction by Mustafa Hadawi in Isfahan: Markaz-i pakhsh, Anjuman-i Himāyat az Khānwāda`hā-yi bī Sarparast, 1369 [1990], and in Qom: Amīr Publishers, 6th edition, 1369 [1990].

After the death of her husband, the first volume of Amin's principles of tafsīr *'Makhzan al-'irfān dar 'ulūm-i Qur'ān'* ('Source of Knowledge. Interpretations of the Qur'an') appeared in 1956 and fourteen other volumes followed during the next fifteen years.[43] The *tafsīr* was originally published as *Kitāb-i kanz al-'irfān dar 'ulūm-i Qur'ān.*[44] Fischer lists Nosrat Amin's *tafsīr* as the key text used in an introductory course on rules of conduct and Islamic law in the Islamic Studies Programme at the University of Tehran prior to the 1979 revolution.[45] Nevertheless, to the extent that it is available, the *tafsīr* hardly seems to be consulted today in Iran or outside. Except for two sole MA dissertations on the *tafsīr*, defended at Islamic Azad University, we have found no scholarly commentaries and analyses of her *tafsīr* in various languages.[46]

Other works include her *Makhzan al-la'ālī dar faḍīlat-i mawlá al-mawālī ḥaḍrat-i 'Alī ibn Abīṭālib* ('The Treasure of the Night in Virtues of Prophet 'Alī

---

[43] Published in Isfahan by Chāp-i Muḥammadī, 1376– [1956]–.

[44] Princeton University Library owns three editions of the *tafsīr*. There is the original edition, of which the first volume was published in 1956. Princeton owns volumes one to five, seven, nine, and twelve. Then there is the edition from 1982 in nine volumes published by Jumhūrī-i Islāmī-i Īrān: Nahḍat-i Zanān-i Musalmān (Tehran), 1361 [1982]. In both the 1956 and 1982 editions, there is a jump between the second and third volumes to the thirtieth *juz'*, which Amin herself undertook, as she was not certain she would be able to complete the *tafsīr* in her lifetime. From the third volume on the *ajzā'* are then presented in reverse. Finally, there is the edition of 1989/1990, again in fifteen volumes, which reversed the original order of volumes, so that the volumes correspond to the order of the *ajzā'*. Different editions of her *tafsīr* are available in about ten libraries in North America. According to worldcat, Princeton is the only library worldwide that owns a copy of the newest (1990) edition. Against this background it is all the more striking that the 1956 edition, and, with the exception of volume I, the 1982 and the 1990 editions had never been checked out from the Princeton library before we started to read her work.

[45] See Fischer, *Iran: from Religious Dispute to Revolution*, 250. Amin even finds mention in *The Koran: A Very Brief Introduction* by Michael Cook, as the woman first known to have authored an entire *tafsīr*. See Michael Cook, *The Koran. A Very Short Introduction* (Oxford/New York: Oxford University Press, 2000), 39. Nevertheless, none of her texts are included in the bibliography of Hossein Modarressi's, *Introduction to Shī'ī Law*, which calls into question the contributions she made to the field of law and jurisprudence. See Hossein Modarressi Tabataba'i, *An Introduction to Shī'ī Law: A Bibliographical Study* (London: Ithaca Press, 1984). On the other hand, Amin's *Al-Arba'īn al-Hāshimiyya* is indeed included in Āqā Buzurg Tihrānī's *al-Dharī'ah ilá taṣānīf al-Shī'a*, which lists authoritative Shi'i commentaries and annotations.

[46] Shayistah Nazri, *Taḥqīq dar Zindagī* and Raziyya Mania, *Ravish-shinasi*. The state-funded Iranian Quran News Agency attempts an overview of the tafsīr, in *Bu'd-i Akhlāqī; Rūḥ-i Ḥakīm bar Tafsīr-i Makhzan al-'Irfān* (The Moral Dimension, The Essence of Interpretation of Makhzan al-'Irfān), second article in a series of articles *Āshnā'ī bā Tafāsīr* (Familiarity with Interpretations), The Iranian Quran News Agency, 24 May 2008 (4 Khurdād 1387), <http://www.iqna.ir/fa/news_detail.php?ProdID=253427>. Amin does not always present her own interpretation. For instance, for Verse 4: 5, she only presents three different viewpoints that past scholars have taken on the verse. Her interpretations also often appear to mirror those of Mohammad Hosayn Tabataba'i, without any accreditation.

ibn Abi Talib') in 1961[47] and *Ma'ād, yā Ākharīn Sayr-i Bashar* ('The Resurrection or Human's Last Journey') on eschatology in 1963/64.[48]

Amin's early works in Arabic are considered to be of greatest importance from the viewpoint of Islamic jurisprudence, whereas her later Persian publications are predominantly concerned with *akhlāq* and *'irfān*. The only work that deals explicitly with gender relations is *Ravesh-e Khoshbakhtī,* directed at a non-expert audience, where Amin lays out ways of a pious life for women.[49] Although delineating women's emotional, intellectual, and physical qualities and abilities, the image that Amin devises of a proper Muslim woman rests on domesticity. Women's greatest responsibility is the peace of the family and the moral education of the children. To fulfil this task, women need to be well-educated themselves, in the sciences and in religious knowledge. The fact, however, that out of nine works (two of which were extremely comprehensive and must have taken her two decades to write) only one deals more explicitly with women's issues and is addressed to women, indicates that women's issues with the usual focus on questions of maturity, hygiene, and so forth were not Amin's primary intellectual pursuit. More important to her were her studies in theology, mysticism, and ethics that kept her intellectually pre-occupied.

An Interview with Nosrat Amin Six Years after the Opening of Maktab-e Fatima[50]

The excerpts below contain some of Amin's responses in an interview conducted in 1971 by members of the Scientific and Educational Society of the World of Islam (Kānūn-i 'Ilmī wa-Tarbiyatī-yi Jahān-i Islāmī). Amin's answers elucidate the *mujtahida*'s views on gender roles. She underlines the necessity of a woman's *hijāb* and female piety, and condemns women's indulgence in this world's materialism, to which, she believes, they fall prey more easily than men due to their innate vanity. The man is seen as the caretaker, attracted by the woman's vanity and beauty (which should be revealed only to the husband). In general, the interview reflects the very conservative viewpoints that Amin also expresses in her book *Ravesh-e Khoshbakhtī* published in 1952, but her emphasis on domesticity seems to

---

[47] Published in Isfahan: Thaqafī, 1380 [1961] under the name 'Yakī az Bānūwān-i Īrānī'.

[48] Published in Isfahan: Thaqafī, 1342 [1963 or 1964]. Note that this website credits Amin's paternal aunt, with a work by the same title: <http://pr.alzahra.ac.ir/artist-women/333-1389-07-04-11-38-23>, last accessed 30 March 2011.

[49] For a closer analysis of *Ravish-i Khūshbakhtī,* the conservative viewpoints on gender expressed therein, and how they compare to Murtaḍá Mutahharī's teachings on gender, see Maryam Rutner, *Changing Authority.*

[50] The interview was first published in *Fursat dar Ghurūb* publications, and reprinted in the official weblog of Eshrat Shayegh, a member of the 7th *Majlis Shūrā-yi Islāmī* (Parliament), <http://shayegh.ir/1387/08/23>, last accessed 13 November 2008.

have receded. To the simplistic question of the interviewer 'Can you say that men are better than women?' Amin replies:

> You cannot under any circumstances say that men are in general better than women. We have women like Fatima (pbuh), Khadija, Maryam and many others who were better than men. The superiority that God has granted men in some issues is a general matter not an individual one. The deficiency mentioned in the Qur'an regarding women is only in one *āya* [verse] which states that women cannot settle disputes [*faṣl-i khuṣūmāt*] . . . and if they are asked to arbiter, they will not be capable of convincing the parties or imposing their judgment. The other deficiency of a woman is that she has a tendency to want to be vain and pays less attention to the perfection of her soul. This is, of course, a characteristic which God has given her, and obviously the reason behind the *hijāb* is based on this principle. However, these are generalized issues as there are women who are void of such deficiencies and *therefore these points are not true of all women*.[51]

With regard to the relations between the sexes, Amin suggests they are 'partners in humanity', but believes 'the foundation of the creation of man and woman differs regarding their cerebral, bodily and emotional strengths'.[52] Notably, this difference does not translate, in her understanding, into inequality in women's and men's suitability for public life. Citing several revered Islamic scholars, she declares that men and women are equal in *'ibādāt* (spirituality) and uses this fundamental observation to deduce the equality of men and women with regard to their social rights: women and men have equal rights and duties in most aspects of society, including earning, working, business, farming, teaching, learning, and even, significantly, defence in the face of an enemy.[53]

Her views on the ability of women to resolve disputes reflect the dominant opinion of her male colleagues. Although Amin does not believe in women's principal incapability to serve as judges, for the sake of public order she believes women could only perform such functions in the confined space of their families. To have women serve as arbiters of disputes outside their homes could lead to moral decay, because women in such visible public roles would attract the attention of men, which in turn would inhibit their ability to function as and be regarded as neutral arbiters. '[For women to serve as judges] is good [acceptable] with those who are *maḥram*

---

[51] Scientific and Educational Society of the World of Islam, *Fursat dar Ghurūb*. Emphasis added.

[52] *Bu'd-i Akhlāqī*. To support her argument on gender relations, she cites a *ḥadīth* from al-Tirmidhi narrated by Abu Hurayrah: 'The best of the men of my nation is the one who is even better to his wife and the best of the women of my nation is one who is better towards her husband. The best of the women of my nation is the one who obtains her husband's consent in what is not sinful. The best of the men of my nation is the one who treats his wife with kindness and understanding, like a mother treating her child, this man has the same rewards as a martyr who has died in the path of God.'

[53] Ibid.

and *ḥalāl* to her [that is, her husband and immediate family], but with others this characteristic should be contested as this attribute could lead to digression and bring about lust (*shahwat*). There is a reason behind God's granting to women such a trait [that is, beauty], this is so that men will desire them and this desire will lead to marriage and offspring. Consequently, women will be taken under the leadership and care of men.' Amin insists, however, that certain women such as the prophet's daughter Fatima or Jesus' mother Maryam have taken their public role, in particular their service to the community, very seriously, and that their examples must be invoked to counter conservative voices that wish to exclude women from the public sphere, in particular from commerce, production, and scholarship.[54]

Asked what the most important struggle (*jihād*) was for women at the time (1971), Amin returned to the perils of materialism.

> What is important for today's women is to fight their desires for gold, jewelry, different clothing items and to avoid wanting to become (fashion) models [that is, objects to be looked at]. Although this may prove difficult, it will direct them at a speedier rate to spiritual perfection. Therefore, the best *jihād* is for women to dress modestly (*ḥifẓ-i pūshish zanān*) . . . True happiness is based on virtue. True happiness will be achieved through faith, belief in one God and piety. If you seek happiness in this world and in the next, if you follow the Qur'an and step toward justice and truth, it is only then that you will feel happiness (*khoshbakhtī*).[55]

Zohreh Sefati: From *Maktab-e Tawḥīd* to *Jāmi'at al-Zahrā'*

In many ways, the life of Zohreh Sefati contrasts with that of Nosrat Amin. While the former witnessed the emergence of the modern state in Iran with the transfer of judicial and educational functions from the religious and clerical sphere to the state, Sefati lived through the opposite: the attempted Islamisation of the legal system and state initiatives to strengthen rather than marginalise institutions of religious learning, including those of women.

Sefati was born in Abadan in 1948. In an interview, Sefati portrays Abadan before the revolution as a 'secular' city with low religiosity, which she links to the considerable presence of Western workers in Abadan's oil industry.[56] It was during the latter years of her secondary education that Sefati read an interview with Nosrat Amin in the journal *Nur Danesh* and was inspired to follow in Amin's footsteps. Sefati began her study

---

[54] *Bu'd-i Akhlāqī.*

[55] Scientific and Educational Society of the World of Islam, *Fursat dar Ghurūb*.

[56] Sefati's family hails from Dezful and her full family name is Sefati-Dezfuli. See Mohammad Bade'i, 'Guftugū bā Faqīh Pazhūhandah Bānū Zuhrah Ṣifātī', *Keyhan Farhangī,* No. 199, April 2003, 5–30, here p. 6. Available online at <http://www.noormags.com/View/Magazine/ViewPages.aspx?numberId=1131&ViewType=1&PageNo=8>.

of Islamic studies in 1966 in the Centre for Islamic Sciences (Markaz-e 'Ulūm-e Islāmī) in her hometown, founded by a student of Ayatollah Khu'i's (1899–1992).[57] After gaining some training in the Islamic sciences, including *fiqh*, she moved to Qom in 1970 together with four other female classmates to further her Islamic education.[58] Sefati describes their move to Qom as difficult due to the opposition they faced from the clergy. The classes took place in a house that Sefati and her four companions had rented. While students had faced the teacher during lectures in her hometown Abadan, in Qom the lecturer would come to the female students' house and teach from behind a curtain (she notes without comment).[59]

Among Sefati's more noteworthy teachers during that time were Ayatollah Meshkini (1922–2007) with whom she and her companions studied *akhlāq*,[60] Ayatollahs Shahidi and Haqqi who taught them *fiqh* and *uṣūl*.[61] Like other members of her family, Sefati spent time in prison under the Pahlavi dynasty.[62]

Since it was difficult to find scholars in Qom willing to teach women, Sefati and her companions from time to time were without teachers.[63] The women's group soon took matters into their own hands and began to offer classes for female students. According to Sefati, soon hundreds of young women flocked to their classes, including Zahra Mostafavi (b. 1940), the daughter of Ayatollah Khomeini. Most women came from clerical households that were reluctant to let their daughters study at the secular universities and welcomed the opportunity for their daughters to study with female teachers. Sefati recalls that at the beginning, these lessons took place

---

[57] The student was Sayyid Hosayn Makki. See *Zendegīnāmeh* (biography), http://www.sefaty.net/Index.asp?HoorRobot=Biography.asp, also Bade'i, 7.

[58] There is no indication that Sefati and Amin ever met. One wonders why Sefati, if indeed inspired by Amin, would never have attempted to meet the latter in Isfahan.

[59] Bade'i, 'Guftugū', 8.

[60] Ayatollah 'Ali Meshkini was one of the founders of the Islamic Republic. He was the chair of the Assembly of Experts until his death in 2007 and in this position succeeded Ayatollah Montazeri. Meshkini was also the head of the Society of Seminary Teachers of Qom and the Friday prayer imam of Qom.

[61] Sefati later married one of her teachers, Ayatollah Muohammad Hasan Ahmadi Faqih (d. 2010). Sefati has four daughters and two sons and in 2006 had three grandchildren.

[62] Sefati's brother Qolam-Husayn Sefati Dezfuli (1952–1977) is known to have been a member of a radical anti-capitalist group named 'Manṣūrān' in the late 1970s (after leaving the Mujahedin-e Khalq). The group, to which Mohsen Rezai and 'Ali Shamkhani also belonged, assassinated businessmen in the oil industry. Qolam-Husayn was responsible for bombing the headquarters of the American firm ATT in Tehran. He died in 1977 and is referred to in the Islamic Republic as a *shahīd* (martyr). It is possible that Zohreh Sefati was imprisoned on account of QolamHusayn's political activities under the Shah. A biographical note on her reads, ' Sefati actively participated in Islamic propagation against the Pahlavi regime.' Her other brother, Iraj Sefati Dezfuli (b. 1940), represented the city of Abadan in the first and fifth Majles, and was a member of the Majles' Supreme Audit Court.

[63] Bade'i, 'Guftugū', 8.

in the same house where she lived, but once the group of students grew beyond the 100s, she and her companions inaugurated *Maktab-e Tawḥīd* in 1974, Qom's equivalent to Amin's *Maktab-e Fatima*.[64]

Today, Sefati is one of the most visible high-ranking female religious authorities, although she has not attained a status comparable to that of Nosrat Amin. While the latter was a scholar independent from political institutions, Sefati owes some of her status to her political activities as well as her connections to regimist clergy through her family and her husband. While she is considered to have a solid training in the Islamic sciences and few would doubt her rightful status as a *mujtahida*, she has published relatively little and may see her calling more in public engagement and teaching than a secluded scholarly life.[65]

Among Sefati's publications are *Pazhūhishī fiqhī pīrāmūn-i sinn-i taklīf* ('A Jurisprudential Inquiry on the Age of Maturity') (1997), *Ziyārat dar partaw-i wilāyat: sharḥī bar ziyārat-i 'Āshūrā*) ('Pilgrimage Under the Rays of Guardianship') (1997), and *Nuāwari-hā-yi fiqhī dar Ahkām-i Bānūwān* ('Jurisprudential Innovations in Women's Rulings').[66]

Sefati received her first permission of *riwāya* from Ayatollah Aqa Asli Ali Yari Gharavi Tabrizi in 1996 and subsequently from Mohammad Fazel Lankarani (1931–2007).[67] She claims that after having read her book *Ziyārat dar partaw-i vilāyat*, Ayatollah Lotfollah Safi Golpaygani (b. 1919)[68] granted her certifications of *riwāya* and *ijtihād*.[69] According to Sefati, she herself has given *ijāzas* of *riwāya* to more than forty male scholars. Until their assassinations,

---

[64] Ayatullahs Qudūsī and Bihishtī were two known supporters of this institution. According to Sefati, soon after the inception of Maktab-i Tawḥīd in 1974, another *maktab* for women was opened, called Qodusiyya (by the suggestion of Ayatollah Qodusi). Both of these institutions are now under the umbrella of Jāmi'at al-Zahrā'. Sefati also speaks of Ayatollahs Qodusi's views on the level of studies women could undertake at *Maktab-e Tawḥīd*. In her words, the Ayatollah, unlike some other scholars who think women need only some familiarity with Islamic sciences in order to engage in *tablīgh*, was of the opinion that they should study at the highest level of understanding of the Islamic sciences.

[65] Her proximity to the regime may also be indicated by the fact that Sefati received (and accepted) a plaque of honour from Iran's president Mahmoud Ahmadinejad in October 2006 as one of 3,000 'exemplary women'.

[66] See Sefati's official website: <http://sefaty.net/Index.asp?HoorRobot=Books.asp>, last accessed 25 July 2009. The publication details are *Pazhūhishī fiqhī pīrāmūn-i sinn-i taklīf* (Tehran: Nashr-i Muṭahhar, 1376 [1997 or 1998]) and *Ziyārat dar partaw-i wilāyat: sharḥī bar ziyārat-i 'Āshūrā* (Qom: Mujtama'-i 'Ulūm-i Dīnī-i Ḥaḍrat-i Walī-i 'Aṣr, 1376 [1997]). See also her 'Sinn-i Bulūgh-i Shar'ī-yi Dukhtarān [The Legal Age of Maturity for Girls]' in *Bulūgh-i Dukhtarān*, ed. Mahdī Mihrīzī, (Qom: Daftar-i Tablīghāt-i Islāmī-i Ḥawzah-i 'Ilmiyya-i Qom [Islamic Propagation Office of the Religious Seminaries Qom]), 1997, 379–390; and 'Juluyihā-yi Ijtihād-i Zan dar Fiqh-i Shī'ī (The Effects of Women's Ijtihād in Shī'ī Fiqh)', *Gulistan-i Qur'an* 30, (1379 [2000]), 32.

[67] Bade'i, 'Goftegū', 6.

[68] Bade'i, 'Guftugū', 6.

[69] <http://www.sefaty.net/Index.asp?HoorRobot=Biography.asp>. Following Safi Golpaygani's *ijāza*, Sefati received another certification of *ijtihād* from Ayatollah Mohammad Hasan Ahmadi Faqih, her husband.

she is said to have enjoyed strong intellectual links to Ayatollahs Beheshti (d. 1981) and Morteza Motahhari (d. 1979).[70]

Sefati taught *fiqh* and *tafsīr* at Jāmi'at al-Zahrā', the largest women's theological seminary in Iran, which was officially founded after the revolution in 1985 as an extension of *Maktab-e Tawḥīd*.[71] However, since the seminary's curriculum was simplified in 1993/1994 and the course of study changed to a four year-degree, the *dars-e khārej*, which Sefati had taught (the third and highest level of the *ḥawza* education) were no longer offered[72] and thus Sefati only taught private lessons henceforth.[73]

In 2006, rumours suggested that Sefati would run in the Assembly of Experts elections, a council of eighty-six clerics who in turn elect and theoretically oversee the actions of the Supreme Leader, the highest political office in the Islamic Republic. Sefati pointed out in a public interview that there were no objections against women running for the Assembly elections. However, she did not submit her candidacy.[74]

Sefati's Views on Politics, Religion and Women in the Public Sphere

In the sections below, we explore Sefati's views on some critical topics such as the relationship between Islamic law and government, women's possibilities in the Islamic Republic, and women's access to theological training.

---

[70] According to Sefati, Ayatollah Motahhari used to stay with Sefati and her family on weekly visits to Qom and offer lectures on Western and Islamic philosophy in their house. She states that these lectures in her house were frequented by Hasan Taheri Khorram Abadi, Hosayn Modarressi, Mustafa Mohaqqeq-Damad, and Ahmad Khomeini.

[71] See Fazaeli and Künkler, *New Opportunities*.

[72] Bade'i, 'Guftugū', 18. Perhaps so that her position is not taken as a critique of the curriculum change that was introduced by Supreme Leader Khamenei, she emphasises that she agrees with the simplification of the curriculum, as not everyone would have the time or the ability for advanced study.

[73] Sefati's private classes are designed to prepare women to become *mujtahids*. She teaches the books of 'Allameh Mohammad Hosayn Tabataba'i, Yusuf Bahrani's *Al-Ḥadā'iq al-nāḍira fī aḥkām al-'itra al-ṭāhira*, and other works of classical Sunni and Shi'i scholars, historians, contemporary scholars, and *aḥadīth*.

[74] The women's organisation *Jāmi'at-i Zaynab* headed by Maryam Behruzi nominated six women candidates for the Assembly of Experts election in 2006, among them Monireh Gorji. None of the women were ultimately included in the list of candidates, however, because the Guardian Council found them insufficiently qualified for the post. Sefati observed that the number of women who meet the qualifications for candidacy set by the Guardian Council was small. 'I personally have not made a decision with regard to running for the Assembly of Expert elections. So far, no political parties or factions have proposed that I nominate myself either.' The scholar did not, however, rule out the possibility of putting forward her name in the future, stating, 'I might decide to take part in the elections.' She is of the opinion that men and women intending to stand for the elections of the Assembly need to be renowned *mujtahids* with a relatively long record of instruction in the *ḥawza*. 'We should stay away from sloganeering about women's candidacy for the Experts Assembly elections since the female scholars have to endeavour for many years to attain such scientific level,' Sefati commented.

On government

Sefati believes that the *velāyat-e faqīh* (the guardianship of the jurist), on which the government of the Islamic Republic is based, needs to operate in full attention to political, social, and economic concerns of society. In delineating political rule from *fiqh* and *ijtihād,* principles of governing should be extracted from the sources and enacted contextually. By this, Sefati suggests that when *fiqh* is used to justify *hokumat* (government), as is currently the case in the Islamic Republic, *hokumat* has to be undertaken in the framework of exigency and context rather than strict adherence to Islamic jurisprudence. Her position on the question of political rule very much reflects the dominant approach to the question of *velāyat-e faqīh* in Iran today, one based on exigency and context rather than strict deductions from the classical sources. After Ayatollah Khomeini underlined the centrality of exigency in rule in 1988, including Islamic rule, this pragmatic approach to what Islamic rule precisely entails, from a legal and exegetical perspective, has become the modus operandi in the Islamic Republic.[75]

On possibilities for women in the Islamic Republic

Sefati's commentary on women's participation in the affairs of government suggests a decisive critique of women's opportunities in the politics of post-Khomeini Iran. 'In the present situation, women's participation in some spheres has become impossible and this is far from Ayatollah Khomeini's teachings', Sefati suggests in an interview in July 2008.[76] Ever since Ayatollah Khomeini incepted certain transformations in the women's domains that effectively empowered women in the 1980s, progress in this direction, according to Sefati, has stalled and there need to be decisive changes in this realm. For example, Sefati, points out, 'When he (Khomeini) sent some ambassadors to the ex-Soviet Union, there was a woman included[77] and when there were discussions over the drafting of the constitution, he saw no obstacles in the inclusion of women.'[78] Sefati, bemoans that the politics of the Islamic Republic today little reflected the visions of Ayatollah Khomeini. 'These are pains which need to be cured by referring to the opinion and philosophy of the Imām . . . Unfortunately, today we witness a certain narrow-mindedness

[75] On the place of exigency in law-making in Iran, see Said Amir Arjomand, 'Shari'a and Constitution in Iran: A Historical Perspective', in *Shari'a: Islamic Law in the Contemporary Context*, eds Abbas Amanat and Frank Griffel (Stanford: Stanford University Press, 2007), 156–164.

[76] See the interview 'Women's Participation in Some Realms has been Transformed to the Forbidden Tree (Shajar-i Mamnū)', Ayunia-yi Tihrān (Sirvis-i Madhābiḥ-yi Andīshah-hā), 12 July 2008, <http://www.ir-women.com/spip.php?article5833>.

[77] This is a reference to Marziyeh Dabbagh who was a part of a delegation sent to Russia to convey Ayatollah Khomeini's message to Mikhail Gorbachev in 1989. The message was an invitation to Gorbachev to study Islam, as Communism, in Khomeini's assessment, had lost its appeal.

[78] Monireh Gorji was the sole female member of the constitution-drafting Assembly of Experts at that time.

towards women at a time when the number of educated and able women is much higher than ever before . . . One of the expectations of women in the society is that since we have women parliamentarians, women should also be better represented in the executive. However, this has not yet happened.'[79]

But, as if not to provoke the resentment of the current Supreme Leader, Ayatollah Khamenei, in response to her criticism, Sefati is quick to suggest, 'I feel that not only are we in practice far from the Imām's thoughts and opinions on women, but in some instances the views of the current Leader [Ayatollah Khamenei] who follows Imām Khomeini's line of thought are not put to practice.'[80] In other words, Sefati proposes that the current situation is not a reflection of Ayatollah Khamenei's views on women in the public sphere either, but rather the result of a lack of implementing the true wishes of the current Leader.

Sefati bemoans the gap between the demands of women's rights advocates on the one hand and the unresponsiveness of the system on the other, which has contributed to discrediting Islam.

> We are at a time of extravagance and dissipation, meaning that, on the one hand, some women's rights advocates are branded 'feminists' and, on the other hand, some of the shortcomings in women's realms have provided the basis for objections to Islam . . . Feminists believe in total equality of genders but the Imām believed in gender justice not equality . . . When Imām Khomeini considered gender justice, it is clear that in his view everything is motioned on justice and on their rightful place and neither the man nor the woman is allowed to oppress the other.[81]

Asked whether she thought it was possible for a woman to become president of the Islamic Republic, Sefati responds, '[O]ur choice is Islam, and in Islam it is not forbidden for a woman to become president.'[82] In fact, Sefati suggests that it would contribute to the deterioration of society if women were excluded from public life. 'Decadence is the result of a society where the level of thought and culture of people is in decline. It is when women in a society are unemployed and feel that they have little to offer, it is then that they will be drawn to decadence.'[83]

---

[79] See *Women's Participation*, Ayunia-yi Tihrān.

[80] This argument is frequently invoked in all sorts of critiques against governmental policies. The one who critiques establishes that his or her position on a given topic is a reflection of Ayatollah Khomeini's position on this topic, that this perspective would lead to specific governmental policies different from those currently enacted, and that current policies do not reflect Khomeini's preferences.

[81] See *Women's Participation*, Ayunia-yi Tihrān.

[82] One of the more telling public interviews Zohreh Sefati has ever granted appeared in the Spanish newspaper *El País* in 2006. See 'Zoreh Sefaty – Ayatolá. "El islam no hace diferencias entre mujeres y hombres"' ('Zoreh Sefati – Ayatullah. "Islam does not differentiate between women and men"'), *El País*, 12 June 2006, 12 June 2006, <http://www.elpais.com/articulo/internacional/islam/hace/diferencias/mujeres/hombres/elpporint/20060612elpepuint_1/Tes>.

[83] See 'Zoreh Sefaty – Ayatolá'.

On the question of maturity and marriage age

In the year 2000, a bill was passed by the reformist-dominated *Majles* (Iranian parliament), which raised the marriage age for girls and boys to eighteen years in accordance with the International Convention on the Rights of the Child (CRC) to which Iran is a signatory.[84] The parliament passed the bill with the provision that a girl of fifteen years who wished to marry could acquire a permit from a local court in order to do so. The conservative Guardian Council (*Shūrā-ye Negahbān*) vetoed the relatively progressive bill and the *Majles* sent the bill on to the Expediency Council (*Majma'-ye Tashkhiṣ-e Maṣlaḥat-e Neẓām*), which functions not unlike a mediation council.[85] In 2002, the bill became a law and included the provision that 'marriage of a girl younger than thirteen or a boy younger than fifteen years of age is dependent on the consent of their guardian and also contingent on the court'.[86] The final version dramatically fell short of the standards set in both the original draft of the *Majles* and the International Convention on the Rights of the Child (CRC). The law was finalised after the Expediency Council consulted Sefati on this matter, whose first book explicitly deals with the question of the age of maturity.[87] In the book as well as her statement to the Expediency Council, Sefati differentiates between the age of *taklīf* – when one gains legal responsibility – and the age of marriage. She criticises some scholars who have mixed these two definitions. According to Sefati, the age of *taklīf* should not be changed and should remain nine years for girls and fifteen for boys based in her knowledge of numerous *riwāyāt* that exist on this issue.[88] To ascertain the difference between the age of *taklīf* and the age of marriage, one should take into account *'aql* (reason) and the *'urf* (custom) of the society one lives in. Having studied 'the statistics' and the *riwāyāt,* Sefati concludes that the minimum marriage age ought to be thirteen years for girls and fifteen for boys. Sefati also highlights that in her studies she took into consideration the age of growth and puberty of girls both in Iran and elsewhere in the world. Sefati adds that the age of marriage is also contingent on the ability and consent of the person.

---

[84] Article 1 of ICCR states 'For the purposes of the present Convention, a child means every human being below the age of eighteen years unless the law applicable to the child, majority is attained earlier.' Iran ratified ICCR on 13 July 1994, with no reservation. See *The Convention on the Rights of the Child,* <http://www2.ohchr.org/english/law/crc.htm>.

[85] If the Guardian Council, which reviews every law passed by the Majles for its 'compatibility' both with the 1979 constitution and its interpretation of Ja'farī jurisprudence, rejects the law, the Majles has the choice of revising it in line with the Guardian Council's commentary, or to vote with a two-thirds majority to pass the bill on to the Expediency Council. The latter council may pass the law as the Majles devised it, or with the changes the Guardian Council demanded, or in a third version of its own.

[86] Shirin Ebadi, *Ḥuqūq-i zan dar qavānīn-i Īrān* (Tehran: Kitābkhānah-i Ganj-i Dānish, 2002).

[87] Bade'i, 'Guftugū', 8.

[88] Note that she does not cite these *riwāyāt.*

The fact that Sefati, as a woman, was consulted by the Expediency Council as a religious authority on the issue is remarkable, and certainly a path foreclosed to her predecessors. At the same time, her interpretation indicates that while some high-ranking male Islamic jurists have developed arguments that buttress the legal standards set in the International Convention on the Rights of the Child (CRC), she occupies a much more conservative position – which rendered her a useful resource for the conservative Expediency Council in this case.[89]

On women in the Islamic seminaries

In an interview with *El País* newspaper, Sefati narrates her experience and motivations for following a religious education. Significantly, she attributes the scarcity of influential female religious authorities in Iran today to women's lack of interest in the profession and commitment to religious studies, rather than socially induced or legal obstacles:

> I started my studies at the time of the Shah. While studying for the final high school exams, I also started to go to a *madrasa*. Why? I noticed that women did not know Islam, and going to the *madrasa.* seemed the best way for me to get to know my religion better. It requires many years of study to understand the Islamic religion. My parents were both religious, but there were no religious scholars (*'ulamā'*) in my family.
>
> At this time, Abadan was a city full of foreigners who worked in the oil industry and the atmosphere was not very Islamic. It was precisely this absence of religion which motivated me to choose the path [of Islamic studies] with the goal of helping women understand Islam, first Iranian women and then women around the world. If you allow me a short excursus: since the birth of Islam and during our entire history, there were always exceptionally accomplished women in religion, in philosophy, in literature, even women poets. And as a *mujtahida,* I want to draw attention to Banu Amin, who was outstanding in philosophy and Islam at the time of the Shah[90]. . . About 10.000 women have gone through the seminary in the last couple of years. Why are there not more? No Islamic law and no restriction [in Islam] keep women from entering the seminary. It is a lack of will and interest.[91]

---

[89] Note also her rejection of the positions of Ayatollahs Bujnurdi and Sane'i on the question of blood money. While the latter have developed arguments for the equalisation of blood money between men and women, Sefati continues to argue that a man's blood is more valuable as he continues to be the breadwinner in most Iranian families today.

[90] Bade'i, 'Guftugū'. Sefati suggests in the same interview that there are only three to four *mujtahidāt* in Iran today.

[91] Ibid.

Can women become sources of emulation *(marāji' al-taqlīd)*?

Sefati explains that although Islamic schools also educate girls, they are facing a shortage of female scholars who are inclined or sufficiently skilled to authoritatively theorise in Islamic matters. 'The number of female scholars capable of making a legal decision through independent interpretation of legal sources, the Qur'an and *Sunna*, is very small.' Women should study for years at the *ḥawza* before they meet the necessary qualifications, she stresses. 'Many female scholars argue that reaching the degree of *ijtihād* has no use for them as long as they cannot be a source of emulation.' In response to this view, Sefati exclaims that the responsibilities of a *mujtahid* are not limited to those of a source of emulation. *Mujtahidāt* could serve society by helping Muslims interpret Islamic principles, she adds. She highlights that there is controversy among Islamic scholars with regard to whether women can become a source of emulation (*marja' al-taqlīd* – the highest level of Shi'i authority). 'A number of renowned Islamic scholars believe Islam does not ban women from becoming sources of emulation.'[92]

> [The] *marja' al-taqlīd* is a person of great knowledge . . . We need someone on the religious level to illuminate our doubts and ignorances and dark spots. This is what the *marja' al-taqlīd* is for, and in Islam there is no difference between man and woman. What counts is one's qualification [for this title] . . . The training [to become a *mujtahida*] is identical to that of men. We undertake the same course of studies. What counts are our achievements and publications.[93]

In light of the force of Sefati's position on the question of a female *marja'*, she is quick to emphasise that men have encouraged her throughout her career. 'I have to point out that men helped me achieve my goals. When I proposed to open a school for women, male *'ulamā'* supported me.'[94]

It is noteworthy how explicitly Sefati criticises perceptions among certain *'ulamā'* that exclude women *a priori* from the *marja'iyya*. Similarly, her critique of social policies in the post-Khomeini era that do not provide sufficient opportunities for women, and her suggestion that women could run for the presidency and the clerical Assembly of Experts, indicate her political independence despite the fact that she is a member of the Islamic Republic's Women's Social and Cultural Council. Compared to Amin,

---

[92] For instance, Ayatollah Yusuf Sane'i declared that women were equal to men in all aspects of political and social life and that a woman could even become the Supreme Leader, the highest political office in Iran, which must be staffed by a *mujtahid*. See *Women's Participation*, Ayunia-yi Tihrān.

[93] *El País*, 'Zoreh Sefaty'.

[94] *El País*, 'Zoreh Sefaty'. Sefati also suggests 'the West does not recognize that Islam does not discriminate between men and women. A woman can attain the same levels of knowledge and distinction as men.'

Sefati is much more concerned with equal opportunities for women than questions of how to preserve healthy gender balances and how to ward off the encroaching cultural influence of materialism. When Sefati speaks of decadence, she locates its roots in unemployment and psychological depression, not in immorality induced by foreign cultural influences. One may make the conjecture – but it is merely this: a hypothesis – that the difference in emphasis between Amin's and Sefati's accounts of the roots of social ills is symptomatic of a larger transformation in worldviews Iranian societal elites have undergone since 1979: the fears of moral decay due to 'Westoxification' have been gradually replaced by the conviction that it is the incapacity of the Iranian state, coupled with a lack of political will on the part of unaccountable elites, that is primarily responsible for the persistence and resurgence of social ills like drug addiction and prostitution.

Female Religious Authority in Iran: Between Female Agency and State-induced Stagnation

With the high involvement of women as transmitters and as scholars of religious knowledge from the classical period through medieval Islam and the Safavid, Qajar, and Pahlavi dynasties, Iran exhibits a strong tradition of female religious authority in the Middle East.[95]

Nosrat Amin and Zohreh Sefati are two female *mujtahidāt* who are both products of the pre-revolutionary system of Islamic learning. Until today, Amin's path remains unrepeated. No woman since has published so prolifically in the realms of *fiqh*, hadith, and *akhlāq*, received as many endorsements by senior colleagues, or granted *ijāzas* to male *'ulamā'* of such high authority.

Both women owe their career predominantly to their own agency. They sought distinguished teachers with whom to study, published on specific realms of Islamic knowledge, and later opened schools and seminaries for women in order to overcome the difficulty in women's access to the *ḥawza* education. The *maktab*s they founded or helped found, in Isfahan and Qom respectively, allowed women to complete the *muqaddimat* cycle, the first of three cycles of learning in the *ḥawza* education, and both scholars offered private lessons for those wishing to study in the advanced *suṭūḥ* and the *dars-e khārej* cycles. Male invitation facilitated Amin's and Sefati's studies in the sense that both of their families permitted, supported, and funded the

[95] See Mirjam Künkler's chapter in this volume.

course the two female scholars had chosen. The openings of the *maktab*s also benefited from the support of male *'ulamā'*, and both *mujtahidāt* emphasise that along their path, male colleagues helped them along at critical junctures. Meanwhile, state intervention, the third explanatory framework mentioned above, accounts little for the furthering of these women's distinction. The effects of the pre-revolutionary Pahlavi regime and the post-revolutionary Islamic Republic, although diametrically opposed on most policy realms, are surprisingly similar in their effect on religious education opportunities for women. Amin opened her *maktab* at a time when the Shah sought to shift religious education out of the *ḥawza* into the Islamic studies programmes of the state-run universities, where the curricula would be subject to state oversight. The opening of the high school and *maktab* in Isfahan was hence in direct contrast to the state educational policies at the time. A decade later, still prior to the 1979 revolution, Sefati and her colleagues initiated the opening of the *Maktab-e Tawḥīd* in Qom with objectives not unlike those of Amin. After the revolution, the Islamic Republic transformed the *Maktab-e Tawḥīd* into a full-fledged women's *ḥawza* called Jāmi'at al-Zahrā', which henceforth became the primary theological seminary for women in the Shi'i world. However, while it was initially devised to offer all three levels of the *ḥawza* education to women, Iran's Supreme Leader Khamenei ordered the simplification of the curriculum in the mid-1990s that demoted Jāmi'at al-Zahrā' to an institution that prepares women for *tablīgh* (Islamic propagation) rather than scholarship. Zohreh Sefati, who had taught *dars-i khārij* at Jāmi'at al-Zahrā', henceforth concentrated on private classes to instruct women at the highest level.

While Jāmi'at al-Zahrā' had initially been incepted to facilitate the training of women up to the *dars-i khārij* level, so that they could acquire *ijāzas* of *ijtihād*, the simplification of the curriculum once again closed that window of opportunity. Like its predecessor, therefore, the current political regime de facto makes for the stagnation of female religious scholarship in Iran by not facilitating and supporting the necessary training opportunities for women to emerge as *mujtahidāt*. Accordingly, although more than 30,000 women have started a *ḥawza* education over the past thirty years, Iran today counts only a handful of *mujtahidāt*.

Apart from lacking training opportunities, there are also few incentives for women to strive towards religious authority. With the revolution, the standards to evaluate religious authority have shifted and today political personalities surround themselves with titles of 'Ayatollah' or even 'grand Ayatollah' who previously may only have been considered a *hojjatoleslam*. A scholar's authority – once depending on theological and legal competence (as recognised by peers and illustrated in publications received by the *'ulamā'*), the number and quality of *ijāzas* collected from other *mujtahid*s, as well as the clerical networks and institutional locations of which one is part – today is much more difficult to establish. Both recognition and reputation remain important constituents of religious authority, but access to political office and state funds has tainted recognition criteria. Today regimist newspapers and a state-sanctioned association in Qom (the *Jāmi'ah-ye Modarresin-e Ḥawza-ye 'Elmiyeh-ye Qom*) have greater say over who counts as an 'Ayatollah' as opposed to a '*hojjatoleslam*' than one's peers and expertise in the Islamic sciences. Formal authority has become a question more of state recognition than theological and legal expertise or peer recognition (although the old criteria are still recognised by those unimpressed by the political proliferation of clerical titles). Formal religious titles today open doors to political patronage and state-funded positions that offer a secure salary. Most of these positions are de facto off limits for women, who even if trained as a *mujtahida* have no chance of being appointed a Friday prayer leader, a judge, a member of any of the political clerical councils, or to attain the level of *marja' al-taqlīd,* where they could collect *khoms* (religious tax) and re-invest it in *ḥawza,* student stipends, or social services (which in turn reproduce one's authority).

Further, while it is widely accepted that women can attain the *ijtihād* degree and become *mujtahidāt,* the position of *marja'* is out of reach. Courageously, Zohreh Sefati publicly argues that no theological or jurisprudential justifications exist that legitimise the exclusion of women from the *marja'iyya,* a position also taken by several of her highest-ranking male colleagues.

Nevertheless, in contrast to most female religious authority in other parts of the Muslim word, Iranian *mujtahidāt* may have legal competence that is publicly invoked, as the example of Sefati shows. The law that was adopted in 2002 concerning the age of marriage reflected Sefati's recommendations. The fact that it set the marriage age much lower than the reformist parliament and women's rights activists would have hoped highlights the instrumental use of the state in jurisprudential opinions. Where jurisprudential commentaries reflect the preferences of the clerically appointed councils that in this case passed the law, the regime invokes such opinions. Sefati is no exception: had she recommended the marriage age of sixteen or eighteen, her scholarly opinion would have been disregarded.

Compared to the demands of contemporary women's rights activists in Iran, the viewpoints on gender of both Nosrat Amin and Zohreh Sefati are very conservative. Yet when contrasting between the two, revealing nuances emerge. While both scholars affirm women's rights to education, women's right to enter marriages only by consent, and the sharing of responsibilities between wife and husband, Amin emphasises the proper place of women at home. Her views on gender are defined by the axiom of domesticity: women hold nearly full responsibility for the domestic sphere, while men do so for all public matters. Her writings are defined by binaries (inside versus outside the home, religiosity versus irreligiosity, a morally corrupt West versus a morally integer Islamic world, and so forth) with few possibilities for shades of grey. Sefati by contrast is hardly concerned with the vices of materialism and moral corruption, or the vanity of women, which in Amin's eyes is women's greatest predicament. Sefati instead speaks of the lacking 'will and interest' of women to advance in Islamic scholarship. Mirroring the conviction of her fellow citizens involved in women's rights advocacy (with whom she otherwise has little to share), Sefati highlights that it is women themselves who are first and foremost responsible for their destiny. To improve their situation they should not wait for male invitation or state intervention. If anything, it is their own agency that will open new doors. Despite their differing viewpoints on gender questions then, Amin's and Sefati's lives underscore the same insight. Even if domesticity characterised Amin's earlier writing about women, she hardly lived by that standard towards the end of her life. She published widely, and overwhelmingly on issues not specific to women and gender questions. She opened schools for female *talabeh*, and did so in defiance of the *Zeitgeist*: against a clerical environment that did not accommodate women, and a political environment that sought to eliminate religious learning outside the state altogether. She became a public figure and a role model that motivated an emerging generation to follow in her footsteps. Religious authority and domesticity only go together so far. The extent to which female religious authority can profess domesticity is limited, because religious authority has an inherently social component. Amin's and Sefati's lives are the best illustrations of this tension. Where they act as religious authorities, the image of female domesticity retreats and female public agency takes its place.

CHAPTER

11

THE OTHER HALF OF THE MISSION: AMINA 'BINT AL-HUDA' AS A REPRESENTATIVE (*WAKĪLA*) OF MUHAMMAD BAQIR AL-SADR

Raffaele Mauriello

Two weeks after the assassination of the renowned Iraqi scholar Ayatollah Muhammad Baqir al-Sadr (1935–1980) and of his sister Amina 'Bint al-Huda' by the regime of Saddam Hussein, perpetrated on 8 April 1980, the victorious leader of the Islamic revolution in Iran, Ayatollah Ruhollah Khomeini (1902–1989), issued the following statement:

> Following a report from the Minister of Foreign Affairs, based on several sources and officials from Islamic countries and based [also] on reports from other sources, I have come to know with utmost grief that the late martyr Ayatollah Sayyid Muhammad Baqir Sadr and his honourable oppressed sister, who was among the teachers of knowledge and ethics and the great scholars and literati, have attained martyrdom under the most heart-rendering circumstances at the hands of the perverse Ba'thist regime of Iraq. Martyrdom is a legacy that these dear characters inherited from their holy ancestors, while crime and oppression is a legacy that [their] oppressors inherited from [their own] history.[1]

Although he never mentioned her by name, Khomeini described Amina as an honourable figure, a teacher of knowledge and ethics, and a great scholar and literati. Indeed, he was aware of the activities of Bint al-Huda[2] and,

[1] Ruhollah Khomeini, 'Vazife-ye Eqshar-e Mellat-e 'Eraq dar Qebal-e Jenayat-e Hezb-e Ba'th: Payam be Mosalmanan-e Iran va-Jahan (Shahadat-e Aqa-ye Sadr va-Khahar-e Mazlumesh)', in *Sahife-ye Emam*, vol. 12 (Tehran: Mo'assase-ye Tanzim va-Nashr-e Athar-e Emam Khomeini, 1378 [SH/1999–2000]), 253–254. www.imam-khomeini.ir/fa/C207_43090/_, last accessed 1 March 2018. All translations are mine.

[2] Personal communication with members of Muhammad Baqir al-Sadr's family and interview with Dr Fatima Tabataba'i (1333– [SH/1954–1955]), the widow of Ahmad Khomeini and daughter-in-law of Ayatollah Khomeini, in her office at the Pajuhishkade-yi Imam Khomeini (5 February 2014, Tehran). For more information on her, see: Raffaele Mauriello, 'Sub-Centres of Power in Shi'i Islam: Women of 'Alid Descent in the Contemporary Near East', *British Journal of Middle Eastern Studies* 45.1 (2018), 79–94.

moreover, more generally held the belief that women, too, can reach the level of *ijtihād*.[3]

Almost forty years have passed since the tragic death of Bint al-Huda (1937–1980), the renowned Iraqi *'ālima* (feminine of *'ālim*, religious scholar), educator, and public intellectual. Particularly following the overthrow of Saddam Hussein's regime (2003), her figure has attracted increasing interest among Shi'i female religious activists both in Iraq and Iran and in the Shi'i diaspora in North America, Europe, and Australia.

This chapter presents an authoritative biography of Bint al-Huda,[4] offering an in-depth case study of contemporary female religious authority.[5] It addresses her figure in the framework of her relationship with her brother, the eminent scholar Ayatollah Muhammad Baqir al-Sadr, advancing the hypothesis that part of this relationship should be interpreted through the prism of the one between a *marja' al-taqlīd*[6] and his *wakīls*.[7]

Female Religious Authority: Sources, Structures and Paradigms

Hilary Kalmbach[8] has offered the following definition of religious authority, which I also use in this chapter:

[3] This at least according to an interview with Dr Fatima Tabataba'i published online on 6 June 2013 by *Jamaran*, http://jamaran.ir/fa/NewsContent-id_27050.aspx, last accessed 28 June 2013.

[4] In Euro-American academia passing references to Amina al-Sadr are largely relegated to a single sentence where the tragic assassination of Muhammad Baqir al-Sadr *and his sister* Bint al-Huda is mentioned. Among the few, notable exceptions are: Chibli Mallat, 'Le féminisme islamique de Bint al-Houdâ', *Maghreb Machrek* 116 (1987), 45–58; Joyce Wiley, "Alima Bint al-Huda, Women's Advocate', in *The Most Learned of the Shi'a: the Institution of the Marja' Taqlid*, ed. Linda S. Walbridge (Oxford: Oxford University Press, 2001), 149–160; Sara Pursley, 'Daughters of the Right Path: Family Law, Homosocial Publics, and the Ethics of Intimacy in the Works of Shi'i Revivalist Bint Al-Huda', *Journal of Middle East Women's Studies* 8.2 (2012), 51–77; and, to a lesser extent, Matthew Pierce, 'Remembering Fāṭimah: New Means of Legitimizing Female Authority in Contemporary Shīʿī Discourse', in *Women, Leadership, and Mosques: Changes in Contemporary Islamic Authority*, eds Masooda Bano and Hilary Kalmbach (Leiden and Boston: Brill, 2012), 345–362.

[5] The exercise of different types of female Islamic religious authority and leadership has received an increasing interest among academia in the recent years. Of particular interest are: Masooda Bano and Hilary Kalmbach (eds), *Women, Leadership, and Mosques: Changes in Contemporary Islamic Authority* (Leiden and Boston: Brill, 2012); Juliane Hammer and Riem Spielhaus (eds), *Muslim Women and the Challenge of Authority*, special issue of *The Muslim World* 103 (2013), 3; Kloos and Künkler, *Studying Female Islamic Authority*. For a list of publications on this topic, see the online collective bibliography available at www.zotero.org/groups/Islamic_authority/items/collectionKey/HEVSU8RS.

[6] Literally: a source of emulation, that is, a religious scholar who is qualified to be followed in religious practice and matters of law by Shi'i believers, alternatively named *ayatollah al-'uzma*. See: Jean Calmard, 'Mardja'-i Taklīd', in *The Encyclopedia of Islam*, vol. 6, 2nd edn, eds Clifford E. Bosworth et al. (Leiden: Brill, 1991), http://dx.doi.org/10.1163/1573-3912_islam_COM_0684, last accessed 3 January 2018.

[7] Representatives of a *marja'*, they play a variety of roles as intermediaries between the *marja'* and his followers.

[8] Hilary Kalmbach, 'Introduction: Islamic Authority and the Study of Female Leader', in *Women, Leadership, and Mosques: Changes in Contemporary Islamic Authority*, eds Masooda Bano and

> [R]eligious authority is linked only with those activities that require explicitly Islamic knowledge, specifically teaching, preaching, interpreting (or reinterpreting) texts, leading worship, and providing guidance on religious matters.

In the case of Bint al-Huda, the historical period and location she lived in made her a female scholar whose religious authority was to be built upon informal training, family ties, reputation for personal piety, charisma, *baraka* (the power to confer blessings), strong commitment to educational work, teaching experience, and uncommon organisational skills.

More to the point, she unquestionably represents a case of a prominent female scholar whose reputation, and indeed very possibility to become an *'ālima*, derived from her being a member of a family of established male religious scholars, the al-Sadr.[9] This element is in line with the female religious scholars (*ahong*) in China studied by Maria Jaschok,[10] who indicates that the most prominent female *ahong* in central China's Hui Muslim communities also come from families of established male religious scholars. A passage in her essay is of particular interest for what concerns the general issue debated here, particularly in light of the wider perspective offered by my research on the 'Alid Shi'i religious establishment of the Near East.[11] She notices:

> Most of the female *ahong* were from religious families and there is evidence, if scant, that as early as the seventeenth century a number of erudite female scholars had emerged from this group of women.[12]

This observation is intriguing in that one of my oral sources, a member of the al-Hakim family – a prominent 'Alid family of the Shi'i religious establishment – during an interview at his house in London, in December 2006, mentioned that his family had counted among its members a *mujtahida*[13] between the end of the nineteenth century and the beginning of the twentieth, in Lebanon. These

---

Hilary Kalmbach (Leiden and Boston: Brill, 2012), 1–27 at 19. See also: David Kloos and Mirjam Künkler, *Studying Female Islamic Authority: From Top-Down to Bottom-Up Modes of Certification*, special issue of *Asian Studies Review* 40.4 (2016), 479–490.

[9] For an overview on the al-Sadr family, see: Raffaele Mauriello, *Descendants of the Family of the Prophet in Contemporary History: A Case Study, the Šī'ī Religious Establishment of al-Naǧaf (Iraq)* (Pisa-Rome: Rivista degli Studi Orientali-Fabrizio Serra Editore, 2011), in particular 57–63.

[10] Maria Jaschok, 'Sources of Authority: Female *Ahong* and *Qingzhen Nüsi* (Women's Mosques) in China', in *Women, Leadership, and Mosques: Changes in Contemporary Islamic Authority*, eds Masooda Bano and Hilary Kalmbach (Leiden and Boston: Brill, 2012), 37–58.

[11] Mauriello, 'Sub-Centres of Power'; Raffaele Mauriello, 'Casate e politica dell'Iraq post-Saddam: il ruolo degli alidi nell'exclusive élite bargain', *Rivista di Politica* 3 (2015), 75–86; Mauriello, Raffaele, 'Genealogical Prestige and Marriage Strategy among the *Ahl al-Bayt*: The Case of the al-Sadr in Recent Times', in *Genealogy and Knowledge in Muslim Societies: Understanding the Past*, eds Sarah B. Savant and Helena de Felipe Rodriguez (Edinburgh: Edinburgh University Press, 2014), 131–148; Mauriello, *Descendants of the Family*.

[12] Jaschok, 'Sources of Authority', 41.

[13] Feminine of *mujtahid*, a scholar who has obtained a level of knowledge sufficient to formulate independent interpretations of the religious law.

elements provide further ground to the evidence that, within established structures of traditional religious authority, support from within the male religious leadership is a key element in helping women win recognition as high-profile religious scholars. The latter element provides common ground between what is described above and observed by Mirjam Künkler and Roja Fazaeli with reference to high-profile experiences of female religious authority in modern Iran. Künkler and Fazaeli indicate that the success of the many women 'who made a name for themselves in fields of Islamic learning' and who counted among them 'dozens who attained the *mujtahid* rank' was in important ways linked to the support they received from within the male leadership.[14] More to the point, but this time partly in contrast to the case of Bint al-Huda, Künkler and Fazaeli indicate that most of these women were *daughters* and *wives* of influential scholars. With Bint al-Huda, we have the case of a *sister*.[15]

In her memoirs,[16] Fatima al-Sadr (1321– [SH/1942–1943]), wife of Muhammad Baqir and sister-in-law of Bint al-Huda (and also first cousin of them), who lived in the same house as Bint al-Huda throughout the latter's entire adult life, lays out some ground for my hypothesis. She describes Sayyida[17] Amina's relation with her brother in the following terms:

> She took upon herself [the responsibility of] the Martyr [Muhammad Baqir al-Sadr] . . . complementing his role and fulfilling his mission with regard to the part where the Martyr was not in a position to [carry out] his role directly: the female believers . . . She let herself become absorbed in the personality of Sayyid the Martyr. She consecrated her life to the service of his project. She assisted him and served him in all the affairs that he was not capable of carrying out, [him or] whoever of his male assistants . . . *She was an emissary (safīra) for him* in [relation to] many arenas, spheres, and individuals.[18]

---

[14] Mirjam Künkler and Roja Fazaeli, 'The Life of Two *Mujtahidahs*: Female Religious Authority in Twentieth-Century Iran', in *Women, Leadership, and Mosques: Changes in Contemporary Islamic Authority*, eds Masooda Bano and Hilary Kalmbach (Leiden and Boston: Brill, 2012), 127–160.

[15] The case of Bint al-Huda and the special relationship with her brother is, interestingly enough, partly replicated within the al-Sadr family and in the same period by the special relationship between Sayyid Musa al-Sadr (1928–1978?) and his sister Sayyida Rubab al-Sadr (1944–). Although Sayyida Rubab was not a religious scholar, she is of interest for the points made at the beginning of this chapter. On Rubab, see: Mauriello, 'Sub-Centres of Power'. Finally, it is worth mentioning that also the case of Sayyid Qutb and his renowned sisters Amina and Hamida occurred *grosso modo* in the same period as those of Bint al-Huda and Muhammad Baqir and of Musa al-Sadr and Rubab al-Sadr.

[16] On these memoirs, see: Mauriello, 'Sub-Centres of Power'.

[17] A peculiar characteristic of the Islamic civilisation is that members of the Prophet's family have played an important role in the history of the Muslim world, and therefore are endowed with a special honorific: *sayyid* (in Arabic, fem. *sayyida*; in Persian *seyyed*). Within this kinfolk, the most important branch is represented by the 'Alids, who claim to descend from the Prophet Muhammad through his daughter Fatima and her husband, the prophet's cousin 'Ali.

[18] Amal al-Baqshi, *Waja' al-Sadr wa-min wara'i al-Sadr Umm Ja'far* (Beirut: Dar al-Ijtihad, 2007), 129; emphasis added. Al-Baqshi's book is largely based on the recollection of Fatima al-Sadr's memoirs. However, it also reports information related to her by other members of the family, in particular by Muhammad Baqir al-Sadr's children.

Although Fatima never uses the word *wakīl* (representative) or *wikāla* (representation) to refer to this relationship, she indicates that Bint al-Huda was Muhammad Baqir's emissary in relation to different arenas, spheres, and individuals, and that she undertook this role in all the matters that he was not able to deal with by himself, complementing his role with regard to 'the other half' of her brother's following, that of the female believers.

Ayatollah al-Sadr reportedly started his *marja'iyya*[19] following the death of Ayatollah al-'Uzma Sayyid Muhsin al-Hakim (d. 1970)[20] – the most important *marja'* of the 1960s in Iraq. Moreover, some of the roles covered by Bint al-Huda in relation to him were exercised by her as a recognised *'ālima*; that is, in terms of religious authority. In addition to this, she had as her almost single teacher and source of higher religious authority her own brother. These different elements allow me to argue that Bint al-Huda may be considered one of the first, if not the first, known cases of a female representative of religious authority (*wikāla*) in Shi'ism.

The Development of a 'Home-schooled' Female Religious Authority

Amina al-Sadr was born in Kazimayn, nowadays a suburb of Baghdad, in Iraq, on 23 March 1937.[21] She was given the same name as the mother of the Prophet Muhammad.[22] She was the fourteenth child of Sayyid Haydar al-Sadr and Batul Al Yasin.[23] Her father, a religious scholar, was the scion of one of the most established and influential families of the Shi'i religious establishment of the Near East, the al-Sadr. Her mother was the daughter of Ayatollah 'Abd al-Husayn Al Yasin (d. 1932), member of a prestigious family of the Iraqi Shi'i religious establishment. Ayatollah al-'Uzma Murtada Al

---

[19] This term indicates both the social role of the *marja'*s as sources of guidance in the spiritual and legal mentorship to their followers together with the informal web of personal relations through that this activity is carried out.

[20] al-Baqshi, *Waja' al-Sadr*, 192.

[21] Fadil al-Nuri, *Uswat al-'Amilin: Fi Rihab al-Imam al-Shahid al-Sayyid Muhammad Baqir al-Sadr wa-'l-Shahida Bint al-Huda* (Beirut: Mu'assasa al-'Arif li-'l-Matbu'at, 2008), 283; Muhammad Reza al-Nu'mani, *Sire va Rah-i Shahide Bint al-Huda*, trans. Najib-Allah Nuri (Qom: Jami'a al-Mustafa al-'Alamiyya, 2009). However, Anisi reports that she was born during the first ten days of the month of Muharram 1358 AH, that is, at the end of February 1939. Most probably, this is an error, as she herself also writes that the date of her birth corresponds to 1937. Fariba Anisi, *Dokhtari az Tabar-e Hedayat: 'Alaviyye Bint al-Huda Sadr dar Ayine-ye Khaterat* (Tehran: Markaz-e Omur-e Zanan va Khanevade Riyasat-e Jomhur, 2012), 16.

[22] Anisi, *Dokhtari az Tabar-e Hedayat*, 16.

[23] al-Nuri, *Uswat al-'Amilin*, 284. They had seven daughters (Anisi, *Dokhtari az Tabar-e Hedayat*, 16) and seven sons. The information is confirmed by an unpublished typescript provided to me by Fatima al-Sadr through the intermediation of Hawra' al-Sadr (11 May 2010, Tehran). The same information is reported by Wiley, who writes that, during an interview with Hanan al-Sadr, a niece of Muhammad Baqir al-Sadr, she told her that, in the period between the birth of Isma'il and the birth of Muhammad Baqir and Bint al-Huda, Sayyid Haydar and his wife lost eleven children. Wiley, "Alima Bint al-Huda', 159.

Yasin, a maternal uncle of Bint al-Huda, was an important *marja'* in Najaf in the 1960s, gone down in history for having delivered an anti-Communist fatwa.[24] Amina's birth came three years after the birth of her brother Muhammad Baqir (b. 1935) and six years after the birth of Isma'il (1921–1969); the other children all died during their infancy.[25] At the age of only six months, she lost her father.[26] The family was reportedly left in a harsh and difficult economic situation.[27]

In 1365 [AH/1945–1946], when she was six years old, her older brother Isma'il was offered the opportunity to start teaching in the *ḥawza 'ilmiyya* (traditional Shi'i seminary) of Najaf, and therefore the family left Kazimayn and settled there.[28] According to the sources, however, this did not mitigate her family's chronic economic problems.[29] As a child, she did not use to play with children of her same age but preferred to spend her time talking with older people.[30] Moreover, after the marriage of her brother Muhammad Baqir, she used to help her sister-in-law (and first cousin) Fatima al-Sadr take care of their children. They both also took care of Batul Al Yasin, Bint al-Huda's mother.[31] Muhammad Baqir's wife, herself a member of the al-Sadr family and a sister of the renowned Shi'i religious scholar-cum social and political leader Sayyid Musa al-Sadr, was born in Iran and from time to time used to go back to her country to spend two or three months with her parents who were living in Qom, leaving their children, who were studying at a madrasa, in Najaf with him and his family.[32]

Bint al-Huda learned how to read and write, and later on studied grammar and logic with her brothers, Isma'il and Muhammad Baqir.[33] She attended neither a traditional Qur'anic *maktaba* nor a modern school.[34] According to the sources, it was traditionally unusual to have women studying in the *ḥawza*

---

[24] Hanna Batatu, *The Old Social Classes and the Revolutionary Movements of Iraq* (London: Saqi, 1978 [2004]).

[25] al-Nuri, *Uswat al-'Amilin*, 284.

[26] Anisi, *Dokhtari az Tabar-e Hedayat*, 16.

[27] Kazim al-Husayni al-Ha'iri, 'Tarjamat Hayat al-Sayyid al-Shahid', in *Mabahith al-Usul, Taqrir li-Abhath Samahat Ayatullah al-'Uzma al-Shahid al-Sayyid Muhammad Baqir al-Sadr*, Vol. 2, ed. Kazim al-Husayni al-Ha'iri (Qom: Markaz al-Nashr – Islamic Information Centre, 1987), 11–168. He reports that, after just a month from the death of Haydar al-Sadr, the family was unable to provide its daily bread.

[28] Anisi, *Dokhtari az Tabar-e Hedayat*, 17.

[29] Muhammad Reza al-Nu'mani, *al-Shahida Bint al-Huda, Siratuha wa-Masiratuha* (Qum: Mu'assasa-ye Isma'iliyan, 2000), 25.

[30] Anisi, *Dokhtari az Tabar-e Hedayat*, 32.

[31] al-Baqshi, *Waja' al-Sadr*, 129; Anisi, *Dokhtari az Tabar-e Hedayat*, 27.

[32] Anisi, *Dokhtari az Tabar-e Hedayat*, 265–267.

[33] Anisi, *Dokhtari az Tabar-e Hedayat*, 22; al-Baqshi, *Waja' al-Sadr*, 131. However, according to al-Nu'mani, Bint al-Huda's very first teacher was her mother Batul. With her, she learned how to read and write, and only later she advanced in her studies with the help of her brothers, in particular Muhammad Baqir. Al-Nu'mani, *al-Shahida Bint al-Huda*, 26.

[34] Anisi, *Dokhtari az Tabar-e Hedayat*, 22.

in Najaf. Bint al-Huda overcame this obstacle by studying with her brothers, in particular Muhammad Baqir.[35] With him, she studied *fiqh*, principles of *fiqh* (*uṣūl al-fiqh*) and theology. [36]

Some experts go so far as to claim that when Bint al-Huda published her religious treatise *al-Huda*, she 'announced herself as a *mujtahida*'.[37] In the written sources, this claim is to be found in the unsigned introduction to 'Bint al-Huda Sadr', a long article published in the section *Shuhada-yi Zan* (Female Martyrs) of a special issue of *Shahide Yaran: Mahname-yi Farhangi-Tarikhi* (Shahide Yaran: A Monthly Cultural-Historical Magazine). There, the unknown author sustains that, having completed her elementary studies, Bint al-Huda moved to the *ḥawza* of Najaf together with her brothers Isma'il and Muhammad Baqir, continuing her higher studies in literature, principles of Islamic jurisprudence, and the hadith and, having studied fiqh, ethics, and Qur'anic exegesis she reached the level of *ijtihād*.[38] This seems to be an exaggeration, since we know that when Amina published *al-Huda* she was still not past the age of twenty and was trained as a scholar solely by her brother Muhammad Baqir. What is certain is that she became a recognised *'ālima*[39] and that more cautious – and better informed – sources sustain that she reached a level close to mastering *al-Makasib*, a famous work on trade and commerce by Murtada al-Ansari (1781–1864) that is studied by students of religious sciences during a stage just before *baḥth al-khārij* (the third and highest level of religious studies in the *ḥawza*), and that there are some ulema who affirm that those who perfectly master this book are entitled to exercise *ijtihād*.[40] Therefore, Bint al-Huda did not become a *mujtahida*. However, the sources clearly describe her as an *'ālima* and they assert that she attained a level of competence that *almost* qualified her to issue fatwas. (She is not known to ever have issued any fatwas.)

Bint al-Huda, an Unmarried and Childless Intellectual?

She lived in the house of her brother Muhammad Baqir, in Najaf, together with their mother, and Muhammad Baqir's wife and children. There, she had

---

[35] al-Nu'mani, *al-Shahida Bint al-Huda*, 28, 103.

[36] Wiley, ''Alima Bint al-Huda', 152. In this respect, also al-Baqshi, who describes the *ḥawza* of Najaf at that time as a society abundant in religious scholars, literati, thinkers, writers, and *marja' al-taqlīd*, but male-dominated in all these 'virtues'. Al-Baqshi, *Waja' al-Sadr*, 132.

[37] Wiley, ''Alima Bint al-Huda', 152. This claim was, moreover, repeated with slightly different words by Pierce, who writes that 'she proclaimed herself a *mujtahida*'. Pierce, 'Remembering Fāṭimah', 359. However, as in the case of Wiley, Pierce does not give any reference to primary sources.

[38] 'Bint al-Huda Sadr', *Shuhada-yi Zan*, special issue of *Shahide Yaran: Mahname-yi Farhangi-Tarikhi*, n.s., 27.35 (2008), 81–92 at 82.

[39] Wiley even describes her as '[o]ne of the clerics in the Islamic movement'. Wiley, ''Alima Bint al-Huda', 149.

[40] al-Nu'mani, *al-Shahida Bint al-Huda*, 28–29.

a small room, where she used to study, pray, and receive her guests.[41] In this respect, a particularly striking element of Bint al-Huda's life is that she did not marry, despite the numerous suitors who reportedly proposed to her family.[42] According to the sources, she decided not to get married because she felt that her religion needed her and she was not ready to be constrained by the limitations of a marital life that the atmosphere of the period she lived in would have imposed onto her.[43] Moreover, as she was the only daughter, she felt a strong responsibility towards her ill mother.[44] Based on interviews with Fatima al-Sadr and Ja'far al-Sadr (Muhammad Baqir's only son), Anisi gives four reasons for Bint al-Huda's decision not to get married: she did not find someone who completely suited her; she did it for the sake of her family; she wanted to take care of her sick mother; and she did not want to interrupt her battle for the faith and missionary activities and feared that she would not be able to balance her marital and listed activities.[45] On a different tone, in her essay on Bint al-Huda, Pursley advances the hypothesis that her decision not to marry simply puts on a line of coherence in Amina's thoughts and actions, in that as a never-married woman she concretely put into practice her 'critiques of the contemporary liberal-secular imaginary that valued the child-centred conjugal family over all other types of human relationality'; critiques that, according to Pursley, are very present in, and central to, Bint al-Huda's writings.[46] Indeed, she even describes Amina as 'an unmarried and childless intellectual'.[47] Clearly enough, the issue of Bint al-Huda's non-marriage was very unusual and has engendered debatable hypotheses, if not some controversy.

The Written Production of Iraq's Bint al-Huda, the First Female Shi'i Religious Public Intellectual

Amina al-Sadr wrote in different fields such as literature, culture, and society. She is considered an important Arab Muslim woman writer. In particular, she reportedly became a successful author of short stories.[48] Her

---

[41] Anisi, *Dokhtari az Tabar-e Hedayat*, 22; al-Nu'mani, *al-Shahida Bint al-Huda*, 76. In this respect, however, Dr Fatima Tabataba'i told me that Bint al-Huda used to receive her guests in the room where her mother used to spend her entire day, as the latter had serious health problems and could not move easily. Interview with Fatima Tabataba'i (5 February 2014, Tehran).

[42] al-Nuri, *Uswat al-'Amilin*, 287; al-Nu'mani, *al-Shahida Bint al-Huda*, 34; al-Baqshi, *Waja' al-Sadr*, 136–137. Tabataba'i (2011: 15, 34) mentions that when in 1968 she visited the house of Muhammad Baqir Bint al-Huda was not married.

[43] Anisi, *Dokhtari az Tabar-e Hedayat*, 33. Based on memories collected from Fatima al-Sadr.

[44] Anisi, *Dokhtari az Tabar-e Hedayat*, 33.

[45] This last element seems to be also favoured by al-Nu'mani (2000: 20, 34). However, he points it out as one of the many cases showing how Bint al-Huda sacrificed her right to get married for her religion.

[46] Pursley, 'Daughters of the Right Path', 52.

[47] Ibid., 58.

[48] al-Nu'mani, *al-Shahida Bint al-Huda*, 106.

pseudonym, 'Bint al-Huda' (Daughter of the Right Path), derives from a juvenile work that she wrote before being twenty years old.[49] As a writer of what we might label 'Islamic edifying fiction', Bint al-Huda's strongest quality arguably is that she had the ability to address important issues linked to her project to build an ideal Muslim woman in a very accessible language and in very simple terms. On the other hand, this element also limited the overall quality of her literary production. In this respect, one can only agree with Mallat in that a critical analysis of Bint al-Huda's written production indicates that this has no particular literary value, and its relevance stems mainly from the very fact that she tried to engage her constituency using short stories, where she addresses basic ethical issues relevant to a young female Islamically oriented readership.[50] In any case, the result is a written production of a unique genre in the contemporary literature of the Orient.[51] Bint al-Huda herself gives us a clear and conscious description of the character of her literary production in the short Introduction to *Sira' min Waqi' al-Hayat* (Conflict with the Facts of Life):[52]

> My dear female readers,
>
> The object of these short stories is to represent the general concepts of the Islamic vision of life. Indeed, I believe that proposing [these] concepts at the theoretical level can neither bring change nor exercise as much influence as it would their representation through events and problems drawn from real life.

When we look at Bint al-Huda's written production from the perspective of Islamic legal practice, her writings locate her within the 'progressist' religious interpretations of her time, although still fully within the limits of an 'Islamist' interpretation of Islamic law:[53] in addition to marrying someone they choose, women can impose their own conditions to the marriage contract and in this respect include into it a clause mentioning their right to divorce or to go to the (Islamic) judge asking for separation when they find out that their husband has a defect as established by the (Islamic) law; Muslim women have the right to the full ownership and independent disposition of their personal property during their entire life (both as daughters and as married women), but when it comes to heritage their share is half that of men. It would have been interesting to know the position of Bint al-Huda as regards polygamy and temporary marriage, but they are not mentioned at all in her writings. This might indicate that she was opposed to them, as they do not exist in her articles and in her literary world. Mallat labels this attitude '*silence constructif*' (constructive silence).[54] More generally, her arguments are always grounded in direct and recurrent quotes from the Qur'an.

---

[49] Wiley, "Alima Bint al-Huda', 152.
[50] Mallat, 'Le féminisme islamique'.
[51] Ibid., 46.
[52] A translation of this passage in French is offered by Mallat. Mallat, 'Le féminisme islamique', 47.
[53] Mallat, 'Le féminisme islamique', 53–55.
[54] Ibid., 54.

Most of Bint al-Huda's written production was collected after her death and published in a three-volume set entitled *al-Majmu'a al-Qasasiyya al-Kamila* (The Complete Works of Fiction) by the Lebanese Dar al-Ta'aruf li-'l-Matbu'at at the beginning of the 1980s. The collected works were for the most part translated into Persian by Mahdi Sarhaddi and published in Tehran in 2007, in two volumes, by the Imam Moussa Sadr Cultural & Research Institute under the title of *Tavallud-i Dubare: Majmu'e-yi Dastanha* (Born Again: Collected Short Stories) and *Bar Bulandiha-yi Makke: Khatirat va-Maqalat* (On the Hills of Mecca: Memories and Essays).[55]

With reference to the Arabic edition, the first volume comprises two novellas, *al-Fadila Tantasiru* (Virtue Triumphs) and *Imra'atan wa-Rajul* (Two Women and a Man), and a collection of ten short stories, *Laytani Kuntu A'lamu* (I Wish I had Known). The second comprises a collection of short stories, *Sira' min Waqi' al-Hayat* (Conflict with the Facts of Life), a novella, *Liqa' fi 'l-Mustashfa* (Encounter in the Hospital), another collection of short stories, *al-Khala al-Da'i'a* (The Lost Aunt), the diary of one of her pilgrimages to Mecca, *Dhikrayat 'ala Tilal Makka* (Memories on the Hills of Mecca), and two poems. Finally, the third comprises a romance, *al-Bahitha 'an al-Haqiqa* (Searching for the Truth), an historical essay, *Batulat al-Mar'a al-Muslima* (The Heroism of the Muslim Woman), a collection of essays, *al-Mar'a ma'a al-Nabi* (Women with the Prophet), and a collection of the articles she wrote for her column in *al-Adwa'*, *Kalima wa-Da'wa* (A Word and an Invitation).

When Bint al-Huda was twelve years old, she began to write for a ten-page journal called in the sources alternatively *Mujtama'* (Society) or *Jama'a* (Community).[56] Later, she wrote articles for the Islamic journals *al-Adwa' al-Islamiyya* (Islamic Lights) and *al-Iman* (Faith).[57]

---

[55] Later, in 1392–1393 [SH/2013–2014–2014–2015], the Foundation published a revised edition of Bint al-Huda's translated works in a different format, a nine-volume collection titled *Majmu'e-yi Asar* (Collected Works), thus offering to the public the possibility of buying just a single or more of the short stories: Vol. 1 *Tavallud-i Dubare* (Born Again), Vol. 2 *Akharin Hadiyye* (The Last Present, originally I Wish I had Known), Vol. 3 *Du Zan va Yak Mard* (Two Women and a Man), Vol. 4 *Nabard ba Zindigi* (Conflict with the Fact of Life), Vol. 5 *Didar dar Bimaristan* (Encounter in the Hospital), Vol. 6 *Didar-i 'Arus* (Meeting the Bride, originally The Lost Aunt), Vol. 7 *Dar Gustugu-yi Haqiqat* (Searching for the Truth); in addition to the diary of one of her pilgrimages to Mecca, Vol. 8 *Bar Bulandiha-yi Makke* (Memories on the Hills of Mecca), and three different works on women in Islam, Vol. 9 *Jaygah-i Zan dar Islam* (Women's Role in Islam, it contains: Words and Guidances, originally A Word and An Invitation; Woman and Civilisation, originally The Heroism of the Muslim Woman; and Women with the Prophet). In three cases (Vols 2 and 6 and two of the three works collected in Vol 9) the title in Persian is different from the one in Arabic, and I therefore both translated the Persian title but also mentioned the translation in English of the original with reference to the Arabic edition to help the reader identify the different works. In addition to her works, also her biography authored by al-Nu'mani was translated into Persian by Najib-Allah Nuri and published by Jami'a al-Mustafa al-'Alamiyya.

[56] Anisi, *Dokhtari az Tabar-e Hedayat*, 87. According to al-Baqshi, Bint al-Huda began writing for this journal when she was eleven. Al-Baqshi, *Waja' al-Sadr*, 132.

[57] The latter published by Musa al-Ya'qubi. Al-Nu'mani, *al-Shahida Bint al-Huda*, 105–106. Moreover, Nizar has a list of the articles published by Bint al-Huda in *al-Adwa'*. Ja'far Husayn Nizar, *'Adhra' al-'Aqida wa-l-Mabda': al-Shahida Bint al-Huda* (Beirut: Dar al-Ta'aruf li-l-Matbu'at, 1985).

Bint al-Huda's collaboration with *al-Adwa'* is of particular interest for what concerns the relation with her brother and the recognition of her status as an *'ālima* within the Shi'i religious establishment. It was established by *Jama'at al-'Ulama' fi 'l-Najaf al-Ashraf* (The Society of the Ulema in Najaf). Amina began to write for the journal since its very first number appeared on 9 June 1960. There, she had her own column, under the heading 'The Voice of the Muslim Woman' (*Sawt al-Mar'a al-Muslima*).[58] In one of the articles, she expresses her great pleasure in meeting her audience 'at the beginning of each month'.[59] She not only was a regular contributor to *al-Adwa'* but, according to many sources, a member of its editorial board. She contributed to the journal for at least two years.[60] It is interesting to note that she continued to write for the journal even after her brother Muhammad Baqir had been constrained to stop his role as de facto editor following disagreements between the senior and junior ulema of the religious establishment.[61] According to Abdul-Jabar, the Society was divided among junior and senior members, and the former were entrusted with executive tasks, the foremost being to run the 'mouthpiece' of the Society, *al-Adwa' al-Islamiyya*.[62] In this framework, Muhammad Baqir gained the position of a de facto editing manager.[63] Both the Society and the journal were exclusively formed by ulema.[64] This element lends credibility to considering Bint al-Huda as a recognised *'ālima* even among the highest members of the Shi'i religious establishment in Iraq. Indeed, the written sources sustain that she was a revered religious scholar 'trusted by the highest sources of religious emulation among the Shi'as, such as Ayatollah al-'Uzma al-Khu'i'.[65] The leader of the *Jama'a* was Murtada Al Yasin[66] and the Society, in addition to Muhammad Baqir al-Sadr, counted Amina's older brother Isma'il among its senior members. In his study on *The Renewal of Islamic Law*, Mallat gives great significance to the existence of what he describes

---

[58] Journal accessed at www.noormags.com/view/fa/articlepage/610034, on 7 February 2014. In this respect, also see: Wiley, "Alima Bint al-Huda', 153; Mallat, *The Renewal of Islamic Law*, 16.

[59] Chibli Mallat, *The Renewal of Islamic Law: Muhammad Baqer as-Sadr, Najaf and the Shi'i International* (Cambridge: Cambridge University Press, 2004), 16.

[60] Pursley, 'Daughters of the Right', 55.

[61] Ibid.; Faleh Abdul-Jabar, *The Shi'ite Movement in Iraq* (London: Saqi, 2003), 119; Mallat, *The Renewal of Islamic Law*, 51.

[62] Abdul-Jabar, *The Shi'ite Movement in Iraq*, 110–127, in particular 112–113.

[63] Ibid., 112–113. In this respect, however, Aziz claims that the editor-in-chief of the journal was Muhammad Husayn Fadlallah. Talib Aziz, 'Fadlallah and the Remaking of the Marja'iya', in *The Most Learned of the Shi'a: The Institution of the Marja' Taqlid*, ed. Linda S. Walbridge (Oxford: Oxford University Press, 2001), 205–215 at 206.

[64] Abdul-Jabar, *The Shi'ite Movement in Iraq*, 110–127.

[65] 'Arif Kazim Muhammad, *al-Shahida Bint al-Huda: al-Sira wa-'l-Masira* (Beirut: Dar al-Murtada, 2004), 19.

[66] He was a maternal uncle of Bint al-Huda.

as 'an openly political journal'.[67] Through a brief analysis of its team of collaborators, he supports the idea that Bint al-Huda was a fully fledged member of a network of Shi'i leaders then being formed in Southern Iraq. In this framework, Bint al-Huda was in charge of what Mallat describes as the 'feminist rubric'.[68] There, she developed and put forward her ideal of a Muslim woman in an ideal Islamic society.

On the other hand, the primary sources – in particular those represented by women – do not shy away from pointing out the difficulties Amina faced in carrying out her role in the journal. Indeed, we know that Bint al-Huda did not pen her articles with her real name, and instead used to sign them as 'AH', the initials of her first name and of that of her father.[69]

Numerous female Islamic activists who claim to have been students or friends of Bint al-Huda stress that Bint al-Huda's short stories were one of the most striking features about her as a leader. However, it is difficult to assess to what extent her writings were read and had an impact on the life of her readership before her execution by the Iraqi regime and her 'canonization' as *the* female protagonist of the Shi'i Islamic revival of the 1960s and 1970s of the last century.

Leading by Example,[70] Bint al-Huda as Founder of Women's Modern Religious Education in Iraq

In an oral history interview recorded by the Imam Moussa Sadr Cultural & Research Institute in Tehran, Ayatollah Muhammad-'Ali Taskhiri (1944–), current secretary general of the World Forum for Proximity of Islamic Schools of Thought in Iran, describes Bint al-Huda as the founder of women's Islamic education in Iraq.[71] Amina al-Sadr is indeed considered among the founders of the al-Zahra' schools in Kazimayn, Baghdad, and Najaf, which were established in about 1967.[72] According to what is reported by Anisi,[73]

---

[67] Mallat, *The Renewal of Islamic Law*, 16.
[68] Ibid., *The Renewal of Islamic Law*, 15–16.
[69] al-Nuri, *Uswat al-'Amilin*, 285–286.
[70] See: Patricia Jeffery et al., 'Leading by Example? Women Madrasah Teachers in Rural North India', in *Women, Leadership, and Mosques: Changes in Contemporary Islamic Authority*, eds Masooda Bano and Hilary Kalmbach (Leiden and Boston: Brill, 2012), 195–216.
[71] Oral history archive of the Imam Moussa Sadr Cultural & Research Institute in Tehran. Interview: Ayatollah Muhammad-'Ali Taskhiri. Archive Number: tsh0282, 10 October 2012 (accessed 4 February 2014).
[72] al-Nu'mani, *al-Shahida Bint al-Huda*, 98; al-Nuri, *Uswa 'l-'Amilin*, 285–286. Al-Zahra' refers to the Prophet's daughter Fatima. In her memoirs, Tabataba'i claims that Bint al-Huda was a teacher at various private Islamic schools in Baghdad, Kazimayn, and Najaf. She also mentions that Bint al-Huda knew Persian fairly well. Fatima Tabataba'i, *Iqlim-i Khatirat* (Tehran: Pajuhishkadih-i Imam Khumayni va Inqilab-i Islami, 2011), 15, 34.
[73] Anisi, *Dokhtari az Tabar-e Hedayat*, 59.

these were under the supervision of Sayyid Murtada al-'Askari (1914–2007), a religious scholar who championed the establishment of Islamic modern education in Iraq[74] and a founding member of the Da'wa party.[75] Among the others, Ayatollah al-'Uzma Abu l-Qasim al-Khu'i was among those who set up the al-Zahra' primary school for girls in Najaf[76] and provided economic support for the establishment of the one in Kazimayn.[77] As supervisor of[78] and teacher in these schools, she reportedly educated hundreds of young girls, female religious activists, and *'ālimāt* (plural of *'ālima*). In this respect, however, the information provided by the primary (and secondary) sources with reference to Amina al-Sadr's role and activities as responsible for some years for different schools for girls in Iraq is contradictory – an element noticeable in many other details of her life. According to al-Baqshi, Bint al-Huda was in charge of four private and state-directed schools for girls: three in Kazimayn and Baghdad, and one in Najaf.[79] Al-Ha'iri (1987: 30) reports that the cities interested by her engagement were in fact only three: Kazimayn, Najaf, and Kut.[80] However, he is the only source to mention the city of Kut. Anisi mentions an unspecified number of schools in Kazimayn and Baghdad linked to the

---

[74] According to Corboz, he did so acting as a *wakīl* of Muhsin al-Hakim. Elvire Corboz, *Guardians of Shi'ism: Sacred Authority and Transnational Family Networks* (Edinburgh: Edinburgh University Press, 2015).

[75] Sheikh M. Khurasani, 'Ayatollah Murtada Al-Askari Buried in Holy Qom', *Jafariyanews*, 21 September 2007, www.jafariyanews.com/2k7_news/sep/21ayatulla_askari_funeral.htm, last accessed 10 August 2017.

[76] Yusuf al-Khoei, 'Abū 'l-Qāsim al-Ḫū'ī', *The Role of the Sādāt/Ašrāf in Muslim History and Civilization*, eds Biancamaria Scarcia Amoretti and Laura Bottini, special issue of *Oriente Moderno* XVIII (LXXIX).2 (1999), 491–500 at 493; Yusuf al-Kho'i, 'Grand Ayatollah Abu al-Qassim al-Kho'i: Political Thought and Positions', in *Ayatollahs, Sufis and Ideologues: State, Religion and Social Movements in Iraq*, ed. Faleh Abdul-Jabar (London: Saqi Books, 2002), 223–230.

[77] This at least according to one of my oral sources, Sayyid Jawad al-Khu'i (interview in his house in Qom, February 2008). Jawad also mentioned that the school in Kazimayn had in fact been established with the economic support of his grandfather, Abu 'l-Qasim.

[78] Wiley and Pursley refer to Bint al-Huda as 'principal' of those schools. Wiley, "Alima Bint al-Huda, 154; Pursley, 'Daughters of the Right Path'. Anisi alternatively refers to her role with the words *mudīr* (director, manager, principal, superintendent, school master), *nezārat* (supervision, superintendence, overseeing), and *sarparastī* (supervision, superintendence). Anisi, *Dokhtari az Tabar-e Hedayat*, 59–60, 136. Al-Baqshi uses the expression *kāna tahta yadihā* (it was under her authority). Al-Baqshi, *Waja' al-Sadr*, 137. In this respect, however, Nu'mani mentions that the director of the al-Zahra' schools was, in fact, Wajihah Al-Saydali. Al-Nu'mani, *al-Shahida Bint al-Huda*, 99. He moreover reproduces an article by al-Saydali, originally published in *al-Minbar*, No. 24, p. 8, in which she claims that Bint al-Huda was among the founders of the schools and had the role of supervisor. Ibid., 99–100. Overall, it seems more probable that Bint al-Huda was more of a supervisor than the director of the schools.

[79] al-Baqshi, *Waja' al-Sadr*, 137–138. With respect to this *madrasa*, al-Baqshi mentions that it was located in the neighbourhood of al-Mishraq, close to the Shrine of Imam 'Ali. Ibid., 137.

[80] al-Ha'iri, 'Tarjamat Hayat al-Sayyid al-Shahid', 30.

Sanduq-i Khayriye-yi Islami (Charitable Islamic Fund) and two schools in Najaf.[81] As regards the schools in Najaf, one was called Jami'a al-Ta'limat al-Islamiyya (Association for Islamic Education) and had been established and was administered under the supervision of Ayatollah al-'Uzma al-Khu'i.[82] Again, one of Anisi's sources, Zahra' al-Ha'iri, daughter of one of the founders of the school, 'Abd al-Rahim al-Ha'iri,[83] mentions that in 1967 she was among the first students to enrol in the al-Zahra' School in Kazimayn.[84] Therefore, it might be possible that it was established in that very year. The other school is alternatively referred to by Anisi as Idare-yi Amuzish-i Dini (Office for Religious Education)[85] or Markaz-i Amuzish-i Dini (Centre for Religious Education).[86] The information and name of the Idare-yi Amuzish-i Dini was provided to Anisi by Umm Furqan, a former student and friend of Bint al-Huda. Umm Furqan, moreover, mentions that Bint al-Huda used to spend the first three days of the week in Baghdad and the remaining days in Najaf. Moreover, according to the same source, who quotes the very words of Bint al-Huda, the latter used to spend the mornings in occupations linked to her responsibility as supervisor, and the second part of the day holding meetings in her house or in the house of her friends. A first-hand source on Bint al-Huda's educational activities is represented by Dr Ashraf Borujerdi, whose memories about Bint al-Huda are available in the oral history archive of the Imam Moussa Sadr Cultural & Research Institute in Tehran. Dr Borujerdi is a former student of the al-Zahra' School in Najaf and a disciple of Bint al-Huda. She left Iraq in 1350 [SH/1971–1972], when she was fourteen years old, after having studied for five years in the Markaz Ta'lim al-Banat (Centre for Girls' Education) – from the second to the sixth term. Having left Iraq for Iran, she continued to be in contact with Bint al-Huda, exchanging with her a written correspondence. Asked about the actual name of her school, that is, al-Zahra' School or Markaz al-Ta'lim al-Dini li-'l-Banat (Centre for Girls'

[81] Anisi, *Dokhtari az Tabar-e Hedayat*, 59, 113–114, 136, 140. In this respect, and with regard to Najaf, Anisi on three occasions (pp. 59, 113–114, and 136) mentions only one school while, on a different occasion (p. 140), mentions the existence of a second school.

[82] Ibid., 59, 113–114. She reports that this information was given to her by Mrs Rashidiyan, who was herself a teacher at the Jami'e-yi Ta'limat-i Islami School in Najaf. Moreover, one of Anisi's sources reports that the Jami'e-yi Ta'limat-i Islami School was not allowed to issue official state-recognised certificates and that the (all female) students who wished to obtain official certificates had to undergo final-year examinations as external private candidates in public institutes. More generally, Anisi offers an interesting insider account on the establishment and early steps of the school. Ibid., 113–114.

[83] According to the same source, the third founder was Zahra's paternal uncle Yusuf 'Abd al-Ghaffar.

[84] Anisi, *Dokhtari az Tabar-e Hedayat*, 118.

[85] Ibid., 136.

[86] Ibid., 140. The information is provided by Umm Furqan.

Religious Education), Dr Borujerdi sustains that there was no such thing as the al-Zahra' School, and that her school was known under the name of Markaz al-Ta'lim al-Dini li-'l-Banat, adding that these centres were known to have been established by Ayatollah al-'Uzma al-Hakim. In this respect, she affirms that most probably some people knew the centres as al-Zahra' schools, but these were known to be administered by the Board of Trustees of the Markaz al-Ta'lim al-Dini li-'l-Banat. She also sustains that the schools had their own principals, but their overall responsibility was under the supervision of Bint al-Huda. In this respect, the role of Amina appears very much as the usual role carried out by 'official' male representatives or envoys of the *marja'iyya*. Dr Borujerdi also sustains that Bint al-Huda used to organise her week in the following manner: she spent two days in Najaf, two days in Kazimayn, and two days in Karbala.[87] Hence, she adds a further city to those touched by the activities of Bint al-Huda. She even mentions that sometimes Bint al-Huda used to go also to Basra. Dr Borujerdi furthermore affirms that 90% of the students of these schools were daughters of ulema, who could not attend public schools, and about 80% of ulema who had come to Iraq from Iran. In this respect, she recalls how the mother tongue of these students was Persian – the language that the students used at home – and that Bint al-Huda had prohibited the use of this language among the students, and insisted they learn and use Arabic.[88] She also mentions that all the teachers were female, and most of them used to work also in the public-school system. Finally, she sustains that the students used to study the same subjects as in public schools, in addition to religious studies. The lessons on religion were delivered by Amina, and consisted of Qur'anic exegesis, Islamic rulings, hadith, and other subjects. At least, this was the case of Dr Borujerdi's own school in Najaf. She evaluates the overall establishment of the schools and Bint al-Huda's role as a 'revolution for the daughters of families of religious scholars'.

The apparent inconsistency of the primary oral sources is partly resolved by an article signed by the very Bint al-Huda and published in the monthly *al-Muntalaq* (The Starting Point) (Bint al-Huda 1980).[89] There, she describes

---

[87] Oral history archive of the Imam Moussa Sadr Cultural & Research Institute in Tehran. Interview: Dr Ashraf Borujerdi. Archive Number: tsh0273, 17 December 2012 (accessed 4 February 2014).

[88] In fact, this affirmation is contradicted by what I was told by Dr Fatima Tabataba'i (5 February 2014, Tehran). In the interview, Tabataba'i recalled how during her permanence in Najaf, where her family was a guest at the very house of Muhammad Baqir al-Sadr for two months, one day she went with Bint al-Huda to the school she supervised in that city. According to what she remembers, the students spoke Arabic and, as she could not understand what they were saying, Bint al-Huda translated it for her. Tabataba'i also mentioned that at that time one of Muhammad Baqir's daughters was a student at the same institute.

[89] Amina Bint al-Huda, 'Hawla Markaz Ta'lim al-Banat wa-Madrasa al-Zahra'', *al-Muntalaq* 11, 11 September 1980, <www.noormags.com/view/fa/articlepage/487985>, last accessed 7 February 2014.

the al-Zahra' School as the sister of Markaz Ta'lim al-Banat, established following the successful experience and with the same aims of the latter.

Bint al-Huda held these responsibilities for seven years, until 1972.[90] In that year, the government nationalised private schools and she resigned in protest.[91] In this respect, however, a source claims that following the closure of the al-Zahra' School in Kazimayn Bint al-Huda continued to be active in the Markaz-i Amuzish-i Dini in Najaf for two years. This because, despite the fact that the school had been closed down, she remained in contact with the female students and used to hold bi-weekly classes of *Shara'i' al-Islam* and programmes in which she taught about Islamic law issues.[92]

Within the framework of her activities with young girls, a last one to be mentioned is the organization of what is known in Persian as *jashn-i taklif* (celebration of puberty or coming-of-age).[93] In Shi'ism, at the age of nine girls stop being children and become *mukallaf* (duty-bound or of age), thus starting to have religious and legal responsibilities such as veiling, daily prayer, fasting, and being marriable. This practice became a major public event in Iran following the establishment of the Islamic Republic, but was not common practice - possibly did not even exist - among Shi'as before the revolution.[94] Once again, it is difficult to evaluate the historical reliability of information related to Amina al-Sadr's life and activities. But once again her image as a 'pioneer' female religious scholar (and activist) is unquestionable.

The Other Half of the Mission, Bint al-Huda as the Female Spiritual Leader of al-Da'wa

Bint al-Huda operated in a socio-political context characterised by an increasing process of 'Ba'thisation' and 'laicisation' of Iraqi society. Women were a major target of this process, and Bint al-Huda's socio-religious activism was particularly aimed at resisting it.[95] In line with her brother Muhammad Baqir, on the one hand she concentrated her efforts on offering alternative Islamic ways of education to new generations of young female Muslims who would

---

[90] al-Nu'mani, *al-Shahida Bint al-Huda*, 102; al-Ha'iri, 'Tarjama Hayat al-Sayyid al-Shahid', 30. In this respect, Wiley affirms that Bint al-Huda's engagement with the madrasas involved only Kazimayn and Najaf. Wiley, "Alima Bint al-Huda, 154.

[91] al-Nu'mani, *al-Shahida Bint al-Huda*, 102; Anisi, *Dokhtari az Tabar-e Hedayat*, 136.
In the case of Anisi, the information was provided to her by Umm Furqan. It, however, contradicts what is related by another source of Anisi, Zahra' al-Ha'iri, daughter of one of the founders of the al-Zahra' School in Kazimayn. Al-Ha'iri affirms that she was among the first students to enrol in the School, in 1967, and that she studied there for six years. Then, in 1975, private schools were closed down and she was obliged to enrol in a public school, also called al-Zahra'. See: Anisi, *Dokhtari az Tabar-e Hedayat*, 126.

[92] Anisi, *Dokhtari az Tabar-e Hedayat*, 140. The information is provided by Umm Furqan.

[93] Ibid., 126.

[94] Azam Torab, *Performing Islam: Gender and Ritual in Iran* (Leiden and Boston: Brill, 2007), 169–193.

[95] al-Nu'mani, *al-Shahida Bint al-Huda*, 109.

have otherwise been lost to the prevailing ideologies of communism and liberalism and, on the other, she tried to develop an alternative vision of the modern Muslim woman. She was among the first Shi'i Muslim women, reportedly the first,[96] to resort to writing short stories as an instrument to attract young girls to religious values and ethics in Iraq in the 1960s and 1970s.[97]

In this context, one should not be surprised to find out that, in the framework of her interviews with Shi'i 'Islamist' activist women of the Iraqi diaspora in Dearborn (United States), and more concretely with an activist at the Kerbala Education Centre claiming to be a former student of Amina al-Sadr, Nadje Sadiq Al-Ali describes Bint al-Huda as 'the spiritual female leader of al-Dawa'.[98] This view was promoted by the English website of the Islamic Dawa Party, where her biography, narrated in the 'Dawa People' section of the website, was available alongside those of her brother Muhammad Baqir and of the (former) Iraqi prime minister party leader Nuri al-Maliki.[99]

Bint al-Huda as Representative (*wakīla*) for Muhammad Baqir al-Sadr? The First and Only Known Female Religious Authority in Contemporary Najaf?

As far as contemporary history is concerned, Bint al-Huda was the first, or in any case among a very few Shi'i women religious activists whose different activities, from writing to teaching, were financed with funds related to the *ḥawza* and *marja'iyya* of Najaf. She was instrumental in Iraq in the 1960s and 1970s in favouring socio-religious activism among women of religious families outside of the 'closed doors' within which they used to live.[100] She was especially active in holding prayer gatherings and religious discussion groups for women, particularly during the month of Ramadan.[101] More generally, al-Nu'mani reports:

> What I can say with certainty is that the martyr Bint al-Huda generally was very well versed in [Islamic] jurisprudential rulings. She was a shelter for many female believers [as a source] of knowledge of [Islamic] law rulings. She also was the female religious leader of women for the hajj, and is it known that the issues of the hajj and its religious law rulings are among the most difficult and vast [in number].[102]

---

[96] Anisi, *Dokhtari az Tabar e Hedayat*, 126. According to al-Nu'mani, this was at least the case of Najaf and of its *ḥawza* and *marja'iyya*. Al-Nu'mani, *al-Shahida Bint al-Huda*, 105.

[97] al-Nu'mani, *al-Shahida Bint al-Huda*, 92–93.

[98] Nadje Sadig Al-Ali, *Iraqi Women: Untold Stories from 1948 to the Present* (London and New York: Zed Books, 2007), 161.

[99] <www.islamicdawaparty.com/?module=home&fname=leaderdesc.php&id=77>, last accessed 2 February 2014. This is not the case, however, of the website of the party in Arabic (www.al-daawa.org) nor, indeed, of main websites in the same language linked to the various offshoots of the party (dawa-party.com, www.islamicdawaparty.org, aldaawa-io.org), all accessed February 2014.

[100] Anisi, *Dokhtari az Tabar-e Hedayat*, 147. See also the Introduction written by Sayyid Husayn al-Sadr to al-Nu'mani. al-Nu'mani, *al-Shahida Bint al-Huda*, 12.

[101] Anisi, *Dokhtari az Tabar-e Hedayat*, 142.

[102] al-Nu'mani, *al-Shahida Bint al-Huda*, 28.

In this chapter, I argue that Amina al-Sadr more concretely acted as a link between the *marja'iyya* of her brother and his female followers. Indeed, in what is commonly referred to as the 'traditional *marja'iyya*', the members of the family of the *marja'*, represented by his sons and sons-in-law, usually are his most important *wakīls*. This is the case, for example, of Ayatollah al-'Uzma Sayyid 'Ali al-Sistani, whose main representative in Iran (and worldwide, in particular Asia and Africa) is his son-in-law Sayyid Jawad al-Shahristani; in London (Europe and the US) is Sayyid Murtada al-Kashmiri (another son-in-law); and in Najaf (and Iraq) is his son Sayyid Muhammad Rida al-Sistani, who even de facto also teaches *baḥth al-khārij* instead of his father and is his main mediator to the Iraqi government.[103] Amina al-Sadr might well be the first known case of an *'ālima* who acted as *wakīla* for a *marja'*, her brother Muhammad Baqir al-Sadr. In this respect, it could be argued that a major reason for this singularity, that is, the absence of other known *wakīlas*, might have been the lack of female religious scholars within families whose members have reached the level of *marja'*.

The functions and roles of the *wakīl* (pl. *wukalā'*[104]) seem to have received little attention or interest among academia. Usually, it is not mentioned even in the works on Shi'ism and, when this is the case, it is rarely accompanied by an explanation or definition.[105] On the other hand, the term is listed in the

---

[103] Mehdi Khalaji, *The Last Marja: Sistani and the End of Traditional Religious Authority in Shiism*, Policy Focus #59 (Washington, DC: Washington Institute for Near East Policy, 2006), 10–12. Al-Sistani reportedly quit teaching in 1999 and never resumed it again.

[104] As far as the *marja'iyya*-linked use of the word is concerned, to the best of my knowledge this is not attested in the feminine form. In this respect, for example, it is not to be found in the glossary of *Terms Describing Female Leaders and Leadership* provided at the end of Bano and Kalmbach. It is worth mentioning that the words *wakīl* (pl. *wukalā'*) and/or *wikāla* are altogether absent in fact from the volume and not to be found at all in the pages covering its two sets of glossaries. Bano and Kalmbach (eds), *Women, Leadership, and Mosques*, 536–556.

[105] For example, *wakīl/wukalā'* is not listed in the glossary of Moomen, nor it is to be found in the Index of Arjomand, nor in Litvak. Moojan Moomen, *An Introduction to Shi'i Islam: The History and Doctrines of Twelver Shi'ism* (New Haven and London: Yale University Press, 1985), xix–xxii; Said Amir Arjomand (ed.), *Authority and Political Culture in Shi'ism* (Albany: State University of New York Press, 1988), 383–393; Meir Litvak, *Shi'i Scholars of Nineteenth-Century Iraq: The 'Ulama' of Najaf and Karbala'* (Cambridge: Cambridge University Press, 1998). In fact, Litvak relevantly mentions that al-Najafi 'used to delegate to his students the authority to judge on his behalf thereby consolidating the function of *marja'iyya* and attaching them to himself', therefore giving a single but useful mention of one of the aspects linked to the issue of the roles of a *marja'*'s representatives. Litvak, *Shi'i Scholars of Nineteenth-Century Iraq*, 67. *The Encyclopaedia of Islam* (EI2 2002, Vol. 11, 57–58) dedicates one entire page to the word *wakāla*. However, it describes *wakāla* almost only in terms of commercial practice and law, without any reference to the issues debated here. Nevertheless, the introductory short definition given in the EI2 is of some interest for my hypothesis: 'It means to commission, depute or authorise a person to act on behalf of another.' In addition to this, one can note that the concept is not even discussed in the *Encyclopaedia Iranica*. The most detailed, or at least longest, description of the functions and roles of the *wukalā'* in contemporary Shi'ism is to be found in a work of political science: Khalaji, *The Last Marja*, 8–9. In addition to Khalaji, see: Robert J. Riggs, 'Partisan and Global Identity in the Historiography of Iraqi Religious Institutions', in *Writing the Modern History of Iraq: Historiographical and Political Challenges*, eds Jordi Tejel et al. (Hachensack: World Scientific, 2012), 303–320.

glossary given by Ahmad Kazemi Moussavi,[106] but the entry is simply given as '*wakīl*: agent, deputy'. Moreover, it is to be found in *Les mondes chiites et l'Iran*, edited by Sabrina Mervin:

> wakîl/vakil: agent d'un *marja'* qui le représente dans un lieu donné, et perçoit pour lui les impôts religieux.[107]

More relevantly to my hypothesis, the role of the *wukalā'* is shortly addressed in Abdul-Jabar.[108] The relevance is given by the fact that this is done in reference to Muhammad Baqir al-Sadr. According to Abdul-Jabar, at the time of the Islamic Revolution in Iran, al-Sadr had about 100 *wukalā'* and they were present in at least twelve towns across the Middle East, including Baghdad.[109] This estimate is mainly based on what was reported by one of al-Sadr's close disciples, al-Ha'iri.[110] In the framework of his socio-political analysis of the Shi'i movement in Iraq, Abdul-Jabar describes the *wukalā'* as

> mostly low-ranking sheikhs [apparently here with the meaning of non-*sayyid* ulema] and *sayyid*s [ulema] or some devout laypeople who act as mediators for the collection of *khums*, the organization of pilgrimages and the like.[111]

As far as the role of Bint al-Huda as representative of Muhammad Baqir al-Sadr is concerned, we have already discussed what is narrated by Fatima al-Sadr in her memoirs. In the same spirit, al-Nu'mani relates:

> Sayyida the Martyr had a big role in connecting Sayyid the Martyr with women. She used to convey directly to Sayyid the Martyr with faithfulness the legal questions that were of concern for women and [that] they were reluctant to direct [to him] because of shyness . . . And this was not the only role she had, rather she used to convey to him the precise exposition of women's problems, affairs, and afflictions, and the suggestions for remedying them and the likes.[112]

---

[106] Ahmad Kazemi Moussavi, *Religious Authority in Shi'ite Islam: From the Office of Mufti to the Institution of Marja'* (Kuala Lumpur: ISTAC, 1996), 319.

[107] Sabrina Mervin (ed.), *Les mondes chiites et l'Iran* (Paris: Karthala-ifpo, 2007).

[108] Faleh Abdul-Jabar (ed.), *Ayatollahs, Sufis and Ideologues: State, Religion and Social Movements in Iraq* (London: Saqi Books, 2002).

[109] Abdul-Jabar (ed.), *Ayatollahs, Sufis and Ideologues*, 228, 230. With reference to studies conducted on the topic of contemporary Shi'i religious and political movements and networks, it is worth mentioning that the word *wakīl/wukalā'* is, for example, found only twice in Louër – a 301-page book largely dedicated to the study of a *marja'*-based network (the one of the al-Shirazi and al-Mudarrisi families). Laurence Louër, *Transnational Shia Politics: Religious and Political Networks in the Gulf* (New York: Columbia University Press, 2008), 75, 290. Interestingly enough, however, one of the two mentions introduces the expression *wakīl muṭlaq*, that Louër translates as 'main representative' of a *marja'* (al-Sistani) in a specific country (Bahrain).

[110] al-Ha'iri, 'Tarjamat Hayat al-Sayyid al-Shahid', 116, 120–121.

[111] Abdul-Jabar (ed.), *Ayatollahs, Sufis and Ideologues*, 230.

[112] al-Nu'mani, *al-Shahida Bint al-Huda*, 108.

More to the point, the heading of the section from which the above-quoted passage is taken is entitled 'The Role of Connecting the *Marja'* with the Requests for Religious Advice'. In terms of religious authority, this role is conveyed by the *wakīl*s of the *marja'*. In this respect, answering to questions about Bint al-Huda's role in relation to Muhammad Baqir al-Sadr, Fatima al-Sadr affirmed that she was authorised by her brother to answer the questions on religious law rulings posed by those requesting them and to provide explanation on religious law rulings.[113] Fatima underlined that Bint al-Huda also provided guidance on religious law rulings to followers of other *marja'*s of her time on the basis of their fatwas.

An important role covered by religious scholars (ulema) in terms of religious authority and function is represented by the religious duties regarding the hajj rituals that Muslim worshippers need to learn in order to perform it. The religious rulings for the hajj are very sophisticated.[114] During the hajj, pilgrims are organised in caravans. The role of the religious scholar in the caravan is to guide each pilgrim to fulfil their ritual duties, which can slightly change in accordance with the interpretation of their *marja'* of choice. Another important role covered by a religious scholar in respect of their caravan or group of believers is to collect religious taxes and donations. Once the caravans arrive in Mecca, pilgrims refer to the local offices representing the different *marja'*s.[115] As we have seen, the requests for religious advice and Bint al-Huda's role and recognised knowledge in religious jurisprudential rules, as 'a shelter for many female believers [in terms of a source] of knowledge of [religious] law rulings', was particularly relevant in relation to her role as a female religious leader for the hajj.[116] In this respect, the sources tell us that every year Bint al-Huda led a group of about 200 women, both married and unmarried, to Mecca and Medina for this purpose.[117] According to Anisi, the presence of unmarried women in the group is particularly significant because, at that time, the conditions of the hajj were harsh and difficult for women, both from a sanitary and from a security perspective.[118] Therefore, the presence of unmarried women might indicate an important level of trust enjoyed by Bint al-Huda. In any case, it should be stressed that the hajj groups were, overall, still led by men, who took care of the most

---

[113] Written communication received from Fatima al-Sadr through the intermediary of Hawra' al-Sadr, February 2014.

[114] al-Nu'mani, *al-Shahida Bint al-Huda*, 28.

[115] Interview with Dr Fatima Tabataba'i.

[116] al-Nu'mani, *al-Shahida Bint al-Huda*, 28, 107.

[117] Anisi, *Dokhtari az Tabar-e Hedayat*, 127. In 1978, Bint al-Huda, moreover, performed the umrah together with her mother and other members of her family. Al-Nu'mani also mentions that he went with them to Mecca and was particularly impressed by how she took care of her sick mother. Al-Nu'mani, *al-Shahida Bint al-Huda*, 50.

[118] In this respect, she mentioned the case of a huge fire in Mecca that in 1975 killed about 200 pilgrims, injuring many others. On that occasion, as Anisi was told by her mother, a number of women died, and others got lost. Phone interview with Fariba Anisi, Tehran, 24 April 2018.

important organizational aspects of the pilgrimage. Within this framework, we can deduce that Bint al-Huda's role was primarily to help women fulfil their religious duties and deal with handling ordinary problems that might occur during the trip. In this last respect, it is worth remembering that Bint al-Huda wrote a small but useful travelogue on the pilgrimage, *Dhikrayat 'ala Tilal Makka* (Memories on the Hills of Mecca), where she relates her own personal experience as a female pilgrim but also addresses concrete matters of religious and ritual practice linked to the hajj. As regards the presence of women more generally, Anisi pointed out that, according to interviews she had with disciples and friends of Bint al-Huda, in particular in the last three to four years, Bint al-Huda insisted very much on the fact that women should be intellectually and economically independent, which might help explain the presence of probably young, unmarried women in the group of pilgrims.

Of particular relevance as regards the main issue being discussed here, is that, answering to questions about Bint al-Huda's role during the hajj, Hawra' al-Sadr (daughter of Muhammad Baqir al-Sadr and niece of Amina al-Sadr) indicates that during the hajj Bint al-Huda also went to a hajj office to represent her brother, to answer to questions on religious law rulings and other issues as representative of her brother. However, she pointed out that, because of his difficult situation in respect to both politics and the *ḥawza,* Muhammad Baqir did not have his own hajj office and instead used the one of the Ayatollah al-'Uzma al-Ya'qubi.[119] Therefore, we can conclude that it is there that Bint al-Huda used to go during the hajj. Moreover, Hawra' pointed out that Bint al-Huda also answered questions on religious law rulings posed by followers of other *marja*'s – information corroborated by what I was told also by her sister-in-law, Fatima al-Sadr. In this respect, it is interesting to mention that al-Nu'mani sustains that when, during the hajj, Bint al-Huda was consulted about issues that were not present in the religious manuals of the *marja*'s followed by the enquirer, she would phone her brother in order to ask him for the religious ruling.[120]

There is a final element important in the role of a *wakīl*, the collection and disposition of the *khums* (a religious 'tax' paid to a *marja'*) or *al-ḥuqūq al-shar'iyya*. This is problematic. My experience with the Shi'i religious establishment of Najaf and Qom indicates that its members rarely mention this issue and, when they indirectly do it, it is only to underline that the money collected in this way is entirely spent for legitimate religious purposes.[121]

[119] Personal written communication I exchanged with Hawra' al-Sadr, February 2014.

[120] al-Nu'mani, *al-Shahida Bint al-Huda*, 107.

[121] Tabataba'i, *Iqlim-i Khatirat*, 100–101; al-Nu'mani, *al-Shahida Bint al-Huda*, 49; Muhammad Reza al-Nu'mani, *al-Shahid al-Sadr, Sanawat al-Mihna wa-Ayyam al-Hisar*, 2nd edn (Qum: Mu'assasa-ye Isma'iliyan, 1997), 116–117.

We know that, at least in the contemporary history of the Near East, it has not been uncommon to have women distribute – and hence possibly collect – Islamic religious taxes and charity – an element noticed by anthropologists as early as the 1950s, 1960s, and 1970s, the period when Bint al-Huda's activities are located.[122] Therefore, it is possible to hypothesise that she might indeed have been a representative of her brother also in this respect. For example, we know that Bint al-Huda had under her supervision some schools and their expenses that were financed, among the others, by the *marja'iyya* of her brother Muhammad Baqir.

The hypothesis put forward above seems to be corroborated by personal written communications I exchanged with Hawra' al-Sadr (daughter of Muhammad Baqir al-Sadr). Answering to a direct question in this respect, she affirmed that 'we do firmly believe that the martyr [Bint al-Huda] was authorised by Sayyid the Martyr [Muhammad Baqir al-Sadr], even though [only] orally'.[123] More concretely, answering questions on the same issue, Fatima al-Sadr affirmed that Bint al-Huda was authorised by her brother to collect *khums*. Moreover, she sustained that Bint al-Huda was also authorised by him to determine the disposition of 30 per cent of those funds.[124]

From what is stated by Hawra' al-Sadr, we can assume that, most probably, this act of representation was not based on a written statement by her brother but instead an oral agreement. This would not have been particularly unusual within the *marja'iyya*. A partly similar case is, for example, offered by Ayatollah Khomeini and his son Ahmad (1945–1995). Although the latter was his father's main representative for a relevant part of the former's *marja'iyya* (and leadership of the newly established Islamic Republic of Iran), he never received a formal written letter of *wikāla* from him. This at least according to Dr Fatima Tabataba'i, who explained this in light of the fact that Ahmad was very close to his father.[125] This is also the case of Bint al-Huda, who lived in her brother's very house.

A Late Episode: Muhammad Baqir al-Sadr's House Arrests and Bint al-Huda's Historical Sermon in the Shrine

Amina was always a companion to her brother Muhammad Baqir, and bore the tremendous burden of its consequences.[126] This was especially the case when he was arrested a first time in 1971 and, then, a second time in 1977.[127]

---

[122] Robert A. Fernea and Elizabeth W. Fernea, 'Variation in Religious Observance among Islamic Women', in *Scholars, Saints, and Sufis: Muslim Religious Institutions since 1500*, pbk edn, ed. Nikki R. Keddie (Berkeley: University of California Press, 1972 [1978]), 385–401 at 390.

[123] Personal written communication I exchanged with Hawra' al-Sadr, February 2014.

[124] Written communication, received from Fatima al-Sadr through the intermediary of Hawra' al-Sadr, February 2014.

[125] Interview with Dr Fatima Tabataba'i.

[126] al-Nu'mani, *al-Shahida Bint al-Huda*, 115.

[127] Ibid., 116–117.

On 16 *Rajab* 1399 (AH/11–12 June 1979), the Iraqi security services arrested her brother Muhammad Baqir for a third time.[128] According to the sources, Bint al-Huda uselessly tried to oppose the arrest. She went out to the street, stood in front of the car where her brother was being held waiting to be brought to prison, and gave a fierce speech – a 'Zaynabian speech', according to the sources.[129] Having been unable to avoid the arrest, she decided to go to the Shrine of Imam 'Ali to publicly denounce it and urge the believers, both men and women, to intervene and demand his liberation.[130] Following her denunciation, the news of Muhammad Baqir al-Sadr's arrest began to spread, and street demonstrations were held in Najaf, to which massive demonstrations followed in Najaf, Karbala, Kufa, and Baghdad.[131] As a consequence of Bint al-Huda's denunciation and of street protests, her brother was soon released and brought back from Baghdad to Najaf.[132] However, the Iraqi authorities de facto posed him under house arrests for nine months. The security services not only barred him, and his entire family, from leaving his house, but reportedly even cut the electricity, water, and telephone lines.[133] After a while, Bint al-Huda was able to get out and started to go at regular times every day to the Shrine of Imam 'Ali and to act as a link between the members of the house and the exterior,[134] and in particular between Muhammad Baqir and his close disciples and followers (via the latter's wives). From this information, it is evident once more that Bint al-Huda was both authorised by her brother to represent him and accepted by people as his representative.

Martyrdom 'On the Path of God', and of Her Brother

Bint al-Huda literally accompanied her brother to the very end of his (and her own) life. On 5 April 1980, the Ba'thist regime once again imprisoned Bint al-Huda's brother, Muhammad Baqir.[135] The day after, they arrested Bint

---

[128] Anisi, *Dokhtari az Tabar-e Hedayat*, 169–172. Anisi's account of the event is largely based on al-Nu'mani, *al-Shahida Bint al-Huda*.

[129] al-Nu'mani, *al-Shahida Bint al-Huda*, 118–124.

[130] Anisi, *Dokhtari az Tabar-e Hedayat*, 173–177; al-Nu'mani, *al-Shahida Bint al-Huda*, 118–124.

[131] Charles Tripp, *A History of Iraq*, 2nd edn (Cambridge: Cambridge University Press, 2002), 220–221.

[132] Anisi, *Dokhtari az Tabar-e Hedayat*, 178–183, 192; al-Nu'mani, *al-Shahida Bint al-Huda*, 124–127.

[133] al-Nu'mani, *al-Shahida Bint al-Huda*, 127–128; Muhammad Reza al-Nu'mani, 'Faratar az Bavar. . .: Vapasin Fasl az Hayat-i Mubarizati Shahid Amina Bint al-Huda Sadr', in 'Bint al-Huda Sadr', *Shuhada-yi Zan*, special issue of *Shahide Yaran: Mahname-yi Farhangi-Tarikhi*, n.s., 27.35 (2008), 83–87. Mentioned also in Anisi, from the same source. Anisi, *Dokhtari az Tabar-e Hedayat*, 192–193; al-Nu'mani, *al-Shahida Bint al-Huda*. However, on the basis of one of her oral sources, Anisi also writes that the duration of the house arrests was (in fact) ten months. Anisi, *Dokhtari az Tabar-e Hedayat*, 211–212.

[134] al-Nu'mani, *al-Shahida Bint al-Huda*, 141.

[135] Ibid., 145. Mentioned also in Anisi from the same source. Anisi, *Dokhtari az Tabar-e Hedayat*, 224.

al-Huda also.[136] Reportedly, her arrest was undertaken in order to avoid the reoccurrence of what had happened during the previous detention of her brother, when she had gone to the Shrine urging the community of believers to intervene and oppose the arrest – and had indeed obtained his release.

On 8 April 1980, she was assassinated by the Iraqi security services together with her brother.[137] According to some sources, they were both killed by bullets fired by Saddam Hussein himself[138] while others only mention the case of Muhammad Baqir al-Sadr, affirming that he had been killed and that his face showed signs of torture.[139] Whatever the case, she became one of the first – and apparently the first – female 'martyrs' of the Shi'i religious revival in Iraq.

On the night of 9 April 1980, at about 9 or 10, the police cut the electricity of the entire city of Najaf and a group of members of the security services went to the house of Muhammad Saqid al-Sadr, Muhammad Baqir's first cousin on the father's side, and told him to follow them to the Provincial Office of Najaf.[140] Once there the accounts related by the primary sources are contradictory. According to some sources, they showed him both the dead bodies of Muhammad Baqir and Bint al-Huda while, according to other sources, they showed him only the dead body of Muhammad Bariq and, then, went with him to an unspecified place in the cemetery of Wadi al-Salam, burying him there.[141] Indeed, according to a majority of sources, the body of Amina was never returned to her family, but there are important differences concerning the events related to Bint al-Huda's dead body. Al-Nu'mani reports that on the night of 9 April 1980 the police showed Muhammad Sadiq al-Sadr the dead bodies of both Muhammad Baqir and Amina, telling him to bury both but not to speak with anyone of the death of Bint al-Huda.[142] By contrast, Aziz, on the basis of information related by members of the al-Sadr family, writes that Amina's body was never given back to her family, and even reports that 'according to one of Sadr's cousins, the family of Sadr still hopes that the regime has spared the life of Amina al-Sadr, but the Islamic movement always refers to her as a martyr'.[143] Indeed, this information is confirmed also by female members of the al-Sadr family I interviewed. Finally, Anisi reports both versions. On the one hand, on the

---

[136] Anisi, *Dokhtari az Tabar-e Hedayat*, 228; al-Nu'mani, *al-Shahida Bint al-Huda*, 146.

[137] Anisi, *Dokhtari az Tabar-e Hedayat*, 228. In her autobiography, Fatima Tabataba'i (2011: 15, 34) writes that in 1980 Amina Bint al-Huda was arrested together with her brother and, after a week of torture, died in prison.

[138] al-Nu'mani, *al-Shahida Bint al-Huda*, 153–154. Mentioned also in Anisi from the same source. Anisi, *Dokhtari az Tabar-e Hedayat*, 233–235.

[139] Anisi, *Dokhtari az Tabar-e Hedayat*, 235.

[140] Ibid., 236.

[141] Ibid., 238.

[142] al-Nu'mani, *al-Shahida Bint al-Huda*, 154–155; al-Nu'mani, *al-Shahid al-Sadr*, 326–327; al-Nu'mani, 'Faratar az Bavar . . .', 87.

[143] Aziz, 'Fadlallah and the Remaking of the Marja'iya', 221.

basis of what is related to her by Fatima al-Sadr 'Umm Ja'far', she reports that the body of Bint al-Huda was not handed back to Muhammad Sadiq al-Sadr and that, up to the year when Fatima al-Sadr and her family left Iraq, they did not have any information about Bint al-Huda's dead body, but knew that she had been martyred.[144] On the other hand, based on what is reported by al-Nu'mani, Anisi mentions that Bint al-Huda's dead body was in fact handed back to the family.[145] Moreover, once again on the basis of information related to her by Fatima al-Sadr, Anisi also mentions that, following the overthrow of the Ba'thist regime, some people informed Fatima that Bint al-Huda's body had been buried in the family tomb of the Al Yasin, in Wadi al-Salam, by a person close to the al-Sadr and Al Yasin families by the name of Khudayyar.[146]

Having received the information of their assassination, on 22 April 1980, Ayatollah Khomeini related the statement denouncing the martyrdom of Muhammad Baqir al-Sadr 'and his honourable oppressed sister' quoted at the beginning of this chapter. He also announced three days of official mourning and one day of public holiday (Khomeini 1378 [SH/1999–2000]).

Conclusions

This chapter argued that an important interpretative key for locating and understanding the emergence, exercise, and impact of the role and figure of Amina 'Bint al-Huda' al-Sadr is represented by her relationship with her brother Muhammad Baqir in his role as *marja'*. In this respect, and with reference to the framework proposed by Khaled Abou El-Fadl[147] on the existence of certain families in the history of the Near East who established 'a virtual tradition of training female transmitters and narrators' of hadith, my wider research on the role of 'Alid women of the Shi'i religious establishment in Iraq, Iran, and Lebanon indicate that at least in the case of some women of the al-Sadr family, and from the second half of the last century,[148] we have the case of a family whose female members had open access to religious knowledge within the walls of their houses and, in some cases, to traditional female *maktabas* (private teaching administered in the home of the educator). Indeed, with Bint al-Huda we have the case of a female scholar whose reputation and very possibility of development as a religious scholar unquestionably derived from her being a member of a family of renowned male religious

[144] Anisi, *Dokhtari az Tabar-e Hedayat*, 238.
[145] Ibid., 236.
[146] Ibid., 244–245.
[147] Khaled Abou El Fadl, 'Legal and Jurisprudential Literature: 9th to 15th Century', in *Encyclopedia of Women & Islamic Cultures*, General Editor Suad Joseph, <http://dx.doi.org/10.1163/1872-5309_ewic_EWICSIM_0006>, last accessed 25 May 2018.
[148] Mauriello, 'Sub-Centres of Power in Shi'i Islam'.

scholars, the al-Sadr. A combination of necessity and opportunity made it possible for one or more women of this family to enter the public sphere and take up new roles, including those traditionally reserved to the male members of the family. In the specific case of Bint al-Huda, it can be argued that the relative absence of male members in her immediate family who could help her brother Muhammad Baqir al-Sadr with his *marja'iyya*, probably favoured her innate inclination. Interestingly enough, her case brings several striking elements of resemblance to that of her first cousin Rubab al-Sadr (1944–) and, to a lesser extent, to the one of Hawra' al-Sadr (1962–) (both of whom, however, did not develop expertise in *fiqh* and *ijtihad*).[149]

If we address the complex set of factors facilitating the emergence, exercise, and impact of contemporary female religious authority in terms of state action, male invitation, or female initiative, a triad proposed by Kalmbach,[150] in the case of Bint al-Huda, these are represented by the creation of modern state-sponsored institutes of education in Iraq – and the consequent challenge and opening of opportunities offered to female members of the religious establishment – by the intellectual and practical opportunities put in place by the very Muhammad Baqir – relevantly in the Shi'i semi-formal structure of Islamic authority – and by Bint al-Huda's undisputable willingness and uncommon capacity to take up these opportunities. It can be argued that with Bint al-Huda we are in the framework of the contemporary phenomenon of 'proliferation' of religious knowledge and actors determined by mass literacy and education, new trends in Islamic thought and practice, and altered social structures as identified by Krämer and Schmidtke.[151] This chapter argued that with Amina and her brother Muhammad Baqir, we also and relevantly deal with one of the responses generated by the previous elements within the modern Shi'i religious establishment, and its efforts at integrating or repelling those elements.

At least part of the relationship between Bint al-Huda and her brother can be understood through the prism of the relationship between a *marja' al-taqlīd* and his *wakīls*. Instead of a phenomenon of 'fragmentation' of Islamic authority and leadership,[152] with Bint al-Huda we should more properly speak of the efforts of one particularly reform-minded ('Alid) family of the Shi'i religious establishment at 'modernizing' and 'differentiating' traditional forms of Shi'i religious

---

[149] Another interesting case is the one of Dr Fatima Tabataba'i, who is regarded as an important expert in the field of Islamic Gnosticism (*'irfān*) and is currently editor-in-chief of the journal *'Irfan* and the Head of the Department of Islamic Gnosticism of the Imam Khomeini and Islamic Revolution Research Centre in Tehran (Mauriello 2018).

[150] Kalmbach, 'Introduction: Islamic Authority'.

[151] Gubrun Krämer and Sabine Schmidtke, 'Introduction: Religious Authority and Religious Authorities in Muslim Societies, A Critical Overview', in *Speaking for Islam: Religious Authorities in Muslim Societies*, eds Gudrun Krämer and Sabine Schmidtke (Leiden: Brill, 2006), 1–14 at 12.

[152] Dale F. Eickelman and James Piscatori, *Muslim Politics*, 2nd ppbk edn (Princeton: Princeton University Press, 1996 [2004]), 131–135.

authority and leadership, integrating the spaces created for women in the modern public sphere and job market within the informal and decentralised structure of authority and job market represented by the *marja'iyya*. The emergence of Amina al-Sadr's role occurred in a historical period that witnessed a crisis of traditional religious authority in Iraq. Religious authority is greatly dependent on the expectations of its 'audience' and on a relationship that involves the followers' recognition of the leader(ship) as legitimate, knowledgeable, and in touch with their demands and necessities.[153] Amina can be described as a female religious leader and authority that developed, or at least established and was in the process of developing, new female parallel spaces of religious authority alongside and integrated with existing male-dominated structures of religious authority. On the one hand, she faced expected criticisms in her efforts at opening the 'closed doors' within the confines of which women of religious families used to live and, on the other hand, a tragic death at the hands of the Ba'thist regime. However, overall she was successful in winning legitimacy in the eyes of the Shi'i religious establishment and, more recently, her memory has generated unexpected interest among the public of female Shi'i religious activists in Iraq and Iran and in the Shi'i diaspora in North America, Europe, and Australia. Indeed, Bint al-Huda and her brother Muhammad Baqir al-Sadr represent a successful case of the Shi'i religious establishment meeting the challenges posed by 'modernity', in particular with reference to the necessities of the ulema and the *marja'iyya* to communicate effectively with, and build consensus among, 'lay' individuals with a modern education, and even more with 'the other half' of their constituency, women.

The present chapter was concerned with formal aspects of contemporary female religious authority in a Shi'i context, and aimed at reconstructing a factual biography of Amina al-Sadr. Despite this, in its conclusions it is unavoidable to acknowledge that the special relationship between Bint al-Huda and Muhammad Baqir delineated above raises unaddressed, and therefore unanswered, questions. The biography of Amina proposed by the primary sources, and reconstructed above, appears to be too linear and saintly to be entirely plausible. It bears few traces of contradiction in Bint al-Huda's life, with one important exception: the absence of marriage. What moved Bint al-Huda to become the intriguing and exceptional figure she became? Was it ambition? Does her significant involvement in social and educational activities betray a want of affection in her private life? What moved her and her brother to develop the unquestionably special relationship delineated in the previous pages? These are all questions that time and better, previously untapped sources, will, it is hoped, allow scholars to address in the near future.

153 Krämer and Schmidtke, 'Introduction', 1–2; Kalmbach, 'Introduction: Islamic Authority', 6–11.

CHAPTER

12

THE *'ĀLIMĀT* OF SAYYIDA ZAYNAB: FEMALE SHI'I RELIGIOUS AUTHORITY IN A SYRIAN SEMINARY

Edith Szanto

Introduction

'There is a difference between reason (*'aql*) and being clever (*shāṭir*)', according to Umm Mustafa al-Shirazi, a senior instructor at the Zaynabiyya seminary in the Syrian shrine-town of Sayyida Zaynab. Sayyida Zaynab is where one of the most important female members of the Prophet's family lies buried: Zaynab, the daughter of the Prophet's son-in-law 'Ali, and his wife Fatimah. 'While Mu'awiya ibn abi Sufyan was *shāṭir* (i.e. sly and cunning), Imam 'Ali and his daughter Zaynab possessed reason.' Umm Mustafa explained that unlike cleverness, reason is necessarily moral.[1] Cleverness connotes self-interest, whereas reason implies virtue and an all-encompassing universalist form of piety. For her, the purpose of seminary education is the inculcation of moral reason, rather than memorisation, critical analysis, or pragmatic materialism. The goal is not to create scholars, but to propagate and promote a particular form of piety. Based on ethnographic research conducted in Syria from 2007 to 2010, this chapter interrogates the specific content of this form of piety (moral reason) as well as the authority of the female teachers who support it.[2]

---

[1] Fieldnotes, autumn 2009.

[2] Umm Mustafa's formulation is markedly Shi'i in its invocation of Imam 'Ali and Zaynab, but it is also typical of pre-Arab Spring grassroots movements, which aimed to engender Islamic piety across the Middle East. The movement in Egypt and Lebanon has been studied by anthropologists such as Saba Mahmood and Lara Deeb, both of whom analyse the cultivation of pious subjects but neglect the teachers who inculcate it. This chapter fills in the gap by looking at female teachers or *'ālimāt* at the Zaynabiyya seminary. For example, see: Saba Mahmood, *Politics of Piety: The Islamic Revival and the Feminist Subject* (Princeton: Princeton University Press, 2005); Lara Deeb, *An Enchanted Modern: Gender and Public Piety in Shi'i Lebanon* (Princeton: Princeton University Press, 2006).

In terms of their authority, the female teachers in Syria can all be classified according to sociologist Max Weber's three categories of religious authority – traditional, charismatic, and legal-rational – or as a combination of categories. Traditional authority is based on customary status as exemplified by hereditary monarchy. This also pertains to teachers who hail from renowned scholarly families. Charismatic authority requires an individual to have charm or strength of character. Legal-rational authority presupposes institutionalised hierarchies and is exercised by office-holders. In contexts such as Bahrain and Lebanon legal-rational authority and authenticated, disciplined piety have recently become the dominant form of Shi'i religiosity.[3] However, in Syria female Shi'i leaders were most effective when they were able to resort to traditional and charismatic forms of authority because seminaries were operating in a state of exception.[4] Moreover, as the following analysis will demonstrate, charismatic and traditional modes of authority among Shi'i *'ālimāt* in pre-revolutionary Syria from roughly 2003 to 2010 were strengthened discursively because *'aql*, which constituted their educational *telos*, emphasises virtue rather than discipline.

The Zaynabiyya, which was founded by Sayyid Hassan al-Shirazi (d. 1983) in 1973, was the first seminary in the shrine-town of Sayyida Zaynab. It offered a four-year programme, as well as non-degree summer courses. Most of the courses were taught by women belonging to the Shirazi family. Graduates of the Zaynabiyya or other nearby seminaries occasionally taught introductory summer courses. Only one young teacher with a degree in Arabic Literature from the University of Damascus taught regular courses, although they mostly consisted of non-essential courses like child rearing. In other words, graduating from a seminary or a university did not always suffice to be appointed as a seminary teacher. This also often required particular familial affiliations and close connections to established male Shi'i authorities. Aside from seminary teachers, ritual

---

[3] Deeb, *An Enchanted Modern*; Sophia Pandya, 'Women's Shi'i Ma'atim in Bahrain', *Journal of Middle East Women's Studies* 6.2 (2010), 31–58. In both Bahrain and Lebanon, similar to Iran, there are institutions of learning and hierarchies of authority. However, unlike in Iran, Shi'is in Lebanon and Bahrain have generally belonged to the underprivileged, uneducated, and often-rural working classes. As such, the appeal of Shi'i institutions to ideas of rationalism and modernity is an attempt to climb up the socio-cultural hierarchy.

[4] Regarding the notion that the shrine town of Sayyida Zaynab constituted a 'state of exception' see: Edith Szanto, 'Sayyida Zaynab in the State of Exception: Shi'i Sainthood as "Qualified Life" in Contemporary Syria', *International Journal of Middle East Studies* 44.2 (2012b), 285–299. Thomas Pierret writes that because the Syrian government tried to marginalise Sunni religious authorities and make them superfluous, their policies inadvertently strengthened traditional forms of Sunni education and scholarly authority. See: Thomas Pierret, *Religion and State in Syria: The Sunni Ulama from Coup to Revolution* (Cambridge: Cambridge University Press, 2013).

mourning gathering leaders or *mullayāt* commanded religious authority in Sayyida Zaynab. Sometimes *mullayāt* were concurrently seminary teachers, as well as members of clerical families. As *mullayāt* were rarely seen as learned authorities, they cannot be classified as female scholars or *'ālimāt*, however.

In what follows below, I examine the authority and efficacy of female seminary teachers, as well as the kind of piety they promoted. I do so by focusing on five individuals. They may not be *mujtahidāt* or famous, innovative scholars capable of independent legal judgments. They may not go down in history as scholars, but they attained the highest degree of knowledge possible considering the time and place. The women who work at the Zaynabiyya seminary include young and old teachers, many but not all of whom belong to the Shirazi family. Two elder Shirazi women are Umm Mustafa and Umm Haydar; they command respect, traditional, and charismatic authority. There is 'Alawiyya 'Aliya, a young Shirazi jurisprudence teacher, whose rulings on marriage and children some of the students dismiss because they think 'Aliya lacks experience and cannot, therefore, speak legitimately. The only one who is not related to the Shirazi family is Salma. Salma draws her legitimacy from her secular university degree and from her scholastic methodology. This chapter will not discuss *mullayāt* at length as they are not scholars per se. Nevertheless, the two most important ones, who will be examined briefly, are Umm Zaynab and Umm 'Isa. Umm Zaynab was only indirectly linked to a scholarly family and Umm 'Isa had no connections at all. Both of these women exemplify the kind of leadership roles that are available to lay Shi'i women in Sayyida Zaynab.

Given the particularity of the context, I begin by introducing the seminaries in the Syrian shrine-town of Sayyida Zaynab, approximately fifteen kilometres south of Damascus (as they existed prior to the 2011 Syrian Uprising). As the seminaries' students and teachers were for the most part transient Iraqi asylum seekers, institutional structures played an extraordinary role in shaping the kind of authority and education women could have. Therefore, I turn to the following questions: What constitutes Shi'i learning and knowledge in this context? How do seminaries engender learning? What makes a Shi'i woman into a leader and an *'ālima*? Can women become *'ālimāt* outside of the seminary and what roles do they play in the public sphere? I answer these questions primarily by examining the teachers and students at the Zaynabiyya seminary. Although the analysis is based on a narrow snap-shot, it makes occasional wider claims about Shi'i female leadership and learning in pre-revolutionary Syria.[5]

---

[5] Notably, the Zaynabiyya seminary continues to operate in Sayyida Zaynab to date. However, many of the Iraqi students have fled since 2011, which means that there are only a handful of students left.

Shi'i Seminaries in Syria

The Zaynabiyya was the first seminary in the Syrian shrine-town of Sayyida Zaynab and was founded in 1973 by the Iraqi Sayyid Hassan Shirazi. A native of Karbala, where his father had founded and led an important seminary, Hassan Shirazi and his brother Muhammad Shirazi (d. 2001) had attained the status of *marj'a al-taqlīd* or legal point of reference relatively early in life.[6] The Shirazi brothers claimed religious authority through their learning and their lineage, which includes several important Shi'i scholars and reaches back to the Prophet Muhammad.[7] Like many other scholars in Iraq, the Shirazis were politically active, which led to Hassan Shirazi's forced exile in the early 1970s. It was then that he came to Damascus and upon finding a group of exiled seminary teachers and students from Iraq in Sayyida Zaynab, he decided to found the Zaynabiyya seminary. Hassan Shirazi then moved to Beirut where he was assassinated in 1983. After that, Hassan's elder brother Muhammad Shirazi led the Shirazi network including the Zaynabiyya, although he did not come to live in Syria, but rather moved to Qom following the 1979 Iranian Revolution.[8]

Sabrina Mervin writes in 1996 that the Zaynabiyya had altogether 200 students.[9] In the years I was there, the number of students varied significantly. During the summer of 2007 there were more than 100 female students. In 2008, there were only about sixty women who attended the summer classes (the Zaynabiyya allowed all girls above the age of six to enrol for summer classes, however, it only admitted girls over the age of sixteen to normal seminary classes; some of the other *ḥawzāt* or seminaries have upper age limits).[10] There are students who enrol at a seminary after they have finished high school. Others enrol in their late twenties or later.[11] The programme for women takes four years, although more than half of those who started did not finish the entire programme. Many Iraqi Shi'is enrolled in religious seminaries such as the Zaynabiyya out of boredom, in order to socialise, or in order to learn while in exile or in transit,

---

[6] The Najaf establishment, which rivalled the seminaries of Karbala since the 1700s, criticised the Shirazis for this. See: Laurence Louër, *Transnational Shia Politics* (New York: Columbia University Press, 2008), 88–89, 91.

[7] Louër, *Transnational Shia Politics*, 90–91.

[8] Sabrina Mervin, 'Sayyida Zaynab, Banlieue de Damas ou nouvelle ville sainte chiite?' *Cahiers d'etudes sur la Mediterranée orientale et le monde turco-iranien: Arabes et Iraniens* 22 (1996), 149–162. <http://cemoti.revues.org/document138.html>, last accessed 23 March 2009.

[9] Ibid.

[10] For example, the *ḥawza* of Khomeini does not accept students above the age of thirty-five.

[11] In Syria, young women typically get married between seventeen and twenty years of age. This means that by the time women reach thirty, their children may already be attending elementary school, freeing up time for seminary classes.

waiting for a chance to move elsewhere. Residency cards, small stipends, and opportunities for social networking or even prestige and authority among one's own family and neighbours may have constituted an added incentive for studying at a seminary.[12]

As of 2009, there were twenty-one seminaries in Sayyida Zaynab. Twelve of these had women's sections. Outside of Sayyida Zaynab in Syria, there are only a few other *ḥawzāt* in Damascus and near Homs. The term *ḥawza* literally means 'corner'.[13] Originally, it referred to the corner of a mosque or *hussayniyya* (halls dedicated to commemorative mourning gatherings or *majālis 'azā'*), where teachers taught students. The *hussayniyya* is still an important part of many *ḥawzāt*, although there are *ḥawzāt* without *hussayniyyāt* and there are *hussayniyyāt* without *ḥawzāt*. *Hussayniyyāt* may consist of *awqāf* properties and thus function independent of a particular group or scholarly affiliation. In contrast, *ḥawzāt* usually belong to a network of institutions (such as other *ḥawzāt*, *hussayniyyāt*, and hospitals) linked to a particular *marj'a al-taqlīd*.[14]

In order to build and maintain large networks of institutions (schools, *hussayniyyāt*, hospitals, and television channels), scholars work together. While the scholarly elite is theoretically an open elite and there are always new scholars who join the ranks of the ayatollahs, the scene is dominated by large scholarly families, such as the Hakims, the Shirazis, the Khu'is, the Ha'iris, and the Sadrs. Families such as the Shirazis typically produce multiple scholars, but not all of them become major ayatollahs. These related scholars may serve in the administration and other aspects of network. Wives and daughters can be involved with the women's section of a *ḥawza* or a *hussayniyya*.

The rise of Shi'i seminaries in Syria with women's sections has created spaces for female leaders and scholars to flourish (at least until 2011 when the Syrian revolution broke out). Yet, given a context wherein Shi'is remained a minority in a state that did not seek to involve itself deeply in domestic religious matters[15] also meant that their leadership remained marginal. Moreover, their leadership was shaped by particular notions of what constitutes an education.

---

[12] The Zaynabiyya generally does not pay students stipends. However, they do help students with Syrian residency by providing letters that confirm their status as students. This became helpful after 2007 when it became increasingly difficult for Iraqis to attain Syrian residency.

[13] Louër, *Transnational Shia Politics*, 73–74; Khalid Sindawi, 'The Zaynabiyya Hawza in Damascus and its Role in Shī'ite Religious Instruction', *Middle Eastern Studies* 45.6 (2009a), 859–879 at 861.

[14] Some seminaries also function as *hussayniyyāt*, spaces dedicated to mourning gatherings. For example, the main hall of the women's section of Shirazi's Zaynabiyya seminary is used as a *hussayniyya* every Tuesday and on other important religious dates.

[15] This is one of the main points discussed by Thomas Pierret in his monograph. See: Pierret, *Religion and State in Syria*, 38.

The Object of Learning

What constitutes an 'education'? The Latin root *educere* means to bring out that which is within. The underlying assumption is that nothing is added to the self. An educated person is but a polished version of herself. In Arabic, there are a number of terms, which fall under the semantic field of education and learning. The terms *'ilm, shi'r, fiqh, ma'rifa,* and *hikma* all share the meaning of 'knowing'.[16] According to the *Encyclopaedia of Islam*, the main philological dichotomy juxtaposes *'ilm* and *ma'rifa* whereby the former refers to universal theological insights and the latter to particulars. The latter *'arafa* carries the connotation of recognising or acknowledging. It is an imperfect version of knowing or *'ilm*.[17] An *'ālima* (or female scholar) is hence someone who understands universals and has wisdom.[18] In a sense, *ma'rifa* can be tied to law as it legislates the details of everyday life. *'Ilm*, in contrast, encompasses law but also exceeds it.

A minimum of both *'ilm* and *ma'rifa* are required of all Shi'is, according to the women I spoke with in Sayyida Zaynab. For example, Umm 'Ali al-Najafiyya, an Iraqi Shi'i in her mid-twenties married to a man thirty years her senior, explained that institutionalised religious learning (*dirāsa ḥawzawiyya*) is *wājib* (a religious obligation). She finished the sixth grade and learned how to sew from her mother. She attended *majālis* (commemorative mourning rituals) at the Zaynabiyya, but did not take classes. Because she has no children to occupy her time, she admitted that she has no excuse. 'I will pay for it on Judgment Day, I really should know the birth and death dates of the *ahl al-bayt*. To know them allows us to feel with them, it ensures healing (*shifa'*) and intercession on Judgment Day (*shafa'a*).'[19] The kind of knowledge, which Umm 'Ali considered crucial, was not religious law, but an uncritical and simplified form of hagiography or *sīra*. For her, it constitutes the relationship with the family of the Prophet, which is important. At the seminaries, *sīra* and *fiqh* are both taught at the elementary level, during the first year and summer courses. By their third year, students no longer study *sīra*, although the study of *fiqh* continues until graduation.

At more advanced stages of seminary learning, the question of the nature and value of different forms of knowledge in itself constitutes a course. At the Zaynabiyya, Umm Mustafa, a Shirazi and the wife of the men's section's

---

16 Paul Walker, 'Knowledge and Learning', in *Encyclopaedia of the Qur'an*, vol. 2, ed. Jane McAuliffe (Leiden: Brill, 2003), 100–104.

17 Walker, 'Knowledge and Learning'; Navid Kermani, 'Intellect', in *Encyclopaedia of the Qur'an*, vol. 2, ed. Jane McAuliffe (Leiden: Brill, 2002), 548.

18 The root *d – r – s*, to learn, from which the noun *madrasa* is derived, originally meant 'studying religious law' more narrowly but then expanded to learning more generally. See: J. Pedersen, Rahman Munibur, and R. Hillenbrand, 'Madrasa', in *Encyclopaedia of Islam*, 2nd edn, vol. 5, eds P. Bearman et al. (Leiden: Brill, 2010), 1,123–1,154.

19 Fieldnotes, Thursday, 31 July 2008.

principal, taught a weekly class on different forms of knowledge, notions of learning and reason in Islamic thought. For the course, she used the book *Uṣūl al-kāfi*, a Shi'i hadith collection by Muhammad al-Kulayni (d. 941 CE). Umm Mustafa was a heavyset woman in her fifties. Like the other elder high-ranking women at the seminary, she wore a black *abaya* over a black dress and a black scarf pulled over her eyebrows and chin.[20] In the autumn semester of 2009, Umm Mustafa al-Shiraziyya began her course on *Usūl al-kāfi* by explaining the importance of *'aql*, or reason, sense, and intellect. In *Uṣūl al-kāfi*, *'aql* is opposed to *jahl*, ignorance, reminiscent of the *jahiliyya*, the pre-Islamic era, and barbarian Arab customs.[21] For Umm Mustafa, *'aql* is what differentiates humans from animals who are unaware of the consequences of their actions. 'Complete reason or intellect', *'aql kāmil*, however, remains reserved for prophets and the fourteen infallibles.[22] Imam 'Ali and his semi-infallible daughter Sayyida Zaynab are nicknamed *'aqīl* (the most reasonable) and *'aqīla* (the most reasonable woman). Being reasonable, however, does not mean being pragmatic or efficient in this case. Imam 'Ali was well-known for his uncompromising idealism. He remained devoted to his pious values, even when it cost him his status and potential allies. As noted in the anecdote in the introduction of this chapter, Umm Mustafa explained that Mu'awiya ibn Abu Sufyan, was intelligent, clever, but lacked 'complete reason'.[23] *'Aql kāmil* requires spirituality linked with a sense of justice. It means doing *ihsān*, that which is beautiful.[24]

In one of her weekly classes on *'sabīl'*, *telos*, or purpose, Umm Mustafa taught that Shi'is should strive to become more sensitive to others and their needs.[25] These specific others include close loved ones, family, and friends. This kind of openness towards loved ones and fellow Shi'is is part of *'aql kāmil*. Based on Ayatollah Muhammad Shirazi's book on *sabīl*, Umm Mustafa explained that the reason for the 'backwardness' of the Middle East, for civil wars, and corruption, is a generalised lack of *'aql kāmil* among Shi'is specifically and also Muslims more generally.[26] If Muslims had *'aql kāmil* they

---

[20] All the teachers at the Zaynabiyya women's seminary generally wore black *'abayāt* over plain loose dresses. Only Anisa Salma, who based her authority on her university degree, deviated from the standard.

[21] Muhammad al-Kulyani, *Usul al-kafi* (Beirut: Alaalami, 2005), 11–20.

[22] The fourteen infallibles included Prophet Muhammad, his daughter Fatima, and the twelve Shi'i Imams.

[23] Fieldnotes, Wednesday, 21 October 2009 and Wednesday, 28 October 2009.

[24] Reza Shah-Kazemi, *Justice and Remembrance: Introducing the Spirituality of Imam 'Ali* (New York: I. B. Tauris and Institute of Ismaili Studies, 2006), 79. Besides these aesthetic and ethical aspects, *'aql* also has more practical or sensible meanings, as in 'to tie (up), a horse' or 'to pay blood money'. None of the forty-nine occurrences of the root *'–q–l* in the Qur'an takes these latter meanings. See also: Shah-Kazemi, *Justice and Remembrance*, 547.

[25] Fieldnotes, autumn 2009.

[26] Sayyid Muhammad Hussayni al-Shirazi, *Al-Sabil ila inhadh al-muslimin* (Kuwait: Dar al-'ulum, 2009).

would understand that corruption and civil war hurt all Muslims. Significantly, her interpretation means that *'aql kāmil* is more concerned with universal ethics than metaphysical questions.

How can lay Shi'is attain *'aql*? According to Umm Mustafa, as well as the *mullaya* Umm Zahra, the transmission of pious knowledge and the inculcation of *'aql kāmil* occurs in two modes: *ḥawza* education and *majālis* (or ritual mourning gatherings).[27] These two modes engage participants on two different but related and even contiguous levels: intellect and affect. *Ḥawza* learning includes not only lectures, but also discussions. It requires students to read and pass examinations. In contrast, commemorative mourning gatherings may or may not include lectures. Instead, the emphasis lies on aesthetics, emotion, crying, and lamenting. The two modes are related both ideologically and spatially as *majālis* often meet at *ḥawzāt*. *Majālis* attendance is encouraged at the seminaries. On the birthdays and death anniversaries of the Infallibles and other important dates, *ḥawza* classes are interrupted and substituted by *majālis*. Seminary teachers and *mullayāt* often quote an expression: *'al-majālis madāris'* ('mourning gatherings are schools'). Women such as Umm 'Ali al-Najafiyya may not make it to seminary lessons. However, she at least tries to attend *majālis* regularly.

Does the fact that mourning gatherings are an important aspect of pious subject formation mean that *mullayāt* constitute Shi'i *'ālimāt*? Not necessarily. They lead ritual gatherings and thereby may convey universal truths and insights. Yet, they are not scholarly authorities. They have charismatic authority. Sometimes, because of familial ties, they may wield traditional authority. But does that make them scholars? This is a question I will return to towards the end of the chapter.

The Subject of Teaching

One morning at the Shirazi seminary, one of the fourth year-students, Umm Ridha, an Iraqi mother of two boys in her late twenties, said that neighbours frequently ask her: 'Why do you study if they don't give you money?' 'As if everything has to be about money! These people don't know what traces the *ḥawza* has had on my marriage and children! I have become a much more patient parent. And my relationship with my husband has improved tremendously.' Sometimes, she tells people that she studies for the sake of an *iqāma*, a residency permit, thereby presenting her studies in terms of a legal and political necessity, which she considers an irrefutable argument.[28]

According to Anisa Salma, a young and unmarried half-Iranian and half-Syrian teacher at the Zaynabiyya, the most important goal of seminary

[27] Fieldnotes, spring 2009 and autumn 2009.
[28] Fieldnotes, Wednesday, 21 October 2009.

education is an eschatological aim.[29] Salma, who is not related to the Shirazis and bases her authority on her master's degree from the University of Damascus, considers becoming more pious to be a preparatory step for becoming a follower and helper of the Hidden Twelfth Imam, the Mahdi. As the Mahdi is expected to lead an army against the anti-Christ, becoming his follower means becoming one of his soldiers. The focus on the self, in other words, allows Shi'is to train for an impending revolution.[30]

For both Umm Rida and Anisa Salma the goal of studying at a seminary is to become a better and more pious Shi'i. However, there is an important difference between what that means for Umm Rida and what that means for Anisa Salma. For Umm Rida, the purpose of studying at a seminary is to become more virtuous, peaceful, and content. In contrast, Anisa Salma thinks the goal of studying is to become more disciplined, militant, and more efficient as an activist. Discipline and virtue are similar, but they are not the same. The former reflects a Foucauldian notion according to which behaviour is shaped by modern institutions. The latter echoes an idealist attitude towards the world that values morality above efficiency. The relationship between discipline and virtue is analogous to the relationship between hygiene and ritual cleanliness. 'Modernist' Muslims such as Muhammad 'Abdu, or 'modern' Shi'is, such as followers of Khamenei in Iran and Hezbollah in Lebanon, like to conflate ritual cleanliness with modern notions of hygiene. Even at the Zaynabiyya, teachers and students often discuss ritual cleanliness (*ṭahāra*) with a connotation of hygiene. However, after major public mourning events, even teachers sometimes commented cynically on the bathrooms at the Zaynabiyya, noting that *ṭahāra* does not require *naẓāfa* or hygienic cleanliness.[31] Umm Mustafa's ideal of *'aql kāmil* encompasses both discipline and virtue, although it emphasises the latter. Similarly, seminary education in Sayyida Zaynab encourages and fosters both, although the emphasis is on virtue rather than discipline, especially for teachers who derive their authority from tradition and personal charisma.

Becoming disciplined through learning and becoming virtuous through purifying the self or *tazkiyat al-nafs* are similar processes in that they are both aimed at producing more pious Shi'is.[32] However, they differ with regard to priorities and the ways in which they envision the relationships between

---

[29] Fieldnotes, Monday, 14 December 2009.

[30] In that sense, it is both 'soteriological' and 'revolutionary' and fits into both modes of the Karbala Paradigm. See, for example: Kamran Aghaie, *The Martyrs of Karbala: Shi'i Symbols and Rituals in Modern Iran* (Seattle: University of Washington Press, 2004); Deeb, *An Enchanted Modern*; Edith Szanto, 'Beyond the Karbala Paradigm: Rethinking Revolution and Redemption in Twelver Shi'a Mourning Rituals', *Journal of Shi'a Islamic Studies* 6.1 (2013), 75–91.

[31] Fieldnotes, spring 2009.

[32] Hans Wehr, *A Dictionary of Modern Arabic*, ed. J. Milton Cowan (Ithaca: Cornell University Press, 1996).

subjects and the world at-large. Disciplined subjects, especially in the Foucauldian sense, are more orderly and productive.[33] Purified or morally refined selves are not necessarily capable of or concerned with economic productivity or progress. The Shirazis' ideal pious self is a beneficent and grateful self, trained in virtues rather than marketable skills. Valuing virtue above discipline helps explain why the Zaynabiyya and many other seminaries continuously offer courses on topics such as *akhlāq* (morals, righteous character), but not English language. Notably, there are a few seminaries that offer courses on more 'secular' forms of knowledge. For instance, the Afghan *ḥawza* Baqir offers morning classes to teenage girls wherein they teach English and computer skills. The students at the Zaynabiyya have repeatedly requested English classes. However, to date, the principal of the Zaynabiyya has not granted them their request.

As noted earlier, the curriculum at the Zaynabiyya is structured such that it takes four years for full-time students to graduate. Most courses are taught by women who are related to the Shirazi family. Advanced students and graduates are sometimes asked to teach a beginner's class, a summer course, or to fill in if a teacher has fallen ill or is otherwise unable to teach for a day. Most courses, such as *manṭiq* (logic), *naḥw* (grammar), Qur'an and *tafsīr* (exegesis), *sīra* (hagiography), *tarbiya* (children's pedagogy), *balāgha* (rhetoric), *khaṭāba* (art of preaching), *madhāhib* (comparative monotheistic religions), and *tablīgh* (missionary activities) are taught intermittently. Only three courses are part of the curriculum every year: *'aqā'id* or creed, *akhlāq* or morals (which is taught by Umm Haydar, the principal of the Zaynabiyya), and *fiqh* or jurisprudence (which is taught by 'Alawiyya 'Aliya whose father teaches in the men's section of the Zaynabiyya). Significantly, two of these three important courses are concerned with orthopraxy, whereas only one is concerned with orthodoxy. All three value virtue above discipline and are mostly taught by women who are related to the Shirazi family and hence possess traditional authority.[34]

The least important of the three continuously taught courses is theology, the class most concerned with orthodoxy. On the one hand, the teachers at the Zaynabiyya argue that *'aqīda* is a crucial subject. For instance, when the daughter of the late Ayatollah Ridha Shirazi (d. 2008) visited the Zaynabiyya in August 2008 she gave a lecture in which she argued that *'aqā'id* is the most important of all *ḥawza* classes. 'When we die, it is our *'aqīda* (i.e. belief or

---

[33] Michel Foucault, *Society Must Be Defended: Lectures at the Collège de France, 1975–76*, eds Mauro Bertani and Alessandro Fontana, trans. David Macey (New York: Picado, 2003). 239–263.

[34] Jurisprudence might be thought of as promoting discipline. However, given that 'Aliya teaches it by reflecting on abstract questions and by insisting on how people should rather than actually act, I would argue that the class stresses virtue, rather than discipline. In other words, 'Aliya prescriptive rather than descriptive method in teaching law emphasises morals, rather than modern notions of progress and productivity. Marginal courses such as logic, child-rearing, and missionary activity could be seen as courses that promote discipline.

dogmatic conviction) which counts. Only having a strong *'aqīda* guarantees that you will remain a Muslim until the end of your life.'[35] On the other hand, *'aqīda* is the only recurrent subject that is not always taught by a member of the Shirazi family and never by any of the senior members. During the summers, it is even regularly taught by a graduate of the Zaynabiyya. Moreover, none of the books that are used for this class is authored by any of the Shirazi *marāji'*. Perhaps the fact that the Shirazis are not competing with Sunni seminaries and share their theological beliefs with other Shi'i institutions has led them to assume that the presentation of *'aqīda* does not need to be backed by any particularly effective form of authority. It is authoritative in and of its own and can thus be taught by anyone at the Zaynabiyya.

Akhlāq and *fiqh*, in contrast to *'aqīda*, are always taught by a Shirazi woman. During the normal school year, *akhlāq* is usually taught by the principal Umm Haydar, the principal of the women's section of the Zaynabiyya. During the summers of 2007 and 2008, she often reminded students of the importance of wearing proper *hijab* and the permissibility of performing *tatbīr* (a bloody form of self-flagellation).[36] In her regular third and fourth year classes, she seldom spoke about specific rules or disciplinary regulations. Instead, Umm Haydar often read from Ayatollah Muhammad Shirazi's book on *akhlāq*. Occasionally, she would drift off-topic and give general advice. For instance, one day she discussed the evils of materialism. She warned that materialism can undermine love and happy marriages. Umm Haydar recounted a story where a young woman complained about her husband's lack of income. This woman had waited for six years to marry her husband, as her family had opposed the marriage, and now that they were finally married, the woman allowed her materialist desires to destroy her happiness.[37] As the principal of the Zaynabiyya and as part of the Shirazi family, Umm Haydar not only exercised traditional but also charismatic authority. Students would come to her with their personal problems and she listened carefully and gave thoughtful advice. She was seen as a wise matriarch whose authority stemmed from her experience and insight, rather than her formal education.

Of all the courses at the Zaynabiyya *fiqh* is the most often taught subject because it is not only important for cultivating pious Shi'is but also for creating and maintaining relationships between lay followers and *marāji' al-taqlīd*. Jurisprudence is the only course that is always taught by in-house teachers who are related and loyal to the absent *'ulama* who are the 'spiritual leaders' of each seminary. Jurisprudence teachers thus become the links between students and *marāji'*. They become personally known transmitters of knowledge and tradition.

---

[35] Fieldnotes, Tuesday, 5 August 2008.

[36] Szanto, 'Sayyida Zaynab in the State of Exception', 290–292.

[37] Fieldnotes, Wednesday, 21 October 2009.

In first-year *fiqh* courses and during the Zaynabiyya's summer sessions, *fiqh* classes focus on the 'jurisprudence' of worship, including prayer, fasting, and ritual cleanliness. On an elementary level *fiqh* classes focus on Sunni–Shi'i differences rather than intra-Shi'i distinctions. For example, Sunnis generally wash their hands, mouth, nose, and face three times before praying, whereas Shi'is only wash once or twice, but not three times. Also, 'Alawiyya 'Aliya encourages her students to combine the noon and the afternoon prayer or the sunset and the evening prayer. Besides sectarian differences regarding ritual, first-year *fiqh* classes often emphasise *hijab* and music. 'Aliya repeatedly points out the importance of covering up to the tip of the chin and the jaw-line. She argues that *manteaus*, popular long coats worn by urban Syrian women are *shar'i*, legally acceptable, but less modest than the Iraqi *'abaya*. The *'abaya* visibly distinguishes Shi'i women from Sunnis, the minority from the majority, insiders from outsiders.

From the second year onward, students study Ayatollah Muhammad al-Shirazi's *fiqh* manual. Occasionally, 'Aliya refers students to the opinions of other scholars when discussing particular legal issues. Thereby, she demonstrates her knowledge of *fiqh*. However, she never gives her own opinion or fatwa on a matter. Students usually respect what she has to say, because the content of her lessons is in itself authoritative. It is, after all, based directly on the authoritative writings of Ayatollah al-Shirazi. Yet when it comes to women's issues, such as questions of marriage, female students feel like they have the right to debate and question both 'Aliya and the text. In the autumn of 2009, the fourth-year students and 'Aliya had a heated debate about polygyny and temporary (or 'pleasure') marriage. When 'Aliya tried to justify Ayatollah Shirazi's permission of polygyny, Samar, an Iraqi mother of six in her mid-thirties, argued against the permission because she had seen her father's second marriage destroy her natal home.[38] 'Aliya claimed that polygyny (or *ta'addud al-zawjāt*) makes things easier for the wife as she has fewer responsibilities. The students disagreed. They pointed out that a husband's absence does not reduce a woman's responsibilities towards the house and the children. Rather, his absence means that he is not there to help. The students felt like they could question 'Aliya with regard to marriage because they – unlike her – were married, had children, and were on average ten years older. 'Aliya was in her mid-twenties, unmarried, and was seen by her students as a bit too idealistic, impractical, and inexperienced. Rather than engaging in the world, she spent her time at the Zaynabiyya women's seminary as a teacher and a *khaṭība*, preacher at *majālis*.[39] Students often voiced the same critique regarding Anisa Salma. Some students admired Anisa Salma's knowledge of

---

[38] Fieldnotes, Saturday, 5 December 2009.

[39] When Amal's husband married a third wife in the Gulf and did not send Amal money for the hospital when she gave birth to their son, 'Aliya simply exclaimed: 'But he must send her money!' She could not come up with any practical solutions for Amal's dilemma. Fieldnotes, Saturday, 12 December 2009.

pop culture and scientific developments, but also critiqued Salma for teaching students about subjects she had no experience in, such as raising children. The seminary teachers' efforts to inculcate piety, therefore, did not remain uncontested.

In short, seminary education generally values both discipline and virtue. Yet, it is useful to distinguish between discipline and virtue, because they require different forms of authority and because seminaries such as the Zaynbiyya actively encourage virtue while they neglect discipline. For example, in January of 2009, Amal, who was a Syrian fourth-year student married to an Indian, complained that the Zaynabiyya administration's inconsistent enforcement of regulations was not conducive to discipline among students.[40] According to an often preached but rarely applied rule, if a student is late, she is forbidden from entering the class until the next break so as to not disrupt the lesson. Amal had asked the principal for permission to come to class late the following day because she planned to accompany her husband to the airport in the morning. When Amal arrived the next morning and stuck her head into the principal's office so that her presence could be marked down on the attendance sheet, the principal told her not to go to class and wait until the break. The very next day, another fourth-year student came in half an hour late and Umm Haydar, the principal who was teaching the class *akhlāq*, did not say a word. Amal was angry: 'There is no point in following the rules!'[41]

Becoming an *'Ālima*

What does it mean to be an *'ālima* in a context that stresses virtue over discipline? What forms of authority can she draw on? While the teachers introduced so far have been representative of all three Weberian authority types, there are crucial trends to be noted. Only one young, unmarried teacher with a university degree – Anisa Salma – exercises legal-rational authority (and only she insists on discipline). 'Aliya is also young and unmarried, but unlike Salma she has no formal university education and belongs to a scholarly family, which means that she holds traditional authority. Salma and 'Aliya resemble each other in the sense that neither holds the same charismatic sway that some of the older female teachers do. Usually, students do not contest their authority on impersonal subjects such as grammar or laws on financial transactions. However, students did question their teachers when it came to topics they felt they had more experience in than Salma and 'Aliya. This was particularly the case in classes on child rearing or when discussing family law. The only teachers whose authority remained uncontested were charismatic and wise matriarchal figures such as Umm Haydar and Umm Mustafa.

---

[40] Interestingly, both of the Shi'i women at Zaynabiyya who were most concerned with discipline were Syrian and not Iraqi refugees.

[41] Fieldnotes, Monday, 26 January 2009.

Does this mean that effective and legitimate religious authority is restricted to elder, charismatic women related to scholarly families? In effect, yes. Structurally, Shi'i women who are not part of scholarly families are restricted with regard to the kinds of subjects they can teach. Most importantly, they do not teach *fiqh*, which requires not only thorough knowledge of jurisprudence and law, but also access to male authorities who are qualified to issue new rulings. Yet, as the example of Anisa Salma proves, a non-Shirazi can become a teacher at a seminary. Salma might be a unique case: a pious young activist with a university degree. Moreover, Salma differs from the other teachers and students who were mainly non-Syrians and who did not expect to stay in Syria for the duration of their lives. She is rooted in Syria and even though one of her parents is Iranian, she has been brought up in Syria. Aside from her stability, her activist zeal, and her secular education, her marital status is another factor that helped her become a teacher at a women's seminary. Will she continue to teach once she marries and has children? None of the teachers at the seminary have young children. They are either elder women with grown-up children or childless and/or unmarried. There is no rule per se stating that women with children cannot teach. However, students explained to me that having small children makes it logistically very difficult to leave one's house and teach. Once a teacher is older and her children can be left alone, she can return – yet only those who belong to scholarly families actually do return to teaching (in addition to taking on administrative responsibilities).

I met a number of older women with university degrees who attended the seminary as students, but they did not aim to teach at seminaries. They attended seminary classes in order to become better Muslims, but did not express a desire to join the institution's faculty. Their reasons included other commitments, such as children. Many tried to find more financially rewarding careers because they, unlike Salma, needed to support their families. I was told that teachers make about 3,000 Syrian Liras (*c.* 60 USD) per month and some receive no pay at all. Those women that did express a desire to teach others, to promote virtue among Shi'is, generally endeavoured to become *mullayāt* or leaders of commemorative mourning gatherings (*majālis 'azā'*). *Mullayāt* are charismatic figures that teach to the extent that they include short sermons in the mourning gatherings they conduct. But they are not recognised as 'teachers' per se and, as such, they do not constitute *'ālimāt* unless, of course, they are simultaneously teachers at seminaries, as in the case of 'Alawiyya 'Aliya or Umm Haydar. There was one exception: Umm Zaynab taught at the *ḥawza* of Imam Khomeini and also served as a *mullaya* at the *hussayniyya* Abu al-Fadl on a weekly basis.[42] She is not related to a scholarly family. However, her husband worked for Ayatollah al-Ha'iri and, as such, she could be considered as an honorary member of the scholarly familial network.[43]

---

[42] Umm Zaynab has since returned to Iraq.

[43] Fieldnotes, January 2009.

Mullayāt did not, except for 'Aliya and Umm Haydar (who were not primarily *mullayāt*), wield legal-rational authority. Sometimes, they held traditional authority, as in the case of 'Alawiyya Umm Hussayn who was an assistant *mullaya* working with Umm Zaynab at the *hussayniyya* Abu al-Fadl.[44] Instead, successful *mullayāt* rely on charismatic authority. Their success is measured by the degree to which they can affectively move the attendees at commemorative gatherings. Their lessons are often aimed at inspiring their audience, although conveying practical knowledge is not anathema to them. In contrast to a seminary class on jurisprudence, the mourning gathering constitutes a liturgical performance that does not permit time for discussion. Like a Catholic priest, the *mullaya* gives sermons. She can be asked questions only after the *majlis* is over. The charismatic authority of a *mullaya* is not necessarily derived from seminary learning, although some have attended seminary classes or have even graduated from a seminary. According to Umm Zaynab, a *mullaya* learns her craft and how to become a pious subject from the *ahl al-bayt*, the family of the Prophet. By studying their lives, a *mullaya* gains pious inspiration and insight into universals.[45] There are numerous *mullayāt* who have not studied at seminaries. Umm 'Isa, for instance, a childless Iraqi woman in her mid-thirties, said that she became a *mullaya* because she felt the need to serve the *ahl al-bayt*. After seeing a dream wherein Imam 'Ali invited her to ascend a *mimbar* (or pulpit), which she interpreted as a calling to become a *mullaya*, she began attending a variety of *hussayniyyāt* and eventually became an assistant to a more established *mullaya* who allowed her to lead parts of mourning gatherings.[46] Umm 'Isa was not the only one chosen by the *ahl al-bayt* in this way. Umm Muhammad, an Iraqi in her mid-thirties with three sons and a student at the Zaynabiyya, had a similar dream and said she attended the seminary and multiple *hussayniyyāt* in order to become a *mullaya*.[47] Becoming a *mullaya* was often described as becoming a *khādima* or servant of the *ahl al-bayt* and was considered to be equally rewarding (in terms of *haṣanāt* or good deeds) as becoming a teacher. Moreover, Umm 'Isa noted that it allowed for more flexibility as it did not require a daily routine that might interrupt family life and domestic responsibilities.

In short, this means that scholarly authority in Sayyida Zaynab remains largely restricted to women who belong to scholarly families. Becoming a teacher at the seminary, for the most part, required familial ties, experience, wisdom, and charisma. (It was expected that young women such as Anisa Salma and even 'Aliya will stop teaching once they marry and have children.) Women who are not related to scholarly families usually chose to serve the *ahl al-bayt* by becoming *mullayāt*, which does not carry the same scholarly authority as teaching at a seminary. This division reserves scholarly authority

[44] 'Alawiyya Umm Hussayn was highly regarded because she was part of the al-Ha'iri family.
[45] Notably, hagiography which both Umm Zaynab and Umm 'Ali al-Najafiyya highly valued constituted only a minor subject at the Zaynabiyya.
[46] Fieldnotes, January 2009.
[47] Fieldnotes, December 2009.

for those who have traditional authority based on family connections. These familial ties, however, not only bestow privileges, but also demand loyalty, such that female seminary teachers generally refrain from challenging the authority of their male relatives. For the female teachers at the Zaynabiyya, female authority is a conservative force that ought to engender piety rather than challenge religious law, which is already marginalised by the state. As legal-rational authority and learning are neither highly valued, nor expected, female teachers do not compete with male religious authorities. Were they to seriously challenge male authority, they would probably lose their teaching posts and the regard of their relatives who are concurrently their colleagues. Furthermore, challenging male authority in the seminary (that is, in public) would mean revealing intra-family differences to outsiders. The 'us versus them' logic (especially in a context where Shi'is as a whole and Shi'i scholarly families in particular, are a minority) hence prevents female teachers from identifying as primarily female in a male-dominated religious context.

Conclusion

I began this chapter by asking: What is learning? I noted that for Shi'i women in Syria, it primarily means having ethical insight. It resembles scholastic pursuits rather than modern academic endeavours. As such, a Shi'i female scholar is someone who is capable of teaching such ethical insights. These insights differ from legal-rational notions of disciplined learning, which explains why students challenge teachers like Salma and why Salma is not representative of teachers in Sayyida Zaynab who in turn are more likely to hold traditional and charismatic forms of authority. Throughout this chapter I analyse how the concept of education is perceived and portrayed at local seminaries, especially the Shirazis' Zaynabiyya. I posited that the formation of pious subjects there emphasises both virtue and discipline, although it values the former over the latter. I showed how virtue is inculcated and what forms of religious authority such subject formation requires. Lastly, I asked what kinds of authority are available to Shi'i women in Sayyida Zaynab. Since the ideal pious subject according to Umm Mustafa is neither a docile subject, nor a disciplined subject, but a subject that possesses *'aql kāmil*, which necessitates understanding, sensitivity, practicality, and ethics, effective female authority must be traditional and charismatic. This means religious authority remains restricted to female members of scholarly families who do not challenge male authority since their own authority derives from their relationship to those men. The reason for this is not that Shi'is in Sayyida Zaynab are inherently anti-modern or traditional, but rather that those forms of authority can coexist with circumstances that were produced by regional socio-political instability.

CHAPTER

13

WOMEN'S RELIGIOUS SEMINARIES IN IRAN: A DIVERSIFIED SYSTEM DESPITE STATE ATTEMPTS AT UNIFICATION AND STANDARDISATION

Maryam Rutner

Introduction

It was in 2005, remembers the director of the women's religious seminary in Estahban in Southwest Iran, that the Management Centre for Women's Seminaries (Markaz-e modiriyat-e ḥouzeh-ye 'elmiyyeh khwāharān) in Qom asked the Friday prayer leader (*emām jom'eh*) of Estahban whether the town was in need of a religious seminary (*ḥouzeh*) for women. The Friday prayer leader answered in the affirmative. He was then asked to recommend someone suitable for the directorship, and he named Mrs Sabedi, a learned lady who had studied Islamic Sciences for about ten years (up to the equivalent of the end of the third level of the women's religious seminary system). Despite the Friday prayer leader's recommendation, Mrs Sabedi had to undergo exams, first in Shiraz, and then in Qom. Eventually, her credentials were confirmed to teach up to the advanced (second) level and to lead the programme. The Management Centre further asked the Friday prayer leader to contribute financially to the founding and maintenance of the seminary, to which, she says, he agreed.[1]

---

[1] Interview on 27 June 2011. I would like to express my gratitude to all those who accompanied and supported me during the summer months of 2011 in Iran. I also thank those individuals at the religious seminaries and at the Management Centre for Women's Seminaries in Shiraz who gave me their trust and confidence for my project. Without their generous cooperation, this study would never have materialised. The head of the Management Centre of Religious Seminaries in Fars, for example, wrote a permission letter for me that I could use to approach and request data from the administration of the Management Centre in Shiraz. The staff there were collaborative and provided data to the extent that was permissible for them. Some names have been changed to protect the privacy of individuals. My gratitude also goes to the Hawza Project at the University of Exeter for awarding me a project grant. Today, in 2018, sadly, I would not be able to frequent the Management Centre or the seminaries or sit in classes at the seminary, nor would I be given access to the material, courses, and the seminaries that was possible in 2011. The political milieu has drastically changed in recent months; authorities in Iran are nowadays extremely wary not only of foreign researchers but also of Iranians living in Iran who seek information about institutions such as religious seminaries.

This study brings into focus the women's religious seminaries (*ḥouzeh-ye 'elmiyeh-ye khwāharān*) of Shiraz, the capital city of Fars Province, and Estahban, a small town about 200 km southeast of Shiraz. By examining their administration, curriculum, and internal organisation in the mid-2010s, it moves away from the conventional focus on Qom in contemporary studies of Iran's religious seminaries (*ḥouzeh* in Persian, *ḥawza* in Arabic).[2] Qom is sometimes misleadingly portrayed as if it were representative of the entire system of religious learning in Iran. The chapter also brings the local dimension of the women's religious seminary in conversation with the national, showing how and to what extent the national Management Centre's[3] designs in regard to curriculum, textbooks, and staff are implemented at the local level, and if and how they are adapted to the local context.

This study draws on oral testimonies and the results of observation during my research at the Rayhaneh al-Nabi seminary in Shiraz and al-Zahra seminary in Estahban in summer 2011 (see Figure 13.1), as well as statistics and information I collected at the local branches of women's religious seminaries during the same year. Most of the information referred to in this study is not available online, nor was it published anywhere at the time I conducted research; data sharing was at the discretion of the contacts I made in Estahban and Shiraz. Accordingly, much data I draw on here has no extant catalogue citation. Most of it was printed or copied for me at the Shiraz office of the Management Centre for Religious Seminaries, the al-Zahra religious seminary in Estahban, or the Rayhaneh al-Nabi seminary in Shiraz. I complement the data from 2011 with statistics from the last two years (2016–2018) wherever possible, drawing on the very few extant publications on lesson plans in the religious seminaries (for women), in Qom or elsewhere.[4]

---

[2] This chapter uses Persian transliteration, unless reference is made to Arabic texts.

[3] See below for further information regarding the Management Centre for Women's Seminaries (Markaz-e modiriyat-e ḥouzeh-hā-ye 'elmiyeh-ye khwāharān).

[4] What this chapter does not capture is information about any religious seminary that has decided against submission and agreement to the supervision of the Management Centre, and thus remains 'independent'. There is at least one such independent (*mostaqel*) religious seminary in Shiraz. These independent religious are typically known to the locals. One can join the study circles through a reference only; they are not open to the public. In an interview with a wife of a well-known Shirazi who wishes to remain anonymous, she entrusted me that the religious seminaries have become 'a very closed environment' and that independent seminaries may still provide an 'open learning space'. The close-mindedness and the many restrictions that were imposed on the learning environment after the 1979 revolution prompted her to quit her studies in Islamic sciences. She herself was part one of the earliest study circles in Shiraz in about 1985. She studied with the ayatollahs 'Ali Mohammad Dastghayb (b. 1935) and Hasan 'Ali Nejabat (b. 1917) in one of the first learning settings in Islamic sciences at which women could participate. The lessons were held at Abu Saleh in the Molla Sadra Street. Later, the institution moved to Zand Street. Lessons took place for both genders and there were about twenty women at the institution. Conversation on 5 July 2011.

This study is structured in the following manner: Section II provides a brief history of the women's Shi'ite religious seminaries in Iran and presents current data on the number and location of the seminaries, as well as the availability of study places. It also briefly explains the pre- and post-revolutionary organisation of studies and provides more detailed data for Fars Province (see Figure 13.2). Section III gives insight into the curricula at the three main levels of seminary education, and also provides an overview of the criteria for entrance into these programmes. Section IV concludes the study.

As will emerge, handouts and statistics alone do not necessarily reveal whether and how the Management Centre's programme or curriculum is implemented in the individual religious seminary throughout the country. The Management Centre in Qom may design and plan curricula, but they may not be realised because of a lack of resources. Furthermore, this study will also show that despite the concern that the current women's religious seminary system does not pursue the goal of training women to become religious authorities, the system does offer a number of opportunities. First, the entry level of the women's religious seminary system provides girls from remote villages and rural areas with the chance to receive any education at all. Second, those female students who are interested in gaining deeper knowledge in the Islamic sciences can apply for the subsequent (higher) level of seminary training. The fourth level of the seminary education specifically trains women in independent legal reasoning, and it may produce a wave of female religious authorities in the coming years. The women's religious seminary system may not necessarily overtly promote women to religious authority positions (especially women as legal scholars, *mujtahedeh*), but it also does not hinder those who strive for such positions.

For religious seminaries to remain autonomous is first and foremost an ideological decision. The librarian at the Rayhaneh al-Nabi declared in a conversation on 27 June 2011 that at the core of this 'submission is the agreement to and belief in the concept of the guardianship of the jurist (*velāyat-e faqih*), basically what the Islamic Republic of Iran is all about'. The concept of guardianship is one of the central tenets of the constitution of the Islamic Republic of Iran. See, on the constitution: A. Schirazi, *The Constitution of Iran: Politics and the State in the Islamic Republic* (London and New York: I. B. Tauris, 1997); A. Schirazi, *Die Widersprüche in der Verfassung der Islamischen Republik: vor dem Hintergrund der politischen Auseinandersetzung im nachrevolutionären Iran* (Berlin: Das Arabische Buch, 1992); S. Tellenbach, *Untersuchungen zur Verfassung der Islamischen Republik Iran vom 15. November 1979* (Berlin: Klaus Schwarz, 1985); and S. Tellenbach, 'Zur Änderung der Verfassung der Islamischen Republik Iran vom 28. Juli 1989', *Orient* 31.1 (1990), 46–66. See, for example, for some of religious scholars' criticism of the concept: M. Kadivar, 'The Rise and Fall of Azari Qomi; The Evolution of Ayatollah Ahmad Azari Qomi's Thought' (2014), <https://en.kadivar.com/2014/02/24/the-rise-and-fall-of-azari-qomi-the-evolution-of-ayatollah-ahmad-azari-qomis-thought/>.

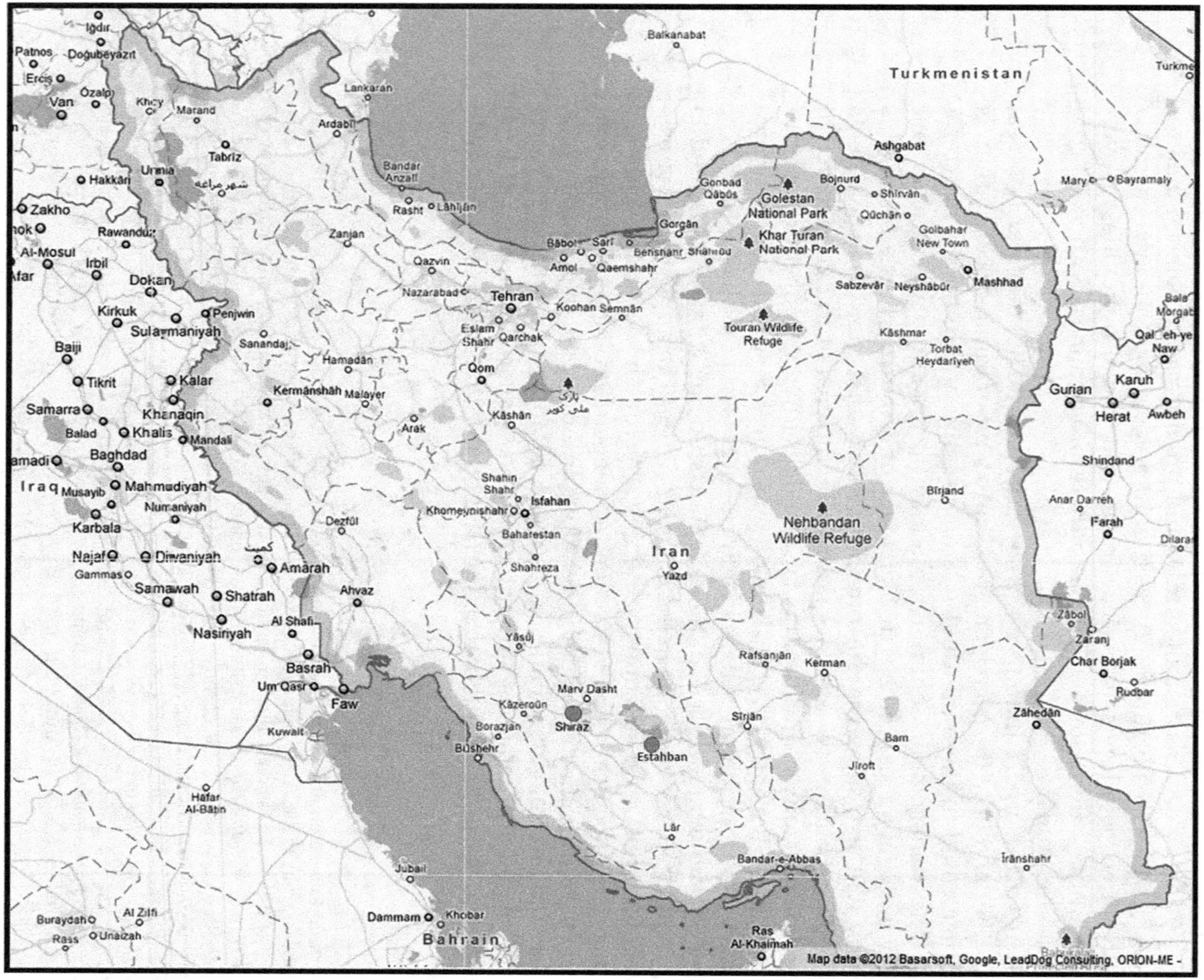

Figure 13.1 Rayhaneh al-Nabi in Shiraz und al-Zahra in Estahban.

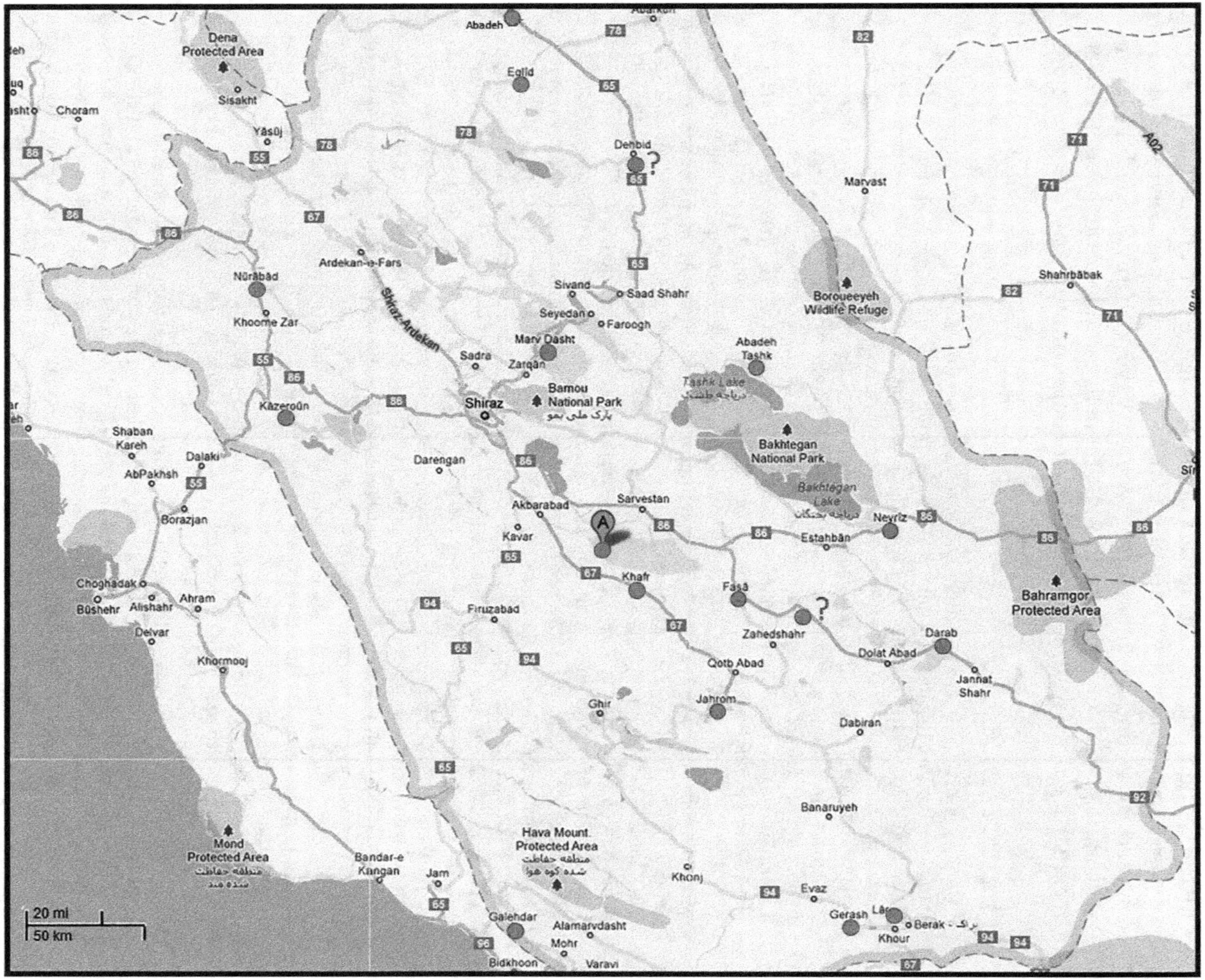

Figure 13.2 Women's Religious Seminaries in 2011.

Women's Religious Seminaries in Contemporary Iran and Fars

Women have been part of religious education from the beginning of Islamic history.[5] Their role as transmitters of knowledge, especially as transmitters of narrations about the Prophet's words and deeds, has been well documented in secondary literature.[6] Women have also functioned as jurists and muftis[7] in the past, even though their lives and works have not been reconstructed as well as those of their male counterparts.[8] Furthermore,

---

[5] Until recently, major surveys on religious seminaries in the Shi'i world, including those in Iran, were limited to those for men. See, for example, R. P. Mottahedeh, 'Traditional Shi'ite Education in Qom', in *Philosophers on Education. Historical Perspectives*, ed. A. Oksenberg Rorty (London: Routledge, 1998), 451–457; M. Litvak, 'Madrasa and Learning in Nineteenth-Century Najaf and Karbalā'', in *The Twelver Shia in Modern Times: Religious Culture & Political History*, eds R. Brunner and W. Ende (Leiden: Brill, 2001), 58–78; K. Sindawi, '*Ḥawza* Instruction and Its Role in Shaping Modern Sh'īte Identity: The *Ḥawza*s of al-Najaf and Qumm as a Case Study', *Middle Eastern Studies* 43.6 (2007), 831–856; A. W. Rasiah, *City of Knowledge. The Development of Shī'ī Religious Learning with Particular Attention to Ḥawzah 'Illmīyah of Qom, Iran*, Doctoral Degree, University of California, Berkeley, 2007; R. P. Mottahedeh, 'The Najaf Hawzah Curriculum', *Journal of Royal Asiatic Society* 26.1–2, 341–351. For further references see also M. M. J. Fischer, *Iran from Religious Dispute to Revolution* (Madison: University of Wisconsin Press, 1980);Mottahedeh, R. P., *The Mantle of the Prophet: Religion and Politics in Iran* (New York: Simon and Schuster, 1985). The study of women's learning in religious seminaries was largely neglected.

[6] See, for a first reference to women as hadith transmitters: Goldziher, I., *Muhammedanische Studien* (Halle: Max Niemeyer, 1889). See for more detailed discussion and analysis on women as hadith transmitters: R. Roded, *Women in Islamic Biographical Collections: From Ibn Sa'd to Who's Who* (Colorado: L. Rienner, 1994); J. Berkey, 'Women and Islamic Education in the Mamluk Period', in *Women in the Middle Eastern History: Shifting Boundaries in Sex and Gender*, eds N. Keddie and B. Baron (New Haven and London: Yale University Press, 1991); M. A. Nadwī, *Al-Muḥaddithāt: The Women Scholars in Islam* (Oxford: Interface Publications, 2007); H. Lutfi, 'Al-Sakhāwī's Kitāb al-nisā' As A Source for the Social and Economic History of Muslim Women during the Fifteenth Century A.D.', *The Muslim World* 71 (1981), 104–124; R. Jacobi, 'Gelehrte Frauen im islamischen Spätmittelalter', in *Nonne, Königin und Kurtisane: Wissen, Bildung und Gelehrsamkeit von Frauen in der Frühen Neuzeit*, eds M. Hohkamp and G. Jancke (Königstein: Ulrike Helmer Verlag, 2004), 225–246. For the most comprehensive monograph on women as hadith transmitters, see A. Sayeed, *Women and the Transmission of Religious Knowledge in Islam* (New York: Cambridge University Press, 2013), but also Sayeed's dissertation: A. Sayeed, *Shifting Fortunes: Women and Ḥadīth Transmission in Islamic History (First to Eight Centuries)*, PhD, Princeton University, New Jersey, 2005.

[7] Muftis are qualified jurists who have the authority to issue legal opinions, termed *fatwā*s.

[8] Despite references to women in positions of religious authority in biographical dictionaries, scholarly and historical engagement with the reconstruction of the life and work of most of such women is non-existent. My dissertation project on the life and work of Nosrat Amin (d. 1983), the most prominent *mojtahedeh* in twentieth-century Iran, may be an exception. See: M. Rutner, *Situating a Female Mojtahed in the Pahlavi Monarchy and the Islamic Republic: Noṣrat Amin (1886/87–1983)*, PhD, New York University, forthcoming. See also on Amin: M. Rutner, 'Religious Authority, Gendered Recognition, and Instrumentalization of Nusrat Amin in Life and after Death', *Journal of Middle East Women's Studies* 11(1) (2015), 24–41; M. Künkler and R. Fazaeli, 'The Life of Two Mujtahidas: Female Religious Authority in Twentieth Century Iran', in *Women, Leadership, and Mosques: Changes in Contemporary Islamic Authority*, ed. H. K. Masooda Bano (Leiden: Brill, 2012), 127–160.

women have not been barred from formal or informal settings of religious education.[9]

As far as Iran is concerned, the seminaries that were founded in the two decades prior to the 1979 revolution can be considered the precursors of today's women's religious seminaries.[10] Those were local and private

---

[9] Biographical dictionaries attest to women who took part in study circles or acted as religious authorities. See, for example, Berkey, 'Women and Islamic Education'; J. Berkey, *The Transmission of Knowledge in Medieval Cairo: A Social History of Islamic Education* (Princeton: Princeton University Press, 1992); I. Schneider, 'Gelehrte Frauen des 5./11. bis 7./13. Jh.s nach dem biographischen Werk des Dhahabi (st. 748/1347)', in *Philosophy and Arts in the Islamic World. Proceedings of the 18th Congress of L'Union Européenne des Arabisants et Islamisants held at the Katholieke Universiteit Leuven (September 3–9, 1996)*, eds U. Vermeulen and D. de Smet (Leuven: Peeters Press, 1998), 107–121; D. Stewart, 'Women's Biographies in Islamic Societies: Mīrzā ʻAbd Allāh al-Iṣfahānī's Riyāḍ al-'Ulamā'', in *The Rhetoric of Biography: Narrating Lives in Persianate Societies*, ed. L. Marlowe (Boston: Ilex Foundation, 2011), 106–139; and R. W. Bulliet, 'Women and the Urban Religious Elite in the Pre-Mongol Period', in *Women in Iran from the Rise of Islam to 1800*, eds G. Nashat and L. Beck (Urbana: University of Illinois Press, 2003), 68–79, esp. 71. These women typically hailed from families with religious scholarly backgrounds.

[10] See, for example, on some of these seminaries that were founded by Fatemeh Amini: A. Kian, 'Gendering Shi'ism in Post-revolutionary Iran', in *Gender in Contemporary Iran: Pushing the Boundaries*, eds R. Bahramitash and E. Hoogland (London and New York: Routledge, 2011)), 24–35 at 26–27. See: M. Künkler and R. Fazaeli, 'The Life of Two Mujtahidas', 136–137, 144–147. See K. Sakurai, 'Women's Empowerment and Irani-Style Seminaries in Iran and Pakistan', in *The Moral Economy of the Madrasa. Islam and Education Today*, eds K. Sakurai and F. Adelkhah (New York: Routledge, 2011), 31–58, esp. 33 on other seminaries, as well as M. Künkler 'The Bureaucratization of Religious Education in the Islamic Republic of Iran', in *Regulating Religion in Asia: Norms, Modes, and Challenges*, eds A. A. Jamal, J. L. Neo, and D. Goh (Cambridge: Cambridge University Press, forthcoming).

Unfortunately, no historical and scholarly study has examined the establishment, function, and purpose of these pre-revolutionary seminaries. For example, whether, which, when, and how long seminaries came under the Pahlavi state's scrutiny and were subject to closure is not clear. Historical reconstruction of these seminaries would be of utmost importance, since our sources and information about them are limited to narratives that have been published in the post-revolutionary era. Some of these narratives have been embellished or tweaked to fit a specific ideological purpose. One such example is Nosrat Amin's Maktab-e Fatemeh in Isfahan. There are contradictory statements between post-revolutionary narratives and information that we can extract from archival sources related to the establishment and purpose of Maktab-e Fatemeh. For example, Persian post-revolutionary sources construct the establishment of Maktab-e Fatemeh as an act of 'opposition' vis-à-vis the allegedly decadent, secular, and irreligious Pahlavi state, and claim that Amin was forced to close down due to pressure from the Pahlavi state. None of these statements are corroborated by pre-revolutionary or contemporaneous sources. For more details, see: Rutner, *Situating a Female Mojtahed.*

Maktab-e al-Zahra in Shiraz has received no attention in secondary literature, even though it might have been one of the earliest founded, if not the earliest founded, women's religious seminaries in Iran, most likely earlier than Nosrat Amin's Ṃaktab-e Fatemeh, which is said to have been the first by Isfahani locals. Al-Zahra is said to have been founded by Simin Mo'ayyedi in 1962–1963. She was a gynaecologist who had studied and lived in France and returned to Shiraz to serve Iranians at her practice in her house. She later established Al-Zahra in the back of her house. She was never married, nor did she have children. Mrs Fallahzadeh also said that she was Minister of Culture in the pre-revolutionary era and got her permission from the Shah to found her secondary school for girls with traditional family backgrounds. Her grandfather was a well-known judge. She was still alive when I was in Shiraz in 2011, but she was already more than ninety years old and had Alzheimer's disease. Mrs Fallahzadeh closed her remarks about Mo'ayyedi by emphasising that she had a strong spiritual bond with God.

institutions in various urban centres such as Qom, Tehran, Isfahan, and Shiraz. The initial impetus for the establishment of those seminaries came predominantly from women who strove to educate themselves or other girls and women in Islamic studies.[11] Their interest was met with support by leading male religious authorities such as the grand ayatollahs Mohammad Reza Golpayegani (d. 1993) or Mohammad Shariatmadari (d. 1986).[12]

The revolution disrupted the natural development and progress of the women's seminaries. Most seem to have closed before, during, or after the revolution. Some of the seminaries re-opened in the post-revolutionary era, albeit with changes in name and structure. For example, Maktab-e Touhid and some other seminaries in Qom were transformed into the prestigious Jame`eh al-Zahra in Qom in 1984, a religious seminary (*ḥouzeh*) for women, the largest of its kind at the time.[13] In the 1990s, the seminary system expanded throughout the country 'under the initiative of the clerical leaders of the state'.[14] The role and function of the Management Centre for Women's Seminaries (Markaz-e modiriyat-e ḥouzeh-hā-ye 'elmiyeh-ye khwāharān) is noteworthy in this regard. It was established in 1997 by the High Council of Seminaries (*shourā-ye 'āli-ye ḥouzeh-hā-ye 'elmiyeh*)[15] to standardise education at all religious seminaries for women in Iran. Since its establishment, it has dictated a unified admissions process and curriculum for each level of seminary training. Seminaries that submit to the supervision of the Management Centre need to follow its guidelines and are not free to choose their curriculum or staff as they wish. On the one hand, the Management Centre helps with financial and logistical issues; on the other hand, it also constrains the seminaries in their choices of programmes, curricula, and teachers. My research indicates that, in addition, the Management Centre helps establish seminaries where none previously existed and tries to convince independent religious seminaries to subordinate themselves to the Management Centre's supervisory administration.[16]

---

11 Such women include Monir Gorji, Ma'sumeh Golgiri, and Zohreh Sefati in Qom, Simin Moa'ayyedi in Shiraz, Nosrat Amin in Isfahan, and Fatemeh Amini in Qom and Tehran.

12 See Sakurai, 'Women's Empowerment'.

13 Sakurai writes that this seminary was established after Ayatollah Khomeini 'issued a sanction (*hokm*) to establish an official women's seminary in order to mobilize women for the consolidation of the newly established Islamic republic'. K. Sakurai, 'Shi'ite Women's Seminaries (howzeh-ye 'elmiyyeh-ye khaharan) in Iran: Possibilities and Limitations', *Iranian Studies* 45.6 (2012), 727–744 at 729. On Jame'eh al-Zahra see also Künkler 'The Bureaucratization of Religious Education'.

14 Sakurai, 'Women's Empowerment', 32.

15 The High Council of Seminaries was established in 1991.

16 The Management Centre is a highly hierarchical institution. See http://public.whc.ir/article/23839/مرکز-مدیریت-حوزه-های-علمیه-خواهران#mo-amoozesh for a more detailed list of the Management Centre's responsibilities and the different branches of the Management Centre (Secretary of Education, Secretary of Research, Secretary of Culture and Advertisement, Secretary of Administration and Finance, Secretary of Communication and

Old and New Levels of Learning

The structure of learning in the women's religious seminaries differs from traditional religious training. The pre-revolutionary old-style learning consists of three cycles: The introductory cycle (*moqaddamāt*) teaches the students grammar, syntax, rhetoric, and logic. The advanced cycle (*soṭuḥ*) teaches jurisprudence (*feqh*) and deductive methodology of jurisprudence (*oṣul-e feqh*). At the highest level of instruction (*dars-e khārej*), students go beyond the textbooks, learn discursive means of argumentation and debate, and engage in independent legal reasoning (*ejtehād*). The new style of learning, introduced since the early 1990s, is divided into four levels. Levels (*saṭḥ*) 1 and 2 are equivalent to the former introductory cycle (they are also called *maqṭa'-e 'omumi*). The second level is a five-year programme; the first and second levels together take seven years. The first level is almost never mentioned or deemed relevant in conversations because its completion is regarded as equivalent to a high-school degree. The degree of the second level is understood to be equivalent to a BA degree. Level 3 (also called *maqṭa'-e 'āli*) at the seminary is equivalent to the advanced cycle of the old-style seminary system and is considered equivalent to an MA degree. This level is a semi-specialised programme.[17] Level 4 (*maqṭa'-e takhaṣṣoṣi*) is equivalent to the third cycle (*dars-e khārej*) of the old-style seminary programme, or a doctoral degree at the university; it is a highly specialised programme, leading students to develop their own abilities in authoritatively interpreting religious law.[18]

Study Place in the Women's Religious Seminaries in Iran

For the year 2012–2013, there were a total of 11,839 places available at the second level, and 1,345 at the third level at religious seminaries that were under the supervision of the Management Centre. These numbers include places for which attendance is required (8,187 for Iran, 462 for Fars), for which attendance is required and dorms available (939 for Iran, 173 for Fars), for which semi-attendance is possible (958 for Iran, 85 for Fars), and for which part-time attendance is possible (1,755 for Iran, 65 for Fars).[19] In the province

---

Seminary Affairs, Centre for technology of information, Centre for Education without Attendance, Centre for Research of Women and Family, Centre for Planning and Supervision, Centre for Development and Renovation, Headquarters of Planning and Composing the Textbooks, Headquarters of Public Communication and International Affairs). More research on the Management Centre, its staff, the background of the staff, or the source of its funding would be invaluable.

[17] 'Semi-specialised' and 'specialised' are terms that the Management Centre uses to describe the programmes at the third and fourth level, respectively. It may be referring to the depth of the content of the courses or the scope of the material to be studied or both.

[18] See handout '*Daftar-e rāh-namā-ye pazireshe-e maqṭa'-e takhaṣṣoṣi-ye (saṭḥ-e chahār) ḥouzeh-hā-ye 'elmi-ye khwāharan*' for the academic year 2018/2019.

[19] Semi-attendance means that students do not have to be present for every class; part-time means that students must be present for all courses, but can either work or stay at home while studying.

of Fars, 785 female students could be admitted to the second level of the seminary system for the same year, and 60 for the third level. These numbers are the total numbers of various types of places: places for which attendance is required (795 for Iran, 30 for Fars), attendance required and dorms available (125 for Iran, 20 for Fars), semi-attendance possible (175 for Iran, 10 for Fars). The third level does not give the students the option to study part-time. Table 1 considers only statistics that require students to attend the programme and places that are available for dorms; semi-attendance and part-time places are not included.

The numbers in Table 1 show that available places are unequally distributed among the provinces. Tehran and Isfahan offered more than 1,000 places for students for the second level, while the other provinces each offered from 25 to 598 places for the 2012–2013 academic year. The distribution of population does not seem to be a deciding factor. Some populous provinces offer fewer places in religious seminaries than provinces with a smaller population. More research is needed to determine the rationale for the distribution. For example, one could ask what role alternative and other forms of educational institutions (public and private universities), the distribution between rural versus urban areas, or poverty play. One may also investigate whether seminaries are considered to be morally, religiously, and culturally more Islamic and conservative than the universities. Some conservative-minded families indeed consider sending their daughters to religious seminaries rather than universities, where they could possibly intermingle with men. At the universities, for example, veiling is not as strict, and the *chador*[20] is not compulsory, as it is in the religious seminaries.

There were no statistics available for the Khorasan Province. Khorasan, as was repeatedly indicated to me during my research, enjoys a special status: it has decided to be independent from the Management Centre and other forms of national centralisation. My informants, while being part of the centralised seminary system, spoke about Khorasan with a certain level of awe. It was often mentioned together with Qom as one of the two best options for religious education on account of the high quality of religious instruction in Iran.[21] Furthermore, places with dormitory availability are either not available or very limited. As we will see below in the case of Fars, students from rural areas and villages especially are highly dependent on dormitory availability.

Detailed statistics equivalent to Table 1 for recent years cannot be located. What makes comparison across years additionally challenging is that the

[20] The *chādor* is a large piece of cloth that veils a woman's entire body except for her face and hands.

[21] No publication addresses the special case of Khorasan; it would be worthwhile to shed light on the reasons for this exception and the way this exceptional role is perceived by the Management Centre.

Management Centre does not collect, store, or publish data retaining the same categories across years. For example, whereas for the academic year 2012–2013 the available places for students was divided into places for full-time students, dormitory students, part-time students, or virtual (or online) students, data for the 2017–2018 academic year does not offer insight into available places, but instead focuses on student status and divides it between those who have graduated from a programme (according to the level) and those who are students (*ṭollāb*) and have a job. A direct comparison is therefore not possible. Table 2 shows that the most recent (and only) data available on the official website of the Management Centre of Women's Religious Seminaries is for the academic year 2017–2018.[22] The centrality of the second level of the seminary education and the wide gulf between the places that are available for women in religious seminaries for the second level on the one hand and the third and fourth levels on the other are striking. Whereas about 50,000 students currently study at the second level, only about 8,000 study at the third level and approximately 330 at the fourth level. In other words, between 80 and 90 per cent of all students of the women's religious seminaries study at or have graduated from the second level. The number of students decreases drastically for the third and even more dramatically for the fourth level. Only between 4 and 14 per cent of all students study at or have graduated from the third level, and less than 1 per cent study at the fourth level.

Women's religious seminaries in Fars: an overview

Before presenting information on women's religious seminaries in Fars, this section introduces the two women's religious seminaries where I conducted research in 2011. The Madreseh-ye 'Elmiyeh al-Zahra in Estahban was founded in 2004; Mrs Sabedi, the director, has been teaching and managing affairs at this seminary since its founding. Estahban is a small town of about 40,000 inhabitants and is known in Fars as 'the City of the Qur'an' (shahr-e Qur'an).[23] Nobody knows why exactly, but inhabitants seem to agree that it refers to the fact that all the women of the town wear the *chador*, and perhaps more importantly because of the many Qur'an reciters who emanated from the town throughout the history of Islam.[24] Mohammad Javad Eslami, author of a biography[25] of the eminent religious scholar Grand Ayatollah

---

[22] See <http://amar.whc.ir>, last accessed 10 April 2018.

[23] Estahban has been referred to in works of history with the names Estahbanat, Estahbanan, Eṣṭahbān, Eṣṭahājān, and Ṣābunāt. In October 1974, the name of the town was changed from Eṣṭahbānāt to Estahbān.

[24] Indeed, compared to the city of Shiraz, Estahban is more 'conservative' in its outer appearance. One hardly encounters women without the *chador* in public places.

[25] See M. J. Eslāmi, *Shokuh-e faqāhat (The Glory of the Knowledge of Religious Jurisprudence)* (Tehran: Setād-e Yādvāreh-ye Sar-dārān va Pānṣad Shahid Estahbān, 2005).

Seyyed Ebrahim Hosayni Estahbanati (known also as Mirza Aqa or Mirza Aqa Estahbanati Shirazi) (d. 1959–1960)[26] claims that Estahban is sometimes referred to as 'the small Najaf' (Najaf-e kuchek), since it has been home to many pre-eminent religious scholars, such as Grand Ayatollah Mohammad Baqer Estahbanati (d. 1900)[27] or Hojjatoleslam Hajj Shaykh Ahmad Faqihi (d. 1981).[28] The small town also has a shrine (*emāmzādeh*) that is believed to be the tomb of Pir-e Morad, the brother of Emām Reza.[29] Outside of Fars Province, this shrine appears to be unknown, however. During my research I encountered a number of Estahbanatis who were working in state institutions of religious but also of political administration such as the seminaries (*ḥouzeh*) and ministries, mostly in Shiraz, but also in Qom and Tehran. This may not be coincidental – in fact, Mrs Sadeq, the administrator of one of the Shiraz seminaries, hailed from Estahban.

The women's religious seminary Rayhaneh al-Nabi in Shiraz was one of the two religious seminaries in Fars that offered lessons at the third level (the other being al-Zahra in Gerash). Shiraz is the capital of Fars Province.[30] For the first time, Rayhaneh al-Nabi was offering classes over the summer months for reasons that will be set forth further below. Both seminaries were located in facilities of old and abandoned secondary schools. Staff and students of both seminaries were excitedly awaiting the new facilities to be built so that they could move. At Rayhaneh al-Nabi, for example, students complained about the extremely noisy, old air-conditioning systems that made

[26] He began his religious training in Estahban, moved to Shiraz, where he studied with eminent scholars such as Shaykh Mohammad Baqer Estahbanati (philosophy, jurisprudence, and the principles of jurisprudence), Mirza Abu al-Hasan Mohaqqeq Estahbanati (jurisprudence and principles of jurisprudence), Shaykh Ja'far Mahallati, and Shaykh Abu al-Hasan Hada'eq Estahbanati. He continued his studies in Najaf with Seyyed Mohammad Kazem Yazdi (jurisprudence), Shaykh Mohammad Taqi Kazem Khorasani (principles of jurisprudence), Mirza Mohammad Taqi Shirāzi (jurisprudence), and Shaykh Mohammad Baqer Estahbanati (philosophy). He obtained a number of *ejtehād* certificates (*ejāzeh-nāmeh*), including certificates from Akhund Khorasani, the author of the authoritative work *Kifāyah al-uṣūl*, and from Grand Ayatollah Mirza Mohammad Taqi Shirazi. Nosrat Amin (d. 1983), a prominent female *mojtahedeh* in twentieth-century Iran, was one of his students and the only female recipient of an *ejāzeh* certificate from Estahbanati.

[27] He began his education in Estahban and moved to Shiraz and then to Tehran to continue his studies. He returned to Shiraz and was soon exiled to Samarra due to a conflict with the political authorities. In Samarra, he studied with Mirza Mohammad Hasan Hosayni Shirazi and earned the degree of *ejtehād*. After the death of his professor, he moved to Najaf. He is also known as the fourth martyr (*Shahid-i Tābi'*) in Shi'i history because he was killed in an uprising.

[28] He began his religious training in Estahban and migrated to Shiraz, Qom, and Najaf to continue his studies. He returned to Fars and became judge in the towns of Fasa, Darab, Yazd, and Estahban under the Islamic Republic of Iran.

[29] On *emāmzādehs* in Iran, see Algar, H., Emāmzāda: Function and Devotional Practice, *Encyclopaedia Iranica, Online Edition* (1998 [2011]); A. H. Betteridge, *Ziārat: Pilgrimage to the Shrines of Shiraz,* Doctoral Degree, University of Chicago, Chicago, 1985.

[30] Shiraz had about 4.5 million inhabitants in 2011/2012.

it hard for them to follow the lessons.[31] Brand new buildings were being constructed for both seminaries.[32]

The issue of dormitories was a crucial one for both the staff and the students. For the academic year 2010–2011, for example, the religious seminary in Estahban had a total of 102 students, thirty-two of whom were from the surrounding villages and the rest from Estahban. The seminary had the capacity to offer housing (two rooms in total) to fourteen students; these were typically offered to students from those villages farthest away. The rest of the villagers had to commute on a daily basis. These students, if they chose to continue their studies at the third cycle, would be dependent on dormitories, since the third cycle was only offered in Shiraz or even further away. The director said that every year she had to turn down applications from students from the surrounding villages, because she was not able to offer these young women housing.

At the time of my research in 2011, there were nineteen women's religious seminaries in Fars that offered lessons for the second level of the seminary programme. Shiraz was the only location that had multiple seminaries (see Table 3). Some changes were made to the seminary system in Fars for the academic year 2012–2013.[33] First, the names of some of the seminaries changed, or seminaries closed down and re-opened under new names. For example, where there used to be Fatemeh al-Zahra in Arsenjan, there was instead seminary Fatemiyeh in 2012–2013. Seminary al-Zahra in Abadeh Tashk closed and seminary Kousar opened. In Shiraz, only two seminaries were listed (al-Zahra and Fatemeh al-Zahra) where there had previously been three.[34] Second, new seminaries were established: al-Zahra in Khorram Bid and Fatemeh-ye Zahra in Marvdasht.

Lessons for the third level were offered in only two towns, at Reyhaneh al-Nabi in Shiraz and at al-Zahra in Gerash.[35] Until 2011, only Rayhaneh al-Nabi

---

[31] The two layers of veiling – through the *maqna'eh*, a type of headscarf, and the *chador* – added to the severity of the problem, for they covered the ears.

[32] Not only seminary students in Estahban and Shiraz enjoy their lessons in a new building now. Other towns in Fars such as Kazerun, too, inaugurated a new building. See 'Aṣr-eKāzerun, Eftetāḥ-e sākhtemān-e jadid-e ḥouzeh-ye 'elmiyeh khwāharān dar Kāzerun, 2015, http://www.asrekazeroon.ir/افتتاح-ساختمان-جدید-حوزه-علمیه-خواهرا/ and the Islamic Republic of Iran Broadcasting (IRIB), Eftetāḥ-e sākhtemān-e jadid-e ḥouzeh-ye 'elmiyeh-ye khwāharān dar Kāzerun, year unknown, http://fars.irib.ir/نمایش-محتوای-صدا?p_p_id=101_INSTANCE_ugRs8EYqvk8c&p_p_lifecycle=0&p_p_state=pop_up&p_p_mode=view&p_r_p_564233524_tag=حوزه%20علمیه%20خواهران.

[33] See document with the title *'Fehrest-e madāres-e 'elmiyeh' keh dar ostān-e Fars az dāvṭalabān dārā-ye madrak-e diplom va bālātar paziresh darand'*.

[34] The reason for omitting Rayhaneh al-Nabi may be that it is now offering lessons at the third level only, rather than at the second and third levels.

[35] In a conversation at the seminary Rayhaneh al-Nabi on 6 July 2011 the librarian disclosed that there are plans to move into a new building together with Fatemeh al-Zahra. One of the issues that still needs to be clarified is how to combine the two seminaries without anyone from the administration losing her job.

offered lessons for the third level. Not one single town in Fars offered lessons for the fourth level. According to the official website of the Management Centre, Fars has thirty women's religious seminaries today; of these, six are in Shiraz – Ghadariyeh, al-Zahra, Fatemeh al-Zahra, Rayhaneh al-Nabi, Ma'sumiyeh, and Jame'eh al-Nur – of which only the last offers lessons for the fourth level. Today, three seminaries in Fars offer lessons for the third level: Rayhaneh al-Nabi in Shiraz, al-Zahra in Gerash, and Fatemeh al-Zahra in Marvdasht.[36]

According to the most recent data, a total of 1,982 female students have graduated from the women's religious seminaries in Fars from 2006 to 2018: 1,939 from the second level and 48 students from the third level. Currently, 2,915 students study at the second level at women's religious seminaries in Fars, 166 at the third level, and 17 students at the fourth level. Furthermore, Fars now offers lessons at twelve additional religious seminaries: in addition to the above-mentioned towns, seminaries were established in the towns of Jannatshahr, Sepidan, Lamard, and Miyanshahr, as well as three further seminaries in Shiraz that are not named.[37]

Not one single seminary offered lessons at the fourth level in Fars for the academic year 2012–2013. Nor were statistics or other data available for the fourth level of seminary training at the time of my stay in 2011. The director of

---

[36] See http://whc.ir/maps. Unfortunately, no date is provided for the update of the website, so I cannot discern whether the list is up to date.

[37] WHC, Āghāz-e paziresh-e ḥouzeh-ye 'elmiyeh-ye khwāharān-e ostān-e Fārs barāye sāl-e taḥṣili-ye 97–98, 2018a, http://fars.whc.ir/news/view/55404/-97-98. -فارس-برای-سال-تحصیلی آغاز-پذیرش-حوزه-علمیه-خواهران-استان. See also Shiraze, Āmār-e bālā-ye jaẓab-e ṭalabeh dar ḥouzeh-ye 'elmi-ye khwāharān dar ostān-e fars, 2017, http://shiraze.ir/fa/news/111634/ -بالای-جذب-طلبه-در-حوزه-علمیه-خواهران-در-استان-فارس : Hojjatoleslam Nouruzi, director of the Service Office for Supplementary Education of the Women's Religious Seminaries, reports that the Management Centre has been offering lessons for the fourth level in a serious way for the third consecutive year. These lessons relate to two 'general (*'omumi*) fields of study' and 'one specialized (*takhaṣṣoṣi*) field of study'. The Management Centre offers lessons for the fourth level in Exegesis and Qur'anic studies, Comparative Exegesis Study, Jurisprudence and Principles of Jurisprudence, as well as Jurisprudence in Family Matters in eleven provinces. He reports that, in 2017, more than 4,000 students applied for the third level and about 622 students applied for the fourth level, but the Management could only accept about one-fifth of the applications for the fourth level. In Fars, only jurisprudence and the principles of jurisprudence with a specialisation in family matters is offered at the fourth level; there are plans to add exegesis and Qur'anic studies for the 2018–2019 academic year. In January 2018, the Management Centre published further data; see Iran News Agency (IRNA), 39 hezār va 217 dāneshju-ye bānu dar ḥouzeh-hā-ye 'elmiyeh-ye khwāharān taḥṣil mikonand, 2018, <http://www.irna.ir/fa/News/82805607>. The deputy director of the Management Centre reported that from 2009 to 2017, 39,217 students have studied at women's religious seminaries throughout the country. Currently, the director continued, 65,636 students are studying at seminaries that are supervised by the Management Centre, of which about 55,000 study at the second level, 9,470 at the second level, and 414 at the fourth level. Excluded from the data are students who study at independent seminaries and those who are at seminaries in Qom and Khorasan-e Razavi, north and south. He also emphasised that the number of applicants has increased compared to previous years.

Rayhaneh al-Nabi explained to me that 'ever since the new seminary system was established in Fars, no student has yet graduated from the third level. Shiraz will have the first graduates [from the third level] next year [2013].' These students, she continued, will then be able to continue their studies at the fourth level in Qom or Mashhad, if they wish. But, she added after a short pause, she was working with the authorities to obtain permission to offer the programme at the fourth level in Shiraz as well. She admitted that this was a crucial step for those women who do not have the means or their family's permission to move to Qom or Mashhad for their studies.[38]

Plans to establish the programme for the fourth level in Shiraz only materialised in 2017: on 29–30 July 2017, fourteen applicants were interviewed for the fourth level for the specialisation jurisprudence and principles of jurisprudence (*feqh* and *oṣul*), with the sub-specialisation of jurisprudence in family matters (*gerāyesh-e feqh-e khānevādeh*).[39] The institution that offers lessons at the fourth level is not Rayhaneh al-Nabi, but Jame'eh al-Nur. At the time of my research stay in Shiraz, no women's religious seminary with the name Jame'eh al-Nur and under the supervision of the Management Centre existed. The establishment of the programme for the fourth level at the seminary beyond the religious prominent centres such as Qom, Isfahan, and Mashhad is a more recent phenomenon. In Qom, for example, the first programme for the fourth level that was designed by the Management Centre was initiated in 2010, and in surrounding areas in 2015.[40]

The Curricula of and Admissions to the Women's Religious Seminaries

This section provides an overview of the curriculum and the textbooks that students at the women's religious seminaries study. The source material for this section stems from documents made available to me by the Management Centre of Women's Religious Seminaries in Fars. The documents include a detailed list of the curriculum for the five-year programme of the second level, which I translate in its entirety in the appendix. While this section presents all the specialisations that are offered at the third level of the

[38] Written permission from the father, if the student is single, and from the husband, if she is married, is necessary for all levels of seminary training. I was told that many parents and husbands would not give their daughters or wives permission to study in a different town.

[39] The three examiners were religious scholars of the rank *hojjatoleslam*, Bazargan, Musavi, and Mrs Kola'i. The results were to be published on the official website of the women's religious seminaries – www.whc.ir – in September 2017 for the applicants.

[40] See: HawzaNews, Paziresh-e saṭḥ-e 4 ḥouzeh vizheh-ye khwāharān, 2010, https://hawzah.net/fa/News/View/82537/پذیرش-سطح-4-حوزه-ویژه-خواهران and MehrNews, Ta'sis-e ḥouzeh-ye 'elmi-yeh-ye khwāharān dar maḥalleh-hā-ye Qom / Paziresh-e saṭḥ-e 4 barā-ye avvalin bār, 2015, https://www.mehrnews.com/news/2479860/تاسیس-حوزه-علمیه-خواهران-در-محله-های-قم-پذیرش-سطح-4-برای-اولین.

seminary system, the appendix translates only the curriculum of the two specialisations for which the Management Centre provides the most study places; these are the fields 'Jurisprudence and Principles of jurisprudence' and 'Qur'anic Studies and Exegesis'. While I have no access to the curriculum to the fourth level, the section below nevertheless draws on documents that offer a glimpse of its organisation and admissions criteria.

It will be shown that the second level aims primarily to provide a general overview of most fields in the Islamic sciences. Graduates are expected to pursue goals other than a career in Islamic sciences. The third and fourth levels of the seminary training move towards a specialisation and prepare students for potential careers as researchers, professors, or even professionals in positions of juristic or interpretative authority. In that respect, women do have the opportunity to gain the necessary training to become thematically focused jurists (*mojtahedeh-ye motejazzi* or *mouḍu'i*). This qualification is to be differentiated from that of absolute jurists (*mojtahed-e moṭlaq*), which is the level available to male students in the men's seminaries.

The section below presents and discusses the curriculum at the second, third, and fourth levels. It sets forth the admissions process for each level. It will also be seen that while the suitability of the background of the candidate is the primary deciding factor for entry into the second level, the main admission requirement for the third and fourth levels is the scholarly credentials of the candidate. This is not to say that the personal background of the candidate is irrelevant. These candidates typically stem from within the seminary system and are already known to the seminary staff; that is, they have already proven themselves to comply with the ethical and political norms of the system.

Curriculum of Level 2

It is important to stress the centrality and significance of the second level. Not only do many more seminaries throughout the country offer lessons at the second level and many more students graduate from the second level than from the other levels (see Tables 2 and 3), but the Management Centre also pursues specific goals with the programme. The second level of the seminary system was not designed primarily to satisfy the thirst for knowledge of women who are interested in Islamic studies. The Management Centre's main goal has been to train propagandists and teachers rather than to prepare the students for a serious career in the religious sciences.[41] According to the handout with general information about the second level that is available on the website of the Management Centre for Women's Religious Seminaries, the five-year training programme is aimed at preparing students

[41] See Sakurai, 'Shi'ite Women's Seminaries'; Künkler, 'The Bureaucratization of Religious Education'.

for the teaching and propagation of Islamic culture and knowledge (*tabligh va-tarvij-e farhang va-ma'āref-e eslām*) or advice (*rāhnamā'i va- moshāvereh*). This is confirmed by the corresponding curriculum design reviewed below. The third and fourth levels of the seminary training have different aims, as will be shown further below. An example of a second-level graduate was a twenty-five-year old woman in Estahban. She taught about ten young children (from five to eight years of age) the important narratives of the Koran in the Basij building of the town.[42] The topic of the session was the creation of Adam and Eve. This young woman is the ideal graduate of such a seminary programme, as the director proclaimed proudly: she had learnt something useful, she was transmitting her knowledge to the next generation, and she was not paid for her lessons but was instead happy and satisfied to be serving the society. It also gave her the option to participate in public life and be outside of home.

From an examination of the curriculum and the list of courses and textbooks for the second level of the seminary training, four main observations can be made based on Table 4. First, a great portion of these books were written specifically for the education of women in the religious seminaries. These are recent (post-revolutionary) publications, predominantly printed with Hajar Publications, which is associated with the Management Centre of Women's Religious Seminaries in Qom.[43] Furthermore, almost all of these books are written and taught in Persian. Arabic texts are typically translated into Persian, such as Mohammad Hosayn Tabataba'i's exegesis of the Qur'an, *al-Mīzān*. The only two exceptions to this first observation are Mohammad Reza Mozaffar's book on logic and Mohammad Baqer al-Sadr's book on the principles of jurisprudence. Interestingly, the second level also includes courses that have political and societal significance, such as the course on 'The Constitution of the Islamic Republic' or 'The Political System in Islam' – topics one may not necessarily expect as part of the curriculum at a religious seminary.

Second, the curriculum of the second level covers the main themes and topics that male students study at the first stage (*moqaddamāt*): morphology, syntax, rhetoric, basic concepts of logic, and Arabic language. The main difference lies in the choice of textbooks. Whereas women primarily read texts that were written in the post-revolutionary era by contemporary religious scholars or politicians in the Persian language and designed specifically for the training at the women's religious seminaries, men read Arabic books, most of which were not written in the contemporary era. Of all the books

---

[42] The Basij is a national mobilisation organisation and is controlled by the supreme leader. Together with the Revolutionary Guards, the Basij is dedicated to guarding the revolution and its principles. See for more information: S. Golkar, *Captive Society: The Basij Militia and Social Control in Iran* (Washington, DC: Woodrow Wilson Centre Press, 2015).

[43] Mrs Sabedi, the director of al-Zahra seminary in Estahban, also revealed that besides Hajar, many of the seminary books are published with Qods Publishers. These books are given to the individual seminaries with a 60 per cent discount. Interview on 27 June 2011.

used in the women's seminaries, *Manṭiq al-Muẓaffar* (Muzaffar's logic) is the only book that is an integral part of the traditional seminary system for men in the first cycle.[44]

Whether the new textbooks necessarily mean a simplification of the curriculum or whether the curriculum aims at training propagandists cannot be established from the list. It is possible to state that the main goal of the second level appears to be to provide foundational knowledge in the most relevant subjects of Islamic studies, such as theology, jurisprudence, Qur'an, exegesis, *Nahj al-balagheh*, or hadith, but with a thematic focus that is determined for them by the Management Centre. Ethics, manners, and family matters are the main foci in these courses, but not exclusively. That being said, only a detailed qualitative analysis of the content of the textbooks (in comparison with those for men) can reveal to what extent the curriculum is simplified and whether the textbooks have an ideological mission or not.

Third, the authors of these works were or are still active in the realm of education in the Islamic sciences or on the political scene in the Islamic Republic. Most are religious scholars who have enjoyed a classical training in the Islamic sciences.[45] Fourth, none of these books is authored by a woman, even though such books do exist and have even been taught previously. For example, *Makhzan al-'erfān*, the exegesis of the Qur'an by Nosrat Amin (d. 1983), the most prominent female religious authority in twentieth-century Iran, was taught in a course on 'Rules of Conduct and Law in the Qur'an' at the Faculty of Theology and Islamic Studies at the University of Tehran before the 1979 revolution.[46] When I asked the directors of both seminaries in Fars why Amin's exegesis was not taught at their seminaries, two different answers were given: The director of al-Zahra seminary in Estahban suggested that Amin's *Makhzan al-'erfān* was too difficult for her students to understand and that she preferred *Tafsir-e nemuneh* by Naser Makarem Shirazi (d. 1927). The librarian at Rayhaneh al-Nabi, who was initially surprised by the question, said, 'It is not the seminary that chooses a textbook, but the Management Centre.' After a short pause, she added, 'But it is a good question, why does the Management Centre not actually assign Amin's *tafsir*?'

Admissions to Level 2

The doors to the religious seminary are not open to any girl or woman interested in Islamic sciences. The admissions process goes beyond a student's

---

44 Sindawi, '*Ḥawza* Instruction', 841.

45 Some examples are Mohsen Hosayn Fallahzadeh, Mahdi Pishva'i, Mohammad Reza Jabaran, and Mohammad Taqi Mesbah Yazdi. See footnotes to Table 4 for more details on these individuals.

46 See Fischer, *Iran from Religious Dispute to Revolution*, 250.

scholarly interest in the subject matter. The directors of al-Zahra in Estahban and at Rayhaneh al-Nabi emphasised the importance of 'motivation' (*angizeh-ye ṭalabi budan*), which is the subject of testing prior to admission. The interview process for the new students for the upcoming academic year at Rayhaneh al-Nabi took place during my stay in Iran. The director disclosed to me that more than seventy students had applied for the twenty-five places available. 'At the interview, we will ask questions to determine someone's motivation. At the same time, we investigate [the background of] the applicant, her relatives, and friends; we also ask her prior teachers [about the applicant's manners and behaviour].' At the centre of attention is the applicant's veiling, she said. She defined 'motivation' in specific terms as the desire to 'strengthen one's faith, learn, and transmit something useful to society'.

The confidential form number three of the evaluation process gives insight into the application process and reveals that 'motivation' and 'veiling' are only a fraction of what makes a good candidate; none of the other points were mentioned or stressed by them in my conversations with the two directors. The students can earn up to fifty points in eight categories and an additional 'special' ten points in three categories. 'Motivation' and 'veiling' make up a maximum of thirteen points. The categories are as follows:

1.) Family situation (matters of education . . .), up to five points
2.) Skills and talents in fields of culture and fine arts, up to three points
3.) Individual characteristics (capability to understand and convey information, communication skills, capability to speak, and so forth), up to eight points
4.) Religious beliefs and religious piety (*bāvar-hā-ye dini va-i'tiqādāt-e mazhabi*), up to ten points
5.) Political and societal views, up to four points
6.) Personal situation, characteristics, and behaviour, up to seven points
7.) Outer appearance (veiling, visage, speech), up to five points
8.) Motivation, up to eight points

Students who earn at least twenty points in the above-mentioned categories can be admitted. They can attain ten more points in three special categories: 1) up to five points for knowing how to recite the entire Koran or *Nahj al-balagheh*[47] by heart; 2) up to three points for being related to martyrs or those injured or imprisoned during the Iran–Iraq war (*ithār-garān*); and 3) up to two points for membership in the Basij. Furthermore, the questionnaire specifies whether the applicant is physically and mentally healthy.

---

[47] The *Nahj al-balagheh* (literally 'The Path of Eloquence') is a collection of the sermons and sayings by Emam 'Ali, the prophet's son-in-law.

The importance of the background of an applicant and her family and friends (for example, whether they wear the veil properly) is held to be intimately linked to the budget for the education at seminaries. Mrs Fallahzadeh reasoned that 'these programs are financed with Imam Zaman's money, *khoms* and other related sources.[48] It is therefore logical and natural that not anyone [who is interested in the seminary training] can benefit from it, that is, get a stipend to study.'[49] She went on to describe the difference between male and female students of religious sciences: the male students typically study with a *marja'*[50] of their choice and receive their salary directly from him that he has collected in the form of *khoms*. Female students, by contrast, 'do not get a salary; they are not even entitled to a salary (*ḥoquq*), because they are not breadwinners.' It is expected or assumed that either fathers or husbands care for them financially. They only get a small stipend to cover the expenses associated with their education, and it is 'ridiculously little'.[51] In other words, entry to the seminary system is highly political and reserved for candidates with a certain religious, political, and cultural background; the Management Centre decides who is entitled to the money that people donate to their local religious authorities as *khoms*. The source of the funds that the Management Centre spends on the salaries of the seminaries' staff was not, or rather could not be, revealed.

[48] Khoms is one-fifth of one's income, a religious tax. See: A. Sachedina, 'Al-Khums: The Fifth in the Imāmī Shī'ī Legal System', *Journal of Near Eastern Studies* 39.4 (1980), 275–289; N. Calder, 'Khums in Imāmī Shī'ī Jurisprudence, from the Tenth to the Sixteenth Century A.D.', *Bulletin of the School of Oriental and African Studies, University of London* 45.1 (1982), 39–47; and A. Zysow and R. Gleave, 'Khums', in *Encyclopaedia of Islam, Second Edition*, eds P. Bearman, T. Bianquis, C. E. Bosworth, E. van Donzel, and W. P. Heinrichs (2012).

[49] Conversation, 6 July 2011. Imam Zaman is Muhammad ibn Hasan al-Mahdi, believed to be the saviour of humankind and the Twelfth and last Imam according to the Shi'is. He will eventually appear to bring peace and justice to the world. See for more information: A. Amanat, *Apocalyptic Islam and Iranian Shi'ism* (London and New York: I. B. Tauris, 2009).

[50] See, for example, on *marja'iyya*, the highest position of religious authority in Shi'ism: L. Walbridge, *The Most Learned of the Shi'a: The Institution of the Marja' Taqlid* (Oxford: Oxford University Press, 2011).

[51] Teachers and administrators at the seminary get their 'money' (she did not use the terminology 'salary') from the Management Centre. Mrs Fallahzadeh disclosed that she gets 380,000 tomans, from which about 100,000 tomans are deducted for insurance. One can earn up to 500,000 tomans as director of a seminary. She compared this to a university professor's salary, which gets two million tomans. She herself also teaches 'Islamic thought' at the university, but she did not disclose her university salary. Both directors emphasised the independence of the religious seminaries from politics. For the first time, the seminaries are independent from both the state and the market (the traditional *bazar*), they declared. They are solely financed by the Management Centre and the Imam's share. While administrators and professors at the seminaries did not complain about their compensation, the students seemed to regard the financial burden as unacceptable. They complained about the expenses such as copying the reading materials for which they had to pay out of their own pockets.

Curriculum and Admissions to Level 3

Questionnaires for applicants to the third and fourth level equivalent to that of the second level do not exist, as suitability of a candidate is not an issue for a candidate applying to the programme at the third and fourth levels. The student is already known to the seminaries since she hails from within the seminary system. Moreover, the applicant to the third level is tested on her knowledge in specific subject matters based on specific books or works. These textbooks are not new to students, since they have been taught at the second level of their religious training. For example, a questionnaire quizzes the candidates about Mohammad Hosayn Tabataba'i's (d. 1981) famous Qur'anic exegesis *al-Mīzān*.[52] Questions relate to the grammatical function of some words, the interpretation of a word, sentence, or verse according to Tabataba'i that the Management Centre expects the candidates to know. The candidates are expected to know Arabic well to read and understand the verses that are referred to in the questionnaire.

Only a small fraction of the graduates of the second level continue their studies at the third level at the women's religious seminaries, that is, an average of about 10 per cent of students. Students can choose from among eleven specialisations: Exegesis and Qur'anic studies, Jurisprudence and Principles of jurisprudence, Islamic theology, Islamic study of women, Islamic philosophy, Theology (focus on the Imamate), Islamic history, Theology (focus on Mahdavism), Arabic literature, Religious sects in Islam, and Ethics and Islamic education. Students cannot really 'choose' the specialisation of their interest; rather, this list represents the total of all specialisations that are offered anywhere in the seminary system. Not all seminaries offer all these specialisations, and most only offer one, two, or three specialisations at most. Very few seminaries offer more than three specialisations. Women typically choose to go to the seminary that is geographically close to their home. The two specialisations that are offered at an overwhelming majority of the seminaries are 'Exegesis and Qur'an studies' and 'Jurisprudence and Principles of jurisprudence'. Of the total 1,905 places that are available for all the specialisations at the third level for the 2018–2019 academic year, 612 places are available for 'Exegesis and Qur'anic studies' and 556 places for 'Jurisprudence and Principles of Jurisprudence'. The available places for the other specialisations range from fifteen places for 'Religious Sects in Islam' to 245 places for 'Islamic Theology'.

Because of the significance of the specialisations of 'jurisprudence and principles of jurisprudence' and 'exegesis and Qur'anic studies', this study focuses on the curriculum of these two specialisations only (see Tables 5 and 6). It is important to mention that the curriculum for the third level

---

[52] The questions are limited to Tabataba'i's interpretation of the first two surahs of the Qur'an *Surat al-ḥamd* and *Surat al-baqarah* up to verse 27.

that the Management Centre in Shiraz gave me for various specialisations is incomplete. The curriculum for the second semester of each of the three years is not included. It was not available for print at the time of my research trip in summer 2011. Despite the missing part of the curriculum, one can predict some of the courses that are offered in the second semester of the first, second, and third years. For example, the course 'Jurisprudence 2' must be offered in the second semester of the first year, because 'Jurisprudence 1' is offered in first semester of the first year, and 'Jurisprudence 3' in the first semester of the second year. Details such as the scope of the reading material, however, is harder, or even impossible, to guess. Despite its incompleteness, the table offers a valuable glimpse into the curriculum of the specialisations on Qur'anic studies and jurisprudence at the third level at the women's religious seminaries in Iran.

At the third level, women read some Arabic works that their male counterparts read in their seminary education at the second cycle, the *suṭuḥ*. These include Shahid Thani's jurisprudential work *Sharḥ al-Lum'a* or Morteza Ansari's (d. 1864) *al-Makāsib* on Islamic commercial law or the *Uṣūl al-Muẓaffar*, a work on the principles of jurisprudence by Mozaffar. Many female students complained that they found the curriculum of the women's religious seminary harder because they had to read many more books in a shorter period of time. However, the scope of the textbooks at the women's religious seminaries seems to be thematically limited; they are not necessarily reading the entire work in the class. Furthermore, despite the fact that these works are written in Arabic, this does not mean that the discussion of the book takes place in Arabic. For example, in the 'Jurisprudence' course at Reyhaneh al-Nabi in Shiraz, Professor 'Edalat, a young *mojtahed*,[53] taught *Sharḥ al-Lum'a* in this manner: he read out one sentence in Arabic, translated and explained it in Persian, and then moved on to the next sentence. When a reference to a specific work was made in the text, he added the name of the author of the work. When the sentences were too long, he dissected them into smaller pieces. Most students worked with the Arabic text and took notes in Persian, but few students worked with the Persian translation, which included explanations as well. The course was dry, there was no discussion about the rules, and the students were expected to become familiar with the rulings, no more.[54]

---

[53] A *mojtahed* has completed the third cycle of the traditional seminary training and is capable of deducing legal rulings based on primary sources such as the Qur'an. Professor 'Edalat wore the traditional garment of the religious scholar. Interestingly, his wife, as it turned out later, was sitting in the same course. Compared to all the other students, she did not take notes, but instead took care of all administrative or organisational questions and matters for the course. In one of the sessions, for example, she distributed a form that needed to be filled out and returned to the main office along with a fee to be paid.

[54] Interestingly, the professor had with him an audio recorder and recorded his own lecture. When students asked clarification questions, he paused the recorder.

Furthermore, women are expected to choose a specialisation at the third level of the seminary training. Men do not choose a specialisation but are instead expected to study a range of disciplines including jurisprudence, philosophy, astronomy, and Qur'an exegesis during their second cycle of religious training (*soṭuḥ*). Despite the thematic specialisation, whether it is jurisprudence, theology or Qur'anic exegesis or something else, women still gain insight into the foundations of other subjects. For example, students with a specialisation in 'jurisprudence and principles of jurisprudence' take classes in hadith, philosophy, or Qur'anic studies. The most relevant question is whether and to what extent these courses are taught according to the curriculum of the Management Centre. Lack of resources and staff is a serious issue in provincial towns, as the following examples demonstrate.

A paucity of suitable professors was a major issue in Estahban and Shiraz. The directors confessed that it was not easy to find professors who are suitable, available, academically competent, and willing to take on teaching appointments. Potential candidates are typically either busy with their primary profession (that is, teaching at a university or somewhere else) or reside in Qom or other relevant religious centres. Only when Qom becomes unbearably hot do some of these scholars return to their home towns and may be available for teaching obligations at the seminaries. Summer 2011 was one such example; the Rayhaneh al-Nabi seminary in Shiraz took advantage of the scholars' local presence and decided to offer classes during the summer months for the first time. Should there be lack of suitable instructors for a given class, the directors of the seminaries are forced to change the curriculum slightly. They usually postpone a lesson until a suitable instructor becomes available or agrees to teach the course. While adjustments to the curriculum are acceptable, the Management Centre would not allow the prescribed material or text for a course to be changed, even if a suitable instructor could teach it. Adherence to the rigid curriculum is obligatory for seminaries under the Management Centre's supervision.

While the class on jurisprudence with Professor 'Edalat worked with the prescribed textbook, the text source for the other classes was not always clear. In the other courses, the professor was either holding lectures, as in the Theology class where Professor Jahanbakhsh spoke freely, without any textbook, about different Islamic religious schools of thought such as the Sunnis, Shi'is, Wahhabis, or Salafis from the point of view of theology. Alternatively, the professor handed out a number of pages out of a book, without proper citation, on the topic of the lesson and started to read it out loud. This was the case in the course 'Philosophy of Religion' with Professor 'Erfanifar, a religious scholar who had prepared to teach about 'the meaning of life'. In his first class, he handed out two pages of a book on 'the meaning of life', read the text out loud, and stopped to explain or invite the students to intervene.

Limited access to necessary resources and course material is yet another challenge in more remote locations such as Estahban. Even though the Management Centre in Qom is expected to equip the seminaries with the same sources and resources, this does not happen. For example, students in Estahban do not get some of the collections of Koranic interpretations, hadith, or other works on CD. In Shiraz, the seminaries do get the CDs, but they cannot use them, because they do not have the necessary computers. The librarian at the Rayhaneh al-Nabi said that they would not allow students to borrow CDs, so at least for now the CDs are being collected on a shelf and need to be dusted once in a while. Sometimes, one of the students in Estahban would take the bus and go all the way to Shiraz just to get a copy of a book that the class needs for the lessons. In Shiraz, the students are less affected by resource challenges, because they belong to a larger environment of knowledge and institutions of learning: numerous libraries and bookstores (especially the Shahid Motahhari bookstore), other seminaries, and the University of Koranic studies were among the most cited institutions at which they could locate additional resources. But even Shirazi students complained about many books that they would not get in Shiraz. Sometimes relatives travelling to Qom would obtain the desired book for them. In Shirazi bookstores, they reported, only works by the most important ulama would be sold. Ordering books online was not as prevalent or as easy as it may be today.

My observations at the seminaries in Shiraz and Estahban indicate that the Management Centre's curriculum may not always be implemented in the way it was designed or expected to be. In order to evaluate the content of the curriculum, it is therefore not sufficient to refer to the Management Centre's handouts or book lists or to analyse the content of the textbooks. One also needs to take local conditions into account. At present, we can conclude that the nationwide unification of the curriculum is an ideal that has not yet been achieved.

Level 4

The fourth and highest level is a fully specialised programme. Most students choose to study jurisprudence, focusing on legal matters related to women and gender, at this stage. As stated above, no data was available about the fourth level at the women's religious seminaries at the time of my research trip in 2011. Today, seven years later, a number of provinces offer lessons at the fourth level (see Table 7). Fourteen women's religious seminaries offer this programme for the academic year 2018–2019 throughout the country.[55]

[55] The information about the seminaries and their specialisations at the fourth level are taken from: WHC, Fehrest-e marākez-e takhaṣoṣi va mo'asesāt-e āmuzesh-e 'āli-ye saṭh-e chahār - sāl-e taḥṣili-ye 97–98, 2018b, http://paziresh.whc.ir/news/view/55129/علمیه-سطح-چهار-98-97-اعلام-فهرست-مدارس. In addition to names of the seminaries and specialisations, the list provides the addresses and phone numbers of the seminaries for interested students.

It is noteworthy that almost all these seminaries are located in the capital cities of the provinces (with the two exceptions of Gorgan and Maybod), for example, Tehran, Qom, Isfahan, Yazd, or Shiraz.

Hojjatoleslam Nouruzi, director of the Service Office for Supplementary Education of the Women's Religious Seminaries, reports that the Management Centre has been offering lessons for the fourth level in a serious way for the third consecutive year. These lessons relate to two 'general (*'omumi*) fields of study' (that is, exegesis and Qur'anic studies as well as comparative exegesis studies) and 'one specialized (*takhaṣṣoṣi*) field of study' (that is, jurisprudence and principles of jurisprudence). He reports that in 2017, about 622 students applied for the fourth level, but the management could only accept about one-fifth of the applications for the fourth level. In Fars, only jurisprudence and the principles of jurisprudence with a specialisation in family matters is offered at the fourth level; there are plans to add exegesis and Qur'anic studies for the 2018–2019 academic year. Currently, about 444 women study Islamic sciences at the fourth level at the women's religious seminaries.[56]

Curriculum

Four different specialisations are offered at the fourth level at fourteen women's religious seminaries. Almost half of these seminaries offer the specialisation 'Jurisprudence and Principles of Jurisprudence'; eight of them offer 'Comparative Qur'anic Studies'. Most seminaries offer only one specialisation, but Fari'eh al-Mostafa in Tehran offers three specialisations ('Comparative Qur'anic Studies', 'Jurisprudence and Principles of Jurisprudence' and 'Transcendent Philosophy' (*ḥekmat-e mote'āliyeh*)), and Ma'sumiyeh in Qom even offer all four (the same three plus 'Islamic Theology').

The programme at the fourth level takes at least eight semesters and at most twelve semesters to complete. Students need to earn a total of eighty credits. One-fourth (twenty credit points) is earned with a thesis (*resāleh-ye 'elmi*). In addition to the thesis, students are also expected to produce and submit at least two articles for publication during their programme.

The handout with general information about the fourth level for the academic year 2017–2018 mentions the following among the goals that the women's programme pursues: establishing proficiency in foundations (*mabāni*), schools (*makāteb*), opinions and methodologies related to the respective specialisation or major (*reshteh*); consolidating and strengthening research capabilities, criticising and voicing opinions on matters related to the respective major; and advancing the capability of responding to

[56] See WHC, Āghāz-e paziresh-e ḥouzeh-ye; Shiraze, Āmār-e bālā-ye jaẓab-e; and IRNA, 39 hezār va 217.

the scholarly necessities and matters of the respective major. Among the objectives that the Management Centre pursues for this level are efforts to 'promote moral and spiritual virtues and character traits', but also 'to emphasize the approach of *ejtehad* in various lessons'. The handout does not specifically state that it aims to produce *mojtahedehs,* but learning the capability of deducing the rulings based on primary religious texts (*ejtehād*), the main qualification of *mojtaheds,* is an integral part of the programme. It remains to be seen whether and how graduates of the fourth level claim authority and what professions they eventually decide to pursue. One foresees, for example, that some of these women will become much-needed professors for the third level of training in women's seminaries. Today, most of these professors are male. During my stay at Rayhaneh al-Nabi, the director confessed that not one single woman taught at the third level. One could furthermore anticipate that some of the graduates of the fourth level will become researchers or work in religious and political institutions where legal reasoning is one of their tools for addressing socially relevant matters. Hence, a woman who studies jurisprudence and principles of jurisprudence at the fourth level is understood to be on her path to becoming a thematically specialised jurist (*mojtahedeh-ye motejazzi* or *mouḍu'i*) in women and family matters. This qualification is to be differentiated from that of an absolute jurist (*mojtahedeh-ye moṭlaq*) trained to deduce the law based on the primary Islamic sources on any subject.[57] The latter rank is the rank typically at the end point of the men's seminary education.

Admissions

Students who wish to enter the programme of the fourth level are expected to respond to questions in jurisprudence, principles of jurisprudence, and the Qur'an based on the textbooks by twentieth-century scholars Baqer Irvani and Mohammad Reza Muzaffar (d. 1964) (although the scope is limited, as Table 8 shows).

The material on which candidates for admission are tested differs depending on the specialisation. For the specialisation in 'Comparative Exegesis', for example, students are expected to be familiar with the exegetical works by the twentieth-century Tabataba'i and twelfth-century Tabarsi; the focus is on the twenty-eighth *juz'* (one-thirtieth part) of the Qur'an (these are the Medinan chapters 55–66). For the specialisation in jurisprudence, candidates are required to demonstrate knowledge of three textbooks by the scholars who have contributed significantly to the field of jurisprudence and principles of jurisprudence, that is, the twentieth-century Iraqi legal scholar Mohammad Baqer Sadr, the prominent nineteenth-century Akhund Khorasani, and the sixteenth-century scholar Shahid Thani, whose texts are widely esteemed

[57] Interview with the director and the professors at the Rayhaneh al-Nabi.

and read in the seminaries.[58] The books the candidates are tested on are either classics (for example, Akhund Khorasani's *Kifāyat al-uṣūl*) or more recent works such as Mohammad Baqer Sadr's *Durūs* that have become part of the seminary curriculum (see Table 9). All are books that are studied at the third level.

At present, dormitories are not available for the fourth level and students must sign a written commitment to reside in the town where the seminary is located for the entire duration of the programme. It seems that the Management Centre expects women to be married by the time they enter the programme, and the natural place for a married woman is at home and not in a dormitory.

Concluding Remarks

Women's religious seminaries in Iran, with their different programmes and specialisations, are too diverse for one to make sweeping statements about the entirety of the system. The four different levels of learning deserve separate attention, as the thematic focus, societal function, and political goal of each level is different. The specialisation and academic focus of Islamic sciences increases with the level. The first and second levels offer access to a broad spectrum of subjects, even non-religious subjects such as the constitution of the Islamic Republic of Iran, and the graduates are not necessarily expected to pursue education or a career in the Islamic sciences. Indeed, less than 10 per cent of the tens of thousands of graduates of the second level have continued their studies at the third level to date. Starting with the third level, women have the opportunity to specialise in various branches of the Islamic sciences, most frequently in jurisprudence and principles of jurisprudence, Qur'anic exegesis, and Islamic theology.

At the fourth level, women may choose to specialise in jurisprudence and principles of jurisprudence, acquire the capability of deducing rulings based on primary religious texts (*ejtehād*), the main qualification of a *mojtahed*. Considering that some seminaries will provide this specialisation with respect to family matters, one may expect graduates of this programme to become thematically focused mojtaheds (*mojtahedeh-ye motejazzi* or *mouḍu'i*). It remains to be seen whether graduates of the fourth level will claim authority as *mojtahedehs* and whether they will qualify for various legal, judicial, and political positions that require the qualification as *mojtaheds* (for example, member

[58] Muhammad Baqer al-Sadr (executed in 1980) authored the most authoritative work in the principles of jurisprudence in the contemporary era, the three-volume *Durūs fī 'ilm al-uṣūl* (Lessons in the Science of Jurisprudence). Mohammad Kazem Khorasani (d. 1911), known as Akhund-e Khorasani, is author of *Kifāyah* (The Sufficiency), one of the most famous textbooks in the principles of jurisprudence. Zayn al-Din b. Nur al-Din 'Ali b. Ahmad al-'Amili al-Juba'i (d. 1559), known as Shahid Thani, is most famous for his jurisprudential work *Al-Rawḍa al-bahīyya fī sharḥ al-lum'ā al-dimashqīyyah*, a commentary on *al-Lum'a al-dimaqshīyya* by Shahi Awwal.

of the Assembly of Experts that has the right to elect the religious leader, *rahbar*). The seminary system, while not overtly proclaiming to produce *mojtahedehs*, does not hinder women from becoming *mojtahedehs* at the end of the fourth level either. While it is too early to evaluate the work of the seminaries at the fourth level, how the programme will be implemented, and what professions the students will pursue after graduation, staff and students of the seminaries have high expectations of it, however.

With regard to women's religious seminary system from a provincial view, one can conclude that the nature of the seminary system is highly hierarchical and centralised. It is not only perceived as such; this fact actually manifests itself in the unequal distribution of available places, resources, staff, and opportunities. Even though the Management Centre in Qom has designed one single concept for all the seminaries, there are differences among them in their curriculum, staff, and resources.

Table 13.1 Student Capacity, Academic Year 2012–2013

Name of province	Population, 2011–2012[a]	Student capacity, second level, for academic year 2012–2013	Student capacity, third level, for academic year 2012–2013	Dorm capacity, second level, for academic year 2012–2013	Dorm capacity, third level, for academic year 2012–13
Alborz	2,412,513	265	20	0	0
Ardabil	1,248,488	110	0	10	0
Azarbayjan-e Gharbi	3,080,576	170	5	15	5
Azarbayjan-e Sharqi	3,724,620	360	20	30	10
Bushehr	1,032,949	110	15	30	0
Chaharmaḥal va Bakhtiyari	895,263	70	5	25	5
Fars	4,596,658	462	30	168	20
Gilan	2,480,874	170		54	
Golestan	1,777,014	230	20	50	15
Hamedan	1,758,268	250	30	5	15
Hormozgan	1,578,183	230	10	55	5
Ilam	557,599	120		22	
Isfahan	4,879,312	1,202	115	40	15
Kahkiluyeh va Buyer Ahmad	658,629	50	0	35	0
Kerman	2,938,988	445	35	45	0

Name of province	Population, 2011–2012[a]	Student capacity, second level, for academic year 2012–2013	Student capacity, third level, for academic year 2012–2013	Dorm capacity, second level, for academic year 2012–2013	Dorm capacity, third level, for academic year 2012–13
Kermanshah	1,945,227	265	5	50	0
Khorasan					
Khuzestan	4,531,720	598	70	42	5
Kordestan	1,493,645	145	0	45	0
Lorestan	1,754,243	280	0	0	0
Markazi	1,413,959	215	30	10	0
Mazandaran	3,073,943	495	15	40	15
Nehbandan	No data	25		10	
Qazvin	1,201,565	75	15	10	0
Qom	1,151,672	65	75	0	0
Semnan	631,218	185	25	20	10
Sistan	2,534,327	285	30	55	0
Tehran	12,183,391	1,000	165	15	0
Yazd	1,074,428	328	40	38	0
Zanjan	1,015,734	80	30	10	0

[a] Data taken from the official website of data and statistics in Iran at <https://www.amar.org.ir/Portals/0/News/1396/chnsanvms95.pdf>, last accessed 10 April 2018.

Table 13.2 Number of Seminaries and Students in Iran for the Academic year 2017–2018

Level of education	Number of seminary sections that offer lessons for that level, 2017–2018	Number of students with a job (*ṭollāb-e shāghel*), 2017–2018	Number of graduated students (*dānesh-āmukhtegān*) 2017–2018
Level 1	No data provided	No data provided	3,070
Level 2 (*'omumi*)	413	48,806	39,423
Level 3 (*'āli*)	57	7,916	1,730
Level 4 (*takhaṣṣoṣi*)	18	330	7

Table 13.3 Women's Religious Seminaries in Fars, 2012–2013[a]

City/Town	Name of seminary	Number of available places	Number of available places with dormitory
Abadeh	Kousar	30	0
Abadeh Tashk	Al-Zahra	20	10
Arsenjan	Fatemeh al-Zahra	15	15
Darab	Fatemeh al-Zahra	20	10
Eqlid	Omm al-A'emeh	20	15
Estahban	Al-Zahra	20	5
Fasa	Fatemiyeh	30	0
Gallehdar	Fatemeh al-Zahra	15	15
Gerash	Al-Zahra*[b]	17	13
Jahrom	Hazrat-e Narges	25	0
Kazerun	Al-Zahra	30	0
Khafr	Fatemeh al-Zahra	20	10
Khorram Bid[c]	Al-Zahra	15	15
Lar	Zahra Athar	15	15
Lorestan	Zahra-ye Athar	No data provided	No data provided
Marvdasht	Fatemeh al-Zahra	30	0
Nayriz	Al-Zahra	25	10
Nurabad-e Mamasani	Narjesiyeh	15	5
Safashahr	Al-Zahra	No data provided	No data provided
Sheshdeh	Al-Zahra	30	5
Shiraz	Al-Zahra	30	20
	Fatemeh al-Zahra	40	10
	Rayhaneh al-Nabi*		

[a] See document with the title '*Asāmi-ye madāres-e ḥouzeh-hā-ye 'elmiyeh-e khwāharān-e ostān-e Fārs*'.
[b] * indicates that the respective seminary offers lessons at the third level as well.
[c] There is no town or village with the name Khorram Bid. Rather, Khorram Bid refers to a county in Fars of which Safashahr is the capital. Whether the al-Zahra seminary in Safashahr and Khorram Bid is the same institution is not clear.

Table 13.4 Five-year Programme, Second Level, 2010–2011

First Year, First Semester

Subject	Text	Scope
Intermediate morphology 1 (*ṣarf*)[a]	*Ṣarf-e motevasseṭeh* (Intermediate morphology)	From the beginning until the end of the chapter on 'verbs'
Reading the Qur'an fluidly (*ravānkhwāni-ye qor'ān-e karim*)	*Ravānkhwāni-ye qor'ān-e karim* (Reading out the Qur'an and reciting the Qur'an) by Habibi and Shahidi[b]	From the beginning of the book until the end of lesson eleven (first part)
General legal rulings 1 (*aḥkām-e 'omumi*)	*Āmuzesh-e feqh 1* (Jurisprudence 1) by Fallahzadeh[c]	From the beginning until the end of lesson twenty-seven (first part) (pp. 25–185)
Legal rulings regarding women (*aḥkām-e vizheh-ye bānvān*)	*Aḥkām-e dokhtarān* (Legal rulings related to girls)[d]	First part (pp. 25–109)
Analytical history of Islam 1 (*tārikh-e taḥlili-ye eslām*)	*Tārikh-e eslām* (Islamic history) by Pishva'i[e]	The entire book
English language 1	Concepts and comments	From the beginning until the end of lesson ten
Islamic ethics 1 (*akhlāq-e eslāmi*)	*Darsnāmeh-ye 'elm-e akhlāq*, vol. 1 (Textbook in science of ethics, vol. 1)[f]	From the beginning until the end of lesson eleven
Persian literature (*adabiyāt-e fārsi*)	*Kelk-e khiyāl angiz* (A pen that inspires to contemplate), vol. 2[g]	The entire book (exceptions apply)
Physical education	General principles of physical education	The entire book (exceptions apply)

[a] The seven-year programme that comprises the first and second level of the seminary training starts with the beginning level of this course. I have disregarded the curriculum of the first level in this chapter.
[b] No information is available about 'Ali Habibi (b. 1958–1959) and Mohammad Reza Shahidi (b. 1958–1959).
[c] Mohsen Hosayn Fallahzadeh (b. 1959–1960) is the director of the Institute for Determining the Themes in Jurisprudence at a religious seminary in Qom, the director of the Headquarters of the Propagation of Religious Rulings in Qom, and a member of the Fatwa Office of Iran's Supreme Leader. I cannot say with certainty whether he is related to the director of Rayhaneh al-Nabi, the women's religious seminaries in Shiraz, but it is very likely, as he lived and studied in Shiraz before he moved to Qom: He went to Madreseh-ye 'Elmiyeh-ye Hakim in Shiraz (under Ayatollah Dastghayb) to start his seminary career.
[d] This refers to the book *Aḥkām-e dokhtarān: raveshi dar dasteh-bandi-ye aḥkām* by Mohammad Vahidi and is published by Nashr-e Hajar, a publisher that is associated with the Management Centre. It has been printed at least fifteen times.
[e] The full title of Mahdi Pishva'i's book is *Tarikh-e eslām: jāheliyat tā raḥlat-e payāmbar-e eslām*. Another of Pishva'i's books, *Sireh-ye pishvāyān*, is also read in the women's religious seminaries. Pishva'i is one of the professors at the Imam Sadeq Institute and the Institute for Teaching and Research of Imam Khomeini in Qom.
[f] This is the two-volume book authored by Mohammad Reza Jabaran (b. 1958–1959), published with the Management Centre. It has been printed at least fifteen times. Jabaran has been active in the fields of propagation and teaching of Islamic sciences. He was director of at least two offices of the Centre of Propagating Islam. As a student of Islamic sciences, he studied with prominent religious authorities such as Naser Makarem Shirazi.
[g] The full title of the book is *Kelk-e khiyāl angiz: āshenā'i bā adabiyāt-e farsi va āmuzesh-e nevisandegi*, is authored by Hamid Basiriyan, and published by the printing house of the Management Centre.

First Year, Second Semester

Subject	Text	Scope
Intermediate morphology 2 (*ṣarf*)	*Ṣarf-e motevasseṭeh* (Intermediate morphology)	The chapter on nouns (*ism*)
Rules governing pronunciation [during recitation of the Qur'an] 1 (*tajvid*)	*Ravān-khwāni va-tajvid-e qor'ān-e karim* (Reading out the Qur'an and reciting the Qur'an) by Habibi and Shahidi	Second part
Learning the Qur'an by heart 1	*Ketāb-e oṣul va-ravesh-hā-ye ḥefẓ-e qor'ān va-ḥefẓ-e joz'-e 30* (Book on principles and methods on learning the Qur'an by heart; thirtieth part)[a]	The entire book and learning the thirtieth part by heart
General rulings 2	*Feqh 1 and 2* (Jurisprudence 1 and 2) by Fallahzadeh	From lesson twenty-eight in the first volume up to lesson thirteen of the second volume
Islamic ethics 2	*Edāmeh-ye dars-nāmeh-ye 'elm-e akhlāq, jeld-e 1* (Continuing with the main text on science of ethics, vol. 1)	From lesson twelve on 'fasting' up to the end of lesson twenty-two on the 'law [regulating the relationship] between wife and husband'
Beginning syntax	*Mabādi, jeld-e 2* (Principles, vol. 2)	The part on syntax
Deductive tenets of faith 1	*Āmuzesh-e 'aqāyed* (Teaching tenets of faith)[b]	From the beginning of the book up to the part on 'issues of the prophethood'
Persian literature 2	*Kelk-e khiyāl angiz 3* (A pen that inspires to contemplate, vol. 3)	The entire book except for lessons nine and ten
English language 2	Concepts and comments	From the beginning of lesson eleven up to lesson twenty

[a] This book might be referring to *Oṣul va-ravesh-hā-ye ḥefẓ-e qor'ān* by Ya'qub Karimi. It features the inclusion of forty hadith, which praise the virtue of learning the Qur'an by heart.

[b] *Āmuzesh-e 'aqāyed* is a three-volume book by Moḥammad Taqi Mesbah Yazdi, a religious scholar and politician in the Islamic Republic.

Second Year, First Semester

Subject	Text	Scope
Advanced syntax 1 (*naḥv-e pishrafteh 1*)	*Kitāb-e Hidāya* (Book of guidance) by Shirafkan[a]	From the beginning up to lesson thirty-two
Qur'anic sciences (*'olum-e qor'āni*)	*Dars-nāmeh-ye 'olum-e qor'āni, level 1* (Textbook in Qur'anic studies, level 1)	The entire textbook
General rulings 3 (*aḥkām-e 'omumi*)	*Feqh* 2 (Jurisprudence 2) by Fallahzadeh	From the beginning of lesson fourteen up to the end of the book
English language 1	Concepts and comments	From the beginning up to the end of lesson ten
Islamic ethics 3 (*akhlāq-e eslāmi 3*)	*Dars-nāmeh-ye 'elm-e akhlāq, j* 2 (Textbook in science of ethics, vol. 2)[b]	From lesson twenty-three until lesson thirty-four
Vocabulary in the Qur'an (*mofredāt-e qor'ān*)	*Mofradāt-e qor'ān* (Qur'anic vocabulary)[c]	From the beginning of the book up to part thirty-two
Analytical history of Islam 3 (*Tarikh-e taḥlili-ye eslām 3*)	*Sireh-ye pishvāyān* (Biography of [religious?] leaders) by Pishva'i	From the part on the life of Imam Baqer up to the end of the book
Physical education (*tarbiyat-e badani*)	*Oṣul-e 'omumi-ye tarbiyat-e badani* (General principles of physical education)	The entire book except for lesson thirteen
Deductive tenets of faith 1 (*'aqāyed-e estedlāli 1*)	*Āmuzesh-e 'aqāyed* (Education of tenets of faith)	From the beginning of the book up to the part on issues of prophethood
Educative discussion of family in Islam (*mobāḥeth-e tarbiyati-e khanevādeh dar eslām*)	*Neẓām-e khānevādeh dar eslām* (The system of family in Islam)[d]	The entire book

[a] The entire title is *al-Hidāyah fī al-nahw taṣḥīḥ* and the book is written by Hosayn Shirafkan (b. 1964–1965). He is a religious scholar and instructor.

[b] The book *Dars-nāmeh-ye 'olum-e qor'āni* is a textbook by Hosayn Javan Arasteh (b. 1962–1963) and published by the publisher of the Office of Islamic Propagation of the Religious Seminary in Qom. It was written for the students at the first and second levels of the women's religious seminaries. Arasteh studied at the seminaries Golpaygani and Haqqani. He later studied with eminent scholars such as Fazel Lankarani Javadi Amoli. He went on to study law at the university in Tehran.

[c] The book *Darāmādi bar dānesh-e mofredāt-e qor'ān* by Seyyed Mahmud Tayyeb Hosayni and Seyyed Reza 'Ali 'Askari was specifically written for students at the second level of the women's religious seminaries.

[d] This book is written by Shaykh Hosayn Ansarian, a religious scholar and a prolific author. In 2017, a new edition of the book was introduced to the public. See, for example, F. N. Agency, Virāst-e jadid-e ketāb-e "Neẓām-e khānevādeh dar eslām" ostād Anṣāriān beh nashr āmad, 2017, <http://www.farsnews.com/newstext.php?nn=13960905000535>.

Second Year, Second Semester

Subject	Text	Scope
Advanced syntax 2 (*naḥv-e pishrafteh*)	*Ketāb-e Hidāyeh* by Shirafkan	From lesson thirty-three up to the end of the book
Deductive tenets of faith 2 (*'aqāyed-e estedlāli*)	*Amuzesh-e 'aqāyed* (Teaching tenets)	From the issue on prophet up to the end of the part on Imamate
History of Shi'ism (*tārikh-e tashayyo'*)	*Tārikh-e tashayyo'* (History of Shi'ism)[a]	The entire book
Islamic ethics 4 (*akhlāq-e eslāmi*)	*Edāmeh-ye dars-nāmeh-ye 'elm-e akhlāq* (Textbook on sciences of ethics)[b]	From lesson thirty-five up to the end of lesson forty-five
English language 2	Concepts and comments	From the beginning of lesson eleven up to the end of lesson twenty
Research methodology (*ravesh-e taḥqiq*)	*Dars-nāmeh-ye ravesh-e taḥqiq* (Textbook on research methodology)	The entire book
Logic 1 (*manṭeq*)	*Durūs fī 'ilm al-manṭiq* (Lessons in the sciences of logic)[c]	From the beginning of the book until the beginning of taṣdiqāt (*taṣdīq* means assent or attestation and constitutes one of two states of knowledge that logic aims to produce in the intellect; the other is *tasawwur*)
Will (*waṣiyyat-nāmeh*)	*Rahnemud-hā-ye jāvdāneh* (Eternal guidance)	The entire book including the commentaries

[a] This book could be one of the following two: it is either the book *Tārikh-e tashayyo'* written by a number of scholars who are affiliated with the Research Centre of the seminary and university (*pazhuhesh-gāh-e ḥouzeh va dānesh-gāh*). Or it is the book *Dars-nāmeh-ye tārikh-e tashayyo'* by Gholam Hosayn Moharami.

[b] *Dars-nāmeh-ye 'elm-e akhlāq* is a two-volume textbook by Mohammad Reza Jabaran, a religious scholar. It is published with the Hajar publisher.

[c] This book is written by the prominent religious scholar Mohammad Reza Mozaffar (d. 1964) and published with the Hajar that is affiliated with the Management Centre. Mozaffar studied with religious authorities such as 'Abd al-Hadi Shirazi (d. 1962). Some of his publications are on the principles of jurisprudence, philosophy, logic, foundation of Shi'i belief and Islamic theology.

Third Year, First Semester

Subject	Text	Scope
Upper level syntax 1 (*naḥv-e 'āli*)	*Mabādī al-'arabiyya* (Foundations of the Arabic language, vol. 4)	From the beginning of the science of syntax up to the beginning of the accusative
Grammar 1 (*tajziyeh va-tarkib*)	*Tajziyeh va-tarkib*, notebook 4[a]	From the beginning of the book up to the beginning of chapter '*naṣr*'
English language 1	Concepts and comments	From the beginning of the book up to lesson ten
The Constitution (*qānun-e asāsi*)	*Āshenā'i bā qānun-e asāsi-ye jomhuri-ye eslāmi* (Introduction to the Constitution of the Islamic Republic)[b]	The entire book
Deductive doctrines (1) (*'aqāyed-e estedlāli*)	*Āmuzesh-e 'aqāyed* (Teaching of the tenets)	From the beginning of the book up to the first part of 'A take-away from the issue of prophethood'
Logic 2 (*manṭeq*)	*Durūs fī 'ilm al-manṭiq* (Lessons in the science of logic)	The chapter on *taṣdīqāt*
Science of hadith (*ḥadith shenāsi*)	*Dars-nāmeh-ye 'elm-e ḥadith* (Textbook on science of hadith)	The entire book except for chapter two
History of Shi'ism (*tārikh-e tashayyo'*)	*Tārikh-e tashayyo'-e pazhuheshgāh-e ḥouzeh va dāneshgāh* (History of Shi'ism of the research centres of the seminaries and the universities)	The entire book

[a] There are a number of books with this title, but this must be *Zabān-e qor'ān: tajziyeh va tarkib* by Hamid Mohammadi, published with Hajar. The author wrote this book by the order of the Management Centre. *Tajziyeh* literally means 'de-composition' and refers to identifying a word in its grammatical function. *Tarkib* literally means 'combination' and refers to the role that a word plays in a sentence.

[b] It is not clear which *Āshenā'i bā qānun-e asāsi-ye jomhuri-ye eslāmi-ye iran* is used at the women's religious seminaries. One such work is written by Mohammad Reza Majidi and published with Nashr-e Ma'āref. Another book with the same title is authored by Mahdi Nazarpur.

Third Year, Second Semester

Subject	Text	Scope
Upper level syntax 2 (*naḥv-e 'āli*)	*Edāmeh-ye mabādi al-'arabiyya* (Continue the book on the principles of the Arabic language, vol. 4)	From the beginning of '*baḥth fī al-manṣubāt*' up to the beginning of '*istighāthah*'
Serial Qur'ānic exegesis 1 (*tafsir-e tartibi*)	*Tafsir-e boshri*[a]	Chapters *Ḥamd* and *Baqarah* up to the beginning of verse 83
Logic 3 (*manṭeq*)	*Durūs fī 'ilm al-manṭiq* (Lessons in the sciences of logic)	*khoms* year[b]
English language 2	Concept and comments	From lesson eleven up to lesson twenty
Islamic Ethics 5 (*akhlāq-e eslāmi*)	*Tafsir-e nemuneh*[c]	Chapter *Ḥijr*
Deductive doctrines 2 (*'aqāyed-e estedlāli*)	*Āmuzesh-e 'aqāyed* (Teaching of tenets)	From the beginning of the part on 'a take-away from matters on prophethood' up to the end of Imamate
Principles of jurisprudence 1 (*oṣul-e feqh*)	*Ḥalaqa ūlā* (Persian translation by Hekmat)[d]	The entire book
Educational psychology (*ravān-shenāsi-ye tarbiyati*)	*Ravān-shenāsi-ye tarbiyati* by Sālārifar (Educational psychology)[e]	Limitations not determined yet

[a] *Tafsir-e bashari: sharḥ-e ravān* is authored by Hamid Mohammadi, Saleh Qanadi, 'Ali Homa'i and is published with Nashr-e Hajar. The work is based on the *tafsir* of 'Allameh Tabataba'i, but parts have been selected and arranged by the Teaching Secretary of the Management Centre (the focus seems to be on the Qur'anic surahs *al-Aḥzāb* (33) and *al-Nūr* (24)).

[b] The *khoms* year is a one-year span in which the *khoms*, one-fifth of one's income, is calculated. The term '*khoms* year' is mentioned in newer works of jurisprudence starting in the second half of the twentieth century.

[c] *Tafsir-e nemuneh* is a twenty-seven-volume Qur'anic exegesis by Naser Makarem Shirazi with the collaboration of some scholars at the religious seminary in Qom. It is written for a broader audience, including non-seminary readers.

[d] *Ḥalaqah* is a multi-volume work by the prominent Iraqi Shi'i scholar Muhammad Baqir al-Sadr. Students at the seminary read a translation of the work by Nasrollah Hekmat.

[e] Mohammad Reza Salarifar is a member of the research group on psychology of the Research Centre of the Seminary and University. He has published extensively on matters related to marriage and family in Islam. No information or reference to a book with the title *Ravān-shenāsi-ye tarbiyati* that he has allegedly authored could be found. The only book of his that includes the term psychology (*ravān-shenāsi*) in the title is *Ketāb-e khānevādeh dar negaresh-e eslām va-ravānshenāsi*.

Fourth Year, First Semester

Subject	Text	Scope
Introduction to the science of rhetoric 1 (*āshenā'i bā 'olum-e balāghi*)	*Āshenā'i bā 'olūm-e balāghi* (Introduction of the science of rhetoric)[a]	From the beginning of the book up to chapter six
Deductive jurisprudence 1 (*feqh-e estedlāli*)	*Durūs tamhīdiyya fī al-fiqh al-istidlālī* (Introductory lessons in the deductive jurisprudence)[b]	The volumes on ritual purity, *khoms* and *zakat*
Principles of jurisprudence 3 (*oṣul-e feqh*)	*Al-mūjaz fī uṣūl al-fiqh* (A short summary of the principles of jurisprudence)[c] and *Ḥalqa thāniyah* (for some seminaries)	From the beginning of *'baḥth al-'umūm wa al-khuṣūṣ'* up to the end of the discussion on *'ḥojiyyat-e khabar-e vāḥed'* (the authority or authenticity of traditions with limited number of narrators) From lesson twenty-one up to the end of lesson forty
Science of hadith (*ḥadith shenāsi*)	*Dars-nāmeh-ye 'elm-e ḥadith* (Textbook on the science of hadith)	The entire book except for chapter two
Introduction to Nahj al-Balagheh (*āshenā'i bā nahj al-balāgheh*)	*Dar maḥḍar-e khorshid* (In the presence of the sun)[d]	The entire book
Introduction to religions (*āshenā'i bā adyān*)	*Āshenā'i bā adyān* by Toufiqi, latest edition (Introduction to religions)[e]	The entire book
Islamic ethics 7 (*akhlāq-e eslāmi*)	*Bar kerāneh sharḥ-e chehel* hadith by Mohadethi[f] (At the shore of forty hadith commentary)	Hadith one up to hadith eighteen, with exception of hadith eight and eleven
Women in Islam 1 (*zan dar eslām*)	*Neẓām-e ḥoqūq-e zan dar eslām* (The system of women's rights in Islam)[g]	From the beginning up to part eleven, with the exception of part four
Thematic teaching methodology 1 (*ravesh-e tadris-e mouḍu'i*)	*Rāhnamā-ye tadris-e qor'ān* by Habibi (A guide of teaching the Qur'an)[h]	The entire book

[a] The full title of the work is *Āshenā'i bā 'olūm-e balāghi: ma'āni, bayān va badi'* and is authored by Baqer Irvani and Hamid Mohammadi. It is published with Nashr-e Hajar. Hamid Mohammadi is a freelance scholar and works with the Islamic Republic of Iranian Broadcasting (IRIB). Irvani is a religious scholar who studied with eminent scholars such as Abu al-Qasim Khu'i (d. 1992) and Muhammad Baqir al-Sadr (d. 1980).

[b] *Durūs tamhīdīyyah fī al-fiqh al-istidlālī* is a three-volume work by Mohammad Baqer Irvāni and relates to the fields of jurisprudence and its principles. The first volume covers issues of worship (*al-ibādāt*), the second volume contracts and unilateral legal actions (*al-'uqūd wa al-īqā'āt*), and the third volume judges' verdicts (*aḥkām*).

[c] This book is written in the Arabic language and is authored by Ja'far Sobhani, a former member of the Society of Seminary Teachers of Qom and founder of the Imam Sadeq Institute in Qom. He founded and edited two magazines, *Maktab-e eslām* and *Maktab-e eslāmi*. His work *Doctrines of Shi'i Islam: A Compendium of Imami Beliefs and Practices* has been translated into English.

[d] Depending on the source of information, this book is authored by Seyyed Jamal al-Din-Pur, but Akbar Asad Alizadeh and Seyyed Mohammad Kazem Tabataba'i are also listed as contributors. It is published by Hajar Publishers, a firm associated with the Management Centre. The themes that recur most frequently in the book are knowledge of God, piety, the material world, daily bread, and means of livelihood. Jamal al-Din-Pur studied with prominent scholars such as 'Allameh Tabataba'i (d. 1981), Hosayn Borujerdi (d. 1961), Mohammad Reza Golpaygani (d. 1993), and Ruhollah Khomeini (d. 1989).

[e] The book *Ketāb-e āshenā'i bā adyān-e bozorg* is authored by Hosayn Toufiqi, who is a scholar and translator at the University Adyān va Madhāheb. He completed his studies at the Haqqani seminary, one of the leading seminaries in Qom.

[f] Javad Mohaddethi (b. 1952–1953) started his seminary career at the Haqqani seminary in Qom. Some of his professors were Yousef Sane'i (b. 1937), Mohammad Taqi Masbah Yazdi (b. 1935), and Ahmad Jannati (b. 1927). Some of his publications deal with ethics, religious culture, and happiness.

[g] This work must be the famous book by Morteza Motahhari (d. 1979), as there is no other book with that title.

[h] The complete title is *Rāhnamā-ye tadris-e ravān-khāni-ye qor'ān-e karim va kholāṣeh-i az rasm va ḍabṭ-e qor'ān-e karim* and it is by 'Ali Habibi.

Fourth Year, Second Semester

Subject	Text	Scope
Introduction to the science of rhetoric 2 (*āshenā'i bā 'olum-e balāghi*)	*Āshenā'i bā 'olum-e balāghi* (Introduction to the science of rhetoric)	From chapter six up to the end of the book
Deductive jurisprudence 2 (*feqh-e estedlāli*)	*Durūs tamhīdiyya fī al-fiqh al-istidlālī* (Introductory lessons in deductive jurisprudence)	The volumes on prayer and fasting
Principles of jurisprudence 4 (*oṣul-e feqh*)	*Al-mūjaz fī uṣūl al-fiqh* (A short summary of the principles of jurisprudence)	From *'al-kalām fī al-ijmā'* up to the end of the book
	and	and
	Ḥalqa thāniya (for some seminaries)	From lesson forty-one up to the end of the book
Philosophy 1 (*falsafeh*)	*Falsafeh-ye eslāmi* by 'Obudiyat (Islamic philosophy)[a]	From the beginning of the book up to the second part (*'ellat va ma'lul*)
Serial Qur'anic exegesis 2 (*tafsir-e tartibi*)	*Tafsir-e Ṣāfi* (Safi's Qur'anic exegesis)[b]	Chapter *Nisā'* up to the verse 113
Introduction to Islamic religions and branches (*āshenā'i bā feraq va madhāheb-e eslāmi*)	*Āshenā'i bā feraq va madhāheb-e eslāmi* (Introduction to the religions and religions of Islam)[c]	The entire book
Women in Islam 2 (*zan dar eslām*)	*Dar āmadi bar neẓām-e shakhṣiyat-e zan dar eslām* (A take-away from the system of women's character in Islam)[d]	From *'mabāni-e eslāmi dar negaresh beh shakhṣiyat-e zan'* up to the end of p. 188
Islamic ethics 8 (*akhlāq-e eslāmi*)	*Bar kerāneh sharḥ-e chehel* hadith by Mohadethi (At the shore of forty hadith commentary)	Hadith nine up to the last hadith, exception hadith twenty-four, twenty-six, thirty-four, thirty-five, and thirty-eight
Methodology in public speaking 2 (*ravesh-e sokhanrāni*)	Practising different approaches to public speaking and propaganda with the use of videotaping	

[a] The complete title of the book is *Dar-āmadi bar falsafeh-ye eslāmi,* and it is by 'Abdolrasul 'Obudiyat, who is a scholar and educator of Islamic philosophy.

[b] *Tafsir-e ṣāfi* is a Qur'anic exegesis by the seventeenth-century scholar Molla Mohsen Fayz Kashani, whose exegesis draws heavily on narrations.

[c] *Āshenā'i bā feraq va-madhāheb-e eslāmi* is written by Hojjatoleslam Reza Berenjkar. The main parts of the book are related to the earliest branches of Islam, Shi'ism, Sunnism, and the 'extremists' (*gholāt*). Berenjkar has been a faculty member at the Tehran University and an instructor of the seminary.

[d] *Dar-āmadi bar neẓām-e shakhṣiyat-e zan dar eslām, barresi-ye moqāyeseh-'i-ye did-gāh-e eslām va-gharb,* by Mohammad Reza Ziba'i Nezhad and Mohammad Taqi Sobhani, was published by the Study and Research Office for Women (Daftar-e moṭāle'āt va-taḥqiqāt-e zanān). Both authors are religious scholars.

Fifth Year, First Semester

Subject	Text	Scope
Serial Qur'anic exegesis 5 (*tafsir-e tartibi*)	*Tafsir al-mizān* (*al-Mizān* exegesis)[a]	Continuing Chapter *Nūr*, verse twenty-seven until the end of the chapter
Deductive jurisprudence 3 (*feqh-e estedlāli*)	*Durūs tamhīdiyya fī al-fiqh al-istidlālī* (Introductory lessons in deductive jurisprudence)	Volumes on pilgrimage (*ḥajj*), struggle (*jihād*), commanding the right and forbidding the wrong (*amr bih ma'ruf*), sale (*bay'*)
Science of hadith (*ḥadith shenāsi*)	*Dars-nāmeh-ye 'elm-e ḥadith* (Textbook on the science of hadith)	The entire book except for chapter two
Philosophy 3 (*falsafeh*)	*Dar sāyeh-ye sār-e ḥekmat* (In the light of wisdom)[b]	From part ten up to part twelve
Islamic ethics 8 (*akhlāq-e eslāmi*)	*Bar kerāneh sharḥ-e chehel* hadith by Mohadethi (At the shore of forty hadith commentary)	Hadith nineteen up to the last hadith, exception hadith twenty-four, twenty-six, thirty-four, thirty-five, thirty-eight
Methodology in public speaking 2 (*ravesh-e sokhanrāni*)	Practising different approaches to public speaking and propaganda with the use of videotaping	
Introduction to religions (*āshenā'i bā adyān*)	*Āshenā'i bā adyān* by Toufiqi (Introduction to religions)	The entire book
Grammar 2 (*tajziyeh va tarkib*)	*Zabān-e qur'ān*, upper level, vol. 5 (The language of the Qur'an)[c]	Twenty pages of chapter one; twenty pages of chapter two; ten pages of chapter three; fifteen pages of chapter four

[a] *Al-Mīzān fī tafsīr al-qur'ān* is a twenty-volume exegesis of the Qur'an by Mohammad Hosayn Tabataba'i (d. 1981).

[b] The full title of the book is *Dar sāyeh-ye sār-e ḥekmat: sharḥ va-touḍiḥ-e 'Bidāyat al-ḥikmah'* and it was authored by Mohammad Hosayn Akhundi and printed by Nashr-e Hajar. Nothing further is known about Akhundi. He does not seem to have authored any other books.

[c] There are several books with *Zabān-e qor'ān* in the title; this book is most likely *Zabān-e qor'ān: tajziyeh va-tarkib* by Hamid Mohammadi and published by Nashr-e Hajar.

Fifth Year, Second Semester

Subject	Text	Scope
New issues in theology (*Masā'el-e jadid-e kalāmi*)	*Kalām-e jadid* by Yousefiyan (New theology)[a]	Scope will be announced
Deductive jurisprudence 4 (*feqh-e estedlāli*)	*Durūs tamhīdiyya fī al-fiqh al-istidlālī* (Introductory lessons in deductive jurisprudence)	Marriage, divorce, oath, vows and allegiance, testament
Introduction to Nahj al-balāgheh (*āshenā'i bā nahj al-balāgheh*)	*Dar maḥḍar-e khorshid* (In the presence of the sun)[b]	The entire book
Educational psychology (*ravān-shenāsi-ye tarbiyati*)	*Ravan-shenāsi-ye tarbiyati* by Salarifar (Educational pscychology)	Scope will be announced
Political system in Islam (*neẓām-e siyāsi-ye eslām*)	*Nezām-e siyāsi-ye eslām* (Political system in Islam)[c]	The entire book except for pp. 29–129
Women in Islam 2 (*zan dar eslām*)	*Dar āmadi bar neẓām-e shakhṣiyat-e zan dar eslām* (A take away from the system of women's character in Islam)	From '*mabāni-ye eslāmi dar negaresh be shakhṣiyyat-e zan*' up to the end of the part
Thematic Qur'anic exegesis (*tafsir-e mouḍu'i*)	*Ahl-e bayt dar qor'ān* by Naqipur (The household of the prophet in the Qur'an)	Scope will be announced
Research for final paper (*taḥqiq-e pāyāni*)	*Erā'eh-ye taḥqiq bar asās-e ā'in-nāmeh-ye khāṣṣ* (Production of research based on special statutes)	

[a] *Kalām-e jadid* is authored by Hasan Yusefian and was written with the cooperation of the Study and Research Centre of Imam Khomeini (mo'aseseh-ye āmuzeshi va pazhuheshi-ye Imam Khomeini). Yusefian graduated from the University of Tarbiyat Modarres.

[b] Depending on the source of information, this book has at least one author: Seyyed Jamal al-Din-Pur, but Akbar Asad Alizadeh and Seyyed Mohammad Kazem Tabataba'i are also listed as contributors. It is published by the Hajar publisher that is associated with the Management Centre.

[c] 'Ali Asghar Nosrati wrote *Neẓām-e siyasi-ye eslām* and published it with Nashr-e Hajar for the Management Centre. Nosrati is a religious scholar who studied with Fazel Lankarani, Javad Tabrizi or 'Abdollah Javadi Amoli. He teaches at the seminary and university.

Table 13.5 Curriculum: Jurisprudence and Principles of Jurisprudence, Third Level, 2011–2012

First Year, First Semester

Course	Text	Themes/Scope
Principles of jurisprudence, prerequisite (*oṣul-e pish niyāz*)	*Durūs fī 'ilm al-uṣūl (ḥalqa thāniya)* (Discourses on the science of the principles of jurisprudence) (by Mohammad Baqer Sadr)	From the beginning of the book up to the chapter on '*al-dalīl al-'aqlī*'
Jurisprudence 1 (*feqh*)	*Durūs tamhīdiyya fī al-fiqh al-istidlālī* (Introductory lessons in the deductive jurisprudence)	Religious obligation (*al-taklīf*), menstruation (*al-ḥayḍ*), childbirth (*al-nifās*), a traveller's prayer (*ṣalāt al-musāfir*), sale (*al-bay'*)
History of principles of jurisprudence (*tārikh-e 'elm-e oṣul*)	*Darāmadi bar tārikh-e 'elm-e oṣul* (A take-away from the science of the principles of jurisprudence) by Mahdi 'Alipur	Importance of the history of the science of the principles of jurisprudence: history beginning with the establishment of this science (up until the lesser occultation); development of the science of the principles of jurisprudence (*touse'eh-ye 'elm-e oṣul*) – from Shaykh Mofid up to Shaykh Tusi; stagnation of the science of the principles (*rokud-e 'elm-e oṣul*) – the century after Shaykh Tusi; new development of the science of the principles (*takāmol-e mojaddad-e 'elm-e oṣul*) – from Ibn Idris up to Mohaqqeq Helli; innovations of theories (*ebdā'-e naẓariyyāt*) – 'Allameh Helli up to Shaykh Baha'i; development and resurgence of the Akhbarism (*shekl-giri va ravāj-e akhbār-gari*) – from Astarabadi up to Yusof Baḥrāni (author of *Ḥadā'iq*); renewal of the science of the principles (*tajdid-e ḥayāt-e 'elm-e oṣul*) – from Behbehani up to Shaykh Ansari; scrutiny in the science of the principles (*zharf-negari dar 'elm-e oṣul*) – from Shaykh Ansari up to Borujerdi; contemporary era (after Borujerdi)
History of jurisprudence and jurists (*tārikh-e feqh va-foqahā'*)		1.) The era of legislation (*'aṣr-e tashri'*) (from the beginning of the Prophetic mission until the fifteenth century), 2.) the era of branching out (*'aṣr-e tafrī'*), Sunni jurisprudence: the era of the companions of the Prophet (*'aṣr-e ṣaḥābeh*), the era of the adherents (*'aṣr-e tābe'ān*), the era of the leaders of the legal schools (*'aṣr-e pishvāyān-e madhhab*), the era of the stagnation of legal reasoning and choosing a legal school (*'asr-e touqif-e ejtehād va gozinesh-e madhāheb*), era of sheer following and jurisprudential decline (*'aṣr-e taqlid-e maḥḍ va inḥeṭāṭ-e feqhi*), era of renewed jurisprudential vitality – contemporary era (*'aṣr-e tajdid-e neshāṭ-e feqhi*)

(continued)

First Year, First Semester (*continued*)

Course	Text	Themes/Scope
		Imami Shi'i jurisprudence Imami, Zaydi and Esma'ili jurisprudence; era of the Imams (*'aṣr-e a'emmeh*); era of composing and developing legal reasoning and the use of hadith (*'aṣr-e tadvin va-takāmol-e ejtehād va estefādeh az ḥadith*) – up to Shaykh Tusi; era of stagnation and following (*'aṣr-e rokud va taqlid*) up to Ibn Idris; era of renewal of jurisprudence (*'aṣr-e tajdid-e ḥayāt-e feqhi*) – up to before Astarabadi; era of appearance and growth of the Akhbari movement (*'aṣr-e ẓohur va-roshd-e ḥarkat-e akhbāri*) – from Astarabadi up to Shaykh Yusef Bahrani; era of stop of growth of Akhbaris and decline of dynamic jurisprudence (*'aṣr-e touqif-e roshd-e akhbāri va-afzāyesh-e puyā'i-ye feqh*) from Behbehani up to Saheb-e Javāher (Muhammad Hasan al-Najafi); era of jurisprudential innovations and universality of their matters (*'aṣr-e ebdā'āt-e feqhi va-jāme'iyat-e masā'el-e ān*) – Shaykh Ansari; era of entering of influential jurisprudence in socio-political (issues) (*'aṣr-e vorud-e mo'ather dar omur-e siyāsi ejtemā'i*) – from Akhund Khorasani up to Borujerdi; era of establishment of jurisprudential government (*'aṣr-e esteqrār-e ḥokumat-e feqhi*) from Khomeini up to today
Grammar (*tajziyeh va-tarkib*)		Composition and de-composition of writings
Shi'i beliefs 1		Imamate; the household of the Prophet (*ahl-bayt*); oneness of worshippers and doubts related to it (*touḥid-e 'ebādi va-shobahāt marbuṭ beh ān*) – for example, visitation of tombs of the sinless (*ma'ṣumin*)
Methodology in writing		Characteristics of a good author, characteristics of a good book

Second Year, First Semester

Course	Text	Themes/Scope
Jurisprudence 3 (*feqh*)	*Durūs tamhīdiyya fī al-fiqh al-istidlālī*	Chapters on: struggle (*al-jihād*), commanding the right and forbidding the wrong (*al-amr bi al-ma'rūf wa al-nahy 'an al-munkar*), donating or endowing (*al-hiba*), deposit (*al-wadī'a*), loan (*al-'āriyah*), two forms of betting agreements (*al-sabq wa al-rimāya*), marriage (*al-nikāḥ*)
Principles of jurisprudence 1 (*oṣul-e feqh*)	*Durūs fī 'ilm al-uṣūl; ḥalqa thālitha*	From the beginning of the book up to matters of proof of devotedness (*ithbāt-e ta'abbodi*)
Hadith texts 2 (*motun-e ḥadithi*)	*Kafī* (Sufficient) by Kolayni[a]	Foundations of belief: chapters on the virtue of knowledge, belief and disbelief, companionship, fasting
	Wasā'il al-shī'a (Means) by Ḥorr 'Amoli[b]	Struggle of soul (*jihad al-nafs*); commanding the right and forbidding the wrong; companionship in travels and town dwellers in the book on pilgrimage
	Kitāb al-wāfī (The abundantly sufficient) by Fayd Kashani[c]	Necessity of pilgrimage, speeches and messages (*al-khuṭab wa-al-rasā'il*), preachings
	Biḥār al-anwār (Seas of light) by Majlesi[d]	Rules of conduct and habitual practice and commands and instructions and prohibitions, sins and guilts (*al-adab, al-sunan, al-awāmir, al-nawāhī, al-kabā'ir, al-ma'āṣī*).
Philosophy 2 (*faslsafeh*)	*Āmuzesh-e falsafeh*	Cause (*'illa*), precedent (*'aṣl*), the relationship between the causes, cause and effect (*ma'lul*), rules governing cause and effect, final cause (*ghā'i*), efficient cause (*fā'eli*)
Methodology in research		Steps of research, evaluation

[a] *Al-Kāfī* (The Sufficient) is one of Mohammad ibn Ya'qob al-Kulayni's (d. 941) works and consists of three parts: *uṣūl al-kāfī, furū' al-kāfī,* and *rawdah al-kāfī*. It is one of the most famous hadith collections in the Shi'i tradition.

[b] *Wasā'il al-shi'ah ilā taḥṣīl masā'il al-shari'ah* is one of Mohammad bin al-Hasan b. 'Ali b. Hosayn al-'Ameli al-Mashghari's, known as al-Horr al-'Ameli's (d. 1624) most prominent works that is widely read in the Shi'i tradition. The work is based on four books of hadiths.

[c] *Al-Wāfī* is a hadith reference by al-Fayd al-Kashani (d. 1680).

[d] Biḥār al-Anwār is a comprehensive collection of hadiths by the Safavid scholar Mohammad Baqer Majlesi (d. 1699), known as 'Allameh Majlesi.

Third Year, First Semester

Course	Text	Themes/Scope
Jurisprudence 5 (*feqh*)	*Durūs tamhīdiyya fī al-fiqh al-istidlālī*	The chapters on judgement (*al-qaḍā'*); testimonies (*shahādāt*); legal punishment (*al-ḥudūd*); retributive justice (*al-qiṣāṣ*); financial compensation (*al-diyāt*)
Principles of jurisprudence 4 (*oṣul al-feqh*)	*Durūs fī 'ilm al-usūl ḥalqa thālitha*	From 'presumption' (*istiṣḥāb*) up to the end of the book
Contemporary Arabic 1	*Nuṣūṣ fiqhiyya*	Students work on at least three pages of texts independently; instructor helps with questions
Qur'anic exegesis	*Al-Mizān* (in Arabic), vol. 4, handout by Management Centre Students also expected to refer to the exegetical works of *Aḥsan al-ḥadīth*,[a] and *Min waḥy al-qur'ān*[b] and *al-Manār*[c]	Verses 4:36 up to 4:71
Legal maxims (of Islamic law) 1 (*qavā'ed-e feqhiyeh*)	*Taḥrir-e qavā'ed-e feqhiyeh*[d]	Rules based on demonstrative power/ authority (*ḥujjiya*); rules for union and disunion, transgression, and purity; rules for causing damage

[a] *Aḥsan al-ḥadīth: ta'ammulāt 'ilmiya wa-adabiya fī kitāb allāh 'azza wa jalla* by the Syrian scholar Muhammad Sa'id Ramadan al-Buti.

[b] I assume that this refers to the multi-volume work by Muhammad Husayn Fazl Allah.

[c] The magazine founded and published by Rashid Rida.

[d] *Taḥrir-e qavā'ed-e feqhiyeh* is originally authored by Hasan Bojnurdi and has been translated into Persian by Maryam Esma'ili. She has translated a number of works in the field of Islamic sciences.

Fourth Year, First Semester

Course	Text	Themes/Scope
Jurisprudence 8	*Al-Rawḍa al-bahiyya fī sharḥ al-Lum'a al-dimashqiyya* (The magnificient garden; a commentary on the radiance of Damascus)	Inheritance (*mīrāth*)
Jurisprudence 9	*al-Makāsib* (Profits) by Shaykh Anṣāri, vol. 1	From the beginning up to occultation (*ghayba*) (exception apply)
Hadith texts 2	*Kitab al-Kāfī* by Kolayni *Wasā'il al-shī'a* by Horr 'Amili *Kitāb al-Wāfī* by Fayd Kashani *Biḥār al-anwār* by Majlesi	The same description as above
Public penal law (*hoquq-e jazā'i 'omumi*)		Historical development of public penal law; crime and elements constituting it as such; retributive accountability; facing a crime
English language 1	Thirty-five pages of an easy English text related to jurisprudence by the choice of the seminary	
Legal maxims (of Islamic law) 2 (*qavā'ed-e feqhiyeh*)	*Taḥrīr al-qawā'id al-fiqhiyya*	Rules related to loss/destruction; safeguard of possession; deception; damage and loss; rules related to dissimulation; obligation

Table 13.6 Exegesis and Qur'anic Studies, Third Level, 2011–2012

First Year, First Semester

Course	Text	Themes/Scope
Qur'anic studies 1 (*'olum-e qor'ān*)	*Talkhīṣ al-tamhīd*, vol. 2	Miracle of the Qur'an
Qur'anic studies 2 (*'olum-e qor'ān*)		Alteration of the Qur'an
Principles of jurisprudence 1 (*oṣūl-e feqh*)	*Oṣul-e feqh-e Moẓaffar*	State (of the field) and controversy; true and false use (*iste'māl-e ḥaqiqi va-majāzi*); signs (*'alā'em*) of truth and falseness; synonymity (*tarādof*) and ambiguity (*eshterāk*); legal truth (*ḥaqiqat-e shar'iyeh*), right and common (*ṣaḥiḥ wa a'amm*); derivatives (*moshtaqq*); intent
Jurisprudence 1 (*feqh*)	*Durūs tamhīdiyya fī al-fiqh al-istidlālī*	Rent contract (*ijārah*), liability (*ḍamān*), sleeping partnership (*muḍāraba*), loan (*qarḍ*), savings (*wadī'a*), gratuitous loan (*'āriya*), endowment (*waqf*)
Grammar (*tajziyeh va tarkib*)		Importance of *tajziyeh* and *tarkib*; their role in translating the Qur'an; meaning and intention of *tajziyeh* and *tarkib*
Complementary syntax 1 (*naḥv-e takmili*)	*Mughnī al-labīb* (Satisfier of the understanding), first section[a]	Students may choose one of the following two exercises: extraction of terminologies from one part of the Qur'an (*ḥizb*) and their analysis from the point of view of Moghni. Or: choosing one important letter such as *hamza* and analysing it in respect to one part of the Qur'an
Translation and interpretation of the Qur'an 1		Chapters 2:80–2:286; 3:1–3:200 and 5:1–5:120.
Writing methodology		Characteristics of a good writer and characteristics of a good writing piece.

[a] *Mughnī al-labīb* is a book of Arabic grammar and authored by Ibn Hisham (d. 1359).

Second Year, First Semester

Course	Text	Themes/Scope
Jurisprudence 3 (*feqh*)	*Durūs tamhīdiyya fī al-fiqh al-istidlālī*	Found property (*luqṭa*), food (*aṭ'ima*) and drinks, inheritance (*irth*)
Principles of jurisprudence 3 (*oṣūl-e feqh*)	*Uṣūl al-fiqh* by Mozaffar	Proof (*ḥujja*); the Qur'an and its abrogation; Sunnism, deeds (*fi'l*) of the Imams, approval (*taqrīr*) of the Imams, narrations reported on the authority of the Imams (*akhbār*)
Advanced research methodology (*ravesh-e taḥqiq-e pishrafteh*)		Research methodology related to exegesis and Qur'anic studies
Qur'anic vocabulary (*mofredāt-e qor'ān*)		Significance of Qur'anic terminology; relationship between Qur'anic terminology and other sciences; alien words in the Qur'an; facets and analogous passages (*wujūh wa-naẓā'ir*); synonymy (*tarāduf wa-ishtirāk*)
Foundation and rules in interpreting the Qur'an 1 (*mabādi va-qavā'ed-e tafsir-e qor'ān*)	*Ravesh-e tafsir-e qor'ān* (Approaches to Qur'anic commentaries) by Mahmud Rajabi	General knowledge: definitions of foundations (*mabānī*), rules (*qawā'id*), interpretation (*tafsīr*), and interpretation (*ta'wīl*); necessity of interpretation (*tafsīr*); conditions of the exegete and the necessary (knowledge of) sciences for interpretation. Exegetical foundation: capability of understanding and interpreting the Qur'an immunity of Qur'an miracle of Qur'an; Qur'anic language; adaptation (*taṭbīq*)
Useful terminologies (*balāghat-e kārbordi*)	*Jozveh-ye ma'āni al-qor'ān* (Handout on the meaning of the Qur'an); sent from the Management Centre	The entire handout
Translating and interpreting the Qur'an 3 (*tarjomeh va-sharḥ-e qor'ān*)		Chapter twelve (*Yūsuf*) up to chapter twenty-two (*al-Ḥajj*)

Third Year, First Semester

Course	Text	Themes/Scope
Jurisprudence 3	*Durūs tamhīdiyya fī al-fiqh al-istidlālī*	Same as above (jurisprudence 1)
Philosophy 1 (*falsafeh*)	*Āmuzesh-e falsafeh* (Teachings in philosophy) by Mesbah Yazdi	Introductory remarks: the history of philosophical thoughts from the beginning until the contemporary era; terminologies in science and philosophy; issues in philosophy; foundation and purpose of philosophy; research methodology in philosophy; necessity of philosophy Cognitive science (*shenākht shenāsi*): definition of cognitive science; a priori principles; divisions of recognition; acquired knowledge (*'ilm ḥuṣūlī*); senses (*ḥiss*); role of intellect and senses in conception (*taṣdīq*) and conceptionalisation (*taṣawwurāt*); value of recognition; evaluation of legal and ethical judgement
Serial Qur'anic exegesis 2 (*tafsir-e tartibi*)	*Majma' al-bayān* (Collection of explanation) by al-Tabrisi[a]	Chapters eighty-one (*al-Takwīr*), eighty-seven (*al-A'lā*), eighty-nine (*al-Fajr*), ninety-two (al-Layl), ninety-three (*al-Duḥā*), ninety-four (*al-Sharḥ*), 100 (*al-'Ādiyāt*), 102 (*al-Takāthur*), 103 (*al-'Aṣr*), 105 (*al-Fīl*), 107 (*al-Mā'ūn*), 108 (*al-Kawthar*), 109 (*al-Kāfirūn*), 111 (*al-Masad*)
Contemporary Arabic texts	Passages from the Qur'an	Students work on the text themselves; instructor's role is only to help when there are specific questions
Thematic Qur'anic exegesis 2 (*tafsir-e mouḍu'i*)	*Ma'āref-e qor'ān* (Qur'anic teachings) by Mesbah Yazdi, vol. 1	Anthropology (*ensān shenāsi*)[b]
Translating and interpreting the Qur'an 4		Chapters twenty-three (*al-Mu'minūn*) up to forty (*al-Ghāfir*), except for twenty-four (*al-Nūr*) and thirty-three (*al-Aḥzāb*)

Third Year, First Semester (*continued*)

Course	Text	Themes/Scope
Qur'an and the two [other] holy books [literally: the two covenants] (*Qur'ān va-'ahdayn*)		General knowledge of the Torah and Bible and what unites them; commonalities and differences of the Qur'an and the two Testaments

[a] *Majma' al-bayān fī tafsīr al-qur'ān* is authored by Fadl b. Hasan al-Tabrisi (d. 1153) and is one of the most important commentaries of the Qur'an (*tafsir*) in the Shi'i tradition. For an analysis of the work, see B. Fudge, *Qur'ānic Hermeneutics: al-Tabrisī and the Craft of Commentary* (New York: Routledge, 2011).
[b] The word reads '*etsān shenāsi*'. I assume this is a typographical mistake and should have been '*ensān shenāsi*'.
[c] It is not clear why chapter twenty-four is excluded from the curriculum as it deals with some regulations for the Muslim community (mainly marriage, modesty, obedience to the Prophet, and appropriate behaviour in the household). The verses related to veiling are also in this chapter.

Fourth Year, First Semester

Course	Text	Themes/Scope
Qur'an and the two other holy books		The same scope as above
Philosophy 3	*Āmuzesh-e falsafeh* (Teachings of philosophy) by Mesbah Yazdi	Guidance to know God; proof of the necessary being (*ethbāt-e wajeb al-wojūd*), oneness (*touḥid*), divine action (*touḥid-e af'āli*), divine characteristics (*ṣefāt-e elāhi*), characteristics of God's essence (*ṣefāt-e dhātiyeh*), characteristics of God's free will (*ṣefāt-e fe'liyeh*), purpose of creation, divine will and decree (*qaḍā' va-qadar-e elāhi*), good and evil in the world
Thematic exegesis 4	*Akhlāq dar qor'ān* (Ethics in the Qur'an) by Mesbah, vol. 1 up to p. 237	Ethics in the Qur'an
Thematic exegesis 5	*Akhlāq dar qor'ān* by Mesbah, vol. 3	Family in the Qur'an; societal discussions in the Qur'an
English language 2	Thirty-five pages, easy text pertaining to the Qur'an	
Final thesis		

Table 13.7 Seminaries, Fourth Level, 2018–2019

Province City/Town: seminary	Jurisprudence/ Principles of jurisprudence	Comparative exegesis	Transcendent metaphysics/ Philosophy	Islamic theology
Isfahan				
Isfahan: Fatemeh al-Zahra		•		
Isfahan: Mojtahedeh Amin[a]	•			
Tehran				
Tehran: Imam Hasan Mojtaba	•			
Tehran: Kousar		•		
Tehran: Rafi'eh al-Mostafa	•	•	•	
Tehran: Qasem b. al-Hasan		•		
Semnan				
Semnan: Fatemeh al-Zahra	•			
Fars				
Shiraz: Jame'eh al-Nur	•			
Qom				
Qom: Ma'sumiyeh	•	•	•	•
Kerman				
Kerman: Rokn al-Hoda		•		
Golestan				
Gorgan: al-Zahra	•			
Mazandaran				
Babol: Hazrat-e Umm al-Banin	•	•		
Markazi				
Arak: Rayhaneh al-Nabi	•			
Yazd				
Maybod: Hazrat-e Zahra		•		
Yazd: Amir al-Mo'menin	•			

[a] The Mojtahedeh Amin seminary in Isfahan that offers jurisprudence and principles of jurisprudence is only named after the renowned mojtahedeh Noṣrat Amin (d. 1983); neither the building, nor the staff nor the curriculum has any link to her. In fact, one of Amin's former students I conversed with quit working there as an instructor because she held the philosophy of the seminary to be contradictory to that of Amin (conversation with Mrs H., 2013).

Table 13.8 General Knowledge for Admission to Fourth Level

Subject	Textbook	Scope
Grammar and translation (*tajziyah va tarkib va tarjomeh*)	*I'rāb al-qur'ān va-bayāneh,' Dar ḥadd-e mabādī al-'arabīyya*, vol. 4 by Muhyi al-Din Darvish	Part 30
Principles of jurisprudence	*Uṣūl al-fiqh* (in Arabic) by Mohammad Reza Mozaffar	Discussion on proof (*al-ḥujja*)
Jurisprudence	*Durūs tamhīdiyya fī al-fiqh al-istidlāli* by Irvani	Chapters on judgement and penal law (*qaḍā' wa-al-ḥudūd*)

Table 13.9 Specialised Knowledge for Admission to Fourth Level

Comparative exegesis

Sub-division	Textbook	Scope
Qur'anic studies	*Talkhīṣ al-tamhīd* (Abridgement of the introduction), 1 and 2 by Mohammad Hadi Ma'refat[a]	Vol. 1: from '*nuzūl al-qur'ān*' (revelation) up to the end of the discussion on '*kitāb al-waḥy*' Vol. 2: from the discussion on '*al-qirā'āt fī 'nash'at-i-hā wa taṭawwur-i-hā*'
Exegesis	*Majma' al-bayān* by Tabarsi	Part twenty-eight (*juz'*) (chapters fifty-five to sixty-six)
Exegesis	*al-Mīzān* by Tabataba'i	Part twenty-eight

[a] Mohammad Hadi Ma'refat (d. 2007) is a twentieth-century cleric who studied in Karbala, Najaf and Qom and eventually stayed in Qom to teach at the seminary. He has mainly written works in Qur'anic studies.

Jurisprudence and Principles of Jurisprudence

Sub-division	Textbook	Scope
Principles of jurisprudence	*Durūs fī 'ilm al-uṣūl (al-ḥalqa al-thālitha)* by Sadr[a]	From '*taḥdīd dalālāt al-dalīl al-shar'ī*' up to '*al-khātima fī ta'āruḍ al-adilla*'
	Or *Kifāyat al-uṣūl* by Akhund Khorasani	From the beginning of the book up to '*al-maqṣid al-sādis*' and from '*al-ijmā' al-manqūl*' up to '*al-maqṣid al-thāmin*'
Jurisprudence	*Sharḥ al-Lum'a* by Shahid Thani	Chapters on inheritance (*mirāth*) and divorce (*al-ṭalāq*)
Jurisprudence	*Makāsib* by Shaykh Ansari	The part on forbidden businesses (*al-makāsib al-muḥarrama*)
The science of critical study of the transmitters and the content of the hadith (*rijāl wa-dirāya*)	*Kulliyāt fī 'ilm al-rijāl* by Sobhāni	The entire book
	Darsnāmeh-ye 'elm-e hadith	Chapter three (on the history of Shi'i hadith) and four (on terminologies of hadith)

[a] *Ḥalaqāt al-uṣūl* (Discourses on the Science of the Principles of Jurisprudence) is held to be a direct criticism of Muzaffar's ideas on morality, rationality, and independent rationality as a source of religious rulings. See A.-R. Bhojani, *Moral Rationalism and Sharī'a: Independent Rationality in Modern Shī'ī uṣūl al-fiqh* (London and New York: Routledge, 2015).

Transcendental philosophy

Sub-division	Textbook	Scope
Philosophy	*Nihāyat al-ḥikma* (in Arabic) (The Ultimate Wisdom) by 'Allameh Tabataba'i	The entire book
Logic	*Al-Jawhar al-naḍīd* by 'Allameh Ḥelli[a]	Chapter five on proof (*burhān*) and definition (*ta'rīf*)
Logic	*Mughālaṭāt* (Fallacies) by 'Ali Asghar Khandan	The entire book
History of philosophy (*tārikh-e falsafeh*)	*Darāmādi bar tārikh-e falsafeh-ye eslāmi* (a take-away from the history of Islamic philosophy) by Mohammad Fana'i Eshkevari[b]	Vol. 1: chapters one, three, four Vol. 3: chapters eleven, thirteen, fourteen

[a] The complete title is *al-Jawhar al-naḍīd fī sharḥ manṭiq al-tajrīd*, a commentary on logic, by 'Abu Mansur Jamal al-Din al-Hasan b. Yusuf b. Mutahhar al-Hilli, known as al-'Allamah al-Hilli (d. 1326). The work is a commentary on the section that is devoted to the issue of logic in *Tajrīd al-i'tiqād* by Naser al-Din al-Tusi (d. 1273).

[b] Eshkevari studied mysticism and philosophy at a religious seminary, before he went to Canada to obtain a master's degree and a PhD from McGill University in philosophy. In 2001, he took on a teaching position at the Imam Khomeini Education and Research Institute in Qom.

Islamic theology

Sub-division	Textbook	Scope
Philosophy	*Nihāyat al-ḥikma* (in Arabic) (The end of wisdom) by 'Allameh Tabataba'i	The entire book except for parts three, five, ten
Logic	*Manṭiq* (Logic) by Mohammad Reza Mozaffar	Demonstration (*burhān*), fallacy (*mughālaṭah*), dialectics (*jadal*)
Theology	*Kashf al-murād* (The discovery of intention) by 'Allameh Helli[a]	From the 'third intention' (*maqṣid thālith*) up to the end of the book
Theology	*Kalām-e jadid bā ru'ikard-e eslāmi* (New theology with an Islamic approach) by 'Abdolhosayn Khosroupanah	The entire book

[a] The full title is *Kashf al-murād fī sharḥ tajrīd al-i'tiqād* and is a commentary on the section on theology in Naser al-Din al-Tusi's (d. 1274) *Tajrīd al-i'tiqād* (Summation of belief). As author of many significant books, 'Allamah Helli (d. 1326) has significantly contributed to the field of Shi'i studies.

INDEX

Abu Bakr (d. 634), 9, 23, 60, 70, 78–9, 83, 86, 88, 93, 96n, 98, 99, 101, 103, 116, 136, 153–4, 161–4
'A'isha 'Abd al-Rahman (b. 1913), 281
'A'isha bt. 'Abd al-Hadi al-Ba'uniyya (d. 1516), 25, 190
'A'isha bt. Hasan Isfahani (d. 1068), 23
akhlaq, 281, 283, 286, 294, 334–5, 337, 371–4, 376–9, 389
'Alasvand, Fariba (b. 1967), 13, 44, 294
'Ali al-Hadi (d. 868), 109
'Ali al-Rida (d. 818), 60, 75, 115, 117–19, 144, 158, 165–6, 177, 179–80, 183, 29n
'Ali b. Abi Talib (d. 661), 9, 63–4, 71, 73, 77, 85, 88, 99, 109, 113–16, 153, 161, 163, 181, 245, 247
'Alid(s), 50, 57, 67, 88, 163, 300–1, 322, 323
'ālima, 11, 299, 300, 302, 304, 308, 310, 315, 325–7, 330, 332, 337, 338
Amin, Nosrat (d. 1983), 13, 39–44, 271–97, 346–7n, 348n, 352n, 358, 380, 390
Amina bt. al-Huda al-Sadr (d. 1980), 11, 13, 298–324
Amina bt. al-Husayn al-Mahamili (d. 987), 25
Amina Khwatun Majlisi (d. early 18th c.), 32
'Amra bt. 'Abd al-Rahman (d. 724), 190
'aqīda, 334–5
'aql, 12, 28–9, 31, 121, 128, 291, 325–6, 331–3, 340, 381
  kamāl al-'aql, 128
'aṣaba, 79, 92
authority
  charismatic, 12, 45, 69, 81, 326f, 332, 335, 337, 399, 340
  juristic, 11, 17, 132,
  legal, 10, 17, 85, 133
  political, 80, 84, 250, 253, 268, 270
  religious, 1–4, 6–10, 12–17, 18–21, 27, 30n, 36–7, 42–3, 45–6, 80–2, 85, 87, 91–3, 97–8, 109, 138, 140, 145, 154, 177–81, 184–5, 187, 190–2, 228, 240, 249, 265, 267–70, 272, 275, 292, 294–7, 299–302, 314, 317, 323–4, 325–8, 338, 340, 343, 346n, 358
  religio-political, 219
  traditional, 326, 332, 334, 337, 339–40

Baraqani, 17, 34, 35–9, 45
al-Barqi, Ahmad b. Muhammad b. Khalid (d. 887), 89, 107, 109, 112n
Behzad of Herat (d. 1535), 193–201

Damascus, 4n, 8, 11, 21, 23–5n, 141, 151, 157n, 160, 202, 325–40, 385
Da'wa party, 310

Fadak, 9, 15, 60, 78–80, 85–8, 91–3, 96–9, 101, 136, 163
Fatima, 47–8, 50–1, 53–6, 59–60, 62, 64–5, 76, 104, 105–11, 116, 136, 162–3, 187, 190, 220, 229–30, 235, 242, 253, 262, 265, 268, 325, 356
  and intercession on Day of Judgement, 83, 330
  and *khuṭba*, 9, 78–104
  and political authority, 15
  and religious authority, 6, 14–16
  as *ḥujja*, 92
Fatima al-Sadr (b. 1942), 301, 303, 305, 316–19, 322
Fatima bt. al-Baghdadi (d. 1144), 23
Fatima bt. Harun b. Musa Al Furat, 111
Fatima Umm Farwah, 109n, 116
Fidda (slave-servant of Fatima), 7n, 14, 16, 187
fiqh, 6n, 27n, 29n, 34n, 42n, 92, 133–5, 266n, 287n, 349, 355, 371–3, 376–87

Gawhar Shad Begum (d. 1457), 8, 26

Hababa al-Walibiyya, 115
hadīth, 3–5, 7–8, 11–15, 20–33, 36, 38, 40, 43n, 46, 47n, 47–77, 80, 82, 89–91, 95, 98, 105–19, 123–4, 126, 130–1, 140, 157, 162–4, 168–70, 183, 185, 188–9, 191, 212, 222n, 226, 232, 237n, 238, 241, 256, 257n, 258n, 260n, 269n, 271, 272n, 274n, 275, 277, 278n, 280, 284n, 288, 294, 304, 312, 322, 331, 346n, 358, 363–4, 372, 375, 377–9, 382–5, 392
Ha'eri Yazdi, Abdulkarim, 6, 40n, 276–7, 352n
ḥajj, 13, 123–4, 314, 317–8, 352, 387
Hakima, 13 75, 117
al-Hasan al-'Askari (d. 874), 75, 109, 181
Hasan b. 'Ali, 53, 77, 184, 257n, 383
ḥawza, 11, 42, 61n, 279n, 318, 328–9, 332, 334, 338, 341n, 342, 346, 358
Hisham b. al-Hakam (d. 807), 112, 151
Hujayma bt. Huyayy al-Awtabiyya (d. 701), 25
ḥujja, 92, 391
Husayn b. 'Ali (d. 680), 53, 71, 75, 77, 88, 99, 154, 163
Husniyya, 10, 14, 16, 138–92

Ibn Abi Tahir Tayfur, Abu al-Fadl (d. 893), 9, 78–80n, 86n, 88–90, 95n, 99n
Ibn Babawayh, Abu Ja'far (al-Shaykh al-Saduq) (d. 991), 48n, 63, 64n, 71n, 75, 80–1, 88–91, 95, 97, 117, 123, 124n, 154, 155n, 226, 228, 234, 242
Ibn Taymiyya (d. 1328), 26, 49n
ijtihād, 5, 6, 11, 17, 30, 37, 40–1, 43, 72, 125, 168n, 272, 276–80, 287, 289, 293, 295–6, 299, 304, 323, 349, 352, 366–7, 381–2
'ilm, 70, 72–3, 82, 115–16, 128, 232, 243, 330, 375–6, 381, 383–4, 388, 392
Imam Moussa Sadr Cultural & Research Institute, 307, 309, 311–12

imāmī, 27–9, 30, 68, 74–5, 80n, 122–3, 125–31, 136–7, 140, 171–2, 179, 226, 234, 360, 382
infallibility, 229, 234, 241
inheritance, 15, 25, 38, 52n, 60, 62, 73, 79–81, 85, 87, 90–5, 99, 101–4, 148, 163, 185, 214, 385, 387, 392
'Isa b. Ja'far b. Mansur, 163
isnād, 31n, 49, 53, 62, 67, 89, 91, 99, 111, 184, 245

Jabir b. Yazid al-Ju'fi (d. 745), 116
Ja'far al-Sadiq (d. 765), 16, 72, 74, 92, 109, 112–13, 116–19, 124, 135n, 140, 166, 168–9, 171, 179, 180–3, 186–8, 191, 222, 229, 264, 268
Jama'at al-'Ulama' fi 'l-Najaf al-Ashraf, 308

Karbala, 34, 36–9, 58, 59, 61–2, 74, 110, 113–14, 116, 164, 179, 225, 264, 312, 314, 320, 328, 333n, 391
Kazimayn, 302–3, 309–10, 312–13
Khadija bt. Muhammad al-Batalyuni (d. 1523), 25
Khamenei, 288n, 290, 295, 333
Khomeini, 133, 245, 286, 289–90, 293, 298, 319, 322–3, 328 n, 338, 348n, 371 fb, 377n, 380n, 382, 393
al-Khu'i, Abu al-Qasim (d. 1992), 108, 310, 377
khums, 15, 17, 296, 316, 318–19, 360, 376–7
Kufa, 107, 118, 242, 320
Al-Kulayni (d. 939), 59n, 75, 89, 110–15 n, 383

Layli, 10, 193–209

al-Mahdi (b. 870), 110, 154
majālis / *majālis 'azā'*, 329–30, 332, 336, 338–9
Majles (Iranian parliament), 42, 286n, 291
Majnun, 10, 197–209
marja' / *marja'īyya*, 6, 11, 13, 17, 40n, 278n, 293, 296, 299, 302–4, 308, 312, 314–24, 328–9, 360
Markaz Ta'lim al-Banat, 13, 311–2
Mashhad, 26, 177, 195–6, 223–5, 236, 254n, 258–9, 262, 355
Maytham al-Tammar, 115
mihrāb, 197–8, 201
Mu'alla b. Khunays, 112
Muhammad al-Baqir (d. 733–737), 54, 17, 72–3, 75, 110–11, 117, 123, 166n, 181
Muhammad Baqir al-Majlisi (d. 1699), 32, 33n, 62n, 64n, 74–6, 80–1, 91, 95, 97, 117n, 145–5, 159–60, 217, 257n, 266, 383, 385
Muhammad Baqir al-Sadr (d. 1980), 11, 80n, 84, 85n, 96n, 97, 298–324, 366, 367n, 376–8, 381
Muhammad Baqir al-Wahid al-Bihbahani (d. 1791), 6, 34–5
Muhammad b. 'Abd al-Rahman al-Sakhawi (d. 1497), 21n, 22, 26, 139, 189, 346n
Muhammad b. Abi 'Umayr, 111, 113
Muhammad b. Muslim (d. 767), 73, 106, 112
Muhammad b. 'Umar al-Kashshi (d. 978), 107
Muhammad al-Taqi al-Jawad (d. 835), 117
Muhammadi of Herat, 193–7, 201, 202, 207, 209
Muhsin al-Hakim, 6, 55, 302, 310n, 312

mujtahid(a), 9, 11, 32, 38–9n, 41, 273n, 279, 281, 287, 292–3, 296, 301, 343, 346, 362, 367
mullaya, 11, 327, 332, 338–9
Murtada al-Ansari (1781–1864), 6, 304,
Musa al-Kazim (d. 799), 144, 166, 179, 181, 228, 269

Najaf, 34, 37n, 38, 39n, 130, 225, 267n, 276, 303, 304, 308–21, 328, 346, 352, 391, 392
al-Najashi, Ahmad b. 'Ali (d. 1058), 107, 109 111, 118–9, 184n
Nishapur, 28, 3, 154

Pari Khan Khanum, 16, 32, 212, 213n, 214, 220, 250–3, 267, 269
patriarchy, 5, 48, 136, 187, 208
patrilineal, 93, 94, 96n
polygyny / polygamy, 306, 336

Qom, 41n, 43–6, 98, 107, 226, 264, 276, 278–9, 286, 288, 294, 294–6, 303, 310n, 318, 328, 341–3, 348, 350, 352, 354–5, 357, 363–5, 368–9, 371, 373, 376–7, 390–2

rijāl, 9, 106–9, 110–11n, 113n, 115–19, 180–1, 183–4, 232, 392

Saddam Hussein, 11, 84, 298–300, 321
Salman al-Farisi (d. 644–647), 49, 116, 188
Samarra, 109, 352n
Sayyida Zaynab *see* Zaynabiyya
Sefati, Zohreh (b. 1950), 13, 41–4, 271–97, 348
shifā', 330
Shifa bt. 'Abd Allah al-'Adawiyya, 25
Shiraz, 11–12, 34n, 37, 44n, 145, 156, 196, 202, 204, 233n, 234, 252, 254, 276–7, 316, 325–36, 338, 340, 341–90
Shirazi, Hasan (d. 1983), 11, 326, 328
Shirazi, Muhammad (d. 2001), 328, 331
al-Suyuti, Jalal al-Din (d. 1505), 21n, 26, 33, 50

tablīgh, 11, 39n, 278, 287, 295, 334, 357
tafsīr, 28, 32, 36, 38–42, 47, 48, 50, 52, 55, 155, 168, 185, 188, 227–8, 326, 237, 282, 334, 358, 376, 378–80, 388–89
taklīf, 42, 291, 313, 381
al-Tall-'ukbari, Harun b. Musa (d. 995–6), 111
taqlīd, 293, 296, 323, 328–9, 335, 381–2
Tehran, 7, 33, 38, 39, 41n, 43n, 44n, 143, 242, 275n, 279n, 282, 309, 311, 317, 348, 350, 352, 358, 365, 369, 373, 390
al-Tusi, Abu Ja'far Muhammad b. al-Hasan (d. 1067), 5, 27–8n, 29, 30n, 47n, 64–5, 74, 85, 107n, 109, 111, 125n, 126–8, 131, 151, 159, 180n, 181, 183n, 232–6, 242, 245, 249, 381–2, 392

'Ulayya bt. 'Ali b. al-Husayn, 118, 119
Umm Ahmad, 118
Umm Aslam, 13, 113–15
Umm Aswad, 119
Umm Hani al-Thaqafiyya, 110–11
Umm Ishaq bt. Sulayman, 111
Umm Sa'id al-Ahmasiyya, 113
Umm Salama, 9, 14, 47–77, 111, 113, 117

Umayyads, 49, 74, 83, 105, 118, 132, 179

wakīl(a) / wikāla, 11, 13, 259n, 302, 310, 315–16, 318–19
Weber, Max, 81, 84, 326, 337

Yasin, Al, 302–3, 308, 322

al-Zahra' School, 309–313
Zayd b. 'Ali (d. 740), 54, 88, 99, 101, 103, 118, 163
Zayn al-'Abidin, 74, 75, 88, 113, 115, 117, 181, 188
Zaynab bt. 'Ali, 16, 22n, 75, 77, 89, 105, 179, 325
Zaynab Begum (d. 1640), 212n, 253–58, 267, 269
Zaynabiyya, 11–12, 325–340
Zurarah, 106, 119

EU representative:
Easy Access System Europe
Mustamäe tee 50, 10621 Tallinn, Estonia
Gpsr.requests@easproject.com

www.ingramcontent.com/pod-product-compliance
Lightning Source LLC
Chambersburg PA
CBHW051554230426
43668CB00013B/1852

* 9 7 8 1 4 7 4 4 2 6 6 1 9 *